Jan Helenus Ferguson

MANUAL OF INTERNATIONAL LAW,

FOR THE USE OF

NAVIES, COLONIES & CONSULATES

Volume 2

Elibron Classics
www.elibron.com

Elibron Classics series.

ISBN 1-4021-9930-9 (paperback)
ISBN 1-4212-9967-4 (hardcover)

This Elibron Classics Replica Edition is an unabridged facsimile of the edition publishedin 1884 by W. B. Whittingham & Co., London.

MANUAL

OF

INTERNATIONAL LAW,

FOR THE USE OF

NAVIES, COLONIES & CONSULATES,

BY

JAN HELENUS FERGUSON,

MINISTER OF THE NETHERLANDS IN CHINA; FORMERLY OF THE NETHERLANDS ROYAL NAVY AND COLONIAL SERVICE.

In Six Parts bound in Two Volumes.

VOL. II.

LONDON:
W. B. WHITTINGHAM & Co., 91, GRACECHURCH STREET.

THE HAGUE:
MARTINUS NYHOFF.

HONGKONG:
NORONHA & Co.

1884.

PART IV.

MUTUAL RIGHTS AND RESPONSIBILITIES OF STATES IN TIME OF PEACE.

CHAPTER XVIII.

General Principles with regard to the Mutual Duties of States in their Intercourse.

§ 128. In Parts II and III we have successively treated the nature and extent of the individual rights and obligations of States and the modifications of these rights and obligations, the origin of which was described in Part I. We must now proceed to follow up the development of these rights and obligations in their bearings on the various conditions of mutual intercourse, which of course present different aspects in time of peace, that is in the normal state of intercourse, and in the state of war. These will be treated, respectively, in the present Part IV and in the succeeding Part V of this work, while Part VI, which concludes the work, will contain the rules with regard to the legal manifestation of a return to the normal state of peace, called the treaty of peace.

General principles of international intercourse.

The basis of all moral and legal intercourse in the case of Nations as well as individuals, is *good faith*, *i.e.*, the respect which civilized men owe to the given word of promise. All mutual agreements, from which obligations result, must fulfil the following conditions, viz.: 1°., that the contracting parties possess the moral and legal capacity to treat; 2°., that the consentment be freely and voluntarily given; 3°., that the agreement be in harmony with the Moral Law of Nature, *i.e.*, in conformity with the Spirit of Law of the highest standard existing between the contracting parties, in other words, the agreement must be based on the standard of national morality and civilization of the party most advanced in morality and civilization, for those who have attained to the higher moral standard cannot under any consideration stoop to the lower one without polluting their moral conscience and retreating on the road to civilization (comp. §§ 11–14). These principles determine the mutual duties of States.

With regard to the attitude which a civilized State ought to assume towards uncivilized Nations and the mutual confidence which ought to exist between equally civilized States, in accordance with the Moral Law of Nature, we cannot give better evidence, in support of our exposition of the general principles given in Part I of this work, than by quoting from the recent remarkable work of Professor Lorimer, the Institutes of the Law of Nations, the following passages.

"The moment that the power to help a retrograde race forward, towards the goal of human life, consciously exists in a civilized Nation, that civilized nation is bound to exert its power; and in the exercise of its power, it is entitled to assume an attitude of guardianship, and to put wholly aside the proximate will of the retrograde race. Its own civilization having resulted from the exercise of a will which it regards as rational, real and ultimate, at least when contrasted with the irrational, phenomenal and proximate will of the inferior race, in vindicating its own proximate will, it is entitled to assume, that it vindicates the ultimate will of the inferior race,—the will, that is to say, at which the inferior race must arrive when it reaches the stage of civilization to which the higher race has attained. But the obligation and the right of a civilized Nation to interfere with a retrograde race, even where such interference might be for the benefit of the latter, is limited by the proviso, that, in so doing, it does not so burden its own resources as to cause a greater loss of the means of progress to itself and others than it confers on the retrograde race. This latter proviso seems more generally to be forgotten in our own day than the duty which it defines."

"But, says Prof. Lorimer further, time is an element, in the action of civilizing influences, the importance of which is not always sufficiently kept in view. Neither warlike nor peaceful contact acts immediately,—nay, the first generation subjected to the influences of either is frequently inferior to that which preceded it. The pagan temple is in ruins, and the Christian Church has not been built. The old rude rule of life has been abrogated, and no better rule has yet taken its place. In many cases it becomes a question of the utmost delicacy, whether appeals to the reason, the conscience, and the self-interest, even of savages, through missionaries, traders and neighbouring settlers, be not more potent than the closer contact and more direct guidance which results from political subjection if unaccompanied by actual colonisation. It is too true that colonisation often acts as an improving influence only by improving those subjected to it off the face of the earth; but its action admits of being so regulated by the mother country as that it shall ultimately assign to her retrograde children the position for which they are suited by the characteristics of the race to which they belong, and the stage of progress which they have reached, or, in the case of old communities, at which they stand for the time being. The great difficulty always consists in understanding those whose circumstances differ from our own often more widely than their characters." *

With regard to the relations of mutual confidence which ought in general to subsist between civilized States, Professor Lorimer makes the following further remarks.

"The normal relations of States are relations neither of hostility nor indifference, as is alleged, not very justly perhaps, to have been the ancient opinion,—nor of mutual jealousy and distrust, which is still too much the modern opinion, but of amity and reciprocal confidence. This is the logical inference from the doctrines of Natural Law which we have elsewhere established. It is on this inference that all the doctrines of the Law of Nations rest, and its conquest, as a conscious starting point, is justly regarded as the greatest achievement of science in this department of inquiry. The much profaned principle of *fraternité*, when thus understood, brings the whole moral hemisphere within the range of scientific vision, and holds out to us a prospect of its practical exploration. Expanding from the person to the family, from the family to the State, and from the State to the community of States, the doctrine that 'love, which worketh no ill to its neighbour,' is 'the fulfilling of the law,' by bringing the law of Nations within the range of ethics, is preparing it gradually to assume the character of a positive jural system. But mutual goodwill by no means implies mutual interference or even co-operation, in ordinary circumstances. On the contrary, the capacity for self-support and self-government being, as we have seen,

* PROF. JAMES LORIMER. LL.D. The Institutes of the Law of Nations. Vol. I. p. 227.

conditions of recognition, non-interference may be enunciated as the primary duty which separate communities, simply as such, owe to each other. That, in the normal relations of jural entities, the negative takes precedence of the positive principle, is a maxim of universal application in jurisprudence, which follows as a corollary from the subjective origin which we have assigned both to rights and duties. As the first subjective right of every separate rational entity is the right to the unfettered exercise of the powers which God has conferred on him, and his first subjective duty is to exercise these powers in his own behalf, so, in like manner, the first objective right which this entity must acknowledge is the right of others to be relieved by his personal efforts of the burden of his support, and the first objective duty towards him is the duty of permitting him to energize for this purpose. Now separate States are such rational and responsible entities. It is on this ground, as we have seen, that their right to recognition rests,—and in their case, consequently, just as in the case of individuals that are *sui juris*, the rule must be in favour of non-interference. As time rolls on, and the experience of ages accumulates, the importance of this rule, not only for the sake of those in behalf of whose liberties it is invoked, but of those on whose ambition, or philanthropy, or restlessness, its restrictions are imposed, comes to be more and more clearly admitted. The interest of each is felt to be the interest of all; and the interest of each, with few and often doubtful exceptions, will be better promoted by leaving him to follow the bent of his own genius than by any rules that we can impose upon him, or even by any aid that we can afford him." *

* PROF. LORIMER. The Institutes of the Law of Nations, Vol. I. p. 230, et seq. IDEM. *Institutes of Law*. p. 101, et seq. 212 and 235.

The interdependence of States.

As explained above, in Chapter III, with regard to States as well as with regard to individuals, every right implies a correlative duty. Accordingly all international rights are bound up with corresponding obligations. Hence proceeds the interdependence of States. *

From the point of view of humanity and civilization, the normal condition of Nations appears to be a relationship of mutual goodwill and peace. From the necessity and the desire to secure this natural relationship, devolve various measures, including even war, when the state of equilibrium is disturbed and all peaceable means are exhausted.

The obligation of a State to render justice to all others, says Halleck, is a *perfect* obligation, of strictly binding force, at all times and under all circumstances. No State can relieve itself from this obligation, under any pretext whatever. It is an obligation, according to Vattel, 'more necessary still between Nations than between individuals; because injustice has more terrible consequences in the quarrels of these powerful bodies politic and it is more difficult to obtain redress.' The same rule applies to all the duties of a State which result from the *perfect* international rights of others, for whatever one Nation has a perfect right to demand of another, that is the other absolutely bound to surrender. The rule is absolute, and cannot be evaded by any technicality, sophistry, or under any other pretext. Whatever one State can claim as its perfect right, that it is the absolute duty of the other to concede. To refuse it, under any pretext whatsoever,

* Souveränität ist nicht absolute Unabhängigkeit, noch absolute Freiheit eines Staates, denn die Staaten sind keine absolute Wesen, sondern rechtlich beschränkte Personen. BLUNTSCHLI. Völkerrecht. § 65. Prof. LORIMER. The Institutes of the Law of Nations. Book III. Chapt. I.

would be a violation of the positive rule and fundamental principle of international jurisprudence, and no civilized Nation can now be found to refuse to another an acknowledged and indisputable right. They may dispute the right itself, and deny its existence as a right, but there is none so low and debased in moral character as to deny the duty and obligation to respect what is a manifest and acknowledged international right of another. Moreover, this obligation of the State is equally binding upon all its rulers, officers, and citizens,—in short upon each and every individual member that belongs to a State or body politic. *

* VATTEL. Droit des Gens. Liv. II. Ch. V. § 63. HALLECK. Intern. Law. Edit. Sir Sherston Baker. Vol. I. p. 392.

CHAPTER XIX.

RIGHT OF LEGATION, NEGOTIATION AND TREATY.

Right of presentation and legation.

§ 129. The measures generally resorted to in order to secure international relationship are in the first place those by which regular international communication is established between the respective Governments as the national organs of the States. This necessity establishes the right of presentation and of legation combined with that of negotiation and treaty.

The institution of permanent diplomatic missions between different States is the natural result of the progress of civilization. Among the ancient classical nations ambassadors were often employed and thus also in the Middle Ages, but permanent missions were first established in Europe after the peace of Westphalia. This is the era *par excellence*, and the starting point of the recognition accorded to permanent international intercourse which, growing more and more indispensable in proportion with the growing commercial and political interests of European States, caused the right of legation to become an established right in International Law. Thus it is now admitted that every independent State has both the right to send a public Minister to any other State with which it wishes to entertain amicable relations, and the duty to receive the public Ministers of other States. This right is however modified in proportion to the means of individual States and the nature of their reciprocal relations. *

With regard to the right of legation *(jus legationis)*, Sir Robert Phillimore makes the following remarks. "The principal rights and duties incident to embassies have been recognized by all communities at all removed from the condition of savages. Every Nation, so far *sui juris* as to be capable of negotiating, in its own name, with another Nation, has the right of sending an embassy *(droit actif, Actives Gesandtschaftsrecht)*. Therefore, not only independent States have this, among other *jura majestatis*, but dependent States which have not an entire sovereignty, may possess this right if the nature of their connexion with the protecting State allows them the liberty of conducting their foreign relations with other States." † *Right of embassy of dependent States.*

The same necessity and reasons have very generally caused the *jus legationis* to be granted to the European governors of American or Asiatic dependencies. The cases of the Governor-General of British India, the Governor-General of Netherlands India and the Spanish Governor-General of the Philippines are examples which readily occur. The great companies of European States, such as the Dutch, the French, and the British East India Companies, have often possessed this power. But this authority cannot be presumed; it must be conferred by the special and express grant of the respective Governments.

"International Law, strictly speaking," says Sir Robert Phillimore further, "is not concerned with cases of rebellion. There is no doubt that *Right of embassy of insurgents or rebels.*

* VATTEL. Droit des Gens. Liv. IV. Chap. V. § 55–65.

† PHILLIMORE. Comm. Intern. Law. Vol. II. p. 156.

rebellious *subjects* are not entitled to the *jus legationis* in their communications with their sovereign; the foundation of right is wanting. Nevertheless, when rebellion has grown, from the numbers who partake in it, the duration of it, the severity of the struggle, and other causes, into the terrible magnitude of a civil war, the emissaries of both parties have been considered entitled to the privilege of ambassadors, so far as their personal safety is concerned. '*In hoc eventu*,' Grotius says, '*gens una pro tempore quasi duæ gentes habetur*.'* Peace and order, under these circumstances, can only be restored, the shedding of blood can only be stayed, through the medium of negotiation: negotiation must be carried on through negotiators, and negotiators cannot act unless their personal security be guaranteed. So far as the State itself, in which the rebellion has broken out, is concerned, it must always be a question of circumstances, and incapable of definition beforehand, when the citizen is to be considered as entitled to the privilege of an enemy rather than the punishment of a rebel."

The right of sending an ambassador involves that of receiving.

"States which have the right to send, have the right to receive (*droit passif, passives Gesandtschaftsrecht*). The active and the passive right of legation are inseparably connected, and, as will be seen, the rule extends generally to the sending and reception of the same grade of diplomatic agents. It is said by Klüber and Miruss that dependent States have not necessarily the latter, because they have the former right. But it does not appear on what principle this position is to be maintained, and no authority is cited in support of it. On the other hand, Vattel, Martens, Wheaton and other writers do not qualify the general principle which has been laid down.

* GROTIUS. L. II. B. 18, 2.

Perhaps, however, where the right to send is exclusively derived from treaty, (as in the now obsolete cases of Moldavia and Wallachia), the right of reception, not being mentioned in the instrument, cannot be inferred as a matter of necessary implication. But, as a general proposition, the right of sending and receiving embassies is inherent in all States; and it therefore follows that to prevent the free exercise, in either way, of this right, would constitute a very heinous violation of International Law, a crime, which, inasmuch as it affected the interests, would justify the interference of all Nations on behalf of the one which had been so injured. A State has a right to receive, as it has to send, an embassy; but a State is not under an obligation of duty to send or to receive an embassy."

"Upon the consideration of this last point, three questions arise, viz.:— *Questions with regard to the obligation of sending and receiving an ambassador.*

1. Is a State bound, as a general proposition, to receive an ambassador at all?

2. Is it bound to receive any ambassador duly commissioned?

3. Is it bound to allow a resident embassy within its territories *(legationem assiduam)?*

"With respect to the first question, the sound opinion appears to be that a State is bound to give audience to an ambassador, and, except under most extraordinary circumstances, to receive him for that purpose within its territories and at its Court. If, however, such circumstances do exist, some place must be specified—Vattel suggests the frontier—at which the ambassador's message must be received. A State may be aware that an ambassador is sent for a mischievous purpose, or, it may be, from a third Nation for a purpose conceived to be inexpedient by the refusing State,

e. g. reconciliation with another State. In these cases, *ex eo ob quod mittitur*, it may refuse the ambassador."

"With respect to the second question, it may be unhesitatingly answered in the negative. It is in the discretion of the receiving State to refuse the reception of a certain diplomatic agent; but it is not altogether an arbitrary discretion. Some reason must be alleged for the refusal. '*Non enim*', says Grotius, '*omnes admitti præcipit gentium jus: sed vetat sine causa rejici.*'"

Ambassadresses. "A State cannot reasonably refuse to receive an ambassador on the grounds of sex. The League of Cambrai in 1508 was signed by Margaret of Austria, in the name of her brother, Charles V. In the same place Louisa of Savoy, mother of Francis, signed a peace, sometimes called Le Traité des Dames. It is said that, in the reign of Henry IV, France sent an ambassadress to Constantinople. In 1645, Louis XIV, sent la Maréchale de Guebriant to conduct to Poland the Princess des Gonzaques, bride to the King of Poland. Wicquefort says, erroneously, that she was the first female diplomatic agent. The Duchess of Orleans negotiated as Plenipotentiary the treaty between France and England, which in Charles II's time detached the latter country from its alliance with Holland. "*Minus frequentari,*" says Bynkershoek, "*mulierum legationes res certa est, sed non minus certa, etiam olim minus fuisse frequentatas. Sed plus minusve sint fuerintue frequentatæ, jus principis non tollit, ejus igitur voluntas, etiam in hac causa, suprema lex est.*" *

* BYNKERSHOEK. De Foro Leg. Chapt. XI. Quest. Jur. Pub. L. II. Chapt. V. .The Questiones Juris Publici were published after the treatise "De Foro Legatorum."

"A State may reasonably refuse to receive one of its own subjects as a foreign diplomatic agent, especially if its constitution forbid the subject ever to put off his allegiance. One very good reason for refusing such a diplomatic agent is the expediency of avoiding the very difficult question which may arise from a possible conflict between his privileges as a foreign ambassador with his present and former obligations contracted as a subject, for it will be seen that a class of these privileges is founded upon the fact that the bearer of them is not a subject of the country in which he is residing as an ambassador. Bynkershoek is of opinion that no objection exists to the employment of a subject; but he builds his opinion on the proposition that there is no reason why a subject should not serve two masters, or rather be actively the subject of one and passively the subject of another. Yet Bynkershoek himself is obliged to qualify his proposition with the condition that the interests of the two masters do not come into conflict, or that, if they do, the ambassador take no part in them. In France, it has been for some time settled as a constitutional maxim that subjects are not admissible as ambassadors. An exception appears to have been formerly made in favour of the ambassador from Malta. The Swedish Law equally forbids the reception of a subject as a foreign ambassador. The old German Confederation refused upon special grounds to receive any Frankfurt Burgher as the representative of any member of the Confederation except of Frankfurt itself."

Reasons for refusing particular individuals as ambassadors.

"As a State may exercise its right of refusal absolutely, it may also exercise it conditionally. A State may declare beforehand the terms under which it will consent to receive its own subject as a foreign diplomatic agent. But if the subject be received without any such previously promulgated stipulation, he will be entitled to the full *jus legationis.*"

"That the exile is in any case, though more especially if his return be forbidden by law, subject to the refusal of his own country, cannot be doubted; the only doubt is whether he can escape, by virtue of his ambassadorial character, punishment in the State which had exiled him, to which he has returned without permission and therefore with an additional offence. In 1697, the English ambassador to France obtained permission from the Government of that country to include among his suit certain Frenchmen and refugees on account of their religion, without which permission Bynkershoek thinks France might have claimed them "*ut reversos exules.*" *

With regard to the question of refusing an ambassador on account of his political nationality, this distinguished author makes the following remarks.

"The fact of the ambassador not being a native of the State which sent him would not alone afford a reasonable cause for refusal. The subject of a third country might be the domiciled citizen of the country which employed him as ambassador, and, even if he were not domiciled, no objection seems to lie against him, on the sole ground of his not being a native. The private rank or birth of the ambassador who is sufficiently ennabled by his Sovereign's choice can constitute no ground of refusal. The King of Spain employed Rubens as ambassador both to England and Holland (1633). A State, however, would for its own honour justly refuse a notoriously scandalous person, and less justly

* PHILLIMORE. Vol. II. p. 176, et seq.

but lawfully, any person known to be personally disagreeable to the head of the State." *

The notification of the refusal to receive ought to be made, if possible, before the ambassador has left his own country, but it may be imparted openly on his arrival, or tacitly by not accepting his letters of credit. †

The same author further states, that the existence of a state of war between two Nations by no means relieves them from the necessity of receiving each other's ambassadors, not of course for the purpose of residence but of audience. It may be necessary to demand a passport or safe conduct, through the intervention of a third State or of a herald, and what it is necessary to demand may be refused; but the refusal cannot lawfully be grounded on the mere existence of a state of war, for the greater the evil, the more stringent is the obligation upon Nations to adopt the readiest means of putting an end to it, and especially those which are most likely to prevent or stay the shedding of blood. ‡

In answer to the third question, whether a State is bound to allow a resident ambassador *(legationem assiduam)* within its territories, Sir Robert Phillimore gives the following opinion. "We have now arrived at the discussion of the third question propounded, viz.—Is a State bound to allow a resident embassy within its territories? The continuous residence of an embassy is, to speak strictly, a matter of *comity* and not of *strict right.* Nevertheless, so long a custom and so universal a consent have incorporated this permis-

* PHILLIMORE. Com. Intern. Law. Vol. II. p. 182.

† MIRUSS. Das Europäische Gesandtschaftsrecht. § 82.

‡ Sir ROBERT PHILLIMORE. Vol. II. p. 183. See VATTEL. Droit des Gens. L. IV. Chapt. V. § 67. Comment on doit admettre les ministres.

sion of continuous residence into the practice of Nations, that the gross discourtesy of refusing it would require unanswerable reasons for its justification, and would place the refusing in so unfriendly an attitude towards the refused State, as to be little removed from a condition of declared hostility. Grotius, indeed, says, *optimo autem jure rejici possunt, quæ nunc in usu sunt legationes assiduæ, quibus quam non sit opus, docet nos antiquitas cui illæ ignoratæ;* but it must be remembered that since this opinion was expressed, a usage of two additional centuries has imparted a character approaching to that of positive law upon this institution of resident embassies. Vattel therefore declares, that even in his time the custom was so deeply rooted as to require excellent reasons for its abrogation by any individual State." * (Comp. § 29).

Right of Negotiation and Treaty.

§ 130. Treaties and conventions between Nations are the means by which international rights are created, modified or extended, by developing or regulating the natural moral obligations between the contracting parties. Whilst moulding these natural moral obligations into practical rules, international agreements impose upon the respective parties special lines of conduct, by specifying the particular supplementary obligations, through mutual agreement, to do or to omit to do or to suffer third parties to do or omit to do certain special acts by which parties calculate to arrive at a certain definite aim.

The constitution of every State determines the authority in which is vested the power to conclude treaties binding on the State as body-politic.

* Sir ROBERT PHILLIMORE. Comm. Intern. Law. Vol. I. p. 41. and Vol. II. Edit. 1882. Part VI. Chapt. II & III. GROTIUS. Liv. II. Chapt. XVIII. § 3, 2. VATTEL. Liv. IV. Chapt. V.

As this power devolves from the Public Law of the State (§§ 37 & 38), international agreements are called public treaties or conventions *(pactum gentium publicum)*, in contra-distinction from private contracts, which the Government of a State sometimes enter into with private individuals or corporations,—whether native or foreign,—with regard to loans, or concessions of territories for agricultural, colonization, mining or any other industrial purposes. It is evident that only public treaties or conventions, as being agreements between States, belong to the domain of International Law. *

Different names given to international contracts.

There is no formula adopted as a standard for international agreements in general. The consent of contracting parties can be given expressly or tacitly. In the first case it is given verbally or in writing. Written consent can be given by way of a formal document, signed by the contracting agents of parties, or by declaration and contra-declaration in the form of letters, despatches or notes exchanged between the parties concerned or their agents. Verbal agreements, called *pourparlers*, must, as soon as practicable, be reduced to writing in order to avoid subsequent misunderstanding and contestation. Tacit consent of an agreement is inferred from undisputed facts of execution or the beginning of execution of the agreement.

Roman juris-consults divided international contracts into three classes, 1°. *pactiones*, 2°. *sponsiones*, and 3°. *fœdera*.

Treaty or Convention.

The *fœdera* were regarded as the most solemn agreement, regulating general principles of intercourse, and are now termed treaties or conven-

---

* VATTEL. Dr. des Gens. Liv. II. Chapt. 12. MARTENS. Précis des Droits des Gens Moderns. § 47. KLUBER. p. 141. ORTOLAN. Dipl. de la Mer. Vol. I. Chapt. V.

tions; such as treaties of peace, of offensive or defensive alliance, of commerce and navigation, for the extradition of criminals and deserters, for the mutual protection of literary, artistic or industrial properties, for uniformity in the monetary system, weights and measures, postal and telegraphic, fishery and railroad conventions, Consular conventions, etc. The term *declaration* is used for supplementary agreements with regard to the interpretation of a treaty or convention.

The *pactiones* are what we now call transitory conventions *(conventions transitoires)*, being agreements to be settled or accomplished within a certain given time or locality, having for their object some special mutual interest in a particular direction.

Sponsions.

The *sponsiones* are provisional or temporary agreements, concluded by agents not expressly qualified by special powers to treat, but who, through their actual position in the exercise of their general functions as officials of rank of the respective Government, are accidentally placed in a position to treat in the name of their respective Governments, on subjects directly or indirectly confided to their discretion. These agreements are invariably subjected to the *conditio sine qua non* of the consent of the respective Governments, when they are contracted without authorisation and when they exceed the authority of one or more of the contracting agents. Such agreements are *per se*, null and void if the consent of the respective power is withheld. If, however, any of the contracting powers has acted in good faith on the supposition that the other party was duly represented, then indemnification is due to that party and restoration to its previous condition. *

* GROTIUS. De Jure belli ac pacis. Liv. III. chap. XXII. §§ 6 & 8. VATTEL. Dr. des Gens. Liv. II. chap. XIV. §§ 209–212. RUTHERFORTH. Instit. Book II. Chap. IX. § 21. WHEATON. Elem. of Int. Law. Part III. Chap. II.

§ 131. There is a special sort of convention; which is the official agreement made between generals or admirals of belligerent powers when, by mutual consent, active hostilities are limited or suspended by land or at sea within the sphere of the respective commands of the contracting authorities. Such suspension of hostilities, called armistice, can be arranged temporarily as for the exchange of prisoners *(cartel d'échange de prisonniers)*, for the removal of the sick or wounded, permission for special commerce under certain conditions;—or indefinitely, as the capitulation of fortresses, towns or provinces. The armistice preceding peace is always ordered by the respective Governments, this being always the result of a preliminary convention which must pave the way to a treaty of peace. The preliminaries are also always negotiated by duly qualified agents appointed by the respective Governments. These preliminaries, forming the basis of peace, require the utmost skill of diplomacy, combined with explicit statements and information from the theatre of war, frankly and accurately provided by the Commanders to their respective diplomatic agent, at the preliminary conference. This is indispensable in order to establish, punctually and with all precision, the *status quo* to be observed during the armistice. *Conventions for the suspension of hostilities (armistices).*

The armistice for the preliminaries of peace having been duly agreed upon by authorized agents of both parties, the conditions of the armistice must at once, be explicitly obeyed and adhered to by the military authorities on both sides, without awaiting any ratification from the respective central Governments. The exchange of places or positions or the capitulations agreed upon, must be faithfully accomplished within the term fixed by the armistice convention, and the *status quo* of the armistice must be brought about without unnecessary delay, in strict adherence to the wording of the convention. In case the respective Government does not come to an agreement on the preliminary basis of peace, the revocation of the armistice must be duly notified by the revoking party to the other, and a day named, within a reasonable period of time, on which hostilities may be resumed. Every well directed negotiation for a preliminary armistice invariably contains the necessary provisions with regard to the above stated cases.

Ratification of Treaty.

§ 132. With the exception of military arrangements, which are of momentary exigence, as stated in the preceeding paragraph, treaties or conventions, in the ordinary sense, do not become binding by the sole signature of the negotiating agents. The confirmation of the agreement, by the executive power of the States concerned, is necessary for the complete validity of the agreements entered into by their agents. This confirmation given to the work of their plenipotentiaries by the contracting States, is called ratification. The reservation of ratification is indispensable in the case of all treaties and conventions concluded in behalf of those Governments which are dependent upon the sanction of their respective legislatures.

As the power to conclude treaties depends of the Public Law or Constitution of each State, the ratification by one party does not alter the right of the other to refuse ratification. With the exception of the case of rejection by the legislature, the Governments never refuse to sanction the agreement of their plenipotentiaries, when these have not exceeded their powers, unless there be exceptional circumstances providing conclusive material reasons for a change of a policy.

With regard to the ratification of treaties, Mr. Woolsey makes the following statements.

"Unless some other time is agreed upon, treaties are binding at the time when they are signed by an authorized agent, and their ratification by their sovereign is retroactive. If then an ambassador, in conformity with a full power received from his sovereign, has negotiated and signed a treaty, is the sovereign justified in withholding his ratification? This question has no significance in regard to States, by whose form of government the engagements made by the executive with foreign powers need some further sanction. In other cases, that is, wherever the treaty-making power of the sovereign is final, the older writers held that he was bound by the acts of his agent, if the latter acted within the full power which he had received, even though he had gone contrary to secret instructions. But Bynkershoek defended another opinion which is now the received one among the text-writers, and which Wheaton has advocated at large with great ability." *

"If the minister has conformed at once to his ostensible powers and to his secret instructions, there is no doubt that, in ordinary cases, it would be bad faith in the sovereign not to add ratification. But if the minister disobeys or transcends his instructions, the sovereign may refuse his sanction to the treaty without bad faith or ground of complaint on the other side. But even this violation of secret instructions would be no valid excuse for the sovereign's refusing to accept the treaty, if he should have given public credentials of a minute and specific character to his agent; for the evident intention, in so doing,

* WHEATON'S. Elements. Book III. 2. § 5. BYNKERSHOEK' Quæst. J. P. II. 7. De MARTENS. § 48.

would be to convey an impression to the other party, that he is making a sincere declaration of the terms on which he is willing to treat. And even when the negotiator has followed his private instructions, there are cases, according to Dr. Wheaton, where the sovereign may refuse his ratification. He may do so when the motive for making the treaty was an error in regard to a matter of fact, or when the treaty would involve an injury to a third party, or when there is a physical impossibility of fulfilling it, or when such a change of circumstances takes place as would make the treaty void after ratification. All questions would be removed if in the full power of the negotiation or in a clause of the treaty itself, it were declared that the sovereign reserved to himself the power of giving validity to the treaty by ratification. This, if we are not deceived, is now very generally the case." *

Interpretation of treaties and conventions.

§ 133. "Treaties of every kind," says Kent, "are to receive a fair and liberal interpretation, according to the intention of the contracting parties, and to be kept with the most scrupulous good faith. Their meaning is to be ascertained by the same rules of construction and course of reasoning which we apply to the interpretation of private contracts." The same general rule is laid down by Wheaton, but he adds: "Such is the inevitable imperfection and ambiguity of all human language, that the mere words alone of any writing, literally expounded, will go a very little way towards explaining the meaning. Certain technical rules of interpretation have, therefore, been adopted by writers on ethics and public law, to explain the meaning of international compacts, in cases of doubts." These rules are most

* WOOLSEY. Intern. Law. Edit. 1879. p. 178, et seq.

fully expounded by Grotius, Vattel, Rutherforth and Paley.*

Halleck gives a brief outline of the principles of interpretation, as laid down by these authors, of which we quote the following.

"Grotius has devoted an entire chapter to the interpretation of difficult and ambiguous terms. He sets out with the saying of Cicero, that, 'when you promise, we must consider rather what you mean, than what you say.' But as inward motives are not in themselves discernible, we can determine what they were only from the *words* used, and *conjectures* drawn from other parts of the treaty, and from the peculiar circumstances of the particular case. These, he says, must sometimes be considered together, and sometimes separately. Words are not to be strictly construed according to their etymology, but according to their common use, as 'use is the judge, the law, and rule of speech.' Technical words, or terms of art are to be construed according to their meaning in such art. Conjectures are to be drawn from the subject matter, the effect of the terms used, and the circumstances under which the engagement was entered into. He divides things promised into three classes, *favourable*, *odious* and *mixed*. Favourable promises are those which carry in them an equality and a common advantage; odious promises are those where the charge and burthen are all on one side; and mixed promises are those which partake of both characters, but in which the favourable predominates. In the first, he says, the words must be taken in their full propriety, as they are generally understood, and if ambiguous, they must be allowed their largest sense. In

* KENT. Com. on Am. Law. Vol. I. p. 174. WHEATON. Elem. Int. Law. Part III. Ch. 2. § 17.

the second, the words are to be taken in a stricter sense, whether they have reference to the subject matter, time, or circumstances. In the third kind of promises, the words are to be taken according to the character of the particular stipulation in which they occur, or of the particular matter or circumstances to which they refer." *

These distinctions are particularly commented on by Vattel, who lays down several maxims for the interpretation of treaties, which may be briefly stated as follows. 1st. It is not allowable to interpret what has no need of interpretation, for when a treaty is conceived in clear and precise terms, and the sense is manifest, and leads to no absurdity, there can be no reason for refusing the sense which is naturally presented and manifest. To go elsewhere in search of conjectures, is to endeavour to elude it. 2nd. If he who could and ought to have explained himself clearly, has not done so, he cannot be allowed to introduce subsequent restrictions for his own benefit. *Pactionem obscuram iis nocere, in quorum fuit potestate legem assertius conscribere.* 3rd. Neither of the contracting Powers is allowed to interpret the treaty at his own pleasure. 4th. As the party which made the promise ought to have known his intention, what he has sufficiently declared must be taken for true against him. 5th. The interpretation should be made according to the rules established for determining the sense in which the parties naturally understood it when the treaty was entered into. He next proceeds to lay down the following particular rules on which the interpretation ought to be formed, in order to be just and right. 1st. We must seek to discover the thoughts of the parties who drew up

* GROTIUS. De Jure Belli ac. Pac. Lib. II. Cap. XVI.

the treaty, and interpret it accordingly. Thus, we must give to a disposition the full extent properly implied in the terms, if such appears to have been the intention of the parties; but its signification should be restrained, if it is probable that the parties at the time so understood it. 2nd. No mental reservations can be admitted. 3rd. Common expressions and terms are to be taken according to common custom. 4th. Technical terms, or terms proper to the arts and sciences, are generally to be interpreted according to the definition given to them by persons versed in such art or science. 5th. We should give to equivocal expressions the sense most suitable to the subject or matter to which they relate. 6th. The same term is not necessarily to be taken in the same sense wherever it appears in the same instrument. 7th. Every interpretation that leads to an absurdity should be rejected. 8th. An interpretation that would render a treaty null and without effect should be rejected. 9th. Vague and obscure expressions should be interpreted in such a manner as to agree with the terms which are clear and without ambiguity. 10th. The whole treaty must be considered together, and an interpretation given to each particular expression so as to agree with the tenor of the whole instrument. 11th. The words of a party should be construed in accordance with the general reasons and motives of the agreement. 12th. The interpretation may be restrictive or extensive, according to reasons and probable intention of the contracting parties. *

" Rutherforth, says Halleck further, has discussed this subject with his usual perspicuity and ability, but in a manner somewhat diffuse.

* VATTEL. Droit des Gens. Liv. II. Chapt. 17. §§ 263–298.

We will attempt but a brief outline of his remarks, referring the reader to his chapter on interpretation, the perusal of which will afford both pleasure and profit. A promise, he says, gives us a right to whatever the promiser designed or intended to make ours. But his design or intention, if it be considered merely as an act of his mind, cannot be known to anyone besides himself. When, therefore, we speak of his design or intention as the measure of our claim, we must necessarily be understood to mean the design or intention which he has made known or expressed by some outward mark; because a design or intention, which does not appear, can have no more effect, or can no more produce a claim, than a design or intention which does not exist. Hence, the way to ascertain our claims, as they arise from promises or contracts, is to collect the meaning and intention of the promiser or contractor, from some outward signs or marks. The collecting of a man's intention from such signs or marks is called *interpretation*."

"The remarks of Dr. Paley, in his work on Moral and Political Philosophy, are well worthy of attention, being as applicable to questions of International Law as to questions in ethics. He says: 'Where the terms of promise admit of more senses than one, the promise is to be performed in that sense in which the promiser apprehended at the time that the promisee received it.' It is not the sense in which the promiser actually intended it, that always governs the interpretation of an equivocal promise, because, at that rate, you might excite expectations which you never meant, nor would be obliged to satisfy. Much less is it the sense in which the promisee actually received the promise; for, according to that rule, you might be drawn into engagements which you never designed to undertake. It must, therefore, be the sense, (for there is no other remaining,) in which the promiser believed that the promisee accepted the promise. This will not differ from the actual intention of the promiser, where the promise is given without collusion or reserve; but we put the rule in the above form to exclude evasion in cases in which the popular meaning of a phrase and the strict grammatical signification of the words differ; or, in general, wherever the promiser attempts to make his escape through some ambiguity in the expressions which he used. Zemures promised the garrison of Sebastia, that if they would surrender, no blood should be shed. The garrison surrendered, and Zemures buried them all alive. Now Zemures fulfilled the promise in one sense, and in the sense, too, in which he intended at the time; but not in the sense in which the garrison of Sebastia actually received it, nor in the sense in which Zemures himself knew that the garrison received it, which last sense, according to our rule, was the sense in which he was, in conscience, bound to have performed it."

"Many efforts have been made by other writers to lay down precise and positive rules, and to frame formulæ for the various modes of interpretation. In order to facilitate this, a nomenclature of classes, modes and species of construction has been attempted, and numerous cases, actual or possible, have been resorted to for the purpose of elucidating these definitions, and of exhibiting the application of these rules. Thus, Leiber distinguishes between interpretation and construction, dividing the former into close, extensive, extravagant, limited or free, predestinated and authentic; and the latter in close, comprehensive, transcendent, and extravagant. The classifications, rules, and arbitrary formulæ which he has given under these heads, are more calculated to astonish and puzzle the reader, as a metaphysical curiosity, than to afford any real assistance in the interpretation or construction of treaties or laws. The same remark is applicable, in a qualified sense, to the numerous rules of the learned Domat. Others, again, as Mackelday and Phillimore, have adopted a more simple classification, and fewer and more general rules."

"The best modern writers on interpretation have confined themselves to stating the general principles which are to guide us in ascertaining the true meaning of a treaty, law or contract, avoiding all metaphysical distinctions, minute subdivision of terms and the use of arbitrary formulæ. Of this character are the rules laid down by Story, in his commentaries on the constitution of the United States. He regards some of the rules of Vattel as erroneous, but speaks in high terms of those given by Rutherforth, a summary of which is found in the preceding pages. Savigny regards the civil law rules of interpretation—which are substantially those of Domat—as affording little aid beyond that which an intelligent and dispassionate consideration of each particular case would fournish. Sedgwick thinks it 'as vain to attempt to frame positive and fixed rules of interpretation as to endeavour, in the same way, to define the mode by which the mind shall draw conclusions from testimony. . . . . Nor do I believe it easy to prescribe any system of rules of interpretation for cases of ambiguity, in written language, that will really avail to guide the mind in the decision of doubts.' But while we fully agree with Savigny and Sedgwick, that metaphysical classifications, minute sub-divisions and arbitrary formulæ, are not calculated to facilitate the interpretation and construction of laws, it must not be inferred that all rules established for that purpose should be rejected. On the contrary, general rules, which restrain from latitudinarian construction, and from extravagant and false interpretation, have received the approval of the most learned jurists and most distinguished publicists of all ages. Indeed, the very necessity and importance of such rules, for the interpretation of constitutional and statutory laws, have led some authors into the extravagant nomenclature and minute classification which are here objected to. Sedgwick, notwithstanding his objection to rules, very justly remarks that 'there must be some general principles to control' the construction and interpretation of laws, the subject being too important 'to be left to the mere arbitrary discretion of the judiciary.'"

"And if the necessity of well-established rules for the interpretation of laws be generally admitted, it certainly will hardly be denied that such rules are equally important in connection with international jurisprudence. Some of the bloodiest wars that have been inflicted upon the human race have originated in a conflict of opinions respecting the interpretation of treaty stipulations. Moreover, it not unfrequently happens, that when one Nation seeks an excuse for quarrelling with another, or for encroaching on another's rights, some old and long forgotten treaty is brought forth from the dusty archives, or some new interpretation is introduced, with corresponding allegations of a violation of its stipulations. It is not pretended that any rules of interpretation, however complete or well established they may be, will entirely prevent such conflicts and aggressions; nevertheless, they will greatly contribute towards such a result, or, at least, will prevent the real aggressor in an unjust war from escaping the odium which should attach to one who disturbs the peace of Nations, under the cloak of a false interpretation of treaty stipulations." *

Interpretation of conflicting agreements.

Where treaties or treaty stipulations are in collision or opposition, that is, where two promises are not contradictory to themselves, but are of such a nature as to render it impossible to fulfil both at the same time, Vattel lays down the following rules for determining which shall have the preference. 1st. If what is permitted is incompatible with what is prescribed, the latter is to be preferred. 2nd. What is permitted must yield to what is forbidden. 3rd. What is ordained must yield to what is forbidden. 4th. Other things being equal, that of the most recent date is to be preferred. 5th. A special promise is to be preferred to a general one. 6th. What, from its nature, cannot be delayed is to be preferred to what may be done at another time. 7th. When two promises or duties are incompatible, that of the highest honesty and utility is to have the preference. 8th. If we cannot perform at the same time two promises to the same person, he may select which he prefers. 9th. The stronger obligation has the preference over the weaker. 10th. What is promised under the higher penalty, has the preference over one with the lesser penalty, or with no penalty at all. †

Rules of Vattel.

Rules of Mr. Hall.

Mr. Hall gives with regard to conflicts occurring between different provisions of a treaty or between different treaties, the following rules:—

* HALLECK. Intern. Law. Edit. Sir Sherston Baker. Vol. I. Chapt. VIII.

† VATTEL. Droit des Gens. Liv. II. Ch. 17. §§ 311–322. PUFFENDORF. De Jure Gent. Liv. V. Cap. 12. § 23.

1. A generally or specifically imperative provision takes precedence of a general permission. Thus if a treaty concedes a right of fishing over certain territorial waters, and at the same time prohibits the persons to whom permission is given from landing to dry or cure the fish which may be caught, the prohibition out-weighs the permission, notwithstanding that the power of curing and drying on the spot may be found to be so essential to the enjoyment of the fishing, that the right to fish is nullified by its absence.

2. On the other hand, a special permission takes precedence of a general imperative provision; that is to say, if a treaty contains an agreement couched in general terms, and also an agreement with regard to a particular matter which, if allowed to operate, will act as an exception from the former agreement, effect is given to the exception.

3. If a penalty for non-observance is attached to one of two prohibitory stipulations and not to the other, or if a more severe penalty is attached to one than the other, preference is given to that which is the better guarded. If a penalty is attached to neither, the stipulation has precedence which has the more precision in its command.

4. When stipulations are of identical nature, that is to say when both are general and prohibitory or special and imperative etc., and no priority can be ascribed to either upon the grounds mentioned in the last rule, that which is the more important must be observed by the party obliged, unless the promisee, who is at liberty to choose that the less important stipulation shall be performed, exercises his power of choice in that direction.

5. When two treaties made between the same States at different dates conflict, the later governs, it being supposed to be in substitution for the earlier contract. It is hardly an exception from this rule that, when of two conflicting treaties the later is made by an inferior though competent authority, the earlier is preferred.

6. When two treaties conflict which are made with different States at different times, the earlier governs, it being of course impossible to derogate from an engagement made with a particular person by a subsequent agreement with another person entered into without his consent. Hence, until all the parties to a treaty have consented to forego their rights under it, no subsequent treaty incompatible with it can be valid; any such treaty is null at least to the extent of its direct incompatibility; and if the incompatible portions are not separable from the remainder, it is null in its entirety. *

Durability of the obligatory force of treaties for which no time of expiration has been stipulated.

§ 134. The validity of a treaty depends essentially on the free will and mutual consent of the contracting parties, so that, as a general rule, mutual consent is likewise required for the dissolution of the contract. However there are circumstances which may afford sufficient grounds upon which a treaty may be repudiated by one of the parties. Woolsey maintains that a treaty in which the treaty-making Power flagitiously sacrifices the interests of the Nation which it represents, has no binding force. In this case the treacherous act of the Government cannot be justly regarded as the act of the Nation and the forms ought to give way to the realities of things.

* GROTIUS. Lib. II. Chapt. XVI. § 29. VATTEL. Liv. II. Chapt. XVII. §§ 321–22. PHILLIMORE. II. Chapt. IX. CALVO. §§ 604–7. W. E. HALL. Intern. Law. p. 285.

Lésion, which is inequality of advantages derived from the contract, does not invalidate a treaty when one of the parties was under a wrong impression, not necessarily through false representations of the other party, but through that party's own want of judgment. When one of the parties acts under a wrong impression or formed a false judgment of the other's power, this other is not responsible, for the consideration is not a real objective good, but the expectation of good which may not be realized. Thus if a garrison capitulates under a mistaken calculation as to the force of the besieging army or the probability of relief, and discovers the mistake before the capitulation takes effect, the capitulation is still binding. *

Relief through invalidity of a treaty on account of fear, fraud or incompetency of the contracting agent, places the relieved party altogether in the same situation in which that party was before the contracting of the obligation, provided that the other party be also replaced exactly into the position in which it previously was. This imposes on the other side the obligation to effect a restitution of all fruits and profits received, as also compensation for all losses. The relief is also of effect against third parties which are benefitted by the contract or obligation.

By fear is meant serious personal apprehensions, as of death, dishonour, great sufferings, imprisonment or ill-treatment of the contracting agent or his family, and in general all individual compulsion which has a definite personal feature. Fraud is an act or instrumentality by which an unfair or unlawful advantage, injuring the interests of another party, is sought to be gained deceitfully.

* WOOLSEY, p. 168.

When any obligation is contracted through fraud perpetrated on both sides, the transaction is void from the beginning. *

Two conspicuous historical incidents with regard to the durability of international treaties, in our time, ought to be mentioned here. We mean the Treaty of Paris of 1856 and the Clayton Bulwer Treaty of 1850. With regard to the Treaty of Paris of 1856, Sir Robert Phillimore makes the following statements.

Opinion of Sir Robert Phillimore.

"Private contracts may be set aside on the ground of the inferences of fraud and unfair dealing arising from their manifest injustice and want of mutual advantage. But no inequality of advantage, no *lésion*, can invalidate a treaty. It is truly said by Vattel, '*si l'on pouvait revenir d'un traité, parce qu'on s'y trouverait lésé, il n'y aurait rien de stable dans les contrats des nations.*' No more dangerous attempt has ever been made than that of Russia in 1870, to escape from the obligations of the Treaty of 1856 on this pretext."

The Treaty of Paris of 1856.

"The International writer may point, with at least some satisfaction, to the refusal of all the other Powers to admit the plea of Russia, and to the Protocol which prefaced the new Treaty of 1871. A Conference was held in London in the early parts of that year, to consider the Treaty of 1856. Earl Granville, President of the Conference, said:—

"The Conference has been accepted by all the "co-signatory Powers of the Treaty of 1856, for "the purpose of examining without any foregone "conclusion, and of discussing with perfect free-"dom, the proposals which Russia desires to make "to us with regard to the revision which she asks "of the stipulations of the said Treaty relative to "the neutralisation of the Black Sea."

* GROTIUS, Introduction to Dutch Jurisprudence, Chapt. XLVIII.

"This unanimity furnishes a striking proof that "the Powers recognize that it is an essential prin-"ciple of the Law of Nations, that none of them "can liberate itself from the engagements of a "treaty, nor modify the stipulations thereof, unless "with the consent of the contracting parties, by "means of an amicable understanding."

"This important principle appears to me to "meet with general acceptance, and I have the "honour to propose to you, gentlemen, to sign a "protocol *ad hoc*."

The protocol in question was then submitted to the Conference and signed by all the Plenipotentiaries, that is to say, Prussia or North Germany, Austria, Great Britain, Italy, Russia, Turkey, and, by subsequent adoption, France. All subscribed to the maintenance of this primary and elementary principle of Internationol Law; and under the circumstances such subscription was most valuable to the welfare of States. *

With regard to this treaty, Mr. Hall makes the following statements.

In 1856 the Crimean war ended by the Treaty of Paris. The object of the treaty was to settle the affairs of the East, so far as possible, in a permanent manner; and in order that this should be done, it was considered necessary to secure Turkey against being attacked by Russia under conditions decidedly advantageous to the latter Power. To this end the prevention of the naval preponderance of Russia in the Black Sea was essential, and the simplest mode of prevention was to forbid the maintenance of a fleet. This course was accordingly fixed upon. But as, without a fleet, Russia would be exposed to

* Sir ROBERT PHILLIMORE. Vol. II. p. 76. VATTEL. Liv. II. Chapt. XII. § 158.

danger in the event of war with a third Power, unless access to the Black Sea were denied to its enemy, and as at the same time, in the absence of a Russian navy, the presence of foreign fleets was unnecessary to Turkey, the Treaty of Paris, while limiting the number of vessels to be kept within the Black Sea by the two Powers respectively, contained also a promise on the part of Turkey to close the Bosphorus to foreign vessels of war except in case of hostilities in which she was herself engaged; and the Black Sea was declared to be neutral. In 1870 the Russian Government seized the occasion presented by the Franco-German war, to escape from the obligations under which it lay, and issued a circular declaring itself to be no longer bound by that part of the Treaty of Paris which had reference to the Black Sea.

Lord Granville, in answering the Russian circular, took it for granted that no breach of the treaty, by the other contracting parties, had taken place which could free Russia from her obligations, and confined himself to the question in whose hand lay the power of releasing one or more of the parties to the treaty from all or any of its stipulations. It has always been held, he says, that the right of releasing a party to a treaty belongs only to the Governments who have been parties to the original instrument. The despatches of the Russian Government appear to assume that any one of the Powers who have signed the engagement may allege that occurrences have taken place which, in its opinion, are at variance with the provisions of the treaty, and though their view is not shared nor admitted by the co-signatary Powers, may found upon that allegation, not a request to those Governments for a consideration of the case, but an announcement to them that it has emancipated itself, or holds itself emancipated, from any stipulations of the treaty which it thinks fit to disapprove. Yet it is quite evident that the effect of such a doctrine and of any proceeding, which, with or without avowal, is founded upon it, is to bring the entire authority and efficacy of treaties under the discretionary control of each of the Powers who may have signed them; the result of which would be the entire destruction of treaties in their essence."

The protest of Lord Granville, says Mr. Hall further, although uttered under circumstances which made its practical importance at the moment very slight, nevertheless compelled Russia to abandon the position which it had taken up. A conference of such of the Powers, signatary of the Treaty of Paris, as could attend was held, at which it was declared that it is an essential principle of the Law of Nations that no Power can liberate itself from the engagements of a treaty, nor modify the stipulations thereof, unless with the consent of the contracting Powers by means of an amicable arrangement. The general correctness of the principle is indisputable, and in a declaration of the kind made it would have been impossible to enounce it with those qualifications which have been seen to be necessary in practice. The force of its assertion may have been impaired by the fact that Russia, as the reward of submission to law, was given what she had affected to take. But the concessions made were dictated by political considerations, with which International Law has nothing to do. It is enough from the legal point of view, that the declaration purported to affirm a principle as existing, and that it was ultimately signed by all the leading Powers of Europe. *

* W. E. HALL. Intern. Law. Edit. 1880. p. 297-301.

The Clayton-Bulwer Treaty.

The Clayton-Bulwer Treaty, A.D. 1850, * concluded between Great Britain and the United States, respecting the future use of the canal in course of construction between the Atlantic and Pacific oceans by way of San Juan de Nicaragua, has undergone discussions which somewhat threatened to affect International Law.

The correspondence which took place between the American Secretary of State (Mr. Blaine) and the English Secretary for Foreign Affairs (Earl Granville), in which suggestions were made by the former for the abrogation or modification of the treaty in question, will be found in the papers respecting the "projected Panama canal," presented to Parliament by command of Her Majesty, 1882. Earl Granville, in his despatch to Mr. West, the British Minister at Washington, states the following conclusions at which the British Government had arrived in this matter:—

* This Treaty concerning the formation of a canal or railway across the Isthmus of Central America, is, both on account of its immediate object, and the principle which it recognizes, of such vast importance that it is not out of our way to reproduce it here in full.

The preamble sets forth that, "Her Britannic Majesty and the United States of America being desirous of consolidating the relations of amity which so happily subsist between them, by setting forth and fixing in a Convention their views and intentions with reference to any means of communication by ship-canal, which may be constructed between the Atlantic and Pacific oceans by the way of the river St. Juan de Nicaragua, and either or both of the lakes of Nicaragua or Managua, to any port or place on the Pacific ocean, &c."

The text runs as follows:—"Art. 1. The Governments of Great Britain and the United States hereby declare that neither the one nor the other will ever obtain or maintain for itself any exclusive control over the said ship-canal; agreeing that neither will ever erect or maintain any fortifications commandi g the same, or in the vicinity thereof, or occupy, or fortify, or colonize, or assume or exercise any dominion over Nicaragua, Costa Rica, the Mosquito Coast, or any part of Central America; nor will either make use of any protection which either affords or may afford, or any alliance which either has or may have, to or with any State or people, for the purpose of erecting or maintaining any such fortifications, or of occupying, fortifying, or colonizing Nicaragua, Costa Rica, the Mosquito Coast, or any part of Central America, or of assuming or exercising dominion over the same. Nor will Great Britain or the United States take

"1. That the differences which arose between the two Governments in regard to the treaty, and which occasioned at one time considerable irritation, but which have long since been happily disposed of, did not relate to the general principles to be observed in regard to the means of inter-oceanic communication across the isthmus, but had their origin in a stipulation which Mr. Blaine still proposes in great part to maintain. He wishes every part of the treaty, in which Great Britain and the United States agree to make no acquisition of territory in Central

---

advantage of any intimacy, or use any alliance, connection, or influence that either may possess with any State or Government through whose territory the said canal may pass, for the purpose of acquiring or holding, directly or indirectly, for the subjects or citizens of the one, any rights or advantages, in regard to commerce or navigation through the said canal, which shall not be offered on the same terms to the subjects or citizens of the other."

"Art. 2. Vessels of Great Britain or the United States traversing the said canal shall, in case of war between the contracting parties, be exempted from blockade, detention, or capture by either of the belligerents; and this provision shall extend to such a distance from the two ends of the said canal as it may hereafter be found expedient to establish."

"Art. 3. In order to secure the construction of the said canal, the contracting parties engage that if any such canal shall be undertaken upon fair and equitable terms by any parties having the authority of the local Government or Governments through whose territory the same may pass, then the persons employed in making the said canal and their property used or to be used for that object shall be protected, from the commencement of the said canal, to its completion, by the Governments of Great Britain and the United States from unjust detention, confiscation, seizure, or any violence whatsoever."

"Art. 4. The contracting parties will use whatever influence they respectively exercise with any State, States, or Governments possessing, or claiming to possess, any jurisdiction or right over the territory which the said canal shall traverse, or which shall be near the waters applicable thereto, in order to induce such States or Governments to facilitate the construction of the said canal by every means in their power; and, furthermore, Great Britain and the United States agree to use their good offices, where-ever or however it may be most expedient, in order to procure the establishment of two free ports, one at each end of the said canal."

"Art. 5. The contracting parties further engage, that when the said canal shall have been completed, they will protect it from interruption, seizure, or unjust confiscation and that they will guarantee the neutrality thereof, so that the said canal may for ever be open and free, and the capital invested therein secure. Nevertheless, the Governments of Great Britain, and the United States, in according

America, to remain in full force, while he desires to cancel those portions of the treaty which forbid the United States fortifying the canal, and holding the political control of it in conjunction with the country in which it is located."

"2. That the declarations of the United States' Government during the controversy were distinctly at variance with any such proposal as that just stated. They disclaimed any desire to obtain an exclusive or preferential control over the canal. Their sole contention was, that Great Britain was bound by the treaty to abandon

---

their protection to the construction of the said canal, and guaranteeing its neutrality and security when completed, always understand that this protection and guarantee are granted conditionally, and may be withdrawn by both Governments, or either Government, if both Governments or either Government should deem that the persons or company undertaking or managing the same adopt or establish such regulations concerning the traffic thereupon as are contrary to the spirit and intention of this Convention, either by making unfair discriminations in favour of the commerce of one of the contracting parties over the commerce of the other or by imposing oppressive exactions or unreasonable tolls upon passengers, vessels, goods, wares, merchandise, or other articles. Neither party, however, shall withdraw the aforesaid protection and guarantee, without first giving six months' notice to the other."

"Art. 6. The contracting parties in this Convention engage to invite every State with which both or either have friendly intercourse to enter into stipulations with them, similar to those which they have entered into with each other, to the end that all other States may share in the honour and advantage of having contributed to a work of such general interest and importance as the canal herein contemplated; and the contracting parties likewise agree that each shall enter into treaty stipulations with such of the Central American States as they may deem advisable, for the purpose of more effectually carrying out the great design of this Convention, namely, that of constructing and maintaining the said canal as a ship communication between the two oceans for the benefit of mankind, on equal terms to all, and of protecting the same; and they also agree, that the good offices of either shall be employed when requested by the other, in aiding and assisting the negotiation of such treaty stipulations; and should any differences arise as to right or property over the territory through which the said canal shall pass, between the States or Governments of Central America, and such differences should in any way impede or obstruct the execution of the said canal, the Governments of Great Britain and the United States will use their good offices to settle such differences, in the manner best suited to promote the interests of the said canal, and to strengthen the bonds of friendship and alliance which exist between the contracting parties."

those positions on the mainland or adjacent islands, which, in their opinion, were calculated to give her the means of such a control. Nor did they in any way seek to limit the application of the principles laid down in the treaty so as to exclude Columbian or Mexican territory, as Mr. Blaine now suggests, nor urge that such application would be inconsistent with the Convention between the United States and New Granada of 1846. On the contrary, they were ready to give those principles their full extension."

"Art. 7. It being desirable that no time should be unnecessarily lost in commencing and constructing the said canal, the Governments of Great Britain and the United States determine to give their support and encouragement to such persons or company as may first offer to commence the same, with the necessary capital, the consent of the local authorities, and on such principles as accord with the spirit and intention of this Convention: and if any persons or company should already have, with any State through which the proposed ship-canal may pass, a contract for the construction of such a canal as that specified in this Convention, to the stipulations of which contract neither of the contracting parties in this Convention have any just cause to object, and the said persons or company shall, moreover, have made preparations and expended time, money, and trouble on the faith of such contract, it is hereby agreed that such persons or company shall have a priority of claim over every other person, persons, or company, to the protection of the Governments of Great Britain and the United States, and be allowed a year, from the date of the exchange of the ratifications of this Convention, for concluding their arrangements, and presenting evidence of sufficient capital subscribed to accomplish the contemplated undertaking; it being understood that if, at the expiration of the aforesaid period, such persons or company be not able to commence and carry out the proposed enterprise, then the Governments of Great Britain and the United States shall be free to afford their protection to any other persons or company that shall be prepared to commence and proceed with construction of the canal in question.

"Art. 8. The Governments of Great Britain and the United States having not only desired, in entering into this Convention, to accomplish a particular object, but also *to establish a general principle*, they hereby agreed to extend their protection by treaty stipulations to any other practicable communications, *whether by canal or railway*, across the isthmus which connects North and South America; and especially to the inter-oceanic communications, should the same prove to be practicable, whether by canal or railway, which are now proposed to be established by the way of Tehnantepec or Panama. In granting, however, *their joint protection to any such canal or railways* as are by this Article specified, it is always understood by Great Britain and the United States, that the parties constructing or owning the same shall impose no other charges or conditions of traffic thereupon than the aforesaid Governments shall approve of

"3. That at a time when the British Government had been induced by the long continuance of the controversy to contemplate the abrogation of the treaty, they were only willing to do so on the condition of reverting to the *status quo ante* its conclusion in 1850; a solution which was at that time possible though, as the United States' Government justly pointed out, it would have been fraught with great danger to the good relations between the two countries, but which is now rendered impossible by the subsequent events."

"4. That a better and more conciliatory conclusion, which for twenty years has remained undisputed, was effected by the independent and voluntary action of Great Britain. The points in dispute were practically conceded by this country, and the controversy terminated in a manner which was declared by President Buchanan to be amicable and honourable, resulting in a final settlement entirely satisfactory to the Government of the United States."

---

as just and equitable; and that the same canals or railways, being open to the subjects and citizens of Great Britain and the United States on equal terms, shall also be open on like terms to the subjects and citizens of every other State which is willing to grant thereto such protection as Great Britain and the United States engage to afford.

"Art. 9. The ratifications of this Convention shall be exchanged at Washington within six months from this day, or sooner, if possible.

"In faith whereof, we, the respective Plenipotentiaries, have signed this Convention, and have hereunto affixed our Seals.

"Done at Washington, the nineteenth day of April Anno Domini One thousand eight hundred and fifty.

(Signed) HENRY LYTTON BULWER.
JOHN M. CLAYTON."*

---

* ANNUAL REGISTER. 1850, pp. 387-390. DE MARTENS. Rec. Gen. II. 219-39.

The question finally remained on the footing of the Clayton-Bulwer Treaty.

Sir Robert Phillimore makes the following statements with regard to this famous question.

"Before the ratifications were exchanged, it was explained by the British to the American Plenipotentiary, that the words 'or any part of Central America' were not to apply to the British settlements in Honduras, or its dependencies. This explanation was fully adopted by the American Plenipotentiary, and the ratifications were exchanged. The treaty was subsequently submitted by the President of the United States to the Senate, and was approved of, after discussion by that deliberative assembly. It was, however, contended by certain persons averse to the conditions of the treaty, that the Senate did not understand that the treaty was to be construed with reference to the American Plenipotentiary's consent, which he had expressed in the reply to the British Plenipotentiary's explanation with respect to the Honduras, and consequently that the Senate had in reality not assented to the treaty so qualified. Though there is no ground for this supposition, the objection evinces how much knowledge of the department of Government, in which the power of making and ratifying treaties is vested by the constitution of each State, is necessary for the security of the foreign relations of all States."

"The reason of the thing would indeed seem to have excluded the Honduras, as the terms were employed in the treaty, even without the subsequent express limitation, from the category of 'Central America,' though geographically and literally within the scope of the expressions. It is true that Great Britain had originally only certain limited *jura in re* with respect to the

Honduras, such as the right of cutting mahogany and logwood conceded to her by treaties with Spain, the right of sovereignty being reserved to the Crown of the latter country; yet, since Spain has ceased to exercised any sovereignty, either at Honduras, or in the circumjacent territory, and the British jurisdiction is exercised there under a Commission of the Crown which has been recognized by the United States, inasmuch as their Consul is received at Belize under the *exequatur* of the British Crown, Honduras, therefore was justly considered as both *de facto* and *de jure* a British settlement; and the terms in the treaty appear, by the ordinary and admitted rules of construction applied with reference to the subject-matter and context of the treaty, not to include the British possession of Honduras." *

"The discordant constructions put by England and the United States upon this treaty did not, as has been shown, receive a satisfactory adjustment until 1859–60, when England, by separate treaties with Honduras and Nicaragua, relinquished the Mosquito protectorate, and recognized the Bay Islands as part of the Republic of Honduras." †

"The neutral character of this ship-canal between the Atlantic and Pacific oceans has been thus recognized and established. The neutrality of what is called the 'Honduras inter-oceanic railway' was guaranteed by a Convention of August 27th, 1856, between Great Britain and Honduras." ‡

* Comp. the Convention between Great Britain and Spain, concluded at London on the 14th of July, 1786. DE MARTENS. Rec. de Tr. IV. (1786), pp. 133–140. Annual Register. 1787, p. 78.

† DE MARTENS. Vol. XLV. p. 374. HERTSLET. Treaties, Vol. XI. p. 367.

‡ WHEATON. Edit. Lawrence. Vol. I. p. 478. HERTSLETS' Treaties. Vol. X. p. 871. The contract between the State of New Granada and the Panama Railway Company is given in the State Papers. Vol. XLII. p. 1187. In 1846 the United States and New Granada entered

§ 135. International contracts are extinguished when their objects are satisfied or when they become by special circumstances, temporarily or definitely, void and cease to be obligatory. *Circumstances under which the obligatory force of a treaty ceases.*

International treaties cease to be obligatory under the following circumstances, viz.:—

1°. By the mutual consent of the parties interested.

2°. By express renunciation of one of the parties by virtue of a power of renunciation expressly reserved.

3°. At the expiration of the term fixed by the treaty, as sometimes is the case with treaties of commerce.

4°. If the object of the treaty is attained; if all the conditions stipulated are accomplished, or when the conditions on which the obligations of the treaty depend cease to exist.

5°. When the execution of the treaty becomes physically or morally impossible. Physical impossibilities are the following cases:—

(*a.*) When a State has concluded treaties of alliance with different States which subsequently become mutually involved in war.

(*b.*) When three States formed a triple alliance of defence, and two of them engage in war.

With regard to the moral reasons through which a treaty becomes extinct, Mr. Hall states, that a treaty becomes void "by incompatibility with the general obligations of States, when a change has taken place in undisputed law or in views universally held with respect to morals."*

---

into a Treaty of Commerce and Navigation. State Papers. Vol. XXXVI. 994. See also Treaty between England and the United States of Columbia, February 16th, 1866. PHILLIMORE. Vol. I. 1879, p. 309, et seq.

* That is when a change has taken place in the standard of international morality, in other words, in the International Spirit of Law.

"If, for example, it were found that, by successive renewals of treaties and incorporations of treaties in others subsequently made, an agreement to allow a State certain privileges in importing slaves into the territory of the other contracting Power was still subsisting, it might fairly be treated as void, and as not protecting subjects of the former State who might endeavour to introduce slaves in accordance with its terms." *

6°. When a treaty is inexecutable through actual collision with other legally existing treaty obligations or through new inevitable engagements caused by *force majeure.*

7°. When certain circumstances, on the supposed existence of which by both parties the treaty is made, have essentially altered, whether such circumstances, which have *de facto* become a *conditio sine qua non* of the treaty, be expressly stated in the treaty or are tacitly implied from the nature of the treaty. When an express condition upon which the treaty is based ceases to exist, the treaty becomes void.

8°. Through defection of one of the parties, violating or refusing the execution of a treaty *in toto* or only of a certain part of the same. Such complete or partial refusal entirely liberates the other contracting parties from all obligations entailed by the treaty in question, as then a new agreement is to be entered into. When a treaty is violated by one party in one or more of its articles, the other can regard it as broken. It is, however, not every petty failure or delay in the fulfilment of a treaty which can authorise the other party to regard it as broken, especially if the intention, to observe the contract in its principal bearings, remains. †

* W. E. HALL. p. 293.

† WOOLSEY. § 112.

9°. Finally the functions of a treaty cease when the acts contemplated by it have been fulfilled, the treaty being then dissolved and gone over into actual facts with the consequences derived from the situation created by the treaty. These are the treaties or conventions, called by Vattel, de Martens and Wheaton *conventions transitoires*, such as regulating boundaries, cession or change of territories, etc. * The object of the treaty is satisfied, but the acts contemplated by it, though done once for all, leave legal obligations behind them. If a treaty stipulates for the cession of territory or the recognition of a new State, the act of cession or of recognition is no doubt complete in itself; but the true object of the treaty is to set up a permanent state of things and not barely to secure the performance of the act which forms the starting-point of that state; the ceding or recognizing country therefore remains under an obligation until the treaty has become void or voidable in one or other of the ways that may be applicable to it. †

Circumstances under which a treaty becomes voidable.

§ 136. The conditions under which treaties cease to be binding, as given in the preceding Section, resolve themselves, as Mr. Hall states, into impossibility of execution, consent of the parties, satisfaction of the object of the compact and incompatibility with undisputed law and morals. With regard to such causes of nullity, there can be no room for disagreement, but it is less easy, says this author, to lay down precisely the conditions under which a treaty becomes voidable; that is to say, under which one of the contracting parties acquires the right of declaring itself freed from the obligation under which it has

* VATTEL. Liv. II. Chapt. XII. § 192. DE MARTENS. Precis, etc. Liv. II. Chapt. II. p. 58.

† W. E. HALL. Intern. Law. p. 293. CALVO. § 550.

placed itself. A clear principle, however, is ready to hand, which, if honestly applied, would generally furnish a sufficient test of the existence or non-existence of the right in a particular case. This principle, which is proposed as a sufficient test of the existence of an obligatory treaty or of the voidability of a treaty at a given moment, Mr. Hall states as follows. "Neither party to a contract can make its binding effect dependent at its will upon conditions other than those contemplated at the moment when the contract was entered into, and on the other hand a contract ceases to be binding so soon as anything which formed an implied condition of its obligatory force, at the time of its conclusion, is essentially altered. If this be true, and it will scarcely be contradicted, it is only necessary to determine under what implied conditions an international agreement is made. When these are found, the reasons for which a treaty may be denounced or disregarded will also be found." * (Comp. §§ 133 & 137).

Beyond the grounds afforded by the conditions stated above, writers on International Law admit no basis upon which repudiation of existing treaty obligations can be placed. With regard to alleged grounds upon which a treaty may be voided, Mr. Hall gives the following opinion. "The other reasons for which it is alleged that States may refuse to execute the contracts into which they have entered, resolve themselves into so many different forms of excuse for disregarding an agreement when it becomes unduly onerous in the opinion of the party wishing to escape from its burden." M. Heffter says that a State may repudiate a treaty when it conflicts with 'the rights and welfare of its people.' M. Haute-

* W. E. HALL. p. 295.

feuille declares that 'a treaty containing the gratuitous cession or abandonment of an essential natural right, such for example as part of its independence, is not obligatory.' M. Bluntschli thinks that a State may hold treaties incompatible with its development to be null, and seems to regard the propriety of the renunciation of the treaties of 1856 by Russia as an open question. * The doctrine of M. Fiore exhibits the extravagancies which are the logical consequence of these views. According to him 'all treaties are to be looked upon as null, which are in any way opposed to the development of the free activity of a Nation, or which hinder the exercise of its natural rights'; and by the light of this principle he finds that if the numerous treaties concluded in Europe are examined, they are seen to be immoral, iniquitous, and valueless. † Such doctrines as these may be allowed to speak for themselves. Law is not intended to bring licence and confusion, but restraint and order; and neither restraint nor order can be imposed by the principles of which the expression has just been quoted. Incapable in their vagueness of supplying a definite rule, fundamentally immoral by the scope which they givc to unregulated action, scarcely an act of international bad faith could be so shameless as not to find shelter behind them. High sounding generalities, by which anything may be sanctioned, are the favourite weapons of unscrupulousness and ambition; they cannot be kept from distorting the popular judgment, but they may at least be prevented from affecting the standard of law." ‡

---

* HEFFTER. § 98. HAUTEFEUILLE. Des Droits et Devoirs des Nations Neutres. Vol. I. p. 9. BLUNTSCHLI. §§ 415–456.

† FIORI. Nouv. Droit Intern. Part I. Chapt. IV.

‡ W. E. HALL. Intern. Law. p. 302.

The durability of international treaties depends upon the International Spirit of Law.

§ 137. A treaty ceases to be efficacious when the moral or material, the speculative or practical object of agreement on which its *raison d'être* was based, ceases to exist. The moral causes of the imperfect observance of international contracts must be looked for in the changes which take place in the standard of international morality.

Moral causes of the imperfect observance of treaties.

Characteristics of international treaties and international customs compared.

International treaties as well as international customs are the manifestations of the International Spirit of Law (§ 14); in other words, they are the indications of the state of progress or of re-action in civilization, with this distinction, that the elasticity of custom renders it a far more sincere interpreter of this Spirit of Law than the formal treaty. Custom rarely mistakes actual circumstances as is the case with treaties which are based on theories or presumed facts or made to satisfy temporary exigencies. Custom being unconsciously guided by the Moral Law of Nature, causes men to follow the true direction without being able to explain to themselves the reason why they have chosen any particular course; while many treaties, which pretend to fix the goal beforehand or to establish the right direction, through premeditating conception of the material object to be attained, make men drift into the wrong way while they intended to go right. * Thus treaties which serve to suit special interests are often serious impediments to progress. Finally, the existence of a custom is the unfailing evidence that its object was possible; while the real objects of many treaties are rarely attainable.

These statements are plainly demonstrated by the scientific investigation of the main source or origin of International Law, as so lucidly stated

* Prof. LORIMER. The Institutes of the Law of Nations, p. 27 et seq.

by Prof. Sheldon Amos, in his work "The Science of Law."

"The scientific study of Law," says the Professor, "seems to attain its highest perfection and its noblest uses when it is directed to what is now generally known as 'International Law,' or the 'Law of Nations.' A preliminary difficulty is here encountered as to whether the rules of reciprocal action, to which the Governments of modern civilized States practically submit themselves with more or less steadiness, can properly be held to constitute a body of Law in the same sense of this term as is involved when the rules for the internal government of any particular State are concerned. There are, no doubt, obvious resemblances between the two sorts of rules, and there are also obvious discrepancies. The question is, whether a new term should be invented to designate the rules practically guiding the mutual action of States in certain respects, or whether it is rather expedient that the meaning of the term Law should be extended to admit of its covering both classes of rules."

"This inquiry opens out another, as to whether the definition of the term Law, as given by the most recent and celebrated school of English legal writers, is not based on too restricted a conception of the phenomena to which it relates; and it is only at the moment of attempting to apply the former definition of law to international uses, that the insufficiency of that definition is discovered."

"Mr. Austin, indeed, endeavoured to escape the necessity of reconstructing his own definition by denying to the rules for regulating the mutual relations of States the name of Law. He styled those rules, in their assemblage, morality. Two inconvenient consequences followed from this innovation. In the first place, the word morality was restricted to expressing the sort of outward and formal acts which alone belong to the well-recognized region of the Law of Nations. In the second place, and following from the former consequence, the field for moral action and for moral rights and duties as between States—so far as that action and those rights and duties do not admit of the precise and logical circumscription demanded in Courts of justice—was entirely ignored. In fact, morality, as between States, was made to exhibit itself in nothing else than in the limited number of precisely ascertained rules hitherto making up the so-called Law of Nations and the name morality was implicitly denied to every other standard of mutual responsibility between States. Had this language prevailed, the indirect influence of it must have been to conflict with one of the most promising tendencies of the present age,—that is, to recognize moral rights and duties as existing between States wholly independently of the strictly legal rights and duties which properly belong to the great structure called the Law of Nations or International Law. Those moral rights and duties, like the moral rights and duties of private life, reach far too deeply, and extend too widely, to be ever made the topic of forensic circumscription or legislative enactment. Legal rights and duties are their signs and buttresses, but not their substitutes. Law is ever the handmaid of morality, but where the notion of morality is limited by that of law, morality and law will soon perish together."

"To return from this apparent, though not real, digression occasioned by Mr. Austin's attempt to make International Law and International Morality convertible expressions, it becomes necessary to consider the true lessons enforced by the seemingly impracticable phenomenon presented by the body of rules forming the bulk of what is called the Law of Nations.

"This lesson is that the distinguishing characteristics of true Law must be sought for somewhere else than in the nature of the authority from whence it proceeds, and in the certainty of the punishment by which its infraction is attended."

"It is not necessary to warn a Continental student of the importance of this lesson. None of the words *Recht*, *droit*, nor *jus*, have ever been restricted to the narrow meaning that, in the hands of Bentham and Austin, the word Law has acquired in England. And yet it is true that the excessive precision by which the use of the word Law has of the late been narrowed in this country has tended to save English students from many of the pitfalls of vagueness and indeterminateness, not to say sentimentality, to which some foreign writers are undoubtedly prone. But precision, valuable as it is, must not be sought at the expense of truth; and the question is now presented, as to whether recent English legal writers have not, in aspiring after clearness and brevity, entailed upon themselves a loss which is not appreciable at the full till the problem of the scientific nature of so-called International Law comes under treatment." *

Material causes of the imperfect observance of treaties.

The practical causes of the imperfect observance of treaties must be looked for in their material and technical imperfections and defects. These causes are indicated by Professor Sheldon Amos, in his late work on the Science of Jurisprudence, as follows:—

"In the first place, treaties are often made to last for an indefinite length of time, during

* Prof. SHELDON AMOS. A.M. The Science of Law. Edit. 1874. p. 322, et seq.

which the parties to them ordinarily undergo remarkable changes in their circumstances, both in relation to each other and to other States, to which there is no parallel presented in the circumstances of parties to a contract in National Law. In order to meet this difficulty, it has been suggested that either no treaty should be made for longer than a very limited period,—say ten years,—or that, if made for longer than that period, it should be known to be open to revision at the end of some such period. The objection to this recommendation is that some treaties, must, from the nature of the case, be intended to endure for a far longer time than others, and that a prospect of a revision of them at a short distance of time would produce the very insecurity in the tenure of all rights under them which it is the main purpose of the treaty to prevent. In the treaties with Great Britain which followed the declaration of American Independence, and which had for one purpose, among others, a definite fixing of the relative claims of American and British citizens to fisheries along the coast of Canada and of the adjoining islands, any prospect of changes after the efflux of a definite period must have seriously qualified the nature of the rights themselves, and any prospect of a revision of the treaties at a fixed time must have not only had a like effect, but have operated very unfavourably in fostering a restless temper of political ambition. It should be admitted that just as a single State can acquire rights by prescription or by continued possession, or by the enduring consent of other States, so between two States certain treaties may be made which must be allowed and expected to operate as long as the two States exist. The responsibility incurred in making any such treaties, and the inexpediency of multiplying them, is sufficiently evident to all."

"Another cause which leads to the imperfect observance of treaties is the fact that the most important treaties, on the strict maintenance of which the peace and order of a complex society of States depends, are constantly made at the conclusion of a war, in order to ascertain and fix the relations of the belligerent States towards one another. A professedly moral engagement made under such circumstances can hardly fail to lack all the elements of choice and freedom which alone can create a personal sense or a general recognition of real responsibility. In all national systems of Law the presence of 'duress,' or *vis* and *metus*, are peremptorily held to invalidate the most formal, and the most apparently voluntary transactions. When terms are imposed by a conqueror, with the terrible alternative to their adoption of a continuance of the war, and when, as it too frequently happens in times of war, opinions and feelings in the vanquished or worsted State are violently distracted, any engagement that can be made as to the future must always contain the suppressed clause that the treaty is only to operate so long as the weaker State is physically forced to tolerate its operation. The very consciousness of this latent infirmity, attaching to every treaty of peace, tends, of itself, to make the customary terms of such treaties harder than they might otherwise be. Thus violence begets distrust, and distrust increases the violence; from which terrible series of reactions springs the lamentable phenomenon that, while all the existing relations of the European States have been mainly determined by treaties of peace, following upon sanguinary wars, and depend, for their stability, upon the rigid observance of those treaties, nevertheless hardly a single State shrinks from breaking,—or, at the least, from clamorously insisting upon a revision of,—any one of those treaties, as soon as it seems conducive to its own interests to do so. A remedy for this cause of the prevailing infirmity attaching to treaties is to be found in multiplying treaties between States at peace with each other, and while each is enjoying a considerable measure of independence and dignity, such treaties would possess all the most hopeful elements of stability and cogency, and the States which were parties to them, instead of writhing under a hard and tyrannical chain,—the memorials of past degradation,—would cherish and honour them with a noble rivalry, as being at once memorials of a worthy ambition and continuing tests of the national honour."

"A third cause of the non-observance of treaties is undoubtedly to be found in the loose and inaccurate form in which they are frequently drawn up, in consequence of which there exists no universal canon of interpretation which is applicable to them. This fact is due partly to the political necessity of the case, and partly to the want of any common juridical language equally accepted by all the States of Europe. A treaty, when once finally agreed upon, is always the result of a series of compromises, especially when following upon a war. These compromises are the product of protracted negotiations, conducted by a body of men proverbially famous rather for deceiving one another in the politest language, than for successfully communicating to one another the real meaning of their language and no more nor less. Those negotiations again are apt to be violently interfered with by all kinds of special influences and of indirect aims irrelevant to the main points at issue, which yet, however, in the general result, are not and cannot be ignored. Again, while there is an avoidance of purely colloquial language in framing a treaty, there is a current dislike to a purely legal style,—founded no doubt on a reminiscence of the narrow system of interpretation, vulgarly, though not altogether unjustly, attributed to professional lawyers. It thus comes about that the style of a treaty runs a risk of having the special defects of a home-made will, and of containing just enough legal phraseology to generate disputes, and not enough to clear them up. It is scarcely necessary to say that the true remedy for this cause of the imperfect observance of treaties will be found in the general culture throughout Europe of the study of International Law. The age of secret diplomacy is passing away with that of autocratic rule. It is probable that the new era will be marked by a race of great and popular statesmen, carrying on the negotiations with foreign States as far as may be in the light of day and on principles which do not shun that light, and by a growing school of international lawyers who will assist to build up a truly humane code, expressed in precise language, to which the terms of every international document will bear explicit or implicit reference."

"The notice of the influence of popular movements in the present day suggests the last or fourth cause which need be noticed of the imperfect observance of treaties. It has always, of necessity, been a matter of the utmost solicitude to determine what amount of ratification, and by what persons, is necessary in order to impart to a treaty its binding force. Treaties are necessarily negotiated and executed by persons who reproduce, in International Law, the character of agents in National Law. As in the case of such agents, the special or general character of the representatives has to be taken into account in estimating the degree of their authority. In all States, ancient and modern, the capacity to make binding treaties with foreign Powers has been held to rest exclusively in the Executive Authority of the State, though,—as in the case of the share in such capacity possessed by the Senate, in the United States,—the Executive Authority has occasionally been, for this special purpose, modified in its constitution. This remarkable and enormous function of the Executive has maintained its ground, no doubt, in part from the traditional notions of the mutual dynastic relationships of the monarchical heads of different States, whereby all foreign transactions peculiarly adhered to the prerogative of the monarch, even where matters of internal government had gradually become encroached upon by the people; and partly to the possibility of sudden emergencies presenting themselves, needing instant settlement by conventions between States under circumstances in which the delay necessary for consulting a public assembly, or the publicity involved in consulting it, would seriously interfere with the accomplishment of the purpose in view. It is possible, however, that the capacity of making important treaties will, in all States, be more and more taken into its own hands by the supreme Political Authority. It is much to be desired that this should be the case, not only to ensure more prudent and deliberate engagements being made, but in such a way to charge the whole

Nation with the joint responsibility as to ensure their being kept." *

But, whatever may be inherent defects or imperfections of international contracts, their obligatory force rests on mutual good faith. All laws which have been formally enacted must be formally repealed, so treaties which have been formally negotiated must be formally renounced or revised, as they do not possess the elasticity and self-regulating characteristic of customs. As long as the material interests are in harmony with the moral reasons, the conscientious fulfilment of the mutual obligations, imposed by the compact, is as natural a task as it is an easy duty to accomplish. But, as we noted in paragraphs 14 and 15, the progress of humanity, in conformity with the Moral Law of Nature, is ever changing and moulding the International Spirit of Law, which manifests itself in the intercourse of Nations and finds formulated utterances in different international transactions. As such, international treaties are the land-marks of the progress or the retrogression of Nations on the road to civilization, and when a treaty does not agree with the actuality of that state of mutual understanding between parties, which is created by and is existing through the International Spirit of Law, the treaty becomes naturally amendable. The natural defect of such a contract must lead sooner or later to its invalidity, and finally to a rupture of the inefficient contract, unless the treaty be in due time abrogated or altered. The aspects under which the successive degrees of inefficaciousness of a treaty and its final peaceable amendment or abrogation present themselves, are conspicuous marks of the progress or retrogression of the

* Prof. SHELDON AMOS. A Systematic view of the Science of Jurisprudence. Ed. 1872. p. 425, et seq.

International Spirit of Law. Thus, when we observe States entering into mutual obligations which afterwards become unduly onerous for one of the parties, so that the contracted obligation "conflicts with the rights and welfare of its people" (Heffter); when we see a Nation, having "inadvertently and gratuitously abandoned an essential natural right such for example as part of its independence, holds treaties incompatible with its development to be null" (Bluntschli), or when we hear that "all treaties are to be looked upon as null, which are opposed to the development of the free moral and material activity of a Nation, and that by the light of this principle, such treaties must be held immoral, iniquitous and valueless" (Fiore), then, in all these cases, the sole way by which it could be ascertained whether reasons given as above are vile excuses of unscrupulousness and ambition, emanating from a powerful party to impose on its weaker neighbours, or whether they are real principles emanating from a progressing International Spirit of Law, is to put them to the test of the Moral Law of Nature, which underlies this Spirit of Law (§ 14). This is done through the practical solution of the question whether the contract under dispute is or is not compatible with the real welfare of the complaining party, as well as with the progress of civilization in general, and thus ought to be adhered to or modified for the benefit of all parties concerned. The solution of this question is the task of impartial arbitration.

When justice and benevolence, which combined constitute the Moral Law of Nature, condemn an existing contract, the obligations emanating from such a pactum, though couched in the most solemn legal forms, are doubtless immoral, iniquitous and valueless, and when, under the disguise of justice or humanity, weapons of vile ambition are used, these are easily detected by unbiassed common sense, as described above in sections 10–15; for nothing is more consistent with our common sense than what Mr. Hall tersely stated in the above quoted pages, viz., that Law (which emanates from the Moral Law of Nature) is not intended to bring license and confusion but restraint and order into all human dealings and transactions. But, as noted above, these dealings and transactions are products of the state of civilization of the respective parties to the transactions, and the changes which these transactions undergo keep pace with the moral progress or retrogression of Nations in their intercourse, in other words, with the International Spirit of Law.

§ 138. Does war abrogate or suspend treaties? *Effect of War upon treaties and conventions.* On this question, opinions are divided as to the classes of treaties which are essentially affected by war and the degree in which they are affected by it. But on the whole, it is the outcome of practice, that, in the case of treaties which are yet in force, their operation must necessarily be suspended when all peaceable intercourse terminates between parties. Such are the treaties of commerce and navigation, of alliance, of succour and subsidy, and, in fine, all conventions regulating acts of peaceable intercourse. Such are also those treaties which have not yet received their full sanction or which have not been fully established, accomplished or carried out to the extent of their final aim. But those treaties which have already passed into established facts and are thus not merely in course of regulating special or general conditions of mutual conduct regarding commercial or political intercourse in time of peace, are not affected by war between the parties. Such are the treaties indicated in subsection 9 of paragraph 135, as treaties of recognition of the independence of a State, of cession or exchange of territories, boundary conventions, and those which create certain permanent servitude rights in favour of a neighbouring State over the territory of another. If, in certain instances, the operation of such treaties might be suspended by war in some special directions, they tacitly resume effect at the conclusion of peace, without their renewal being expressly mentioned in the treaty of peace, unless they have been the vital cause of the war or form special conditions of peace.

Treaties which are made in time of peace to secure some mutual interest in time of war between parties, have the state of war for their *raison d'être* and are consequently suspended in time of peace, as having only effect between belligerent States. Such are conventions regarding the time allowed reciprocally, to the respective nationalities, for quitting the enemy's territory with their moveables; regarding exemption from confiscation with reference to property left behind, whether personal or real. Such are also all regulations made with regard to the laws of war, or stipulations which are meant to provide for the event of an intervening war, as stipulations relating to prizes, prisoners of war, blockades, contraband of war, inviolability of private property, etc. These agreements are, by their nature, liable to be annulled only by new agreements or in the manner provided in the treaties themselves. *

Opinion of Mr. Hall.

In his elaborate and clear treatment of this question, Mr. Hall gives the following opinion.

* VATTEL. Liv. III. Chapt. X. § 175. KENT. Com. on American Law. Vol. I. p. 177. HALLECK. Edit. Sir Sherston Baker. Vol. I. p. 242.

"It is not altogether settled what treaties are annulled or suspended by war, and what treaties remain in force during its continuance or revive at its conclusion. According to some writers all treaties are annulled except in so far as they are concluded with the express object of regulating the conduct of the parties while hostilities last." * Wheaton considers that so-called 'transitory conventions,' which set up a permanent state of things by an act done once for all, such as treaties of cession or boundary, or those which create a servitude in favour of one Nation within the territory of another, generally subsist notwithstanding the existence of war, 'and although their operation may in some cases,' which he does not specify, 'be suspended during war, they revive on the return of peace without any express stipulation; other treaties, as of commerce and navigation, expire of course, except such stipulations as are made expressly with a view to a rupture.' † De Martens is of the same opinion, except that he thinks that transitory conventions may always be suspended and sometimes annulled. ‡ Other writers and the English and American Courts hold that 'transitory conventions' are in no case destroyed or suspended by war, they being, according to Sir Travers Twiss, less of the nature of an agreement than of a recognition of a right already existing, or, as the same view was put in the form of an example by an American judge, 'if treaties which contemplate a permanent arrangement of territorial or other national rights were extinguished by the event of war, even the treaty of 1783, so far as it fixed our limits and acknowledged our independence, would be gone, and

* VATTEL. Liv. III. Chapt. X. § 175.

† WHEATON. Part III. Chapt. II. §§ 9–10.

‡ DE MARTENS. § 58.

on the occurrence of war between England and the United States we should have had again to struggle for both upon original revolutionary principles.' * Others again think that all treaties remain binding unless their terms imply the existence of peace, or unless the reason for their stipulations is destroyed by the war; or else that treaties of the last-mentioned kind, such as treaties of alliance, are annulled, but that treaties of commerce, postal conventions, and other arrangements of like character, are suspended only, and that treaties or provisions in them, such as those ceding or defining territory, which are intended to be permanent, remain in force; or finally that treaties are put an end to or suspended only when or in so far as their execution is incompatible with the war itself." †

"A like divergence of opinion is suggested by the conduct of States at the conclusion of recent wars. By the Treaty of Paris, which ended the Crimean war, it was stipulated that, until the treaties or conventions existing before the war between the belligerent Powers were renewed or replaced by fresh agreements, trade should be carried on on the footing of the regulations in force before the war, and the subjects of the inter-belligerent States should be treated, as between those States, as favourably as those of the most favoured Nation. Under this provision, not only were fresh treaties of commerce concluded, but it seemed necessary to Russia and Sardinia to exchange declarations to the effect that a convention for the abolition of the *droit d'aubaine*, than which no agreement could seem to be more thoroughly made in view of a permanent arrange-

* TWISS. I. §§ 225–6. Sutton v. Sutton. I. Russell and Mylne. 663.

† HEFFTER. §§ 122 and 180–1. CALVO. § 729. BLUNTSCHLI. § 538.

ment of rights, was to be considered as having recovered its force from the date of the exchange of ratifications of treaty. Again, as between Austria and Sardinia in 1859, all treaties in vigour upon the commencement of the war of that year were confirmed, that is to say were stated by way of precaution to be in force, by the Treaty of Zurich, and among those treaties seem to have been a treaty of commerce and postal convention; but as between Austria and France, no revival or confirmation of treaties was stipulated, although agreements of every kind existed between them. In 1866 the Treaty of Vienna between Austria and Italy confirmed afresh the engagements with which the Treaty of Zurich had dealt, and the Treaty of Prague revived, or in other words re-stipulated all the treaties existing between Prussia and Austria in so far as they had not lost their applicability through the dissolution of the German Confederation. In 1871, the Treaty of Frankfurt revived treaties of commerce and navigation, a railway convention having reference to the customs, copy-right conventions and extradition treaties, without making any mention of other treaties by which France and Germany were bound to each other."

"Looking at the matter apart from authority and from practice, treaties and other conventions, except those made in express contemplation of war, or articles so made forming part of more general treaties, as to the binding force of which during hostilities there is no question, would seem to fall naturally for present purposes under the following heads :—

"1. Treaties, such as great European territorial settlements and dynastic arrangements, intended to set up a permanent state of things by an act done once for all, in which the belligerent parties have contracted with third Powers as well as with each other."

"2. Treaties also binding the belligerent States with third Powers as well as to each other, but unlike the former class stipulating for continuous acts or for acts to be done under certain contingencies, such for example as treaties of guarantee."

"3. Treaties with political objects, intended to set up a permanent state of things by an act done once for all, which have been concluded between the belligerent parties alone, such as treaties of cession or of confederation."

"4. Treaties concluded between the belligerent States only, and dealing with matters connected with the social relations of States, which from the nature of their contents appear to be intended to set up a permanent state of things such as conventions to abolish the *droit d'aubaine.*"

"5. Treaties concluded between the belligerent States only, whether with political objects or not, which from the nature of their contents do not appear to be intended to set up a permanent state of things, such as treaties of alliance, commercial treaties, postal conventions, etc."

"With regard to the first of these classes of treaties it is obvious that the fact of war makes no difference in their binding force, since each party remains bound to another with whom he is not at war. There is also no difficulty in observing them, since they merely oblige to an abstention from acts at variance with their provisions. The second class remain equally obligatory, subject to the condition that there shall be a reasonable possibility of carrying out their provisions; but as those provisions require performance of acts, and not simply abstention from them, compliance may readily be inconsistent with the state of war or with the incidents of the particular war. Treaties of this kind therefore must be viewed according to circumstances, as continuing or as being suspended. Compacts of the third kind, on the other hand, must in all cases be regarded as continuing to impose obligations until they are either supplanted by a fresh agreement or are invalidated by a sufficiently long adverse prescription. Suppose, for example, that a province belonging to one of two States is held under a treaty of cession from the other. On the outbreak of war between them, if the treaty were annulled by the occurrence of hostilities, the former owner would re-enter the province as his own, or if it were suspended he would be able to exercise the rights of a sovereign there as against those of an occupant in the remainder of his enemy's territory. Neither of these things however takes place. The rights of a belligerent in territory which he has formerly ceded are identical with those which he has in territory which has never belonged to him. In both he has merely the rights of a military occupant; he may appropriate both; but neither become definitively his until the conclusion of a peace assigning the territory to him, or if his enemy refuses to treat until a due term of prescription has elapsed."

"As regards treaties of the fourth class, it would seem reasonable that they should continue or be suspended at the will of either of the belligerents. They are intended to be permanent arrangements so long as peace shall exist, and there is nothing in the fact of war to prevent them from recommencing their operation automatically with the conclusion of peace; there is therefore no reason for supposing them to be annulled. But as all social relations are suspended for the time of war, except by express or tacit permission of the sovereign, it is impossible to look upon treaty modifications of the normal social relations which are thus interrupted as being compulsorily operative during the progress of hostilities."

"Treaties of the fifth class are necessarily at least suspended by war, many of them are necessarily annulled, and there is nothing in any of them to make them revive as a matter of course on the advent of peace,—frequently in fact a change in the relations of the parties to them, effected by the treaty of peace, is inconsistent with a renewal of the identical stipulations. It would appear therefore to be simplest to take them to be all annulled, and to adopt the easy course, when it is wished to put them in force again without alteration, of expressly stipulating for their renewal by an article in the treaty of peace. In all cases in which war is caused by differences as to the meaning of a treaty, the treaty must be taken to be annulled. During hostilities the right interpretation is at issue; and it would be pedantry to press the analogy between war and legal process so far as to regard the meaning ultimately sanctioned by victory as representing the continuing obligation of the original compact. Whether the point in dispute be settled at the peace by express stipulations, or whether the events of the war have been such as to render express stipulations unnecessary, a fresh starting point is taken; a peace which, whether tacitly or in terms, gives effect to either of two interpretations, has substituted certainty for doubt, and thus has brought a new state of things into existence." *

* W. E. HALL. Intern. Law. Edit. 1880. p. 322, et seq.

§ 139. Contracts of guarantee are applicable to all conditions that may arise in the intercourse of Nations. *Treaties of guarantee.*

"Unhappy experience," says Vattel, "having shown that the faith of treaties, sacred and inviolable as it ought to be, does not always afford a sufficient assurance that they shall be punctually observed, mankind have sought for securities against perfidy, for methods, whose efficacy should not depend on the good faith of the contracting parties. A guarantee is one of those means. When those who make a treaty of peace, or any other treaty, are not perfectly easy with respect to its observance, they require the guarantee of some powerful sovereign. The party who guarantees promises to maintain the conditions of the treaty and to cause it to be observed." *

The ancient custom of taking hostages *(otages)* as guarantees for the due observance of treaty obligations, has been done away with in modern time with regard to ordinary treaties concluded in time of peace, but is sometimes resorted to in time of war to secure the accomplishment of capitulations and other military arrangements. † The security for the fulfilment of international agreements, in time of peace, are conventions of guarantee. These consist of engagements by which a State promises to give material help to another if this other is threatened in its existence or in the peaceable enjoyment of its rights by a third Power. The convention of guarantee is also often supplementary to a treaty of peace, in which case third Powers, who have not been parties to the treaty to be guaranteed, undertake to secure its proper accomplishment. Material guarantee or surety for the fulfilment of tran-

* VATTEL. Droit des Gens. Liv. II. Chapt. XVI. §§ 235, 241-244.
† WENCK. Codex juris gentium. Vol. II. p. 352.

sitory engagement is the temporary occupation of territories, which of course ought to be restored as soon as the debt is paid or the contract is accomplished. *

Halleck's opinion. "Treaties of guarantee and of surety," says Halleck, "are engagements by which a State promises to aid another against any interruption of certain specified rights, such as boundaries, territory, constitution or form of government, etc. A distinction is made between guarantee and surety; where the matter relates to things to be done by the party for whom the obligation is contracted, the surety is bound to make good the promise in default of the principal, while the guarantee is only obliged to use his best endeavours to obtain its performance from the principal himself. How far a State may legally contract this class of obligations, must depend first upon its own constitution, and, second, upon the nature of the stipulations with respect to any interference with or infringement of the sovereign rights of other independent States. † The guarantee may be to all the contracting parties equally, or only to one of them. It is an agreement to cause the fulfilment of the conditions of the treaty, but it in no way affects the conditions themselves; the party guaranteeing, therefore, has no right to

* VATTEL. Droit des Gens. Liv. II. Chapt. XVI. § 235–244. KLUBER. Droit des Gens. Mod. §§ 155–158. DE MARTENS. Précis, etc., § 63. WHEATON. Elem. Intern. Law. Part. III. Chapt. II.

† FLASSAN. Hist. de la Dip. Tome VIII. p. 195. PHILLIMORE. Comm. Intern. Law. Vol. II. §§ 56, et seq. The Protestant succession to the throne of England is guaranteed by Austria, France, Holland, and Spain. In the treaty of 1713, entitled: "The treaty of guarantee of the Protestant succession and of the Dutch Barrier," the British Statute 12 and 13, Will. III. Chapt. II. is recited. Examples of modern guarantees are supplied by the treaty of 1832, concluded between Bavaria, France, Great Britain, and Russia, when the monarchy and independence of Greece was guaranteed, also by the treaty of 1839 concluded between Austria, Belgium, France, Great Britain, Holland, Prussia, and Russia, when the independence and perpetual neutrality of Belgium was guaranteed.

interfere between the contracting parties, and decide upon the interpretation which should be given to its stipulations. But, if called upon by one of these parties, for assistance to enforce the treaty against the other, he must judge for himself whether such assistance is justly due as against the party complained of. We have pointed out, in this chapter, the distinction between guarantee and surety, where the engagements relate to things to be done by the party for whom the obligation is contracted. Sometimes one of the contracting parties puts some of its property or possessions into the hands of another, for the security of its promises, debts, or engagements. Movable things thus remitted are called *pledges*, towns and provinces are given in *pawn* or *mortgaged*, and if the revenues are ceded as an equivalent for the interest of the debt, it is the fact called *antichresis*. But these securities have no effect upon the obligations of the treaty. The party giving the security is no more excusable for refusing or neglecting to perform his engagements than if no securities whatever had been given." *

"Questions have sometimes arisen with respect to the duration of the guarantee, and the withdrawal or release of the security. The guarantee naturally subsists until the stipulations guaranteed are performed, unless a certain time has been agreed upon for its termination. A general and indefinite treaty of guarantee may be changed or modified, the same as any other treaty. As soon as the debt is paid, or the particular engagement is accomplished for which the security was given, the security ends, and the pledge should be returned, or the towns or provinces, held in pawn

* VATTEL. Droit des Gens. Liv. II. Ch. XVI. §§ 235, 241. GUNTHER. Europ. Völkerrecht. B. II. p. 154.

or under mortgage, should be restored in the same condition in which they were received, so far as depends upon the holder." *

With regard to the effect of a collective guarantee, Mr. Hall gives the following opinion.

Opinion of Mr. Hall.

"When a guarantee is given collectively by several Powers, the extent of their obligation is not quite so certain. M. Bluntschli lays down, that they are bound, upon being called upon to act in the manner contemplated by the guarantee, to examine the affair in common for the purpose of seeing whether a case for intervention has arisen, and to agree, if possible, upon a common conclusion and a common action; but that, if no agreement can be arrived at, each guarantor is not only authorized but bound to act separately according to his view of the requirements of the case. A very different doctrine was put forward by Lord Derby in 1867, when explaining in the House of Commons the opinion held by the English Government as to the nature of the obligations undertaken by it in signing the Luxemburg convention of that year. According to him, a collective guarantee means, that, in the event of a violation of neutrality, all the Powers who have signed the treaty may be called upon for their collective action. No one of those Powers is liable to be called upon to act singly or separately. It is a case so to speak of limited liability. We are bound in honour—you cannot place a legal construction upon it—to see, in concert with others, that these arrangements are maintained. But if the other Powers join with us, it is certain that there will be no violation of neutrality. If they, situated exactly as we are, decline to join, we are not bound single-handed to make up the deficiency. Such a guarantee has obviously rather

* HALLECK. Edit. Sir Sherston Baker. Vol. I. pp. 235 & 240.

the character of a moral sanction to the arrangements which it defends than that of a contingent liability to make war. It would no doubt give a right to make war, but would not necessarily impose the obligation.* It is in favour of the latter construction that a collective guarantee must be supposed to be something different from a several, or a joint and several guarantee, and that if it imposes a duty of separate intervention in the last resort it is not very evident what distinction can be drawn between them."

"On the other hand, a guarantee is meaningless if it does no more than provide for common action under circumstances in which the guaranteeing Powers would act together apart from treaty, or for a right of single action under circumstances which would provoke such action as a matter of policy. The only objects of a guarantee are to secure that action shall be taken under circumstances in which a State might not move for its own sake, and to prevent other States from disregarding the arrangement, or attacking the territory, guaranteed by holding up to them the certainty that the force of the guaranteeing Powers will be employed to check them. On the construction given to a collective guarantee by Lord Derby, neither end would be attained. Whichever view be adopted, the word collective is inconvenient. If it imposes a duty, but the extent of the duty is not at least clearly defined. If it can be held to prevent a duty from being imposed, it would be well to abstain from couching agreements in terms which may seriously mislead some of the parties to them, or to avoid making agreements at all which some of the contracting parties may intend from the beginning to be illusory." †

* BLUNTSCHLI. § 440. HANSARD. 3rd Ser. 187, 1922.

† W. E. HALL, Intern. Law, Edit. 1880, p. 289.

CHAPTER XX.

TREATIES AFFECTING INTERNATIONAL LAW.

§ 140. With regard to the history of International Treaties, Sir Robert Phillimore makes the following observations.

History of International Treaties.

"History is a record of the injustice, evil passions, and folly, as well as of the justice, virtues, and wisdom of Nations. The necessities of the epoch in which Grotius wrote left him little or no choice in selecting his examples and precedents chiefly from the antiquity of Greece and Rome. This is not the case with his successors; they have far ampler and far apter materials. But the edifice is not the weaker for the breadth and depth of the classical foundations laid by the first architect; and the principle which guided him is in this, as in most other instances, most valuable to the later and, in spite of their advantages, inferior builders. Secondly, the consent of Nations is evidenced by the contents of treaties, which for this, as well as for other reasons, constitute, a most important part of International Law."

"Upon this point there is one observation which merits, from its importance, precedence over all others. It is this: No treaty between two or more Nations can affect the general principles of International Law prejudicially to the interest of other Nations not parties to such covenant; at the same time, the contracting parties may introduce into a treaty expressions so generally worded as to be either explanatory of a previously contested point of law, or declaratory of the future interpretation of it, or in other ways frame the covenants of the treaty between themselves so as to lay down an universal principle binding on them, at least, in their intercourse with the rest of the world. Nowhere will this important doctrine be found laid down with greater precision or more irresistible argument, than in Lord Granville's speech delivered in the House of Peers, upon the motion for an address to the Throne approving of the convention with Russia in 1801. Among the many attributes of a statesman possessed in rare excellence by that minister, was his intimate acquaintance with International Jurisprudence in all its branches. His opinion is, therefore, of very great authority. He argued that, by the language of that convention, a new sense, and one hitherto repudiated by Great Britain, with respect to contraband of war, would be introduced, so far at least as Great Britain was concerned, into general International Law; that, inasmuch as some provisions of the treaty with respect to what should be considered contraband of war were merely prospective, and confined to the contracting parties, England and Russia, while other provisions of the same treaty were so couched in the preamble, the body, and certain sections which contained them, as to set forth, not the concession of a special privilege to be enjoyed by contracting parties only, but a recognition of one universal pre-existing right, they must be taken as laying down a general rule for all future discussion with any Power whatever, and as establishing a principle of law which was to decide universally on the just interpretation of the technical term contraband of war."

"The constant consent of various Nations to adopt a particular interpretation of a particular term is, generally speaking, strong evidence that such is the true international meaning belonging to it. Bynkershoek was in the habit of placing great stress upon the language of treaties, as evidence of the universal consent of Nations and especially on this point. Nor, in this respect, is he at variance with other jurists; it is their universal opinion that not only the particular provisions, but the general spirit of treaties to which at different periods many Nations have been parties, is of great moment and account as the evidence of their consent to the doctrine contained in them. So Lord Stowell, in his judgment in *The Maria*, arguing for the universal right of the belligerent to visit neutral merchant ships, says: 'The right is equally clear in practice, for practice is uniform and universal upon the subject; the many European treaties which refer to this right refer to it as pre-existing, and merely regulate the exercise of it.' " *

When, however, it is said that the consent of Nations may be gathered in some degree from the conventions of treaties, it is not meant that every kind of treaty can furnish even this degree of evidence. Many, says Sir Robert Phillimore further, are concerned with matters of no general interest to other than the contracting parties; many contain stipulations wrong from the necessities of one party, compelled to admit claims to which by the general law its adversary was not entitled. From treaties of this description no argument of the consent of Nations can be fairly deduced. But there are certain great and cardinal treaties in which, after long and bloody wars, a re-adjustment of international relations

* *The Maria.* Rob. Adm. Rep. Chapt. I. p. 360. Sir ROBERT PHILLIMORE. Comm. on Int. Law. Vol. I. p. 46, et seq. BYNKERSHOEK. Quest. Juris Publ. Liv. I. Chapt. X. p. 113.

has taken place, and which are therefore more especially valuable, both from the magnitude and importance of their provisions, which have necessitated a recurrence to, and a restatement of, the fundamental principles of International Law, and also from the fact, that frequently the greater number of European States, and lately some American and even Asiatic communities, have been parties thereto. *

The following are treaties which have principally affected International Law.

Some of the most important treaties which affected International Law, beginning with the Treaty of Westphalia.

I. The Peace of Westphalia, 24th October, 1648, consisting of two treaties, of Münster where the French, and of Osnabrück where the Swedes negociated with the German Emperor. This peace put an end to the Thirty Years' War and adjusted the relations of a large part of Europe. †

"The Peace of Westphalia," says Wheaton, "established the equality of the three religious communities, of Catholics, Lutherans, and Calvinists in Germany, and sought to oppose a perpetual barrier to further religious innovations and secularizations of ecclesiastical property. At the same time it rendered the States of the Empire almost independent of the Emperor, its federal head. It arrested the progress of Germany towards national unity under the Catholic banner, and prepared the way for the subsequent development of the power of Prussia,—the child of the Reformation,—which thus became the natural head of the Protestant party, and the political rival of the house of Austria, which last still maintained its ancient position as the temporal chief of the Catholic body. It introduced two foreign elements into the internal constitution of the Empire,—France and Sweden, as guarantees

* Sir ROBERT PHILLIMORE. Com. on Intern. Law. Vol. I. p. 48.

† DUMONT. VI. 1,450, 469.

of the peace, and Sweden as a member of the federal body,—thus giving to these two Powers a perpetual right of interference in the internal affairs of Germany. It reserved to the individual States the liberty of forming alliances among themselves, as well as with foreign Powers, for their preservation and security, provided these alliances were not directed against the Emperor and the Empire, nor contrary to the public peace and that of Westphalia. This liberty contributed to render the federative system of Germany a new security for the general balance of European power. The Germanic body thus placed in the centre of Europe, served, by its composition, in which so many political and religious interests were combined, to maintain the independence and tranquillity of all the neighbouring States."*

While the peace of Westphalia was still in agitation, Spain and the United Provinces of North-Netherlands made a separate peace at Münster on the 30th January, 1648. By this treaty, (1), the freedom and sovereignty of the United Provinces were recognized. (2.) Each party retained the places in its possession. Thus the Republic gained Bois-le-Duc or Hertzogenbosch, Bergen-op-Zoom with Breda in Brabant, Hulst, Axel, etc., in Flanders; certain joint rights in Limburg, etc. (3.) The Scheldt and certain water-cources connected with it were closed. (4.) Places won by the Dutch Republic from Portugal were renounced by Spain. Important commercial concessions were made to the Republic in the East and West Indies. †

II. Next in importance with regard to the chart of Europe is the Treaty of Utrecht, 1713,

---

* WHEATON. History. Introduction to Part I. SCHOELL. Histoire abrégée des Traités de Paix. Vol. I. p. 182. HEGEL'S Werke. Band 9. § 434. Philosophie der Geschichte.

† DUMONT. VI. 1,429 (in French).

and Rastadt, 1714, by which the war of succession to the crown of Spain, which began in 1701, was ended.

The Peace of Utrecht consists of separate treaties made by France with Great Britain, Portugal Prussia, Savoy, and the United Provinces of the Netherlands (April 11th, 1713), and by Spain with Great Britain (July 13), and with Savoy (August 13), which were followed by treaties of Spain with the United Provinces (June 26, 1714), and with Portugal (February 6, 1715), all signed at Utrecht. The treaty of Rastadt (March 6, 1714), made by the German Emperor for himself and the Empire, with France, was modified slightly and concluded at Baden in Switzerland, September 7, 1714.

By the Peace of Utrecht and its auxiliary treaties, (1) a barrier was erected in favour of Holland against France, by giving the Spanish Netherlands to Austria; (2) France and Spain could never be united under one monarch by the Public Law of Europe; (3) the Emperor recovered some of the old Germanic influence in the affairs of Italy; (4) the Duke of Savoy, with an accession of power as king of Sardinia, became a stronger check against any designs of France upon Italy, and against Austrian predominance in that peninsula. The remaining minor differences between the Emperor and Spain were discussed at the Congress of Cambray (from 1722, onward). *

III. The Peace of Paris, between France, Spain, England and Portugal, 10th February, 1763, and the Peace of Hubertsburg (a hunting château near Meissen in Saxony) of 15th February of the same year. By the first, the great contest between

* WOOLSEY. Intern. Law. Edit. 1879. p. 446.

France and England, to which Spain and Portugal became parties, was closed, greatly to the advantage of England; and by the second, the seven years' war which had been waged by Austria and its powerful allies against Prussia.

IV. The declaration of Russia, of 28th February, 1780, introducing the first armed neutrality. *

V. Recognition by Great Britain of the independence of the United States of North-America. Preliminaries were arranged on the 30th November, 1782, and on the 3rd September, 1783; the definite treaty of peace was signed at Paris, in which Great Britain acknowledged the independence of the United States, and conceded certain rights of fishery. Boundaries were fixed, debts incurred before the war could be collected, etc. †

VI. The Peace of Versailles. Preliminary treaties were concluded on the 20th January, 1783, between Great Britain on the one part, and France, Spain, and (September 2nd, 1783) the Netherlands on the other. Definitive treaties of Versailles, September 3rd, 1783, between Great Britain, France, and Spain. To France, Great Britain restored the islands of St. Pierre and Miquelon with full right of property, reaffirmed the French rights of fishery near and on Newfoundland, as mentioned in the treaty of Utrecht, restored St. Lucia, and ceded Tobago in the West-Indies, and restored Grenada, St. Vincent, St. Dominique, St. Kitts, Nevis, and Mountserrat. In Africa, Senegal was ceded back to France, and Goree restored. In the East Indies there was a general restitution of conquests made from France in the war. The articles of the treaty of Utrecht and of other subsequent treaties relative to Dunkirk were

* MARTENS. III. 707.
† MARTENS. III. 495–553.

abrogated. To Spain, Great Britain ceded Minorca and Florida; Spain restored Providence Island and the Bahamas, and re-affirmed the right of the English to cut logwood (see Peace of Paris, 1763), settling the limits within which it could be exercised. Between England and Holland the final peace was signed on the 20th of May, 1784. The *status quo ante bellum* was its basis, excepting that Holland ceded Negapatam on the coast of Coromandel. *

VII. The treaties for the pacification of Europe and the re-adjustment of the different States which have been incorporated or subjected by the Napoleonic wars. The following immediate arrangements, consequent upon the downfall of Napoleon, were made:—

1814, May 30th. At the first Peace of Paris, consisting of treaties, nearly identical, between France, now under Louis XVIII, and each of the four great Powers. †

1815, June 9th. Final act of the Congress of Vienna, the most important document of modern times, in an international respect. The Peace of 1814, just spoken of, provided for the meeting of such a Congress within two months, in order to complete the arrangements there begun, but it was not opened until November 1st, 1814. It closed June 11th, 1815; eight Powers composed the Congress, viz., Great Britain, Russia, Austria, Prussia, France, Spain, Portugal and Sweden. In March the alarming news reached the Congress that Napoleon had left Elba, that he had landed in France, that he had recovered his throne without a struggle. He was put under the ban of Europe, a new compact was made by the four great Powers with many accessories, on the 25th

* MARTENS. III. 503, et seq.

† See MARTENS. Nouv. Rec. II. 1, 18.

of March, for the maintenance of the Peace of Paris, and in June the field of Waterloo baffled this attempt of the wonderful man to regain his lost power. The Congress of Vienna was a meeting of dictators for arranging the affairs of Europe according to their arbitrary views, and in effect required the smaller Powers to submit to their decrees, without a share in their deliberations. To perfect the arrangements which appear in the final act, a multitude of special compacts had to be made, some of which were annexed to that instrument, and declared to be a part of it. *

For the final act see Martens, II., 379; Martens and Cussy, III., 61; Wheaton's Int. Law, Appendix; Klüber's Acten des Wiener Congress; Flassan, Hist. du Cong. de Vienne, 3 Vols., Paris, 1829. For the arrangements of the Congress in regard to river navigation, comp. Martens, u. s. 434. For its rule touching the rank of ambassadors, Martens, u. s. 449.

The second Treaty of Paris, after Napoleon's final downfall, was signed on the 20th November 1815, and consists of four separate instruments of the same tenor, between France and each of the four great Powers. By this treaty, the limits of France towards Belgium, Germany, and Savoy, were made somewhat narrower than the Peace of 1814 had made them, being brought back nearly to the line of 1790.

Congress of Aix-la-Chapelle, in Autumn, 1818, of the four allies and France. By an agreement dated October 9, the troops of the allies are to evacuate France on or before the last day of November, and to give up the forts, as they were then when the occupation began. By the Protocol of 21 November, 1818, the class of *Minister-*

* WOOLSEY. Intern. Law. Edit. 1879, p. 466, et seq.

Resident ranking between *Ministers Plenipotentiaries*-and *Chargés d'Affaires* was created. *

VIII. Treaty with regard to the separation of Belgium from the Netherlands, signed at London on the 15th November, 1831, between the five Powers on the one part, and Belgium on the other. †

IX. 1832, May 7. Convention of London, between France, England and Russia on the one part, and Bavaria on the other. The Crown of Greece, now made a kingdom, is offered, with the authorization of the Greek Nation, to the king of Bavaria, to be worn by his second son, Frederic Otho, and accepted. The limits of the kingdom are to be fixed by treaty with Turkey, according to a protocol of September 26, 1831. A loan to the King of Greece is guaranteed by Russia, and, if the consent of the Chambers and of the Parliament can be obtained, by France and England. ‡

X. 1842, August 9. Treaty of Washington, for adjustment of the boundary between the United States and the British possessions on the north-east. §

XI. 1848, February 2. Treaty of Guadalupe-Hidalgo, by which Texas, New Mexico, and Upper California were ceded to the United States, which agreed to surrender all other conquests, to pay Mexico fifteen millions of dollars, and to assume all claims of its citizens against Mexico, decided or undecided, arising before the signature of the treaty. ‖

XII. 1856, March 30. Treaty of Paris after the Crimean War, between Austria, France, Great

---

* MARTENS. Nouv. Rec. IV. pp. 549–566.
† MARTENS. Nouv. Rec. XI. 390.
‡ MARTENS. Nouv. Rec. 550.
§ MARTENS. Nouv. Rec. Gen. (continuing Nouv. Rec.) III. 456.
‖ MURHARD. XIV. 7.

Britain, Russia, Sardinia, and the Ottoman Porte, Prussia also being invited to participate. By this treaty among others, the Black Sea was neutralized and opened to the commerce of all Nations, but interdicted to flags of war, excepting that a certain force can be kept on foot for revenue purposes by Turkey and Russia, who pledge themselves to maintain no naval arsenals on its coasts. In accordance with this, the old Turkish principle is to be maintained of admitting no vessels of war into the Dardanelles and the Bosphorus; the only exceptions being those of light vessels in the service of the legations of friendly Powers, and of the Powers who have a right under the treaty to station certain vessels at the mouth of the Danube (Articles XI–XIV). The Danube is thrown open to commerce (Articles XV–XIX). The limits of Bessarabia are somewhat altered, with the intention of taking away from Russia the command of the mouth of the Danube, and the tract thus ceded by Russia is added to Moldavia (Articles XX–XXVI). Austria, France and Great Britain guarantee the independence and integrity of the Ottoman Empire. *

XIII. By a declaration of April 16, 1856, certain important rules of Maritime International Law are adopted by the parties to this peace. †

Modifications of the rule neutralizing the Black Sea, were agreed to at London on March 13, 1871, by the Powers participating in the Treaty of 1856, in consequence of the following circumstance as noted on page 36, *et seq.* In October, 1870,—soon after the fall of the second Empire,—the Russian Government declared to the other signatory Powers, that the Emperor could no longer hold himself to be bound by the restrictions of

---

* MARTENS. Nouv. Rec. Gen. XV. 770 & 791.

† MARTENS. Nouv. Rec. Gen. XV. 790.

1856, on his right of sovereignty in the Black Sea, nor by the special convention then made with Turkey, which determined the number and size of the vessels which these two riparian Powers allowed each other to maintain in these waters. The reasons brought forward for this step were:—(1.) An inconsistency between the main treaty of 1856 and the convention of the Straits attached to it. (2.) That the treaty had been violated by the great Powers, in its letter and spirit, by their acquiescence in the revolutionary union of the Danubian Principalities. (3.) That the Straits had been opened to foreign vessels of war against the terms of the treaty. (4.) That naval warfare had been altered by the use of the iron-clads, which exposed the Russian ports in the sea to sudden attacks of enemies forcing their way through the Straits.

A conference, held at London in January, 1871, to consider this declaration resulted in annulling Articles XI., XIII., and XIV., of the Treaty of Paris, together with the Convention concerning the Straits between Turkey and Russia. The following Article was put in their place: "The principle of the closure of the Straits of the Dardanelles and of the Bosphorus established by the special Convention of March 30, 1856, is maintained, with the right, on the part of His Imperial Majesty the Sultan, of opening said Straits in time of peace to ships of war of friendly Powers, in case the Sublime Porte should find it necessary in order to secure the Treaty of Paris of March 30, 1856." A Convention between Russia and Turkey abrogating the convention of the Straits of the same date, accompanies this treaty.

Thus Russia has recovered the national right of maintaining her fleets of whatever size in the Black Sea, and Turkey can lawfully open in peace the Straits to her friends who are enemies of Russia, in order to observe the treaty and protect herself against Russia. *

XIV. The Treaty of Prague, 1866, was made at the close of the war between Austria and Prussia, by which the old German *Bund* was dissolved and a new North-German Confederation created.

XV. The amalgamation of the various Italian States into the Kingdom of Italy is not recorded in any treaty or treaties. The union of Lombardy with Piedmont is recorded in the Treaty or Treaties of Zürich, November 11, 1859, between Austria, France, and Sardinia. Austria adopted the course with respect to Lombardy which she afterwards pursued with respect to Venetia,—namely, that of ceding the territory to France, who transferred it to Sardinia. Events, subsequent to the Treaties of Zürich, led to the formation of the present Italian Kingdom, which has been recognized by all Powers. †

A well selected list of the principal treaties since the Reformation, with a brief statement of their provisions, is inserted as Appendix. II, in the fifth edition of Mr. Woolsey's work on International Law. ‡

---

* WOOLSEY. Intern. Law. Edit. 1879. Appendix II. p. 482.

† Sir ROBERT PHILLIMORE. Vol. I. p. 46. et seq.

‡ Most civilized Nations have special Collections of their own diplomatic transactions.

Collections of Treaties of the principal States are :—

1. Austria, edited by L. Neumann, from 1763. 2. Belgium, De Garcia de la Vega. 3. France, De Clercq. From 1713 to the present time, published under the auspices of the Minister of Foreign Affairs. 4. Germany, Deutsches Reichs-Archiv. J. C. Lünig. Leipzig 1710–12. 24 Vols. folio. Recueil, Martens, established in 1791 by G. Fr. de Martens; continued by his nephew Ch. de Martens and by Saalfeld and Murhard, by Murhard and Pinhas, and, from the 14th Vol., by Samwer and J. Hopf. Göttingen. Libr. of Dieterich. 1881. 5. Great Britain, Herstlet. Complete collection of treaties, etc. London. 6. Greece, Soutzo, 1858, Athens. 7. The Netherlands, E. G. Lagemans. From 1813 to the present time. 8. Poland, Angeberg, Rec. des Traités concernant la Pologne, Paris, 1862. 9. Portugal, De Castro,

These treaties, says Sir Robert Phillimore, furnish one of the many reasons why the science of International Law has made such progress since the treaty of Westphalia, which is usually considered as the first great adjustment of International relations on the Continent of Europe. It is, then, a sound maxim that a principle of International Law acquires additional force from having been solemnly acknowledged as such in the provisions of a public treaty. *

From 1640. Lisbon, 1856. 10. Russia "Recueil des Traités," etc., published by order of the Minister of Foreign Affairs by F. Martens, in Russian and French. 11. Savoy, House of, from Peace of Château Cambresis in 1559. Turin, 1836–1861, 8 Vols. 4to. 12. Spain, "Tratados de Paz," etc., 1700–1843. Madrid, 1843. 13. United States of America. Treaties, etc., since 1776. Washington, 1871, with an appendix, 1873. "American Diplomatic Code," containing treaties of the United States between 1778 and 1834. Washington, 1834. The Seventh Volume of Public Statutes at Large of the United States of America edited by R. Peters, Boston 1848, contains in two parts, treaties with foreign States and Indian tribes (Vols. VII and VIII, new edit.). 14. Spanish and Portuguese States of America. Ch. Calvo. Rec. des Traités de tous les Etats de l'Amerique. Latine, from 1493 onward. In three parts: the first in II Vols., 800 to 1807; the second in 5 Vols., 1808–1819; the third to the present time, Paris.

* Sir ROBERT PHILLIMORE. Comm. Intern. Law. Vol. I. p. 53.

CHAPTER XXI.

INTERNATIONAL AGENTS.

PUBLIC MINISTERS, THEIR RIGHTS AND DUTIES.

§ 141. In Chapter XIX., we have given a sketch of the right of legation and embassy and the rights and duties incident to the sending and receiving of ministers, ambassadors or envoys (Gesandte.—§ 129). We must now proceed to treat of the status which international usages ascribe to those sent and received as agents for the management of international intercourse.

This status, says Sir Robert Phillimore, is composed of rights *stricti juris*, resting upon the basis of Natural Law and therefore immutable, and of privileges, originally not immutable, but so rational in their character, and so hallowed by usage, as to be universally presumed, and to become matter of strict right if their abrogation have not been formally promulgated (a case almost inconceivable) before the arrival of the ambassador. The former are usually described under the title of *inviolability*, the latter under the title of *exterritoriality*. * The right of sending embassies being established, the personal inviolability (*inviolabilitas*, *inviolabilité*, *Unverletz-*

* VATTEL. I. IV. Chapt. V. § 55, ib. Chapt. VII. § 81, and § 103. Nous avons déduit l'indépendance et l'inviolabilité de l'ambassadeur des principes naturels et nécessaires du droit des gens ces prérogatives lui sont confirmées par l'usage et le consentment général des nations.

HEFFTER. § 204. "Ein so von selbst sich verstehendes Recht." § 205. "In der Natur der Sache ist nun ein mehreres nicht begründet," etc. KLUBER. § 203. "Den Gesandten räumt theils das natürliche Völkerrecht, theils das positive der europäischen Staaten, besondere Vorrechte ein."

barkeit) of the ambassador follows as a necessary consequence. Every foreigner, indeed, is under the protection of the State in which he is commorant, and is so far inviolable. But this attribute is in a special manner ascribed to the representative of a foreign State, in whom the image of his sovereign and the majesty of his country are as it were visibly present; therefore the expression of sanctity *(sanctitas, personne sacré, Heiligkeit)* is often applied by jurists, philosophers and historians, of all ages and countries, as applicable to the bearers of an embassy. Any offence committed against their person is or ought to be considered by the State as an offence against the State itself *(crime d'état).*" *

"The injury done to an ambassador is not merely an injury done to the sovereign and country which he represents, but a violation of the common welfare and general safety of all Nations. Therefore there is a peculiarity incident to this right, viz.: that an infringement of it, unlike the invasion of particular national interest, becomes immediately and directly a matter of general international concern, and entitles all Nations to demand and enforce atonement for the offence and punishment of the offender. The atonement and punishment, moreover, are to be measured by a standard different from that which might satisfy an injury done to a private subject."†

"An ambassador, it will be seen, may, with, but not without, the consent of his master, waive his privilege of exemption from the local tribunals; but if wrong has been done, or an insult offered to him, he cannot appear as a common

* VATTEL. I. IV. Chapt. VII. § 81 and § 92. "L'inviolabilité du ministre public, ou la sureté qui lui est due, plus saintement et plus particulièrement qu'a tout autre étranger ou citoyen." MARTENS. § 214. KLUBER. § 203.

† MIRUSS. § 337.

person demanding satisfaction in a Court of justice; he has a right to demand that the State in which he is residing prosecute the wrongdoer as a public criminal." *

"There is another peculiarity incident to this right which requires observation. The Civil Law of Rome expressed a sound principle of jurisprudence, in declaring that it was competent to a person to waive any advantage which had been introduced, for his sake only, into a covenant."

"The sovereigns, therefore, of the State may waive the rights due to them in person of their ambassadors, but the ambassadors themselves have no such liberty, because these rights are not incident to their office for their own private convenience, but for the honour of their sovereign, the good of their country, and the welfare of all Nations. These rights of inviolability, flowing from the Law of Nature and the reason of the thing, are applicable to all societies, and therefore unalterable by any individual member of the community of Nations. These rights have been acknowledged and respected since the dawn of civilization in all ages, and are not without vestiges of their recognition even among barbarous tribes."

Grotius, at the outset of his excellent chapter *De legationum jure*, observes that the sanctity of ambassadors, the sacred rights of embassies, the inviolability of treaties, are topics abounding in the works of writers of all ages. †

The status of inviolability which International Law ascribes to those who are delegated by their respective Governments to act as agents in international intercourse, extend to all classes of

* VATTEL. I. IV. Ch. VIII. § 3.

† GROTIUS. Liv. 2. Chapt. 18. § 1. Sir ROBERT PHILLIMORE. Vol. II. p. 186.

public ministers who duly represent their sovereign or their State.

This right of inviolability attaches to all those who really and properly belong to the legation, *i.e.* those who accompany the minister as members of his family and his suite; the councellors *(Conseillers de Legation, Gesandtschafts-räthe)*, secretaries and attachés of the embassy *(Gesandtschaft)* and all persons attached in any official capacity to the embassy or legation; besides the domestic servants belonging to the nationality of the minister and living within the precincts of his hotel or legation.

The inviolability extends to all that is necessary for the discharge of ambassadorial functions, the private effects of the minister and of every member of his legation aforementioned, and, above all, the papers, the archives and the correspondence of the minister and of the members of the embassy are inviolable. *

This right of inviolability, says Sir Robert Phillimore, attaches from the moment the minister sets foot in the country to which he is sent, if previous notice of his mission has been imparted to it or in any case as soon as he has made his public character officially known. It extends at least so far as the State to which he is accredited is concerned, over the time occupied by the minister in his arrival, his sojourn and his departure. Lastly, the right is not affected by the breaking out of war between his own country and that to which he is sent. †

* GROTIUS. Liv. II. Chapt. XVIII. § IX. KLUBER. § 203. MIRUSS. § 335. DE GARDEN. Traité complet de la Diplomatie. Vol. II. p. 86, et seq.

† GROTIUS. Liv. II. Chapt. XVIII. § VI. VATTEL. Liv. IV. Chapt. VII. § 83. MARTENS. Liv. VII. Chapt. V. § 214. HEFFTER. §§ 204–210. KLUBER. § 203. MIRUSS. §§ 335 & 336. Sir ROBERT PHILLIMORE. Vol. II. p. 199, et seq.

Immunities of the Public Minister. Sir Robert Phillimore's Opinion.

§ 142. From the status of inviolability of the minister *(Gesandte)* result several personal immunities of which we quote in the first place the exemption from all criminal proceedings and freedom from arrest in all civil suits.

With regard to the question whether the inviolability of the minister *(Gesandte)* shields him from responsibility with regard to the criminal law of the State to which he is delegated, Sir Robert Phillimore gives the following opinion.

"With respect to criminal offences against the Private Law, these may be of two classes, *i. e.* against the property, or against the life of individuals. With respect to the former, the reason of the thing and the nature of the ambassador's function unquestionably demand his exemption from the criminal tribunals of the country. The sovereign may, according to the gravity of the offence, signify, in various ways, his displeasure, or demand his recall; but he can neither be punished nor arrested."

"In 1763, the Ambassador of Holland at the Court of the Landgrave of Hesse-Cassel was accused of mal-administration of a testamentary trust. The Government of Cassel called upon him to render an account, which he refused to do, whereupon he was arrested with a view to to obtain from him the necessary documents connected with the trust. But the Landgrave was obliged to send a special embassy to Holland to make apology and reparation for this infraction of International Law."

"With respect to graver offences against the Criminal Law, such as murder, the question is more difficult; but the true proposition of International Law upon this subject is, as laid down by Grotius, namely, that the guilty person cannot be tried by the foreign tribunals. This doctrine is also supported by Wicquefort, Zouch, Bynkershoek, and Vattel. Great authorities in the English law, Coke, Comyns, Hale, Foster, held a contrary doctrine; but Blackstone correctly states that, whatever may have formerly been the opinion, this country follows, as others do, the opinion of Grotius. With respect to crimes against the majesty of the State, such as conspiracies against the Government or the sovereign thereof, it appears to be now the clear law that no judicial process in the State against which the offence has been committed can be put in motion against the representative of a foreign sovereign. Such appears to be the best and most generally received opinion. There are not, however, wanting writers who draw a distinction between the commission of *mala prohibita* and *mala in se*, and between *privata* and *publica delicta*. But the reasons of exemption apply to both cases; namely first, because the nature of the ambassador's functions demands the most absolute freedom in every case that may arise, *securitas legatorum utilitate quæ ex pœna est præponderat.* Secondly because the ambassador represents the person of another, and is recognized in that capacity by the tacit compact by which he is admitted into the country; it has been nobly said: *ils sont la parole du Prince qui les envoie, et cette parole doit être libre.*"

"It is not meant, however, to convey the impression, either that the ambassador is to escape without punishment, or that the State in which he is discharching his functions is powerless to resist his open violence, or to stay his secret machinations against her public safety, or to redress the rights of a subject whom he may have criminally injured. It is the duty and the right of the injured State, under these circumstances, to oppose force to force, and in the event of secret machinations, to secure the person of the ambassador and remove him from her borders, and in the case of the *privatum delictum*, to insist upon his being tried by the tribunals, or the proper authorities, of his own country." *

"It has been held by high judicial authority, says Sir Robert Phillimore further, that if a foreign minister commit an assault, he is so far deprived of his privilege that battery committed on him, by way of self-defence, is legal, though even such conduct on the part of a foreign minister will not justify an arrest on process."

"It is clear that Courts of Justice cannot inquire whether a person recognized by the Government as a foreign minister was duly appointed as such or not. The recognition of the Government is conclusive upon the judicial tribunal. Courts of Law have considered that the reasons which necessitate the inviolability of the person of the foreign minister apply to those of his train or suite, and therefore, that an assault upon, and that threats used towards, a secretary of legation are punishable as a criminal violation of International Law." †

Right of Exterritoriality. Droit d'Asile. Prof. Lorimer's Opinion.

§ 143. The right of exterritoriality (described under § 46) of the public minister is merely another aspect of the status of inviolability. The right of exterritoriality involves the exemption, to a certain extent, of his house or legation buildings from the operations of territorial jurisdiction.

---

* GROTIUS. Liv. II. Chapt. XVIII. 4, 5, 7. MONTESQUIEU. De l'Esprit des Lois. Part II. Chapt. XXVI. § 21. WARD. Vol. II. pp. 515–16. ZOUCH. Solut. Quest. De Leg. del Ind. Comp. BYNKERSHOEK. De Fore Leg. Ch. 17, 18, 19. VATTEL. Liv. II. §§ 94–96.

† KLUBER. § 211. STEPHENS.' (Blackstone's) Comm. Edit. 1858. II. p. 498. BYNKERSHOEK. De Foro Leg. Chapt. VI. WICKEFORT. L'Ambassadeur et ses functions. Liv. I. Chapt. XXVII. PHILLIMORE. Common International Law. Vol. II. pp. 202–214.

Prof. Lorimer gives the following opinion on this head.

"Amongst the conditions which experience has indicated as inseparable from the right of legation in the existing conditions of society, and which thus become subsidiary rights in themselves, the most peculiar is the right of the international agent to exemption from the municipal jurisdiction of the State in which he resides, or through which he passes. A sharp distinction is here rightly drawn between his character as an international agent and as an individual foreigner. In the former character, and in it alone, he is held to carry the municipal laws of his own State along with him. An English ambassador, with his family and his suite, whilst abroad in the public service, is domiciled in England and his house is English ground. Beyond the necessities of self-protection, the State in which he resides can deal with him only diplomatically, even in the event of his transgressing its laws, *i. e.* it must call on his own State to deal with him through its agent there resident; and debts, incurred in his public capacity, must be sued for in England. In his character of a private individual, on the other hand, if that character be deliberately assumed by him, for example, by entering into private speculations, or by purchasing property in the country of his residence, that country deals with him as a private foreigner, the exterritorial gives way to the territorial jurisdiction. It was towards tracing this line that the work of Bynkershoek, *De foro legatorum*, offered such important contributions. But even in Bynkershoek's hands it was found scarcely to admit of definition; and its necessity has been evaded by the prohibition which most States impose on their diplomatic and even their higher consular agents to enter into private transactions in the States in which they reside."

"The right of exterritoriality extends not only to the person of the international agent but to his house and his suite. It cannot be entered and they cannot be arrested."

"The privileges accorded to ambassadors led to many scandalous abuses in former times, none of them greater than those which arose out of the inviolability of their residences, or what was technically known as the *franchise de l'hôtel.* Whole quarters of populous cities—Rome, Venice, Madrid, and Frankfurt, during the assembly for the election of the emperor—were taken possession of by foreign ministers under this guise. By the simple expedient of placing the arms of their sovereigns over the doors of as many houses as they thought proper to hire, and letting them out as asylums for offenders against the laws of the countries in which they dwelt, enormous profits were realised. Even Callières, who was not scrupulous, was shocked at the practice. 'It is impossible,' he says, 'sufficiently to blame foreign ministers who abuse the right of asylum by sheltering criminals and bandits condemned to death for atrocius crimes, and make a shameful traffic of the protection they afford them.'"*

"Grotius declares that the *droit d'asile* has no warrant in International Law, and Bynkershoek limits it to the person, the family, and the suite of the minister. Such, in recent times, has come to be the universal rule, with this additional proviso, that the ambassador is required to furnish to the minister for foreign affairs a list of the names of the persons in favour of whom he claims the privilege. Even as regards his own domes-

* Page 161.

tics, it is scarcely consistent with modern usage for the minister to exercise magisterial functions; and in criminal cases he either sends the delinquents for trial to their own country, or delivers them to the local tribunals."

"One of the privileges of the *hôtel*, however, is still maintained,—viz., that of holding religious worship within its precincts, in accordance with the national faith of the ambassador; and this not only for the benefit of his household, but for that of his other countrymen resident in the place. The use of external rites—such as processions, bells, and the like—for obvious reasons, is generally interdicted."

Marriages in Legation chapels.

"Marriages which take place in the chapels of English embassies, are held, in English law, to have taken place in England, and to be valid independently of the local law; but the point of their international validity is one on which grave doubts exists, both in this country and in America and which has been decided in the negative in France. *

Halleck's opinion on the immunities of the Public Minister.

On the immunities of the public minister with regard to the right of extraterritoriality and the *droit d'asyle*, the opinion of Halleck is as follows.

"The act of sending a minister by the one, and of receiving him by the other, amounts to a tacit compact between the two States, that he shall be subject only to the authority of his own Government. The inviolability of the minister is founded upon mutual utility, growing out of the necessity that such officers and agents should be entirely independent of the local authority, in order to properly fulfil the duties of their mission. Hence, the fiction of exterritoriality has been invented, by which the minister, though actually

* Prof. LORIMER. p. 248, et seq. FRASER. Husband and Wife, Vol. II. pp. 1312 & 1529.

in a foreign country, is considered still to remain within the territory of his own State. He continues subject to the laws of his own country, both with respect to his personal status, and his rights of property; and his children, though born in a foreign country, are considered as natives. A respect due to sovereigns, says Vattel, should reflect on their representatives, and chiefly on their ambassadors, as representing their master's person in the first degree. Whoever affronts or injures a public minister, commits a crime the more deserving a severe punishment, as thereby the sovereign and his country might be brought into great difficulties and trouble. It is just that he should be punished for his fault, and that the State should, at the expense of the delinquent, give a full satisfaction to the sovereign affronted in the person of his minister. If a foreign minister offends a citizen, the latter may oppose him without departing from the respect due to the character, and give him a lesson which shall both efface the stain of the outrage, and expose the author of it. The person offended may further prefer a complaint to his sovereign, who will demand of the minister's master a just satisfaction. The great concerns of the State forbid the citizen, on such occasions, to entertain those thoughts of revenge which the point of honour might suggest though otherwise allowable. Even according to the maxims of the world, a gentleman receives no disgrace by an affront for which it is not in his power, of himself, to procure satisfaction. The necessity and right of embassies being established, the inviolability of ambassadors and other public ministers is a certain consequence of it; for if their person be not protected from violence of every kind, the right of embassies becomes precarious, and the success very uncertain. A right to the end, is the right to the necessary means. Embassies, then, being of such great importance in the universal society of Nations, and so necessary to their common well-being, the person of ministers charged with this embassy is to be *sacred and inviolable* among all Nations." *

"It is proper to distinguish between the inviolability of the public minister and the legal fiction of his exterritoriality. The former is not a consequence of the latter, but the latter was invented for the purpose of giving security to the former. The mere fact of a public minister being regarded as a foreigner, resident in a foreign country, would not, of itself, necessarily exempt him from local jurisdiction. Article fourteen of the Code Napoleon provides for bringing before the French tribunals *a foreigner resident in a foreign country*, even for engagements contracted *in a foreign country* with a Frenchman. If, therefore, the exemption of the minister depended upon his exterritoriality, or implied foreign residents, he might still be subject to local jurisdiction. The true basis of all diplomatic privilege consists in the idea of inviolability which international jurisprudence attaches to his person and his office, and from which it cannot be severed. This idea of inviolability is an inherent and essential quality of the public minister, and the office cannot exist without it. International Law has conferred it upon the State or Sovereign which he represents. and to divest him of that quality, is to divest him of his office, as the two are inseparable. Not so

* VATTEL. Droit des Gens. Liv. IV. Chapt. IX. § 81. WICQUEFORT. De l'Ambas. Liv. I. § 27. MARTENS. Précis du Droit des Gens. §§ 214–218. HORNE. On Diplomacy. Sec. III. §§ 20–22. It was decided by the English Parliament, that the slaying of the Genoese ambassador in England in the reign of Richard III. was high treason, for ambassadors should be protected like princes (Stat. Pap. 3 R. 3, num. 18).

with respect to the fiction of exterritoriality. * So far as that is necessary to the exercise of his functions, or in other words, to secure his inviolability, it is not an essential quality of the public minister, and therefore may be dispensed with by renouncement or otherwise. It will be seen, hereafter, that this distinction, which is made by the best writers on Public Law, leads to very important results. As a consequence of the sacredness and inviolability of the person of a public minister, he is entitled to an entire exemption from the local jurisdiction, both civil and criminal. This exemption commences the moment he enters the territory of the State to which he is sent, and continues, not only during the whole time of his residence, but until he leaves the country, or at least till he loses his official character, and the protection due to his office. The State to which he is accredited may at any time require him to leave, either before or after his recall by his own Government. Sometimes the period within which he must leave is designated in his letter of dis-

* BLUNTSCHLI. Droit International, p. 112. "La fiction de l'exterritorialité n'est pas la cause de l'immunité dont les personnes ci-dessus joissent en pays étranger ; elle en est simplement l'application a une personne déterminée : la vraie cause c'est le respect de l'indépendance de ceux qui sont chargés de représenter les états. Cette fiction n'a donc que des effets relatifs ; sa portée est réglée par les causes réelles de cette immunité. . . . . La personne qui jouit de l'exterritorialité n'est pas soumise à la jurisdiction des tribunaux criminels de l'étât ou elle réside. . . . . Cette disposition, comfirmée par l'usage universal des peuples civilisés, est de droit singulier, parce qu' elle arrête le cours régulier de la justice. Elle a quelque chose analogue á l'irresponsabilité des Souverains en droit public. Il est, du reste, prudent de rappeler qu' il serait dangereux de mettre á l'essai la valeur de ces fictions des juris-consultes . . . Il est, en général, dangereux de pousser trop loin les conséquences du principe de l'exterritorialité ; le respect des lois et l'ordre public peuvent en souffrir. Le Droit International se borne á exiger qu'on protège la liberté et l'honneur des états dans la personne de leurs représentants ; il ne veut pas qu'on laisse impunis les mefaits de certains individus,"

One of the earliest applications of the word extra-territorium to ambassadors is to be found in Grotius (De Bell. Lib. 2. Chapt. 18).

missal; and, at the termination of that period, the protection due to his office necessarily ceases." *

The public minister himself, says Halleck further, can afford no protection; it is the law which gives a public character to his family, domestics and servants. Hence, a mere appointment by a minister of any person as a member of his household, is, in itself, no protection to such person. It must be shown that he is *bonâ fide* the officer or servant of such household, and that he performs the duties corresponding to the position or office which he pretends to hold. A Court will inquire if his appointment is a fair *bonâ fide* transaction, and if not, the privilege claimed will not be allowed. The same may be said of the goods of persons claiming such privilege; if they are not *bonâ fide* members of such household, or are engaged in other business or trade, their goods are not exempt from process for debts, rents, &c. Ministers have not unfrequently attempted to protect the persons and property of their friends from arrest or attachment, or execution, by pretended appointments to positions in their household but the Courts have very properly refused to give any countenance to such frauds." †

No right of asylum to refugees in the house of the Public Minister.

In the opinion of Grotius, Wicquefort, Bynkershoek and Merlin, no right of asylum to refugees

* HALLECK. Edit. Sir Sherston Baker. Vol. I. p. 277, et seq. WHEATON. Elem. Intern. Law. Part III. Chapt. I. § 14. PHILLIMORE. Vol. I. § 219. Vol. II. § 153. GROTIUS, de Jur. Bel. ac Pac. Lib. II. Chapt. XVIII. §§ 1–6. RUTHERFORTH. Institutes, B. II. Chapt. IX. § 20. KLUBER. Droit des Gens Mod. p. II. tit. II. § 203. BYNKERSHOEK. De Foro Legat. Chapts. 17–19. BLACKSTONE. Commentaries, Vol. I. p. 253. FŒLIX. Droit Intern. Privé. §§ 169, 188, 210, et seq. HEFFTER. Droit International §§ 204, 205, 212–215. VILLEFORT. Priviléges Diplomatiques, p. 7, et seq.

† HALLECK. Vol. I. p. 276, et seq.

in the house of an ambassador is founded on the Law of Nations. *

Passage through a third State, in peace and war.

§ 144. Has the public minister the right of inviolability and extraterritoriality in the territory of a third State, where he is passing through or temporarily staying on his way to the State to which he is accredited? As such a case must frequently occur, this question can arise at any time. Vattel is of opinion that it is a reciprocal obligation, imposed by the comity of Nations, that the authorities of the country through which a public minister is passing cannot reasonably refuse him all the privileges due to the representative of a Foreign Power, at all events, perfect safety and protection must be accorded to him. † Wheaton states that he is entitled to respect and protection, though not invested with all the privileges and immunities which he enjoys within the dominions of the Sovereign to whom he is sent. ‡ Kluber says, "Persönliche Sicherheit ist das mindeste worauf alsdann der Gesandte Anspruch zu machen hat." ||

Opinion of Sir Robert Phillimore.

Sir Robert Phillimore gives the following opinion.

"The sound rules which ought to govern this question appear to be :—

"1. That, in time of peace, the ambassador is of right inviolable in his transit through a third

* See Heathfield v. Chilton 4 Burr. 2016 as to the registration in England of the names of the servants of an ambassador. In the present century, in the case of the coachman of Mr. Gallatin, the United States minister in London, the British Government claimed the right to arrest him on a criminal charge for an assault committed outside the residence, and to make the arrest within the limits, admitting, however, the propriety of first giving notice to the minister that he might deliver him up or make arrangements with the police as to the time and manner of their entering to search and seize. WHEATON. Dana's Edit. 303. note.

† VATTEL. Liv. IV. Chapt. VII. § 84.

‡ WHEATON. Vol. I. p. 269.

|| KLUBER. § 176.

country, but cannot claim the privileges of ex-territoriality as a matter of tacit compact, though they would probably be acceded to him by the Courts of all Nations—and to ambassadors to a Congress they are accorded. The diplomatic agents of foreign Powers at Frankfurt-on-the Main were allowed the same privileges, on their transit, as the members of the German Confederation." *

"2. That, in time of war, he cannot be secure from imprisonment without a previously obtained permission to pass through the territory; but that his life can in no case be taken, unless, indeed, he actually exercises hostilities in the country through which he passes."

"The true international rule would be, that the ambassador should be allowed, in all cases, the *jus transitus innoxii*. This was the law of Holland at the beginning of the eighteenth century. The Mexicans are said to have adopted a similar principle of law; their practice was to mark out a certain route out of which it was not lawful for the hostile ambassador to deviate."

"It is well remarked by Zouch, that both the State which sends the ambassador, and that to which he is sent, are injured by harm or insult inflicted upon him by a third country." †

The Minister of Foreign Affairs and his department.

§ 145. In conformity with the Public Law of the State (§§ 37 & 38), the political affairs of international intercourse are directed by a State department, called the department of Foreign Affairs *(ministère des affaires étrangères)* and the officer presiding over that department is styled the Minister or Secretary of State for Foreign

---

* GROTIUS. Liv. II. Chapt. XVIII. 5.

† ZOUCH. De Judicio inter Gentes. P. 2. §§ 4 & 18. FŒLIX, in his Droit Intern. Priv. p. 279, states the enactments contained in various municipal codes with reference to the treatment and protection of ambassadors. PHILLIMORE. Vol. II, p. 217.

Affairs *(ministre des affaires étrangères* or *chancelier d'état)*. The attributes of this high functionary, upon whose knowledge, experience and sound policy in the management of political affairs, depends the maintenance of friendly relations between his Government and foreign Powers, are manifold. All business relating to ceremonials of reception, audiences, presentation of credentials or letters of recall of and conferences with foreign diplomatic agents, the discussion of reciprocal interests, the negotiation and drawing up of treaties and conventions, and the issue of all documents and despatches relating to external political affairs, letters of credence and instructions for the diplomatic agents going abroad, belong to his department.

This department has in a large State such a preponderant influence, that the Minister or Secretary for Foreign Affairs in the government of large States is, as such, the Prime Minister, or chief leader of the Cabinet.

At the seat of every Government the Minister of Foreign Affairs is thus, next to the Sovereign or Chief Magistrate of the State, the first personage in the eye of the foreign diplomatic agent, for whom he is the constituted authority, representing the whole external sovereignty of the State (§ 24).

He represents his Government in dealing with all foreign agents, accredited to his Government or Sovereign, and he does so both in relation to individual agents and in relation to them in the aggregate called the *corps diplomatique*.

All political transactions and communications with other States emanating from or addressed to the Sovereign or Chief Magistrate of the State, regarding external State affairs, pass through the hands of the Minister of Foreign Affairs. The right of direct personal communication with the

Sovereign, which nominally belongs yet to the privileges attaching to the rank of an Ambassador, is falling more and more into disuse through the general adoption of the principles of constitutional representative government which enhance the position of responsible Ministers or Secretaries of State.

§ 146. There are two classes of international or so-called diplomatic agents. *Mutual ranking of International Agents.*

1°. Those with credentials from the Sovereign or Chief Magistrate of their State representing the whole Government and external sovereignty. They are accredited direct to the Sovereign or the Chief Magistrate of the State to which they are sent. These are called Ambassadors, Envoys Extraordinary, Ministers Plenipotentiary and Ministers-Resident *(Gesandte)*.

2°. Those who have no letters of credence to the Sovereign or Chief Magistrate, representing only the foreign department of their State and are accredited as agents of that department to the foreign department of the other State. These are *chargés d'affaires (Geschäftsträger, Zaakgelastigden)* and, in some instances, Consular officers.

The rank of a Public Minister has nothing to do with the transaction of affairs, but only with the ceremonials of the Court. As the capacity to represent the external sovereignty of the State is restricted to the first class, viz. to those provided with credentials from their Sovereign or the Chief Magistrate of the State, it is not legal to have treaties or conventions concluded by the political agents of the second class, as treaties and conventions can be made only by the constituted authorities of a State and those who represent its whole Government. Formerly, says Mr. Woolsey, there was but one class of Public Minister or at most two, Ambassadors *(Gesandte)* and agents *(chargés* *d'affaires)* known to Europe, but since the beginning of the eighteenth century there have been three grades. Moreover, sometimes extraordinary ministers have claimed precedence over ordinary ministers of the same class. *

Nominal ranking of International Agents by the Congress of Vienna in 1815 *and that of Aix-la-Chapelle* 1818.

Differences about rank among diplomatic agents accredited at the same Court led to some regulations in the protocol of the plenipotentiaries of the eight principal Powers, concerned in the Congress of Vienna, dated March 19, 1815, which is to the following effect:—

"To prevent the embarrassments which have often occurred, and which may yet arise from the claims to precedence between different diplomatic agents, the plenipotentiaries of the Powers signing the Treaty of Paris, have agreed to the following articles; and they feel it their duty to ask those of other crowned heads to adopt the same regulations:—

Art. I. Diplomatic employés are divided into three classes:—

That of ambassadors, legates, or nuncios;

That of envoys, ministers, or others accredited to sovereigns;

That of chargés d'affaires accredited to ministers charged with foreign affairs.

Art. II. Ambassadors, legates, or nuncios alone have the representative character.

Art. III. Diplomatic employés on an extraordinary mission have not, for that reason, any superiority of rank.

Art. IV. Diplomatic employés shall take rank among themselves, in each class, according to the date of the official notification of their arrival.

The present rule shall bring with it no innovation in regard to the representatives of the Pope.

* WOOLSEY, p. 156.

Art. V. There shall be in each State a uniform mode, determined upon for the reception of the diplomatic employés of each class.

Art. VI. The ties of relationship or of family alliance between Courts give no rank to their diplomatic employés. The same is true of political ties.

Art. VII. In the acts or treaties between several Powers which admit of the *alternat*, the lot shall decide between the ministers, as to the order to be followed in signatures." *

In the protocol of the Congress of Aix-la-Chapelle, dated November 21, 1818, a new class of ministers was constituted by the plenipotentiaries of the five great Powers, in the following terms.

"To avoid the disagreeable discussions which may arise in the future on a point of diplomatic etiquette, which the rule, annexed to the *recès* of Vienna, by which questions of rank were regulated, does not seem to have provided for, it is decided between the five Courts, that *resident ministers* accredited with them shall form, in respect to their rank, an intermediate class between ministers of the second order and *chargés d'affaires*."

According to these rules, there are, nominally, four classes of diplomatic agents. The first are ambassadors of temporal Powers, together with legates *a* or *de latere* and nuncios of the Pope. †

---

* By the *alternat* is intended the practice, sometimes adopted in signing conventions, of alternating in the order of priority of signature, according to some fixed rule, so as to cut off questions of rank. The lot has also been used. KLUBER. §§ 104-106.

† There is no distinction between legates *a* and *de latere*. These are cardinals, nuncios or not. Internuncios form an inferior grade of papal diplomats, belonging to the second or third class. HEFFTER. §§ 201-209.

To the second class belong all diplomatic employés accredited to Sovereigns, whether called envoys, ministers, ministers plenipotentiary, or internuncios. To the third class belong resident ministers also accredited to Sovereigns. The fourth class is constituted by chargés d'affaires accredited to ministers of foreign affairs, with whom would be reckoned consuls invested with diplomatic functions. *

In regard to the rank of the minister who shall represent a State at a particular Court, Mr. Woolsey remarks that the general rule is "that one of such rank and title is sent, as has been usually received from the other party; and that the Sovereigns having a royal title neither send ministers of the first rank to, nor receive them from inferior Powers." †

In regard to diplomatic etiquette, Dr. Wheaton observes, that while it is in great part a code of manners, and not of laws, there are certain rules the breach of which may hinder the performance of more serious duties. Such is the rule requiring a reciprocation of diplomatic visits between ministers resident at the same court.

"As for the ceremonial of courts Mr. Woolsey says further, an ambassador is to regard himself the representative of national politeness and good-will, but to submit to no ceremony abroad which would be accounted degrading at home; for nothing can be demanded of him inconsistent with the honour of his country. A question somewhat agitated among us (United States of America), who have no distinct costume for the chief magistrate, or for those who wait on him, is, in what costume should our diplomatic agents appear at foreign Courts? In none other, it may

* Comp. Heffter, § 208.

† See also HEFFTER. § 209.

be answered, than such as is appropriate when we pay our respects to the President of the United States, unless another is expressly prescribed. The rule is to emanate from home and not from abroad." *

With regard to the ranking of public ministers, Sir Robert Phillimore states the following: —

Sir Robert Phillimore on the ranking of International Agents.

"The Romans, and indeed the ancients generally, recognized but one class of diplomatic agents whom they usually designated by the terms *oratores* or *legati*. In Europe these terms found their translation at first in the generic term of ambassadors †, or in some equivalent designation of a single class. Since the fifteenth or sixteenth century, the refinements and the vanity of European Courts have introduced various grades of diplomatic agency into the positive Law of Nations, which are only so far of importance as different ceremonial privileges are attached to the different degrees of legation. But to the accredited public minister of every State, whatever be his designation, the rights of inviolability and the privileges of exterritoriality appertain with equal certainty and strength."

"Equally unknown to the ancients was the modern distinction of ordinary, or resident and extraordinary ambassadors. The Romans safe, as they reasonably concluded, in the vastness of their empire, from foreign invasion, and having but little commerce with other Nations, neither required nor instituted any resident embassy in foreign countries. The breaking up of this vast empire into various kingdoms introduced that necessity, which under the gigantic domination of Rome had not existed."

---

* WOOLSEY. Intern. Law, Edit. 1879, p. 158.

† *Ambassadeurs, Embaxadores, Ambasciatori* or *Ambactus (Botschafter, Gesandte).*

"It was not, however, till after the Peace of Westphalia (1648), that the institution of permanent embassies, (though beginning, contemporaneously with standing armies, to take root soon after the fifteenth century), can be said to have become the established practice of Nations. It was about this period that the rights of legation began to be ascertained with the careful minuteness which distinguishes this part of positive International Law. Before the close of the fifteenth century, a second order, and during the eighteenth century, a third order, of diplomatic agents appears to have sprung up; and since the Congress of Vienna, in 1815, and the protocol of Aix-la-Chapelle, in 1818, to which Austria, France, Great Britain, Prussia, and Russia were parties, the diplomatic hierarchy has consisted, technically speaking, of four orders." *

All diplomatic agents, says Sir Robert Phillimore further, enjoy in the fullest manner, the privileges incident to what is universally called the representative character, by virtue of which they represent their Sovereign or State, not only in the conduct of affairs at a foreign Court, but they also represent the person of the Sovereign or State, and are by usage entitled, speaking generally, to the honours which the Sovereign or the State (if it could be conceived to be present) would receive. This idea of the full representative character in the agent, had no doubt its origin in the fundamental constitution of monarchical States, because it was possible to represent the person of the monarch; but Republican States, nevertheless, have imitated the example. Legates *a latere* must not be confounded with other

* VATTEL. Liv. IV. Chapt. VI. § 73. WARD. Vol. II. p. 413. HEFTER. §§ 199 & 357. MIRUSS. §§ 85–89. KLUBER. § 170. DE MARTENS. § 193. Sir ROBERT PHILLIMORE. Vol. II. p. 248.

classes of Papal agents designated Nuncios. The legates *a latere* are sent by the Pope into Roman Catholic countries, to exercise, in his name, the spiritual functions which depend upon his recognition as Head of the Church. The nuncios are ambassadors sent to foreign Courts to represent the Pope in the conduct of his affairs, of whatever kind they may be. The division of ambassadors and nuncios into ordinary and extraordinary had its origin in the distinction between permanent or indeterminate missions and those which had for their object the transaction of an extraordinary, particular, and determinate business.

"In modern practice, however, the title 'extraordinary' is given occasionally, as a title of greater honour, even to ambassadors destined to a residence, for an indeterminate period, at the Court to which they are sent. Diplomatic agents of this first class, are sent by States, whether monarchical or republican, entitled to royal honours. That is to say, if an inferior State accredit an ambassador of the first class, he will not be received by the great European Powers. It is impossible, however, to maintain, as has been attempted, that the right to send ambassadors is confined to monarchies, or to deny that the rank of the ambassador, abstractedly speaking, depends upon the sending and not upon the receiving State."

"The second class comprises envoys *(envoyés, ablegati, prolegati, inviati)* ordinary and extraordinary; ministers plenipotentiary *(plena potentia muniti, ministres plénipotentiaires, bevollmächtige Gesandte)*. The Austrian Minister at Constantinople, who appears to be by custom exclusively designated as *Internuncius* The Internuncio of the Pope."

"The third, or intermediate class, created by the Conference of the Five Powers at Aix-la-Chapelle, in 1818, is composed of what are called *ministres résidents*, accredited to the Sovereign."

"The fourth, usually denominated the third class, includes *chargés d'affaires (Geschäftsträger)* accredited to the minister of foreign affairs; either such as are originally sent and accredited *ad hoc*, or who have been nominated, either verbally or by writing, *ad interim*, during the absence of the minister, or accredited to Courts to which it is not customary to send a formally constituted minister. The ceremonial honours to which this class may be entitled appear doubtful, but they are entitled to the immunities of recognized diplomatic agents, though without the formal character of ministers. To this class belong consuls, being accredited as diplomatic agents or public ministers, such as are maintained by the Christian Powers of Europe and America at the Courts of the Barbary States or in Egypt."

"These different orders of ministers, it must be observed, can only be distinguished by the ceremonial honours accorded to them; and, in fact, these divisions, which make the difference of order depend upon the difference of ceremonial are strictly speaking, illogical. * For if upon this principle of distinction, it were asked why the ambassador enjoyed greater honours than the envoy, it must be answered, because the former belongs to the first, and the latter to the second class; and if it were asked why the former belonged to the first, and the latter to the second class, it must be answered, because the former is an ambassador and the latter an envoy. The only sound and logical division is that which is

* DE MARTENS. § 192. Note of Mr. Pinheiro Ferreira.

founded on the true principle of general International Law, viz., as regard the character of the affair, evidenced by his credentials *(mandatum, Mandat)*, entrusted to the management of the agent, whatever be his title. There is a clear distinction, according to the nature of things between agents *(plénipotentiaires)* accredited by one Sovereign to another Sovereign, and agents *(chargés d'affaires)*, accredited by one Minister for Foreign Affairs to another Minister for Foreign Affairs."

"According to the fourth article of the Congress of Vienna (1815) the rank of diplomatic agents, between themselves, was to be determined by reference to the date of the official notification of their arrival at the Court to which they are accredited; and by the sixth article, all distinctions of rank between diplomatic ministers, arising out of the ties of consanguinity and the domestic or political relations of their respective Courts, are abolished."

"Every State may determine for itself what rank it will confer upon its diplomatic agents, nor is it restricted by International Law as to their number, their sex, their religion, or their station, whether lay or clerical, military or civil, unless in cases opposed to a fundamental law of the receiving State. It is usual for States to send and receive diplomatic agents of equal rank."

"A diplomatic agent may be accredited at one and the same time to various States. A diplomatic agent may be fully empowered to negotiate with foreign States, as at a Congress of different Nations, without being accredited to any particular Court: or he may be accredited by a third State to mediate between two other States."

"The legal status of mere agents employed, on behalf of Governments or princes, in foreign countries, is not very clearly defined by any writer upon International Jurisprudence. It is clear, however, that agents employed in adjusting private claims of the Sovereign or negotiating a loan, commissioners to settle boundaries, and the like, are not *virtute officii* clothed with the immunities of a diplomatic agent. The same remark applies to secret emissaries of a State, though sent with the permission of the foreign State into its territory. These commissioners or emissaries, though furnished perhaps with letters of recommendation from their Sovereign, and therefore entitled to more consideration than private individuals, are not accredited, and therefore cannot claim the *jus legationum*. If, however, the State clothe them with diplomatic powers, and accredit them to a foreign State, they become entitled to the immunities of a diplomatic agent. This is also the case with deputies sent to a Congress on behalf of a Confederation of States, if they be accredited."

"The whole question depends upon whether or no the constituent body has been competent, and has intended to clothe them with a ministerial character." *

Letters of Credence.

§ 147. The mission of the public minister begins as soon as he receives his letters of credence *(lettres de créance, creditia, Credentialien, Beglaubigungs-schreiben)* from his Sovereign or the Chief Magistrate of his State accompanied with his instructions, through the Minister or Secretary of State for Foreign Affairs. The letters of credence are addressed by the Sovereign or Chief Magistrate of the sending State to that of the receiving State. In the case of a *chargé d'affairs*

* DE MARTENS. §§ 193–203. VATTEL. Liv. IV. Chapt. VI. §§ 75–78. KLUBER. §§ 171–187. HEFFTER. §§ 208–222. Sir ROBERT PHILLIMORE. Vol. II. Edit. 1882. p. 248, et seq.

the credentials are addressed by one Minister of Foreign Affairs to another. *

The letters of credence contain the general purport of the mission and the name and class of the diplomatic agent with the request that faith may be given to his representations on the part of his principal; to which is added "especially when he (the agent) gives you the assurance of our friendly feelings, high consideration and esteem;" sometimes being variated by the terms "inviolable attachment," "perfect friendship," or the like complimentary clause. †

The Full Power. (plein pouvoir).

The full power *(plein pouvoir, Vollmacht)* is a separate instrument distinct from the letters of credence. It is drawn up in the form of letters patent *(mandatum procuratorium)* empowering the diplomatic agent to negotiate.

It is the full power, says Robert Phillimore, whether it be a separate instrument or contained in the letters of credence, which founds the authority of the diplomatic agent as the representative of his Sovereign, and the terms of it are binding on him and his principal, though at variance with secret instructions.

The full power may be general or special. The general full power *(mandatum illimitatum)* capacitates the holder of it for all the usual diplomatic functions, or for negotiating generally with a foreign State. The special full power *(mandatum limitatum)* authorizes the holder of it to transact only a particular business; the limits of his authority are defined, and out of these he cannot travel. If these powers be granted to several persons, it should be expressed in the document,

* DE MARTENS. § 202.

† BARON CHARLES DE MARTENS. Guide Dipl. Vol. II. p. 516, et seq.

whether they may act severally or only jointly in the execution of their office. *

Audience for the delivery of the Letter of Credence.

With regard to the ceremonials connected with the arrival and audience of an accredited diplomatic agent, Sir Robert Phillimore states the following as international usage and practice.

"Every diplomatic agent must notify his arrival to the Minister for Foreign Affairs. If the diplomatic agent be of the first class, his arrival is communicated through the secretary of the embassy, or some other gentleman *(Gesandtschaftscavalier)* attached to the mission. He delivers a copy of the letters of credence to the Minister for Foreign Affairs and requests an audience for his principal with the Sovereign. This audience may be either public or private; diplomatic agents of the first class are alone entitled to the former. But this audience is not a necessary preliminary to entering upon the performance of his functions. † This public audience used to be preceded by a solemn entry *(entrée solennelle)*; this ceremony has now fallen into general desuetude. ‡ At the audience, which is now usually private, the letters of credence are delivered, a complimentary speech is made by the ambassador and replied to by the Sovereign."

"If the diplomatic agent be of the second or third class, his arrival is notified by a letter to the Minister for Foreign Affairs, who is requested to take the orders of his Sovereign respecting the delivery of the letters of credence. The Sovereign usually receives them at a private audience, at which the Minister for Foreign Affairs restores to them their letters of credence. ||

---

* PHILLIMORE. Vol. II. p. 257.

† MARTENS. § 206. MIRUSS. § 307. WHEATON. I. 270.

‡ "Au reste, said Martens, toute cette pénible cérémonie de l'audience solennelle est peu nécessaire, même à un ambassadeur, pour entrer en fonctions," &c.

|| MARTENS. § 207. MIRUSS. § 311.

"If the diplomatic agent be of the fourth class, that is a *chargé d'affaires* not accredited to the Sovereign, his arrival is notified by letter to the Minister for Foreign Affairs, of whom alone an audience is requested, for the purpose of delivering the letters of credence."

"In Republican States, Mr. Wheaton observes, the diplomatic agent is received in a similar manner by the Chief Executive Magistrate or Council charged with the foreign affairs of the Nation." *

Rules of Diplomatic Etiquette.

The rules of etiquette which long usage has established between diplomatic agents resident at the same foreign Court, and towards the members of the foreign Government, occupy many pages of some works upon International Law; but these rules, though their observance on the ground of convenience be very desirable, and their non-observance would denote ill-breeding in the State renouncing them, do not arrive at the dignity of laws, or attain the character of rights. †

Merlin's remark is sound and just, says Sir Robert Phillimore, that there is but one general rule on this subject: namely, that public ministers should receive all the distinctions which etiquette and the manners of each Nation have determined, as marks of that estimation which is befitting." ‡ It must be remembered that custom may impart a value to a ceremony in itself indifferent, but which has become significant of the estimation in which the object of the ceremony is held. We have seen an instance of this in the honours of the salute paid to the flags of Nations. When usage has attached a

* WHEATON. I. 270. MARTENS. § 206. Sir ROBERT PHILLIMORE. Vol. II. p. 259, et seq.

† WHEATON. I. 272.

‡ MERLIN. S. IV.

real value to a point of etiquette, the omission of it is not justifiable by any principle of International Law. Nevertheless, it must always be competent to a Sovereign to make alterations in the ceremonies of his Court; he must of course be prepared for two consequences—one would probably be, that foreign Nations will refuse to accredit diplomatic agents to him to be received upon the footing of these alterations; another, in all likelihood, would be, that he must submit himself to retaliatory alterations, in the persons of his own representatives at foreign Courts." *

Ending of the mission. Recall or death of the Diplomatic Agent. Sir Robert Phillimore's statement.

The international usages and practices with regard the altering, suspending and ending of the mission of the public minister by his promotion, replacing, recall or death, are described by Sir Robert Phillimore as follows. "The mission of a public minister may be :—

1. Altered in its rank or character.
2. Suspended.
3. Entirely closed or ended."

"It is altered in its character when the grade of the agent is heightened or lowered, when an envoy becomes an ambassador or *vice versâ*, or when an ambassador, sent on an affair of ceremony, becomes a resident ambassador. By such changes as these the embassy is not *suspended* or *ended*, but only *changed*, as to its diplomatic rank or character. Various events may happen which suspend the functions of the agent; for instance the death of his Sovereign may have this effect only, though it may also *end* his mission. During this interval, however, he enjoys all the privileges of inviolability and exterritoriality which appertain to his office. These remain until his embassy be *bonâ fide* terminated,

* MERLIN. S. IV. See also MARTENS, S. 184.

and until he has left the territory of the State to which he has been accredited." *

"The mission is *ended* by:—

1. The lapse of a particular period, as in the case of an agent appointed *ad interim*, when the regular ambassador returns to his post.

2. By the accomplishment of the particular object of the mission, as in the case of an embassy sent for the purpose of congratulation, or to represent a State at a particular ceremony; or when there has been a special and limited object to the mission, which has either been attained or has failed.

3. By the death, abdication, or dethronement of the Sovereign accrediting the agent, or by the death of the Sovereign to whom he is accredited. In both these cases, according to international usage and practice, the agent must be accredited anew by his Sovereign; though, in cases in which it is known that his mission is only suspended, and that he will be re-accredited, it is usual to continue to transact business, *sub spê rati*, with him.

4. By the formal declaration of the agent, on account of some injury or insult, or of some pressing urgency, that his mission must be considered as closed.

5. By the act of the Court to which he is accredited, when that Court on the ground of his misconduct, or of a quarrel with his Government orders the agent to leave the territory, without waiting for his formal recall.

6. By the voluntary resignation of his office by himself.

* MARTENS. I. IV. Chapt. 3. S. 148. MIRUSS. SS. 366–370. KLUBER. SS. 228–230. WHEATON. Dr. Int. I. SS. 23, 24. GROTIUS. Liv. III. Chapt. XXI. 16.

7. By his recall by the Government which accredited him."

"In the last-mentioned case it is usual for the agent to request an audience, more or less formal according to circumstances, with the Sovereign to whom he is accredited, and to deliver to him the order or letter recalling him *(lettres de rappel, Züruckberufungsschreiben)*. He afterwards usually receives, in return, letters or papers to facilitate his return (what are termed *lettres de recréance, recreditio*), and his passport, and sometimes a present; but the Republic of the United States of America follows the example of the ancient Republic of Venice, and forbids her representatives to accept any such present."

"At the death of a diplomatic agent, the first step that the secretary of legation—or, in his default, some minister of an allied Power—takes, is to affix a seal upon his official papers, and, if necessary, upon his moveables. It is only a case of necessity that warrants the interference of the local authority. His corpse is entitled to a decent burial at the place of his death, or it may be removed for the purpose of interment elsewhere; and it is exempted from any mortuary dues usually payable in the country. All questions relating to his moveable property, whether he died testate or intestate, are, by a long established rule of international comity, determinable only by the laws of his domicile or of his own country. His moveables are also exempt from any kind of tax or impost *(droit d'aubaine, detractis)*. It is usual also to continue to the widow, family, and suite of the deceased, the privileges and immunities incident to his office, for such limited period as may reasonably suffice to enable them to leave the country." *

* Sir ROBERT PHILLIMORE. Vol. II. p. 262, et seq.

CHAPTER XXII.

CONSULAR OFFICERS.

§ 148. The Consular mission was originally a consequence of the state which is ordinarily called exterritoriality and dates from the earliest period of commercial intercourse among Nations. It is traced historically as far back as the time of the Grecian colonisation on the shores of the Mediterranean. *Origin of the Consular mission.*

In the sixth century the laws of the Visigoths admitted of a sort of exterritoriality by stating that differences between resident strangers should be adjudicated by judges of the respective nationality in conformity with the respective foreign law. This system was more generally developed during the crusades which brought a general migration in their wake. Emperor Alexis conceded, in 1100, to the subjects of Pisa the right to establish in the Levant Consulates which were qualified to decide differences which might occur among subjects of the said nationality. This privilege was confirmed successively by Frederick I. in 1161, Otho IV. in 1209 and Frederick II. in 1220. The first Consul of the Venitians was sent to Aleppo in 1229, at the time of the Sixth Crusade. It was however not till the fall of the feudal system in Southern Europe and the revival of municipalities, with the consequent free commercial intercourse, that Consular institutions were brought into prominence and altered so as to be of more direct practical utility. This took place principally in the Mediterranean and Adriatic ports, but Consular attributes acquired more of the commercial aspects of the present time in the States of Italy, France and Spain, which after the feudal yoke was thrown off, constituted themselves into republics and commercial towns, as Amalfi, Venice, Geneva, Pisa, Marseilles, Sicily, Barcelona, Ancona. Here the first official commercial agents and Consular missions were established, with power to administer the commercial and maritime laws of their respective countries.

Regular Consular missions were established in Spain and Genoa since the 14th, and in Portugal and England about the 16th century.

The diversity of the commercial laws and usages in force in different countries, engaged in active commercial relations, as also the difficulties which travellers and foreign merchants encountered in those days, caused the establishment of Consular conventions based on the system of mutual reciprocity. By such conventions foreigners were allowed to bring with them their own legal advisers or magistrates as general agents for the purpose of administering justice among the subjects of their respective nationalities, in conformity with their own commercial laws and usages. * The ships of foreign merchants, says Sir T. Twiss, were held to be navigated under the jurisdiction of the Nation whose flag they carried, and the general practice was for vessels engaged in long sea voyages, some of which occupied a period of not less than three years, to have on board a magistrate whose duty it was to administer the law of the country of the flag, amongst all on board, not merely whilst the vessel was on the high seas, but while she

* Don. ANTONIO BERNAL DE O'REILLY. Elementos para el ejercicio de la Carrera Consular, Cap. I.

was in a foreign port, loading or unloading cargo. This magistrate was termed the alderman in the ports of the Baltic and the North Sea, whilst in the Mediterranean ports he was designated by the familiar name of Consul, and was the precursor of the resident commercial Consul, who continues at the present day to exercise, in the case of merchant ships of his own nationality, notwithstanding their being within the territorial jurisdiction of another State, a portion of the personal jurisdiction formerly exercised by the ship's Consul. The exercise of this Consular jurisdiction requires no fiction of exterritoriality to support it. Its limits are either regulated by commercial treaties, or, where it has originated in charter privileges, it is now held to rest upon custom. *

With regard to the origin of the Consular mission, Prof. Lorimer makes the following statements.

" Like the other institutions of the middle ages which had the protection of commerce for their object, that of the Consulate originated with those merchant communities which at an early period sprang up around the shores of the Mediterranean. The best authority on the early history and development of the Consulate is Alexander von Miltitz, whose *Manuel des Consuls* appeared in London and Berlin in 1837; following upon the *Essai sur les Consuls* of Herr von Steck, published in Berlin in 1790. The work of Miltitz consists of five thick volumes, executed with all the fidelity and something of the prolixity of German *Gelehrsamkeit*,—a statement which will explain the impossibility of my even attempting a resumé of it here. I shall endeavour, however, to state, in a few sentences, the view which he takes of

* Sir T. TWISS. Law Magazine. Feb., 1876.

the history of the office,—a subject on which nothing satisfactory is to be found in the popular treatises."

"And first, I refer to the name. Having been continued by the emperors of the West, as a mere empty title, long after it had lost its ancient significance, and adopted by their rivals and successors at Constantinople, the name to which so many magnificent associations cling was arrogated to themselves for a time by the kings of France and Italy and Germany. Even the Saracen princes in Spain coveted it; and it became a most incongruous addition to their other titles. The consequence of its popularity was that it fell into entire disrepute. 'Having lost its eclat,' says Miltitz, 'from the multitude of little princes who adorned themselves with it, the Greek emperors, and in imitation of them the other great monarchs, abandoned it, towards the commencement of the tenth century. When thus repudiated by sovereign princes, the title of Consul was adopted by the chief magistrates of the free towns of Italy. On the establishment of the Commune in France, in the twelfth century, municipal officers were appointed who, in the southern provinces, were called Consuls, and who corresponded to the maires, echevins, jurats, and conseillers de l'hôtel de ville, elsewhere.'"

In his preface to Haliburton's Ledger (p. XLVIII) Professor Innes says: "The Consuls and prudhommes in Southern France, the maires and echevins in the Langue d'Oil, the schout and schepens of the Low Country cities, and many another name of magistrature, hardly differ in essentials from our own aldermen, provosts, bailies, and councillors."

"Many other examples might be given of the generic sense in which the term was used, corresponding to a certain extent to the loose and general way in which we ourselves often speak of a magistrate. But some of the uses thus made of the term might disturb the complacency of the present dignified holders of a title at the mention of which once 'the world grew pale.' From the learned pages of Miltitz, one may learn that in the fourteenth century the tailors and the broom-makers of Montpelier had each a Consul of their own. On board ship, the officer under whose charge the provisions were placed, and who thus corresponded to the modern steward (an epithet, by the way, of great historical dignity amongst ourselves), was known as the Consul. The eleventh section of the Consulato del Mare provides that if this dignitary should be guilty of cheating the owners (whether sole or part owners), he should be branded on the forehead with a hot iron. But enough of antiquarianism, by which, as by statistics, it would often seem that anything can be proved."

"The next step, by which the title of a Consul was specially appropriated to domestic judges in maritime affairs, was an easy and natural one. The statutes of the city of Pisa of the year 1169 vest, it is said, in the *consules marinariorum et mercatorum*, authority to counsel, to advise, and to judge in all matters relating to the interests of the mercantile community, and impose upon them the duty of advancing, by every means in their power, the maritime and commercial interests of their country. These latter judges were the *consules maris*, out of the recorded decisions of whose Courts the maritime codes of the middle ages grew. The last stage in the transition of the word from its ancient to its modern signification, presents us with the institution of the Consulship pretty nearly in its completed form. In foreign ports Consuls were appointed whose functions very closely resembled those of the domestic magistrates whom I have just mentioned. Of these Consuls *d'outre mer*, or Consuls *à l'étranger*, traces appear at a very early period. Their first establishment was probably a consequence of the wise policy which induced the barbarian Conquerors of the Western Empire to recognize the municipal laws of Rome as governing the city communities; and accordingly we find in the Codex Visigothorum a distinct recognition of the right of seafaring strangers and foreigners to be judged by magistrates and arbitrators of their own Nation, and according to their own laws. But though such was probably the origin of the Consular office in Europe in mediæval times, there can be little doubt that it has existed whenever and wherever a permanent foreign trade has been established. Whether Heeren and Miltitz may or may not have succeeded in finding traces of it in the very remote ages in which they have sought them, I shall not hesitate to believe that there were Phœnician Consuls at any rate, of whose Courts the Rhodian and other earlier maritime codes were the digested decision, just as the codes of the middle ages were the decisions of the Courts of their successors."

"The popular view of the matter assigns to them, however, a far shorter pedigree. The prevailing opinion appears to be that foreign Consuls were first appointed during the Crusades, in consequence of permission granted by the Franks to the trading towns of Italy, France, and Spain, to send magistrates into Asia to protect the commercial interests of their own citizens, and to act as judges amongst them. The advantages resulting from these appointments induced several States of Europe, towards the commencement of the thirteenth century, to obtain from each other the privilege of sending Consuls. Martens gives examples, ranging from 1256 to 1201; and Miltitz mentions the existence of a diploma bearing date 9th May, 1190, by which the city of Naples conferred on the merchants of Amalfi the power of naming Consuls to judge in such disputes as might arise amongst them. Whether the so-called table of Amalfi, if it ever existed, was the code by which these judges were guided, is a subject on which Miltitz speculates, but into which we cannot follow him. In Pardessus, and in Reddie, who repeats him, there will be found clear indications of the existence of a Consulate at Genoa in 1250, and at Pisa in 1298; and it seems probable that the trading communities of Spain were not slow, in this and in other respects, to follow the example of their Italian rivals, if, indeed, from their more extensive connections with Phœnicians and Carthaginians in early times, they did not precede them."

"But, though the origin of the Consular office is thus of venerable age, it was not till the beginning of the fifteenth century that the practice of sending Consuls to foreign ports became general; and in many instances, both as between different European States and between these and the partially recognized States in other portions of the globe, it is much more recent. The first foreign Consul appointed by England, according to Tuson, was Leonardo Strozzi, at Pisa in 1485, or as Lindsay, in his History of Merchant Shipping, says, in 1490. Two other Italians were appointed in the earlier part of the following century, one at Candia in 1522 and one at Scio in 1531; and Mr. John Tipton was 'Commissary' at Algiers in 1584.

But it was by the Hanseatic League that the Consular system was chiefly developed; and it is said that, at one time, this great trading body maintained more than a hundred foreign Consuls in different parts of the world."

"Foreign Consuls were originally elected by the merchants of their Nation at the port at which their duties were to be performed. Such was the case with those appointed at Naples by the merchants of Amalfi; and such appears to have been the case also with Lawrence Pomstrat, who was a burgess of Slusa, and was appointed by the merchants, with consent of the magistrates of Aberdeen. But it soon became apparent, that in order to strengthen their authority and give efficacy to their decisions, it was necessary to obtain the approbation of the prince to whom they were subject. Subsequently Governments began to see that it belonged to their interest and their dignity to choose Consuls for themselves; and examples are frequent of their reserving the right of establishing them in treaties." *

Consular officers, their rights and duties.

§ 149. The Consular organization of several States comprehends four classes of Consular Officers, viz.: Consuls-General, Consuls, Vice-Consuls and Consular agents.

Consuls-General exercise their functions over several placês and sometimes over a whole State, in which case the functions of Consul-General are sometimes intrusted to the Public Minister accredited to the respective Government. It is sometimes pretended, mostly through the one-sided view of the *ésprit de corps* among members of the Corps Diplomatique, that a Public Minister, to be properly called a diplomatic agent, must be employed about political or State affairs exclusively and not incumbered with affairs of commerce,

* Prof. LORIMER. Vol. I. p. 290, et seq.

the supervision of which belongs exclusively to the attributes of the Consular officer. But it is obvious that commerce, which is the most prominant international concern, can never be regarded as of lesser consequence than the so-called political affairs which from time to time happen to fall more particularly within the range of duties of a diplomatic agent. Trade is as much a matter of State as any other international affair, and being of the utmost concern to every civilized State it unquestionably partakes of an international political nature and is consequently the proper subject of employment for an Ambassador or Public Minister. In negotiating treaties of commerce the Public Minister, who is at the same time Consul-General, has all the advantage of the knowledge and experience of a throughly practical and useful position. *

He who is charged by his Government with the service of the State and to watch over the interests of its subjects or citizens in a foreign country, is certainly a public officer. Whatever may be his rank in the bureaucratic order with regard to other officers of the diplomatic class, and though subordinate to another higher officer accredited as the direct representative of his Government, the Consul is not the less a public functionary of his Government and as such entitled to certain immunities regulated by treaty, provided he be delegated from his country as a *bonâ fide* Government official to the State in which he is to exercise his functions by virtue of his exequatur.

Consular officers, having no representative or diplomatic character, have no right of exterritoriality and therefore cannot claim the privileges of exemption which by this fiction of

* PHILLIMORE. Vol. II. p. 269. BLUNTSCHLI. Introd. p. 28.

law are accorded to diplomatic agents who are considered as representing, in a greater or lesser degree, the sovereignty of the State which appoints them. Consular officers who have no diplomatic character whatever, are, when not expressly otherwise stipulated by treaties, amenable, generally speaking, to the civil and criminal jurisdiction of the country in which they reside, their property and effects are subject to the recourse of execution and process of the local Courts, and they may be either punished for their offences by the laws of the State where they reside or be sent back to their own country at the discretion of the Government which they have offended. Consular officers are subject to the payment of taxes and mnnicipal imposts and duties or charges, when not otherwise stipulated by treaty. *

But although Consuls do not enjoy the immunities accorded by international usages to diplomatic agents, they are nevertheless entitled to certain rights of comity and to certain privileges of exemption from local and political obligations which cannot be claimed by private individuals.

Their official papers and archives are exempt from seizure and detention and soldiers cannot be quartered in their Consular residence.

The immunities and privileges secured to the Consular officer by treaties are:—

1°. The Consular officer, after the granting of an exequatur, may raise the flag and place the arms of his country over his gates and doors.

2°. Inviolability of the Consular office and dwelling.

3°. Inviolability of the archives and papers of the Consulate which are exempted from seizure or detention.

---

* HALLECK, Edit. Sir Sherston Baker, Vol. I. p. 310, et seq.

4°. If the Consular officer is not a subject or citizen of the country in which his Consulate is situated, and if he do not hold real estate or engage in business in the country of which he has the exequatur, he is exempt from arrest for debts (but not for crimes).

5°. Exemption from liability to appear as a witness, under the same conditions as mentioned under sub-section 4°. In such case the testimony may be taken in writing at his dwelling. If the Consular officer claims this privilege, he should offer to give his evidence in the form prescribed by the convention and should throw no impediment in the way of the proper administration of justice.

6°. Under the same conditions as stated above in sub-sections 4°. and 5°., the Consular officer can be secured by treaty stipulations against liability to taxation.

7°. Also, under the same conditions as stated above, the Consular officer can be granted exemption from military service.

The right secured to the Consular officer by conventions, are:—

1°. The right to correspond officially with local authorities in cases of infraction of treaties.

2°. The right to take depositions at his Consulate.

3°. Jurisdiction over disputes between masters, officers and crew of vessels of his nationality including questions of wages, etc.

4°. The right to reclaim deserters (comp. §§ 44, 110 & 111).

5°. The right to settle salvage claims for damages at sea with regard to vessels of his nationality.

6°. The adjustment of intestate estates within his jurisdiction.

7°. Exterritorial Jurisdiction such as conceded by treaties between Western Nations and China, Japan, Turkey and other Eastern States.

Exemptions and immunities of Consuls regulated on the principle of perfect reciprocity.

Exemptions and immunities are granted by every State to foreign Consular officers on the international principle of perfect reciprocity. *

With regard to the international status of a Consular officer, Sir Robert Phillimore makes the following statements:—

Statement of Sir Robert Phillimore with regard to the international status of Consular officers.

"Consuls in Christian countries are not, legally speaking, public ministers of the State to which they belong, though, having a public character, they are under a more special protection of International Law than uncommissioned individuals. This protection they have a right to claim both

---

* In the Netherlands the exemptions and immunities of foreign Consuls are regulated on the principle of reciprocity by Royal Decree of 5th June, 1822, and by the Laws of 29th March, 1833, Art. 24, § 7, in connection with Art. 13 of that of 24th April, 1843. We William, etc. Having seen, etc. Have decreed and decree.

The principle of perfect reciprocity, with respect to the granting of exemptions and immunities to Consuls of foreign Powers, shall be generally adopted upon the footing and in the manner determined by the following articles.

Art. 1. Netherland subjects to whom permission has been or shall be given to exercise Consular functions for foreign Powers or States, shall in general be liable to the payment of all taxes and contributions of whatsoever nature; should they. however, so desire they may be exempted from service to be rendered personally in the towns, saving their obligation, in the event of their being called up for service in the militia, of providing a fit substitute if required, and provided moreover they can show that the Powers from whom they received their appointment allow similar facilities to those of their subjects who act as Netherland Consuls in their dominions.

Art. 2. Consuls who are not natives of the Netherlands or recognized Netherland subjects, or at the time of their appointment are not established as inhabitants of this country, for so far as they do not carry on any profession or occupation other than their Consular functions, shall be exempt from providing lodging for soldiers, from serving in or contributing to the militia, and also from personal taxes, and further from all public or municipal imposts which might be regarded as being of a direct and at the same time personal nature; but this exemption shall in no case extend to any indirect taxes or imposts upon real property. The above being subject to the condition that they shall produce satisfactory proof that the Governments from which they derive their commissions grant similar exemptions and immunities to Consuls who are natives or subjects of this Kingdom, whenever such Consuls may at any time be resident in their dominions.

from the State which sends, and from the State which admits them. But they are not the representatives of their State, nor entitled to any of the privileges and immunities accorded to such representatives, whether they be full ambassadors or simple *chargés d'affaires*, and for these more especial reasons.

1. They are not, except in cases where they are also *chargés d'affaires* furnished with credentials *(lettres de créance)*, but with a mere commission *(lettres de provision)* to watch over the commercial rights and privileges of their Nations.

2. They cannot enter upon the discharge of their functions without the permission and confirmation of their commission by the Sovereign of the country to which they are deputed. That commission is termed the *exequatur* and may, at any time, be revoked by such Sovereign.

3. As a general rule, they are amenable to the civil and criminal jurisdiction of the country in

---

Art. 3. Consuls who are not natives of the Netherlands or recognized Netherland subjects, shall, if during their residence in the Netherlands, they carry on any business or profession other than and besides their Consular functions, from that moment and for so long as they continue to do so, be regarded as inhabitants and shall be obliged to bear and to pay the said taxes, imposts and contributions upon the same footing as all other subjects and inhabitants, unless they can furnish satisfactory evidence that Consuls, being natives or recognized subjects of this Kingdom, situated in like circumstances in the dominions of the Powers to whom they are commissioned, enjoy any privileges with respect to the billeting of soldiers, to municipal services, including service in the militia, to contributions for the same, and to personal taxes; in which case similar immunities shall be accorded to them.

Art. 4. These, etc.

Given at the Hague, on the 5th June of the year 1822, and the ninth of our reign.

WILLIAM.
By command of the King,
J. G. de Meij van Streefkerk.

N.B.—According to the Law of the 29th March, 1833, Art. 24, § 7, in connection with Art. 13 of that of the 24th April, 1843, foreign Consuls, who practise any profession or carry on any business for which a licence is required, can, in no case, be exempted from the personal tax. Art. 3 of above decree is modified to that extent.

which they reside. Vattel's position that they are exempted from the latter, is wholly unsupported by the requisite proof.

4. They are subject to the payment of taxes.

5. The permission to have places of worship in their houses is very rarely accorded to Consuls.

6. They have no claim to any foreign ceremonial or mark of respect, and no right of precedence except among themselves according to the rank of the different States to which they belong, but they have a right to place the arms of their country over the door of their residence."

De Martens is of opinion that, unless they are engaged in trade, or become owners of immovable property in the country, Consular officers cannot be arrested or incarcerated for any less offence than a criminal act.

The privileges of Consuls, so far as they are derived from the country to which they are sent, are, generally speaking, an exemption from any personal tax, and generally from the liability to have soldiers quartered in their houses; and in cases where the ambassadors are absent, or non-resident, they have a right of access to the authorities of the State in which they reside. They are usually allowed to grant passports to subjects of their (the Consuls') own country, living within the range of their Consulate, but not to foreigners. As a general rule, the muniments and papers of the Consulate are inviolable, and under no pretext to be seized or examined by the local authorities.

As a general rule, too, Consuls in Christian countries have no contentious jurisdiction over their fellow-countrymen, but simply a sort of voluntary jurisdiction—a power of arbitration *(jurisdiction arbitrale)* in disputes, more especially those relating to matters of commerce. Their functions must, in great measure, depend upon the Municipal Law of their own country. No contentious jurisdiction can be exercised over their fellow-countrymen without the express permission of the State in which they reside; and no Christian State has as yet permitted the criminal jurisdiction of foreign Consuls. But usage and the rule adopted in most treaties concede to the Consul the assistance of the local police when it may be necessary for the exercise of his functions over the seamen of merchant-vessels belonging to his own country."

"In England it has been decided that in a suit for wages by seamen on board a foreign vessel, the Court of Admiralty has jurisdiction, but will not exercise it without first giving notice, in accordance with the directions of the tenth of the Rules and Orders of 1859 for the practice of the High Court of Admiralty, to the Consul of the Nation to which the foreign vessel belongs; and if the Consul, by protest, objects to the prosecution of the suit, the Court of Admiralty will determine whether it is fit and proper that the suit should proceed or be stayed. Such protest does not, *ipso facto*, operate as a bar to the prosecution of the suit, as the foreign Consul has not the power to put a veto on the exercise of jurisdiction by the Court of Admiralty. In such a suit it makes no difference that the plaintiff is a British subject; it is the nationality of the vessel, and not the nationality of the individual seaman suing for his wages, that regulates the course of procedure."

The cases in the American Courts may be also consulted on this subject; they contain the following propositions:—

"A suit cannot be brought in a State Court against a Consul of a foreign Government, admitted as such by the Government of the United States. He does not waive his privileges by appearing in the State Court, and pleading to the merits." *

"A Consul represents the subjects of his Nation, if they are not otherwise represented." †

"A Consul of a foreign Power, though not entitled to represent his Sovereign in a country where the Sovereign has an ambassador, is entitled to intervene for all subjects of that Power interested; and though he should not set forth the particulars of his claim, still it will be sufficient if they can be fully gathered from the allegations of the libel, and the case it sets forth." ‡

"A Consul, though a public agent, is supposed to be clothed with authority only for commercial purposes; he has a right to interpose claims for the restitution of property belonging to the subjects of his own country, but he is not entitled to be considered as a minister, or diplomatic agent of his Sovereign, intrusted, by virtue of his office, with authority to represent him in his negotiations with foreign States, or to vindicate his prerogative." ||

"Although a foreign Consul is admitted to interpose a claim in the Admiralty for unknown subjects of his Nation, yet before restitution can be decreed, proof of the individual proprietary interest must be exhibited." ¶

"A foreign Consul has a right, without special authority from those for whose benefit he acts,

---

* *Valarino* v. *Thompson*. 3 *Seldon* (N.S.) 576.

† *Gernon* v. *Cochran*. *Bee*. 209.

‡ *Robson* v. *The Huntress*. 2. Wallace Junior, 59.

|| *The Anne*. 3. Wheat. 435.

¶ *The Antelope*. 10. Wheat. 66.

to institute a proceeding *in rem*, where the rights of the property of his fellow-citizens are in question." *

"It has been observed, says Sir Robert Phillimore further, that the institution of the Consulate is a result of international comity; and that the refusal to receive a foreign Consul is no breach of strict International Law. But a Consul, admitted without any express stipulation, is entitled to the same privileges as his predecessors have enjoyed, upon the general principle mentioned in a former chapter, that every Nation is presumed to follow custom and usage in its treatment of foreigners, and is bound to give previous warning of its intention, if it have any, of adopting a different course with respect to them. As a general rule, and in the absence of any treaty upon the subject, the Consul looks for his authority and functions to the diplomatic instrument by which he is appointed to his office, to the *exequatur* which empowers him to exercise them, and to any modification which the particular law or custom of the country in which he is placed may apply to them; and he must always remember, that the principal end and object of the Consulate is to protect the external commerce and the national navigation of his own country in the rights secured to them by usage or treaty."

"Some Nations permit, and others forbid, their Consuls to trade; a trading Consul is, in all that concerns his trade, liable to the local authorities in the same way as any native merchant. In fact, sometimes natives of the place itself, in which Consular services are required, are appointed Consuls; and thus are, at one and the same time, the subjects of the country in which they dwell and agents of a foreign State. The prero-

* *The Bella Corrunes*. 6, Wheat, 152.

gatives of such Consuls are limited to the enjoyment of exemption from lodging soldiers and from personal service in the civic guards or militia." *

The Regulations for the Consular Service of the United States of America of 1881, sustain the following principles with regard to the privileges and powers of Consular officers under the Law of Nations.

Consular privileges under the Law of Nations.

"In the early middle ages, and before the establishment of more or less permanent legations, Consuls appear to have enjoyed the right of exterritoriality, and the privileges and immunities now accorded to diplomatic representatives. In non-Christian and semi-civilized countries these privileges have, to a large degree, been preserved to them, and they have the sanction both of treaty and usage. Upon the establishment of legations, however, the exemptions and immunities granted to Consuls came to be regarded as a limitation of the territorial rights of the Sovereign, and they have in the process of time been restricted to such as are necessarily incident to the Consular office, or have been provided for by treaty, or are supported by long established customs, or the particular laws of the place. A Consular officer in civilized countries now has, under public law, no acknowledged representative or diplomatic character as regards the country to which he is accredited. He has, however, a certain representative character as affecting the commercial interests of the country from which he receives his appointment; and there may be circumstances, as, for example in the absence of a diplomatic representative, which apart from usage, make it proper for him to address the local government upon subjects

* DE MARTENS. Le Guide Diplomatique. I. 398.

which relate to the duties and rights of his office and which are usually dealt with through a legation."

Ground and extent of the Consular powers.

"Although Consuls have no right to claim the privileges and immunities of diplomatic representatives, they are under the special protection of International Law, and are regarded as the officers both of the State which appoints and the State which receives them. The extent of their authority is derived from their commission and their *exequatur;* and it is believed that the granting of the latter instrument, without express restrictions, confers upon the Consul all rights and privileges necessary to the performance of the duties and the Consular office; and generally, a Consul may claim for himself and his office not only such rights and privileges as have been conceded by treaty, but also such as have the sanction of custom and local law, and have been enjoyed by his predecessors or by Consuls of other Nations, unless a formal notice has been given that they will not be extended to him."

General privileges and rights.

"A Consul may place the arms of his Government over his doors. Permission to display the national flag is not a matter of right, though it is usually accorded, and it is often provided for by treaty. He may claim inviolability for the archives and official property of his office, and their exemption from seizure or examination. He is protected from the billeting of soldiers in the Consular residence, and he may claim exemption from service on juries and in the militia, and from other public duties. It is probable, however, that all these privileges could not be claimed for subordinate officers, especially for those who are citizens or subjects of the foreign State. The jurisdiction allowed to Consuls in civilized countries over disputes between their countrymen is voluntary and in the nature of arbitration, and it relates more specially to matters of trade and commerce. A Consul is, however, under public law, subject to the payment of taxes and municipal imposts and duties on his property in the country or on his trade, and generally to the civil and criminal jurisdiction of the country in which he resides. It is probable, if he does not engage in business, and does not own real estate, that he would not be subject to arrest or incarceration except on a criminal charge, and in the case of the commission of a crime he may either be punished by the local laws or sent back to his own country. In the absence of a diplomatic representative, a Consul doubtless has the right of access to the authorities of the State in all matters appertaining to his office."

Trading Consuls.

"The privileges of a Consul who engages in business in the country of his official residence are, under International Law, more restricted, especially if he is a subject or citizen of the foreign State. If his *exequatur* has been granted without limitations, he may claim the privileges and exemptions that are necessary to the performance of the duties of the office; but in all that concerns his personal status or his status as a merchant, it is doubtful that he can claim any rights or privileges not conceded to other subjects or citizens of the State."

Consular Power in countries where they enjoy the right of exterritoriality.

"In Mohammedan and semi-civilized countries, the rights of exterritoriality have been largely preserved, and have generally been confirmed by treaties to Consular officers. To a great degree they enjoy the immunities of diplomatic representatives, besides certain prerogatives of jurisdicton, together, with the right of worship, and, to some extent, the right of asylum.

The immunities extend to an exemption from both the civil and criminal jurisdiction of the country to which they are sent, and protect their household and the effects covered by the Consular residence. The personal property of Consuls is exempt from taxation, though it may be otherwise with real estate or movables not connected with the Consulate. Generally, Consuls are exempt from all personal impositions that arise from the character or equality of a subject or citizen of the country. The Consular jurisdiction in these countries is both civil and criminal, and has in most cases been provided for by the stipulations of treaties. The extent of its exercise as well as the penalties and punishments to be enforced, depend generally upon the laws of the Consul's own country to the exclusion of the jurisdiction of all local tribunals."

"Consuls have no claim, under International Law, to any foreign ceremonial, and no right of precedence except among themselves, and in their relation to the military and naval officers of their own country. This precedence, as to officers of the same grade in the Consular Body of the place, depends upon the date of the respective exequaturs." *

---

* Regulations for the Consular officers of the United States; 1881, Sections 75–82.

The privileges and powers of Consular officers of the United States of America, which are secured by that country under treaties and conventions with foreign Powers, are stated in the above mentioned Consular regulations as follow.

1°.—*Inviolability of the Archives and Papers of the Consulate.* This is secured by treaties with Austria-Hungary, the Argentine Confederation, Bolivia, Belgium, Columbia, Denmark, Dominican Republic, Ecuador, France, Germany, Greece, Hayti, Mexico, the Netherlands (and Colonies), Orange Free State, Peru, Portugal, Salvador, Sweden and Norway, Switzerland, Muscat, and New Grenada.

2°.—*Inviolability of the Consular Office and Dwelling.* This is secured by treaties with Belgium, Bolivia, France, Germany (of Consuls not citizens), Italy, Muscat, and Salvador; but the dwelling cannot be used as an asylum. It is agreed with Columbia that the persons and dwellings of Consuls are to be subject to the laws of the

Mutual ranking of Consular officers.

§ 150. The rank of the Consular officer has not yet been made an object of international understanding like the mutual ranking of the diplomatic agents noted in paragraph 146. Nevertheless international usages have ascribed to Consular officers the same right to marks of respect and on

---

country, except as specially exempted by treaty. The Consulates in Germany are not to be made asylums for the subjects of other Powers.

3°.—*Exemption from Arrest.* By convention with Belgium, Germany, Netherlands, and Italy, the Consul is exempted from arrest, except for crimes. By treaty with Turkey he is entitled to suitable distinction and necessary aid and protection. In Muscat he enjoys the inviolability of a diplomatic officer. In Austria-Hungary and France he is to enjoy personal immunities; but in France, if a citizen of France or owning property there, or engaged in commerce, he can claim only the immunities granted to other citizens of the country who own property or to merchants. In Austria-Hungary, if engaging in business, he can be detained only for commercial debts. In Columbia the Consuls of the United States have no diplomatic character. In Great Britain, Liberia, Netherlands (and colonies), Nicaragua, and Paraguay, they are regarded as appointed for the protection of trade.

4°.—*Exemption from Obligations to appear as a Witness.* This is secured absolutely by convention with France; and, except for defence of persons charged with crime, by conventions with Austria-Hungary, Belgium, Italy, and Salvador. In such case the testimony may be taken in writing at his dwelling. If the Consul claims this privilege, he should, in such case, offer to give his evidence in the mode prescribed by the particular convention, and should throw no impediment in the way of the proper administration of justice in the country of his official residence.

5°.—*Exemption from Taxation.* When the Consul is not a citizen of the country in which the Consulate is situated, and does not own real estate therein, and is not engaged in business therein, he is secured against the liability to taxation by treaties or conventions with Austria-Hungary, Belgium, Bolivia, Denmark, Ecuador, France, Germany, Hayti, Italy, the Netherlands (and colonies), Peru, Salvador, Columbia, and Mexico; and in Germany the official income of a Consul is not taxable; but in the Dominican Republic, the Orange Free State, Persia, Portugal, the Hawaiian Islands, Russia, and Switzerland, if Consuls engage in business, they are subject to the laws of the country. And in general, if a Consular officer engages in business or owns property in the country of his official residence, he cannot claim other exemptions in respect of such business or property than are accorded to citizens or subjects of the country.

6°.—*Exemption from Military Billetings or Service and Public Service.* If not citizens of the country of their Consular residence, or domiciled at the time of the appointment in it, the exemption from military billetings or service is secured by conventions, with Austria-Hungary, Belgium, France, Germany, Netherlands, and Italy; and the same system as such is customary among diplomatic agents accredited at the same Court. As by the Law of Nations all sovereign States are considered equal in rank, with respect to ceremonials and precedence, Consular officers of the same rank in the Consular service, admitted by

---

the exemption from all public service is secured by treaties with Denmark, Germany, Peru, San Salvador, Columbia, New Granada, and Mexico. In Columbia, the exemption also extends to officers, secretaries, and attachés.

7°.—*Infraction of Treaties.* The right in such case to correspond with the local authorities is secured by conventions with Austria-Hungary, Belgium, Columbia, France, Germany, Italy, Netherlands (and colonies), and Salvador; and in case the local authorities fail to give redress, and there be no diplomatic representative, the Consul may apply to the Government.

8°.—*The Use of the National Arms and Flags on Offices and Dwellings.* The right to place the national arms and the name of the Consulate on the offices is given by treaties with Austria-Hungary and the Netherlands (and colonies); on their offices or dwellings by treaty with Belgium and Germany; the right to place the national flag on their dwellings, except where there is a legation, by treaties with Austria-Hungary, Belgium and Germany; the right to place the arms, name, and flag on their offices or dwellings, by treaties with France and Salvador; and on their offices, by treaty with Italy; and the right to place the name and flag on their dwellings, by treaty with Columbia.

9°.—*Depositions.* The right to take depositions is secured by conventions with Austria-Hungary, Belgium, France, Germany, Italy, Netherlands, New Granada, and Salvador. Objection has been raised by the German Government to the taking of testimony by Consular officers of the United States in Germany, except as provided by Article IX of the treaty of 1871. Efforts have been made to induce the German authorities to permit testimony to be taken with the same freedom as in the United States, but without effect, it being stated that the laws of Germany provide for letters-rogatory in such cases.

10°.—*Jurisdiction over Disputes between Masters, Officers and Crews.* Exclusive jurisdiction over such disputes in the vessels of the United States, including questions of wages, is conferred by treaties or conventions with Austria-Hungary, Belgium, Columbia, Denmark, Dominican Republic, France, Germany, Greece, Italy, the Netherlands (and the colonies), Portugal, Russia, Salvador, Sweden and Norway, and Tripoli.

11°.—*Right to reclaim Deserters.* The right to reclaim deserters from the vessels of the United States is conferred by treaties or conventions with Austria-Hungary, Bolivia, Belgium, Columbia, Denmark, Ecuador, France, Greece, Germany, Hanseatic Republics, Hawaiian Islands, Hayti, Italy, Japan, Mexico, Madagascar, the

the same Government, have precedence among themselves, according to the dates of their respective exequaturs.

Assimilation with Naval officers' rank.

The official relations which Consular officers entertain with Naval officers made it necessary to assimilate their rank with those of the Navy.

Netherlands (and colonies). Peru, Portugal, Russia, Salvador, Sweden and Norway, Dominican Republic, and Siam; but if the deserter has committed a crime against local law, the surrender will be delayed until after punishment.

12°.—*Salvage and Wreck.* The powers to adjust damages suffered at sea and in matters of wrecks and salvage are settled by treaties with Austria-Hungary, Belgium, Bolivia, Borneo, China, New Granada, Dominican Republic, Ecuador, France, Germany, Greece, Guatemala, Hawaiian Islands, Hayti, Honduras, Italy, Japan, Lew Chew, Liberia, Madagascar, Morocco, Muscat, Netherlands (including colonies), Ottoman Porte, Paraguay, Peru, Salvador, Siam, Spain, Sweden and Norway, Tripoli, Tunis, and Venezuela. In Muscat and the Ottoman Dominions they have the right, in the absence of the owner or agent, to receive the property of American citizens wrecked or captured from pirates.

13°.—*Estates of Citizens of the United States, Deceased.* In Austria-Hungary, Belgium, Germany, Italy, and the Netherlands (and colonies), the local authorities are required to inform Consuls of the death of their countrymen, intestate, or without known heirs. In Germany, Consuls have the right to appear for absent heirs or creditors until regularly authorized representatives appear. In Peru, Salvador, Tunis, Morocco, Muscat, Persia and Tripoli they may administer the property of their deceased countrymen. In Columbia they may do so, except when legislation prevents it. In Costa Rica, Honduras, and Nicaragua they may nominate curators to take charge of such property, so far as local laws permit. In Paraguay they may become temporary custodians of such property. In Germany they may take charge of the effects of deceased sailors.

14°.—*Extradition of Fugitive Criminals.* Provision has been secured in the treaties with certain countries under which the requisitions for the surrender of fugitives from justice may be made by Consular officers, in the absence of a diplomatic representative. In such cases the requisition is made by the superior Consular officer. Treaties of this character have been concluded with Belgium, the Dominican Republic, Ecuador, Italy, Netherlands, Nicaragua, Orange Free State, Ottoman Empire, Salvador, Siam, Spain, Sweden and Norway, and the Swiss Confederation.

15°.—*Jurisdiction over Offences and Crimes.* Consuls have exclusive jurisdiction over crimes and offences committed by citizens of the United States in Borneo, China, Japan, Madagascar, and Siam. In Morocco, Tripoli, and Tunis the Consuls are empowered to assist in the trial of citizens of the United States accused of murder or

This assimilation is however not the same in all States, but with most nationalities Consuls-General are assimilated with the rank of Commodore, Consuls with Captains *(Capitaine de vaisseau)* and Consuls of the second class and Vice-Consuls with that of a Commander *(Capitaine de frégate).*

The rank which they hold among officers of their own State, civil, naval or military, being

---

assault. In Persia citizens of the United States committing offences are to be tried and judged in the same manner as are the subjects or citizens of the most favored Nation. Americans committing offences in Turkey should be tried by their Minister or Consul, and are to be punished according to their offence, following, in this respect, the usage observed toward other Franks; but, in consequence of a disagreement as to the true text of the treaty, Consuls in the Ottoman Dominions are instructed to take the directions of the Minister of the United States at Constantinople in all cases before assuming to exercise jurisdiction over criminal offences. In China and Japan the question of the judicial authority of Consuls of the United States over persons serving on American vessels has been construed as authorizing Consular officers to assume jurisdiction where offences are committed on shore by foreigners serving on board American merchant vessels, when such foreigners are citizens or subjects of countries having no treaty engagements upon the subject with China and Japan, or when, being subjects or citizens of treaty powers, their own Consuls decline to assume jurisdiction. Under other circumstances a Consul of the United States in China cannot entertain a criminal charge against a citizen or subject of another Power.

Seamen serving on board public vessels of the United States, who have committed offences on shore in Japan and China, are held to be subject to the jurisdiction of the Consul of the country under whose flag they are serving.

16°.—*Civil Jurisdiction.* Jurisdiction over civil disputes is conferred by treaties with Borneo (Brunei), China, Japan, Ottoman Porte, Madagascar, Siam, Morocco, Muscat, Persia, Tripoli, Tunis, and the Samoan Islands. This jurisdiction is exclusive in disputes between citizens of the United States. In Persia suits and disputes between Persian subjects and American citizens are to be heard before the Persian tribunals where the Consul is located, and in the presence of an employé of the Consul. In Japan it extends to claims of Japanese against Americans. In China, Siam, and Samoa the jurisdiction is joint in controversies between Americans and Chinese, Siamese or Samoans. In Madagascar the exclusive jurisdiction extends to disputes between citizens of the United States and subjects of Madagascar. In Turkey there can be no hearing in a dispute between Turks and Americans unless the dragoman of the Consulate is present.

Regulations for the Consular officers of the United States of America, 1881, Sections 83–101.

regulated by the laws of their State, says Halleck, is not a matter of international jurisprudence, nor does it come within the province of the State where they reside, to interfere in any differences between officers of a foreign Government, with respect either to relative rank among themselves or to their authority over each other. *

---

* DE CLERCQ et DE VALLAT. Guide Pratique des Consulates. Ed. 1868. Vol. I. p. 45. HALLECK. Edit. Sir Sherston Baker. Vol. I. p. 314. PHILLIMORE. Int. Law. Vol. II. § 246.

The British Foreign Office Instructions of 1868 contain the following regulations, with respect to the ranking etc., of British Consular officers.

British Consular officers take rank in their respective grades among their colleagues at the port of their residence, in conformity with the rules prescribed by the Congress of Vienna for diplomatic agents, viz.: seniority according to official title and to priority of recognition. The rights and privileges of Consular officers are of two kinds: those defined by treaty and those regulated by local law or custom. Consular officers should maintain their right to privileges or exemptions which by treaty or by custom they may be fully entitled to demand but they must not aim at more; and in any case of difference of opinion between them and the officers of other Governments, they must avoid giving offence and should conduct the controversy in a spirit of conciliation calculated to render unnecessary the reference which, if the difference cannot be arranged, must be made by the Consular officer to the British Secretary of State.

In the countries where it may be the custom for foreign Consuls to hoist the national flags of their respective Nations over their residences, the flag to be hoisted by British Consular officers is the Union Jack. If the regulations of the country or of the place in which the Consular officer resides do not permit a display of this kind, and if such regulations are applicable to foreign Consuls generally, the British Consular officer should not hoist the British flag.

The interchange of visits in foreign ports between British Naval officers and British Consuls is arranged as follows:—

On the arrival of a British ship of war at a foreign port, the first visit is made by the Naval or Consular officer who may be subordinate in relative rank; but the senior Naval officer present is on all occasions to arrange to provide a suitable boat for Consular officers to pay their official visits afloat, and to reland them, on the said officers notifying their wish to have a boat sent for their accommodation.

The above ceremonial is dependent on the relative rank accorded to certain Naval and Consular officers and such relative rank having undergone several changes since the Naval Regulations were established, the following scale of precedence between Naval and Consular officers has been substituted:—

Agents and Consuls General.—To rank with, but after, Rear-Admirals.

Consuls General.—To rank with, but after, Commodores.

§ 151. The Consular functions are of three classes, viz., judicial, administrative and magistratic. *The Consular functions.*

Exterritoriality (described in §§ 45, 46 & 47), as stated above, is granted by special treaties and, in such case, the Consul's attributes are extended to that of civil and criminal jurisdiction over his countrymen, in conformity with the laws and regulations of his country. *Judicial functions.*

The extraterritorial jurisdiction, criminal and civil, in countries which have ceded the right of extraterritoriality to resident foreigners, is thus exercised by virtue of express treaty stipulations with special prerogatives. The judicial powers of Consular officers in Oriental, non-Christian and uncivilized countries, are regulated by special legislation of the State to which the Consular officer belongs and based on the respective treaties.

Concurrent jurisdiction (referred to in § 49), is the amount of jurisdiction allowed to the Consular officer, by international treaties and usages, in countries where foreigners have no right of exterritoriality.

Consuls.—To rank with, but after, Captains R.N. of 3 years' standing and before all other Captains R.N.

Vice-Consuls.—To rank with, but after, Lieutenants and Navigating Lieutenants of 8 years' standing.

Consular Agents.—To rank with, but after, all other Lieutenants and Navigating Lieutenants R.N. (British F. O. Instr. 1868).

The Consular Officers of the United States rank with their own Naval officers as follows :—

Agents and Consuls General,	with Commodores.
Consuls General,	do.
Consuls and Commercial Agents,	with Captains.
Vice-Consuls,	with Lieutenants.
Deputy-Consuls,	do.
Consular Agents,	do.
Commercial Agents,	do.

The precedence is determined among officers of the same rank by the date of commission (U. S. Consular Regulations 1881. Sections 430–434).

Administrative functions.

The administrative functions of the Consular officer are as follow.

1°. General vigilance of the Consul over the interests of commerce and shipping of his country and over the interests of its subjects or citizens. He is bound to assist compatriots who are in need of his help with the authorities of the country. He sees that the laws are properly administered and communicate with his Government if injustice is done with respect to its subjects or citizens.

2°. His relations to the department of Foreign Affairs of his country and its diplomatic representative accredited to the country where the Consulate is established.

3°. His relations to the Naval officers and the public vessels of his country.

4°. His right to reclaim deserters in conformity with usage or treaties.

5°. The relief and sending home of shipwrecked and unemployed seamen of his nationality and of other nationalities serving on board vessels of his country.

6°. The relief and sending home of destitute persons of his nationality and of other nationalities enjoying the Consular protection of his State *in loco*.

7°. Transportation of persons, charged with crimes committed on board vessels of his nationality on the open sea, mutiny and the like, and of condemned prisoners, in countries with conditions of exterritoriality.

8°. His periodical reports and special official informations to his Government upon commercial, economical and political matters.

9°. Registration of the subjects or citizens of his State residing within his jurisdiction.

10°. His accounts and returns, periodical and special.

11°. Proper arrangement and care for all that belongs to the official archives of the Consulate.

The magisterial functions of the Consular officer, as being invested with some part of the executive government of his State, in certain branches of the department of a public civil officer, of the Justice of Peace and of the Notary Public are comprehended in the following duties. *Magistratic functions.*

1°. His function with regard to the registration and authentication of births, deaths, marriages and divorces.

2°. The administration of properties of intestate deceased subjects or citizens of the State. (See, with regard to deceased seamen, § 70, subs. 31°).

3°. His duties with regard to the registration of bills of sale and the certificate to be granted to that effect to subjects or citizens of his country, being purchasers of foreign vessels within his jurisdiction. The provisional sea-pass to be issued to permit the vessel to use the national flag pending its formal registration.

4°. Passports to subjects or citizens of his State in conformity with his instructions.

5°. The right to claim the extradition or surrender of fugitive criminals. His duties with regard to *commissions rogatoires* (as described in § 87), in the absence of a diplomatic representative, in conformity with treaties.

6°. The arbitration in the case of differences which are voluntarily brought before the Consular officer by his fellow-countrymen, especially in matters relating to commerce, to disputes which have taken place on board ship, and those with regard to wages of seamen on board vessels of the Consul's nationality.

7°. The settlement of disputes between masters, officers and crews of national vessels.

8°. Disciplinary jurisdiction over crews of national vessels in conformity with treaty stipulations (comp. §§ 110 & 111).

9°. The duties of the Consular officer with regard to the shipment and discharge of seamen and, in particular cases, the appointment of masters (comp. §§ 68 & 70).

10°. His duties with regard to protests and reports of masters of vessels of his Nation (comp. § 68, sub-sections 15–38).

11°. The appointing of and administering of oaths to surveyors and experts in order to certify the seaworthiness of vessels, to assess certain damages incurred through sea or collision and for extra-repairs in foreign ports (comp. § 68, subsection 5°. and §§ 69, 77 & 117).

12°. The duties of Consular officers with regard to salvage and wrecks, wrecked and stranded vessels and surveys (comp. §§ 78 & 117).

13°. Duties as emigration officer.

14°. Duties with regard to the revenue and customs regulations of his country, manifests, etc.

15°. Duties with regard to the National Board of Health, bills of health, etc.

The duties and attributes of Consular officers are determined by special treaties and by the laws of their own country. As their functions are public, their instructions are all made public, as well as the rules which regulate the details of their respective duties.

In the next section some of these rules are noted which are found, with little variations, in almost all Consular Regulations.

Rules for the Consular Office.

§ 152. 1°. Consular officers require the exequatur or visum of the Government of the country in which they are established to the commission conferred upon them, before they can enter upon their functions, unless permission for the provisional exercise of the Consular functions be there granted to them, immediately after the receipt of their appointment. *The Exequatur.*

They shall give immediate notice to the Legation or Consulate General and to the Ministry of Foreign Affairs, under which they serve, of any difficulty which may arise respecting their recognition or admission to the exercise of their functions.

2°. The Consular officers, after their recognition as such, may place their arms over the door of their residence; always bearing in mind, in so doing, that this permission has for its object simply the convenience of subjects or citizens of their country and, by no means, serves to elevate the Consulate or the Consular residence into a place of refuge, in the countries where this is at variance with law or custom. *The National Arms.*

They should strictly abstain from all connection with or support of political parties in the country in which they are established.

3°. They should always act with the greatest caution in their communications with the local authority and other officials, so that, on the one hand, the consideration and the privileges attached to their office be preserved inviolate, but also, on the other hand, no occasion be given for just complaint by exaggerated claims. *Relations with local authorities.*

4°. The Consuls General and Consuls can appoint Vice-Consuls and Consular agents in *Appointment of Vice-Consuls and Consular agents.*

places within their districts, if the necessity thereof is shown by them and the approval of their Government has been obtained for the persons selected. In no case may such appointment be made without having first obtained that approval. In proposing persons, they will give preference to subjects or citizens of their country and to persons not carrying on any profession or occupation directly connected with shipping.

The Vice-Consuls and Consular agents, thus appointed, act under the responsibility of the Consuls General or Consuls. They can be suspended and discharged by the latter, provided that immediate notice thereof be given to their Minister of Foreign Affairs.

If, however, Vice-Consuls or Consular agents are appointed directly by the Home Government, they do not perform their functions under the responsibility of the Consul in whose district they are stationed, and they cannot be suspended or discharged by the latter.

General attributes attached to the Consular mission.

5°. The mission of a Consular officer is to watch over the interests of the citizens, the trade and the industry of the country which he represents and to promote these interests whenever he has an occasion to do so within his Consular districts. In order to comply with these obligations, the Consular officer will find it, in the first place, of the utmost necessity to be well versed in all the laws and regulations, which he has to observe, in the fulfilment of his duties, with regard to the reports and communications which he is expected to make on all matters connected with trade, navigation and industry; the protection and help he is to afford, within the limits of his jurisdiction, to all his countrymen in the pursuance of their lawful trade in accordance with treaty rights. He must also fully understand his relations with the mercantile navy of his country, and the Consular jurisdiction and police which bring him into concurrent jurisdiction with the respective local authorities.

6°. The chief result which is hoped to be obtained from the Consular reports is that the commercial public shall thereby be furnished with a basis or source enabling it to make more special enquiries and obtain such subsequent data as may be necessary for its operations. These reports may also prove of utility to the respective Government by indicating the measures which it may be in position to take, either alone or concurrently with other Governments, in favor of commerce, navigation and industry. *Consular reports and communications.*

Keeping therefore these various ends in view, Consular officers will consider the drawing up of the communications which they transmit to their Government in matters of trade, shipping and manufactures, as among their most important duties.

These communications and reports are usually addressed and transmitted to the Diplomatic Agent or to the Consul General, to whom the Consuls, Vice-Consuls and Consular agents generally refer in any case he wants instructions.

In cases when a communication is deemed by the Consular officer of sufficient importance to be made speedily known to the Home Government, for instance, as soon as any epidemic disease or symptoms of such appear at the port, where the Consul resides or in its neighbourhood, he forwards such communication directly to his Minister for Foreign Affairs and also to the Government or local authority of the colonies or ports of his country which are in communication with his port. At the same time the Consul *Express communications.*

shall send the communication to his immediate superior Consular officer or his Diplomatic Agent.

Direct communication must also be made, as aforesaid, in cases of an outbreak of rebellion among the natives or any serious disturbances between foreigners and natives, principally when such disturbances have a general scope or tendency to licence not properly controlled by the local authorities. At the same time, a complete report containing all particulars must be sent to the Diplomatic Agent of his country.

The Consular Seal. 7°. The Consular officer uses in official correspondence and for sealing all documents signed in his official capacity, a Consular seal, as directed by his Government.

National Arms and Ensign. The Consul is entitled to place the coat-of-arms of his country, in moderate size, above the entrance of his Consulate, and to fly his national ensign, where such is customary.

Consular Memorandum. The Consul officer keeps a memorandum of all his official transactions, and copies of all reports, communications, certificates and other documents. The letters and instructions received must be carefully filed, numbered and registered. *Consular Archives.* The Consular Archives and seal are to be kept together in proper places, and the Consul shall make the necessary provision that the registers, letters, documents and seal be handed over in complete order, together with the inventory, to his successor or substitute in case of any vacation of the Consulate.

The Annual Trade-report. 8°. The Consul will be required to furnish annually a report on the trade of the past year, at the port of his Consulate; which report shall be sent in, as soon as may be compatible with necessary completeness and exactitude, in the manner directed by his Government. It is recommended to the attention of Consuls, not to defer all the steps necessary for the making of their annual report, until the year be actually expired, but rather to collect the materials, of which the reports must be composed in the course of the year. The report in question must treat separately, as far as the place of residence of the Consul will allow, of the following particulars:—

I. Agriculture, manufactures, ship-building and mines.

II. Commerce, export and import.

III. Navigation.

IV. Emigration.

V. State of the crops and sundry particulars.

Non-periodical communications.

9°. Independently of the information, which may be specially asked from the Consul on particular subjects and besides the communications alluded to above, it will be the duty of the Consul, at his own instigation, and at as early a period as possible, to communicate to the Diplomatic Agent of his country all matters bearing upon the interest or the trade of his country, having reference to questions not included in his periodical trade-reports. Of such occurrences or facts the Consul shall at once give notice, without waiting for the time when the annual statements have to be sent in.

Shipping Statistics.

10°. The compilation of statistics of navigation renders it necessary that tables of shipping intelligence be sent in by the Consular officers to their respective Government and that they reach in time for the General Annual Trade Statistics of the State, which have to be made up at the end of every year. The annual shipping lists of which the forms are supplied by the respective Government are to be drawn up at the end of the year, in triplicate, one copy to be forthwith dispatched directly to the Department of Foreign Affairs, one for the Consulate General or to the Legation, as the case may be, and one to remain in the archives of the respective Consulate for future reference to parties concerned. On the back part of this shipping list are specified the goods entered and exported by the reported vessels with approximate value of each sort. When there are no vessels to be reported, the columns are filled in with the word Nil, and the document nevertheless despatched as above mentioned. In the column for observations are mentioned the rates of freight and the best chances far sailing vessels or steamers of obtaining cargo for coast navigation or to and from national ports.

Annual list of national subjects.

Together with the annual reports, the Consul forwards yearly to his Diplomatic Agent, a list of all his countrymen and subjects of foreign States under his official protection, residing within his jurisdiction, with all the data of registration. If there be none, he will mention this in his report.

Mutual observance of treaties.

11°. The treaty being the basis of commercial intercourse, the Consul has not only to look that it is observed by his countrymen in all cases, but he shall also watch that it be fully carried out by the local authorities.

Duties of the Consul towards the subjects or citizens of his country.

12°. The powers and duties of Consular officers in regard to their fellow-citizens depend in a great measure upon the Municipal Law of their country. No civil jurisdiction can be exercised by them over their countrymen without express authority of law, or by treaty stipulation with the State in which they reside, and no criminal jurisdiction is permitted to them in Christian States. They are particularly cautioned not to enter into any contentions that can be avoided, either with their countrymen or with the subjects or authorities of the country. They should use every endeavour to settle, in an amicable manner, all disputes in which their countrymen may be concerned, but they should take no part in litigation between citizens. They should countenance and protect them before the authorities of the country in all cases in which they may be injured or oppressed, but their efforts should not be extended to those who have been wilfully guilty of an infraction of the local laws. It is their duty to endeavour, on all occasions, to maintain and promote all their rightful interests, and to protect them in all privileges that are provided for by treaty or are conceded by usage. If representations are made to the local authorities and fail to secure the proper redress, the case should be reported to the Consul-General, if there be one, or to the Diplomatic Representative, if there be no Consul-General, and to their Department of Foreign Affairs. *

Commercial affairs. Most favoured nation clause.

13°. It being the principal duties of the Consular officer to protect and to promote the lawful commerce of his country and to maintain the rights of its traders in foreign countries, it is his official obligation, that, whenever it may happen that subjects, products, shipping or cargoes of any other nation obtain new facilities or favours at the hands of the local Custom-house authorities or any other rights from local institutions, which are not also granted or extended to his countrymen, when they may be entitled to claim them under the clause of treaties known as "the most favoured nation clause," to report this, at once to his chiefs and to the Diplomatic Representative of his country.

Notice must also be given by him to his Government of all special occurrences of a public nature in the domain of commerce and industry in his district, such as the modification of tariffs of

* Consul. Reg. of the U. S. of America. § 460.

import and export, excises, Custom-house regulations, and the like.

He will communicate any useful and interesting information relating to agriculture, manufactures, population, and public works. In all that relates to scientific discoveries, to progress in the useful arts, and to general statistics in foreign countries, Consular officers are expected to communicate freely and frequently with their department, and to note all events occurring within their Consular districts which affect beneficially or otherwise the navigation and commerce of their country; the establishment of new branches of industry; the increase or decline of those before established; and communicate all the information which they may be enabled to obtain calculated to benefit the commerce and other interests of their country, and the best means of removing any impediments that may have retarded their advancement.

Information as to Lighthouses, Buoys, Shoals, etc.

14°. Consular officers are expected to report to their Government all matters that may come to their knowledge affecting the navigation of waters in their districts, or that may be of public interest or advantage to shipping. All notices of the erection of new light-houses, removals or changes in those established, the discovery or survey of shoal and reefs, changes in channels, the fixing of new buoys and beacons, and all subjects that concern the interests of navigation, should be communicated promptly to their Government. If published notices are sent, two copies should be furnished; and if they are in a foreign language, they must be accompanied by accurate and trustworthy translations.*

Ascertaining of nationality before giving protection.

15°. In all cases wherein his Consular protection is claimed, the Consular officer shall make

* Consul. Reg. of the U. S. of America, §§ 436 & 438.

strict inquiries after the proofs of nationality. The passports and other documents constituting these proofs shall be registered, signed and sealed by the Consul and returned to the owner. If the Consul entertains any doubt that the claimed nationality is not *bonâ fide* proved, he will submit the affair to the Diplomatic Agent, after having given due notice to the claimant, to send up his request, with all documents relating to the same.

Register of Nationality.

All foreigners, in order to be entitled to Consular protection, must have their names duly registered in the register of nationality at their respective Consulate. This registration contains :—

a. The names and surnames in full.

b. The birthplace, indicating the province or the colony in which the birthplace is situated.

c. The date of birth or approximate age.

d. The community in which the persons in question had their last domicile in the mother country or its colonies, indicating also the province in which this lies.

e. What was their last profession in the mother country or one of its colonies.

f. What date they left their last residence in the mother country or one of its colonies.

g. Their present profession, and, in the case of a mariner, his last vessel and rank, and when and where he left the vessel.

h. For a minor, (that is, a person who has not completed the age fixed by law for majority), besides the above stated points, also, the names, in full, of his father and mother and their present residence and profession, and, if both be dead, the name, in full, the present residence and profession of the guardian.

Every registration must be signed by the registered person and the Consul, in the register of nationality.

In cases of birth or death, at a port where the Consul is not specially appointed as Registrar of Civil State, in conformity with the Laws of his country, the declaration of birth or death of a subject or citizen of his country is noted in the register of nationality.

16°. When a subject dies abroad, the administration of his property at the place of his decease must, as a rule, be left to his heirs or the executors of his will. The Consular officer shall protect such property, if necessary. If, however, the heirs or executors are absent or unknown, the Consular officer shall take the requisite steps for the security of the estate, so far as the laws of the land are not opposed thereto. If a convention, by which the intervention of the Consul in the matter of unadministered estates is regulated, exists between his country and the country where the death has taken place, he will act in accordance with the stipulations of that convention.

The Consul shall never omit to report to his Department of Foreign Affairs, and, in so doing, to add all such information as may be necessary to explain the case or may serve to trace out unknown heirs. The Consular function with regard to the sealing up, taking inventories, taking care of property, etc., is only indispensable in case no heir or executor of the deceased is present or duly represented on the spot; unless the Consular officer is expressly requested by the heirs or executors to perform these functions.

17°. The Consular officer shall render the necessary services to ships of war of his nationality entering his district, and shall assist the commanders in everything that can promote the object of their missions. When a public vessel of his country arrives within the waters of his consular district, the Consular officer shall send to the captain, as soon as practicable, the respective harbour and pilotage regulations and the quarantine laws. If any contagious disease should be at the place, the Consul shall send to the captain all informations on this head. He shall also send to the captain the respective regulations of the port concerning leave for mariners and sailors to come on shore, and further, all information which the Consul may judge to be useful for the commanding officer to be acquainted with during his stay in those waters. Thus, the Consul will contribute, as much as lies within his sphere, to the security of his country's public vessels, in time of war or danger as well as in time of peace, and for this purpose shall give all information, with regard to the safety of navigation and local security in ports, including such as refers to the existing local regulations or customs respecting the Navy. He shall offer the commander his services as soon as possible, and shall continue them during the whole time the ships of war remain within his district. *Duties with regard to the Navy.*

Consular officers are authorized to call in the aid of the commanding officers of the naval forces, upon the responsibility of the latter and in accordance with the existing regulations, also with respect to the transport of accused and indigent persons.

To a Consular officer of the rank of Consul-General or Consul, the officer in command generally pays the first visit, unless the latter has the rank of Commodore or Admiral, in which case the first visit shall be paid by the Consular officer. Vice-Consuls and Consular agents pay the first visit to the commanders of their country's vessels of war.

Claiming deserters.

18°. Whenever members of the crews of his national vessels, whether merchant vessels or ships of war, desert in a foreign port, the Consular officer, within whose district the desertion has taken place, shall take the necessary steps to have the deserters arrested and surrendered by the authorities of the country, attention being paid to the stipulations of conventions when these exist, in order to act in strict accordance with treaty stipulations and international usages (comp. § 44).

Deposit of ship's papers at the Consulate on the arrival of merchant vessels.

19°. Within the time stipulated by local regulations, after the arrival of a merchant vessel, the ship's papers, that is the certificate of register, shipping articles and crew-list, shall be deposited with the Consul, who gives the master a receipt in due form for the same. Immediately after receiving the ship's papers, the Consul or the master reports the vessel to the Custom-house, giving her name, tonnage and nature of her cargo.

The Captain is held responsible for the correctness of the manifest, which shall contain a true and full account of the cargo on board. The Consul shall request the master to procure for the Consulate all information with regard to goods imported and exported, such as is required to make up the annual shipping list, as mentioned above in sub-section 10.

The Consul shall not fail on his part, to comply, as soon as possible, with all that is requisite under the Custom-house regulations, in order to avoid all disagreements between the Consulate and the Custom-house, by which unnecessary delay or trouble might be caused to vessels of his nationality entering his port.

What constitutes an arrival.

To constitute an arrival within the intent of the law, it is necessary that it should be such as involves an entry and clearance at the Custom-house of the foreign port. If the vessel enters the foreign port conformably to the local law or usage, her coming amounts to an arrival, independently of an ulterior destination or the time she may remain or intend to remain; or of the particular business to be transacted there. A vessel putting into a foreign port to get information only, and not entering or breaking bulk, or discharging seamen, or requiring new seamen, or needing the aid of the Consular officer in any respect, cannot be said to make an arrival at that port within the meaning of the law. Vessels driven into a port are not required to deposit their papers with the Consular officer, unless formal entry be afterwards made or Consular services required. *

When all dues and duties on ship and cargo shall have been paid, the Custom-house having granted a port clearance, the Consular officer will, on exhibition of this clearance, return the ship's papers, after having signed them, to the master, in exchange for the receipt mentioned above. After this the ship is lawfully allowed to leave the port.

Bills of health.

20°. To vessels bound to a national port,—and in any other case when required by the captain,—the Consul shall hand to the captain a bill of health.

* Consul Regulation, U. S. of America, §§ 178 & 182.

Declarations before the Consul at arrival.

21°. The declarations to be made by masters of merchant vessels with the Consul, at their arrival in port, may be classed as ordinary and extraordinary. The first is the usual report of the voyage, obligatory to be made at every port of arrival. The second is the sea-protest, in all cases of accidents to ship or cargo, or compelled deviation from the usual course of the voyage, and must serve as legal proof of average.

Masters of merchant vessels are bound, if they stay more than 24 hours, to have their registers or permits endorsed at each Consulate. Vessels which leave again within that time are exempt from this obligation. In the case of regular steam-service, with generally known dates of sailing, the notice to the Consulate of the first arrival and departure exempts the ship from giving any further notice during the same year, provided that no neglect be occasioned thereby in the payment of the Consular fees fixed by the tariff.

Certifying the log-book and other papers.

Before receiving any report, the Consul shall cause the log-book *(journal)* of the vessel to be exhibited to him, on which he shall put his *visa*, dated and sealed, at the end of the last entry, after the signatures of the master and chief-mate. The Consul will ask the master to point out to him all erasures and additions made in the log-book *(journal)* and, if any, these erasures and additions must likewise be signed by the Consul, after the signature of master and mate.

The Consul shall inquire from the master if during the passage any person died or was lost overboard; also if any child-birth occured on board during the voyage, and act *in casu*, as directed by his instructions. After this exhibition, of which the Consul shall keep note, the log-book *(journal)* shall immediately be returned to the master. Before returning the ship's papers, the Consul shall put the certificate of exhibition on the ship's register, and date and sign and seal it himself. The Consul shall also put his visa on the ship's articles. All alterations, changes, and new engagements on the crew list must be certified on the ship's articles.

Ship's report. The ordinary declaration, which is the customary ship's report on arrival, is made by the master at the time of exhibition of his log-book *(journal)* and contains a report of his voyage stating :—

a. The place he comes from, the place he left last, the port that was made if any, and the port of his destination.

b. The course taken by the vessel according to wind and weather, and all circumstances which influenced the voyage, especially stating the reasons for all deviations from ordinary courses.

c. The dangers met with and other remarkable occurrences respecting ship, cargo, crew and passengers.

The ordinary declaration does not require to be made on oath.

The sea-protest. 22°. Extraordinary declaration is the sea-protest made in cases of shipwreck, damage to ship or cargo, or throwing overboard of goods, or when during the voyage the master has been compelled, through stress of weather, or causes of war, or any other imperative reasons, to enter a port of refuge. The sea-protest is made by the master, when arriving at a port where there is a Consular officer of his nationality, as soon as possible after his arrival. This extraordinary declaration or sea-protest is generally made within twenty-four hours after arrival, by the master and the whole crew and must be duly sworn by all before the Consul. The sea-protest must contain a detailed report, beginning from the time that cargo was first taken in, at the place of departure, up to the day of arrival in the port, where the declaration is made, —including the refuge taken in those ports where no opportunity existed to make the necessary declaration before a Consul. Further, all accidents caused by the sea and weather and those measures taken for the sake of mutual safety, as slipping of anchors or cables, cutting of masts, throwing overboard of goods, extra expenses for lighters, etc., putting the vessel ashore and all voluntary acts, in behalf of ship and cargo. In drawing up the declaration it is desirable to follow, as closely as possible, the text of the log-book *(journal)* of which it should nearly be a reproduction with such additions and observations as may prove necessary (Comp. § 68, sub-sections 35–38).

In taking down the declarations of the master and crew, the Consul is not obliged to limit himself to the statements made; he may interrogate the master, the crew and even the passengers, in order to arrive at a complete and true narrative of the case.

Under the declaration as given by master and crew, the Consul shall write the certificate of his having received the protest as directed by law. Under this certificate all who can write must sign their names, and thereunder the Consul shall sign also and affix his Consular seal.

The sea-protest is to be made up in duplicate, one copy is handed by the Consul to the master, and one remains in the archives of the Consulate.

When the above stated formalities are not observed, there is danger of the sea-protest being wholly or partially set aside at law, and though the initiative to be taken in making the declaration of sea-protest devolves on the master, yet it is desirable that the Consul should remind him of the provisions of the law as laid down by the respective *lex mercatoria*. (Comp. §§ 63 & 68, sub-sections 35–38).

23°. When a vessel of his nationality enters a port with accidents to the vessel or with damages to cargo, the Consul shall, after the sea-protest mentioned above is made, on a written request of the master, appoint the necessary surveyors with instructions to state:— *Surveying damaged ships and cargoes.*

a. What damages have occurred to ship and cargo. What goods are damaged. The sort and marks of the damaged goods and their present condition to be clearly specified and stated.

b. Whether the damage has been caused by voluntary acts to save ship and cargo or by accidents of sea and weather. And, on the other hand, whether the damage was the consequence of unseaworthiness of the vessel, or was caused through neglect of the master or crew.

c. What is the value of the vessel in its present damaged state.

d. What would have been the value of the vessel, if she had arrived at the place of survey in a seaworthy state, able to sail for her destination.

e. By what means the repairs can be effected in the present port or must the vessel be sent to another harbour, and which —to undergo repairs. And, in the last case, what are the necessary provisional repairs required and what their cost to put her in a state to reach the indicated port for complete repairs.

f. What will be the cost of repairs to put the vessel in a state of complete seaworthiness.

g. What would have been the market value of the goods, if they had arrived in good condition at the place of destination, and what is their value in the present damaged state. Whether it is advisable in the interest of the owners, to send the goods in their present damaged state to their destination or to sell them on the spot in behalf of parties concerned.

The Consular disposition containing appointment of surveyors, with the injunctions above stated, must be written under the request of the master. The names, surnames and professions of the surveyors and the time fixed for them to be sworn in, must be mentioned in the appointment, of which a copy is transmitted to the appointed.

In cases of surveying damaged goods alone, only the injunctions mentioned under *a*, *b* and *g* are applicable, but the form of the document is always the same.

At a time fixed, the surveyors will appear at the Consulate to be sworn in by the Consul and accept their charge, and to fix the day on which they will begin the survey. Of this formality a separate document is drawn up, signed by the surveyors and the Consular officer.

The ship's log-book *(journal)* and the sea-protest are placed at the disposal of the surveyors, and all necessary information is afforded to them for the due fulfilment of their task.

They have to give their report in writing, clearly treating every subject as specified in their instructions and distinctly separating the damages caused by voluntary acts and those by accidents of sea and weather, with the respective costs of repairs.

The surveyors' report must be made up in duplicate and both copies, dated and signed by the three surveyors, handed to the Consul who, after having certified the signatures and affixed his Consular seal, gives one copy to the master, and deposits the other in the archives.

The surveyors shall hand in to the Consul, together with their report, a specified statement of the costs, in duplicate, upon which the Consul, after due examination and verification, shall add the declaration: that the costs are in accordance with the generally adopted usage of the place to the amount to be written in full,—which declaration shall be signed and sealed by the Consul, and the statement of costs affixed, with Consular seal, to the surveyors' report.

24°. When the necessity, the amount and the nature of repairs have been proved, the master shall apply in writing to the Consul for his authority, when, in conformity with his law, he cannot have the repairs executed otherwise than with the authorization of the Consul. *Repairs with authorization of the Consul.*

This authorization may be given separately, or it may be proved by the Consul signing the general account of the expenses, certifying that the repairs have been made according to the permission asked and granted, in conformity with law.

The repairs must be paid with the money which may be on board the ship, and if this be not sufficient, by bills on the owners. If the master cannot negotiate bills on the owners, he may, with the authorization of the Consul, raise money on bottomry. This is done by a written request of the master, stating the circumstances on which the Consul writes the disposition, granting the request in conformity with law, after having assured himself of the facts.

Consular attributes with regard to the raising of money for repairs in a port of refuge; with regard to bottomry and respondentia.

25°. When during the voyage, the vessel being in a port of refuge, it happens that the master is in want of money, for ordinary ship's repairs and equipment, or for the supply of provisions, and that he is not able to negotiate any bills on the owners, he can likewise resort to the borrowing money on bottomry or respondentia. In this case the situation and the necessity for the supply must be investigated and proved by the Consul, on the written request of the master, to which must be added a declaration signed by the officers or principal men of the crew, testifying the necessity of the expenses,—all in the manner prescribed by law.

The form of the bottomry-bond must be drawn up in conformity with the general usage of the place, duly certified and legalized by the Consul. (Comp. § 75).

Idem, with regard to the selling of cargo.

26°. In case the master, being in a port of refuge, is obliged to meet indispensable expenses, to enable the ship to proceed on her voyage, and can neither get bills on the owners negotiated nor bottomry on ship and cargo, he is entitled, with the consent of the Consul, to sell as much of the goods on board as cargo as is necessary to procure the amount required to put the vessel in a proper state to proceed to her destination. The same formalities of written request by the master, as prescribed by law, must be observed and the Consul shall give the necessary authorization after investigation.

27°. When it is proved by the report of surveyors, that the cargo, or a part of it, is in such a state that it cannot be transported any farther, and surveyors in their report advise the sale of it, in the interest of parties concerned, the master shall ask the Consul for permission to sell the same, with indication of sort, quantity and marks all clearly specified in a written request; on which document the Consul shall write the permission required, after having satisfied himself regarding the necessity and urgency of the case. *Consular attributes with regard to condemned cargo.*

The goods must be sold at public auction. The account sale shall be legalized by the Consul with the declaration: that the sale has been effected at public auction, in conformity with the general usage of the place, in his presence, that the fees and expenses are those customary and the net proceeds of the sale amount to ...... (the sum to be written in full).

28°. All documents and accounts concerning the sale must be duly legalized by the Consul, and the report and cost of surveying annexed.

29°. The vessel being legally condemned by sworn surveyors, appointed in conformity with law, and neither owners nor underwriters being represented at the port, the master shall make a written request to the Consul, stating the circumstances and the reasons for the condemnation of the vessel and ask for authorization to sell the vessel in the interest of the parties concerned. The Consul shall give this permission after having satisfied himself that all formalities have been duly attended to, in a disposition written on the master's request and in conformity with law. *With regard to condemned vessels.*

The sale must be effected at public auction, in conformity with the general usage of the place, which must be certified by the Consul on the account sale with the declaration as stated above.

Cancelling ship's register of condemned vessel.

30°. The Consul shall not fail to cancel the ship's register and the coasting-permit of the condemned vessel, forwarding it to his Government, and give the master a receipt for the same. Together with the register, the Consul shall forward the crew list with a Consular certificate stating that the crew have been duly paid off before him, and mentioning the name of each man.

Consular authority with regard to experts' or surveyors' certificates.

31°. With regard to the receiving of ships declarations and appointing of surveyors or experts, the Consular officer bears in mind that he is not authorized to issue certificates of unseaworthiness or to condemn a vessel or cargo *ex officio*, and much less, as such, to grant authority for the sale thereof, except in cases provided for by their respective national laws and always in conformity with the formalities prescribed by those laws. (Comp. § 68 sub-section 5 and §§ 69, 77 & 117). With regard to the question, how far Consuls are empowered to grant authorization for the sale of vessels or cargo condemned by surveyors, it is advisable that, when no ground for that power is to be found in the respective law and when they are called upon to interfere in such cases, the Consular officers will do well to confine themselves to simply granting attestation or certificate of the result of the investigations, without adding any authority, opinion or direction with regard to the vessel condemned by the surveyors or experts.

Consular attributes with regard to salvage and wrecks.

32°. In cases of stranding of vessels of his nationality within his jurisdiction, the Consular officer shall, in absence of owners or underwriters and their agents, take proper measures for saving such vessels with cargo and appurtenances. As to storing and securing the effects and merchandises saved, and as to inventories thereof, all is to be done in accordance with the provisions of the respective treaties, or as the laws or usages of the country permit.

The duties of Consular officers with regard to salvage in general and the concurrent Consular jurisdiction and attributes in cases of wrecks have been noted above, in section 78.

Consular legalizations and certificates.

33°. Consular officers are authorized to attest or legalize all commercial documents, declarations and other papers, issued within their districts by the competent authorities, which are intended to serve as legal proofs, in conformity with the respective laws.

Consular certificates and attests are always sealed with the official Consular seal.

Forwarding and serving of documents, administrative and judicial.

34°. The Consular officers shall take care that the copies of judicial documents sent to them by their proper authorities, in pursuance of the law, are delivered or legally served by competent persons to the parties concerned. In general it is one of the Consular functions to transmit or forward to its destination all that is directed to their Consulate for that purpose by competent parties.

Unofficial services.

35°. Consular officers are authorized to perform private commissions, in places within their Consular district, where parties cannot procure any proper agent for the performance of business, provided such private services to their countrymen do not infringe on their instructions or do not interfere or clash with their official duties.

Notary acts.

36°. When authorized by the laws of their country and allowed by Consular Convention, Consular officers are entitled to perform any notarial act or acts, such as any notary public is required or authorized by the laws of his country to do or perform, and with the same formalities as prescribed by those laws.

Depositions. 37°. Consular officers are authorized to receive the protests and declarations which masters, crews, and passengers of national vessels and any private individual of their nationality may respectively choose to make before them, and also such as any foreigner may choose to make, relative to the interests of subjects or citizens of the Consul's nationality. Copies of such acts, duly authenticated by the Consular officer, under his official seal, will receive faith in law with the Courts of their country and, in conformity with conventions, also with the tribunals of the country where the respective Consulate is established, in conformity with the nature of the case which is produced by the particular facts, with regard to which the protest was entered or the deposition made.

Letters rogatory (commissions rogatoires). 38°. In countries where law or comity provides with regard to letters rogatory *(commissions rogatoires)* from foreign tribunals, the Consular officer transfers the judicial commission received from a tribunal of his country (in cases when this cannot be accomplished through the respective Diplomatic Agent) to the competent local tribunal, as prescribed by conventions or in comformity with the *lex fori* (comp. §§ 85–87).

Consular duties with regard Emigration. 39°. It is the duty of the Consular officer, not alone to watch over the strict observance of the laws of his country regarding emigration by national vessels, but also to report to his Department all violations of these laws by masters of foreign vessels bound with emigrants from a foreign port to a port of his country or its colonies. *

* The Regulations for American vessels engaged in the transport of Emigrants, contained in the Consular Regulations of U. S. of America, are as follow. "It is made illegal by statute for citizens of the United States to participate with their vessels in the transportation of *coolies*, and the provisions of two obsolete Acts were revived, and were made to apply to vessels of the United States, engaged in the transportation of passengers from one port without the United States to another port without the United States. Consuls will, at once, report all

40°. The Consular officer, while devoting special care to the interests of the shipping of his country, regards it as his first obligation under this head, to cause his Nation's flag to be used on private vessels in strict conformity with the existing regulations. These regulations prescribe the steps to be taken by the Consular officer in the event of transgression of enactments. *Misuse of the flag by ships masters.*

41°. The Consular officer is entitled to verify, at any time, the ship's papers and the signature of the master or his successor, as it appears on the register. *Master's signature on Register.*

42°. When a vessel, sailing under the Consul's national flag, comes into a port without her ship's register, the Consul shall inquire into the affair and all circumstances attached to it, and report the case to his Government. The master of such vessel shall give a written declaration concerning the reason why he cannot show his register, *Vessels without Register or with doubtful Register.*

---

violations of these statutes coming to their notice. It is understood that British Courts at Hongkong have held that the traffic in coolies is the slave-trade in another form, and therefore piracy. The Courts of the United States probably could not find justification in the statutes for adding it to the list of acts punishable as piracy; but the statute warrants the State Department in urging upon Consuls to endeavour in every way to prevent it, not only by proceeding against every American citizen engaged in it, but by using their influence in every possible manner to prevent it."

"The statute is not intended to apply to the free and voluntary emigration of Chinese subjects. It is made the duty of the Consular officer of the United States, residing at the port from which a vessel with such voluntary emigrants takes her departure, to give the master of such vessel a permit or certificate, containing the names of such persons, and setting forth the fact of their voluntary emigration from such port or place. Such certificate will not be given until the Consular officer has personally satisfied himself, by evidence produced, of the truth of the facts therein contained. By a later statute it is also made the duty of a Consul, before delivering the permit or certificate above referred to, to ascertain whether the emigrant has entered into any contract or agreement for a term of service, within the United States, for lewd and immoral purposes, and if such a contract exists, to refuse to deliver the permit or certificate. The importation into the United States of women for the purposes of prostitution is forbidden, and all contracts relating thereto are declared void; and the attempt to hold them under such a contract is declared a felony. By the same act also it is made unlawful for which declaration the Consul shall forward together with his report. If the ship's other papers are in order, and her nationality is sufficiently proved by other legal documents, the Consul shall proceed to treat the vessel as a national vessel, pending the decision of his Government.

The same course shall be followed in case a master produces a register the validity of which is not proved to the Consul's satisfaction.

Fitting out vessels for war purposes.

43°. Whenever it comes under the notice of a Consul that the master of a vessel of his nationality is misusing his flag, by fitting out his vessel for warlike purposes without special permit of Government, or is acting in violation of neutrality, he shall at once report the case with all the particulars to his Diplomatic Agent, and take the necessary steps to withdraw and cancel the misused register.

---

persons who are undergoing a sentence for conviction in their own country of felonious crimes, other than political, or whose sentence has been remitted on condition of their emigration, or for women imported for the purpose of prostitution, to emigrate into the United States. Provision is also made for the return of such persons to the countries from which they came, and for proceedings against the vessel bringing them to the United States."

"Consuls will be rigid in exacting a compliance with these provisions. It is not necessary to point out to Consuls how easily the crime of transporting involuntary emigrants may be veiled under the form of a voluntary emigration, nor to impress upon them the importance of rigid personal examination of all such classes of emigrants, in order to insure that there shall be no violations of the law."

"Application is sometimes made to a Consul for a certificate showing the admeasurement of vessels engaged in transporting Chinese emigrants, in order to ascertain the number of passengers that may lawfully be carried. It is held that the responsibility of determining the legal number of emigrant passengers that his vessel may carry is devolved entirely upon the master, under Title XLVIII of the Revised Statutes, who is to ascertain the vessel's capacity in any manner he may see fit. The law makes no provision for the issue of a certificate of such capacity by a Consular officer to the master or owner of an American vessel in a foreign port, and applications for such certificates should be refused." (Sections 347–353 of the United States Consular Regulations of 1881. The regulations prohibiting Mormon immigration are contained in Sections 379–381 of said Consular Regulations).

44°. The Consul shall remind the masters to have the names of their vessels and the place where they are registered exhibited in the usual manner at the outside of their vessels, in compliance with the respective shipping laws. *Ship's name to be exhibited outside ship.*

45°. The attributes of the Consular officer in connection with concurrent jurisdiction and protection in behalf of vessels of his nationality in foreign territorial waters, and the Consular jurisdiction with regard to foreign members of crews of such vessels and other foreigners under his Consular protection, have been noted above in paragraphs 110 & 111. *Concurrent Jurisdiction. Foreigners under Consular protection.*

46°. The discipline on board merchant vessels in foreign territorial waters is maintained by the master of the vessel. It is necessary that he should be supported in so doing by his Consular officer as well as that this officer should take under his official protection the rights and interests of the crew as regards the master. Consular officers have therefore no power to dismiss masters of merchant vessels, irrespective of the legal causes as laid down by the respective shipping laws, even at the request of the owners or managers of such vessels. Nor are Consular officers authorized to order the discharge of any member of the crew outside the provisions of said laws. When owners of vessels or their agents think fit to discharge a master, or any officer or member of the crew of their ships, they do this on their own responsibility, subject to the law, and therefore cannot shield themselves behind the authority of the Consular officer, whose magistratic functions, with regard to the proper execution of the laws of his country, must ever be maintained free from any tincture of partiality. *Masters, officers and members of the crew cannot be discharged under Consular authority except in strict conformity with the law. The impartiality of the Consular magistratic decisions to be rigidly maintained.*

CHAPTER XXIII.

BALANCE OF POWER AND INTERVENTION.

The Right of Convenience (droit de convenance).

§ 153. Political considerations, sometimes called reasons of State, are generally based on one-sided arguments prompted by selfishness and rapacity, and put forth in support of political claims which have nothing to do with Law *(Jus, droit, Recht)* and can therefore only appeal to the so-called right of convenience *(droit de convenance)*. It is on this right that powerful States sometimes insisted in matters regarding their so-called natural or military frontiers, basing thereon their claims for the rectification of these frontiers. These proceedings caused continual uncertainty with regard to the peace of the Continent, which includes different States of unequal power with contiguous frontiers.

To counterbalance and, to a certain extent, to neutralize this *droit de convenance*, in the absence of more cogent causes of war, the spirit of modern civilization, prompted by innate abhorrence of war, created an argument of restraint in the theory called the balance of power *(équilibre politique)* which also sustains à right, viz., that of intervention *(droit d'intervention)*. But there is neither for this system of balance of power, nor for the right of intervention which it implies, any foundation in the Law of Nations, unless expressly stipulated by international treaties. *

* See KLUBER. Droit des Gens Mod. de l'Europe. Edit. Ott. 1861. § 42. VON OMPTEDA. Literatur des Völker-rechts. II. 484. HEEREN. Handbuch der Geschichte des Europ. Staaten Systems. Ed. 1811. p. 13. WHEATON. Hist. de Progrès du Droit des Gens. 2nd Edit. Vol. I, p. 110.

Balance of Power versus Balance of Justice.

This doctrine of a balance of power or political equilibrium essentially differs from that equilibrium of justice *(équilibre de droit)* which forms the ground work of International Law. The former is merely the offspring of a false principle of utility; based on ideas of might and preponderance, it offers, whether it be viewed politically or judicially, but a vague, ill-defined, and uncertain calculation of material interests. An equal distribution of countries or Nations in proportion to their political importance *(lex agraria gentium)*, says Kluber, will never be accomplished. Nevertheless, on this principle of utility, which constitutes the *droit de convenance*, many arbitrary systems of a pretended balance of power have been built up or imagined among the leading Powers of Europe. This system was at one time applied to the politics of Europe in general as well as to the navigation of the ocean and of certain seas, with special reference to commerce. At another time the system was limited in its application to a certain portion of the Continent, viz., to Northern, Eastern and Western Europe, Germany and Italy. This was done moreover, with the understanding, that the smallest deviation from these arbitrary rules of equilibrium was to be regarded as a just cause of war. But, at the bottom of this pretentious system of utility, there were feelings of jealousy and mutual distrust which in all cases formed the main spring of action.

On the other hand, the *équilibre de droit*, as above stated, which is strict justice combined with genuine solicitude for the welfare of peoples, has established not merely the indisputable right but the sacred duty, to maintain a balance of justice instead of a mere balance of power, by vigourous opposition to all unjust tendencies on the part of any Power to acquire dominion and aggrandizement or any undue preponderance at the expense of weaker neighbours. In this sense was the treaty of alliance between Austria, Great Britain, Prussia, Russia and Naples, concluded at Tœplitz, on the 9th September, 1813, with the view to assure to Europe *son repos futur par le rétablissement d'un juste équilibre des puissances.* *

On this principle the genuine right of intervention must be based.

Principles of Intervention.

§ 154. Intervention in the internal or domestic affairs of an independent State, is but usurpation if attempted by any foreign Government without the clear force of the logic of events.

Imperative necessity may compel one State to interfere in the affairs of another, when the internal tranquillity of the latter State forms an all-important link binding up its condition with the interests of the interfering State. It may happen in the case of any State, that it becomes a matter of the highest importance affecting even the question of its existence, how affairs are conducted in another State. In such a case it becomes impossible for a State to allow another country, intimately connected with its interests, to fall a pray to anarchy or to the domination of other Powers. Thus by a series of steps, caused in the first instance by a condition of unrestrained anarchy in the case of one State, another State may at last be compelled by the obligations of self-preservation, to assume complete authority over the disturbed State as the logical result of the policy pursued by the latter. Such a measure may be the best solution after all, provided that all available agencies, by which order could be established, have previously been exhausted. In settling the affairs of such a country, the guiding principle

* KLUBER. p. 63.

must be based on facts as they are and not on the assumption of facts as they ought to be. What form of administration could be established with the best chance of permanence and with the least interference with conditions which must perforce be taken into consideration, this is the first question to be solved by the interfering State, which *nolens volens* is compelled to take the lead and to try to enter upon such a line of action as can be pursued with safety and honour.

With regard to the doctrine of intervention we take the following quotations from Sir Robert Phillimore.

Sir Robert Phillimore's statement with regard to the doctrine of Intervention.

"In all systems of private jurisprudence, provision is made for placing upon the abstract right of individual property such restrictions as the general safety may require. The maxim *expedit enim reipublicæ, ne quis sua re male utatur*, belongs to the law of all countries. * The prætorian interdict of the Roman, the injunction of the English Law, give effect to this principle by preventing the mischief from being done, instead of endeavouring to remedy it when done. Some analogous right or power must exist in the system of international jurisprudence. 'Neither,' says Lord Bacon, 'is the opinion of some of the schoolmen to be received, that a war cannot justly be made but upon a precedence of injury or provocation; for there is no question but a just fear of an imminent danger, though there be no blow given, is a lawful cause of a war.' † The right of self-defence, incident to every State, may, in certain circumstances, carry with it the necessity of intervening in the relations, and, to a certain

* INST. Lib. I. VIII. 22. Chaque droit a ses limites: il est limité par les droits analogues de tous membres d'une société. AHRENS. Cours de Droit Naturel ou de Philosophie du Droit, p. 296. Brux. 1841.

† Essay on Empire.

extent, of controlling the conduct of another State; and this where the interest of the intervener is not immediately and directly, but mediately and indirectly, affected. This remark brings us to the considerations of the doctrine of intervention.* And first of all it should be clearly understood that the intervention of bodies of men armed or to be armed, uncommissioned and unauthorised by the State to which they belong, in a war, domestic or foreign, of another State, has no warrant from International Law. It is the duty of a State to restrain its subjects from invading the territory of another State; and the question when such an act on the part of subjects, though unauthorized by the State, may bring penal consequences upon it, has received some consideration. It is a question to which the events of modern times have given great importance, and as to which during the last half-century, the opinions of statesmen especially of this country (England) have undergone a material change. That this duty of restraining her subjects is incumbent upon a State, and that her inability to execute it cannot be alleged as a valid excuse or as a sufficient defence to the invaded State, are propositions which, strenuously contested as they were in 1818, will scarcely be controverted now. The means which each State has provided for the purpose of enabling herself to fulfil this obligation form an interesting part of public and constitutional jurisprudence, to the province of which they, strictly speaking, belong. The question, however, borders closely upon the general province of International Law."

English and American Neutrality Statutes.

"The United States of America began their career as an independent country under wise and

* GUNTHER. I. 287, §§ 8–12. HEFFTER. 90. WHEATON. Droit Intern. Vol. I. pp. 77, 92. MANNING. Law of Nations, p. 97.

great auspices, and it was the firm determination of those who guided their nascent energy, to fulfil the obligations of International Law as recognized and established in the Christian commonwealth of which they had become a member. They were sorely tried at the breaking out of the war of the first French Revolution, for they had been much indebted to France during their conflict with their mother country, and were much embarrassed by certain clauses relating to privateers in their Treaty with France, 1778; but in 1793, under the presidency of Washington, they put forth a proclamation of neutrality, and, resisting both the threats and the blandishments of their recent ally, took their stand upon sound principles of International Law, and passed their first Neutrality Statute of 1794. The same spirit induced the Government of these States at that important crisis, when the Spanish colonies in America threw off their allegiance to the mother country, to pass the amended Foreign Enlistment Statute of 1818; in accordance with which, during the next year, the British Statute, after a severe struggle and mainly by the great power of Mr. Canning, was carried through Parliament. * Public feeling, however, was generally averse to it, and a notion that it assisted the despotic Powers of Europe in repressing the efforts of their subjects to obtain constitutional liberty prevailed. It is a very remarkable fact that no public prosecution of an offender against the provisions of the Statute appears to have been formally conducted, by the order of the Government, in a Court of justice, until the period of the recent American civil war; that is, nearly fifty years after the passing of the Act. Public opinion upon the subject had then undergone a revolution. The Statute when put to a practical

Foreign Enlistment Statute of 1819.

Foreign Enlistment Act of 1870.

* 59 Geo. III. Chapt. 69 (July 3, 1819).

test was found to be badly constructed, and to bear in its loose phraseology and disjointed sentences marks of the compromise which had enabled it to become law. In substance, though not without variations judicially considered important, it agreed with the American Statute, which it was designed to follow. The machinery has been much improved by the Statute of 1870, which is calculated to strengthen the hands of the Executive." *

"It appeared from evidence laid before the English Neutrality Laws Commission, appointed by the Queen in 1867 (the recommendations of whose report are mainly incorporated in the present and recent Statute), that European States generally were furnished by their municipal law with the means of fulfilling their international obligations in this respect. The question whether the powers originally given by the Statute 59 Geo. III. c. 69 (July 3, 1819), to our Government, and by that of the preceding but almost contemporaneous Statute of Congress (April 20, 1818), to the Government of the United States, are in excess or are in fulfilment of the International obligations of the neutral, receives a different solution from two schools of opinion as distinct upon this point as upon that of contraband. If the former school was correct in its opinion, then the English Government was already more than sufficiently armed with authority for the discharge of the international duty incident to a neutral. If the latter school was correct in its opinion, then there was, to say the least, a doubt whether the Statute, as at present interpreted by English judges, did confer on our Government the requisite authority." †

* 33 and 34 Vict. Ch. 90.—An Act to regulate the conduct of her Majesty's Subjects during the existence of hostilities between foreign States, with which her Majesty is at peace. (Aug. 9, 1870).

† See Report of Neutrality Laws Commission, 1868.

"In considering this subject it is to be remembered that International Law is not stationary, and that precedents of history, taken from a period when the mutual relations of States were less clearly defined than at present, cannot be considered as decisive on the point at issue. Precedents may be found in the time of Queen Elizabeth, and later, in which large bodies of English subjects were enlisted under the authority of the Government in this country, and, displaying the English or Scotch standard, took a part in the civil war of a foreign State, without open war being declared between that foreign State and England. But for more than a century, at least, such a state of things has been considered as inconsistent with the duties of a neutral State.* And although the only alternative suggested by the United States has been in favour of a relaxation of the stringency of the provisions of their Municipal Act, I rejoice that the English Government has, by the last Statute, strengthened the hands of the Executive and given greater force and prominence to the maxim, that, with respect to the external relations of the State, the will of the subject is bound up in that of his Government. At all events, those who are interested in the progress of international justice may look with satisfaction upon the general state of feeling and usage throughout the civilized world upon the much-vexed question of foreign enlistment. There is no international subject perhaps in which, during the last thirty years, so decided an improvement has taken place. The axiom that to enlist foreign subjects without the consent of

---

* At the time of the Crimean War the British Government took into their pay large bodies of mercenaries, designated Foreign Legions, and composed chiefly of natives of Germany and Switzerland, countries then at peace with Russia. See HANSARD. Parl. Deb. Vol. CXLII. p. 1152.

their Governments is a grave breach of the rights of States, is now, it may be reasonably hoped, firmly incorporated in the code of International Law." *

"To preserve the balance of power, says Sir Robert Phillimore further, 'was the real object of the terrible and desolating war of the Thirty Years. The creation of the federal system of the Germanic empire, and the recognition of the two new independent States—the United Netherlands, and the Swiss Cantons—guaranteed by France and Sweden in the treaties of Westphalia (1648) and the Pyrenees (1659), were intended and supposed to form an effectual barrier to the undue preponderance of Austria, and to have secured the equilibrium and thereby the peace of Europe. The independence and liberties thus secured to the States of Southern Europe, were, about the same time, guaranteed by the treaties of Copenhagen (1658), and Oliva (1660), to the States of Northern Europe, which composed, in some sort, a distinct system. The equilibrium of power in the North, which had been endangered by the ambition of Sweden, was adjusted by the treaties between Sweden, Denmark, Poland, and the Electorate of Brandenburg under the guaranteeship of Austria, France, England, and the United Provinces. Before the close of the century in which these treaties were made, the aggrandisement and ambition of France united against her the same Powers which had formerly, for like causes existing elsewhere, leagued themselves with her, and to those Powers were now added Great Britain and the United Provinces."

"The principal object of the treaties of Utrecht (1713), Rastadt and Baden (1714), was to secure

* Sir ROBERT PHILLIMORE. Com. Vol. I. Edit. 1879, p. 553, et seq.

Europe against the universal dominion of France. By the fundamental articles of these treaties, the second great landmark of modern history, it was declared that the kingdoms of France and Spain should never be united under one sceptre; and that the Spanish Netherlands should be transferred to the House of Austria, to which Milan and Naples, with less reason, were also assigned. The avowed object of the memorable wars which preceded this treaty, and of the convention itself, was the restoration of the balance of power in Europe. * This treaty may in some degree be said to have 'called in the New World to balance the Old' †; the balance being partly adjusted by the cession and transference, from one European Power to another, of colonial possessions in other parts of the globe ‡; in other words, positive International Law was carried beyond the limits of Europe. This treaty was made, to borrow its own language, || *ad conservandum in Europa equilibrium;* indeed the recognition of the system of balance may be dated from this epoch, and if we accept a partial deviation from it by the treaty of Vienna in 1738, which seated a younger branch of the Spanish monarchy upon the throne of the two Sicilies, it continued to govern the territorial arrangements of the South of Europe till the first French Revolution, and is mentioned in every treaty of peace till that of Luneville in 1800. So late as 1846–47 the treaty of Utrecht was invoked by England when protesting against the ill-omened marriage of the Duke de Montpensier; and though

---

* WHEATON. Hist. p. 125.

† Mr. Canning's Speech on sending the troops to Portugal. Speeches. Vol. VI. p. 61.

‡ WHEATON. Hist. p. 87.

|| KOCH. II. 92.

the doctrine of non-revival, by express mention in subsequent treaties, may be held to have annulled the binding force of its specific provisions, the principle of European policy, namely that the crowns of France and Spain shall never rest upon the same head, is put on record for ever by a treaty of this description."

"The doctrine of the balance of power has of late years been attacked and ridiculed. It certainly is liable to great abuse, but fairly explained means no more than the right of timely prevention of a probable danger. As a matter of fact, it has been, as has been shown, directly recognized as a principle to be maintained by the great European Powers in recent conventions of great importance." *

Halleck's opinion. "But, unfortunately, says Halleck, historians and jurisconsults are too apt to draw their arguments from the fact to the right, and to infer the right of interference from the numerous examples of its actual exercise, without testing the legality of the usage by reference to fundamental principles. If foreign interference in the internal affairs of a sovereign State (except in cases of imminent and actual danger to the general or particular security, freedom and independence of Nations) is contrary to Natural Law and the fundamental principle of international jurisprudence, usage and custom cannot make it justifiable or lawful, for no length of usage can justify a wrong." †

"That the general rule of Natural Law is opposed to all interference in the internal affairs of another State, cannot be doubted. It is confirmed by reason, and the concurring opinions of

* PHILLIMORE. Com. Int. Law. Vol. I. p. 578, et seq.

† WHEATON. Hist. Law of Nations, pp. 80, 88. VATTEL. Droit des Gens. Liv. II. Ch. I. § 7. BYNKERSHOEK. De Foro Legatorum. Cap. II. §4; Idem. Quaest. Jur. Pub. Lib. I. Cap. XXV. Edinburgh Review. No. 156. p. 329. Le Louis. 2 Dod. R. 257.

the most eminent publicists of all ages and all Nations. It must nevertheless be admitted that there are exceptions to this rule. The principal difficulty is in confining the exceptions so as not to infringe upon the principle of the rule. The general rule, and the possible exception to it, were both very clearly stated by M. de Chateaubriand in his speech in the French Chamber, on the Spanish war of 1823. 'Has,' said he, 'a Government of one country a right to interfere in the affairs of another? This great question of International Law has been solved in different ways, by different writers on the subject. Those who incline to the natural right such as Bacon, Puffendorff, Grotius, and all the ancients, mention that it is lawful to take up arms in the name of the human race against a society which violates the principles on which the social order reposes, on the same ground on which, in particular States, you punish an individual malefactor who disturbs the public repose. Those who consider the question as one depending on civil right, are of opinion that no one Government has a right to interfere in the affairs of another. I adopt, in the abstract, the principles of the last. I maintain that no Government has a right to interfere in the affairs of another Government. In truth, if this principle is not admitted, and above all by all people who enjoy a free constitution, no Nation could be in security. It would always be possible for the corruption of a minister, or the ambition of a king to attack a State which attempted to ameliorate its condition. In many cases wars would be multiplied; you would adopt a principle of eternal hostility, a principle of which every one would constitute himself judge, since every one might say to his neighbour, 'your institutions displease me;

change them, or I declare war.' But when the modern political writers rejected the right of intervention, by taking it out of the category of natural to place it in that of civil rights, they felt themselves very much embarrassed at the result; for they saw that cases will occur in which it is impossible to abstain from intervention without putting the State in danger. At the commencement of the revolution, it was said, 'perish the colonies rather than sacrifice a principle,' and the colonies perished. Shall we also say, 'perish the social order rather than sacrifice a principle,' and let the social order perish? In order to avoid being shattered against a principle which they themselves had established, the modern jurists have introduced an exception. They said, no Government has a right to interfere in the affairs of another Government, except in the case where the security and immediate interests of the first Government are compromised." *

"Another ground of foreign interference in the internal affairs of a sovereign State, advocated by some text-writers, is the obligations of treaty stipulations. There can be no doubt that a sovereign State may guarantee a particular form of government to one of its component parts, as the constitution of the United States of America guarantees a republican form to each State of the federal union; or, in case of a protectorate, the protecting State may guarantee or direct a particular form of government for the dependent or protected State. But neither the component nor the protected States are in these cases to be regarded as independent sovereignties; they have

* DE CUSSY. Précis Historique. Ch. IV. ALISON. Hist. of Europe, Ch. XII. § 41, et seq. Moniteur. Feb. 15, 1823. Mons. De Chateaubriand's despatch to Mr. Canning, Jan. 23, 1823, and the answer of Mr. Canning; Annuaire Historique (Leseur). 1823, p. 708. Ann. Reg. 1823, Pub. Doc., 110.

parted with some of the essential qualities of sovereignty and independence, and consequently are not entitled to the full rights incident to their primary condition as equal members of the society of Nations. The same doctrine may apply generally to treaties of unequal alliance. But, in treaties of equal alliance, between independent and sovereign States, will a stipulation of mediation or guaranty justify generally the interference of one State in the internal affairs of another, contrary to the wishes of the latter? If the interference is in itself unlawful, can any previously existing stipulation make it lawful? We think not: for the reason that a contract against public morals has no binding force, and there is more merit in its breach than in its fulfilment."

"Another ground of foreign interference, in the internal affairs of a sovereign State, is that of humanity, it being done for the alleged purpose of stopping the effusion of blood caused by a protracted and desolating civil war in the bosom of the State so interfered with. If such interference be in the nature of a pacific mediation, one State merely proposing its good offices for the settlement of the intestine dissensions of another State, there can be no doubt of its lawfulness." *

A rough outline of what is lawful and what is unlawful in the interference of States might be suggested in the following rules.

Interference in the internal affairs of a State is unlawful; in cases of civil war, or of war between two States, other States may lawfully interfere, but such interference is not interference in the true sense of the word, it is an act of hostility, and a State so interfering loses at once all claim of neutrality. See speech of Lord Palmerston, Parl.

* HALLECK. Intern. Law. Vol. I. p. 83, et seq.

Deb. xxviii. p. 1,163. If civil war or internal commotion prevails in a State, and menaces the tranquillity or interests of another State, in a substantial, distinct, and immediate manner, that latter State may interfere with amicable negotiations, or even with arms; and when two States are at war, other States may interfere in a similar manner for the purpose of preserving the balance of power, should it in reality be menaced. See Canning's Despatch, March 31, 1823. Ann. Reg. 1823. Pub. Doc., 140. *

---

* Sir SHERSTON BAKER'S Edition of Halleck's Intern. Law. Vol. I, note on page 83.

CHAPTER XXIV.

THE LAWS OF PEACE.

Settlement of International Differences. Amicable Arrangement and Compromise. Mediation and Arbitration. Conferences and Congresses.

§ 155. The accidental or momentary disturbances which are often observed in the economical system of nature, both in the physical and in the moral organism, are those phenomena, caused by occasional perturbations in the regular operation of the Laws of Nature, which are called variations. They are observable through all stages of creation (§ 1), from inorganic matter up to the social organism of man, which latter, as noted above (§ 2), is governed by the Moral Law of Nature. *The phenomena of physical and moral varieties of the Laws of Nature.*

The variations in the dominion of the Moral Law of Nature produce the phenomena which we call the Spirit of Law, as described above in paragraphs 10–15. * The causes of disturbances in the physical laws, or, in other words, of varie-

---

* The Moral Law of Nature, being the perfect harmony of Justice and Benevolence, represents a state of perfection which the rules regulating the social relations of men, in the actual development of their Moral-Mental organism, have naturally not yet reached. These rules, which are called Law *(jus, droit, Recht)*, represent the basis on which societies of human beings are founded in their actual state of development, and, having grown out of the influence of the Moral Law of Nature on the Moral Mental organism of man, but moulded by the actual imperfect state of that organism, they can be regarded as a variation of the said law of Nature. It is this variation of the Moral Law of Nature, in which we cannot fail to recognize the Spirit of the Law of Nature, which is described above (§§ 10–15) under the name of Spirit of Law.

ties in species, are often hidden to our senses ; in fact, of laws of variation the naturalist knows next to nothing; the inadequacy of his physical senses to perform proper observations among the milliards of active factors which cause the deviation of some particularly conspicuous physical law into the channel of another or several other laws combined, will remain a serious impediment to natural science, notwithstanding the most skilful contrivances made to bring to perfection the test of experiments. Under these circumstances our perception of physical causes must necessarily be deficient. This is however not the case, to the same extent, with regard to our conception of moral perturbations, provided we try to discover the causes of the variations of the Moral Law of Nature through our moral senses Conscience and Sympathy (§ 2), which, when combined, represent in our mind this Law of Nature, and form our judgment through genuine common sense, which is Reason and Feeling combined, as described above in paragraphs 2–15.

The moralist who accepts the Moral-Mental organism as part of the economical system of Nature, will not fail to obtain, through a well developed moral common sense, a sufficiently clear conception of the causes of the variations of the Moral Law of Nature called Spirit of Law and International Spirit of Law (§§ 11 & 15), for, judging the history of mankind through that genuine common sense, he will easily comprehend the immediate factors which produced these variations. *

* La perturbation accidentelle et momentanée de l'harmonie qui doit présider à tout système régulier, est un fait de l'ordre physique et de l'ordre moral. Ce fait s'observe dans la matière inerte et dans les corps organisés, chez les êtres animés dépourvus de raison, et chez l'homme, être essentiellement raisonable. Dans l'ordre physique, la

We have noted above, in paragraph 18, how civilized States, in their mutual intercourse in time of war as well of peace, invariably appeal to public opinion for the justification of their acts and how it is proved by history that civilized Nations of all ages have recognized the Moral Law to be binding upon them as the basis of mutual duties, however poorly the state of the Spirit of Law, which governed those mutual duties, might now appear to us by the light of a progressing civilization. This Spirit of Law, emanating from the Moral Law of Nature, of which it is the manifestation in the practical life of Nations as well as individuals, shows itself in different aspects, not unlike the different varieties of species produced in the sphere of the physical laws, which are caused by the manifold influences of social life at every stage on the road to civilization made by the subject whose immanent phenomenon it is (§ 11).

Monstrosities of the Moral Law of Nature.

Differences, disputes and war between Nations or States are abnormal variations of the Spirit of Law, or in other words of the natural law which governs social relations. They are not natural varieties of the Moral Law of Nature but simply irregular perturbations of that law, which, as all other deformed products of Nature are called monstrosities; the degree of monstrosity being defined by the greater or lesser deviation from the respective Spirit of Law, which latter, as noted above, is a natural variety of the Moral Law of Nature.

---

découverte des lois qui président à cette pertubation est souvent un problème insoluble pour la raison de l'homme; les effets se perçoivent, tandis que les causes demeurent cachées. Dans les institutions humaines de l'ordre moral, l'interruption de l'harmonie prend sa source dans le conflit des intérêts individuels, dans l'antagonisme des droits de chacun et des obligations ou devoirs qui répondent à ces droits. ORTOLAN. Diplomatie de la Mer. Edit. 1864. Vol. II. p. 2 Cause et objet de la guerre.

In international jurisprudence, as in civil jurisprudence, a distinction must be made between the rights of parties and the legal means they employ to maintain and justify these rights and for the termination of the differences. Justice and Benevolence, which are the two elements of the Moral Law of Nature, are ever influencing the human mind, to bring the latter in harmony with that Law of Nature. The standard by which the rights of parties must be regarded by an unbiassed mind can therefore not be disputed; it is the means of adjudication which constitute the difference between civil and international jurisprudence.

But as between independent Nations or States, there is no supreme judge on earth, their differences or disputes, when not capable of being settled by amicable arrangement,—compromise, arbitration or other means of rectification through the Moral Law of Nature, are apt to throw them back into that state of semi-barbarism in which only brute force constitutes an acknowledged verdict, that is, into a state of war. * In the first instance, the rules applied in order to arrive at a solution of the question in a peaceable way are called the laws of peace, while in the other instance, when parties have drifted into a state of mutual violence, this state is yet subjected, as far as possible, to certain rules of restraint acknowledged by International Law, which are called laws of war.

The intermediate state between peace and war. There is however an intermediate condition between peace and war, a medium state, in which a crisis is formed by the alternative of adopting the one or the other course. In this state arbitrary acts are often committed, by one or both of

* G. F. DE MARTENS. Précis de Droit des Gens, Edit. Vergé. 1858. Vol. II. p. 19. KLUBER. Edit. Ott. 1861, p. 405.

the contending parties, in order to hasten the termination of the crisis. This brings parties into a condition of enmity, often accompanied by acts of violence, which fall short of actual war only by being more or less limited to a certain defined line of action or field of operation in conformity with the predominating social, political or moral conditions which the respective parties occupy in relation to each other. This intermediate condition between peace and war is the state of retortion or reprisal which is treated in the next chapter.

§ 156. The laws of peace, which we have now under consideration, give several remedies at hand to terminate differences among contending States. In the first place, the principles of the laws of peace require that the facts which have caused the difference or contest must be clearly established. In the means which parties employ to establish these facts lies not only the test of the sincerity of their appeal to the laws of peace, but these proceedings form a genuine standard by which one may judge their respective national morality.

The Laws of Peace. Confirmation of international facts.

When Great Britain, with the magnanimity really worthy of a great Nation, acknowledged the misconceptions of facts which had led to the Transvaal war, and ceased the bloody contest with those few brave sons of *het oude Vaderland*, which the colossus could have easily crushed but never made to yield, her great statesmen never displayed a truer sense of the appreciation in which they hold inborn national-moral sense of justice and benevolence. Thus it was also in the case of the Alabama arbitration, when two great Nations avoided a bloody contest between kindred nationalities, by submitting to a sincere investigation of facts, and proved that, when the International Spirit of Law has attained to a high moral standard, bloody conflicts between States are almost sure to be prevented. Alas! that history could not have recorded the same of the latest differences between two of the most civilized Nations of the earth, which, without any serious attempt at a peaceable solution, hurried two friendly neighbouring populations into a war, which filled Europe with consternation and dread. But fortunately again, the chariot of the conqueror was checked by the genuine appreciation of justice and benevolence, worthy of the great Sovereign under whose sceptre a great people has succeeded to combine tribal nationality with political unity, and through the moderation of the great statesman, who, while taking all responsibility on his great mind, yet never quailed in any difficulty, nor never overstepped the limits of his great task to venture on feats of ambition which would have thrust back the civilization of Europe for more than a century into a course of retrogression,—leaving all the great and good minds, which have so zealously pleaded for the recognition of international morality, in profound despair of ever finding a clue to the problem of human destiny. And yet, it was the ever self-rectifying power of the Moral Law of Nature which, regaining its sway over the human mind, caused the good sense and moderation of leaders and people to prevail over the rapacious selfish inclinations of the animal nature of man (§ 3).

But to return to our subject, it must be kept in mind that, although the ascertaining of the facts which gave occasion to the difference is logically the first stage of process in every attempt to discuss a matter of dispute between reasonable beings, yet, unfortunately, facts cannot always be proved to such an incontestable degree of certainty as to convince the party who is in the wrong, even presuming that he really and *bonâ fide* wishes to be convinced. And how seldom does this latter case happens; how often the so-called leading newspapers of the day stoop to become, maliciously, misleading chronicles of history, refusing all rectification that could remove the national prejudices to which it is their interest to pander. Thus, each party tries to establish such a statement of the facts complained of as would tell in its own favour, in which process almost invariably a one-sided subjective conception of the facts in dispute or their effects, is, with all the characteristics of an *ex parte* statement, substituted for actual occurrences which may in themselves have been very innocent acts, caused by *force majeure* or by some peculiar position of the parties. In this case an unprejudiced Court alone can clearly establish the undeniable facts and this indispensable requisite is to be found in the system of arbitration, which is treated in the next sections.

With regard to the moral obligation, resting on both parties, to ascertain the facts with moderation, Halleck says:—

"The precepts of morality, as well as the principles of public law by which human society is governed, render it obligatory upon a State, before resorting to arms, to try every pacific mode of settling its disputes with others, whether such disputes arise from rights denied or injuries received. This moderation is the more necessary, as it not unfrequently happens that what is at first looked upon as an injury or an insult, is found, upon a more deliberate examination, to be a mistake rather than an act of malice or one designed to give offence. Moreover, the injury may result from the acts of inferior persons, which may not receive the approbation of their own Government. A little moderation and delay in such cases may bring to the offended party a just satisfaction; whereas rash and precipitate measures often lead to the shedding of much innocent blood. The moderation of the Government of the United States, in the case of the burning of the American steam-boat *Caroline*, 1837, by a British officer, led to an amicable adjustment of the difficulties arising from a violation of neutral territory, and saved both countries from the disasters of a bloody war. The moderation of the British Admiral in the affair at St. Juan Island is deserving of the highest praise." *

Means of peaceable settlement of international disputes.

§ 157. When the facts are clearly established, it yet remains the moral duty as well as sound policy in the case of every State to try to settle differences in a peaceable manner before resorting to the decision of arms.

The means for peaceable settlements are:—1°. Amicable arrangement or compromise between the two interested parties, without the direct or open interference from any other Government. 2°. Mediation or arbitration which takes place through the good offices of one or more friendly Power, to which may be added Conferences or Congresses on general political questions. We shall proceed to note in this and the next paragraph, these remedies of the laws of peace.

Amicable arrangement and compromise.

The solution of international questions through amicable arrangement or compromise may in some cases be a mere palliative postponing open rupture and war, as the main question is then often left undecided, yet the peace is preserved, though it be only for the moment, and at all events it is a marked proof of the spirit of moderation and of

* HALLECK. Intern. Law. Edit. Sir Sherston Baker. Vol. I. p. 413.

good faith which prevails in the respective counsels of the parties interested. *

The difference between an amicable arrangement and a compromise consists in this that the former indicates the settlement of the dispute by a mutual agreement to abandon the question, while a compromise implies an understanding arrived at, on some definite object of contention, by mutual concessions in the same sense as in a case in civil law. Thus a compromise partakes also of the nature of an amicable arrangement, but an amicable arrangement is not necessarily a compromise. For the amicable arrangement of disputes between Nations, a settlement by negotiation or compromise is not always involved or necessary.

" Amicable arrangement or accommodation, says Halleck, is where each party candidly examines the subject of dispute, with a sincere desire to preserve peace, by doing full justice to the other. In such cases, all doubtful points of etiquette will be yielded, and all uncertain and imaginary rights will be voluntarily renounced, in order to effect an amicable adjustment of differences. If no compromise of the right in dispute can be effected, the question will be avoided by the substitution of some other arrangement which may be mutually satisfactory. Such conduct is worthy of great and magnanimous Nations; weaker States seldom act with so much moderation. An example of amicable accommodation is found in the adjustment, by the treaty of Washington, in 1842, of the differences between the United States and Great Britain, with respect to the right claimed by the latter to visit the vessels of the former in search of slavers on the coast of Africa.

* CALVO. Le Droit Intern. Vol. I. Edition 1870. § 661, p. 785. HEFFTER. Droit. Intern. Trad. Bergson. § 107.

Compromise is where the two parties, without attempting to decide upon the justice of their conflicting pretentions, agree to recede on both sides, and either to divide the thing in dispute, or to indemnify the claimant who surrenders his share to the other. For examples of compromise we may refer to the negotiations terminating in the treaty of 1842, by which the Maine boundary question was satisfactorily adjusted, and to the negotiations terminating in the treaty of 1846, by which the Oregon difficulty was formally disposed of. Accommodation is a peculiar kind of compromise, and has therefore been deemed by some to be improperly classed as a distinct measure." *

Measures via amicabili and via facta. The latter often preferred to the former.

§ 158. Judgment not being admissible when independent States are litigants, other modes of terminating disputes between Nations must be resorted to, whether by peaceable measures, taken *viâ amicabili*, or by forcible measures, *viâ facta*. To come to a solution of the question by the first mode of procedure, the disposition and full consent of both parties to a peaceable settlement are indispensable, while forcible measures to decide the contest *viâ facta* are invariably resorted to against the declared wish of both actors, at least such as can be drawn from diplomatic notes, manifests and proclamations which are cast about at the approach of war like dry leaves before the stormwind. And yet with all this loudly proclaimed wish to maintain the blessing of peace, we have to witness throughout the history of civilization the strange fact that amicable arrangements of international disputes are but seldom preferred to war.

* U. S. Statutes at Large. Vol. VIII. p. 582, etc. HALLECK, Vol. I. p. 414.

The main cause of such an abnormal state of the Spirit of Law is that the mutual consent to an arrangement, should it have any effect at all, must be sincere, and necessarily entails moral restraint and probably some material sacrifice. Besides, to rush into war with an equal antagonist is a sensation agreeable to inflated imagination when this fruitful source of evil is fostering the passionate brutish propensities of certain parties in the State, while in the case of forcing a weaker State, against its interest, into war, it is found easier to keep timid Conscience aloof and to damp the weak voice of Sympathy, than to sacrifice some material interest on the altar of Justice and Benevolence (§ 3). *Physiological causes of the inclination to war.*

At the Congress of Paris, in 1656, the following recommendation was passed by the representatives of the Powers there treating for peace. "The plenipotentiaries do not hesitate to express in the name of their Governments, the wish that States, between which a serious disagreement should arise, would, before appealing to arms, have recourse, as far as circumstances admit, to the good offices of friendly Powers." That this safe recommendation has not been followed during the differences which led to the recent wars in Europe, might be explained by the foregoing observations.

The different modes of adjusting international disputes *viâ amicabili* have been variously enumerated by text-writers. Besides the mutual arrangement between parties in direct dealing, as noted in the preceeding section under the heads of amicable arrangement or accomodation and negotiation or compromise, there are the various processes of mediation, arbitration and conferences in which the good offices of third parties are invoked. *Mediation.*

Mediation may be solicited or offered. When offered by a third party, it includes not seldom, in disguise, a threat of intervention, the intervenor offering his good services for the purposes of an accommodation which would suit his own individual interests.

Principal duty of a mediator. When mediation is asked by parties, it takes the form of arbitration.

When real and impartial reconciliation is intended, the mediator submits his impartial propositions, calculated to enable the contending parties to arrive at an accommodation, which he simply offers, leaving the parties entirely free with regard to their acceptance or not.

"*Le devoir du médiateur*, says Vattel, *en interposant ses bons offices pour engager les parties à s'entendre, est de garder une exacte impartialité; il doit adoucir les reproches, calmer les ressentiments, rapprocher les ésprits. Son devoir est de favoriser le bon droit, de faire rendre à chacun ce qui lui appartient; mais il ne doit point insister scrupuleusement sur une justice rigoureuse. Il est conciliateur et non pas juge: sa vocation est de procurer la paix, et il doit porter celui qui a le droit de son côté à relâcher quelque chose, s'il est nécessaire, dans la vue d'un si grand bien.*" *

Arbitration. Arbitration is the solemn settlement of a dispute, when two States, by common consent, refer the questions in dispute to the decision of a third party, on the condition that they will abide by his decision. Generally the scope and conditions of the reference are settled by special understanding. Mediation and arbitration are closely connected, but with this difference, that the former resembles more the above mentioned amicable arrangement between parties and the other takes the form of compromise. In the case of media-

* VATTEL, Le Droit des Gens. Liv. II. Chapt. XVIII. § 328.

tion, parties retain their complete liberty to accept the proposed arrangement or not, while in the case of arbitration parties having, beforehand, submitted themselves to the decision of the arbiter, the award must be for them the rule of conduct, provided the arbitrators have given a judgment which is not manifestly contrary to all reasonable justice.

Mr. Halleck gives the following opinion with regard to mediation and arbitration.

Halleck's opinion with regard to Mediation and Arbitration.

"Mediation is where a common friend interposes his good offices to bring the contending parties to a mutual understanding. As this friend acts the part of a conciliatior, rather than a judge, he may, while favouring the well-founded claims of one party, seek to induce him to relax something of his pretensions, if necessary, in order to secure peace. The mediator is essentially different from the arbitrator, although he frequently assumes the latter office also; he does not decide upon any of the matters in dispute, but merely seeks to reconcile conflicting opinions and to moderate adverse pretensions. By thus calming the minds of the disputants, and disposing them to a reasonable accommodation or compromise, the mediator may often avert the evils and calamities of a resort to war. The task is a very delicate one, and the office of mediator requires great integrity and strict impartiality, for unless he possess these qualities in a pre-eminent degree, his efforts will not be likely to bring about the desired reconciliation of of the disputants. Hübner deems it incumbent, upon neutrals generally, to act the part of mediators, in order to prevent, if possible, the breaking out of war. But Galiani is of opinion that, although the post of mediator may be accepted, the office is rather to be avoided than sought, on account of the danger to the mediator of compromising his neutrality. Phillimore prefers the Christian principle of Hübner to the more safe expediency of Galiani, but adds that much must depend upon the subject of dispute, the character of the disputants, and upon the position and authority of the State which tenders the good offices."

"Arbitration is where the decision of a dispute is left to arbitrators chosen by common agreement. If the contending parties have agreed to abide by the decision of these referees, they are bound to do so, except in cases where the award is obtained by collision, or is not confined within the limits of the submission. It is usual to specify, in the agreement to arbitrate, the exact questions which are to be decided by the arbitrators, and if they exceed these precise bounds and pretend to decide upon other points than those submitted to them, their decision is in no respects binding. Thus, the award of the king of the Netherlands, on reference by treaty, in 1827, of the question of the North-Eastern boundary of the United States, not being a decision of the question submitted to him, but a proposal for a compromise, was not regarded as binding either upon the United States or Great Britain, and was rejected by both, the dispute being afterward amicably settled by the parties themselves."

Rules of Arbitration as proposed by Halleck.

"The following rules, mostly derived from the civil law, have been applied to international arbitrators, where not otherwise provided in the articles of reference. If there be an uneven number, the decision of a majority is conclusive. If there be only two, and they differ in opinion, they cannot call in a third as umpire. The arbitration is dissolved by the death of any one of the referees. A decision once formally delivered cannot be reconsidered without a new agreement, for when the opinion is delivered, the arbitration is *functus officio*. The arbitrators do not guarantee the execution of their award, and have no power to enforce it. Where the question is territorial, they cannot determine the possession as distinguished from the right of property; for, by the Law of Nations, the right of property draws after it the right of possession, and the owner is not to be prejudiced by the possession of another, nor is the possessor to be disturbed in his possession till the question of ownership is determined. But this does not preclude the arbitrators from inquiring into all the circumstances of possession as part of the evidence of title. In other words, they must determine the question of ownership from which follows the right of possession, and not upon the latter as a right distinct from the former.

"Offers to arbitrate are not always accepted, nor is the State, declining the proposal, bound to give any reasons in justification for rejecting the proposal of the other disputant, or the proffer of a third Power to act as arbitration. 'It cannot,' says Phillimore, 'be laid down as a general and unqualified proposition, that it is the duty of States to adopt this mode of trial. There may, under the circumstances, be no third State willing, or qualified in all respects, for so arduous and invidious a task. Moreover, a State may feel that the contested right is one of vital importance, and one which she is not justified in submitting to the decision of any arbiter or arbiters.' By refusing either to arbitrate, or to accept an offered arbiter, we do not justly incur the suspicion that our intentions are unreasonable or our demands exorbitant. Nevertheless, if the question is not one of vital or of very serious importance, and we refuse to resort to this or any other amicable mode of settlement, such suspicion will be most likely to arise. The refusal to accept the mediation of a third party, not acting as arbiter or judge, but simply as a conciliator, would very seldom be justified." *

Political Conferences and International Congresses.

§ 159. When mediation between contending States is arranged or with the consent of both parties entrusted to the decision of two or more States, the respective representatives of the latter come together to discuss the facts and merits of the case and the best mode to arrive at an amicable settlement between the parties concerned. When the contending States are admitted, by mutual consent, to take part in the discussions, on a preliminary basis agreed upon, these meetings between the mediators or arbitrators and the parties concerned constitute what is styled in diplomatic language a Political Conference. When a Conference involves questions affecting the interests of third parties or questions which might infringe on general political conditions, these third parties and the Great Powers which are interested in the questions under discussion or in the general political status, called, as noted above, the balance of power, are then invited to take part in the Conference. Such a general political Conference is then styled an International Congress. Questions not included in the treaty of peace after the termination of a general war, are often finally settled in a Congress.

Political discussions in Conference or in Congress, having for their aim the facilitating of a general mutual understanding between States,

* HALLECK. Vol. I. p. 415, et seq. Sir ROBERT PHILLIMORE. Comm. Intern. Law. Vol. III. Chapt. I.

the parties interested in the affairs under discussion, who have sent their representatives to the Conference or Congress, are regarded to have done this in response to a mutual invitation, although the first proposals for the meeting of representatives may have originated with one or more particularly interested State or States.

The questions to be brought under discussion at the meetings are previously agreed upon by all parties and also the place where the Conference or Congress shall meet. From these agreements no departure is legally admissible unless sanctioned by all the parties interested.

The choice of the place of meeting is generally left to the party which proposed the meeting. The place selected is always one which is most favourable to freedom of deliberation and most conveniently situated with regard to the respective seats of Government. *

Perfect equality among all the members of the Conference or Congress, with regard to the rights of discussion and as to sharing in the deliberations, is an essential characteristic of every political meeting, be it a Conference or Congress, unless some special stipulation is made before hand with the consent of all parties concerned, as to the casting vote at each meeting.

Verification of the Pleins-pouvoirs.

At the political Conference or Congress each State which is a party to the preliminary agreements with regard to the points to be discussed, sends one or more representatives, who are called delegates, duly provided with letters of credence and full powers *(pleins-pouvoirs)*, as stated above in paragraph 147. At the first meeting of the representatives a president or chairman is elected and the *pleins-pouvoirs* are mutually exchanged and re-exchanged, in order to ascertain, recipro-

* DE MARTENS. Guide Dipl. Vol. I. p. 145.

cally, the legal character of each member of the Conference or Congress. Generally the representative of the State in whose territory the Conference or Congress meet, is elected as chairman or president.

The *pleins-pouvoirs* being reciprocally pronounced in proper order, with regard to form as well as contents, the chairman opens the deliberations with a speech, in which the objects of the present meeting of the represented States are enumerated and explained. Previous to this solemn opening of the Conference, the representatives settle by mutual agreement, whether the question to be discussed should be presented or proposed for deliberation by the chairman, or whether each of the delegates shall bring forward the statement he has to make in behalf of his Government, in the regular order of procedure to be previously agreed upon.

The Protocols or Procès-Verbaux.

The diversity of affairs to be proposed, discussed, negotiated and compromised at the various meetings, and the manifold aspects under which the discussions are apt to bring the questions in deliberation, render it highly necessary that a careful record should be kept of all that is transacted at each separate meeting. These records of the meetings are called *protocols* or *procès-verbaux.* They contain, as nearly as possible, a verbatim account of the proceedings of the Conference or Congress.

At the beginning of each meeting the protocol of the preceding one is read and enacted. At the close of the Conference copies of the whole collection of protocols are sent by the delegates present at the Conference to their respective Governments.

With regard to Conferences and Congresses, Halleck makes the following statement.

"Conferences and International Congresses have frequently been resorted to where differences exist between several States, and where they are willing to discuss them in a spirit of conciliation in order to bring them to an amicable settlement. They are also often resorted to after the termination of a general war, for the purpose of discussing and settling questions growing out of the operations of war, and not included in the stipulations of the treaty of peace. Other States than those who are parties to the dispute, being interested in the determination of the questions submitted, or at least in the preservation of peace, are most usually invited to take part in these Conferences. In order to afford a prospect of success in these deliberations, the plenipotentiaries sent to these Congresses should be actuated by a sincere desire to effect a just and amicable settlement of the questions to be discussed. This, however, has not often been the case. The Congresses of Cambray, in 1724, and of Soissons, in 1728, are characterised by Vattel as 'dull farces played on the political theatre in which the principal actors were less desirous of producing an accommodation, than of appearing to desire it.' Moreover, they have generally been under the control of the great European monarchical States and republics, or the smaller sovereignties have had very little weight in their deliberations. Thus, the Congresses of Paris and Vienna, in 1814 and 1815, were mainly meetings of conquerors, for dividing among themselves the spoils of conquest, and for mutually agreeing among themselves to what extent each of the greater Powers should be permitted to rob its weaker neighbours. 'We know from history,' says Phillimore, 'that Congresses of crowned heads have not always proved themselves to be impartial or competent tribunals of International Law.' For this reason, smaller States seldom willingly submit their disputes to the decision of such tribunals. The Congress of Paris, in 1856, by the justice of its acts, somewhat redeemed the general reputation of European conventions of Nations." *

Rules proposed by the Institut de Droit International for the pacific solution of international differences.

§ 160. We cannot conclude this chapter on the Laws of Peace better than by quoting the rules proposed by the Institut de Droit International in its sessions at Geneva and the Hague, in 1874 and 1875, for the pacific solution of international differences, as stated in the following *Projet de règlement pour la procédure arbitrale internationale.*

L'Institut désirant que le recours à l'arbitrage, pour la solution des conflicts internationaux, soit de plus en plus pratiqué par les peuples civilisés, espère concourir utilement à la réalisation de ces progrès en proposant pour les tribunaux arbitraux le règlement éventuel suivant. Il le recommande à l'adoption entière ou partielle des États qui concluraient des compromis.

Article 1.—Le compromis est conclu par traité international valable.

Il peut l'être :

a. D'avance, soit pour toutes contestations, soit pour les contestations d'une certaine espèce à déterminer, qui pourraient s'élever entre les États contractants ;

b. Pour une contestation ou plusieurs contestations déjà nées entre les États contractants.

Art. 2.—Le compromis donne à chacune des parties contractantes le droit de s'adresser au tribunal arbitral qu'il désigne pour la décision de la contestation. A défaut de désignation du nombre et des noms des arbitres dans le compromis, le tribunal arbitral se règlera selon les dispositions prescrites par le compromis ou par une autre convention.

A défaut de disposition, chacune des parties contractantes choisit de son côté un arbitre, et les deux arbitres ainsi

* HALLECK. Vol. I. p. 418, et seq. Sir ROBERT PHILLIMORE. Vol. III. Chapt. I.

nommés choisissent un tiers arbitre ou désignent une personne tierce qui l'indiquera.

Si les deux arbitres nommés par les parties ne peuvent s'accorder sur le choix d'un tiers arbitre, ou si l'une des parties refuse la co-opération qu'elle doit prêter selon le compromis à la formation du tribunal arbitral, ou si la personne désignée refuse de choisir, le compromis est éteint.

Art. 3.—Si dès le principe, ou parce qu'elles n'ont pu tomber d'accord sur les choix des arbitres, les parties contractantes sont convenues que le tribunal arbitral serait formé par une personne tierce par elles designée, et si la personne désignée se charge de la formation du tribunal arbitral, la marche à suivre à cet effet se règlera en première ligne d'après les prescriptions du compromis. A défaut de prescriptions, le tiers désigné peut ou nommer lui-même les arbitres ou proposer un certain nombre de personnes parmi lesquelles chacune des parties choisira.

Art. 4.—Seront capables d'être nommés arbitres internationaux les souverains et chefs de gouvernements sans aucune restriction, et toutes les personnes qui ont la capacité d'exercer les fonctions d'arbitre d'après la loi commune de leur pays.

Art. 5.—Si les parties ont valablement compromis sur des arbitres individuellement déterminés, l'incapacité ou la récusation valable, fût-ce d'un seul de ces arbitres, infirme le compromis entier, pour autant que les parties ne peuvent se mettre d'accord sur un autre arbitre capable.

Si le compromis ne porte pas détermination individuelle de l'arbitre en question, il faut, en cas d'incapacité ou de récusation valable, suivre la marche prescrite pour le choix originaire (§§ 2, 3).

Art. 6.—La déclaration d'acceptation de l'office d'arbitre a lieu par écrit.

Art. 7.—Si un arbitre refuse l'office arbitral, ou s'il se déporte après l'avoir accepté, ou s'il meurt, ou s'il tombe en état de démence, ou s'il est valablement récusé pour cause d'incapacité aux termes de l'article 4, il y a lieu à l'application des dispositions de l'article 5.

Art. 8.—Si le siège du tribunal arbitral n'est désigné ni par le compromis ni par une convention subsequente des parties, la désignation a lieu par l'arbitre ou la majorité des arbitres.

Le tribunal arbitral n'est autorisé à changer le siège qu'au cas ou l'accomplissement de ses fonctions au lieu convenu est impossible ou manifestement périlleux.

Art. 9.—Le tribunal arbitral, s'il est composé de plusieurs membres, nomme un président, pris dans son sein, et s'adjoint un ou plusieurs secrétaires.

Le tribunal arbitral décide en quelle langue ou quelles langues devront avoir lieu ses délibérations et les débats des parties, et devront être présentés les actes et les autres moyens de preuve. Il tient procès-verbal de ses délibérations.

Art. 10.—Le tribunal arbitral délibère tous membres présents. Il lui est loisible toutefois de déléguer un ou plusieurs membres ou même de commettre des tierces personnes pour certains actes d'instruction.

Si l'arbitre est un État ou son chef, une commune ou autre corporation, une autorité, une faculté de droit, une société savante, ou le président actuel de la commune, corporation, autorité, faculté, compagnie, tous les débats peuvent avoir lieu du consentement des parties devant le commissaire nommé *ad hoc* par l'arbitre. Il en est dressé protocole.

Art. 11.—Aucun arbitre n'est autorisé sans le consentement des parties à se nommer un substitut.

Art. 12.—Si le compromis ou une convention subséquente des compromettants prescrit au tribunal arbitral le mode de procédure à suivre, ou l'observation d'une loi de procédure déterminée et positive, le tribunal arbitral doit se conformer à cette prescription. A défaut d'une prescription pareille, la procédure à suivre sera choisie librement par le tribunal arbitral, lequel est seulement tenu de se conformer aux principes qu'il a déclaré aux parties vouloir suivre.

La direction des débats appartient au président du tribunal arbitral.

Art. 13.—Chacune des parties pourra constituer un ou plusieurs représentants auprès du tribunal arbitral.

Art. 14.—Les exceptions tirées de l'incapacité des arbitres, doivent être opposées avant toute autre. Dans le silence des parties toute contestation ultérieure est exclue, sauf le cas d'incapacité postérieurement survenue.

Les arbitres doivent prononcer sur les exceptions tirées de l'incompétence du tribunal arbitral, sauf le recours dont il est question à l'art. 24, 2me. al., et conformement aux dispositions du compromis.

Aucune voie de recours ne sera ouverte contre des jugements préliminaires sur la compétence, si se n'est cumulativement avec le recours contre le jugement arbitral définitif.

Dans le cas ou le doute sur la compétence, dépend de l'interprétation d'une clause du compromis, les parties sont censées avoir donné aux arbitres la faculté de trancher la question, sauf clause contraire.

Art. 15.—Sauf dispositions contraires du compromis, le tribunal arbitral a le droit:—

1. De déterminer les formes et délais dans lesquels chaque partie devra, par ses représentants duement légitimés, présenter ses conclusions, les fonder en fait et en droit, proposer ses moyens de preuve au tribunal, les communiquer à la partie adverse, produire les documents dont la partie adverse requiert la production.

2. De tenir pour accordées les prétentions de chaque partie qui ne sont pas nettement contestées par la partie adverse, ainsi que le contenu preténdu des documents dont la partie adverse omet la production sans motifs suffisants.

3. D'ordonner de nouvelles auditions des parties, d'exiger de chaque partie l'éclaircissement de points douteux.

4. De rendre des ordonnances de procédure (sur la direction du procès), faire administrer des preuves, et requérir, s'il le faut, du tribunal compétent les actes judiciaires pour lesquels le tribunal arbitral n'est pas qualifié, notamment l'assermentation d'experts et de témoins.

5. De statuer, selon sa libre appréciation, sur l'interprétation des documents produits et généralement sur le mérite des moyens de preuves présentés par les parties.

Les formes et délais mentionnés sous les numeros 1 et 2 du présent article seront déterminés par les arbitres dans une ordonnance préliminaire.

Art. 16.—Ni les parties, ni les arbitres ne peuvent d'office mettre en cause d'autres États ou des tierces personnes quelconques, sauf autorisation spéciale exprimée dans le compromis et consentement préalable du tiers.

L'intervention spontanée d'un tiers n'est admissible qu'avec le consentement des parties qui ont conclu le compromis.

Art. 17.—Les demandes reconventionnelles ne peuvent être portées devant le tribunal arbitral qu'en tant qu'elles lui sont déférées par le compromis, ou que les deux parties et le tribunal sont d'accord pour les admettre.

Art. 18.—Le tribunal arbitral juge selon les principes du droit international, à moins que le compromis ne lui impose des règles différentes ou ne remette la décision à la libre appréciation des arbitres.

Art. 19.—Le tribunal arbitral ne peut refuser de prononcer sous le prétexte qu'il n'est pas suffisamment éclairé soit sur les faits soit sur les principes juridiques qu'il doit appliquer.

Il doit décider définitivement chacun des points en litige. Toutefois, si le compromis ne prescrit pas la décision définitive simultanée de tous les points, le tribunal peut, en decidant définitivement certain points, réserver les autres pour une procédure ultérieure.

Le tribunal arbitral peut rendre des jugements interlocutoires ou préparatoires.

Art. 20.—Le prononcé de la decision definitive doit avoir lieu dans le délai fixé par le compromis ou par une convention subsequente. A défaut d'autre détermination, on tient pour convenu un délai de deux ans à partir du jour de la conclusion du compromis. Le jour de la conclusion n'y est pas compris; on n'y comprend pas non plus le temps durant lequel un ou plusieurs arbitres auront été empêchés, par force majeure, de remplir leurs fonctions.

Dans le cas ou les arbitres, par des jugements interlocutoires, ordonnent des moyens d'instruction, le délai est augmenté d'une année.

Art. 21.—Toute décision définitive ou provisoire sera prise à la majorité de tous les arbitres nommés, même dans le cas où l'un ou quelques uns des arbitres refuseraient d'y prendre part.

Art. 22.—Si le tribunal arbitral ne trouve fondées les prétentions d'aucune des parties, il doit le déclarer, et, s'il n'est limité sous ce rapport par le compromis, établir l'état réel du droit relatif aux parties en litige.

Art. 23.—La sentence arbitrale doit être rédigée par écrit et contenir un exposé des motifs, sauf dispense stipulée par le compromis. Elle doit être signée par chacun des membres du tribunal arbitral. Si une minorité refuse de signer, la signature de la majorité suffit, avec déclaration écrite que la minorité a refusé de signer.

Art. 24.—La sentence, avec les motifs s'ils sont exposés, est notifiée à chaque partie. La notification a lieu par signification d'une expédition ou représentant de chaque partie ou à un fondé de pouvoirs de chaque partie constituée *ad hoc*.

Même si elle n'a été signifiée qu'au représentant ou au fondé de pouvoirs d'une seule partie, la sentence ne peut plus être changée par le tribunal arbitral.

Il a néanmoins le droit, tant que les délais du compromis ne sont pas expirés, de corriger de simples fautes d'écriture ou de calcul, lors même qu' aucune des parties n'en ferait la proposition, et de compléter la sentence sur les points litigieux non décidés, sur la proposition d'une partie et aprés audition de la partie adverse. Une interprétation de la sentence notifiée n'est admissible que si les deux parties la requièrent.

Art. 25.—La sentence duement prononcée décide, dans les limites de sa portée, la contestation entre les parties.

Art. 26.—Chaque partie supportera ses propers frais et la moitié des frais du tribunal arbitral, sans préjudice de la décision du tribunal arbitral touchant l'indemnité que l'une ou l'autre des parties pourra être condamnée à payer.

Art. 27.—La sentence arbitrale est nulle en cas de compromis nul, ou d'excès de pouvoir, ou de corruption prouvée d'un des arbitres ou d'erreur essentielle. *

To the above "Projet" is to be added the "clause compromissoire," voted by the Institut in its session of 12th September, 1877, at Zurich, worded as follows :—

L'Institut de droit international recommande avec instance d'insérer dans les futurs traités internationaux une clause compromissoire, stipulant le recours à la voie de l'arbitrage en cas de contestation sur l'interprétation et l'application de ces traités.

L'Institut propose en même temps, en considération de la difficulté que les parties pourront avoir à s'entendre préalablement sur la procédure à suivre, l'addition, à la clause compromissoire, de la disposition qui suit :

Si les Etats contractants ne sont pas tombés d'accord préalablements sur d'autres dispositions touchant la procédure à suivre devant le tribunal arbitral, il y a lieu d'appliquer le règlement consacré par l'Institut dans sa session de La Haye, le 28 Août, 1875. †

* Annuaire de l'Institut de Droit Intern. 1877, p. 126 et seq.

† Annuaire. 1878, p. 160.

CHAPTER XXV.

THE CONDITION BETWEEN PEACE AND WAR.

Measures of Constraint falling short of War. Retortion and Reprisal.

The Right of Redress. General principles of the right to apply measures of constraint.

§ 161. From the right of redress, which emanates from the sovereignty rights of existence and self-preservation (§ 26), devolves the right to apply measures of constraint. When an injury has been done to a State by another, whether by the commission of an unjust act or by non-fulfilment of treaty obligations, and the injured State cannot get redress by amicable means, and if the injury committed is not of a nature or of sufficient magnitude to justify an immediate declaration of war, the injured State can exercise its right of constraint, by putting material stress upon the wrong-doing State. This material stress may consist of such measures of constraint as may be likely to secure a material guarantee, or of such other pressure brought to bear on the defaulter as may be thought expedient under the particular circumstances of the case in order to obtain redress.

Though being, in fact, acts of war, these measures of constraint do not always constitute a *casus belli*, as the intention is not to make direct war against the other State, but merely to place the latter on the horns of a dilemma, viz., either to make good the wrong done by injury or neglect, or to take the chances of open warfare, so that it devolves in such a case on the State towards which the measures of constraint are directed to determine whether it will regard them as constituting any *casus belli* or not. If the State affected regards the stress or constraint put upon it as a challenge and proceeds to declare war, the state of war and its legal consequences may be regarded to have begun from the time when the measure, which is declared to be a *casus belli*, took effect. If, however, the constrained State, for exceptional reasons, does not regard the acts committed as necessarily entailing war, the aggrieved State is bound to content itself with the special measures of constraint, when these are reasonably calculated to afford sufficient material guarantee, until the whole question can be settled by amicable arrangement or arbitration.

When measures of constraint are reciprocally applied, they are usually of identical nature with or analogous to the act by which they have been provoked.*

The measures of constraint, the principles of which are expounded above, are of two classes, viz., retortion or retaliation, and reprisal. They are applied in different forms which take in practice different names.

§ 162. The right of a State to defend itself or its subjects from injuries *(lésion)*, and even to take measures to prevent such lesions, being indisputable, measures of constraint are not only legitimate, but, when justly and properly applied, they are sometimes beneficent means to avoid the graver alternative of war. "It is this, says Mr. Hall, which justifies their employment. They are supposed to be used when an injury has been done, in the commission of which a State cannot be expected to acquiesce, for which it cannot get

Legality of measures of constraint.

* W. E. HALL. Intern. Law. Edit. 1880. p. 306, et seq.

redress by purely amicable means, and which is scarcely of sufficient magnitude to be a motive of immediate war. A means of putting stress, by something short of war, upon a wrong-doing State, is required; and reprisals are not only milder than war, since they are not complete war, but are capable of being limited to such acts only as are the best for enforcing redress under the circumstances of the particular case. It of course remains true that reprisals are acts of war in fact, though not in intention, and that, as in the parallel instances of intervention and of acts prompted by the necessities of self-preservation, the State affected determines for itself whether the relation of war is set up by them or not." *

To justify measures of constraint, the lesion must be real or material, injuring sovereign or natural rights, or rights acquired by treaties; besides, there must be no other means of obtaining reparation without violence or constraint, after representations, remonstrances and even threats have remained without the desired effect. Another essential condition for the justification of measures of constraint is that they do not surpass in extent or violence the object aimed at or the injury sustained, and must cease as soon as the reparation of the injury is fully obtained. "*Le but pour lequel la violence est employée*, says Kluber, *en prescrit les bornes. La réparation obtenue, elle doit cesser ausitôt.*" In these two sentences the whole principle is contained and the act defined. †

Measures of constraint are not justifiable when taken by one independent State in the name or in behalf of a third independent State, without a previous existing public treaty of alliance, or

* W. E. HALL. Intern. Law. Edit. 1880, p. 309.

† KLUBER. Edit. Ott. § 233.

acting under conditions of openly declared intervention, after all attempts to mediate have failed. In such cases the intervening State enters into all the rights and obligations of the originally injured State and takes the responsibility of the measures also with regard to third parties.

Retortion or retaliation.

§ 163. When the subjects or citizens of a State are treated in a different way from other foreigners in the same circumstances, with regard to civil or criminal laws, property, trade or personnal status, by another State within whose territory they are temporarily residing or domiciled, the aggrieved State answers such breach of comity by equal acts with regard to the subjects of the first which are called retortion or retaliation. Simple difference of civil or criminal laws or modes of legal proceedings between States give no right to retortion. Retortion does not suppose the lesion of a real or formal right but simply a refusal to acknowledge the so-called imperfect obligations.

Difference between retortion and reprisal.

§ 164. Retortion or retaliation, from *retorquere* or *rétorquer*, to retort, is distinct from reprisal, as the former is simply the appropriate return made with reference to acts which are not compatible with the general usages of international comity or of Private International Law (§ 50), and which, though not due *stricti juris* through treaty obligations or other pacta, yet constitute a reciprocal exercise of politeness, good will, or convenience, whether being matters of mere courtesy based on the general principles of the right of respect (§ 29) or serving to facilitate the interest or internal policy of either party, while *reprisal* is an act of retaliation for specific wrongs and consists of different forms of constraint put upon the State which has acted in a manner contrary to acknowledged obligations.

Woolsey's definition.

"Retortion or retaliation, says Prof. Woolsey, is to apply the *lex talionis* to another Nation,—treating it or its subjects in similar circumstances according to the rule which it has set. Thus, if a Nation has failed in comity or politeness, if it has embarrassed intercourse by new taxes on commerce or the like, the same or an analogous course may be taken by the aggrieved Power to bring it back to a sense of propriety and duty. The sphere of retortion ought to be confined within the imperfect rights or moral claims of an opposite party. Rights ought not to be violated because another Nation has violated them. Reprisals, (from *reprendere* in Latin, *reprśaliæ* in mediæval Latin, *représailles* in French), consist properly in recovering what is our own by force, then in seizing an equivalent, or, negatively, in detaining that which belongs to our adversary. Reprisals, says Vattel, are used between Nation and Nation to do justice to themselves, when they cannot otherwise obtain it. If a Nation has taken possession of what belongs to another ; if it refuses to pay a debt, to repair an injury, to make a just satisfaction; the other may seize what belongs to it, and apply it to its own advantage, till it has obtained what is due for interest and damage, or keep it as a pledge until full satisfaction has been made. In the last case it is rather a stoppage or a seizure than reprisals; but they are frequently confounded in common language" (Lib. II., § 342). Reprisals differ from retortion in this, that the essence of the former consists in seizing the property of another Nation by way of security until it shall have listened to the just reclamations of the offended party, while retortion includes all kinds of measures which do an injury to another similar and equivalent to that which we have experienced from him." *

Halleck gives the following definition of retortion and retaliation. *Halleck's definition.*

"Retortion, called by some amicable retaliation, and *rétorsion de droit*, is where one Nation applies, in its transactions with the other, the same rule of conduct by which that other is governed under similar circumstances. Thus, if one State should make aggressive laws respecting the property, or trade, or personal rights of the citizens of another State, the latter may retort by enacting similar laws against the citizens of the former. There is nothing in this contrary to justice and sound policy, so long as it does not degenerate into cruel and barbarous treatment of private individuals. This kind of retaliation usually follows the breach of what are called imperfect obligations, and which do not justify a resort to forcible measures." †

"Retaliation, or, as it is sometimes called, vindictive retaliation, or *retorsio facti*, is where one State seeks to make another, or its citizens, suffer the same amount of evil which the latter has inflicted upon the former. Retaliation should be limited to such punishments as may be requisite for our own safety and the good of society; beyond this it cannot be justified. We have no right to mutilate the ambassador of a barbarous Power, because his sovereign has treated our ambassador in that manner, nor to put prisoners and hostages to death, and to destroy private property, merely because our enemy has done this to us; for no individual is justly chargeable with the guilt of a personal crime for the acts of the community of which he is a member. Retaliation of this kind

* WOOLSEY. Intern. Law. Edit. 1874. p. 188.

† DE MARTENS. Precis de Droit des Gens. § 254.

should be confined, as a general rule, to the individuals who have committed the violation of public law. There may be extraordinary cases which constitute an exception to this rule, but these must be judged according to the peculiar circumstances by which they are attended. Instances of resolutions to retaliate on innocent prisoners of war, says Kent, occurred in this country during the revolutionary war, as well as during that of 1812; but there was no instance in which retaliation, beyond the measure of secure confinement, took place in respect to prisoners of war. Vindictive retaliation is sometimes applied to the property of the offending State or individuals, but such acts are usually of a belligerent character." * "Reprisals are resorted to for the redress of injuries inflicted upon the State, in its collective capacity, or upon the right of individuals to whom it owes protection in return for their allegiance. They consist in the forcible taking of things belonging to the offending State or of its subjects, and holding them until a satisfactory reparation is made for the alleged injury. If the dispute is afterwards arranged, the things thus taken away by way of reprisal are restored, or, if confiscated and sold, are paid for with interest and damages; but if war should result, they are condemned and disposed of in the same manner as other captured property taken as a prize of war. As reprisals bring us to the awful confines of actual war, it is proper to inquire what kind of injuries, inflicted upon the State collectively, or upon its individual members, justify a resort to so dangerous a measure of redress. It is only in cases where justice has been plainly denied, or most unreasonably delayed, that a sovereign State can be justified in authorizing reprisal

* KENT. Com. on Am. Law. Vol. I. pp. 93-94.

upon the property of another Nation. Moreover, the delay must be of such a character as to render it tantamount to a denial of justice. Thus, if the claim be a national one, it must be properly demanded, and the demand refused. If it be the claim of an individual, the claimant must first exhaust the legal remedies in the tribunals of the State from which compensation is demanded, and after an absolute denial of justice by such tribunals, his own Government must address the demand to the sovereign authorities of the offending Nation. Although the presumption of law is clearly in favour of the decisions of the lawfully constituted tribunals of a State, yet, if it is plain that justice has been administered partially, and in a different manner to the foreigner than to the subject, the Government of the injured party may, notwithstanding such decision, demand justice, and if it be refused resort to reprisals. It was a doctrine of the Roman law, that an unjust sentence does not extinguish a just debt. Subjects must submit to the authority of the law, however great the injustice; but foreigners are under no such obligations, for their own State may, by force, compel the execution of justice on their behalf." *

Different acts of reprisal, short of war, admissible by International Law.

§ 165. Reprisals being measures of material constraint can be applied in different forms. Any acts of reprisal short of actual war are permissible, provided they do not go beyond the limits of a due proportion to the provocation received. "Remedies, says Mr. Hall, must vary in stringency with the seriousness of the injuries which call for their application. If, however, on the one hand, the acts which may be done by way of reprisals cannot be kept within any precise bounds, on the other they stray so widely from the ordinary rules

* HALLECK. Vol. I. p. 422.

of peace, that the burden of showing their necessity, and still more the necessity that they shall be of a given severity, is thrown upon the State making use of them. To make reprisals either disproportioned to the provocation, or in excess of what is needed to obtain redress, is to commit a wrong, and, to judge from the amount of feeling which has been shown with respect to some cases in which it was commonly thought that the action taken was in excess of the occasion, it may be added that the wrong is one which there is less disposition to judge leniently than there is to pardon offences of a much more really serious nature." *

The most generally admitted forms of reprisal are directed against the properties and rights of the State. It occurs but seldom that the property of private individuals is seized or sequestrated, innocent private individuals not being answerable for the wrong done by their Government or by some particularly offending countrymen. † "*En droit naturel*, says Massé, *nul est tenu du fait d'autrui: c'est une règle de bon sens. Ce qui est du par un corps par une universalite, n'est même pas du par les membres qui les composent.*" ‡

Acts of reprisal, short of war, which may be regarded as sanctioned in the present state of International Law, are the following measures:—

1°. Suspension of the operation of treaties, when the reprisal is directed against arbitrary repudiation of treaty obligations.

2°. Embargo on ships in port, belonging to the offending State, to be kept in sequestration pending the crisis.

---

* W. E. HALL. p. 311.

† PINHEIRO FERREIRA. Note on § 255 of De Martens. Précis du Droit des Gens.

‡ MASSÉ. Droit Comm. dans ses rapports avec le Droit des Gens. Edit. 1874. Vol. I. § 127.

3°. Seizure, taking possession of, or occupying the thing or territory in dispute.

4°. Pacific blockade.

5°. Seizure and confiscation of public vessels and other public property of the offending State.

6°. Bombarding of military works or public establishments of the State.

Special reprisal (lettres de représailles).

Special reprisal against private individuals as a means of redress, called *lettres de représailles*, formerly granting authority to the citizens of one State against those of another, to take the law into their own hands, are no more in use now-a-days in time of peace. Injuries inflicted by subjects or citizens of one State upon private individuals belonging to or under the protection of another State, are now no more left to be fought out by the private individuals concerned, but the claims are reciprocally taken up by the respective Governments, to be settled in conformity with the present state of International Law. General reprisal is the general state of mutual enmity equal to actual war.

General reprisal.

" Special reprisal, says Halleck, is where one State awards to particular injured persons licences, authorizing them to indemnify themselves upon the property of the subjects of the offending State wherever found, have almost entirely fallen into disuse, and the term itself is now somewhat differently applied ; the commissions issued to privateers in time of actual war being ordinarily denominated letters of marque. These are not to be confounded with letters of reprisals. General permission to all the citizens of one State to make reprisals upon the property and persons of all citizens of another State, is little short of actual war, although considered in International Law as without the pale of the rules applicable to war. The captors are not entitled to exercise the rights of war either toward the subjects of the offending State, or toward neutrals, nor are the persons or goods captured subject to the rules applicable to belligerent captures. Such matters are regulated by the law or authority authorizing the reprisals, and the acts of the parties making them are to be regulated and judged of by such law or authority, but they must, in no case, be in violation of the rules of International Law which may be applicable." *

Passive and active reprisal. Seizure. Reprisals are sometimes classified by making a distinction of negative or passive and positive or active reprisals. The former class consists of acts of refusal to comply with engagements by the denouncing or suspension of treaty obligations. Positive or active reprisals consist often of seizures of property belonging to the wrongdoing State, made with a view to obtain satisfaction, or to establish a *fait-accompli*, by taking possession of or occupying a territory in dispute, when forced by the necessity of securing one's good right against an aggressive party (comp. § 33). †

Halleck's opinion. "Reprisals are negative, says Halleck, when a State refuses to fulfil a perfect obligation which it has contracted or to permit another Nation to enjoy a right which it claims; they are positive when they consist in seizing the persons and effects belonging to the other Nation, in order to

* HALLECK. Vol. I. p. 425.

It was an ancient custom in England, when a merchant had been robbed at sea or despoiled of his property, for the King to issue a commission, under the great seal, to inquire into the robbery, and to punish the offenders, or to give damages in the case of fraud in the mercantile contract. This commission proceeded in conformity with three laws, *i. e.* the law and custom of England, the Merchant Law and the Maritime Law.—50 Eliz., 3 par. 2 Dors. 24 de audiend. et terminand, mercatoribus super mare deprædatis.

† DE MARTENS. Edit. Vergé. Vol. II. § 259. WHEATON. Elem. Int. Law. Part IV. Chapt. I. § 2. KLUBER. Droit des Gens Mod. § 234. POLSON. Law of Nations. Sec. VI. DUVERDY and PISTOYE. Traité des Prises. Tit. I. Chapt. III. Sec. III.

obtain satisfaction. The same rule applies to both of these classes, that is, neither should be resorted to except where the cause is manifestly just, and after all milder means have proved ineffectual. Negative reprisals, however, are, in general, less likely to produce an immediate rupture than those of a positive character. Nations are more ready to repel force than to employ it."

"Seizure is a general term applicable to the forcible taking of the persons or property of others, and is applied alike to reprisals and belligerent captures made in war. But in its more restricted sense, as applied to measures taken *viâ facti*, or forcible means of settling international disputes, the term is limited to taking forcible possession of the thing in dispute, or of the persons by whom the offence is committed. The seizure of the thing in controversy is generally regarded as the preliminary step toward the commencement of a war. It is, nevertheless, neither an actual nor a formal declaration of hostilities, and there is, therefore, still a possibility of a settlement of the dispute, before entering into a state of solemn and public war. In other words, it does not make the subjects of the two States public enemies, or give to either the rights of war, as against the other, or with respect to neutrals. If however, war should immediately follow such seizure, it would be classed as a belligerent act in all its consequences. Thus, the seizure of San Juan Island, in 1859, was, unquestionably, an act of hostility, but not, in its results, an act of war. But before taking such forcible possession, it is necessary for us to prove clearly our right to the thing in dispute, and also that we have already tried the milder modes of adjustment, for other people are not obliged to respect that title any further than we show its validity, nor will they justify us in resorting to a measure of so much rigour, and one, too, so likely to produce the most serious consequences to society, until we justify our conduct on the ground of its absolute necessity. The possessor may, therefore, remain in possession till proof is adduced to convince him that his possession is unjust. 'As long as that remains undone,' says Vattel, 'he has a right to maintain himself in it, and even to recover it by force, if he has been despoiled of it. Consequently, it is not allowable to take up arms in order to obtain possession of a thing to which the claimant has but an uncertain or doubtful right. He is only justifiable in compelling the possessor, by force of arms, if necessary, to come to a discussion of the question, to accede to some reasonable mode of decision or accommodation, or, finally to settle the point by articles of agreement upon an equitable footing.' And where the title to the things seized seems indisputable, to attempt to gain forcible possession against the actual occupant, without first resorting to the milder modes of adjustment, is equally as objectionable as it would be to declare war under the same circumstances. Indeed, it may be regarded as even more objectionable, for the reason that such seizures are sometimes made, by subordinate authorities, without consulting the war-making power of the State." *

"It is a well-settled principle of International Law, that reprisals, strictly speaking, affect the persons as well as the property of the subjects of the Government, against which they are granted; but, in modern times, they have been chiefly confined to goods. In executing the right of reprisal upon vessels, the persons of the com-

---

* VATTEL. Droit des Gens. Liv. II. Chap. XVIII. § 337.

manders and crews are necessarily affected, although it is usual to release them immediately on bringing into port of the vessel taken by the way of reprisal. Nevertheless, the right of reprisal extends also to all persons of the offending Nation. Vattel very justly remarks that 'as we may seize the things which belong to a Nation in order to compel it to do us justice, we may equally, for the same reason, arrest some of its citizens and retain them till we receive full satisfaction. This is what the Greeks called *androlepsia.*' The practice of ancient times, in this respect, is not often followed by modern civilized Nations, except by way of retaliation, or in the case of taking vessels on the high seas. It is proper to remark that all subjects of the injuring Government are liable to reprisals, whether they be native, naturalised, or domiciled, but travellers and passing guests are, in general, excepted from such liability.* But the seizure and punishment of the individuals offending is an act not unusual on the part of the offended State. Where such persons are found within the jurisdiction of the State, and they are duly tried and condemned by the lawfully constituted tribunals of the country, the act is nothing more than the ordinary and legitimate exercise of the authority of sovereign and independent States. But such offenders are sometimes seized upon the high seas, or elsewhere beyond the jurisdiction of the offended Nation, an exercise of force which is justifiable only in case of offences most manifest and palpable, and where the Government of the offender plainly refuses, or most unreasonably delays, to inflict punishment, to surrender the criminal, or to afford satisfaction.

* VATTEL. Droit des Gens. Liv. II. Chapt. XVIII. § 351. *Le Louis.* 2 Dod. R. 245.

Such forcible seizure beyond the jurisdiction of the State is an act, not of war, but in violation of pacific international rights, and is sometimes followed by war, although more usually by a demand for explanation and satisfaction. And such diplomatic discussion, if properly conducted, will generally lead to an arrangement both of the original offence and of the consequent forcible seizure. The act, however, is, in its character, hostile." *

Sir Robert Phillimore gives the following opinion on reprisal.

Opinion of Sir Robert Phillimore.

"An injury done to the rights *stricti juris* of a State may be vindicated by the employment of a kind of force, which nevertheless falls short of war, and the use of which is, and has always been held to be, compatible with the maintenance of general pacific relations. Such a vindication may be sought and obtained through the medium of reprisals." † It must be remembered that, as the rights of a State partly have respect to the collective capacity of the State, its Government or its Representative, partly to the individuals of which it is composed, a State may be injured in two ways,—either directly, by a violation of the right affecting its collective capacity, or indirectly ‡ by a violation of the right of the individual to whom it owes protection in return for his allegiance. For it is to be borne in mind that individuals have committed the defence of themselves to the State of which they are members, and, having done so, they are not entitled to enforce for themselves redress of their injuries, or, to use a common but expressive phrase, to take the law into their own hands. The principle

* ORTOLAN. Dip. de la Mer. Liv. II. Chapt. XVI. HALLECK. Intern. Law. Edit. Sir Sherston Baker. Vol. I. p. 413, et seq.

† BYNKERSHOEK. Quest. Jur. Publ. Liv. II. Chapt. X.

‡ KLUBER. § 231.

of law which forbids this course is thus laid down in the digest: "*Non est singulis concedendum, quod per magistratum publice possit fieri, ne occasio sit majoris tumultus faciendi.*" * This important doctrine is enforced by a judgment of Lord Stowell, in which he says, 'It is wild conceit, that wherever force is used, it may be lawfully resisted. A lawful force cannot be lawfully resisted. The only case where it can be so, is in the state of war and conflict between two countries, where one party has a perfect right to attack by force, and the other an equal right to resist by force. But, in the relative situation of two countries at peace with each other, no such conflicting rights can possibly co-exist.' † It most commonly happens that reprisals are resorted to for the purpose of redressing injuries inflicted upon the right of individuals." ‡

"As we are now drawing very near to the borders of actual war, and are discussing a redress which is to be enforced *viâ facti*, it is expedient to consider what kind of injuries inflicted upon individuals justify a recourse to reprisals. With respect to injuries upon States in their collective capacity, it may be laid down as acknowledged law, that reprisals, according to the modern understanding of International Law, cannot, and ought not to be, granted. General

---

* Dig. L. T. XVII. § 176.

† The *Maria*, 1 Robinson. Adm. Rep. pp. 360–1. The *Marianna Flora*, 11 Wheaton's (Amer.) Rep. 56.

‡ GROTIUS. L. III. Chapt. II. *Quomodo jure gentium bona subditorum pro debito imperantium obligentur: ubi de repressaliis*, §§ 4–7. WOLFF. Jus Gentium. Chapt. V. §§ 589–606. BYNKERSHOEK Q. J. P. Chapt. XXIV. See, also, the notes to Mr. Du Ponceau's (American) translation. Philadelphia, 1810. Ibid. De For. Leg. Chapt. XXII. VATTEL. Liv. II. Chapt. XVIII. §§ 342–354. VALIN. Ordonnance de la Marine. Liv. III. Chapt. X. Des Lettres de Marque ou de Représailles. DE MARTENS. Liv. VIII. Chapt. II. § 260. WHEATON. Elem. Vol. I. Part. IV. Chapt. II. KENT. Comm. I. pp. 56–8.

reprisals, that is, a general permission accorded to the subjects of one State to seize the goods and attack the lives of the subjects of another, do, in fact, constitute a state of war, and are yet considered to be without the pale of the rules of law applicable to war. De Witt was quite correct in saying that he could discover no distinction between general reprisals and open war. The two are now, by the practice of Nations, synonymous. In the late war between England and Russia, an order of the English Council issued on the 29th of March, 1854, in these terms:—"Her Majesty having determined to afford active assistance to her ally, His Highness the Sultan of the Ottoman Empire, for the protection of his dominions against the encroachments and unprovoked aggression of His Imperial Majesty the Emperor of all the Russias, Her Majesty is therefore pleased, by and with the advice of her Privy Council, to order, and it is hereby ordered, that general reprisals be granted against the ships, vessels, and goods of the Emperor of all the Russias, and of his subjects, or others inhabiting within any of his countries, territories, or dominions, so that Her Majesty's fleets and ships shall and may lawfully seize all ships, vessels, and goods," etc. *

Embargo. § 166. The most usual measures of constraint, short of direct violence, are embargo and so-called pacific blockade.

Embargo (from the Spanish and Portuguese *embargar*, to hinder or detain, the root of which is the same as that of *bar*, *barricade*) is the act

* Sir ROBERT PHILLIMORE. Comm. Int. Law. Vol. III. Ed. 1873. p. 18, et seq. Order in Council, March 29, 1854.

With regard to measures of constraint, short of war, see also HEFFTER. Intern. Law. §§ 110–112. KALTENBORN. Zur Revision der Lehre von den internationalen Rechtsmitteln. Tübinger Zeitschrift. 1861.

of detaining, by order of a State, all vessels within its ports, whether they be vessels owned by its own subjects or by foreigners, the detention amounting however simply to a prohibition against leaving port for a certain time, without imposing upon the vessels thus detained any special charge or forcing them into any special service. Embargo is called civil embargo, when it is applied indiscriminately to all vessels in port, for the purposes of national safety or generally in the interest of the public welfare of the State, on the authority of its Public Law and as a measure of internal policy. * Hostile embargo is the same act, but with this modification that the detention is enforced, as a measure of reprisal by one State against those vessels within its ports which belong to another State. † When vessels are detained for the special service of the State, in time of war, it is an application of the *droit d'angarie*, which will be treated hereafter.

With regard to embargo enforced as a measure of reprisal, the effect varies in conformity with the final issue of the dispute, in the course of which this measure of constraint is used. In the case of an amicable arrangement being arrived at, the detained vessels are released, but if war is the result, they are confiscated.

* According to the law of England, a Sovereign may prohibit any of his subjects from leaving the realm; a proclamation, therefore, forbidding this in general for three weeks, by laying an embargo upon all shipping in time of war, will be equally binding as an Act of Parliament, because founded upon a prior law. But a proclamation to lay an embargo in time of peace upon all vessels laden with wheat (though in a time of public scarcity), being contrary to law, and particularly to Statute 22. Car. II., c. 13; the advisers of such a proclamation, and all persons acting under it, deemed it necessary to be indemnified by a special Act of Parliament, viz., 7 George III., 7.—Blackst. Comm. II. See Phillimore. Com. Intern. Law. Vol. III. Chapt. III.

† HAUTEFEUILLE. Des droits et des dévoirs des nations neutres. 2nd Edit. Vol. III. pp. 427–439. Sir ROBERT PHILLIMORE. Comm. Intern. Law. Vol. III. Chapt. III. WOOLSEY. Intern. Law. Edit. 1879. § 118.

Mr. Hall's definition.

"Embargo, says Mr. Hall, is merely a sequestration. Vessels subjected to it are consequently not condemned so long as the abnormal relations exist which have caused its imposition. If peace is confirmed, they are released as a matter of course, but if war breaks out they become liable to confiscation. It is not necessary that vessels, or other property, seized otherwise than by way of embargo, should be treated in a similar manner. They may be confiscated so soon as it appears that their mere seizure will not constrain the wrong-doing State to give proper redress. In recent times, however, instances of confiscation do not seem to have occurred, and probably no property, seized by way of reprisal, would now be condemned until after the outbreak of actual war." *

Judment of Lord Stowell.

When an embargo was laid on Dutch property in the ports of Great Britain, on the rupture of the peace of Amiens, 1803, Sir William Scott (Lord Stowell) described the character of such sequestration as follows. "Upon property so detained the declaration of war is said to have a retro-active effect, and to render it liable to be considered as the property of enemies taken in time of war. The property is seized provisionally; an act hostile enough in the mere execution, but equivocal as to its effects, and liable to be varied by subsequent events, and by the conduct of the Government, the property of whose subjects is so detained. This first seizure is equivocal, and if the matter in dispute terminates in reconciliation, the seizure is converted into a mere civil embargo, so terminated. This would be the retro-active effect of that course of circumstances. On the contrary, if the transactions end in hostilities, the retro-active effect is directly the other way. It

* W. E. HALL. Page 310.

impresses a hostile character upon the original seizure. It is declared to be embargo; it is no longer an equivocal act, subject to two interpretations; there is a declaration of the *animus*, by which it was done, that it was done *hostili animo* and is to be considered a hostile measure *ab initio*. The property taken is liable to be used as the property of persons, trespassers *ab initio*, and guilty of injuries which they have refused to redeem by any amicable alteration of their measures. This is the necessary course, if no particular compact intervenes for the restitution of such property taken before a formal declaration of hostilities.*

"It may be questioned," says Mr. Hall of the above quoted decision, "whether this doctrine is not unnecessarily artificial. To imagine a hostile animus at the moment of capture is surely needless when the property has undoubtedly acquired an enemy character at the time of condemnation through the fact that war has broken out." †

This species of reprisal, says Kent (I. 61), "is laid down in the books as a lawful measure according to the usage of Nations, but it is often reprobated, and cannot well be distinguished from the practice of seizing property found in the territory upon the declaration of war." *Judge Kent's opinion.*

"Although such a measure, says Woolsey, might bring an adversary to terms, and prevent war, yet its resemblance to robbery, occurring, as it does, in the midst of peace, and its contrariety to the rules according to which the private property even of enemies is treated, ought to make it disgraceful, and drive it into disuse." ‡ *Dr. Woolsey's opinion.*

* *The Bæde's Lust.* 5 Rob, Admir. Rep. 245-246.

† W. E. HALL,—note on page 310.

‡ WOOLSEY. Intern. Law. Edit. 1879. p. 187.

Halleck's statement. Halleck's definition of embargo, as reprisal, is as follows:—"An embargo is a species of reprisal upon the property of the offending Nation, found within the territory of the injured State, by prohibiting the departure of vessels, or the removal of goods. An embargo may, or may not, be followed by the sequestration of the goods and property detained. If war follows, it is said to have a retro-active effect, and the detained goods are considered as the property of enemies taken in war. But if the difficulty which led to the embargo is amicably arranged, they are released upon the terms which the parties may stipulate in such an arrangement. In maritime embargos, persons as well as goods are usually seized and retained, to be subsequently released, or treated as prisoners of war, according as the embargo results in peace or solemn war. An embargo is more usually resorted to in contemplation of hostilities than as a mode of settling disputes between States. It is therefore classed by Phillimore as a measure of redress, 'midway between reprisals and war.'" *

Pacific Blockade. § 167. Pacific Blockade is a reprisal against the commerce of the constrained State. This measure of constraint has been applied to Turkey, during the Greek independence war, by Great Britain, France and Russia, to compel the Porte to conclude an armistice. Pacific blockade has subsequently been applied as a measure of constraint by France on the Tague in 1831, by Great Britain on New Granada in 1836, by France on Mexico in 1838, on Buenos-Ayres from 1838–1840 by France and from 1845–1848 by France and Great Britain.

* HALLECK. Vol. I. Edit. Sir Sherston Baker. p. 433. PHILLIMORE. On Intern. Law. Vol. III. §§ 24–26. VALIN. Traité des Prises. Liv. III. Tit. X.; the 'Theresa Bonica,' 4 Rob. 245; the 'Bœdes Lust,' 5 Rob. 245. VATTEL. Droit des Gens. Liv. II. Chapt. XVIII. § 342.

Third Powers have respected all the above mentioned cases of pacific blockade in time of peace, but it is by no means an undisputed principle of International Law. "Uninterrupted commercial intercourse in time of peace, says Woolsey, is now regarded almost as an absolute right, and the injuries inflicted in such a way on friendly States would cause third Powers to protest with energy or to retaliate." *

§ 168. It was probably to respect the above mentioned right of third Powers to uninterrupted commercial intercourse, that France, when applying measures of constraint on China in her recent disputes with regard to Tonquin, limited herself to the bombardment of forts and arsenals and the engagement of Chinese war vessels. Bombarding military works or public establishments of a State and attacking vessels of war, seem to become now the only acts of reprisal short of war which stand the best chance of being looked on by third Powers without protest. *Bombardment as reprisal short of war.*

The bombardment of open towns or villages, in any case, even in war, is condemned in warfare between civilized Nations, while in all cases of bombardment previous notice is invariably given and a sufficient time allowed to enable all the non-combatant population to withdraw.

* WOOLSEY. § 118. KLUBER. Edit. Ott. § 234. HAUTEFEUILLE. Vol. II. p. 272.

PART V.

WAR AND ITS APPURTENANCES.

CHAPTER XXVI.

GENERAL OBSERVATIONS WITH REGARD TO WAR BETWEEN NATIONS.
PRINCIPLES OF THE LAWS OF WAR.

§ 169. War between civilized Nations is that abnormal social condition which is produced by the temporary degeneration of the respective International Spirit of Law (§§ 14 & 155), the latter having ceased to be susceptible of conceiving the practicability of any means of settling differences otherwise than by force. *The abnormal social condition of war.*

Degeneration or retrogression of the moral-mental organism of man is a condition he plainly feels to be contrary to his nature and he strives therefore hard to raise himself above it, into his normal state of existence, in harmony with the Moral Law of Nature, which is perpetually urging the moral-mental organism to complete this harmony. Hence the strange phenomenon that, in the midst of the uncontrollable passions of their brutish propensities, civilized human beings, *i. e.*, those which have reached the stage in creation called the moral-mental organism (§ 1), are imbued with a longing, an innate desire to bridle these passions. This is the manifestation of the influence which the Moral Law of Nature exercises on the moral-mental organism of man and this influence is the origin of the usages which are called Rules or Laws of War (comp. § 155). *Origin of the Laws of war.*

Thus war, though being a state of litigation between Nations in which the force of arms must act as judge and decide, is yet subject to rules which prevent it from degenerating into indiscriminate massacres of human beings on either side, to end, as in the barbarian ages, with the extermination of one of the contending parties.

It is due to the influence of the Moral Law of Nature on the human organism, which causes the development of civilization, that Justice and Benevolence, the two elements of that Law of Nature, though far from being as yet predominant in the human mind, are becoming more and more conspicuous in the present stage of creation on earth (§ 1). Hence the possibility of laws between Nations, in warfare as well as in peaceable mutual intercourse.

Origin of the obligations of neutrals and of the belligerent right of search and adjudication.

Whilst in this condition of carrying on litigation by force of arms, the parties acquire, through the Laws of War, certain accidental rights (§ 26) called belligerent rights, which impose also certain obligations on third parties, called obligations of neutrality. These obligations of neutrality are based on the principle of strict impartiality towards parties in litigation and impose on neutrals the obligation,—when called upon in certain doubtful cases to prove their impartiality,—of granting belligerents, in special cases, the right of investigation and adjudication in matters, which, in a normal state of affairs, would be entirely outside their jurisdiction. Among the rights granted to belligerents, is that to visit and search neutral vessels or conveyances, which are suspected to be in unfair relation with an enemy, provided these proceedings take place in conformity with the generally acknowledged rules, which we termed above the Laws of War.

The investigation of the condition, rights and obligations of belligerents towards each other, as well as towards neutrals, form the subject-matter of the present fifth Part of this work.

CHAPTER XXVII.

THE CONDITION OF WAR AND ITS EFFECT ON PRIVATE INDIVIDUALS.

§ 170. In paragraph 155 we have noted the relation in which war stands with regard to civilized societies, or rather to the natural laws governing these societies or States, and in paragraph 169 we stated our views with regard to the origin of those restraints placed by civilization on the ravages of war, which are called the Laws of War. We must now proceed to note the status which the condition of war is apt to create for the contending as well as for third parties. *War affects in a direct manner States only, not individuals.*

War is a relation between States alone, and States being the only subjects of International Law, that Law takes cognizance of the individual solely through his State and as belonging to it, so that, except as a member of his State, the private individual has, in the eye of International Law, neither personal nor propriety rights. From this principle,—which is acknowledged by almost all writers on the Laws of War,—it naturally follows that where neither personal nor property rights are acknowledged, there can neither exist any personal obligations nor any responsibility.

War affects, in a direct manner, States only, not individuals, for States are the sole international units. "The community and its members," says Mr. Hall, "except in their State form, being internationally unrecognized, any rights which belong to them must be clothed in the garb of State rights, before they can be put forward internationally." *

If this is the case with rights, it is a natural consequence that such must be also the case with obligations. As individual members of a State have no recognized international rights, the private individual cannot be involved in the international obligations of his State.

The state of war entails no *jus in personam* against every private individual in the State, for whose liabilities any human creature belonging to the Nation indiscriminately,—widows and minors and their properties not excepted,—may be sued *in solidum* and compelled *ad dandum aut faciendum.*

The principle of the *jus in personam* is founded on the free will of men and results especially from the power which every individual has over his own acts, and nobody can ever possess such power over the acts of any body else so as to bind the latter to any obligations without his free consent,—for no one can acquire through another a *jus in personam* without distinct transfer. Thus the private individual can, *per se*, never be identified with the international acts for which his State as body politic and its agents of all descriptions are solely responsible, in conformity with the principle of International Law, consequently in war, there exists a relation of a State to a State and not of individuals *versus* individuals. The savage maxim that when war is declared between the two Nations, every individual member of the one is on the warpath against every person belonging to the other, is happily banished from the usages of warfare between civilized States and what is still

* W. E. HALL. Intern. Law. Edit. 1880, p. 39.

left of the individualism of those tribal wars of mutual massacre and plundering, is gradually giving way before the progress of civilization.

The inevitable imperfection of our moral-mental organism entails the same condition of imperfection in social life, for States are collections of human beings and, as such, partake of their imperfections, but the National Spirit of Law, which is the outcome of the influence of the Moral Law of Nature on the individual man, is distinct from the International Spirit of Law (§§ 11 & 14), which latter is the effect of said Law of Nature on aggregates of individuals in their combined condition called States or Bodies-Politic. It would be therefore contrary to the Moral Law of Nature to refer actions and transactions of States, which are distinct unities, governed by the International Spirit of Law, to the responsibility of private individual members of these unities, which latter follow, in their mutual relations, the clearer and better defined rules of the National Spirit of Law. Their respective obligations can therefore not be identical. In the former condition the individual has no direct or active share as such, while in the latter he exercises a direct and active influence, being then in a position to obey the injunctions of the Moral Law of Nature, through the direct control of his individual moral senses, Conscience and Sympathy (§§ 2–7). It is, on the other hand, impossible for the private individual to exercise any control over the actions of a body in the management of which he has no share. Hence the distinction of the two different Spirits of Law as described in paragraphs 11 and 14, and the palpable injustice inflicted in making private individuals, who have no part whatever in the direction of the affairs of a State and who do not possess any leading or executive functions, suffer for the result of actions beyond the control of their individual moral sense (comp. § 165).

The place of war in International Law. § 171. War, as described in § 155, is an abnormal variation of the International Spirit of Law, or, in other words, of the Natural Law which governs international relations, and produces phenomena which are classed as monstrosities of the Moral Law of Nature, as being deformities of the International Spirit of Law. The place of war in International Law is defined by its relation to the normal state of society. This normal state is under the control of the rules of International Law, but this law has only an indirect influence on the abnormal condition caused by war, by giving prominence to the immorality of this condition, when compared with the rules, emanating from the Moral Law of Nature, as manifested to the human moral senses, conscience and sympathy. This disagreement between the normal and abnormal state of intercourse between Nations or States, made conspicuous and defined by International Law, serves not alone to strengthen man's moral conception when comparing the two states, but is, at the same time, a moral check upon war itself. Hence the important place which war occupies in all treatises on the Law of Nations.

With regard to the state of legality of war, Mr. Hall makes the following statement.

Mr. Hall's statement. "When differences between States reach a point at which both parties resort to force, or one of them does acts of violence which the other chooses to look upon as a breach of the peace, the relation of war is set up, in which the combatants may use regulated violence against each other until one of the two has been brought to accept such terms as his enemy is willing to grant. As International Law is destitute of any judicial or administrative machinery, it leaves States, which think themselves aggrieved, and which have exhausted all peaceable methods of obtaining satisfaction, to exact redress for themselves by force. It thus recognizes war as a permitted mode of giving effect to its decisions. Theoretically therefore, as it professes to cover the whole field of the relations of States which can be brought within the scope of law, it ought to determine the causes for which war can be justly undertaken; in other words, it ought to mark out, as plainly as Municipal Law, what constitutes a wrong for which a remedy may be sought at law. It might also not unreasonably go on to discourage the commission of wrongs by investing a State seeking redress with special rights and by subjecting a wrong-doer to special disabilities. The first of these ends it attains to a certain degree, though very imperfectly. It is able to declare that under certain circumstances a clear and sufficiently serious breach of the law, or of obligations contracted under it, takes place. But in most of the disputes which arise between States the grounds of quarrel, though they might probably be always brought into connection with the wide fundamental principles of law, are too complex to be judged with any certainty by reference to them; sometimes again they have their origin in divergent notions, honestly entertained, as to what they consist in, and consequently as to the injunctions of secondary principles by which action is immediately governed; and sometimes they are caused by collisions of naked interest or sentiment, in which there is no question of right, but which are so violent as to render settlement impossible until a struggle has taken place. It is not therefore possible to frame general rules which shall be of any practical value, and the attempts in this direction, which jurists are in the habit of making, result in mere abstract statements of principles, or perhaps of truisms, which it is unnecessary to reproduce." *

"The second end International Law does not even endeavour to attain. However able law might be to declare one of two combatants to have committed a wrong, it would be idle for it to affect to impart the character of a penalty to war, when it is powerless to enforce its decisions. The obedience which is paid to International Law must be a willing obedience, and when a State has taken up arms unjustly, it is useless to expect it to acquiesce in the imposition of penalties for its act. International Law has consequently no alternative but to accept war, independently of the justice of its origin, as a relation which the parties to it may set up if they choose, and to busy itself only in regulating the effects of the relation. Hence both parties to every war are regarded as being in an identical legal position, and consequently as being possessed of equal rights." †

* AYALA. De Jure et Officiis Belli. Lib. I. Chapt. II. § 34. GROTIUS. De Jure Belli et Pacis. Lib. I. Chapt. III. § 4, and Lib. III. Chapt. III. § 1, and Chapt. IV. VATTEL. Liv. III. Chapt. XII. §§ 190–2. DE MARTENS. Précis § 265. HALLECK I. 472.

† W. E. HALL. p. 51.

CHAPTER XXVIII.

DIFFERENT KINDS OF WAR. LAWFUL AND UNLAWFUL WARS.

§ 172. Writers on International Law often exert themselves to give a definition of war and the different sorts or classes of war, but all agree in this that the condition in which the state of war places the mutual relations of parties is an abnormal condition, *i. e.*, as we have noted above (§§ 155, 156, 169), a condition abnormal in the view of the Moral Law of Nature. "Peace, says Dr. Woolsey, is the normal state of mankind, just as society and orderly government are natural; and war, like barbarism, must be regarded as a departure from the natural order of things." *

The main or natural object of war.

The main or natural object of war, as the etymology of the word indicates, is, in the original acceptance of the term, nothing else than a lawful defence by means of force against injustice. The German word *wehr* derived from the ancient Teutonic language, signifies defence; such is the case also with the Dutch term *weer* and the Anglo-Saxon *war*. The means of defence, or the principal arms, have the terms *gewehr* (German) and *geweer* (Dutch) applied to them, being derived from the primitive term *wehr* or *weer*. The latinised derivations gave *werra*, *gwerra* and *guerra*, which latter is yet the common term in Southern Europe. †

* WOOLSEY. p. 182.

† ORTOLAN. Vol. II. p. 2. GROTIUS. Liv. II. Chapt. I. § 3.

Thus war may be defined, in conformity with Dr. Woolsey's views, to be an interruption of a state of peace for the purpose of attempting to procure good or prevent evil by force; and a just war is an attempt to obtain justice or prevent injustice by force, or in other words, to bring back an injuring party to a right state of mind and conduct by the infliction of deserved evil. A justifiable war, again, is only one that is waged as a last resort, when peaceful means have failed to procure redress, or when self-defence calls for it. We have no right to redress our wrongs in a way of violence, involving harm to others, when peaceful methods of obtaining justice would be successful. * For a war to be called just, it is necessary that its origin be traced to the wilful infringement of a legally acknowledged right, in other words to the violation of a principle of the Moral Law, and such whatever the parties concerned may claim in the subjective appreciation of their cause. †

Vattel divides wars between States into two sorts, lawful and unlawful. Unlawful wars are those undertaken without apparent cause and merely for havoc and pillage, such as the warfare carried on by cruisers of filibusters without commission and in time of peace, and the depredations of pirates, etc. ‡

Justifiable and unjust wars.

Wars are lawfully waged against foreign States belonging to the same political system, or Nations

---

* WOOLSEY. Edit. 1879, pp. 182 & 183.

† The conditions under which war is just are explained in the following works. GROTIUS. Lib. II. Chapts. I. and XXII–VI. PUFFENDORF. Bk. VIII. Chapt. VI. § 3. WOLFF. Jus Gent. §§ 617, 646. VATTEL. Liv. III. Chapt. III. HALLECK. Chapt. XV, and FIORE. II. 238. The conditions of a just war are summarily dealt with in the following works. FRANCISCUS DE VICTORIA. Eclect. Theol. VI. AYALA. Lib. I. Chapt. II. § 12. ALBERICUS GENTILIS. De Jure Belli. Lib. I. Chapt. III. DE MARTENS. Précis. § 265. KLUBER. § 237. HEFFTER. § 113. BLUNTSHLI. §§ 515–518.

‡ VATTEL. Droit des Gens. Lib. III. Chapt. IV. § 67.

out of the pale of Christian civilization, against savages, against pirates, or by the parts of a State against each other. Wars are also distinguished as defensive and offensive wars. An offensive war might, under certain circumstances, turn out to be merely a defensive one, for a wronged Nation, or one fearing sudden wrong, may be the first to attack, and that is perhaps its best defence. Offensive wars, however, have usually some pretext of justice to urge in their favour.

In summoning up the causes of justifiable wars, Dr. Woolsey makes the following statements.

Dr. Woolsey's statements.

"A war may be waged to defend any right which a State is bound to protect, or to redress wrong, or to prevent apprehended injury. And (1.) a State may go to war to defend its sovereignty and independence, that is its political life, and its territory. This reason for war is analogous to the individual's right of self-preservation, and of defending his house when attacked."

"(2.) The State, being bound to protect the individual inhabitant in all its rights, is his only defender against foreign violence, and may redress his wrongs even by war. But here it is reasonable to consider the extent of the injury, and the greatness of the evil which the remedy may involve. A State may forbear to redress its own public wrongs, much more the smaller ones of individuals."

"(3.) A State may engage in war to obtain satisfaction for violations of its honour, as for insults to its flag or its ambassadors, or its good name. We have seen that a State has a right of reputation, that this right is extremely important, and that infractions of it cannot fail to arouse a deep sense of wrong in a high-minded people. Redress, therefore, is here as just and natural as suits for libel or slander between individuals. It is plain, however, that every small want of comity or petty insult does not warrant hostile measures, though it may call for remonstrance."

"(4.) Violations of those rights which Nations concede to one another by treaty may call for the redress of war. A contract is broken,—a contract to pay money for instance,—and there is no court before which the party doing the injury can be summoned."

"(5.) The prevention of intended injury is a ground of war. This indeed is a case of self-defence, only the injury must be not remote nor constructive, but fairly inferable from the preparations and intentions of the other party. The injury, again, which is to be prevented may not be aimed directly against a particular State, but may affect the equilibrium of a system of States. Thus the ambition of a leading State, it is now held, may, by disturbing the balance of power in Europe, provoke the interference of others upon the same continent."

"(6.) In some rare cases a great and flagrant wrong committed by another Nation, against religion for instance or liberty, may justify hostile interference on the part of those who are not immediately affected. And this not only because the wrong, if allowed, may threaten all States, but also because the better feelings of Nations impel them to help the injured." *

With regard to the legality and the different kinds of war, we quote the following from Halleck's work.

Halleck's statement.

"A public war is one carried on under the direction, or at least with the sanction, of the supreme authority of the State. 'If it is declared in form,' says Wheaton, 'or is duly commenced,

* WOOLSEY. Edit. 1879, p. 184, et seq.

it entitles both the belligerent parties to all the rights of war against each other.' The voluntary or positive Law of Nations makes no distinction in this respect between a just and an unjust war. A war in form, or duly commenced, is to be considered, as to its effects, as just on both sides. Whatever is permitted by the laws of war to one of the belligerent parties, is equally permitted to the other." *

"A private war is one carried on by individuals, or united bodies of individuals, without the authority or sanction of the State of which they are subjects. Such contests may take place between individuals of the same State or of different States. The first are not the objects of International Law, but of the local laws and jurisdiction of the particular State. The second may or may not belong to international jurisprudence, according to the circumstances of each particular case. As has already been said, every State is, in general, responsible for the acts of its subjects while within its control and jurisdiction ; so, also, is it bound to protect its subjects in all their just rights, and to procure indemnity for any wrongs that may be inflicted on them. But the acts of private individuals, whether citizens or foreigners are, as a general rule, to be judged of and punished by the tribunals, and according to the laws of the place where they are committed. Grotius has devoted considerable space to prove that some kinds of private war are not repugnant to the Law of Nature, and therefore may be lawfully waged. But his reasoning is not applicable to the present system of international jurisprudence." †

* WHEATON. Elem. Intern. Law. Part IV. Chapt. I. § 6.

† GROTIUS. De Jur. Bell. ac Pac. Lib. I. Cap. III. § I. BELLO. De recho International. Part. II. Cap. I. § 1. DE FELICE. Droit de la Nature, etc. Tome II. Lec. XXII. BURLAMAQUI. Droit de la Nat. et des Gens. Tome V. Part. IV. Chapt. III.

"A contest by force between different members of the same society or State has sometimes been called a mixed war. Grotius regards such a war as public on the side of the established authorities, and private on the part of those who resists such authorities. Such a contest on the part of invividuals against the established Government may be a mere insurrection or rebellion, and the acts of such individual insurgents, or rebels, in resisting or opposing the authority of the Government, may, as already stated, be punished according to the municipal laws which they have violated ; but where the contest assumes the character of a public war, as refined and recognized by the Law of Nations, it is the general usage for other States to concede to both parties the rights of war, so far as regards the law of blockade, of contraband, etc. It must be remembered, however, that every insurrection or rebellion is by no means a public war, and a State which recognizes it as such, does so under the responsibilities which are imposed by the laws of international comity. It should, also, be remarked that, in such cases, belligerent rights may be superadded to those of sovereignty, that is, the contending parties may exercise belligerent rights with regard to each other and to neutral Powers, while at the same time, the established Government of the State may exercise its right of sovereignty in punishing, by its municipal laws, individuals of the insurgent or revolting party, as rebels and traitors." *

"Hostile collisions of States have sometimes been divided into perfect and imperfect wars. A perfect war is where the whole State is placed in the legal attitude of a belligerent toward another State, so that every member of the one Nation is authorized

* GROTIUS. supra. VATTEL. Droit des Gens. Liv. II. Chapt. IV. § 56. Rose v. Himeley, 4 Cranch R.. 272.

to commit hostilities against every member of the other, in every place, and under every circumstance, permitted by the general laws of war, and subject only to the limitations and exceptions prescribed by such laws. An imperfect war is limited as to places, persons, and things. Such was the character of the hostilities authorized by the United States against France in 1798." *

"Grotius divides public wars into solemn wars and wars non-solemn. The former include all those which are waged under the authority of the State, and are duly commenced or declared in form. Both the authority and the formality are requisite to constitute a solemn war. 'But a public war, less solemn,' says Grotius, 'may be without those formalities (of a solemn war), and be made against private men, and have for its authority any magistrate. And, indeed, if we consider the thing without respect to the civil law, every magistrate seems to have the power of making war, as in the defence of the people entrusted to him, so, also, to exercise that jurisdiction, if violence be offered. But, since by war the whole city or State is endangered, therefore it is provided, by the laws of almost all Nations, that war be not made but by the authority of him who has the sovereign power in the State. There is such a law in Plato's last book, *de legibus*. And by the Roman laws he was reckoned guilty of high treason, who without commission from the prince, presumed to make war, muster soldiers, or raise an army; and the Cornelian law, enacted by L. Cornelius Sylla,' adds: 'without commission from the people.' In the code of Justinian there is a constitution extant, made by Valentinian and Valens, thus.

* POLSON. Law of Nations. Sec. 6. Miller v. Ship 'Resolution,' 2 Dall. R., 21. Bas v. Tingy, 4 Dall. R., 37.

'Let no man dare to raise an army without our knowledge and advice.' To this we may refer the remark of St. Austin, 'natural order, accommodated to the peace of mankind, requires this, that the authority and counsel of raising war should be in the power of princes. . . . But if the danger be so pressing, that time will not allow to consult the supreme magistrate, here necessity grants an exception.' L. Pinarius, governor of Enna, a Sicilian garrison, presuming on this right, upon certain information that the townsmen designed to revolt to the Carthaginians, preserved the place by putting them to death. Franciscus de Victoria has pretended to transfer the right of making war to the citizens even beyond such a necessity, to revenge those injuries which the king neglects to adjust, but his opinion is justly rejected by others." *

"International jurisprudence must distinguish between unlawful and unjust wars. When war is duly declared or begun and carried on by the proper authority of the State, it is, in the eye of International Law, a lawful war, so far as the belligerent rights of the parties are concerned."

"From the independence of Nations, says Woolsey, it results that each has a right to hold and make good its own view of right in its own affairs. When a quarrel arises between two States, others are not to interfere because their views of the right in the case differ from those of a party concerned; or at least they are not to do this unless the injustice of the war is flagrant and its principle dangerous to the general welfare of Nations. If a Nation, however, should undertake a war with no pretext of right, other States

---

* BURLAMAQUI. Droit de la Nat. et des Gens. Tome V. Part IV. Chapt. III. GROTIUS. De Jur. Bel. ac Pac. Lib. I. Cap. III. § 4. HALLECK. Ed. Sir Sherston Baker. Vol. I. p. 467, et seq.

may not only remonstrate, but use force to put down such wickedness." *

Vattel compares the State that carries on an unjust war with the individual who refuses to pay his honest debts, on the ground of prescription. This rule of civil law is made for the general benefit of the community, although it may at times enable the individual to offend against his duty. So of the Law of Nations. In order to avoid, as far as possible the evils of human society, it is agreed to regard every lawfully declared war as just on both sides. But, says Vattel, "we are never to forget that this voluntary Law of Nations, which is admitted from necessity, and to avoid greater evils, does not give to him whose arms are unjust a genuine right, capable of justifying his conduct, and acquitting his conscience, but only the external effect of the law and impunity among men." †

---

* WOOLSEY. p. 183.

† VATTEL. Droit des Gens. Liv. III. Chapt. XII. §§ 188–192.

On August 9, 1864, Prince Bismark addressed a note to the Prussian Minister in London, in which, alluding to the preliminaries of peace which had been signed at Vienna, he said he hoped the British Government would recognize the moderation and placability displayed by Prussia and Austria towards Denmark. To this Earl Russell replied that, "challenged by M. de Bismarck's invitation to admit the moderation and forbearance of the great German Government, Her Majesty's Government feel bound not to disguise their own sentiments upon these matters. Her Majesty's Government have indeed from time to time, as events took place, repeatedly declared their opinion that the aggression of Austria and Prussia upon Denmark was unjust, and that the war as waged by Germany against Denmark had not for its groundwork either that justice or that necessity which are the only bases on which war ought to be undertaken. Considering the war, therefore, to have been wholly unnecessary on the part of Germany, they deeply lament that the advantages acquired by successful hostility should have been used by Austria and Prussia, to dismember the Danish Monarchy, which it was the object of the Treaty of 1852 to preserve entire. Her Majesty's Government are also bound to remark, when the satisfaction of national feelings is referred to, that it appears certain that a considerable number—perhaps two or three hundred thousand—of the Danish population are transferred to a German State, and it is to be feared that the complaints hitherto made respecting the attempts to force the language of Denmark upon the German subjects of a Danish sovereign, will be succeeded by complaints of the attempts

CHAPTER XXIX.

THE DECLARATION OF WAR.

The formality of declaring war before the commencement of hostilities.

§ 173. From the natural duty of a State to maintain the integrity of its territory, its institutions and all its rights, and to protect the interests of its subjects in their lawful trade, emanates the right to demand redress for the infringement of any of these rights by other States. This right is so natural, so generally acknowledged by all civilised States, and of so frequent occurrence in the history of Nations, that the exercise of the same need not and very seldom does give rise to unfriendly feelings between the interested parties, provided the demand for redress has been preceded by a demand for explanation, couched in the proper language of respect and decorum.

But after this amicable demand for redress has failed, the injured State has, as noted in paragraph 161, the right to apply measures of constraint, which give rise to the condition intermediate between peace and war called the state of reprisals. This intermediate condition of international relations has been treated in chapter xxv. The proceeding by which the mutual condition of the contending States, if not settled amicably, enters into a new phase is the notification of war.

to force the language of Germany upon the Danish subjects of a German sovereign . . . . If it is said that force has decided the question, and that superiority of the arms of Austria and Prussia over those of Denmark was incontestable, the assertion must be admitted. But in that case, it is out of place to claim credit for equity and moderation."—See Ann. Reg. C. VI. 231. HALLECK. Edit. Sir Sherston Baker, note on page 472.

The moral and material effect which war has, not only on the contending parties but on third parties in the mutual intercourse of Nations, proves the necessity of a public announcement of the state of war by the contending parties, through their respective Governments. The right of making war, says Halleck, as well as the right of authorizing retaliations, reprisals and other forcible means of settling international disputes, belongs, in every civilized Nation, to the supreme power of the State, whatever that supreme power may be, or however it may be constituted. As States are known to each other only through their constituted authorities, so all other relations, whether peaceful or hostile, must be settled by their recognized Governments. *

The mere formality of the so-called declaration of war is not requisite to make a war justifiable in the eye of International Law. A formal or public declaration is however necessary with regard to neutrals, in order to have the right to claim, from the time of such public announcement of the state of war, the usual rights of belligerents accorded by all friendly States. The former usage of formally declaring the state of war to the opposite party, as a sort of chivalrous challenge served on him through the *hérauts d'armes*, or other outward solemn performances, has gradually come to be regarded as superfluous, unless a certain mode of entering upon hostilities has been previously laid down in treaties.

The ultimatum. Recall of the ambassador or negotiator.

The old usage of formally declaring the state of war is now replaced by the more practical notification to the enemy of the day on which some special act of hostility shall take place, unless, within a certain fixed time, the claims of the active party have been satisfactorily settled.

* HALLECK. Edit. Sherston Baker. Vol. I. p. 474.

This notification of a pending hostile State is called an ultimatum and may be followed by acts of constraint as described in chapter xxv, or by the general state of war and recall of the ambassador or negotiator, in conformity with the conditions *sine qua non* laid down in the ultimatum.

The proclamation of war.

The actual state of war with regard to third Powers is acknowledged to commence with the proclamation of war *(publicatio belli)*, which consists of a general notification or manifest addressed by each party to its own subjects and to third Powers, in which the causes of the war are, on each side, explained in conformity with the respective appreciation of facts, and the reasons for going to war are defended. These manifests give sometimes occasion to counter-manifests of one or both parties, and not seldom a debate in justification of the war on both sides is going on simultaneously with acts of hostility.

Dr. Woolsey's opinion.

"War between independent sovereignties, says Dr. Woolsey, is, and ought to be, an avowed open way of obtaining justice. For every State has a right to know what its relations are towards those with whom it has been on terms of amity, —whether the amity continues or is at an end. It is necessary therefore, that some act show in a way not to be mistaken that a new state of things, a state of war, has begun." *

Mr. Hall's statement with regard to the declaration of war.

"It is not necessary, says Mr. Hall, to adopt the artificial doctrine that notice must be given to an enemy before entering upon war. The doctrine was never so consistently acted upon as to render obedience to it at any time obligatory. Since the middle of last century it has had no sensible influence upon practice. In its bare form it meets now with little support, compared with that which it formerly received. In the

* WOOLSEY, p. 194.

form of an assertion that a manifesto must be published, it is so enfeebled as to be meaningless. To regard a manifesto as the equivalent of a declaration, is to be satisfied with a fiction, unless it be understood that hostilities are not to commence until after there is a reasonable certainty that authenticated information of its contents has reached the enemy Government. The use of a declaration does not exclude surprise, but it at least provides that notice shall be served an infinitesimal space of time before a blow is struck. A manifesto, apart from the reservation mentioned, is quite consistent with a blow before notice. The truth is that no forms give security against disloyal conduct, and that when no disloyalty occurs, States will always sufficiently know when they stand on the brink of war. Partly for the convenience of the subjects of the State, and partly as a matter of duty towards neutrals, a manifesto or an equivalent notice ought always to be issued, when possible, before the commencement of hostilities; but to imagine a duty of giving notice to an enemy, is both to think incorrectly and to keep open a door for recrimination in cases, which may sometimes arise, when action, for example on conditional orders to a general or admiral, takes place under such circumstances that a manifesto cannot be previously published. If the above views are correct, the moment at which war begins is fixed, as between belligerents, by direct notice given by one to the other, when such notice is given before any acts of hostility are done, and when notice is not given, by the commission of the first act of hostility on the part of the belligerent who takes the initiative." *

---

* HALL. Edit. 1880. p. 321.

"As between belligerents and neutrals however, says Mr. Hall further, the case stands differently. Neutrals are affected by duties and are exposed to liabilities. It is due to them as friends that a belligerent shall not, if possible, allow them to find out incidentally and perhaps with uncertainty that war has commenced, but that they shall be individually informed of its existence. Hence it is that it has long been a common practice to address a manifesto to neutral States, the date of which serves to fix the moment at which war begins; and it is evident that, when practicable, the issue of such a manifesto is not only convenient, but is as obligatory as an act, which after all is one of courtesy, can well be. Where war breaks out at a moment which is not determined by the respective Government engaged, or by that which has just done acts of war, as for example when it results from conditional orders given to an armed force, or from an act of self-preservation on pacific intervention being regarded as hostile, a manifesto cannot of course be issued. In such cases it is the clear duty of belligerents to give every indulgence to neutrals; and where war breaks out through the performance of an act which one of the two parties elects to consider hostile, the date of its commencement, though carried back as between the belligerents to the occurrence of the hostile act, must be taken as against neutrals to be that of the manifest through which third Powers become acquainted with the fact of war." *

"But if a declaration of war is no longer necessary, says Woolsey, a State which enters into war is still bound, (1.) to indicate, in some way, to the party with whom it has a difficulty, its

* HALL, p. 496.

altered feelings and relations. This is done by sending away its ambassador, by a state of non-intercourse, and the like. (2.) It is necessary and usual that its own people should have information of the new state of things; otherwise their persons and property may be exposed to peril. (3.) Neutrals have a right to know that a state of war exists, and that early enough to adjust their commercial transactions to the altered state of things; otherwise a great wrong may be done them. Such notice is given in manifestos. * These documents, says Vattel, never fail to contain the justificative reasons, good or bad, for proceeding to the extremity of taking up arms. The least scrupulous sovereign would be thought just, equitable, and a lover of peace; he is sensible that a contrary reputation might be detrimental to him. The manifesto implying a declaration of war, or the declaration itself, which is published all over the State, contains also the general orders to his subjects relative to their conduct in the war." †

The authority competent to declare war.

§ 174. As stated before (§ 24), the internal and external sovereignty of a State is represented by its Government, the organ through which the intercourse, which a State as body-politic has with other States, must take place. Thus a lawful war between civilized Nations can only be waged in the name of the supreme power which, in conformity with their respective constitution or public law (§§ 24, 37 & 38), represents the Government of the respective States. Colonial Governments receive, by special enactments of the public law of the mother country, the power to wage war against uncivilized Nations or tribes.

---

* WOOLSEY. p. 201.

† VATTEL. Book III. 4. § 64.

Effect of the declaration of war on mutual peaceable intercourse between private individuals of the belligerent States.

§ 175. The effect of war upon treaties and conventions has already been described under paragraph 138 in chapter XIX, dealing with treaties and conventions. Besides abrogating or suspending certain kinds of treaties, as noted above, war puts practically an end to many mutual peaceable transactions between private individuals of the belligerent States, but legally only so far as the suspension or extinction of private or commercial contracts is the legal result of the necessary suspension or abrogation of treaties and conventions, through the state of war, or the consequence of expressly notified prohibition of all intercourse with the enemy. War can therefore not be regarded as putting, *per se*, legally an end to all pacific and innocent relations between the private individual subjects or citizens of hostile States.

Dr. Woolsey's statements.

"If each and all on the one side, says Dr. Woolsey, were enemies to each and all on the other, it would seem that every person had a right, so far as the municipal code did not forbid, to fall upon his enemy wherever he could find him; that, for instance, an invading army had a right to seize on all the property and persons within reach, and dispose of them at discretion. But no such unlimited enmity is now known in the usages of Nations."

"The old strict theory in regard to a state of war was that each and every subject of the one belligerent is at war with each and every subject of the other. Now as it was also a received rule that the persons and goods of my enemy belong to me if I can seize them, there was no end to the amount of suffering which might be inflicted on the innocent inhabitants of a country within the regular operations of war.* It is needless to say that no Christian State acts on such a theory, nor did the Greeks and Romans generally carry it out in practice in its extreme rigor. In particular there is now a wide line drawn between combatants and non-combatants, the latter of whom, by modern practice, are on land exempted from the injuries and molestations of war, as far as is consistent with the use of such a method of obtaining justice." †

In a note at the end of § 124 of his work above quoted, Dr. Woolsey makes the following remarks.

"In the Letters of Camillus, written by Alexander Hamilton just after Jay's treaty in 1795, this subject is considered at length, particularly in letters 18–20 (Works, vol. vii). In letter 19 he examines the right to confiscate or sequestrate private debts or property on the ground of reason and principle. He admits at the outset the proposition that every individual of the Nation with which we are at war is our enemy, and its property is liable to capture. To this there is one admitted exception respecting enemy's property in a neutral State, but this is owing to the right of the neutral alone. 'Reason,' he maintains, 'suggests another exception. Whenever a Government grants permission to foreigners to acquire property within its territories, or to bring and deposit it there, it tacitly promises protection and security. The property of foreigners placed in another country, by permission of its laws, may justly be regarded as a deposit of which the society is a trustee. How can it be reconciled with the

* Comp. KENT, I., 64, MANNING, 2nd Ed. p. 166, has a somewhat opposite view, which depends on a quasi legal theory. If war is a condition of non-peace, there may be active and passive persons in this condition. The latter are the inhabitants who have no share in hostilities.

† WOOLSEY. Edit. 1879. pp. 201 & 207.

idea of a trust, to take the property from its owner when he has personally given no cause for the deprivation?' Goods of enemies found elsewhere differ from those which are in our country, since in the latter case there is a reliance on our hospitality and justice. And the same argument which would confiscate the goods, would seize the persons of enemy subjects. The case of property in the public funds is still stronger than that of private debts. The result which Hamilton reaches is sound, but if we admit the principle that every individual belonging to the belligerent nation is an enemy, and every enemy's property liable to capture, we must deny the validity of exceptions, unless treaty or usage has established them. The foreigner brought his property here, it can at once be said, knowing the risk he might run in the event of a war. Why should he not incur the risk? He should incur it, say the older practice and the older authorities. He should not, says the modern practice, although International Law in its rigor involves him in it. He should not, according to the true principle of justice, because his relation to the State at war is not the same with the relation of his sovereign or Government; because, in short, he is not in the full sense an enemy." *

If each individual subject of the one State were in justice the enemy of every individual subject of the hostile State, it would be lawful for the Government of any belligerent State to excite its subjects to treacherous murder and plunder, by promising recompence for the indiscriminate injuring to body and property of every member of the enemy State. Whether this would be or

* WOOLSEY. Intern. Law. Edit. 1879, pp. 206 & 207.

not against the recognized principles of the laws of war, as noted in paragraphs 155 & 169, can safely be left to the verdict of the moral senses, conscience and sympathy, of every civilized human being.

The subjects of enemy States are enemies in so far as the actual state of hostility and the exigencies of war render the continuation of innocent intercourse inconsistent with active warfare. Thus when private individuals, as noted above, have no direct legal influence on the declaration of war, a theory of direct individual liability cannot be legally maintained. It would not only be immoral, but the State which, at the present condition of general international intercourse and universal commerce between civilized Nations, would adhere to the old barbaric usages of causing war to affect the relations subsisting between private individuals, would simply expose his own people to unnecessary inconvenience, while exciting a spirit of retaliation which is destructive to both parties and in no way conducive to the termination of the war.

When passions have been roused on both sides, there can be no more question of principles of law, hence the manifold divergences from these principles; which deviations are sometimes mistaken for the legal status of war. But the gradual amelioration of these conditions, as recorded by history, shows plainly enough that usages of such origin did not and could not become established principles of the laws of war for the present generation, for this would be contrary to the Moral Law of Nature, whose persistent action on the moral-mental organism of man is here not less manifested than in the laws of peace, described in chapter xxv.

CHAPTER XXX.

THE ENEMY AND HIS ALLIES.

Enemy character. § 176. The hostile character of the public enemy *(hostis)*, which is distinct from that of the private enemy *(inimicus)*, results from political ties and not from personal feelings or personal wrongs. "Their status," says Halleck with reference to public enemies, "is that of legal hostility and not of personal enmity. Private enemies have hatred and rancour in their hearts and seek to do each other personal injury. Not so with public enemies; they do not as individuals seek to do each other personal harm, and even where brought into actual conflict as armed belligerents, there is usually no personal enmity between the individuals of the contending forces. So far from this, when peace is declared, the military forces of the opposing belligerents are usually personal friends, and vie with each other in politeness and mutual kindness." *

The Ally of the enemy. § 177. The hostile character of a public enemy extends to his allies.

States are in mutual friendly relations when they simply respect, reciprocally, each other's rights and comply mutually with treaty obligations. They are called allied when there exists between them some express compact or agreement which imposes, reciprocally, the obligation to act conjointly in the maintenance of their respective rights with regard to third parties and to give

* HALLECK, Vol. II, p. 52.

each other, mutually, moral and material assistance in certain cases and under certain conditions as stipulated in the contract, when any of them may be threatened by third Powers. This mutual assistance may be conditional or unconditional, partial or unlimited, passive or active; it can be given once for all or be claimable as long as necessary,—all in conformity with the treaty of alliance which binds the parties as allied States.

Treaties of alliance *(fœdera, ligues)*, which are concluded with a view to the eventuality of war *(alliances de guerre)*, are those by which the contracting parties promise each other, reciprocally, help and assistance, moral as well as material, against the enemy. They are known as defensive alliances, having for their object the common defence of rights and territory and the guarding of the frontiers *(traités de barrière, fœdera limitum custodiendorum)* against aggressions from without; and offensive alliances which constitute a union for combined aggressive action in a definite direction. An offensive and defensive alliance *(alliance générale)* includes both conditions. Treaties of subsidy *(traité de subside)* are a sort of passive alliance, promising, in case of war, a limited help in money or war materials or permission to recruit troops in the ally's territory or to pass troops through his territory. The occupation of fortresses or colonies during a war by special agreement to protect them against an enemy is called a partial alliance. A passive as well as a partial alliance entails the character of enemy, and consequently the loss of neutrality, but does not, *per se*, place such an ally in the position of belligerent and at the conclusion of peace he is not necessarily a party to the treaty. * *Different kinds of Alliances.*

* KLUBER. §§ 149 & 268-272. VATTEL. Liv. III. Chapt. VI.

Treaties of Alliance are subjected to the moral and legal rules of contracts.

Treaties of alliance are subjected to the moral and legal rules of contracts, and those for the eventuality of war are naturally made under the tacit condition that the war will be just and legal, for no one can be supposed to bind himself and others to commit injustice (comp. chapt. XIX).

Halleck's statement.

With regard to the enemy character of allies, Halleck makes the following statement.

"The question here arises, how are we to know whether an enemy's ally is himself to be regarded as an enemy, and to be treated in the same manner as the principal belligerent? In the first place, if he has made common cause with our enemy in beginning or carrying on hostilities against us, we have toward him the same belligerent rights as toward the principal in the war, for both are equally our enemies. There is no need of proving him an enemy, for his own conduct has made him such. Again, even where there are no obligations of treaty, if he freely and voluntarily declares in favour of his ally and against us, he, of his own accord, becomes our enemy, and is to be treated in every respect as the principal. But the simple fact of there being an alliance between our enemy and other Nations would not justify us in treating such Nations as belligerents." *

"Alliances, for warlike purposes, are divided into two classes, offensive and defensive. In the former the State unites with its ally for the purpose of jointly waging war against a third party; but in the latter, the State engages to defend its ally in case of an attack. Some alliances are both offensive and defensive; others are only defensive; but there is seldom an offensive alliance which is not also a defensive one. Some are against all opponents, and without restriction; while others

* VATTEL. Droit des Gens. Liv. III. Chapt. VI. §§ 96–8.

are only against a particular State, and on specified conditions, with limitations and exceptions." *

With regard to the legal effect of alliances on belligerent rights, Halleck makes the following further remarks.

"Warlike alliances, made at the commencement of or during a war, are necessarily binding, for the contracting parties then know the character of the war and the exact nature of the obligations which they have assumed. Alliances, made under such circumstances, are acts of hostility which make the ally an enemy equally with the principal belligerent. It is important, however, to satisfy ourselves as to the character of such alliances, to see whether or not they are really warlike compacts which make the contracting parties also parties to the war. The alliance between France and the English revolted colonies in North America, being made during the war of the American revolution, was very properly regarded by Great Britain as tantamount to a declaration of war on the part of France, and as justifying immediate hostilities against this ally of the revolted colonies. † A warlike alliance made by a third party before the war with a State, then our friend, but now our enemy, will not, as a general rule, be of itself, a sufficient cause for commencing hostilities against such third party; for there may be good reason why he should not regard himself as bound by the obligations of the alliance. It would certainly be very impolitic, as well as improper, for us to treat as a belligerent one who may not be disposed to become our enemy. The character

* HALLECK. Vol. II. p. 55.

† RIQUELME. Derecho Pub. Int. Lib. I. Tit. I. Cap. XI. BYNKERSHOEK. QUAEST. Jur. Pub. Lib. I. Cap. IX. PHILLIMORE. On Int. Law. Vol. III. § 73.

of the alliance, and the peculiar circumstances of the case, must serve as guides for our conduct, always keeping in mind the maxim, that it is better to have a friend than an enemy, and the rule of International Law, that we are justifiable in engaging in hostilities only so far as may be necessary for our own security and the protection of our just rights. In case of alliances made before the war, the question is to determine whether the actual circumstances are such as were contemplated in the engagement, whether they are such as were expressly specified, or tacitly supposed in the treaty. This is what the civilians call *casus fœderis*, or the cause of the alliance. Whatever has been promised, either expressly or tacitly, in the treaty, is due in the *casus fœderis*. But if not so promised, it is not due. If the war is not such a case as the treaty contemplated, the ally does not become a party to it; for the *casus fœderis* does not take place." *

"In an offensive alliance, made before the war, the ally engages generally to co-operate in hostilities against a specified Power, or against any Power against whom the other party may declare war. Where an alliance is made in general terms, without any specified conditions, limitations, or exceptions, does the *casus fœderis* take place the moment the other party declares war? In other words, does such an offensive alliance differ in its binding effect from one contracted with a party already engaged, or on the point of engaging, in a war, the character of which is already known? Vattel says: 'As it is only for the support of a just war that we are allowed to give assistance or contract alliances, every alliance, every war-

* VATTEL. Droit des Gens. Liv. III. Chapt. VI. § 88. WHEATON. Elem. Int. Law. Pt. III. Chapt. II. § 15. MARTENS. Précis du Droit des Gens. § 299. MOSER. Versuch, &c. Book. IX. Pt. I. p. 24. GARDEN. De Diplomatie. Liv. VI. § 2. and Liv. VII. § 1.

like association, every auxiliary treaty, contracted by way of anticipation in time of peace, and with no view to any particular war, necessarily and of itself includes this tacit clause, that the treaty shall not be obligatory except in case of a just war. On any other footing the alliance could not be validly contracted.' Mr. Wheaton says, 'To promise assistance in an unjust war, would be an obligation to commit an injustice, and no such contract is valid.' It would seem to follow from this fundamental principle, that where one of two parties to an offensive alliance, made before the war, declares war against its enemy, even though that enemy be the very Nation against which the alliance was formed, the other ally is to be allowed time to examine into the causes of war; if it be a just war, all his engagements come into force; but if it be unjustly declared, his treaty obligations cease to be binding. * So, also, in a defensive alliance made before the war, the *casus fœderis* does not take place immediately on one of the parties being attacked by an enemy. The other contracting party has the right, as indeed it is his duty, to ascertain if his ally has not given the enemy just cause of war, for no one is bound to undertake the defence of an ally, in order to enable him to insult others, or to refuse them justice. If he is manifestly in the wrong, his co-ally may require him to offer reasonable satisfaction; and if the enemy refuse to accept it, and insists upon a continuance of the war, the co-ally is then bound to assist in his defence. But without such offer of reasonable satisfaction, the war continues to be aggressive in character, and therefore unjust, and the ally may properly refuse to render the promised assistance, for the tacit condition on which such

* BELLO. Derecho International. Pt. II. Chapt. IX. § 1.

assistance was stipulated to be given has not been observed, or, in other words, the *casus fœderis* has not taken place. If, on the contrary, a party to the defensive alliance, could call upon his ally to assist him whenever he was assailed, and without regard to the justice of the war, or the circumstances of the attack, there would be no difference between a defensive and an offensive alliance, for many wars which are defensive in their operations are essentially offensive in their character and principles. In the words of Wheaton, where attack is the best mode of providing for the defence of a State, the war is defensive in principle, though the operations are offensive. Where the war is unnecessary to safety, its offensive character is not altered because the wrong doer is reduced to defensive warfare. So, a State, against which a dangerous wrong is manifestly meditated, may prevent it by striking the first blow, without thereby waging a war in its principle offensive. Accordingly, it is not every attack made on a State that will entitle it to aid under a defensive alliance; for if that State had given just cause of war to the invader, the war would not be, on its part, defensive in principle." *

Personal union (unio personalis) of States is no reason for alliance in war.

§ 178. As stated above (§ 24), the condition created by a union of crowns,—*i. e.* when the sovereign of one State is, at the same time, the sovereign of another and the union of such crowns depends solely upon the person of the sovereign *(unio personalis)*,—by no means implies a political union *(unio civitatum)*, as each State preserves its complete independence and all its sovereignty

---

* WILDMAN. Intern. Law. Vol. II. p. 166. GROTIUS. De Jur. Bell. ac Pac. Lib. II. Chapt. XV. § 13. GARDEN. De Diplomatie. Liv. VI. Sec. II. § 2. BURLAMAQUI. Droit de la Nat. et des Gens. Tome. V. Pt. IV. Chapt. III.

rights; each having therefore an unrestricted right to declare and wage war or remain neutral, independently of the other. Whatever may be their mutual co-operation in other respects, when there is no special treaty of alliance (as described in the preceding paragraph), a union of crowns does not imply alliance in war.

"States joined by a personal union, says Mr. Hall, are wholly separate States, which happen to employ the same agents for the management of their affairs, and they are not responsible for each other's acts. It is the clear rule therefore that either may remain neutral during a war in which the other engaged. It is only necessary so far to qualify this statement, as to say that any suspicion of indirect aid given by the neutral State, or of any fraudulent use of the produce of its taxes or other resources, gives the enemy of the belligerent Power a right to disregard the character which the associated State claims to possess. The connection between the two States is such, wherever at least the common sovereign may happen not to be trammelled by a constitution, that a right of ceasing to respect a neutrality though it be unreal may fairly be held to arise upon less evidence of non-neutral conduct than would be required in the case of two wholly separate countries." *

* W. E. HALL. p. 440.

CHAPTER XXXI.

Rights and Duties of Belligerent States with regard to each other. The Usages of War.

1°. *General Remarks on the Usages of War (Coutumes de la guerre. Kriegsgebrauch).*

The place of Usages of War in International Law.

§ 179. After having noted the moral principles of the Law of War *(jus belli droit de la guerre, Kriegsrecht)*, in paragraphs 155 & 169–172, it is now our task to proceed with the enumeration of the practical usages which have been the most generally adopted between civilized States in their hostile conditions. The principles of the Law of War, as established above, may then serve as a base from which to measure the variations from the acknowledged standard of civilization which render the usages of war so conspicuous in International Law.

Usages of war *(coutumes de la guerre, Kriegsgebrauch)*, though theoretically based on the principles of the Law of War, are only the practical effects of these principles, which latter are, as noted above (§§ 155 & 169), the rules laid down by human conscience and sympathy, in their striving to bring the practical acts of warfare up to the standard of the existing International Spirit of Law (§ 14).

As Mr. Hall so judiciously remarks, in the passage of his work quoted above (§ 171), "International Law which has no alternative but to accept war, independently of the justice of its origin, as a relation which the parties of its may set up if they choose, has only to busy itself in regulating the effects of the relation." Thus the task of international jurisprudence is limited to the regulation of the usages of war, through utilizing the effect which the Moral Law of Nature may produce on the moral senses of belligerents, in conformity with the standard of the International Spirit of Law, *i.e.*, in conformity with the present state of civilization (comp. § 171).

Prof. Amos' statement with regard to the influence of the Moral Law on usages of warfare.

With regard to the influence of the Moral Law on the usages of war, Professor Sheldon Amos, makes the following statement. "The restrictions imposed by an increasing conscientiousness and by a more and more enlightened sense of general expediency among the Nations of Europe upon the extreme exercise of the physical powers actually in the hands of a belligerent State, and the corresponding claims to such a remission or indulgence recognized as belonging to the other belligerent, could only by a very metaphorical extension of the terms be styled "duties" and "rights." Nevertheless, the gradual introduction of this restriction has marked the main historical stages in the development of International Law, and indeed, has been one of the most directly stimulating causes of that development in its existing form. The treatment of prisoners of war,—which at one time knew no mitigation but such as might be due to the accidental tenderness of the capturer,—gradually progressed to the general practice of only retaining the prisoner till he was ransomed; then to the imposition of limits upon the exaction of exorbitant ransoms; and, finally, to the modern practice of simply guarding the prisoners, with every show of consideration and even of confidence, till an exchange of prisoners is possible or till the conclusion of the war. The general principles on this head have advanced as far as the severest claims of humanity could demand, and as far, indeed, as is compatible with the resort to war at all. This statement does not, of course, imply that the practice is invariably consistent with the principle." *

2°. *Usages of War with regard to the relations between private individuals of enemy States.*

Non-intercourse with the enemy. Edicta dehortatoria, avocatoria and inhibitoria.

§ 180. Governments of belligerent Powers are in the habit of proclaiming, at the outbreak of war, the line of conduct which they will think proper to follow with regard to the relations of their respective subjects or citizens towards those of the enemy State and the amount of mutual commerce they will allow with the enemy.

To this effect it is sometimes through municipal legislation, or by proclamation of the executive Government, declared punishable by law to continue any relations with the enemy which could be in a direct or indirect manner useful to him in the carrying on of the war *(edicta dehortatoria)*.

This proclamation is generally accompanied by the recall *(edicta avocatoria, décrets de rappel)*, of the military classes or of all the male subjects or citizens of the belligerents abroad, to rejoin the service or to help in the defence of the mother-country.

Sometimes the Government of a belligerent State may find it expedient to forbid under penalty all relations whatever with the enemy *(edicta inhibitoria)*. In this case all commerce between the subjects of the belligerents is unlawful for the subjects of the State which has issued

* Prof. SHELDON AMOS, M.A. A Systematic View of the Science of Jurisprudence, Edit. 1872. p. 438.

the prohibition, unless expressly licensed; so that, if not expressly permitted, all partnerships with subjects of the enemy State are suspended; insurances and all contracts for account of the enemy are invalid, as the legal power of prosecuting claims through the Courts of the prohibiting State or through that of the enemy State is suspended during the war. In a case where the business is conducted by a neutral partner, his share in the concern alone is protected.

Licence to trade with the enemy. Postal—and telegraph communications.

It is, however, often found necessary for a belligerent to grant to its own subjects a licence to carry on a certain specified trade with the enemy, which, if the other party allows it, becomes a safe and legitimate traffic; such as the postal service and a regulated telegraph communication (comp. chapter XVI). It is common also for the subjects of one belligerent to obtain such a a licence from the other, but of course, this of itself will not protect them against the laws of their own country.*

It is obvious that this general prohibition of trade with an enemy *(edicta inhibitoria)* does not apply to subjects or citizens of the belligerent State who are temporarily or permanently residing or carrying on trade in a foreign country, as no State has the right to regulate the trade or the political acts of its subjects or citizens under the jurisdiction of another State. This would be tantamount to legislating for the foreign State and thus to infringement on its sovereignty rights.

3°. *Usages of War with regard to Enemy's subjects and Enemy's property within a belligerent country.*

Enemy's subjects.

§ 181. Modern usages of war do not allow any sort of violence against private individuals

* WOOLSEY. p. 202. EMERIGON. Traité des assurances. Vol. I. p. 556. KLUBER. § 240.

of the enemy State, who, at the outbreak of war are found in a belligerent's country, as long as they take no part, direct or indirect, in political affairs in favour of their mother-country. When, for political reasons, their residence or further stay in the belligerent's country is prohibited, they are allowed a proper fixed time to leave the country, after having made proper arrangements with regard to their business and property.

Enemy's property. All public property of the enemy State is *per se* hostile, but private property, *i. e.*, property of private individuals, is only rendered hostile by the acts of its owners, by the circumstances of its use or dispositions with relation to the war, or by the interdict mentioned in the preceding paragraph.

Woolsey's statement. "The usage is now general, says Woolsey, if not fixed, with the single exception of measures of retortion, to allow the subjects of the enemy to remain within the territory during good behaviour, in the enjoyment of their property, or to give them, by public proclamation, reasonable time to remove with their effects from the country. The English and French in the late Crimean war allowed Russian vessels six weeks' time to leave their ports and reach their destination. In many cases treaties have given additional security to the goods, claims, and persons of enemies' subjects so situated. The treaty of 1794, between the United States and Great Britain, often called in the United States Jay's, from its American negotiator, declared it to be unjust and impolitic to confiscate debts due to the subjects of a Nation that has become hostile. * It was also stipulated

* In Article X. it is provided that "neither debts due from individuals of the one Nation to individuals of the other, nor shares nor monies which they may have in the public funds or in the public or private banks, shall ever, in any event of war or national difference, be sequestered or confiscated; it being unjust and impolitic that

in this instrument that the citizens of either Power might remain unmolested, during war, in the dominions of the other, so long as they should behave peaceably, and commit no offence against the laws; and that, if either Government desired their removal, twelve months' notice should be given them to this effect. Of treaties containing similar provisions, 'a list lies before me,' says Mr. Manning, 'too long for insertion, but even the Barbary Powers have in a great number of instances concluded such agreements.'† With regard to the shares held by a Government or its subjects in the public funds of another, all modern authorities agree, we believe, that they ought to be safe and inviolate. To confiscate either principal or interest, would be a breach of good faith, would injure the credit of a Nation and of its public securities, and would provoke retaliation on the property of its private citizens. 'The Emperor Napoleon I., during his stay at Posen, imagining that the cabinet of London had the intention of confiscating stock in the public debt belonging to Frenchmen, ordered his minister of finance to examine whether, in case they should so act, it would not be necessary to have recourse to the same rigour. The matter is a very delicate one, said he; I am not willing to set the example, but if the English do so, I ought to make reprisals. M. Mollien replied that such an act was so contrary to English policy that he could not believe it, that he wished the Cabinet of London would commit such a mistake, but that results

debts and engagements, contracted and made by individuals having confidence in each other and in their respective Governments, should ever be destroyed or impaired by national authority on account of national differences and discontents." This clause of the treaty is in conformity with the natural principles of the Law of War, noted above in paragraphs 169–172.

† Comment. p. 126.

would be the more disastrous for them if it were not imitated. On this occasion he sent to the Emperor the memoir of Hamilton,* the friend, counsellor and minister of Washington, on the question whether the political more even than the moral rule did not forbid every Government, not only to confiscate capital which had been lent to it by the subjects of a Power with which it was at war, but even to suspend, as far as they were concerned, the payment of interest. Napoleon did not insist further on the matter.' "†

"The true theory, says Dr. Woolsey further, seems to be that the private persons on each side are not fully in hostile relations, but in a state of non-intercourse, in a state wherein the rights of intercourse, only secured by treaty and not derived from natural right, are suspended or have ceased; while the political bodies to which they belong are at war with one another, and they only. Of course until these political bodies allow hostile acts to be performed, such acts, save in self-defence, may not be performed; and accordingly the usages of war visit with severity those who fight without a sanction from their Governments. The plunder which such persons seize belongs not to themselves but to the public, until public authority gives them a share in it."‡

4°. *Means and Instruments of carrying on war.*

The Conference of Brussel of 1874.

§ 182. In this and the following sections, we have mainly taken over the rules adopted by the International Conference held at Brussels, in July

---

* Probably the letters of Camillus. (See above § 175. p. 269 of this Volume).

† From a biography of Count Mollien, contributed by Michel Chevalier to the Revue des Deux Mondes, in the year 1856, cited by Vergé in De Martens, § 258. Ed. of 1858.

‡ WOOLSEY. §§ 124–125.

and August 1874, to discuss a set of international rules for military warfare, proposed by Russia. This Conference was attended by delegates of Austria-Hungary, Belgium, Denmark, France, Germany, Great Britain, Greece, Italy, The Netherlands, Portugal, Russia, Spain, Switzerland, Sweden and Norway and Turkey.

At the close of this Conference, the president, the Russian delegate, Baron Jomini, proposed that the delegates should attach their signatures to a final protocol, which contained the following terms :—

" The Conference assembled at Brussels, on the invitation of His Majesty the Emperor of Russia, for the purpose of discussing a project of international rules regarding the laws and usages of war, has examined the project submitted to it in a spirit in accordance with the elevated sentiment which had led to its being convoked, and which all the Governments represented had welcomed with sympathy. This sentiment had already found expression in the declaration exchanged between several Governments at St. Petersburg, 1868, with reference to the exclusion of explosive bullets. It had been unanimously declared, that the progress of civilization should have the effect of alleviating, as far as possible, the calamities of war; and that the only legitimate object which States should have in view during war, is to weaken the enemy without inflicting upon him unnecessary suffering. These principles met, at that time, with unanimous approval. At the present time the Conference, following the same path, participate in the conviction expressed by the Government of His Majesty the Emperor of Russia, that a further step may be taken by revising the laws and general usages of war, whether with the object of defining them with greater precision, or with the view of laying down, by a common agreement, certain limits which will restrain, as far as possible, the severities of war. War being thus regulated, would involve less suffering, would be less liable to those aggravations which produce uncertainty, unforeseen events, and passions excited by the struggle; it would tend more surely to that which should be its final object, viz., the re-establishment of good relations, and a more solid and lasting peace between the belligerent States."

"The Conference could respond to these ideas of humanity in no better way than by entering in the same spirit into the examination of the subject they were to discuss. The modifications which have been introduced into the project, the comments, the reservations and separate opinions which the delegates have thought proper to insert in the protocols, in accordance with instructions, and the particular views of their respective Governments or their own private opinions, constitute the *ensemble* of their work. It is of opinion that it may be submitted to the respective Governments which it represents, as a conscientious inquiry of a nature to serve as a basis for an ulterior exchange of ideas and for the development of the provisions of the Convention of Geneva of 1864, and of the Declaration of St. Petersburg of 1868. It will be their task to ascertain what portion of this work may become the object of an agreement, and what portion requires still further examination."

"The Conference, in concluding its work, is of opinion that its debates will have, in every case, thrown light on those important questions, the regulation of which, should it result in a general agreement, would be a real progress of humanity." *

§ 183. The following general principles form the basis of modern warfare, with regard to the means and instruments of carrying on war.

General principles with regard to the means and instruments of carrying on war.

1°. Operations of war must be directed exclusively against the forces and the means of making war of the hostile State, and not against its subjects, so long as the latter do not themselves take any active part in the war.

2°. In order to attain the object of the war, all means and all measures in conformity with the laws and customs of war, and justified by the necessities of war, shall be permitted.

3°. The laws and customs of war forbid not only useless cruelty and acts of barbarity committed against the enemy; they furthermore require from the competent authorities the immediate punishment of those guilty of such acts, provided they have not been provoked by absolute necessity.

4°. The necessities of war cannot justify either treachery or bad faith towards the enemy, or declaring him an outlaw, or the employment of violence and cruelty towards him.

5°. In the event of the enemy not observing the laws and customs of war, the opposing force may resort to reprisals, but only as an inevitable evil and without ever losing sight of the duties of humanity.

§ 184. At the third meeting of the committee, held, on the 1st August, General Arnaudeau, the French delegate, during the discussion on the treatment of "spies," pointed out the desirableness of introducing uniformity into the penal le-

Proposition at the Brussels Conference with regard to uniformity in the penal legislation of the different countries concerning violation of the laws of war.

* Report of the British Delegate, Sir A. Horford, dated 4th September 1874. Parliamentary Papers, 1874–5.

gislation of different countries on these and similar questions.

At the twelfth meeting of the committee, on the 14th August, the Russian delegates announced that they were authorized by their Government to support the proposition of General Arnaudeau, and at the fourth meeting of the Conference the subject came up for discussion.

It was remarked by General Arnaudeau that in the Russian project often occur the words, "shall be delivered to justice." This phrase, he observed, does not convey a fixed idea either as to the nature of the justice or of the tribunal which administers it. At one place, moreover, a particular act renders the offender liable to the penalty of death, at another to simple imprisonment. He therefore proposed, as a commencement of the desirable work of constructing a uniform code for dealing with all instances of infringement of International Law, that the various States should come to an agreement as to the penalties to be inflicted for the undermentioned crimes committed in the field:—

Pillage, whether committed by bands of men or by individuals.

Thieving from an inhabitant.

Violence to the wounded.

Violation of parole given by a prisoner of war.

Acts of espionage.

Continuation of hostilities beyond the time fixed for their cessation.

Armed assaults.

Hostilities on neutral territory, or on that of allies.

In conclusion, the General proposed the adoption of the following resolution:—

"The Powers represented at the Conference shall come to an understanding for the purpose of establishing an agreement regarding the modes of repression actually prescribed by their military codes. They will give a wider bearing to this first improvement by seeking afterwards the bases of an agreement for assimilating the penalties applicable to crimes, offences, and contraventions committed in violation of International Law."

This declaration received the support of the greater part of the delegates.

In connection with the same object, Baron Jomini, the Russian delegate and President of the Conference, expressed a desire, that in order to insure the observance of the laws and customs of war proposed by the Conference, the Governments, if they adopt these principles and make a declaration to that effect, should take the necessary steps in order that these rules may become part of the military instructions of their respective armies.

5°. *The living Instruments of War. Combatants and Non-Combatants.*

§ 185. As war cannot be carried on without soldiers, says Vattel, "it is evident that whoever has the right of making war, has also naturally that" of raising troops.* *Right of belligerents to raise troops.*

The general right of the State to raise troops is a part of the *jus eminens*, or superior right, which the entire body may, for the common good, exercise over the individual members of which it is composed.

Foreigners, who voluntarily serve a State for stipulated pay, are called *mercenaries*.

"The right of citizens of one State, says Halleck, to be so employed by another, and of this other to so employ them, has often been discussed

* VATTEL. Droit des Gens. Liv. III. Chapt. II. § 10; Chapt. VIII. § 145.

by publicists. * That any citizen, with the consent of his own State, may serve another cannot be denied. But, in doing this, he changes his nationality, and must thereafter look for support and protection to the State in whose service he has engaged. The right of a State to permit its citizens to be employed in the military service of another, is very questionable, but the right of this other to so employ them (with such permission), cannot be doubted. The *policy* of doing so, is a very different question. Mercenaries enlist voluntarily, for no State has a right to require such service of undomiciled foreigners. Domiciled foreigners may be required to do duty in the militia, or the civic and national guards, for the preservation of order and the enforcement of the laws, within a reasonable distance of their place of domicile. But such duty is rather of a civil than a military character. It does not include service against a foreign enemy, nor general military service in a civil war." †

"The British Government, in 1862, informed Mr. Stewart that as a general principle of International law, neutral aliens ought not to be compelled to perform any military service (*i.e.* working in trenches), but that allowance might be made for the conduct of authorities in cities under martial law, and in daily peril of the enemy; and in 1864, the British Government saw no reason to interfere in the case of neutral

* By 33 & 34. Vict. Chapt. 90. (Foreign Enlistment Act). If any person, without the licence of Her Majesty, being a British subject, within or without Her Majesty's dominions, accepts any commission from a foreign State at war with any foreign State at peace with Her Majesty, or, whether a British subject or not, within Her Majesty's dominions, induces any other person to accept any such commission, he is liable to fine and imprisonment. (See Appendix E).

† BYNKERSHOEK. Quaest. Jur. Pub. Lib. I. Chapt. XXII. BELLO. Derecho International. Pt. II. Chapt. I. § 5. WARD. Law of Nations, Vol. II. p. 301. HEFFTER. Droit International, § 62.

foreigners directed to be enrolled as a local police for New Orleans. By the United States Act, April 14, 1802, naturalized aliens are entitled to nearly the same rights, and are charged with the same duties, as the native inhabitants; and aliens not naturalized, if they have at any time assumed the *right of voting at a State election*, or held office, are according to the opinion of Mr. Attorney-General Bates, liable to the Acts for enrolling the national forces. (See also Act, 3 March, 1863, and Act, 24 February, 1864; proclamation of President, May 8, 1863). This was acted on during the American civil war, and tacitly acquiesed in by the British Government." * (Comp. § 40. Nationality of domicile.) *Mercenaries Enlistment of foreigners domiciled in belligerent States.*

The laws, rights, and duties of war are applicable not only to the army, but likewise to militia and corps of volunteers complying with the following conditions:— *Militia and Volunteers of land forces.*

1. That they have at their head a person responsible for his subordinates;

2. That they wear some settled distinctive badge, recognizable at a distance;

3. That they carry arms openly; and

4. That, in their operations, they conform to the laws and customs of war.

In those countries where the militia form the whole or part of the army, they shall be included under the denomination of "army."

The population of a non-occupied territory, who, on the approach of the enemy, of their own accord take up arms to resist the invading troops, without having had time to organize themselves into a regularly commissioned army, shall be considered

* HALLECK. Volume II. p. 6.

as belligerents, if they respect the laws and customs of war.

Naval volunteers (Seewehr).

With regard to maritime war, it is generally acknowledged that, besides the regular Military Navy, the *Sea-Militia (Seewehr)* and *Naval Volunteers* are admissible as legal forces of war when they are placed, with duly commissioned vessels, under the immediate orders of chiefs of the regular Navy and are subjected to the Naval Military Code and discipline. *

The four rules with regard to maritime warfare, as established by the treaty of Paris in 1856, called the Declaration of Paris, are the following:—

1°. Privateering is and remains abolished.

2°. The neutral flag covers enemy's goods, with the exception of contraband of war.

3°. Neutral goods, with the exception of contraband of war, are not liable to capture under an enemy's flag.

4°. Blockades in order to be binding must be effective.

These rules are treated in chapters XXXIII–XXXVI.

Combatants and Non-combatants.

The armed forces of the belligerents may be composed of combatants and non-combatants. In the event of being captured by the enemy, both of them shall enjoy the rights of prisoners of war.

---

* In the Franco-German war, the German Government, having called up the *(Seewehr)* volunteers and invited the owners of private German vessels and mariners to place themselves and their vessels at the disposal of the Government, to be used against the enemy's navy, France protested and denounced these steps as a return to the system of privateering, in violation of the Declaration of Paris, to which Germany had pledged itself. England declared, however, that the complaint of the French Government had no foundation, as the vessels of the *Seewehr* were placed under the orders of the regular Navy and subject to the discipline of that corps. Bluntschli. Droit Intern. Cod. § 670, note 4. Ann. de l'Institut de Droit Intern. 1870–1880. Vol. I. pp. 130 & 136.

6°. *Of the means of inflicting bodily injury to the enemy.*

§ 186. The laws of war do not allow to belligerents an unlimited power as to the choice of means of injuring the enemy. *Forbidden means.*

According to this principle are strictly forbidden:—

a. The use of poison or poisoned weapons.

b. Murder by treachery of individuals belonging to the hostile nation or army.

c. Murder of an antagonist who, having laid down his arms, or having no longer the means of defending himself, has surrendered at discretion.

d. The declaration that no quarter will be given.

e. The use of arms, projectiles, or substances *(matières)* which may cause unnecessary suffering, as well as the use of explosive balls of less than 400 grammes weight charged with inflammable substances.

f. Abuse of the flag of truce, the national flag, or the military insignia or uniform of the enemy, as well as the distinctive badges of the Geneva Convention.

g. All destruction or seizure of the property of the enemy which is not imperatively required by the necessity of war.

Stratagems *(ruses de guerre)*, and the employment of means necessary to procure intelligence respecting the enemy or the country *(terrain)* are considered as lawful means. *

* Declaration of St. Petersburg of 1868.

7°. *Military Occupation.*

Definition of military occupation. §187. Military occupation is analogous to blockade and can only be exercised where it is effective. The occupier must always be in sufficient strength to repress an outbreak. He proves his occupation by this act. An army establishes its occupation when its positions and lines of communication are secured by other corps. If a territory frees itself from the exercise of this authority, it ceases to be occupied. Occupation cannot be presumptive.

Rules with regard to military occupation. The following rules were adopted by the Conference of Brussels in 1874 (see §182), with regard to military occupation.

1°. A territory is considered as occupied when it is actually placed under the authority of the hostile army.

The occupation only extends to those territories where this authority is established and can be exercised.

2°. The authority of the legal power being suspended, and having actually passed into the hands of the occupier, he shall take every step in his power to re-establish and secure, as far as possible, public safety and social order.

3°. With this object he will maintain the laws which were in force in the country in time of peace, and will only modify, suspend, or replace them by others if necessity obliges him to do so.

4°. The functionaries and officials of every class who, at the instance of the occupier, consent to continue to perform their duties, shall be under his protection. They shall not be dismissed or be liable to summary punishment *(punir disciplinairement)*, unless they fail in fulfilling the obligations they have undertaken, and shall be handed over to justice only if they violate those obligations by unfaithfulness.

5°. The army of occupation shall only levy such taxes, dues, duties, and tolls as are already established for the benefit of the State, or their equivalent, if it be impossible to collect them, and this shall be done as far as possible in the form of and according to existing practice. It shall devote them to defraying the expenses of the administration of the country to the same extent as was obligatory on the legal Government.

6°. The army occupying a territory shall take possession only of the specie, the funds, and bills &c. *(valeurs exigibles)*, which are the actual property of the State, the depôts of arms, means of transport, magazines, and supplies, and, in general, all the personal property of the State, which may be of service in carrying on the war.

Railway plant, land telegraphs, steam and other vessels, not included in cases regulated by maritime law, as well as depôts of arms, and generally every kind of munitions of war, although belonging to companies or to private individuals, are to be considered equally as means of aid in carrying on a war, which cannot be left at the disposal of the enemy. Railway plant, land telegraphs, as well as the steam and other vessels above mentioned, shall be restored, and indemnities be regulated on the conclusion of peace.

7°. The occupying State shall only consider itself in the light of an administrator and usufructuary of the public buildings, real property, forests, and agricultural works belonging to the hostile State, and situated in the occupied territory. It is bound to protect these properties *(fonds de ces propriétés)*, and to administer them according to the laws of usufruct.

8°. The property of parishes *(communes)*, of establishments devoted to religion, charity, education, arts and sciences, although belonging to the State, shall be treated as private property.

Every seizure, destruction of or wilful damage to such establishments, historical monuments, or works of art or of science, should be prosecuted by the competent authorities.

8°. *Sieges and Bombardments.*

Rules with regard to sieges and bombardments.

§ 188. With regard to sieges and bombardments the Conference of Brussels has adopted the following rules.

1°. Fortified places are alone liable to be besieged. Towns, agglomerations of houses or villages, which are open and undefended, cannot be attacked or bombarded.

2°. But if a town or fortress, agglomeration of houses, or a village be defended, the commander of the attacking forces should, before commencing a bombardment, and, except in the case of surprise, do all in his power to warn the authorities.

3°. In the like case all necessary steps should be taken to spare, as far as possible, buildings devoted to religion, arts, sciences and charity, hospitals and places where sick and wounded are collected, on condition that they are not used at the same time for military purposes.

It is the duty of the besieged to indicate these buildings, by special visible signs to be notified beforehand by the besieged.

4°. A town taken by storm should not be given up to the victorious troops to plunder.

9°. *Prisoners of War.*

Rules for the treatment of Prisoners of War.

§ 189. Prisoners of war are lawful and disarmed enemies. They are in the power of the enemy Government and not of the individuals or of the corps who made them prisoners.

The following rules with regard to prisoners of war were adopted by the Conference of Brussels.

1°. Prisoners of war should be treated with humanity.

Every act of insubordination authorizes the necessary measures of severity to be taken with regard to them.

All their personal effects, except their arms, are considered to be their own property.

2°. Prisoners of war are liable to internment in a town, fortress, camp, or in any locality whatever, under an obligation not to go beyond certain fixed limits; but they may not be placed in confinement unless absolutely necessary as a measure of security.

3°. Prisoners of war may be employed on certain public works which have no immediate connection with the operations on the theatre of war, provided the employment be not excessive, nor humiliating to their military rank, if they belong to the army, or to their official or social position, if they do not belong to it.

They may also, subject to such regulations as may be drawn up by the military authorities, undertake private work.

The pay they receive will go towards ameliorating their position, or will be put to their credit at the time of their release. In this case the cost of their maintenance may be deducted from their pay.

4°. Prisoners of war cannot be compelled in any way to take any part whatever in carrying on the operations of the war.

5°. The Government in whose power are the prisoners of war, undertakes to provide for their maintenance.

The conditions of such maintenance may be settled by a mutual understanding between the belligerents.

In default of such an understanding, and as a general principle, prisoners of war shall be treated, as regards food and clothing, on the same footing as the troops of the Government who made them prisoners.

6°. Prisoners of war are subject to the laws and regulations in force in the army in whose power they are.

Arms may be used, after summoning, against a prisoner attempting to escape. If retaken, he is subject to summary punishment *(peines disciplinaires)* or to a stricter surveillance.

If, after having escaped, he is again made prisoner, he is not liable to any punishment for his previous escape.

7°. Every prisoner is bound to declare, if interrogated on the point, his true names and rank; and in the case of his infringing this rule, he will incur a restriction of the advantages granted to the prisoners of the class to which he belongs.

8°. The exchange of prisoners of war is regulated by mutual agreement between the belligerents.

9°. Prisoners of war may be released on parole, if the laws of their country allow of it; and in such a case they are bound on their personal honour to fulfil scrupulously, as regards their own Government as well as that which made them prisoners, the engagements they have undertaken.

In the same case their own Government should neither demand nor accept from them any service contrary to their parole.

10°. A prisoner of war cannot be forced to accept release on parole, nor is the enemy Government obliged to comply with the request of a prisoner claiming to be released on parole.

11°. Every prisoner of war liberated on parole, and retaken carrying arms against the Government to which he had pledged his honour, may be deprived of the rights accorded to prisoners of war and may be brought before the tribunals.

12°. Persons in the vicinity of armies, but who do not directly form part of them, such as correspondents, newspapers-reporters, *vivandiers*, contractors, &c., may also be made prisoners of war.

These persons should, however, be furnished with a permit, issued by a competent authority as well as with a certificate of indentity.

10° *Belligerent troops on Neutral territory.*

§ 190. The neutral State receiving in its territory troops belonging to the belligerents' armies, will intern them, so far as it may be possible, away from the theatre of war.

Belligerents interned, and wounded treated in neutral territory. The Geneva Convention applicable.

They may be kept in camps, or even confined in fortresses or in places appropriated to this purpose.

It will decide whether the officers may be released on giving their parole not to quit the neutral territory without authority.

In default of a special agreement, the neutral State which receives the belligerent troops will furnish the interned with provisions, clothing, and such aid as humanity demands.

The expenses incurred by the internment will be made good at the conclusion of peace.

The neutral State may authorize the transport across its territory of the wounded and sick belonging to the belligerent armies, provided that the trains which convey them do not carry either the *personnel* or *materiel* of war.

In this case the neutral State is bound to take the measures necessary for the safety and control of the operation.

The Convention of Geneva (see chapt. XXXIX) is applicable to the sick and wounded interned on neutral territory.

11°. *The Rights of Belligerents with respect to Private Individuals and their property.*

Inviolability of private non-combatants, and of private property. Pillage forbidden.

§ 191. The population of an occupied territory cannot be compelled to take part in military operations against their own country.

The population of occupied territories cannot be compelled to swear allegiance to the enemy's power.

The honour and rights of the family, the life and property of individuals, as well as their religious convictions and the exercise of their religion, should be respected.

Private property cannot be confiscated.

Pillage is expressly forbidden. *

With regard to the private property on the open sea, we refer the reader to chapter XXXII.

12°. *Spies.*

Persons to be regarded as spies and punishable as such.

§ 192. No one shall be considered as a spy, but those who, acting secretly or under false pretences, collect or try to collect information in districts occupied by the enemy, with the intention of communicating it to the opposing force.

A spy, if taken in the act, shall be tried and treated according to the laws in force in the army which captures him.

If a spy, who rejoins the army to which he belongs, is subsequently captured by the enemy,

* Art. 36–39 of the Brussel Conference.

he is to be treated as a prisoner of war, and incurs no responsibility for his previous acts.

Military men *(les militaires)* who have penetrated within the zone of operations of the enemy's army, with the intention of collecting information, are not considered as spies, if it has been possible to recognize their military character.

In like manner, military men (and also non-military persons carrying out their mission openly), charged with the transmission of despatches either to their own army or to that of the enemy shall not be considered as spies if captured by the enemy.

To this class belong also, if captured, individuals sent in balloons to carry despatches, and generally to keep up communications between the different parts of an army or of a territory. *

13°. *Non-hostile relations between belligerents.*

§ 193. An individual authorized by one of the belligerents to confer with the other, on presenting himself with a white flag, accompanied by a trumpeter (bugler or drummer), or also by a flag-bearer, shall be recognized as the bearer of a flag of truce. He, as well as the trumpeter (bugler or drummer), and the flag-bearer, who accompany him, shall have the right of inviolability.

Modes of communication between belligerents.

The commander to whom a bearer of a flag of truce is dispatched, is not obliged to receive him under all circumstances and conditions.

It is lawful for him to take all measures necessary for preventing the bearer of the flag of truce taking advantage of his stay within the radius of the enemy's position, to the prejudice of the latter; and if the bearer of the flag of truce is found guilty of such a breach of confidence, he has the right to detain him temporarily.

* Art. 19–22 of the Brussel Conference.

He may equally declare beforehand that he will not receive bearers of flags of truce during a certain period. Envoys presenting themselves after such a notification from the side to which it has been given, forfeit their right of inviolability.

The bearer of a flag of truce forfeits his right of inviolability, if it be proved, in a positive and irrefutable manner, that he has taken advantage of his privileged position to incite to or commit an act of treachery.

14°. *Capitulation.*

Convention of Capitulation.

§ 194. The conditions of capitulations shall be settled by the contracting parties.

These conditions should not be contrary to military honour.

When once settled by a convention, they should be scrupulously observed by both sides. (Comp. § 131. Conventions for the suspension of hostilities).

15°. *Armistices.*

General Rules with regard to suspension of hostilities.

§ 195. An armistice suspends warlike operations by a mutual agreement between the belligerents. Should the duration thereof not be fixed, the belligerents may resume operations at any moment; provided, however, that proper warning be given to the enemy, in accordance with the conditions of the armistice.

An armistice may be general or local. The former suspends all warlike operations between the belligerents; the latter only those between certain portions of the belligerent armies, and within a fixed radius.

An armistice should be notified officially and without delay to the competent authorities, and to the troops. Hostilities are suspended immediately after the notification.

It rests with the contracting parties to define in the clauses of the armistice the relations which shall exist between the populations.

The violation of the armistice by either of the parties gives to the other the right of terminating it *(le denoncer)*.

The violation of the clauses of an armistice by private individuals, on their own personal initiative, only affords the right of demanding the punishment of the guilty persons, and, if there is occasion for it, an indemnity for loses sustained. (Comp. § 131, Conventions for suspension of hostilities).

16°. *Retaliation in War.*

Rules for Retaliation in war cannot be settled before hand.

§ 196. At the Brussels Conference the Russian delegates proposed the following rules for Reprisals in war.

1°. Reprisals are admissible in extreme cases only, due regard being paid, as far as shall be possible, to the laws of humanity, when it shall have been unquestionably proved that the laws and customs of war have been violated by the enemy, and that they have had recourse to measures condemned by the Law of Nations.

2°. The selection of the means and extent of reprisals should be proportionate to the degree of infraction of the law committed by the enemy. Reprisals that are disproportionately severe are contrary to the rules of International Law.

3°. Reprisals shall be allowed only on the authority of the Commander-in-Chief, who shall likewise determine the degree of their severity and their duration.

The Conference, however, felt itself compelled to decline to discuss the subject, and the first

Russian delegate, in agreeing to the suppression of this chapter on reprisals in war, made the following remarks:—

"I regret that the uncertainty of silence is to prevail with respect to one of the most bitter necessities of war. If the practice could be suppressed by this reticence, I could but approve of this course. But if it is still to exist, this reticence may, it is to be feared, remove any limits to its exercise. Nevertheless, I believe that the mere mention in the protocol that the committee, after having endeavoured to regulate, to soften, and to restrain reprisals, has shrunk from the task before the general repugnance felt with regard to the subject, will have a most serious moral bearing. It will, perhaps, be the best limitation we have been able to affix to the practice, and especially to the use which may be made of it in future." *

Retaliation in war cannot be settled beforehand, as it would indicate the admittance of rules entirely outside the acknowledged usages of war.

"That retaliation in war is sometimes admissible, says Woolsey," all agree: thus if one belligerent treats prisoners of war harshly, the other may do the same; or if one squeezes the expenses of war out of an invaded territory, the other may follow in his steps. It thus becomes a measure of self-protection, and secures the greatest amount of humanity from unfeeling military officers. But there is a limit to the rule. If one general kills in cold blood some hundreds of prisoners who embarrass his motions, his antagonist may not be justified in staining himself by similar crime, nor may he break his word or oath because the other had done so before. The limits

* Protocols of the Conference of Brussel of 1874.

of such retaliation it may be hard to lay down. In the case of Captain Asgill, a prisoner drawn in order to retaliate for the killing of Captain Huddy, Washington had military right on his side. Asgill, however, was finally set free. Yet any act of cruelty to the innocent, any act especially, by which non-combatants are made to feel the stress of war, is what brave men shrink from, although they may feel obliged to threaten it." *

17°. *Of the sick and wounded. The Geneva Convention.*

The sick and wounded to be treated as agreed by the Geneva Convention.

§ 197. The duties of belligerents, with regard to the treatment of sick and wounded, are regulated by the Convention of Geneva, of the 22nd August, 1864, subject to the modifications which may be introduced in the rules of that Convention.

The Geneva Convention is treated in chapter xxxix, neutral aid in war.

* WOOLSEY. § 132.

CHAPTER XXXII.

USAGES OF WAR WITH REGARD TO THE SEIZURE OF THE ENEMY'S PRIVATE PROPERTY ON THE HIGH SEAS.

1°. *The Doctrine of Inviolability of the Private Property of Individual Members of the Enemy State on the High Seas.*

The principles of the Law of War considered in the light of civilization.

§ 198. The principles of the Law of War *(jus belli)*, as described above, in paragraphs 155 and 169–175, are established under the influence of the International Spirit of Law (§ 14), but the usages of war *(coutumes de la guerre, Kriegsgebräuche)*, as we have seen from their description in the preceeding chapter, are not always in conformity with the principles of the Law of War, as laid down by human Conscience and Sympathy in their striving to bring the practices of actual warfare up to the acknowledged normal standard of civilization, *i.e.*, to bring about conformity with the existing International Spirit of Law (Comp. § 179). But there exists nevertheless a certain correspondence between these principles and the usages or accepted practices of war. This is sufficiently perceptible to serve as a guide that will enable us to find out what may or may not be deemed justifiable practices of war.

One of the most conspicuous deviations of the usages of war from the principles of the Law of War is the peculiar custom, which yet exists, to seize and confiscate all private property of the enemy on the high seas,—a custom which on land is called pillage, and as such banished from the practices of war among civilized Nations.

This anomaly in the usages of war of a civilized generation is due to the tenacity with which some Nations persist in adhering to the ancient practices sanctioned at one time by the barbaric propensities of former generations. This anomalous practice is the more surprising as it is maintained side by side with a military code characterized by the most conspicuous marks of an advanced civilization. The cause of this partial barbarism is to be looked for in certain influences predominating in State government, which are maintained by traditional national prejudices, and fostered by narrow minded selfishness, and this notwithstanding all the most able and conscientious efforts made, from within and without, with a view to overcome these prejudices. *

All barbaric practices in war are the result of the mischievous assumption that war is a relation between individual members of the belligerent States, and not simply a relation between States only, as we have endeavoured to explain in paragraphs 170 & 175.

---

* The writers of the last and present centuries, who have most effectually opposed the usage of capturing private property on the high sea are the following:—

MABLY. Le Droit Public de l'Europe, fondé sur les traités. Vol. II. p. 310. LINGUET. Annales politiques. Anno 1779. Vol. V. p. 506. Prof. F. MARTENS. De la propriété privée en temps de guerre. Dr. AEGIDI & KLAUHOLD. Frei Schiff unter Feindes Flagge. 1867. ERCOLE VIDARI. Del rispetto della proprieta privata fra gli Stati in Guerra. Pavia. 1867. EUGÈNE CHAUCHY. Du respect de la propriété privée dans les guerres maritimes Paris, 1866. BLUNTSCHLI. Du droit du butin en général et spécialement du droit de prise maritime. Revue de Droit Intern. Vol. IX. (1877) p. 539 and Vol. X (1878). p. 60. E. DE LAVELEYE. Du respect de la propriété privée sur mer en temps de guerre. Revue de Droit Intern. Vol. VII (1875). p. 560. PIERANTONI. Les prises maritimes d'après l'école et la législation Italienne. Revue de Droit Intern. Vol. VII (1875). p. 618. FIORE. Nouv. Droit Intern. Part II. Chapts. VII, VIII. G. MASSÉ. Le Droit commercial dans ses rapports avec le droit des gens. Paris

It is true, that there are instances in which private citizens have taken an active share in a war waged between their respective Governments, and many may sacrifice their fortune on the altar of the common country and give freely their life-blood in its defence, thus contributing, at their own private risk, to the success of their country's cause, but can these single cases of heroism and devotion be used as arguments to upset all principles of Justice and Benevolence, or as motives to arrive at the conclusion that the war must be waged against every individual member of the enemy State? If this were so, there could be no legal reason against admitting the belligerent right to murder every single member of the enemy State, to plunder indiscriminately and to declare all that we can lay hand on, belonging to our enemy, to be legal prize, and this in order to reduce the whole enemy population; thus securing peace through the extermination or at least utter prostration of the enemy. A doctrine from which such conclusions could be derived is really intolerable. Its principal argument, that war will be the sooner terminated if the enemy is mercilessly attacked in his home industry, in his foreign trade and in every private interest of the individual members of the enemy, has no reasonable ground. All the wars which during this century have devastated Europe serve more or less to prove that general hatred and animosity on the part of the mass of a people

---

1874. Vol. II. Livre II. ERNEST NYS. La Guerre Maritime. Etude de Droit International. Brussels, 1881. In Chapter VIII of this valuable essay we find a very clear and instructive review of the different efforts made, during the last and the present centuries, to establish the rules of maritime warfare, with regard to the private property of the individuals of an enemy State, in conformity with the usages of war as waged on land. "La contradiction est flagrante," says the learned Judge of the Brussel Tribunal, "et il n'est pas besoin de démontrer que l'état actuel des chôses réclame impérieusement une réforme." (l. c. p. 134.)

is invariably the natural result of hardship unjustly inflicted on the private individuals and that a general desire to make peace is not brought about by cruel reprisals. * Truly, Goethe was inspired by his good genius when he conceived it as characteristic of Mephistopheles to rejoice in the doctrine that commerce was ever a fruitful source of war and piracy. When tempting Faust by exhibiting before him the glorius array of plunder which his piratical crafts had collected through war waged against peaceable commerce, Mephistopheles used, with a cleverness worthy of an evil spirit, the ingenious expedient of placing the victim on the same level of morality occupied by its spoilers. "*Krieg, Handel und Piraterie, dreieinig sind sie, nicht zu trennen,*" is the doctrine of a Mephistopheles. How often do we not find this Mephistopheles policy practised, under different forms, when plunder of the defenceless is advocated.

But whence comes this desire, as unjustifiable as it is inefficient, to plunder peaceable commerce? For both parties are unavoidable sufferers in the long run, for there exists in reality no such thing as an exclusively enemy commerce amongst civilized Nations. † Are the merchants of the belligerent States the most clamorous for war? Are they the instigators to upset the state of peace which is the element of their existence? No, certainly not. With the exception of individual speculators fond of hazards, the body of the commercial population is naturally adverse to war. But the politicians, backed by those who prefer to fish in troubled water, the aggressive military

* RAYNEVAL. Liv. III. Chapt. V. § 1. PORTALIS, Le père Discours au conseil des prises du 14 flor. an. VIII. MASSÉ. Le Droit Comm. etc. Vol. I. p. 221. Lord Palmerston's speech at Liverpool on the 7th November, 1856.

† MASSÉ. I. p. 221.

party, and those who are fattened by the plunder of commerce, through privateering, prize-money or lawyer-fees,—they are the instigators of war, for they alone have nothing to lose but all to gain, whether in glory or in the shape of other more substantial acquisitions, reaped by plunder, through the prize court or from the public treasury.

Is it then to be wondered at, that at the present stage of development reached by the European International Spirit of Law, which has worked already such marked progress in the manner of waging war, that we still find the capturing of private property on the high seas an acknowledged usage of war? The cause of the persistency of this usage of war is to be looked for, not so much in the exigencies of war *(Kriegsraison)* as in the tenacity of national prejudice fostered by individual selfishness.

Dr. Woolsey says, "there has long been a difference between the treatment of enemy property, —including in this term the property of individual subjects of the hostile State,—on land and on the sea, or more generally between such as falls within the power of invading armies, and such on the sea and along the coast as falls within the power of armed vessels. The former is to a certain extent protected. The latter, owing to the jealous feelings of commercial rivalship, hardened into a system by Admiralty Courts, has been extensively regarded as lawful prey." *

Make commerce as free in times of war as is possibly consistent with the actual means of defence and with an effective carrying on of the war, abolish completely the ignominious systems of booty and prizes, as not worthy a place in the procedure of modern civilization, lop the excrescences of aggression from the noble stem of Na-

* WOOLSEY. Edit. 1879, p. 207.

tional Defence,—you will then have cut off the main stays of the instigators of war, and the object of war, which is peace, will be more speedily accomplished.

Attack the arch-instigators of war, and not the noble apostles of peace, who, as your own conscience ever tells you, are leaders on the right road to true civilization, such as the Moral Law of Nature indicates, though they be perhaps too far in advance of the present generation, to serve as practical guides.

When narrow-minded jealousy aroused by the enemy's progress in commerce,—which has been the only cause of so many maritime wars of the last century, and is not less threatening in our days,—has no chance of enforcing its malevolence, when the military creed is purified from notions of aggression, when prize-money is no more to be easily pocketed as the reward for the hunting down of defenceless merchant vessels on the high seas, and lawyers desert the prize courts,—you will be nearer to peace than ever Nations were in the golden age of plunder, general reprisals and privateers, enhanced by prize court lustration.

Instances of practical application of the doctrine.

§ 199. In conformity with the principles noted in the preceding paragraphs, we find in modern history several instances of practical application of the doctrine, that the private property of individual members of the enemy State should be regarded as inviolable, on the high seas as on land.

In the treaty between the then newly formed republic of the United States of North-America and Frederic the II of Prussia, signed at The Hague on 10th September, 1785, * (called, after its negotiator, the treaty of Franklin), the principle of inviolability of peaceable commerce was

* Recueil, Martens. II, 566.

upheld by the stipulation (art. 23) that, in the case of war between the contracting parties, pacific merchant vessels and traders should be left unmolested by either belligerent party. It is now a century ago, that between two independent States the principle was established (as Dr. Woolsey puts it), "that all private property on the sea, engaged in a lawful trade to permitted ports, should be allowed to cross the seas in safety." * This principle is thus no pious chimæra, as it has been called, † and it is expected, ere long, to be recognized, as an established rule of International Law, even by those who are its most ardent opposers. Even Ortolan, who is regarded as the best modern defender of the practice of capturing private property when employed in peaceable commerce on the high seas, rejects the doctrine of personal liability in war of private individual members of belligerent States, and gives the following basis for the usages of war.

"*En général, on peut dire que les règles observées par les peuples belligérants, à l'égard les uns des autres, sont basées sur les principes suivants.*"

"*La guerre est une relation d'État à État et non pas une relation d'individus à individus isolés.*"

"*C'est une lute violente entre des corps collectifs, pendant laquelle chacun d'eux est autorisé à s'approprier par la force les biens et les droits de son ennemi; mais les biens et les droits des membres individuels, étant distincts de ceux du corps entier, doivent être respectés.*" ‡

After the treaty of 1785 between the United States and Prussia, it was France that next proclaimed and brought into practice the immunity of private property at sea. In 1792 the

* WOOLSEY. p. 248.

† HEFFTER. Droit Intern. de l'Europe § 139.

‡ ORTOLAN. Régles Intern. et Dipl. de la Mer. Edit. 1864, p. 27.

Legislative Assembly of France, on the motion of Kersaint, member for Paris, voted, on 30th of May, the following decree. "*Le Pouvoir Executif est invité a négocier avec les puissances étrangères, pour faire supprimer, dans les guerres qui pourraient avoir lieu sur mer, les armements en course, et pour assurer la libre navigation du commerce.*" On the 19th of June, 1792, the Minister of Foreign Affairs of France, Mr. de Chambonas, sent a circular note to the representatives of France at foreign Courts, with instructions to open negotiations, for the carrying out of the decree of 30th May afore-mentioned. Only the United States of America responded unconditionally favourable to these generous propositions, through its Secretary of State, Mr. Jefferson, relating the principles contained in the recent treaty with Prussia.

During the Franco-Spanish war of 1823, Mr. de Chateaubriand, Minister of Foreign Affairs, announced by his circular note of April 12 of that year, to the representatives of France at the Courts of Maritime Powers, that France would abstain from giving letters of marque to privateers and that the Royal Navy would fight only Spanish war-vessels; all private property at sea, whether enemy or neutral, would be left unmolested. Subsequently, in December, 1823, President James Munroe, wishing to consolidate this good example displayed by France into an established code of international rules, proposed to France, Great-Britain and Russia an international convention to regulate the principle of general commercial neutrality on the basis of the United States' treaty with Prussia of 1785, but only Russia gave an efficient answer to the American project, * and, in spite of the efforts of indi-

* See WHEATON. Elem. of Int. Law. Edition of William Beach Lawrence, p. 430, note.

vidual members of Legislative bodies, the best portion of the Press, Scientific Academies and different Chambers of Commerce, it was not until 1856, after the Crimean war, that decided progress was made in maritime warfare, by the well-known Declaration of Paris, when the old barbaric doctrine of *bellum omnium contra omnes*, with the system of privateering built on it, was for ever abandoned. (See Chapter XXXIII).

The most decided step in the right direction was the sound position taken up by the Italian Legislature, which, on the proposal of the Government, adopted in Art. 211 of the Maritime Code of 1865, the principle of general immunity of enemy commerce on the just basis of reciprocity. This principle was carried out in the war waged by Prussia and Italy against Austria in 1866 and in the Franco-German War of 1870, and it was also introduced into the treaty of Italy with the United States of America, of 26th February, 1871.

Halleck's statement.

With regard to the existing differences between war on land and maritime warfare, Halleck makes the following statements. "Several of the ablest continental writers oppose this distinction on principle. The Abbé Mably advocated an entire freedom of commercial intercourse in war, even between the subjects of the belligerent Powers; and Emerigon, yielding to the arguments of the Abbé, expresses an earnest desire that the laws of war may be modified or changed accordingly. Others, again, think that the change should extend only to the adoption of the principle that private property on the high seas should be subject to the same rules in war as private property on land; without any modification of the law of war respecting the commercial intercourse of subjects of the belligerent Powers. Napoleon

I. in his Memoirs, dictated at St. Helena, says: '*Il est à désirer qu'un temps vienne, ou les mêmes idées libérales s'étendent sur la guerre de mer, et que les armées navales de deux puissances puissent se battre sans donner lieu à la confiscation des navires marchands, et sans faire constituer prisonniers de guerre de simples matelots du commerce*,' etc. The great advantages which England, by means of her naval superiority, has derived from the capture of private property upon the high seas, have tended very much to the maintenance of the rigour of the ancient rule of commercial warfare, while other Nations have adopted more liberal principles and views in war on land, whereby the interests and happiness of the human race have been greatly promoted." *

The government of the United States proposed to add to the first article of 'the declaration concerning maritime law,' made by the Conference of Paris, April 16, 1856, the following words: 'and the private property of the subjects or citizens of a belligerent on the high seas shall be exempted from seizure by public armed vessels of the other belligerent, unless it be contraband.'

This proposition was favourably received by several Cabinets, but European civilization seems not to have arrived, as yet, at that stage of development which would secure the general adoption of this rule of equity and simple fairness in maritime warfare.

The arguments of the opposite doctrine.

§ 200. After having noted, in the preceding paragraphs, the principles of the Law of War, with regard to the inviolability of inoffensive private property of individual members of enemy States, which principles are corroborated by the

* MABLY. Droit Public, etc. Chapt. XII. p. 308. NAPOLEON. Mémoires, etc., tome III. Chapt. VI. HALLECK, Vol. II. p. 125.

actual usages of war, in dealing with private property on land, as described in paragraphs 180–191, we must now proceed to investigate the arguments, which the supporters of the opposite doctrine bring forward in defence of the capturing of inoffensive private property at sea, as a necessary and indispensable practice of war. *

The principal argument on which this right of capture at sea is based, is the difference which is said to exist between private property on land in an occupied territory and that on the high seas. Ortolan, whom Dudley Field (Draft outlines, etc. p. 527) regards as having advanced the best arguments in defence of the practice of capturing inoffensive private property at sea, states his argument in the following words.

Ortolan's arguments.

"*L'assimilation complète qu'on prétend établir, pour la solution de cette question, entre les relations des peuples par la voie de mer et leurs relations par la voie de terre, aboutit souvent à des consequences erronées. La mer et la terre son des éléments si différents, que tout ce qui se passe sur l'un et sur l'autre, bien que basé sur les mêmes principes généraux, doit présenter nécessairement dans l'application des differences notables. Ces différences sont nombreuses à l'état de paix; elles le sont plus encore à l'état de guerre.*

On ne peut pas assimiler le commerce maritime au commerce pacifique et sédentaire qui a lieu sur terre; on ne peut pas dire qu'un navire marchand

* The writers on International Law of the present century, who, on various grounds, more or less decidedly defend the theory of booty and prizes, are the following.
ORTOLAN. Règles Intern. et Dipl. de la Mer. (Ed. 1864) Vol. II. p. 40, et seq. HAUTEFEUILLE. Des Droits et des Devoirs des Nations neutres. Edit. 1858. Vol. I. p. 160, et seq. Sir ROBERT PHILLIMORE. Comm. on Intern. Law. Vol. III. Edit. 1873. p. 361, et seq. Sir TRAVENS TWISS. The Law of Nations in time of war. Edit. 1863. Chapts. 6 & 9. W. E. HALL. Intern. Law. (Edit. 1880), pages 60 & 61, and p. 375, et seq.

soit comme un magasin de marchandises établi à terre. On ne peut pas nier qu'il existe une grande difference entre le fait de capturer et de confisquer un navire et sa cargaison et le fait de s'approprier par la capture les marchandises renfermées dans une boutique, ou les objets servant à l'usage d'un habitant paisible dans le domicile particulier où il a son foyer domestique." *

Whatever argument might be brought forward in favour of private property on land must, theoretically at least, serve equally to defend the inviolability of inoffensive private property at sea, for the principles of Justice and Benevolence are the same at sea as on land.

But the seizure of private property at sea appear, in the light of the principles of the Law of War, to be far less defensible than the seizure of private property on land, if we take the respective hostile character of the owners into consideration.

We have seen above (§ 181) that private property of the individual members of the enemy State is only rendered hostile by the acts of its owners, by the circumstances of its use or by the dispositions made with relation to the materiel used in carrying on the war, or by interdict of all commerce *(edicta inhibitoria*, § 180*)*. When an invading army invests the enemy's territory, the inhabitants are always hostile to the invaders and are all, more or less, directly or indirectly, opposed to the enemy. In so far, therefore, it would be possible to regard the property of those inhabitants as hostile and liable to confiscation in consequence of the hostile demeanor of the owners. Howsoever futile such an excuse may in all ordinary circumstances be, it has nevertheless the prestige of logical reasoning

* ORTOLAN. Règles Intern. et Dipl. de la Mer. Edit. 1864. Vol. II. pp. 40 & 43.

in its favour. But to protect the property of the invaded country, when situated on land, and to declare it hostile when, far from the scene of war, it is simply carried between distant neutral ports, along the neutral highways of the ocean, is a procedure palpably inconsistent with all logical reasoning. It would be absurd to defend the capture of enemy property at sea on the ground that private property on land has sometimes to suffer from the enemy by the occupation of a territory. If there be any difference with regard to belligerent rights in relation to inoffensive private property in an invested or occupied place and in relation to that on the free ocean, it would certainly be in favour of the inviolability of the latter, as being far less liable to become hostile property in conformity with the principles of the Law of War, than the former.

Ortolan continues his argument in the following words.

" *Mais pour nous, les seuls motifs déterminants, ceux auxquels nous voudrions réduire la démonstration, parce qu'ils sont concluants, parce qu'ils simplifient singulièrement la difficulté et nous paraissent peu susceptible de controverse, ces motifs sont:*

1°. *Que la marine marchande, soit dans son personnel, soit dans son matériel, est un moyen de puissance navale toujours prêt à venir en aide à l'état belligérant dont elle relève, à recruter sa marine militaire; en un mot, à se transformer à la première réquisition en instruments de guerre. A ce titre, elle tombe directement sous le coup des forces navales enemies qui pourront l'atteindre.*

2°. *Que si la marine marchande et les marchandises qu'elle porte étaient reconnues libres et inviolables, quoique appartenant à l'ennemi, il serait libre à une puissance belligérante, en ne mettant en mer aucun bâtiment de guerre, de rendre illusoire à son* *égard les effets de la guerre maritime, de continuer à exploiter par ses navires de commerce les mers et les continents, et de puiser ainsi des moyens même de soutenir la lutte, dans les opérations de cette marine marchande, soit par les impôts, soit par l'accroissement de la fortune privée, dont l'ensemble, en définitive, constitue la fortune de l'état.*" *

These arguments are also embodied in the wellknown speech of John Stuart Mill, and may be answered at the same time with the latter.

The speech of John Stuart Mill.

"Mr. John Stuart Mill, who will not be accused of illiberal or retrograde tendencies," says Sir Robert Phillimore, "had the courage and patriotism thus to speak in 1871. 'I should be heartily glad if I could in my conscience believe that we can do without an army, and trust solely to our fleet. But no country is safe with only one line of defence; and we cannot be sure of always keeping our command of the sea without a day's intermission, which would be necessary if our only force were afloat. We must remember that our navy has a great deal to do. We have possessions all over the world, which, in case of war, we are bound to protect as well as our own islands. We may have to contend, not against one Maritime Power only, but against several; and if we persist in sanctioning, by our silence, the act of our late Foreign Minister, done on that authority in 1856 and never ratified, the abandonment of our chief defensive weapon,—the right to attack an enemy in his commerce, the fleets of a Power at war with us will have nothing to do but to watch for an opportunity of landing an army on our shores, and we should not know where the blow would fall. Our fleet has only to be two days out of the way, in search of prey of commercial vessels and our first line

* ORTOLAN. Dipl de la Mer. Edit. 1864. Vol. II. p 47.

of defence is gone. This is not probable, but we must remember it is possible." *(The Times, March 11, 1871. Speech of Mr. John Stuart Mill.)* *

Mr. John Stuart Mill might, without sinning against the rules of logic, fairly have drawn from the premises of British national defence and commerce, the following conclusion to his speech.

If the British fleet had not to trouble itself with the capture of inoffensive private property at sea, thus spending its best powers in inflicting purposeless injury to commerce,—which is sure indirectly to effect British interests all over the world,—its full strength could be concentrated for an essential defence of the British coasts; but, if Great Britain sends her best sailors to privateering, where are the necessary complements for the much needed war-vessels to be got from? As the British Navy has such a great deal to do in defending the extensive national commerce and the colonies and the coasts of the British Isles, it cannot afford to spare any able British seamen for privateers; thus it is obviously expedient that privateering be abolished, so that our seamen may not be enticed from their noble duty in the defence of their country to the more profitable but less honourable work of plundering defenceless vessels to enrich enterprizing speculators, (who might be all, or for the most part, foreigners, for ought one knows,)—who, while filling their pockets, cause the regular Navy to perform a double task, viz., that of watching these privateers, that they might not turn freebooters, plundering their own country's commerce on the high seas, and at the same time, of keeping off the enemy's privateers

* PHILLIMORE. Vol. III. Ed. 1873. p. 361.

and war-vessels, to which British commerce, spread as it is over the whole world, is game in every corner of the earth. So, after all, privateering seems to be for the British Nation not a defensive but rather a most dangerous weapon, cutting on all sides and without a handle to grasp. So let us abandon this treacherous help and look upon our regular Navy as our chief support in war, and, in order to keep this weapon ready for home and colonial defence, avoid spreading our war-vessels over the high seas, only to capture harmless private property in the hope of, somehow or the other, indirectly to damage the enemy's commerce, with the risk of causing ourselves direct injury, for if we drive the enemy's merchant vessels out of a harmless trade (which cannot do us any direct harm), we send these traders' crews to man war-vessels and thus, by our own act, we strengthen the enemy's hands to oppose us in regular warfare, while she can use her idle merchants vessels to carry her troops to our coasts. All this is not only quite possible but most probable if we do not abandon the chase of harmless private property on the high seas, as well as privateering. To stick to these usages of the barbaric ages at the present stage reached by British commerce, when nine tenths of the commerce of the world are directly or indirectly concerned with British interests, would not alone be radically unsound but also unpatriotic and suicidal. * Can the political and commercial condition of Great Britain, in any way, be more like those of Spain or Mexico than of the Great

* At the mere rumour of a prospect of war between Great Britain and France, in 1859, the effect on British shipping in China waters was that the freightning of second class American vessels was 50 per cent. more than that of first class British vessels. (MUNRO BUTLER JOHNSTONE. Hand-book of maritime rights and the Declaration of Paris considered).

European Powers who have abolished privateering, or of the United States of America and Russia who both agree that private property at sea must be viewed in the same light as that on land?

We may fairly close this argument on British trade by quoting the opinion of Mr. Hall on the policy which it is advisable for Great Britain to follow with regard to the system of capturing private property on the high seas. Mr. Hall says:—

Mr. Hall's advice.

"The question whether it is wise for States in general, or for any given State, to agree as a matter of policy to the abolition of the right of capture of private property at sea, is of course entirely distinct from the question of right. It may very possibly be for the common interest that a change in the law should take place; it is certainly a matter for grave consideration whether it is not more in the interest of England to protect her own than to destroy her enemies' trade. Quite apart from dislike of England, and jealousy of her maritime and commercial position, there is undoubtedly a good deal of genuine feeling on the continent of Europe, against maritime capture. It is not clear how far the latter is strong and general, but it is not unlikely that there is enough of it to afford convenient material for less creditable motives to ferment; and contingencies are not inconceivable in which, if England were engaged in a maritime war, European or other States might take advantage of a set of opinion against her practice at sea to embarrass her seriously by an unfriendly neutrality. The evils of such embarrassment might perhaps be transient, but there are also conceivable contingencies in which the direct evils of maritime capture might be disastrous. English manufactures are dependent on the cheap importation of raw material, and our English population is becoming yearly more and more dependent on foreign food. In the Contemporary Review for 1875 (vol. XXVI, p. 737–51) I endeavoured to show that there are strong reasons for doubting whether England is prudent in adhering to the existing rule of law with respect to the capture of private property at sea. The reasons which were then urged have certainly not grown weaker with the progress of time." *

The right to blockade an enemy port, with the correlative rights of visit and search, and the condemning of all trade with the blockaded port, together with the right of prohibiting all trade in contraband of war with the enemy, are the legitimate and necessary restrictions on commerce in time of war, and will, well carried out, answer all the exigencies of maritime warfare. The cruiser which must be detached for the capturing of harmless private property on the high seas, could be more effectually employed in blockading the great commercial ports of the enemy, which are the sources of supply. The war between the two Great American parties was not terminated by capturing private property at sea, but by an effectual blockade, combined with land expeditions, especially through General Sherman's army-corps occupying the sources of supply in Georgia and Carolina.

It is not difficult for an unbiassed mind to perceive that the so-called doctrine of the right of capture of private property at sea is built up on a false basis, not only with regard to the Moral Law, to whose influence the softening of modern manners and civilization is due, but also with regard to the real practical value of the practice itself as a usage of war, as being, by no

* W. E. HALL. Intern. Law. Edit. 1880. Note on page 380.

means, calculated to bring war to a speedy termination. This proves the viciousness of this practice as being based simply on the rapacity of human nature,—a source from which actions flow which generally defeat the main object in view. Rapacity is the mainstay of the practice of plunder in all its forms.

Rules proposed by the Institut de Droit International.

§ 201. The Institut de Droit International, in its assiduous efforts to bring the usages of war in conformity with the acknowledged Spirit of civilization, has exhibited the most praiseworthy activity with regard to questions of maritime warfare and in particular with respect to inoffensive private property at sea. In its sessions held at Zurich, in September, 1877, the Institut adopted the following resolutions with regard to the rules advisable to be followed in modern maritime warfare.

L'Institut constatant les progrès faits par la conscience publique, * progrès attestés par des faits nombreaux et notoires, propose les règles suivantes, comme réformes nécessaires du droit des gens.

1°. La propriété privée neutre ou ennemie naviguant sous pavillon neutre ou sous pavillon ennemie est inviolable.

2°. Sont toutefois sujets à saisie: les objets destinés à la guerre ou susceptibles d'y être employés immédiatement. Les gouvernment belligérants auront, à l'occasion de chaque guerre, à déterminer d'avance les objets qu'il tiendront pour tels. Sont également sujets à saisie les navires marchands qui ont pris part ou sont en état de prendre immédiatement part aux hostilités, ou qui ont rompu un blocus effectif et déclaré.

3°. Un blocus est effectif, lorsqu'il a pour résultat d'empêcher l'accès du port bloqué au moyen d'un nombre suffisant de vaisseaux de guerre stationnés, ou ne s'écartant que momentanement de leur station. Il y a rupture de blocus lorsqu' un navire marchand, informé de l'existence du blocus a tenté par force ou par ruse de pénétrer à travers la ligne blocus.

4°. La course est interdite.

---

* The International Spirit of Law.

5°. Le droit de visite peut être exercé par les vaisseaux de guerre de puissances belligérantes sur des vaisseaux marchands en vue de vérifier leur nationalité, de rechercher les objets destinés à la guerre et de constater une rupture de blocus. Le droit de visite peut être exercé depuis le moment où la déclaration de guerre a été notifiée jusqu' à la conclusion de la paix. Il est suspendu pendent une trève ou une armistice. Il peux s'exercer dans les caux des belligérents comme sur la haute mer, mais non sur les vaisseaux de guerre neutres ni sur ceux qui appartiennent ostensiblement à un état neutre. Le commandant d'un vaisseau qui opère la visite doit se borner à l'inspection des papiers de bord. Il n'est autorisé à se livrer à une recherche du navire que si les papiers de bord donnent lieu de soupçonner la fraude ou fournissent la preuve de celle ci, ou s'il y a des motifs sérieux de présumer la présence à bord d'objets destinés à la guerre. (Session de Zurich 1877. Vote de nouvelle resolution sur le rapport de M. Bulmerincq.) *

2°. *The Right of Capture.*

Principles of the Right of Capture.

§ 202. The right of capture *(droit de prise)* is a belligerent right, applicable to the property of neutrals as well as to that of the enemy. This right is exclusively a belligerent right and can thus be exercised only during actual war.

As States are the belligerent parties, by the principle of the Law of War (§§ 170–181), it

* Annuaire de l'Institut de Droit International. 1878. p. 111. The Institut de Droit International is constantly occupying itself most zealously with the study of the best means of introducing useful reforms in the legislation and usages affecting naval prizes in war. The following numbers of the Annuaire and of the Revue of the Institut contain the principal works of this body and its individual members on this topic. The Annuaire of the Institut of 1877 devoted to this question pages 48–50, 115–119, and 138 and the Annuaire of 1878 also pages 55–113. There are also reports of the sessions held at Geneva, in 1874, at the Hague in 1875 and at Zurich in 1877, where deliberations took place and resolutions were adopted on propositions of committees appointed to report on questions of maritime war, especially with regard to private property. The papers contributed to the Revue de Droit International on questions regarding private property in Maritime warfare are principally the following, by Mr. ÉMILE DE LAVELEYE, in Revue Vol. VII. (1875) pages 559–602. M. ALBERIC ROLIN. Revue. Vol. VII. (1875) pages 603–618. Mr. AUGUSTE PIERANTONI. Revue. Vol. VII. (1875) pages 619–656. Dr. BLUNTSCHLI. Revue. Vol. IX. (1877) pp. 508–557, concluded in Vol. X. (1878) pp. 60–82.

follows, 1°., that no capture can be made except on an authority derived from the State; 2°., that a legal title of property on captured goods cannot be acquired by private individuals except after adjudication of the prize by Prize Courts, in conformity with the laws of the respective State.

The rules and proceedings with regard to capture and recapture are established by the regulations made regarding prizes by every Maritime State and sometimes also in special international treaties or conventions. With regard to the latter, the rules laid down by the Declaration of Paris, in 1856, form the generally acknowledged basis for international agreements on the questions settled therein, viz., privateering and the conflicts which may arise through the occasionally mixed condition of enemy and neutral property, and which, before the rules of 1856 were adopted by almost all Maritime Powers, were settled on different principles by special international conventions. (Comp. chapter XXXIII).

Capture of private property has disappeared from warfare on land, as stated above (§§ 170–181), but is yet existing as maritime usage of war. Neutrals as well as enemies are subjected to this belligerent right.

"The same humane principles," says Dr. Woolsey, "which have put a stop to it on the one element are at work to abridge its sphere on the other. The rule already adopted by the principal European Powers, that free ship engaged in lawful trade makes free goods, has already become nearly universal; and if so, the hostile property exposed to the cruisers of the other belligerent may become so inconsiderable, that the trade of plundering on the sea will be hardly worth carrying on. Meanwhile, the only specious pretexts for marine capture are these two, that the enemy's commerce furnishes him with the means of war, so that it may justly be obstructed, and that the captured vessels are pledges for the reparation of injuries. The former pretext will amount to nothing, if hostile trade can be conducted in such a way as to exempt it from capture. The other pretext would require that ships and goods captured be regarded, until peace settles all questions between Nations, as simply detained to be restored, or have an equivalent paid for them if necessary. We must confess, however, that we indulge in that pious chimæra, as it has been called, that all private property on the sea, engaged in a lawful trade to permitted ports, ought to cross the seas in safety; we have the sanction of the authority of Franklin and of sober propositions made by our own Government (the United States of America), for regarding such a rule as both desirable and practicable; we must esteem it nearer to justice, and certainly to humanity, than the present inequality of risk on the two elements; and it will probably be found, owing to the new rule in favour of neutrals, that marine capture will not be worth retaining." *

The fact, meanwhile, is that, on the sea, the private as well as the public property of the enemy is lawful prize, and all mariners, found on every description of vessel under the enemy flag, whether public, or private, whether combatants or non-combatants, are detained as prisoners of war. This practice has been carried out even against such vessels as have had no notice of the commencement of hostilities, and everywhere except in neutral waters. Recent practice, however, as noted in §§ 180 & 181, tends to the rule that a proper time is allowed to the enemies' vessels in port to withdraw at the declaration of war, and that private

* WOOLSEY. International Law. Edit. p. 248.

enemy property entering innocently territorial waters after the outbreak of hostilities, but without knowledge thereof, is granted the same privilege.

With regard to enemy's public property in the same condition, it is legally liable to confiscation, as it could not be reasonably expected of any State to remit to the enemy any of its means of waging war, whether these came accidentally in the party's territory or were expressly captured by him. "The only exceptional practice which claims to be of some authority, says Mr. Hall, is one of exempting from capture ship-wrecked vessels and vessels driven to take refuge in an enemy's port by stress of weather or from want of provisions. There are one or two cases in which such exemption has been accorded. In 1746 an English man-of-war entering the Havana, and offering to surrender, was given means of repairing damages and was allowed to leave with a passport protecting her as far as the Bermudas; in 1799 a Prussian vessel called the Diana, which had taken refuge in Dunkirk, was restored by the French Courts; and a few years afterwards an English frigate in distress, off the mouth of the Loire, was saved from ship-wreck and allowed to leave without being captured. But a French Ordinance of the year 1800 prescribed a contrary conduct, and in the same year the precedent of the Diana was reversed and a vessel which had entered a French port under like circumstances was condemned. Some writers, without asserting that a rule of exemption exists, think that justice, or humanity, or generosity demand that a belligerent shall refuse to profit by the illfortune of his enemy. Whether this be so or not,—and in the case of a ship of war at any rate a generosity would seem to be somewhat misplaced which furnishes arms for an adversary, and puts them in his hands, without making any condition as to their use,—it is clear that a belligerent lies under no legal obligations in the matter." *

---

* PISTOYE ET DUVERDY. II. 89. ORTOLAN. Dip. de la Mer. Liv. III. Chapt. VIII. HALLECK. II. 152. CALVO. § 932. W. E. HALL. Intern. Law. Edit. 1880. p. 374. MASSÉ. Vol. I. Edit. 1874. p. 316.

In 1854, at the commencement of the Crimean war, it was proclaimed by an order in Council, that all Russian vessels in British ports should be allowed six weeks for loading their cargoes and for departing therefrom, and further, that, if met with at sea by any British ships of war, they were to be permitted to continue their voyage, if from their papers it was evident that their cargoes had been taken on board before the expiration of the above term. The French Government also issued a similar order. The British Government on the same occasion ordered all Her Majesty's subjects who might be resident in Russia to return to their own country within the term of six weeks.

In 1870, at the commencement of the Franco-German War, the North German Confederation declared, that French merchant vessels should not be subject to be captured or seized as prizes of war, by vessels of the Navy of the Confederation, but that this rule should not apply to those vessels, which might be subject to capture or seizure, if they were neutral vessels. The *Staats-Anzeiger*, July 19, 1870, announced that French merchant vessels would be allowed six weeks, from the date of the declaration of war, to clear out of German ports, and would be permitted, during that period, to load or unload. The German Government, at the request of England, gave a formal recognition to the Declaration of Paris, 1856, respecting the right of navigation in time of war. The French Government did the same, and added that, although Spain and the United States did not adhere to the Declaration of Paris, the Government would not seize enemy's property on board a vessel of those Nations, unless such property was contraband of war; nor would the Government confiscate the property of the subjects of those Nations which might be found on board an enemy's vessel. (*Journal Officiel, July* 25, 1870). The French Government, moreover, directed that merchant vessels, belonging to the enemy, which might actually be in the ports of that Empire, or which might enter such ports in ignorance of the state of war, should have a delay of thirty days for leaving these ports; that safe conducts should be delivered to them to enable them to return freely to their ports of dispatch, or to the port of their destination; that the vessels, which might have taken in cargoes destined for France and on French account, in enemies' or neutral ports, before the declaration of war, should not be subject to capture, and that they would be allowed to freely disembark their freights, in the ports of the Empire, and would receive safe conducts, in order to return to their ports of despatch. (Journal Officiel, July 21, 1870.) The French Government strictly limited the last-mentioned advantage to such vessels, when bound to French ports with French cargoes, and refused the request of England that a temporary exemption from capture should be granted to such enemy vessels when bound with neutral cargoes to neutral ports (*i.e.*, to British ports, with British owned cargoes). In the opinion of the English law officers this refusal did not involve any violation of neutral right, by reason of France having granted such an exemption to enemy's vessels, bound with French cargoes to French ports. (HALLECK. Vol. II. p. 127).

Questions arising from the right of capture.

§ 203. The exercise of the right of capture entails the following principal questions, viz.:

1. What may be captured?
2. What constitutes capture?
3. Where may capture be made?

What may be captured?

As to the first question, what may be captured, we have seen above that, by the present usages of maritime war, all property, private as well as public property, belonging to the enemy and found afloat on the high seas, is regarded as lawful prize. The property belonging to neutrals who have violated their neutrality is, under the circumstances of the particular transaction which caused the breach of neutrality, considered to be hostile property and may be lawfully captured, as will be explained in the following chapters.

What constitutes capture?

What constitutes capture? With regard to this question, Sir Robert Phillimore gives the following rules, founded on various decisions of Prize Courts.

"An act of taking possession is not indispensably necessary to a capture; an act of obedience to the summons of a hostile attack or hostile force, though none of the enemy's crew be on board, is sufficient.* The attack on an enemy's ship and the compelling her to run into the port of an ally amounts to legal capture. †

"But if one party take a vessel and afterwards abandon her, and then another take the same vessel, the last seizor is in law the only captor.‡ The inability, however, of the prize master to secure the captured vessel against a rescue, should

* *La Esperanza.* 1 Haggard's Adm. Rep. p. 91. The *Edward* and *Mary.* 3 Rob. Adm. Rep. p. 305. The *Hercules.* 2 Dodson's Adm. Rep. p. 363. The *Resolution.* 6 Rob. Adm. Rep. p. 13. The *William* and *Mary.* 4 Rob. Adm. Rep. p. 386.

† *La Esperanza.* 1 Haggard's Adm. Rep. p. 91.

‡ The *Diligentia.* 1 Dodson's Adm. Rep. p. 405. The *Polly.* and the *Marguerітte.* Note to the *John* and *Jane.* 4 Rob. Adm. Rep. p. 217. The *Lucretia.* 1 Hay and Marriott's Adm. Rep. p. 227.

one be attempted, his inability to bring in the vessel without the aid of the hands belonging to her, is, in reason, no proof of abandonment. If the circumstances of the captured vessel be such as to do away all apprehension of rescue, and inspire confidence that the crew will bring her into port, the property of the captor may be retained as well by a prize-master alone, as by a considerable detachment from his crew. *

"The real surrender *(deditio)* of a vessel is to be dated from the time of striking the colours. †

"Restitution after a first seizure does not bar a second by another seizor; though, if judicially recorded, it would bar the first seizor; but otherwise a second seizure by the same seizor is lawful, though it is made under peril of costs and damages. ‡

Where may capture be made?

As to the question where captures may be made, it must be borne in mind that it is not competent to a belligerent to exercise any right of war within the territorial jurisdiction of a neutral State. As stated above in §§ 90–94, the territorial jurisdiction of a State extends, beyond the actual territory, to a recognized distance at sea from the shore. Captures made by belligerents within the neutral territorial waters thus described are invalid. On the same principle a capture made by boat or launch sent out from a belligerent vessel, lying, stationed or cruising within neutral territorial waters, is invalid, even when the capture by such boat or launch is made outside the neutral territory; for no belligerent is allowed to use neutral territory as his basis of operation. No use of a neutral territory, says

* The *Alexander*. 8 Cranch's (Amer.) Rep. p. 180.

† The *Rebeckah*. 1 Rob. Adm. Rep. p. 233.

‡ The *Mercurius*. 1 Rob. Adm. Rep. p. 80. The *Woodbridge*. 1 Haggard's Adm. Rep. p. 74. Sir ROBERT PHILLIMORE. Vol. III. Edit. 1873. p. 560.

Sir Robert Phillimore, for purposes of war is to be permitted. No proximate acts of war are in any manner to be allowed to originate on neutral grounds. Neither can you without leave carry prisoners or booty into a neutral territory, because such an act is an immediate continuation of hostility." *

The invalidity of captures within these limits, however, can only be claimed by the neutral State, whose territorial sovereignty has been violated, for, as between belligerents, a capture made within neutral waters is deemed lawful. † "It is only by the neutral sovereign, says Sir Robert Phillimore, that the legal validity of such a capture can be called in question, and as to him, and him only, it is to be considered void." The enemy has no right whatsoever, and if the neutral Sovereign omits or declines to interpose a claim, the property is condemnable *jure belli* to the captors. Now it is an established rule of law, that a claim of neutral territory can be made by the neutral Government only, ‡ Lord Stowell says. "This, says Mr. Justice Story, is the clear result of the authorities, and the doctrine rests on well-established principles of public Law." ‖ It is not as Wheaton suggests, "a technical rule," but, as Dana observes, "a direct and paramount question of right." ¶

Duty of the neutral State whose territorial waters have been illegally used by belligerents.

§ 204. It may or may not be, according to the circumstances, a ground of complaint on the part of a belligerent that the neutral declines to make such a claim, but it is obvious that a State which refuses to make a claim for the restitution

* PHILLIMORE. Vol. III. Edit. 1873. p. 562.

† MERLIN. Rep. Vol. XIII. pp. 111–114. Pris maritime, § IV.

‡ The *Deligentia*. I. Dodson's Adm. Rep. p. 412.

‖ The *Anne*. 3 Wheaton's (Amer.) Rep. p. 447.

¶ DANA'S WHEATON. p. 527, note. PHILLIMORE. Vol. III. Edit. 1873. p. 563.

of a prize, captured, in violation of the right of asile, within its neutral territorial waters, can be regarded as having forfeited the right of neutrality. The State in question is bound to protest against the violation of its neutrality and to claim, through its diplomatic agent at the Court of the agressive belligerent, the restitution of the prize through the agency of the respective Court of Admiralty. But that State is not held materially responsible for the restitution of the illegally captured prize or to make compensation, if all the means in its power had been used and failed in their effect. *

Illegal use of a neutral flag by belligerents.

The same principle is applicable in case a belligerent uses the flag, or any other official distinctive token, of a neutral State to surprise and capture an enemy, whether this is done within or outside the territorial waters of the neutral State.

Vessels pursued on the high seas entering neutral territorial waters are safe.

§ 205. With regard to the case in which a vessel, pursued on the high seas, enters, during the chase, into neutral limits, there is no acknowledged exception to the general rule of the immunity of neutral territory. Bynkershoek expresses his private opinion that, in such a case, the continuance, *dum fervet opus*, of the pursuit and capture within the neutral jurisdiction is lawful. †

"True it is," Lord Stowell says, "that that great man (Bynkershoek) does intimate an opinion of his own to that effect; but with many qualifications, and as an opinion which he did not find to have been adopted by any other writers. I confess I should have been inclined to have gone along with him to this extent, that if a cruiser, which has before acted in a manner entirely unexceptionable, and free from all viola-

* WHEATON. Elem. Int. Law. Edit. Lawrence. p. 496, et seq.

† BYNKERSHOEK. Quest. Jur. P. L. I. Chapt. VIII.

tion of territory, had summoned a vessel to submit to examination and search, and that vessel had fled to such places as these, entirely uninhabited, and the cruiser had, without injury or annoyance to any party whatever, quietly taken possession of his prey, it would be stretching the point too hardly against the captor to say that, on this account only, it should be held an illegal capture. If nothing objectionable had appeared in the conduct of the captors before, the mere following to such a place as this is, would, I think, not invalidate a seizure, otherwise just and lawful." *

D'Abreu, Valin, Emerigon, Vattel, Azuni and Sir Robert Phillimore maintain the sounder doctrine that from the moment when the fugitive enemy enters neutral territory he is forthwith placed under the protection of the neutral Power.

"The same broad principle, says the latter, that would tolerate a forcible entrance upon neutral ground or waters, in pursuit of the foe, would lead the pursuer into the heart of a commercial port. It certainly appears, says Sir Robert Phillimore, further, a much safer and juster construction of International Law altogether, to reject the private opinion of Bynkershoek, which he himself admits to be at variance with usage and authority, and to preserve strictly, under all circumstances, the sacred immunity of the neutral territory and to say, with Mr. Chancellor Kent, that there is no exception to the rule that every voluntary entrance into neutral territory, with hostile purposes, is absolutely unlawful." †

---

* The *Anna*. 5 Robinson's Adm. Rep. p. 385. d.

† KENT. Comm. I. (120), p. 125. VATTEL. Liv. III. Chapt. VII. § 133. EMERIGON. Traité des Ass. I. p. 449. AZUNI. Vol. II. p. 223. PHILLIMORE. Comm. Vol. III. Edit. 1873. p. 568, et seq.

3°. *Ransom of Captured Vessels.*

§ 206. The term ransom was formerly applied to the redemption of all captured property, on land as well as at sea, but at present it is usually understood to apply exclusively to the redemption of ships and property captured on the high seas. *The ransom contract.*

When, for various reasons, the captor finds it inconvenient to send the captured vessel into a safe port, it is usual, under the present state of Maritime International Law, to liberate the prize under an engagement to pay a ransom. This is a sort of repurchase the amount of which must, of course, be fixed at a lower sum than the prize would be worth when carried into a proper port. To this end a contract of ransom is drawn up, and signed by the captor and the owner or master of the ransomed vessel, which document serves at the same time as a safe-conduct. The contract is made out in duplicate; one copy, called the ransom-bill, is to remain in the possession of the captor, and the other is given to the master of the ransomed vessel to serve him as safe-conduct for his vessel, with cargo and crew, to prevent her being interrupted on her voyage or retaken by other cruisers of the captor's State or its allies.

The safe-conduct also prescribes the route and limits a time within which the ransomed vessel must reach a designated port, whether neutral or her own. The amount of the ransom-bill is payable to the captor, in accordance with the conditions stipulated therein.

Dr. Woolsey makes, with regard to ransom-bills and hostages, the following statements, which combine most of what has been said on this head by other text-writers.

Dr. Woolsey's statements.

"The receipt for the ransom is of the nature of a passport or safe-conduct, and contains a permission, good against all cruisers of the belligerent or his ally, to pursue a certain voyage. Only in cases of necessity can the route and time laid down be departed from without violating the contract. The contract insures against molestation from other cruisers, but not against other kinds of hazard, and the ransom would still be binding, if nothing were said to the contrary, in case the vessel perished by the perils of the seas."

Hostages to secure the ransom.

"As it is difficult to enforce the payment of ransom during war, the custom has prevailed more or less to deliver over to the captor hostages, who might be detained until the liquidation of the contract, and whose expenses were provided for in the ransom-bill. The hostage being only collateral security, his death or flight cannot release from the contract. If the master or owners refuse to fulfill their stipulation, the hostage's remedy lies in an appeal to the Courts of the captor's or owners' country."

"If a ransomed vessel is captured out of her course and condemned, the ransom is deducted from the proceeds of the vessel, and only the remainder goes to the second captor. If the captor's vessel is recaptured, with the ransom contract, or with the hostages, or with both on board, there is held to be a complete end to all claim for payment. If, on the other hand, the captor's vessel is taken after putting the ransom-bill and hostage in a place of safety, the contract continues unimpaired; nay, it is held so to continue, if the captor's vessel is taken, and the securities for the payment of ransom are concealed so as not to come into the actual possession of the second captor. And, again, when a captor's vessel was captured with the hostage and the ransom-bill on board, in which there was an agreement that payment should be binding notwithstanding a possible second capture, the English Courts decided, that the first captor, being an alien, could not by their laws bring a suit for the recovery of a right acquired in actual war. But in this case the hostage might sue, or, in case of his death, the captor after the end of the war."

"The master of a vessel being an agent for the owners, they are bound by his act, when not fraudulent nor contrary to usage. But if the ransom should exceed the value of ship and cargo, it is held that the owners by surrendering these may be free from obligation."

"A ransom contract is not invalid under the Law of Nations, although made in war, since it contemplates a state of war which it seeks to mitigate. Nevertheless, no Nation is bound to allow its citizens to give or receive ransom-bills. By a French Ordinance of 1756, privateers were forbidden to ransom a vessel until they had sent three prizes into port. The power of granting ransom has been taken away by Acts of Parliament from English cruisers, except in extreme cases to be allowed by the Courts of Admiralty. The reason alleged for this legislation is, that captors might abuse their power of ransoming vessels and injure neutral trade. To this it may be added that ransom is forbidden by Sweden in a regulation of 1788, by Denmark in one of 1810, by Holland in an Ordinance of 1781, by Russia apparently since 1787, and by Spain, so far as neutral vessels are concerned, since 1782. In France no neutral ship can be ransomed, nor can an enemy's vessel be ransomed without a certain authorization and certain formalities. Our law (the United States') permits ransom both of hostile and of neutral vessels, on the ground that in both cases it is a mere remission of the rights of the captors to what they take in war, so that every prohibition of it must expressly depend on the regulations of each particular country. *

Hautefeuille opposes the ransom of captured neutral vessels on the following grounds.

Opinion of Hautefeuille and Gessner with regard to ransom of neutral vessels.

1. The seizure of neutral property ought to be pronounced lawful by a decision of a prize-court; hence neutrals would be injured by demanding a ransom from them before such a decision. Gessner's reply to this argument is perfectly convincing; for he argues that "the neutral consents to it, and no one takes from him the right of demanding that his vessel shall be seized and tried. Moreover, the ransom does not deprive him of the eventual benefit of a favourable sentence. The proceedings follow their course none the less, and if they end in clearing the vessel, the captor, of course, must pay the ransom back. The neutral, then, has in this case the advantage of avoiding seizure and of freely continuing his voyage with his cargo."

2. Hautefeuille's other objection is, that by granting ransom to neutral vessels, a Nation and its cruisers are accessories, so to speak, to their carrying contraband to the other belligerent. But the belligerent will be likely to provide for his interests in directions given to his vessels of war; and, besides, the ransom does not permit the neutral vessel, if it has contraband on board, to take it to a blockaded port. It still has another gauntlet to run. Most German and French publicists agree in pronouncing ransoms of neutral property permitted by International Law. †

---

* WILDMAN. Vol. II. pp. 273–275. WOOLSEY. Edit. 1879. p. 253.

† HAUTEFEUILLE. IV. pp. 262–264. GESSNER. pp. 338–343. PISTOYE et DUVERDY. I. p. 287. PHILLIMORE. Vol. III. Edit. 1873. p. 644. WOOLSEY. p. 255.

4°. *Recapture. Right of the original Owner. Jus Postliminii.*

§ 207. As stated above (§ 202), it is a principle of the Law of War that no capture can be made except on the authority derived from the State which is the belligerent party. The captor's right comes to him from the State, so that the State must also decide the proceedings by which the capture is to be pronounced valid. To this end each State establishes Courts of Justice with jurisdiction in matters pertaining to captures at sea, called Prize or Admiralty Courts. If this Court pronounces the capture legal in conformity with the principles of the Law of War, the prize becomes the legal property of the captor, *i. e.* of the State to which the captor belongs. If the capture is declared illegal, the property is restored to its original owner, with or without compensation, as the Court may decide. From this principle it naturally follows that all private title in the case of prizes must be derived from the laws of the respective belligerent State to which the captor belongs and, as no capture can be regarded as legal prize until the sentence of adjudication is obtained from a competent Court, private individuals or third parties cannot obtain a legal title to the captured property except through adjudication of the prize by Prize Courts acting in conformity with the laws of the State. With regard to the captor's right, it should also follow from these principles, that a complete title to a prize taken at sea cannot be acquired by the captor or through him by the State in any other way than through the decision of a Prize Court, so that the exclusive right on the property captured does not commence until the judicial sentence declaring the *Right of property after recapture.*

captured property, whether it have been taken from the enemy or from neutrals who violated the laws of war, to be good prize.

When does the right of the captor commence? When do others than captor or owner acquire an interest in the property?

§ 208. When does the right of the captor commence? This question arises when persons other than the captor or the owner acquire an interest in the property through recapture, or through transfer to a neutral third party. In the former case a legal relation is created between the original owner and the recaptor, through the *jus postliminii;* in the latter instance, between the original owner and the neutral transferee. Thus, as no one can convey an interest which he does not possess himself, it becomes necessary to determine when the captor is legally entitled to the possession.

The propositions stated in the preceding paragraph seem to answer the question, theoretically at least, quite satisfactory. But with regard to the relation created between the captor and the original owner, the rule is applicable that the effectual seizure of such property, being a belligerent right, constitutes in itself a title of ownership or possession, and the fact of the captor having shewn his ability to maintain the seizure is sufficient evidence that appropriation has been performed. As to matters of practice, considerable differences exist in dealing with the question how and when property in prizes commences, and different rules have been adopted at different times and by different Nations. " Some have said, says Dr. Woolsey, that a title commences at the moment of capture, or of taking possession, as though the vessel taken were a *res nullius;* others after twenty-four hours' possession; others when the prize is carried *infra præsidia* and is thus secure against recapture; and others, finally, when a Court has adjudged it to the captor."

"The question, says Kent, never arises except between the original owner and a neutral purchasing from the captor; and between the original owner and the recaptor. If a captured ship escapes from the captor, or is retaken, or the owner ransoms her, his property is thereby revested. But if neither of these events happens, the question, as to change of title, is open to dispute, and many arbitrary lines have been drawn, partly from policy, to prevent too easy disposition of the property of neutrals, and partly from equity, to extend the *jus postliminii* in favour of the owner. * Thus there is no settled view or principle as to the time when a title from capture begins. Perhaps no definite rule can be laid down any more than in answering the question when occupation ends in ownership, which the laws of different States will determine differently. The State's title begins in the fact of seizure according to the rights of war, that is, when the battle is over and the *spes recuperandi* is gone. † But the title can be contested under certain circumstances by neutral Governments, as on the ground that capture was made in their waters; or by private subjects of neutral Governments, as in the various cases of seizure of neutral goods and ships; or by subjects of the enemy, as where licenses to trade were not respected by the captor. If, now, a neutral buys the prize immediately after capture, he buys it subject to the claims of injured parties, and has his remedy in the captor's Courts, provided the latter conveys that for which he had no good title. If the owner ransoms her, he extinguishes the captor's title of whatever kind it be, good or bad. The laws of the State determine the steps which the captor, as the State's agent,

* KENT. I., p. 101. Sect. V.

† PHILLIMORE. III., p. 460.

must take in regard to the property, and especially at what time he is allowed to have an entire or partial interest in the things taken. It is the first duty of the captor, says Mr. Wildman (II., 176), to bring in his prize for adjudication, but if this is impossible, his next duty is to destroy the enemy's property. If it be doubtful whether it be the enemy's property, and impossible to bring it in, no such obligation arises, and the safe and proper course is to dismiss. Of course, if this doctrine, based on English decisions, be true, destruction of neutral ships or property by mistake must be made good by the cruiser's Government." *

Jus Postliminii.

§ 209. *Jus postliminii*, with regard to conditions arising from maritime warfare, is the just claim which the owner of captured property has, to be placed in full possession of all his rights to the property when it is recaptured from the enemy,—whether by his own State or by its ally. If a vessel taken by an enemy escapes from the enemy or is retaken, the property, which by the usage of war was obtained by the captor, is thereby revested in the original owner.

The questions which govern the *jus postliminii* are the following:—1°., To whose benefit does the capture inure? and 2°., when does it so inure? These questions have been treated in the preceding paragraphs, 207 & 208.

With regard to the doctrine of the *jus postliminii*, Dr. Woolsey gives the following explanations.

Recapture. Right of the original owner.

"If, according to the received right of war, a thing taken from the enemy becomes the property of the captor, it might seem that, when retaken, it ought to become the property of the second captor. But since the captor's right comes to

* WOOLSEY. Edit. 1879, p. 242, et seq.

him from the State, the State may decide how far he shall be rewarded, if at all, for his risks and labour in retaking what had belonged to a fellow-subject. It seemed inequitable that the original owner should wholly lose his right to what had been recently his own, while the recaptor, an inhabitant of the same, or of a friendly country, at the end of two acts of violence, came into possession of the same property. And yet, policy as well as justice should hold out a prospect of reward for a recapture, which the cruiser would otherwise be apt to shrink from, and which brought with it its hazards. We are led, then, to the question, when, and how far the rights of the original owner revert to him, and to the right of salvage or the premium granted for recapture." *

The return of property to its first owner appears in the shape of the Roman doctrine of the *jus postliminii.* †

"It must be regarded as a striking illustration of the sway of Roman law over the European mind, says Dr. Woolsey, that the lawyers have taken this road to help the first owner to his property after recapture. For the application of modern postliminy is quite different from that of the Roman. (1.) As to person,—freemen, to whose status it applied by Roman law more than to anything else, do not lose their status in modern times by captivity in war. They are absent, like travellers or merchants, and their rights and obligations go on, as far as personal presence is not necessary for their exercise. It

* WOOLSEY. Edit. 1879, p. 256.

† Probably from *post* in the sense behind, and *limen* the threshold. Compare *postscenium, postsignani.* As *postscenium* denotes the space behind the scene, so might *postliminium* originally have signified the space behind the threshold; thence the fact of a return behind the threshold or into the house.

is true, indeed, that a prisoner of war, escaping from a vessel in a neutral port, is protected against recapture by this right, as he would be among the Romans. But two Nations might, if they pleased, agree to give up such escaped captives; and that this is not done, may be best explained on the ground that the laws of one country do not extend into the territory of another, and especially that the laws of a war in which I have no part, ought not to affect my friend or subject within my borders,—the principle, in short, which makes express conventions of extradition necessary. And, again, Roman postliminy applied to slaves, but as slavery is not sanctioned by the modern Law of Nations, it can obtain no application in regard to them. As for the private relations of returned captives, the Roman law held marriage to cease with captivity, which is abhorrent to Christian doctrine. Public personal relations by modern law continue after captivity, but the laws of each State determine how far their advantages, like salary during absence, for example, can be claimed on return to one's own country. The Roman law refused to admit such claims. (2.) As to the limit of time within which the *jus postliminii* takes effect, we are not aware that Roman law contains any definition. Modern usage gives complete possession of booty to the enemy on land, after he has held it for twenty-four hours, so that the former owner cannot claim it again from the purchaser; the reason for which limit is the difficulty of identifying such articles after a lapse of time. On the other hand, land is restored to its original owner, until peace or destruction of national existence has transferred sovereignty to a conqueror. (3.) By modern law, captured ships with the goods on board, carried *infra præsidia* by the enemy and condemned, become absolutely his, so that, if they are afterwards recaptured or repurchased by a neutral, the former owner has nothing to do with them: their connection with him has wholly ceased. It is only in the interval between capture and complete possession, that the right of postliminy continues. This was otherwise by Roman law; the right affected all those kind of things which were under its operation at all, when they came into the power of the enemy, and the more, the more clearly they had passed into his *dominium*. (4.) As to limit of place, modern postliminy takes effect only within the territory of the captor or his ally, with the single exception, already mentioned, of captives escaping ashore in a neutral port. But the Roman law, it seems most probable, took effect within the borders of any friendly Nation. A Nation may make what laws it pleases in regard to the recapture of the goods of one of its subjects by another, but is bound to follow the *jus postliminii* in cases affecting the property of neutrals." *

5°. *Salvage for Recapture.*

§ 210. Salvage, as noted before (§ 78), is the allowance or compensation made to those by whose exertions ships or goods have been saved from the dangers of the seas, from pirates or enemies. The laws of different Nations vary in the amount of reward which they assign to recaptors from the enemy. The national law decides in cases of salvage between vessels of the same nationality, as treaties must settle the condition between allies in cases of joint capture. † *Reward for recapture. Salvage.*

---

* WOOLSEY. Edit. 1879, p. 256, et seq.

† See Convention between Great Britain and France on joint capture. Lushington's Manual, p. 118.

The law of the United States of America, with regard to the salvage to be paid by foreign owners, is stated by Dr. Woolsey as follows.

"In regard to the salvage to be paid to our recaptors by the owners of foreign vessels and goods, the law of the United States adopts the principle of reciprocity, measuring the amount by that which is paid by the law of the State to which the vessel belongs. In regard to the amount to be paid by citizens or resident foreigners, the law contains various provisions, of from one half to one twelfth of the value; more being granted for the salvage of an armed vessel recaptured than of an unarmed, and more to a private vessel recapturing than to a public armed vessel. In no case is salvage allowed if the recapture occurs after condemnation by a competent authority, since the property is regarded as having passed over from the original owner to the captor. Nor is a crew of a public vessel entitled to salvage for the recapture of another public vessel of the same nationality. *

The provisions of the law of the most important Nations are given at length by Dr. Wheaton. (Elements, IV. 2, §§ 367 & 384.)

6°. *Abandonment of Captured Property.*

Loss of the right of property in the captured goods.

§ 211. Loss of the right of property in the booty or prize, acquired through actual seizure by a belligerent from the enemy, takes place through recapture or rescue, whether by a recaptor or through the action of the crew of the prize itself, or by voluntary discharge or abandonment by the captor.

By voluntary abandonment of the captor the title revests to the original owner, but in the case

* WOOLSEY, page 260.

of salvage by a neutral it is doubtful whether the effect of this abandonment is conclusive. On this point Sir Robert Phillimore gives the following opinion.

"Where the captors abandon their prize, and she is afterwards brought into port by neutral salvors, it has been holden that the neutral Court has jurisdiction to decree salvage, but cannot restore the property to the original belligerent owners: for, by the capture, the captors acquired such a right of property as no neutral Nation could justly impugn or destroy, and consequently the proceeds (after deducting salvage) belong to the original captors, and neutral nations ought not to inquire into the validity of a capture as between belligerents. * But if the captors make a donation of the captured vessel to a neutral crew, the latter are entitled as salvors; but after deducting salvage, the remaining proceeds will be decreed to the original owner. † And it seems to be a general rule, liable to but few exceptions that the rights of capture are completely divested by a hostile recapture, escape, or a voluntary discharge of the captured vessel. ‡ And the same principle seems applicable to a hostile rescue; but if the rescue be made by a neutral crew of a neutral ship, it may be doubtful how far such an illegal act, which involves the penalty of confiscation, would be holden in the Courts of the captor's country to divest his original right in case of a subsequent recapture. ||

7°. *Fishingboats.*

§ 212. An exception to the usage of capturing enemy's private vessels at sea is the coast fishery. *Immunity of fishing-boats.*

* The *Mary Ford*. 3. Dallas's (Amer.) Rep. p. 188.
† The *Adventure*. 8. Cranch's (Amer.) Rep. p. 227.
‡ HUDSON. V. *Guestier*. 4. Cranch's (Amer.) Rep. p. 293.
|| PHILLIMORE. Vol. III. Ed. 1873. p. 640.

The immunity of fishingboats is based on the principle that seafishery is an object of international protection, as stated above in paragraph 121. This privilege they enjoy also during war, so long as they do not abuse their position nor become instruments in the hands of the enemy.

This principle of immunity from capture of fishingboats is generally adopted by all maritime Powers, and in actual warfare they are invariably spared as long as they remain harmless, for it is not to be expected that any State will accord immunities under circumstances of danger to itself. In fact, the present usages of maritime war, with regard to fishing-vessels in general, are based on the true principles of the Law of War, which are invoked on the same grounds in behalf of all inoffensive private property at sea, by the doctrine of inviolability of inoffensive private property of individual members of the enemy State, as described in paragraph 198. *

8°. *Lighthouse Tenders. Pilotboats. Telegraph and Postal Vessels. Vessels on Scientific Expeditions.*

Vessels exempt from capture.

§ 213. Lighthouses, pilotboats, telegraph vessels and all vessels belonging to institutions which are established exclusively for the convenience, security and public safety of navigation, and for the general benefit of all nationalities, are entitled to international protection also during war, as long as interference with them is not absolutely necessary in connection with stringent measures of war.

---

* HEFFTER. § 137. BLUNTSCHLI. § 667. CALVO. Vol. II. § 932. ORTOLAN. Règles Intern. et Dipl. de la Mer. Edit. 1864. Vol. II. p. 51.

Regarding mailboats *(paquebot poste, Post-dampfer)*, we have noted above, in paragraphs 109 and 122, that the privileges which they enjoy result from international postal conventions or special treaties.

If lighthouse tenders are captured, the belligerent captor is bound to provide in the lighthouse service.

Lighthouse tenders are exempt from capture. If the belligerent has not actually occupied the lighthouse, the regular supply by the lighthouse-tender must be allowed to go on in the usual way for the benefit of navigation at large. When the belligerent cuts off the supply of a lighthouse situated on a blockaded coast or on outside islands or shoals, by capturing the means of communication, he is bound to continue the maintenance of the light and its supply by his own means by reason of the general international utility attached to the objects thus occupied or captured by him.

Immunity from capture of vessels on scientific expedition.

§ 214. On the same principle of general international utility, vessels sent out on scientific expeditions, on voyages of discovery, exploration and survey, or for the examination of unknown seas, islands and coasts, are, by tacit general consent of civilized Nations, exempt from the contingencies of war and from capture. "Like the sacred vessels which the Athenians sent with their annual offerings to the temple of Delos, says Halleck, they are respected by all Nations, because their labours are intended for the benefit of all mankind. Thus, when Captain Cook sailed from Plymouth, in 1776, in the ship 'Resolution,' accompanied by the 'Discovery,' M. de Sartine, the French Minister of Marine, despatched a letter to the Admiralty and to the chambers of commerce throughout the kingdom, to be communicated to the owners and captains of vessels cruising as privateers or otherwise, directing them, in case they met him at sea, to treat him and his vessels as neutrals and friends, provided that he, on his side, abstained from all hostility. This praiseworthy example has since been followed by all civilized Powers toward vessels similarly employed." *

It has also invariably been the practice with European Powers, to grant safe conducts to ships sent to explore the Arctic regions against being captured by ships of war on their return, in the event of war breaking out during such absence.

It is, however, usual and proper for the Government sending out such expeditions, to give formal notice to other Powers, describing the character and object of the expedition, the number of vessels employed, the nature of their armament, etc., in order that they may issue the proper instructions to their own vessels on the high seas. Such expeditions must confine themselves most strictly to the object in view; if they commit any act of hostility, they forfeit their exemption from capture. †

9°. *Ownership of Goods at the Time of Capture.*

Rules of Prize Courts to establish the ownership of private property at sea.

§ 215. The legality or illegality of a capture depends upon the ownership of the goods at the time of capture; for, when goods are found in a captured enemy vessel, it must be proved whether such goods belong to the enemy and are confiscable or to neutrals and consequently free in conformity with the Declaration of Paris of 1856.

The neutral violates none of his duties towards either belligerent by carrying on a lawful trade with the opposing party. The only question is that of *bonâ fide* ownership of the goods.

---

* HALLECK. II. p. 151.

† EMÉRIGON. Traité des Assurances. Ch. XII. § 19.

The following rules have been established by Admiralty Courts.

1°. All goods found in an enemy vessel are considered enemy property, unless the contrary can be proved.

2°. The captor comes in place of the enemy and capture is considered as delivery of the goods at the destination expressed in the respective bills of lading. If the goods are, on arrival at their place of destination, to be the property of an enemy, they are confiscable at the capture. *

3°. Goods shipped, from an enemy port by enemy subjects or domiciled residents to neutral consignees, are exempt from capture and confiscation. This rule, however, has often been the source of much sophistry in legal proceedings. (Comp. § 216).

4°. As against captors, the ownership of property cannot be changed while it is *in transitu.* †

5°. A change in the national character of the owner, taking place during the voyage, is not allowed to change the hostile character of the property *in transitu.* If he was an enemy at the commencement of the voyage, the property is condemned even in case he should have become a subject of the capturing Power previous to the capture. ‡

6°. Although the character of the property, as noted above, is not permitted to be changed *in*

* The *Sally.* 3 Rob. 300, note. The *Anna Catharina.* 4 Rob. 107. The *Carl Walter.* 4 Rob. 207.

† The *Sally* Magee. 3 Wall. 451.

‡ A Dutch ship, owned and claimed by merchants residing at the Cape of Good Hope, was captured on a voyage from Batavia to Holland, nearly two months after the inhabitants of the Cape of Good Hope had, under the capitulation, sworn allegiance to the British Crown, and had become British subjects. Their ship was condemned on the sole ground that 'having sailed as a Dutch ship, her character during the voyage could not be changed.' The *Diana.* 5 Rob. 60. *Baede's Lust.* 5 Rob. 233–250.

transitu from hostile to friendly or neutral, so as to exempt it from capture and confiscation, nevertheless, if it be neutral or friendly at the commencement of the voyage, its character may be so effectually altered before its termination as to ensure its condemnation. No matter what its character was at the commencement of the voyage, if its owner is the subject of an enemy State at the time of the capture, it is a lawful prize.

From the above mentioned rules the following general rule evolves. The liability of goods to capture at sea by belligerents is determined :—

a. by the real or constructive character of their ownership at the time of seizure ;

b. by their real character, if hostile at the time of capture ;

c. by their constructive character, if neutral or friendly when seized, but hostile at the commencement of the voyage.

7°. The rights of the captor are vested at the time of the seizure and cannot be divested by any subsequent change in the national character of the owner. Previous to the adjudication by the Prize Court, the owner may have become a neutral, an ally or a subject, but in neither capacity can he claim exemption from confiscation of property seized while he was an enemy.

8°. To warrant a condemnation, it is not in all cases necessary that the owner should be an actual enemy at the time of capture. If the seizure is provisionally made, in contemplation of hostilities, a subsequent declaration of war has a retro-active effect, converting the neutral or friendly owner into a public enemy. "If, said Sir William Scott, the dispute terminates in a reconciliation, the seizure is regarded as a mere civil embargo, but if war follow, it impresses upon the original seizure a direct hostile character." * (Comp. § 166).

9°. The interest or expectancy of neutral creditors in enemy property arrested as prize, even though amounting to a lien upon it, does not exempt it from capture as prize. †

"To permit goods in time of war, says Halleck, to be considered the property of the neutral consignor, instead of the enemy consignee, merely on the ground that the former had assumed the risk of transportation, would at once put an end to captures of enemy's property on the high seas. On every contemplation of a war, in the consignments of goods from neutral ports to an enemy's country, the risk of transportation would be laid on the consignor, and the right of capture would be completely frustrated. Hence, says Sir William Scott, that part of the contract laying the risk of transportation, in time of war, upon the neutral consignor, is invalid; or rather, as the captor has all the rights which belong to the enemy, his taking possession is considered equivalent to an actual delivery to the enemy consignee. The foregoing rule of the Prize Courts of England, that property consigned to and to become the property of an enemy, upon arrival, cannot be protected by the neutrality of the shipper, has been explicitly recognized and acted upon by the Prize Courts of the United States, and approved by American writers of the highest authority. No case directly in point has yet been

* The *Bœde's Lust*. 5 Rob. 245–246. The *Diana*. 5 Rob. 60. DUER. On Insurances. Vol. I. p. 441, et seq. PHILLIMORE. Vol. III. § 21.

† The *Mary Clifton*. Blatchf. Pr. Cas. 556. HALLECK. II. p. 136, et seq.

decided by the Supreme Court of the United States, but the doctrine has been affirmed in analagous cases, resting substantially on the same grounds; and Mr. Justice Story, in the United States Circuit Court, says, that in time of war, property shall not be permitted to change character in its transit, nor shall property, consigned to become the property of an enemy upon its arrival, be protected by the neutrality of the shipper. Such contracts, however valid in time of peace, are considered, if made in war, or in contemplation of war, as infringements of belligerent rights, and calculated to introduce the grossest frauds. In fact, if they could prevail, not a single bale of enemy's goods would ever be found upon the ocean. Chancellor Kent, in his commentaries, says, that 'property shipped from a neutral to the enemy's country, under a contract to become the property of the enemy on arrival, may be taken, *in transitu*, as enemy's property; for capture is considered as delivery. The captor, by the rights of war, stands in the place of the enemy. The Prize Courts will not allow the neutral and belligerent, by a special agreement, to change the ordinary rule of peace, by which goods ordered and delivered to the master, are considered as delivered to the consignee. All such agreements are held to be constitutionally fraudulent, and, if they would operate, they would go to cover all belligerent property while passing between a belligerent and a neutral country; since the risk of capture would be laid alternately on the consignor or consignee, as the neutral factor should happen to stand in one or other of these relations.' A contrary doctrine has been held by the Courts of the State of New York, but as the decisions of State Courts are not of authority in questions of prize, the rule, as decided by Justice Story, must be regarded as established in the United States." *

Goods shipped by an enemy consignor to a neutral consignee

§ 216. With regard to the cases when the goods are shipped by an enemy consignor during the war, and under a prior sale or an unconditional contract of sale, the property so shipped vests absolutely in the neutral consignee, and is thus exempted from capture during the voyage.

But, says Halleck, as a neutral cover is the common device by which belligerent interests are sought to be protected, shipments of this character are watched with peculiar jealousy, and the clearest evidence of ownership in the consignee is not unreasonably required. 'It is not sufficient,' says Mr. Duer, 'to establish the title, that the bills of lading and the invoice are in the name of the consignee, and express the shipment to be made on his account and risk; for these documents are indispensable to give even the appearance of neutral ownership. It must be shown by what means the title was acquired. If it is alleged that the goods had been paid for, the payment must be proved. If the goods are claimed under a contract of sale, containing provisions for future payment, or under an order for their shipment, the contract or order must be produced, and must appear to be absolute and unconditional, so as to bind the consignee positively to the acceptance of the goods, and to take from the consignor any right or power to reclaim them (unless in the sole event of the insolvency of the consignee), previous to their arrival. If any elec-

* KENT. Comm. on Am. Law. Vol. I. pp. 86–87; the 'Ann Green,' I. Gallis R. 291 ; the 'Frances,' I Gallis R. 450; Ludlow v. Bowne, I John R. I; De Wolf v. N. Y. Ins. Co., 20 John R. 214; the 'Venus,' 8 Cranch. 253–275 ; the 'Merrimack,' 8 Cranch. 317-327 ; the 'Mary and Susan,' I Wheaton R. 25; the 'San José Indiano,' I Wheaton R. 208–212; the 'Frances,' 8 Cranch 183; Ilsley v. Stubbs, 9 Mass. R. 65: Chandler v. Sprague, 5 Met. R. 306. HALLECK. Vol. II. p. 130, et seq.

tion is given to the consignee, or any power of direction or control is retained by the consignor, the goods continue, in the judgment of law, the property of the consignor and, as such, are liable to capture during the voyage. This doctrine has been clearly established by the British Courts of Admiralty, and affirmed by the Supreme Court of the United States. Thus where an American merchant had ordered certain goods from Holland, then at war with England, and the Dutch merchant, instead of sending the goods to him directly, shipped them on his own account to a third person, and directed his correspondent not to deliver over the bill of lading unless payment was provided for in a satisfactory manner, it was held that the goods, which were captured on the voyage, remained the property of the consignor, and as such were liable to condemnation. So, where the goods were shipped under a positive order from the claimant, but the shippers, with a view to their own security, had the bill of lading altered so as to be transferable to their own order, Sir William Scott held that the goods, being still under the dominion of the shipper and subject to his control, the ownership was not legally changed, and upon this ground condemned the cargo as the property of the enemy shipper.' *

Stoppage in transitu in time of war to prevent capturing.

§ 217. With regard to stoppage *in transitu*, the general rule of the British Admiralty Court is that, in time of war, the national character of property cannot be changed by a transfer to a neutral during the transportation. "That which was enemy's property at the commencement of the voyage, says Halleck, remains liable to capture, until its arrival at the port of destination.

* DUER. On Insurance. Vol. I. pp. 427 & 428; the 'Aurora.' 4 Rob. 219; the 'Noydt Gedacht,' 2 Rob. 13, note; the 'Josephine,' 4 Rob. 25; the 'Carolina,' 1 Rob. 304; the 'Merrimack,' 8 Cranch. 328; the 'Venus,' 8 Cranch. 275. HALLECK. Vol. II. p. 133, et seq.

Nor is the application of the rule confined to a transfer in actual war. If it appear that the immediate motive of the transfer, although made in time of peace, was the expectation of war, and that this fact was known to the purchaser, the contract is held to be equally invalid, as against the belligerent whose right of capture was meant to be evaded. 'These rights, however, says Mr. Duer, are an apparent difference in the mode of applying the rule in these cases. In the latter, positive evidence of the intentions of the parties is plainly required; but, in the first, the fact of a transfer is regarded as conclusive proof of the intended fraud.' This doctrine seems to have been adopted in its full extent by the Supreme Court of the United States." *

The rules of ownership, as noted in this and the two preceding paragraphs, are deviations from Common and Civil Laws, but they have been arbitrarily adopted by Admiralty Courts, as necessary to protect the belligerent right of capture of private property at sea.

10°. *Trade with the Enemy subject to Capture.*

§ 218. On the principle of the *edicta inhibitoria* (§ 180), the property of subjects seized in any trade with the enemy, not expressly licensed, is liable to confiscation. † *Capture on the principle of edicta inhibitoria.*

---

* HALLECK. Vol. II. p. 136, et seq.

† During the Crimean War licences to trade were not issued by the British Government, but it was declared by Order in Council of the 15th April, 1854, that all vessels under a neutral or friendly flag, being neutral or friendly property, shall be permitted to import into any port or place in Her Majesty's dominions all goods and merchandise whatsoever, to whomsoever the same may belong; and to export from any port or place in Her Majesty's dominions, to any port not blockaded, any cargo or goods,—not being contraband of war or not requiring a special permission,—to whomsoever the same may belong; and save and except only, as aforesaid, all the subjects of Her Majesty, and the subjects or citizens of any neutral or friendly State shall and may, during and notwithstanding the present hostili-

An exception to the rule which confiscates all goods imported from the enemy's country during the war, is when the goods were purchased under an order given previous to the commencement of hostilities and when it was not in the power of the owner to countermand the order in time to prevent the shipment. *

But the produce of the soil of the hostile country, engaged in the commerce of the hostile Power, is legitimate prize, without regard to the domicile of the owner. †

A vessel guilty of an unlawful trade with the enemy is liable to capture, at any time, during

---

ties with Russia, freely trade with all ports and places wheresoever situate, which shall not be in a state of blockade, save and except that no British vessel shall under any circumstances whatsoever, either under or by virtue of this order or otherwise, be permitted or empowered to enter or communicate with any port or place which shall belong to, or be in possession or occupation of Her Majesty's enemies.

An Ionian subject was held to be in the same position as a British subject, and his vessel was condemned by an English Prize Court, for trading with Russia during the above-mentioned war. The *San Spiridione*. 2 Jur. N. S. 1238. See Esposito v. Bowden (7 E. and B. 763), and the *Odessa* (Spinks Pr. R. 208), as to the effect of the above Order in Council (and of other similar proclamations), on the trade of a British subject with the enemy, also the *Teutonia* (1 Aspin. Mar. Cas. 32).

A voyage from an enemy to a neutral port, but with directions to put into a British port to obtain a licence, the proof of such directions and consequent intention being clear, was held not to be illegal, or a breach of a certain prohibitive Order in Council of January, 1807; restitution accordingly, with captors' expenses. The *Mercurius* (Edwards, 53) and the *Minna*, therein cited.

The conveyance of passengers for hire held equivalent to the conveyance of goods for freight, and therefore to be a trading within the prohibitions prescribed by the Orders in Council of April 26, 1809, prohibiting all trade by neutrals with France. The *Rose in Bloom*. I Dodson, 58.

During the war waged by Great Britain and France against China, 1858–1860, the principle that all trade with the enemy is hostile was entirely abandoned by the allied Powers, granting their respective subjects, British and French, during and notwithstanding the hostilities with China, all the rights and immunities of neutrals as laid down in the Declaration of Paris of 1856, in all inoffensive trade with the enemy. (*Bulletin des Lois*, 819, No. 7856).

* The *Jufvrouw Catharina*. 5 Rob. 141. The *Fortuna*. 1 Rob. 211. The *Freedom*. 1 Rob. 212. HALLECK. Vol. II., p. 156 and p. 163.

† The *Mary Clifton*. Blatchf. Pr. Cas. 556.

the voyage in which the offence is committed, but not after the voyage is completed. If, however, the voyage is continuous and entire, although broken by visits to separate ports, she is liable to capture while any portion of the voyage remains to be performed, even when that portion of the voyage during which the offence was committed has been completed. *

The same principle applicable to the subjects of an ally.

§ 219. These principles are also applicable to the subjects of an ally. Where two or more States are allied in a war, the relations of the subjects of the ally toward the common enemy are precisely the same as those of the subjects of the principal belligerent. "In this respect, says Halleck, there is no distinction between the two; and if the Courts of their own country do not enforce the rights and duties of war, those of the principal or co-belligerent may do so, for the tribunals of all have an equal right to enforce the Laws of War, and to punish any infraction, whether committed by the subjects of their own Government or of that of an ally. As neither of the allies in a common war can relax, in favour of his own subjects,—without the consent of his co-belligerent,—the general rule which prohibits all commercial intercourse with the common enemy, it is held that the subjects of one State cannot plead in the prize courts of its ally the permission of their own sovereign to engage in such prohibited trade, and that such permission will not exempt from condemnation the property so employed. Sir William Scott makes the following remarks on this point. 'It is of no importance, he says, to other Nations, how much a single belligerent chooses to weaken and dilute his own rights.

* The *Memphis*. Blatchf. Pr. Cas. 260. The *Joseph*. Cranch. 454, 455. WILDMAN. Intern. Law, Vol. II., pp. 20-23. HALLECK. Edit. Sir Sherston Baker. Vol. II., p. 165.

But it is otherwise when allied Nations are pursuing a common cause against a common enemy. Between them, it must be taken as an implied if not an express contract, that one State shall not do anything to defeat the general object. If one State permits its subjects to carry on an interrupted trade with the enemy, the consequence may be that it will supply that aid and comfort to the enemy, especially if it is an enemy depending very materially on the resources of foreign commerce, which may be very injurious to the prosecution of the common cause, and the interests of its ally.' He therefore concludes, that it is not enough to say that one State has given its permission, but that it should also appear that the trade has the allowance of the confederate State, or that it can, in no manner, interfere with the common operations." *

11°. *The Effect of Domiciliation in the Enemy Country on the National Character of Property.*

Effect of the nationality of domicile in war.

§ 220. As noted before (§ 40), domiciliation or permanent abode in a foreign country entails nationality of domicile, which is different from the political nationality, the latter emanating from the State to which an individual owes national allegiance, through birth or naturalization, as described in paragraphs 39 and 40. As most questions of private rights to property or of commercial or political privileges and exemptions, whether in peace or war, are, in the first place, judged by the circumstances of domiciliation, it follows that the nationality of domicile often suspends the claims which the individual has on the protection of his native State, as long as the condition of domiciliation abroad does last.

* HALLECK. Edit. Sir Sherston Baker. Vol. II. p. 155.

An individual settled in a foreign country, where he finds his daily bread or the comforts or pleasures of life, must naturally, during a war to which his native State is a party, share the fate of the hostile or neutral character of the foreign country in which he has fixed his domicile. When he has more than one domicile, as a merchant carrying on commerce in different countries, he is regarded, in time of war, to have the nationality of domicile of all his places of business, and his property, found on the high seas, can be treated by the enemy of any of the countries in which he is domiciled as it may suit the objects of the respective captor,—unless he had by positive declaration, corresponding with overt acts done before the outbreak of hostilities, designated one of his business residences as his principal abode and legal domicile. No changing of domicile by the subject of a belligerent Power is acknowledged by International Law, if this is done after the outbreak of hostilities, with a view to protect his interests by deserting his legal allegiance in time of war. *

From the above stated principles it follows, that property belonging to subjects or neutrals, which are residing in the enemy's country, is, when found on the high seas, liable to be captured as enemy property. Notwithstanding the individual opinion or sympathies of the owner, and although he may be the subject of a neutral Nation or of the capturing belligerent, and may have expressed no disloyal sentiments towards his native country, nevertheless his residence in the enemy's country impresses upon his property

* With respect to the determination of nationality, and as to the question what is to be regarded as that legal domicile from which nationality of domicile is acquired, we refer the reader to paragraphs 39 and 40, in Vol. I. pp. 117–125.

engaged in commerce and found on the high seas a hostile character, and subjects it to belligerent capture.

"A distinction must be here noticed, says Halleck, between the property of a citizen resident in a foreign country, and that of one domiciled in the belligerent State. The property of a citizen domiciled in a foreign country, when that country becomes involved in a war with that of his allegiance, is at once liable to be condemned as that of an enemy. But that of a citizen simply resident in the belligerent State, if condemned on his attempt to withdraw it from the enemy's country, must be condemned as that of a citizen engaged in an unlawful trade with the enemy. The Supreme Court of the United States has decided that the property of American citizens domiciled in an enemy's country, although shipped by the owners before they had knowledge of the war, was, by that event, irredeemably stamped with a hostile character, and the goods were condemned as a lawful prize. But the case of a citizen, merely resident in the enemy's country, presents a very different question. * If it be admitted that it is the duty of a Government to facilitate the withdrawal of its own citizens and their property from an enemy's country, the question next to be considered is the propriety of requiring the citizens to procure a licence from their own Government for the transportation of such property. On this question Mr. Duer makes the following remarks. 'It is doubtless right and necessary that a merchant, not resident in an enemy's country, who desires, at the commencement of a war, to withdraw his

---

* WHEATON. Elem. Int. Law, Pt. 4. Ch. I. § 17; the *Venus*, 8 Cranch. 253.

property and effects, should obtain a licence from his own Government. He is guilty, otherwise, of voluntary trading. The good faith of a person who has the power to apply for a licence and neglect the duty, is liable to just suspicions; and the express permission of the Government is, in such cases, the only adequate security against abuse and fraud. But the propriety of requiring a person, who is seeking to escape from a hostile country, to continue a residence that exposes his person to imprisonment and his property to seizure, until a licence from his own Government can be obtained, so far from being evident, can, by no means, be admitted. His ability to return—to save himself and his property—may depend upon measures, that, to be effectual, must be immediate; and the necessary delay in procuring a licence would operate, in most cases, to defeat the execution of the design.' Mr. Duer, therefore, adopts the conclusion that a licence is not in all cases necessary, and that the property of subjects withdrawing themselves, in good faith, from a hostile country, within a reasonable time after obtaining knowledge of the war, is not stamped with the illegal character of trading with the enemy, but is to be considered by a just exemption from the general rule, as exempt from confiscation. Such would be the probable decision of the question in English prize courts; nor is it by any means certain that an opposite determination would be made in those of the United States. The exact question has not yet been determined by the supreme tribunal; nor is its decision involved as a necessary consequence in the cases that have hitherto occurred." *

* DUER. On Insurance. Vol. I. pp. 564–566. The 'Madonna delle Gracie.' 4. Rob. 198. HALLECK. II. p. 160, et seq.

12°. *Sale of Vessels to Neutrals in Contemplation of War or after the Declaration of War.*

Sale of vessels imminente bello and flagrante bello.

§ 221. The sale of vessels by enemy subjects to those of neutral Powers, in the anticipation of war *(imminente bello)* or even during the war *(flagrante bello)*, is legal, on the principle that inoffensive commercial transactions are allowed between neutrals and the enemy. The only question, as in all cases of property claimed as neutral (§ 215), is the actual *bonâ fide* ownership. In 1857, it was determined by the Privy Council of Great Britain, that the sale of a ship absolutely and *bonâ fide* by an enemy to a neutral, *imminente bello* or even *flagrante bello*, is not illegal. But liens, whether in favour of a neutral on an enemy's ship, or in favour of an enemy on a neutral ship, are, as in the case of goods (mentioned in paragraph 215, rule 9°.), generally equally disregarded by Prize Courts. *

The purchase by neutrals of public or State vessels from a belligerent, *flagrante bello*, is not in

* A Russian subject, immediately before the war between Russia and England, 1854, sold, absolutely and *bonâ fide*, a ship, the *Ariel*, to a subject of a neutral State. Part only of the purchase money was paid at the time of the purchase, the remainder being agreed to be paid out of the earnings of the ship. Before the whole stipulated price was paid, the ship was seized, in a British port, as a prize; and was condemned by the High Court of Admiralty, on the ground that the enemy's interest in the ship was not divested, as the residue of the purchase money was to be paid out of the earnings. This condemnation was reversed by the Privy Council, because the non-payment of part of the purchase money did not create a lien on the freight and ship in favour of the seller, so as to render the ship, in possession of a neutral owner, liable to seizure by a belligerent.

There were six other vessels seized, all belonging to the same appellant. After the delivery of the above judgment, the Crown officers restored these vessels, with the exception of one, the *Bellica*, which they retained on the ground, that the sale of that ship was distinguishable from the others, her sale haven taken place *in transitu*. On appeal, again to the Privy Council, that Court decided that the sale, though *in transitu*, was valid, as the *transitus* had ceased when the vessel had come into possession of the purchaser, which took place before the seizure, and that no distinction could be made between the case of that vessel and the case of the *Ariel*.—Sorensen v. Reg., 11 Moore, Privy Council Cas. 119.

conformity with the principle of strict neutrality. If, for instance, a public vessel, the property of a belligerent State, shelters herself from hostile pursuit in a neutral port and, on account of the difficulty or impossibility of escape, is there sold, it is a violation of the belligerent rights of the opposing party.

It has also been held by British Courts of prize, that ships, like goods (§ 115, rule 5°.), cannot change their character *in transitu.* This rule applies also in cases where the sale is ostensibly absolute, but the vessel continues under the control and management of her former owner and in the same trade and navigation in which she was previously employed, or where the neutral vendee, although residing himself in a neutral country, continues to employ the vessel in the hostile trade to which she belonged. These circumstances are deemed conclusive evidence of a fraudulent intent to cover, under the name of a neutral, the property of an enemy, and the contract is considered to be invalid, because the sole object of the transfer would appear to be to enable the vessel to carry on the enemy's trade without the liabilities connected therewith. *

" The transfer, in time of war, of the vessel of an enemy to a neutral, says Halleck, is a transaction, from its very nature, liable to strong suspicion, and consequently is examined with a jealous and sharp vigilance, and subjected to rules of a peculiar strictness in the Prize Courts of the opposite belligerent. Nevertheless, neutrals have a right to make such purchases of merchant vessels, when they act with good faith, and, consequently, the belligerent Powers are not justified by the Law of Nations, in attempting to prohibit such transfers by a sweeping interdiction, as was

* The *Poglasie*. 2 Spinks, 101.

done in former years by both the French and English Governments. Ordinances of this character form no part of the Law of Nations, and, consequently, are not binding upon the Prize Courts, even of the country by which they are issued. Nevertheless, where the sale is claimed to have been made by an enemy to a neutral, in time of war, it is not unreasonable that its motives, nature and terms, should be an object of the most searching inquiry. The temptation to fraud, in such cases, is so great that the entire transaction should be most strictly examined, otherwise the opposing belligerent might be deprived of his right of capture. * Hence Courts of Admiralty have established very severe rules respecting such transfers. So far as these rules conform to the rules of evidence and logical proof, established by the practice and consent of the nations of Christendom, they are obligatory and can neither be resisted nor disputed. But beyond this they have no force as rules of International Law. For no belligerent Nation can impose upon a neutral its regulations, or dictate to such neutral unusual rules of evidence or arbitrary means of proof. In other words, if a neutral, who has purchased a vessel from a belligerent, holds such vessel by a title valid by the Law of Nations, he cannot be deprived of it by a Prize Court, because he does not prove his ownership according to the arbitrary and unusual rules of evidence which that Court may adopt. If the sale be valid, it cannot be annulled by any rules which a belligerent Nation may see fit to prescribe for itself, but which by the Law of Nations are not obligatory upon neutrals." †

---

* HAUTEFEUILLE. Droit des Nations Neutres. Tit. XI. Ch. II.

† WILDMAN. Intern. Law. Vol. II. p. 84, et seq. PHILLIMORE. Vol. III. p. 448. DUER. On Insurance. Vol. I. p. 446, et seq. KLU-

13°. *Documents to prove a Vessel's Nationality and Ownership.*

§ 222. Vessels are to share the condition of the State under whose flag and pass they sail, whether hostile, friendly or neutral; consequently it is of the utmost importance for all parties concerned, to be able to prove the nationality of a vessel in any given condition. With regard to the documents which must serve to prove the national character of private or merchant vessels, called the ships papers *(papiers de bord ou lettres de mer, Schiffs-papiere)* we refer to chapter xv, treating of the national character and jurisdiction of vessels, and more particularly to paragraphs 102–104 (Vol. I. pp. 433–438), where the conditions of nationality and the papers proving it are described. *Vessels' nationality and ownership.*

In order to be protected, as neutral, against hostile capture, the master must have on board all documents and proofs of the neutral character of the vessel as required by the law of the flag under which she sails or by the special stipulations, *casu quo*, of international treaties. Where the ship appears to be of hostile built, the bill of sale is an important document as a proof of nationality. The rules applicable to registration and transfer of sea-going vessels, as proofs of ownership, such as are generally adopted by the *lex mercatoria* of the principal maritime Nations, are noted in paragraph 66 (Vol. I. p. 278).

"It is stated by Mr. Wheaton, writes Halleck, that, in addition to the certificate of registry, which is the proof naturally to be looked to

---

BER. Droit des Gens. § 234. RAYNEVAL. Droit de la Nat. et des Gens. Liv. III. Chapters XIV & XV. HALLECK. Edit. Sir Sherston Baker. Vol. II. pp. 138 & 141.

for the national character of the ship, the following proofs of property in a vessel and cargo are usually required. 1°. The passport, or sea-letter. This is a permission from the neutral State to the master of the vessel to proceed on the intended voyage, and usually contains his name and residence, the name, description and destination of the vessel, with such other matters as the local law and practice require. 2°. The muster roll, or *role d'équipage*, containing the names, ages, quality and national character of every one of the ship's company. 3°. The charter-party; if the vessel has been let to hire. 4°. The bills of lading, by which the master acknowledges the receipt of the goods specified therein, and promises to deliver to the consignee or his order. 5°. The invoices, which contain the particulars and prices of each parcel of the goods with a statement of the charges thereon. 6°. The log-book, or ship's journal which contains an accurate account of the vessel's course, with a short history of the occurrences during the voyage. 'As the whole of these papers may be fabricated, says Mr. Wheaton, their presence does not necessarily imply a fair case; neither does the absence of any of them furnish a conclusive ground of condemnation, as has been most unjustly provided by the Ordinances of certain belligerent Powers. As they furnish presumptive evidence only of the property in the vessel and cargo belonging to those to whom it purports to belong, so, on the other hand, their absence affords only presumptive evidence of the existence of enemy interests, which may be rebutted by other proof of a positive nature, accounting for the want of them, and supplying their place, according to the circumstances of each particular case.' At one period it was customary for the Government of the United States to issue sea-letters and certificates of ownership to vessels owned by American citizens, whether entitled or not to registry and enrolment. But since the Acts of March 26, and June 30, 1810, these particular documents are not often issued. With respect to ships which have been transferred abroad, a bill of sale is the proper evidence of ownership. A bill of sale, says Lord Stowell, is the proper title to which the Maritime Courts of all countries would look. It is the universal instrument of the transfer of ships in the usage of all maritime countries.* There seems to be some difference in the laws of different States, as well as in the decisions of their Courts and in the opinions of their text-writers, with respects to the character of the documents requisite to prove the neutrality of a vessel, and with respect to the effect of those documents even when their genuineness is unimpeached. Bello is of opinion that the passport, or sea-letter, is absolutely indispensable for the security of the vessel. Article 2 of the French Ordinance of July 26, 1778, requires that neutral vessels shall prove their neutral character by '*passe-ports, connaissements, factures et autres pièces de bord, l'une desquelles au moins constatera la propriété neutre*,' *etc*. And Article 6 of the Ordinance of 1681, says: '*Seront encore de bonne prise les vaisseaux, avec leur chargement, dans lesquels il ne sera trouvé chartes-parties, connaissements, ni factures*.' Abreu was of opinion that these words were to be taken collectively and not distributively. But this is evidently erroneous, for another provision of the Ordinance is (Article

---

* KENT. Com. on Am. Law, Vol. I. p. 130. WHEATON. On Captures, pp. 65 & 66. DUER. On Insurance. Vol. I. pp. 550 & 551. The *Sisters*, 5 Role, 155; the *Pizarro*, 2 Wheaton R. 227; the *Amiable Isabella*, 6 Wheaton R. 1; the *Nereida*, 9 Cranch, 388.

13), that no friendly or neutral vessel is to be made prize, if the captain produces the '*charte-partie ou police de chargement*,' which latter word signifies the same as *connaissement*. Massé

* MASSÉ. Droit Commercial. Liv. II. Tit. I. § 343. HAUTEFEUILLE. Des Nations Neutres. Tit. XII. MERLIN. Repertoire, verb. Prises Maritimes. § 3. ABREU. Traité des Prises. Pt. I. Ch. II. § 17. HALLECK. Vol. II. p. 143, et seq.

The following list, extracted from Mr. Godfrey Lushington's Manual of Naval Prize Law, is taken over by Halleck, as specifying what are the various papers in addition to the Custom House clearance, the manifest of cargo, and the bills of lading which may usually be found on board the vessels of the principal Maritime States viz.:—

AUSTRIA.

Scontrino ministeriale (Certificate of registry).
Patente sovrana (royal licence).
Giornale di navigazione (official log-book).
Scartafaccio, giornale di navigazione cotidiano (ship's log-book).
Charter-party, if vessel is chartered.
Ruolo dell'equipaggio (list of crew).
Bill of health.

BRAZIL.

Passaporte de navigacion. Acta de propriedad del buque. Rol. Conocimientos.

DENMARK.

Royal passport, in Latin, with translation (available only for the voyage for which it is issued, unless renewed by attestation).
Certificate of ownership and registry.
Build-brief (certificate of build).
Admeasurement-brief.
Burgher-brief (certificate that the master is a Danish subject).
Charter-party (if vessel is chartered).
Muster-roll.
The letters D. E. (Dansk Eiendom) burnt into the mainbeam in the after part of the main hatchway.

FINLAND.

Materbref (certificate of measurement).
Belbref (certificate of build).
Journalen (ship's log-book).
Charter-party (if vessel is chartered).
Volkpass (crew list).

FRANCE.

L'acte de francisation (certificate of nationality).
Le congé (sailing licence).
Le journal timbré (stamped log-book, signed by consul on clearance of vessel).
Le Journal du bord (ship's log-book).
National flag.
Charter-party (if vessel is chartered).
Le rôle d'équipage (list of crew).
Bill of health.

GERMANY.

Certificate of nationality.
Messbrief (certificate of measurement).

seems to think that the absence of a passport is a necessary cause of confiscation, and that it cannot be replaced by any other document. But Hautefeuille, Pistoye and Duverdy and others,

---

Beilbrief (builder's certificate).
Seepass (sailing licence).
Journal (ship's log-book).
Charter-party (if vessel is chartered).
Musterrolle (muster-roll).

GREAT BRITAIN.

Certificate of Registry.
Official log-book.
Ship's log-book.
National flag.
Code of signals and numeral flags.
Charter-party (if vessel is chartered).
Shipping articles.
Muster-roll.
Bill of health.

Where a vessel, not on the register, becomes at a foreign port the property of persons qualified to be owners of a British vessel, the British consular officer there may grant a provisional certificate, to be in force for six months or until she arrives at some port where there is a British registrar; and this certificate is to contain the name of the vessel, the time and place of her purchase, and the names of her purchasers, the name of her master, and the best particulars as to her tonnage, build, and description that he is able to obtain. (17 and 18 Vict. C. 104, Sec. 54.)

A pass, with the force of certificate within the time and limits mentioned therein, may be granted in the case of a British vessel before registry, to proceed from any one port or place to any other, both being in Her Majesty's dominions. (Ibid. sec. 98.)

ITALY.

Scontrino ministeriale (certificate of registry).
Patente sovrana (royal license).
Giornale di navigazione (official log-book).
Scartafaccio, giornale de navigazione cotidiano (ship's log-book).
Charter-party (if vessel is chartered).
Ruolo dell' equipaggio (list of crew).
Bill of health.

MEXICO.

La patente de navigacion (sailing license).
El diario de navigacion (ship's log-book).
El rol (list of crew).

NETHERLANDS.

Meetbrief (certificate of tonnage).
Bylbrief (certificate of ownership).
Zeebrief (sailing license).
Journaal (ship's log-book).
National flag.
Charter-party (if vessel is chartered).
Monster-rol (Muster-roll).
Bill of health.

do not consider it as indispensable, and such has been the decision of the French Courts. According to English and American decisions, the neutral character of a vessel may be sustained with-

---

NORWAY.

Bülbrev (certificate of build).
Maalebrev (certificate of measurement).
Nationalitets brevüs (certificate of nationality).
Journal (ship's log-book).
Charter-party (if the vessel is chartered).
Muster-roll or mandskabsliste, or volkelist (list of crew).
Vessels purchased by Norwegian subjects in foreign ports are permitted for two years to sail without a bülbrev or maalebrev.

PORTUGAL.

Passaporte di navigacion. (Sea pass.)
Acto de propiedad del buque.
Rol conocimentos.
Recibos de fletes y despacho.
A copy of the code of commerce.

RUSSIA.

L'acte de construction ou d'acquisition du navire (builder's certificate).
La patente portant authorisation d'arborer le pavillon marchand Russe (certificate of nationality).
Journal du capitaine (ship's log-book).
Charter-party (if vessel is chartered).
Le role d'equipage (crew list).

SPAIN.

La patente real (royal license).
El diario de navigacion (ship's log-book).
National flag.
Charter-party (if vessel is chartered).
El rol (list of crew).
Bill of health.

SWEDEN.

A passport from a Chief Magistrate or Commissioner of Customs.
Bilbref (builder's certificate).
Mätebref (certificate of measurement).
Fribref (certificate of registry).
Journalen (ship's log-book).
Charter-party (if vessel is charrered).
Volkpass or sjemansrubla (muster-roll).
Vessels purchased by Swedish subjects in foreign ports are permitted, on application to the Board of Commerce, to sail for one year without a fribref.

UNITED STATES.

Certificate of registry.
Certificate of Consular record of ownership, is to be issued to citizens of the United States being purchasers of American or foreign built vessel's in a foreign port. (This certificate is attached to the respective bill of sale).
Ships log book.
National flag.

out her having on board either register, or passport; although, in the absence of both, the presumption would be against her." *

Charter-party (if the vessel is chartered).
Shipping articles.
Muster-roll.
Bill of health.

To enable the owners of foreign vessels (whether originally American or foreign built) purchased in a foreign port, to protect their rights, if molested or questioned, a Consular Officer, though forbidden by law to grant any marine document or certificate of ownership, may lawfully make record of the bill of sale in his office, authenticate its execution, and deliver to the purchaser a certificate to that effect; certifying, also, that the owner is a citizen of the United States. Before granting such certificate, the Consular officer will require the tonnage of the vessel to be duly ascertained in pursuance of law, and insert the same in the description of the vessel in his certificate. These facts thus authenticated, if the transfer is in good faith, entitle the vessel to protection as the lawful property of a citizen of the United States; and the authentication of the bill of sale and of citizenship will be *primâ facie* proof of such good faith. (United States Consular Regulation of 1881. Art. XX. § 340. Form No. 35).

CHAPTER XXXIII.

THE DECLARATION OF PARIS OF 1856. PRIVATEERS. NON-COMMISSIONED VESSELS.

The Declaration of Paris. § 223. At the commencement of the last war, waged by Great Britain and France against Russia, the allied Maritime Powers consented to waive the assertion of some often contended practices of maritime warfare. * At the conclusion of that war, Great Britain, France, Austria, Russia, Prussia, Sardinia and Turkey concurred in settling these practices by a formal declaration, as follows :—

Declaration respecting Maritime Law, signed by the Plenipotentiaries of Austria, France, Great

* The concurrent declarations of England and France, issued under date of March 28–29, 1854, were as follows :—

Her Majesty, the Queen of the United Kingdom of Great Britain and Ireland, having been compelled to take up arms in support of an ally, is desirous of rendering the war as little onerous as possible to the Powers with whom she remains at peace.

To preserve the commerce of neutrals from all unnecessary obstruction, Her Majesty is willing, for the present, to waive a part of the belligerent rights appertaining to her by the Law of Nations.

It is impossible for Her Majesty to forego the exercise of her right of seizing articles contraband of war, and of preventing neutrals from bearing the enemy's despatches, and she must maintain the right of a belligerent to prevent neutrals from breaking any effective blockade, which may be established with an adequate force against the enemy's forts, harbours, or coasts.

But Her Majesty will waive the right of seizing enemy's property laden on board a neutral vessel, unless it be contraband of war.

It is not Her Majesty's intention to claim the confiscation of neutral property, not being contraband of war, found on board enemy's ships, and Her Majesty further declares that, being anxious to lessen, as much as possible, the evils of war, and to restrict its operations to the regularly organized forces of the country, it is not her present intention to issue letters of marque for the commissions of privateers.

Britain, Prussia, Russia, Sardinia and Turkey, assembled in Congress at Paris, April 16, 1856.

The Plenipotentiaries who signed the Treaty of Paris of 30th of March, 1856, assembled in Conference,—considering:

That Maritime Law, in time of war, has long been the subject of deplorable disputes;

That the uncertainty of the law, and of the duties in such a matter, gives rise to differences of opinion between neutrals and belligerents, which may occasion serious difficulties, and even conflicts;

That it is consequently advantageous to establish a uniform doctrine on so important a point;

That the Plenipotentiaries assembled in Congress at Paris cannot better respond to the intentions by which their Governments are animated, than by seeking to introduce into international relations fixed principles in this respect:

The above mentioned Plenipotentiaries, being duly authorized, resolved to concert among themselves as to the means of attaining this object; and, having come to an agreement, have adopted the following solemn Declaration:—

I. Privateering is and remains abolished.

II. The neutral flag covers enemy's goods, with the exception of contraband of war.

III. Neutral goods, with the exception of contraband of war, are not liable to capture under enemy's flag.

IV. Blockades, in order to be binding, must be effective, that is to say, maintained by a force sufficient really to prevent access to the coast of the enemy.

The Governments of the undersigned Plenipotentiaries engage to bring the present Declaration to the knowledge of the States which have not taken part in the Congress of Paris, and to invite them to accede to it.

Convinced that the maxims which they now proclaim cannot but be received with gratitude by the whole world, the undersigned Plenipotentiaries doubt not that the efforts of their Governments to obtain the general adoption thereof will be crowned with full success.

"The present Declaration is not and shall not be binding, except between those Powers who have acceded, or shall accede, to it."

"Done at Paris, the 16th of April, 1856."

(Signed)

BUOL-SCHAUENSTEIN.	HATZFELDT.
HUBNER.	ORLOFF.
WALEWSKI.	BRUNNOW.
BOURQUENEY.	CAVOUR.
CLARENDON.	DE VILLAMARINA.
COWLEY.	AALI.
MANTEUFFEL.	MEHEMMED DJEMIL.

This Declaration is, of course, a formal treaty obligation, not only binding upon the subscribers to it, but paving the way for the complete abolishing of the capture of inoffensive private property at sea.

The proposition of the United States of America, with regard to the immunity from capture of inoffensive private property at sea.

"It is not to be wondered at, says Sir Robert Phillimore, that close upon this innovation should have followed the demand for another, namely, the total abolition of the right of capture and search, on the ground that war is made between armies and not the subjects of belligerents, and that the free commerce of the latter would lighten the pressure and the evils of war." *

This is quite natural, and the United States of America, true to their old principles, declined to concur in the present arrangement, unless on the

* PHILLIMORE. Intern. Law. Vol. III. Edit. 1873. p. 361.

further concession that the inoffensive private property of an enemy on the high seas should be allowed the same exemptions from the liabilities of war as by the present Declaration is granted to enemy goods on board neutral vessels. The United States adopted the second third and fourth propositions, independently of the first, offering to adopt that also, with the following amendment or additional clause "and the private property of the subjects or citizens of a belligerent on the high seas, shall be exempted from seizure by public armed vessels of the other belligerent, except it be contraband of war." This proposition, to which Russia acceded, was, however, not accepted by all the original signers of the Declaration (see § 199).

All the other Powers were invited to accede to the Declaration, but with the understanding of solidarity and not separately. In Europe, all except Spain, and on the other side of the Atlantic all but Mexico and the United States subscribed to the new rules. The latter, however, for the reason that the Declaration was not complete.

This is stated by Dr. Woolsey as follows :—

"The United States, among other Powers, were invited to become a party to this declaration. The Secretary of State, Mr. Marcy, in a letter of July 28, 1856, addressed to M. de Sartiges, minister of France at Washington, declined the proposal, although it secured what this country had so long been wishing for,—the greater freedom of neutral vessels. The reluctance to adopt the principles of the Declaration, was owing to a cause already suggested,—that the relinquishment of privateering would be a gain to Nations which keep on foot a large naval force, but not to the United States, where a *Dr. Woolsey's statement.*

powerful navy is not maintained, on account of its great cost, and its danger to civil liberty. On the breaking out of a war, therefore, with a Nation powerful at sea, the United States must rely, to a considerable extent, on merchant vessels converted into vessels of war. The secretary, however, declares that our Government will readily agree to an arrangement, by which the private property of the subjects or citizens of a belligerent Power shall be exempted from seizure by public armed vessels of the enemy, except it be contraband of war, and that 'with this proviso we will consent to the placing of privateering under the ban of the Law of Nations.' It will be the policy of our Goverument, hereafter, it may be presumed, in all treaties, to couple the abolition of privateering with the entire immunity of merchant ships engaged in a lawful trade." *

"The true policy of the United States, says Dr. Woolsey further, is to come under the operation of the four articles as soon as possible. The refusal was based on the utility of privateers in saving the expense of maintaining a large navy. But if a war should break out between the United States and any of the Nations which signed the four articles, that is with any, excepting one or two, of the important civilized Nations of the world, we could have no benefit from the four articles, and privateers could swarm the sea in pursuit of our merchant vessels. Nor could we, if we were neutrals, carry the goods of either enemy upon our vessels, for the four articles do not apply except to the signers of them. In war, especially with a leading commercial Power, that would happen again which happened in the late war of the secession, when 715 vessels, measuring

---

* WOOLSEY. p. 218.

480,882 tons, were transferred to British capitalists. Such was the result of a paltry naval force upon our shipping interest. On the other hand, by acceding to the four articles, we should be in a better position to aid in carrying through the principle of the entire exemption of all private property from capture, which should be engaged in innocent commerce. And that point, once reached, what should we want of privateers, or of a large regular navy? Our position in relation to the Powers of Europe would generally be neutral, but now we cut ourselves off from the advantages of neutrality, which are constant, on account of a possible advantage of a very questionable character." *

Mr. Ch. Vergé, the annotator of De Martens (edition 1858), in treating of this proposition of the United States' Government, expresses himself as follows. "In the usages of war on land, *The opinion of Ch. Vergé.* the soldiers of belligerent Powers have no right, and can, in the way of fact, exercise no control over the private property of the subjects of the hostile Power. Why should not the same principles be applicable to maritime war? The additional proposition of the cabinet of Washington is evidently logical. Vainly has it been contended (in the *Journal des Débats* of October 22, 1856), that the claim of the United States, that land and sea warfare should be put on the same footing, is not admissible, nor just, nor good even, since the calamities of war afforded this advantage, that in acting on the population of countries, they render war shorter and more unfrequent. It seems in all cases difficult to maintain the proposition that the pillage of private property by privateers is just, rational and legitimate. One

* WOOLSEY. p. 324.

cannot admit that private property, which is free even in the enemy's land itself, on the soil invaded by an army, victorious and invested with the right of conquest, can be justly taken and plundered on the sea, on that element free by its nature, which is neither friendly nor hostile territory. Let us hope that the initiative so gloriously adopted by the Congress of Paris, will be fruitful for the future, and that diplomacy will one day reach the point of rendering commerce free for belligerents as for neutrals, that private goods and citizens, who are strangers to the profession of arms, will be freed from the disasters of war, and that private property will remain outside of contests exclusively concentrated in armies acting in the name and under the direction of the public Power." *

Not long after the adoption of the rules of 1856, in a meeting of the Chambers of Commerce of Hamburg and Bremen, resolutions were passed to memorialize a Congress, expected to meet at Paris, in favour of the exemption of private property on the sea from capture. The resolution passed at Bremen, on December 2, 1859, is as follows. "Resolved, that the inviolability of person and property in time of war on the high seas (extended also to the subjects and citizens of belligerent States, except so far as the operations of war necessarily restrict the same), is imperatively demanded by the sentiments of justice universally entertained at the present day." They then request the Senate of Bremen to support this principle, and to lay the subject before the German Confederation or the proposed Congress.

The history of the Declaration of Paris and the controversies it called forth by the United

* Ch. Vergé's note to § 289, de Martens, Vol. II.

States of America, is most clearly set forth in the able written brochure of Messrs. Aegedi and Klauhold, in which work all the documents relating to the famous Declaration are reprinted. *

Privateering. Letters of marque.

§ 224. Privateering is the capturing on the high seas of the property of private individuals of the enemy State by private individuals of the opposing belligerent State, to whom are delegated the belligerent rights of the sovereign Powers of the State, together with the profits made out of the captured property. The term privateer applies therefore to the private armed vessels, owned, manned and officered by private persons under commissions from the Government of the belligerent State, called letters of marque *(lettres de marque, Kaperbrief)*. †

This system of attacking and injuring an enemy is one of the practices of maritime warfare, handed down from barbaric ages by the tenacity with which rapacity keeps its hold on the human mind. Although modified and brought under control by an advancing civilization, privateering was at all times regarded by cultured minds as an unfair and irregular usage of war.

"Privateering, says Chancellor Kent, under all the restrictions which have been adopted, is very liable to abuse. The object is not fame or chivalric warfare, but plunder and profit. The discipline of the crews is not apt to be of the highest order, and privateers are often guilty of enormous excesses, and become the scourges of

---

* Frei Schiff unter Feindes Flagge. Urkundliche Darstellung der Bestrebungen zur Fortbildung des Seerechts seit 1856, auf Veranlassung der Bremer Handelskammer, herausgegeben von LUDWIG KARL AEGEDI und ALFRED KLAUHOLD. Beilage zum Staatsarchiv. Hamburg, 1866. Compare also GESSNER. Le Droit des Neutres sur Mer. Edit. 1865. p. 55.

† From the signification, *border, the marches,* it is said, as being letters of licence to go across the boundary and make reprisals. (WOOLSEY. p. 209, note.)

neutral commerce. Under the best regulations the business tends strongly to blunt the sense of private right, and to nourish a lawless and fierce spirit of rapacity." * Dr. Wheaton observes, that "this practice has been justly arraigned, as liable to gross abuses, as tending to encourage a spirit of lawless depredation, and as being in glaring contradiction to the more mitigated modes of warfare practised by land." † Dr. Franklin expressed his feelings in regard to privateering, in the treaty of 1785, between the United States and Prussia, which he drew up. In this treaty (at the conclusion of Article 23) it was provided that neither of the parties should grant or issue any commission to any private armed vessels against the other, empowering them to take or destroy its trading vessels, or to interrupt commerce. (See above, § 199). Lord Nelson said privateers were only one degree removed from pirates, and complained that he had no power over them. The right to use them has now almost disappeared from the world, says Mr. Hall. It formed part of the Declaration adopted at the Congress of Paris, in 1856, with reference to Maritime Law, that privateering is and remains abolished, and all civilized States have since become signataries of the Declaration, except the United States, Spain and Mexico (as noted in the preceding paragraph). Privateers can therefore not be used by signataries of the Declaration of Paris in a war between each other, but during war with States which have not adopted the rules of the Declaration it should be legal to use privateers on the principle of reprisals. ‡

---

* KENT. I. 97. Lect. 5.

† Elements. IV. § 10.

‡ HALL. Intern. Law. Edit. 1880. p. 453.

Lord Nelson, writing to the British Minister Plenipotentiary at the Court of Sardinia, in 1804, says:—"With respect to the history of

§ 225. Private vessels, without any commission or authorisation of their Government, are not allowed to wage war or to attack any enemy at sea, without classing themselves in the category of pirates. It is a different case, however, when they act in self-defence. If private individuals confine themselves to simple defence, says Chancellor Kent, they are to be considered as acting under the presumed order of the State, and are entitled to be treated by the adversary as lawful enemies; and the captures which they make, in such a case, are allowed to be lawful prize. But they cannot engage in offensive hostilities, without the express permission of the sovereign; and if they have not a regular commission, as evidence of that consent, they run the hazard of being treated by the enemy as lawless banditti, not entitled to the mitigated rules of modern warfare. Hautefeuille says, 'It is admitted by all Nations that, in maritime wars, every individual who *Non-commissioned vessels.*

---

the French privateers from Ancona, and the conduct of the English privateers at Fiumesino, I believe you are correct, but our enemies never adhere to it. They go in and out of the Spanish and Sicilian ports at all times, night and day in short, to examine all vessels passing. But all privateers are very incorrect, and I sincerely wish there were no such vessels allowed. They are only one degree removed from pirates; but I believe an English armed vessel never yet trusted her cause to any Court but an English Court of Admiralty. However, I have no power over them. But certainly, if the custom of the Government of Fiumesino has invariably been not to allow any corsair to sail out of the port until the 24 hours after the sailing of a neutral, then our privateers ought to have been forced to conform. But I dare say the French go in and out of Ancona as they please, and, if so, the Court of Rome has no great cause of complaint. I can only again repeat that over privateers I have no control."

For the history of privateering, see KATCHENOASKY'S Prize Law, particularly with reference to the duties and obligations of belligerents and neutrals. HALLAM. L'Europe au moyen age. Vol. IV. Sir TRAVERS TWISS. The Law of Nations considered as independent political communities. On the rights and duties of Nations in time of war. ROTTECK & WELCHER. Staats-lexicon. Art. Prise. C. DE KALTENBORN. Geschichte der Kaperei im Seekriege. PÖLITZ und BULAU. Nene Jahrbücher fur Geschichte und Politik. 1849. Vol. II. BLUNTSCHLI. Du droit de butin en général et spécialement du droit de prise maritime. Revue de l'Institut de Droit International. Vol. IX. (1877) p. 508, et seq. and Vol X. (1878), p. 60, et seq.

commits acts of hostility, without having received a regular commission from his sovereign, however regularly he may make war, is regarded and treated as guilty of piracy.' In the British naval regulations, established by the King in Council, published 1826, it is declared that 'if any ship or vessel shall be taken, acting as a ship of war or privateer, without having a commission duly authorizing her to do so, her crew shall be considered as pirates, and treated accordingly.' Nevertheless a capture made by such vessel from an enemy is regarded as good prize, and condemned as a *droit* of Admiralty. All agree that defensive hostilities on the high seas, as well as on land, without a commission or public authority, are not criminal acts, but acts fully authorized by the laws of war. *

Mr. Hall makes the following statements with regard to the belligerent rights of non-commissioned vessels. "Non-commissioned vessels, says he, have a right to resist, when summoned to surrender to public ships or privateers of the enemy. The crews, therefore, which make such resistance, have belligerent privileges; and it is a natural consequence of the legitimateness of their acts, that, if they succeed in capturing their assailant, the capture is a good one for the purpose of changing the ownership of the property taken and of making the enemy prisoners of war. †

* KENT. Com. on Am. Law. Vol. I. pp. 94–96. VATTEL. Droit des Gens. Liv. III. Ch. XV. § 226. MARTENS. Essai sur les Armateurs. Ch. I. §§ 5–7. HEFFTER. Droit International. § 124. HAUTEFEUILLE. Des Nations Neutres. Tit. III. Ch. II. MASSÉ. Droit Commercial. Liv. II. Tit. I. Ch. II. WHEATON. Elem. Int. Law. Pt. IV. Ch. II. § 9. ROBINSON. Collectanea. p. 21. SPARKS. Dip. Correspondence. Vol. I. p. 443; Journals of Congress, Vol. VII. p. 187. The *Georginia*, L. I. Dod. Rep. p. 397. The *Dos Hermanos*, 10. Wheaton Rep. p. 306. The *Nereide*, 9. Cranch. Rep. p. 449; The *Amiable Isabella*, 6 Wheaton Rep. p. I. *Brown* v. the U. S. 8 Cranch Rep. p. 132.

† KENT. I., 94. HALLECK. II., 12; Mr. Justice STORY, in Brown v. the United States, VIII. Cranch, 135.

By some writers it is asserted that a non-commissioned ship has also a right to attack. * If there was ever anything to be said for this view, and the weight of practice and of legal authority was always against it, there can be no question that it is too much opposed to the whole bent of modern ideas to be now open to argument. There is no such reason at sea as there is on land for permitting ill-regulated or unregulated action. On the common ground of the ocean, a man is not goaded to leave the non-combatant class, if he naturally belongs to it, by the peril of his country or his home. Every one's right to be there being moreover equal, the initiative in acts of hostility must always be aggressive; and on land irregular levies only rise for defence, and are only permissible for that purpose. It is scarcely necessary to add that non-commissioned ships offer no security that hostilities will be carried on by them in a legitimate manner. Efficient control at sea must always be more difficult than on land; and if it was found, that the exercise of due restraint upon privateers was impossible, *a fortiori* it would be impossible to prevent excesses from being indulged in by non-commissioned captors." †

* WHEATON. Part IV. Ch. II. § 9.

† W. E. HALL. p. 456.

CHAPTER XXXIV.

THE RELATIONS BETWEEN BELLIGERENTS AND NEUTRALS.

1°. *General Principles of Neutrality.*

The principle of neutrality and the duty of impartial conduct.

§ 226. A war between two States, as members of the general community of Nations, creates special international relations not only for the belligerents but also for those who do not take part in the contest. This is the natural result of the interdependence of States, as noted above, in § 128.

Whilst in the act of carrying on a contest by force of arms, the parties engaged acquire, through the acknowledged rules of the Law of War, certain conditional rights (§ 26), called belligerent rights. These belligerent rights impose on third parties, who are unable or unwilling to interfere or to take part in the contest, certain obligations, called obligations of neutrality. The state of neutrality is therefore not a voluntarily adopted position of any State, but the consequence of the belligerent relations of the parties at war. Accordingly neutrality needs not to be declared. If a State does not depart from its usual or normal pacific intercourse with both belligerents or does not show any partiality towards any of them, its condition of neutrality is indubitably proved. Neutrality is impartiality in attitude and action. Kluber says, a neutral State is neither judge nor party. *

* Ein neutraler Staat ist weder Richter noch Partei. KLUBER § 284.

Abstinence and impartiality must be combined in the character of a *bonâ fide* neutral, says Sir Robert Phillimore. *

It does not make any difference as regards the state of neutrality, whether a neutral State carry on a greater amount of trade with one belligerent than with the other, provided it does not violate its neutrality by any act of hostility, whether covert or open (Comp. § 235). But commerce in those articles which are contraband of war (as described in the next chapter) constitutes an illegal intercourse between belligerents and neutrals, punishable in conformity with the usages of war. Neutrality being based on the principle of strict impartiality, it imposes on neutrals the obligation, when called upon in certain doubtful cases to prove their impartiality, of granting belligerents, in these special cases, the right of investigation and adjudication within the sphere of acknowledged usages of war,—proceedings which in a normal state of affairs would be strictly confined to the attributes of the respective State's jurisdiction. Hence arise the belligerent rights of visit and search of neutral vessels or conveyances, when these are suspected to be in unfair relations with the enemy (Comp. § 236).

The occurence of a war between two States, says Professor Sheldon Amos, cannot possibly be a matter of indifference to other States, and it is as much the interest of the belligerents themselves as of all other States, that the precise legal relations of these so-called neutral States to the belligerent States should be definitely circumscribed and rigidly maintained throughout the war. †

* PHILLIMORE. Com. Intern. Law. Vol. III. Edit. 1873. p. 225.

† SHELDON AMOS. Science of Jurisprudence. Edit. 1872. p. 431.

With regard to the principle of neutrality and the duty of impartial conduct, Mr. Hall makes the following statement.

Mr. Hall's statement.

"It is a reasonable and indeed a necessary deduction from the principle that a State is bound to respect the right of free action possessed by other States, that it must not allow feeling of friendship for a country to betray it into embarrassing an enemy of the latter in the exercise of his legitimate rights of war. It has been mentioned as an incident of sovereignty, that every people possessing sovereignty has the right of determining what kind and amount of intercourse it will maintain with foreign Nations, and that it may choose to mark out one as an object for greater friendship than another. In time of peace it is easy to accord such preference and to remain, nevertheless, on terms of perfect amity with less favoured countries. But during war, privileges tending to strengthen the hands of one of two belligerents help him towards the destruction of his enemy. To grant them is not merely to show less friendship to one than the other; it is to embarrass one by reserving to the other a field of action in which his enemy cannot attack him; it is to assume an attitude with respect to him of at least passive hostility. If therefore a people desires not to be the enemy of either belligerent, its amity must be colourless in the eyes of both; in its corporate capacity as a State it must abstain altogether from mixing itself up in their quarrel." *

Perfect and qualified neutrality.

§ 227. Neutrality is perfect or qualified. Perfect neutrality is either permanent or accidental. It is permanent when the neutrality of the State is an object of international treaties as noted above

* W. E. HALL. Page 63.

(§ 24. Vol. I. p. 83). Accidental neutrality is the general condition created, at the outbreak of war, for all States which do not take part with either of the contending parties (as described in the preceding paragraph). Whatever may be the state of neutrality, whether it be permanent or accidental, to be perfect neutrality must be general, absolute and complete; it cannot be limited to certain actions only, but must embrace the whole unconditional state of impartiality, without reserve, with regard to the relations to be observed towards belligerents.

The attitude which might be called qualified neutrality devolves from treaty agreement, entered into before the war, as in the case of anterior engagement to provide certain supplies, to a limited extent, to one of the belligerent parties. Such an agreement, without being in fact an alliance, can yet partake sufficiently of this nature of liability, to make the agreement subject to the option of the other belligerent to whom it is left to decide whether he will regard the State in question as neutral or as an ally of his enemy. If the assistance to be rendered is trifling and has no reference to a war with any particular Nation, it is generally overlooked when strictly limited to the stipulations of the anterior compact. *

§ 228. There may be circumstances under which *Neutral alliance.* a State finds itself powerless to make its neutrality respected; in such a case any other neutral State may come to the rescue of the threatened neutral State, without renouncing its own neutrality, by acts of interference or demonstration, with the object of a temporary occupation of that part of the neutral territory which is threatened by an aggressive belligerent party.

* WOOLSEY. § 163. HEFFTER. § 144.

Armed Neutrality.

Neutrality rights may be defended by armed forces and by an alliance between neutral States which are likely to suffer from aggressions of belligerent parties. This is called an armed neutrality. The armed neutrality of the Baltic Powers of 1780 and 1800 were leagues formed to defend the maritime rights of neutrals.

2°. *Neutral Commerce.*

Conditions with regard to neutrality in commercial relations with belligerents.

§ 229. The law of neutrality is summed up by Vattel as follows. "Generally, we may say, no act on the part of a Nation which falls within the exercise of her rights and is done solely with a view to her own good without partiality,—without a design of favouring one Power to the prejudice of another,—no act of that kind can, in general, be considered as contrary to neutrality; nor does it become such, except on particular occasions, when it cannot take place without injury to one of the parties, who has then a particular right to oppose it." * This definition would well meet the case of passive neutrality, but the duties of a neutral State involve a more active lookout to stear clearly between the dangerous cliffs of a neutral course, than a simple innocent drifting with the tides prompted by a calm indifference as to the interests of all parties but one's own. Breaches of neutrality are not necessarily committed intentionally to favour or injure any particular belligerent, nor are they tested only by the direct actual injuries sustained by the belligerent. The true criterion of a breach of neutrality is whether in doing certain acts, though in themselves quite defensible, in the prosecution of the neutral's own commercial affairs, without direct regard to the good or bad effect

---

* VATTEL. Droit des Gens. Liv. III. Chapt. VII.

upon any of the belligerents, the neutral has in any way, intentionally or otherwise, stepped out of his proper sphere of impartiality in favour of any one belligerent.

The more the laws of war become binding upon belligerents, the more delicate grow the duties of neutrals, and a sharp lookout and a certain measure of self restraint in the search for profit is indispensable to the neutral to comply with his active duties of neutrality, viz., to prevent either of the belligerents being injured by acts for which the neutral may be justly supposed to be responsible.

This is the principle on which neutrals can have commercial intercourse with belligerents. But this does not necessarily include that a neutral State must be held responsible for all acts done by strangers or even his own subjects within his territories which might prove in their consequences particularly injurious or beneficial to one or other of the belligerent parties. There are limits to the responsibility of the neutral Government. When these limits are not traced beforehand by treaties or conventions or by the acknowledged rules of International Law concerning neutrality, or where any act does not directly violate acknowledged usages of war or infringe on belligerent rights, the responsibility of a State ceases when the act is simply one of impartial public commerce, that is to say, of commerce open to belligerent parties indiscriminately.

Thus the Government of a State cannot be held responsible with regard to the exportation of arms or contraband of war from its territory by private individuals, whatever may be the ultimate destination of these goods outside its jurisdiction, provided the market in these articles of commerce is open to all parties without distinction. On the other hand the State is bound, as much as practicable, to prevent acts being committed, by whomsoever, within its jurisdiction, which may constitute any direct material help to any or even equally to both belligerent parties, if such were possible. A State is not at liberty to throw open its territory as a common place for warlike preparations of any kind between Nations in relation to which that State ought to preserve a strictly neutral attitude. Nor is a State at liberty to allow its country or territorial waters to be used by the belligerents as scenes of hostile actions or as bases of hostile expeditions. Such equal friendship would not only cast suspicions on the sincerity with which the real state of neutrality is adhered to, but the Nation which, in violation of all principles of morality, endeavours to foment war between other States by systematically aiding both parties for motives of purely commercial gain, willfully places its rights of neutrality at the caprice or convenience of both belligerents and has no reason for complaint when these rights are violated by either party. By acting for both belligerents such a State makes each its enemy (Comp. §§ 230–232).

3°. *The Distinction between State acts and acts of individuals in cases of neutrality.*

Public and private breach of neutrality.

§ 230. When determining the facts which constitute a breach of neutrality, a distinction must be made in the appreciation of acts, between public and private acts, that is to say acts incompatible with neutrality might be regarded as the acts of the State or as the acts of private individuals outside the direct control of the State. From the same principle that war is a relation between States only and not of individual towards individual (§ 170), it follows also that acts by which a State commits a breach of neutrality are to be brought home to that State alone and not to its individual members. On the other hand, when any act is committed by an individual in contravention of the respective regulations of neutrality issued by his Government, the culpable individual cannot claim the protection of his State and must suffer the consequences of his personal deeds alone, without the whole State, to which he happens to belong, being involved in his private misdemeanor. (See *Abandoned Jurisdiction*, § 48).

Hence the distinction which exists between acts incompatible with neutrality with which the State is identified and commercial acts done by an individual which are affairs to be settled between him individually and the belligerent who suffers by the act.

With regard to the distinction made between State acts and commercial acts of the individual, Mr. Hall gives the following opinion.

Mr. Hall's opinion with regard to the distinction between State acts and acts of private individuals in neutrality.

"An act of the State which is prejudicial to the belligerent is necessarily done with the intent to injure; but the commercial act of the individual only affects the belligerent accidentally. It is not directed against him; it is done in the way of business, with the object of getting a business profit, and however injurious in its consequences, it is not instigated by that wish to do harm to a particular person which is the essence of hostility. It is prevented because it is inconvenient, not because it is a wrong; and to allow the performance by a subject of an act not in itself improper, cannot constitute a crime on the part of the State to which he belongs. Trade between a neutral individual and a belligerent, which is prejudicial to the operations of a country at war, not being in itself wrong, even in the qualified sense in which non-neutral national acts can be said to be wrong, the belligerent right to interfere with it is theoretically a derogation from the strict rights of the neutral State, which refrains in so far as its subjects are affected by the belligerent from protecting them in the performance of innocent acts. The justification of this usage lies in its convenience."

"By existing custom the belligerent has the right of hindering neutral commerce when it is noxious to him, either because it supplies his enemy with articles of direct use in war, or because it diminishes the stress which he puts upon his enemy; or even because it is tainted by association with hostile property. In all these cases the neutral trader is left face to face with the belligerent Nation. It alone determines whether he has infringed its privileges, and in its Courts alone can he in the first instance find a remedy for wrongs done to him by its agents. The neutral State cannot interfere until the belligerent has overstepped the boundary of his rights. When he has done this by rendering unjust decisions, the question transfers itself to another head of International Law. The belligerent has practically committed an act of war, and the neutral State can demand and exact such reparation as may be needful. It appears then, that international usage as between belligerents and neutrals consists of two branches, distinct in respect of the parties affected, of the moral relation of these parties to each other, and of the means by which a breach of the accepted rules can be punished. In the one case the parties are sovereign States. Both of these are affected by the same duties as in peace time. The belligerent therefore remains under an obligation to respect the sovereignty of the neutral; the neutral is under an equal obligation not to aid directly or indirectly, and within certain limits to prevent a State or private persons from aiding, in places under his control, the enemy of the belligerent in matters immediately bearing on the war. If a wrong is done, the remedy is of course international. In the other case the parties are the belligerent State and the neutral individual. They are, and can be, bound by no obligations to each other. The only duty of the individual is to his own sovereign; and so distinctly is this the case, that acts done even with intent to injure a foreign State are only wrong in so far as they compromise the Nation of which the individual is a member. At the same time, the only duty of the belligerent State is to beings of like kind with itself; and it is merely bound to behave in a particular manner to the neutral individual, because of the international agreement which sets limits to the severity which may be used in repressing his noxious acts. But within these limits the belligerent is irresponsible. He exacts in his own prize-courts the penalty for infraction of the rules which he is allowed to enforce; and if he inflicts a wrong, it is for him to repair it." *

Responsibility of the State for breaches of neutrality by private individuals.

§ 231. As with the usages of war, so with regard to the belligerent rights in relation to the obligations of neutrals, the liabilities of the private individual is often confused with those of the State, which latter alone is a party in an international dispute, and the natural distinction between national and private acts is not always kept clearly in view.

Some writers on International Law regard States and private individuals as occupying in common the same position with regard to bellig-

* W. E. HALL. Pages 67-69.

erent rights in the condition of neutrality as in war. Others are less consistent and proclaim the solidarity of the State and the individual only in war, which suits the purpose of defending the capture of inoffensive private property on the high seas,—while in the case of neutrality they accept the doctrine of the separability of the individual from the State, and they put this forward as an argument in favour of free neutral commerce on the part of private individuals. But it is obvious that one and the same theory must govern the relation between States and private individuals with regard to the liabilities entailed by neutrality as well as with regard to belligerent rights in war. The same principle which protects private property in war, when not engaged for any hostile purpose, condemns it when, in the case of neutrals, it partakes of the hostile character of contraband of war. *

Mr. Hall's opinion.

"This distinction between usages affecting national and private acts, says Mr. Hall, is deeply rooted in the habits of Nations. At no time since the rules which make up International Law assumed definite shape, has there been any room for question as to the existence or nature of an authoritative practice in the matter. But the usage was shaped in the first instance by the blind working of natural forces, and its permanence is more due to their continued operation, than to the clearness with which its principle has been defined by legal writers. It has been, and still is, usual for them to confuse neutral States and individuals in a common relation towards belligerent States; and in losing sight of the sound basis of the established practice, they have necessarily failed to indicate any clear

* HEFFTER. § 148. BLUNTSCHLI. §§ 779 and 780. CALVO. Vol. II. § 169.

boundary of State responsibility. This want of precision is both theoretically unfortunate, and not altogether without practical importance. For it has enabled Governments, from time to time, to put forward pretensions, which, though they have never been admitted by neutral States and have never been carried into effect, cannot be often made without endangering the stability of the principles they attack. But the common sense of statesmen has generally met such pretensions with a decided assertion of the authoritative doctrine, and state papers are not wanting in that clearness which is deficient in the writings of jurists." *

4°. *State Responsibility for Acts of Private Individuals. The Treaty of Washington of 1871.*

§ 232. In the preceding paragraphs we have noted that private individuals of neutral States are allowed to continue their commerce with belligerents without involving the responsibility of their respective States and this on the principle of the distinction which is admitted to exist between national or State acts and the doings of private individuals. As a general rule, State acts do not *per se* always bind the private in-

State responsibility regulated by Municipal Law and International Treaties.

* W. E. HALL. International Law. Edit. 1880. p. 69.

"Or de même que l'état de guerre ordinaire n'est qu'une relation de gouvernement à gouvernement, et non une relation de particulier à particulier, de même aussi, l'état d'hostilité qui résulte de la rupture de la neutralité, opérée par le fait d'un gouvernement neutre, ne doit, dans la vérité des principes, réagir que sur ce gouvernement et non sur les particuliers. Si les particuliers inoffensifs sont dès lors traités en ennemis et cessent d'être protégés par les lois de la neutralité, c'est par une suite de l'abus de pouvoir qui impose le même traitement aux sujets inoffensifs du gouvernement ennemi. Réciproquement, de ce qu'un sujet neutre aurait rompu la neutralité et se serait mis en état d'hostilité personnelle contre un belligérant, on ne doit pas en conclure que la neutralité est rompue à l'égard du gouvernement neutre qui n'a pas pris fait et cause pour sont sujet, et qui ne s'est pas approprié le fait d'où vient la rupture. Le sujet neutre peut seul dans ce cas être traité en ennemi par le belligérant. MASSÉ, Droit Commercial. Ed. 1874. Vol. I. p. 168.

dividual; neither can acts of private individuals compromise the State unless there be special circumstances. By this principle the limits of State responsibility in neutrality is theoretically laid down, and the liability of the private individual in war is in the same way defined. But, in the same manner as in war, the property of private individuals of belligerent States may under certain circumstances be involved in the belligerent acts of the State and then partake of the enemy character, which, in ordinary circumstances, is inherent in State or public property only, so in neutrality the State, though distinct from the private individual, can sometimes be compromised by private acts. Hence the practical uncertainty which always remains with regard to the limits of State responsibility in relation to acts of private individuals. Beside municipal laws, as the United States neutrality laws of 1838 * and the British Foreign Enlistment Act of 1870 (see Appendix E) †, the *modus vivendi*, during neutrality, is often regulated beforehand by international treaties. An instance of this mode of international agreement with regard to the responsibility of the neutral State, when the other party is engaged in war, is the Treaty between Great Britain and the United States of America called the Treaty of Washington.

This Treaty contemplated the adjustment by arbitration of the differences occasioned by the wellknown cases of the Alabama and other vessels of the Confederate Government, which preyed on the commerce of the Federal States during the late civil war in the United States. This latter Government brought a claim against that of Great

* KENT. Vol. I. Lect. VI. 122.

† PHILLIMORE. Vol. I. Edit. 1879. p. 553, et seq., quoted above, in this Volume, on pages 183, et seq.

Britain for alleged breaches of neutrality of the latter State in allowing certain vessels to be built and equipped and also in assisting the progress of those vessels. To meet these claims, after various negotiations, on the conclusion of the civil war, the Treaty of Washington (having a retrospective effect) was signed at Washington, 8 May, 1871, between Great Britain and the United States, referring the various questions to five arbitrators, one being chosen to each of the following Governments, viz. Great Britain, the United States, Italy, Switzerland, and Brazil. These arbitrators met at Geneva in Switzerland, on December 15, 1871.

It was stipulated by Art. VI of the above Treaty as follows:—

"In deciding the matters submitted to the arbitrators, they shall be governed by the following three rules, which are agreed upon by the high contracting parties as rules to be taken as applicable to the case, and by such principles of International Law not inconsistent therewith, as the arbitrators shall determine to have been applicable to the case:—

"A neutral Government is bound—

"First. To use due diligence to prevent the fitting out, arming, or equipping within its jurisdiction of any vessel which it has reasonable ground to believe is intended to cruise or carry on war against a Power with which it is at peace, and also to use like diligence to prevent the departure from its jurisdiction of any vessel intended to cruise or carry on war as above, such vessel having been specially adapted, in whole or in part, within such jurisdiction, to warlike uses.

"Secondly. Not to permit or suffer either belligerent to make use of its ports or waters as the base of naval operations against the other, or for the purpose of the renewal or augmentation of military supplies or arms, or the recruitment of men.

"Thirdly. To exercise due diligence in its waters, and as to all persons within its jurisdiction to prevent any violation of the foregoing obligations and duties."

"Her Britannic Majesty has commanded her High Commissioners and Plenipotentiaries to declare that Her Majesty's Government cannot assent to the foregoing rules as a statement of principles of International Law, which were in force at the time when the claims mentioned in Art. I. arose; but that Her Majesty's Government, in order to evince its desire of strenthening the friendly relations between the two countries and of making satisfactory provision for the future, agrees that in deciding the question between the two countries, arising out of those claims, the arbitrators should assume that Her Majesty's Government had undertaken to act upon the principles set forth in these rules."

"And the high contracting parties agree to observe these rules as between themselves in future, and to bring them to the knowledge of other maritime Powers, and to invite them to accede to them." *

5°. *Loans of Money by Neutrals.*

Loans as ordinary financial operations of commerce, and as subsidy to the belligerent.

§ 233. Loans of money by a neutral State to a belligerent constitute undoubtedly a breach of neutrality when such a loan partakes of the character of a subsidy to enable one party to carry on the war against the other. Thus also, in the

* With regard to these rules Lord Chief Justice Cockburn, in his reasons for dissenting from the award, made the following observations.

"With these rules before it, the tribunal is directed to determine, as to each vessel, whether Great Britain has, by any act or omission, case of a civil war, when one of the parties purposes to raise money to overthrow the other.

---

failed to fulfil any of the duties set forth in such rules, or recognized by the principles of International Law not inconsistent with such rules. The effect of this part of the Treaty is to place this Tribunal in a position of some difficulty. Every obligation, for the non-fulfilment of which redress can be claimed, presupposes a prior existing law, by which a right has been created on the one side and a corresponding obligation on the other. But here we have to deal with obligations assumed to have existed prior to the Treaty, yet arising out of a supposed law created for the first time by the Treaty. For we have the one party denying the prior existence of the rules to which it now consents to submit as the measure of its past obligations, while the other virtually admits the same thing, for it agrees to observe the rules as between itself and Great Britain in future, and to bring them to the knowledge of other maritime Powers, and to invite them to accede to them, all of which would plainly be superfluous and vain if these rules already formed part of the existing law recognized as obtaining among Nations. It is, I cannot but think, to be regretted that the whole subject-matter of this great contest, in respect of law as well as of fact, was not left open to us, to be decided according to the true principles and rules of International law in force and binding among Nations, and the duties and obligations arising out of them, at the time when these alleged causes of complaint are said to have arisen. From the history of the Treaty of Washington, we know that it was proposed by the British Commissioners to submit the entire question, both as to law and fact, to arbitration; but the Commissioners of the United States refused to consent to submit the question of the liability of Great Britain to arbitration, unless the principles which should govern the arbitrators in the consideration of the facts could be first agreed upon. In vain the British Commissioners replied that they should be willing to consider what principles should be adopted for observance in future, but that they were of opinion that the best mode of conducting an arbitration was to submit the facts to the arbitrator, and leave him free to decide upon them after hearing such arguments as might be necessary. The American Commissioners replied that they should be willing to consider what principles should be laid down for observance in similar cases in future, but only with the understanding that any principles which should be agreed upon should be held to be applicable to the facts in respect to the Alabama claims. The British Commissioners and Government gave way, possibly without fully appreciating the extent to which the principles, of which they were thus admitting the application, would be attempted to be carried in fixing them with liability."

The following is the decision of the arbitrators, preceded by the Protocol of the last Conference.

PROTOCOL No. XXXII.

"*Record of the proceedings of the Tribunal of Arbitration at the Thirty-second Conference, held at Geneva, in Switzerland, on the 14th of September, 1872.*

The Conference was held with open doors, pursuant to adjournment. All the arbitrators and the agents of the two Governments were present.

The negotiating of any loan by a belligerent party with terms which are made to depend upon

---

The Protocol of the last Conference was read and approved, and was signed by the President and Secretary of the Tribunal.

The President then presented the decision of the Tribunal on the question of the Alabama Claims, and directed the Secretary to read it, which was done, and the decision was signed by Mr. Charles Francis Adams, Count Frederick Sclopis, M. Jacques Staempfli, and Viscount d'Itajubá, arbitrators, in the presence of the agents of the two Governments. A copy of the decision thus signed, was delivered to each of the agents of the two Governments respectively, and the Tribunal decided to have a third copy placed upon record; they further decided that the decision should be printed and annexed to the present Protocol.

Sir Alexander Cockburn, as one of the arbitrators, having declined to assent to the decision, stated the grounds of his own decision, which the Tribunal ordered to be recorded as an annex to the present Protocol.

The Tribunal resolved to request the Council of State at Geneva to receive the archives of the Tribunal and to place them among its own archives.

The President, Count Sclopis, then directed the Secretary to make up the record of the proceedings of the Tribunal at this thirty-second and last Conference, as far as completed; which was done, and the record having been read and approved, was signed by the President and Secretary of the Tribunal and the agents of the two Governments.

Thereupon the President declared the labours of the arbitrators to be finished and the Tribunal to be dissolved.

(Signed) FREDERIC SCLOPIS.
TENTERDEN.
J. C. BANCROFT DAVIS.
ALEX. FAVROT, *Secretary*.

Decision and Award made by the Tribunal of Arbitration constituted by virtue of the 1st Article of the Treaty concluded at Washington the 8th of May, 1871, between Her Majesty the Queen of the United Kingdom of Great Britain and Ireland and the United States of America.

Her Britannic Majesty and the United States of America having agreed by Article I of the Treaty concluded and signed at Washington the 8th of May, 1871, to refer all the claims, generally known as the "Alabama claims," to a Tribunal of Arbitration to be composed of five Arbitrators, named—

One by Her Britannic Majesty, one by the President of the United States, one by His Majesty the King of Italy, one by the President of the Swiss Confederation, one by His Majesty the Emperor of Brazil;

And Her Britanic Majesty, the President of the United States, His Majesty the King of Italy, the President of the Swiss Confederation, and His Majesty the Emperor of Brazil, having respectively named their Arbitrators, to wit:

Her Britannic Majesty, Sir Alexander James Edmund Cockburn, Baronet, a Member of Her Majesty's Privy Council, Lord Chief Justice of England;

the decision of arms or the final issue of the contest, is a breach of neutrality of the neutral

---

The President of the United States, Charles Francis Adams, Esquire;

His Majesty the King of Italy, His Excellency Count Frederic Sclopis of Salerno, a Knight of the Order of the Annunciata, Minister of State, Senator of the Kingdom of Italy;

The President of the Swiss Confederation, M. Jacques Staempfli;

His Majesty the Emperor of Brazil, His Excellency Marcos Antonio d'Aranjo, Viscount d'Itajuba, a Grandee of the Empire of Brazil, Member of the Council of His Majesty the Emperor of Brazil, and his Envoy Extraordinary and Minister Plenipotentiary in France.

And the five Arbitrators above named having assembled at Geneva (in Switzerland) in one of the Chambers of the Hotel-de-Ville on the 15th of December, 1871, in conformity with the terms of the 2nd Article of the Treaty of Washington, of the 8th of May of that year, and having proceeded to the inspection and verification of their respective powers, which were found duly authenticated, the Tribunal of Arbitration was declared duly organized.

The Agents named by each of the High Contracting Parties, by virtue of the same Article II, to wit,—

For Her Britannic Majesty, Charles Stuart Aubrey, Lord Tenterden, a Peer of the United Kingdom, Companion of the Most Honourable Order of the Bath, Assistant Under-Secretary of State for Foreign Affairs;

And for the United States of America, John C. Bancroft Davis, Esquire;

whose powers were found likewise duly authenticated, then delivered to each of the Arbitrators the printed Case prepared by each of two Parties, accompanied by the documents, the official correspondence, and other evidence on which each relied, in conformity with the terms of the 3rd Article of the said Treaty.

In virtue of the decision made by the Tribunal at its first session, the Counter-case and additional documents, correspondence, and evidence, referred to in Article IV of the said Treaty were delivered by the respective Agents of the two Parties to the Secretary of the Tribunal on the 15th of April, 1872, at the Chamber of Conference, at the Hotel-de-Ville of Geneva.

The Tribunal, in accordance with the vote of adjournment passed at their second session, held on the 16th December, 1871, re-assembled at Geneva on the 15th of June, 1872; and the Agent of each of the Parties duly delivered to each of the Arbitrators and to the Agent of the other Party the printed Argument referred to in Article IV of the said Treaty. The Tribunal having since fully taken into their consideration the Treaty, and also the cases, counter-cases, documents, evidence, and arguments, and likewise all other communications made to them by the two Parties during the progress of their sittings and having impartially and carefully examined the same, has arrived at the decision embodied in the present Award:

Whereas, having regard to the 6th and 7th Articles of the said Treaty, the Arbitrators are bound under the terms of the said 6th Article, in deciding the matters submitted to them, to be governed by three Rules therein specified, and by such principles of International Law, not inconsistent therewith, as the Arbitrators shall determine to have been applicable to the case;

State within whose jurisdiction such a loan is publicly negotiated.

And whereas the 'due diligence' referred to in the first and third of the said rules ought to be exercised by neutral Governments in exact proportion to the rules to which either of the belligerents may be exposed, from a failure to fulfil the obligations of Neutrality on their part;

And whereas the circumstances out of which the facts constituting the subject-matter or the present controversy arose, were of a nature to call for the exercise on the part of Her Britannic Majesty's Government of all possible solicitude for the observance of the rights and duties involved in the Proclamation of Neutrality issued by Her Majesty on the 13th day of May, 1861;

And whereas the effects of a violation of Neutrality committed by means of the construction, equipment, and armament of a vessel are not done away with by any commission which the Government of the belligerent Power, benefited by the violation of Neutrality, may afterwards have granted to that vessel: and the ultimate step, by which the offence is completed, cannot be admissible as a ground for the absolution of the offender, nor can the consummation of his fraud become the means of establishing his innocence;

And whereas the privilege of exterritoriality accorded to vessels of war has been admitted into the Law of Nations, not as an absolute right, but solely as a proceeding founded on the principle of courtesy and mutual deference between different Nations, and therefore can never be appealed to for the protection of acts done in violation of neutrality;

And whereas the absence of a previous notice cannot be regarded as a failure in any consideration required by the Law of Nations, in those cases in which a vessel carries with it its own condemnation;

And whereas, in order to impart to any supplies of coal a character inconsistent with the second rule, prohibiting the use of neutral ports or waters, as a base of naval operations for a belligerent, it is necessary that the said supplies should be connected with special circumstances of time, of persons, or of place, which may combine to give them such character;

And whereas, with respect to the vessel called the *Alabama*, it clearly results from all the facts relative to the construction of the ship at first designated by the number 290 in the port of Liverpool, and its equipment and armament in the vicinity of Tèrceira through the agency of the vessels called the *Agrippina* and the *Bahama* despatched from Great Britain to that end, that the British Government failed to use due diligence in the performance of its neutral obligations: and especially that it omitted, notwithstanding the warnings and official representations made by the diplomatic agents of the United States during the construction of the said Number 290, to take in due time any effective measures of prevention, and that those orders which it did give at last, for the detention of the vessel, were issued so late that their execution was not practicable;

And whereas, after the escape of that vessel, the measures taken for its pursuit and arrest were so imperfect as to lead to no result, and therefore cannot be considered sufficient to release Great Britain from the responsibility already incurred;

And whereas, in despite of the violations of the neutrality of Great Britain committed by the 290, this same vessel, later known as

With regard to Government loans negotiated and brought in the market in behalf of a bellig-

---

the Confederate cruiser Alabama, was on several occasions freely admitted into the ports of Colonies of Great Britain, instead of being proceeded against, as it ought to have been, in any and every port within British jurisdiction in which it might have been found;

And whereas the Government of Her Britannic Majesty cannot justify itself for a failure in due diligence on the plea of the insufficiency of the legal means of action which it possessed:

Four of the Arbitrators for the reasons here assigned, and the fifth for reasons separately assigned by him, are of opinion:

That Great Britain has in this case failed, by omission, to fulfil the duties prescribed in the first and the third of the rules established by the 6th Article of the Treaty of Washington.

And whereas, with respect to the vessels called the *Florida*, it results from all the facts relative to the construction of the *Oreto* in the port of Liverpool, and to its issue therefrom, which facts failed to induce the authorities in Great Britain to resort to measures adequate to prevent the violation of the neutrality of that Nation, notwithstanding the warnings and repeated representations of the Agents of the United States, that Her Majesty's Government has failed to use due diligence to fulfil the duties of neutrality;

And whereas it likewise results from all the facts relative to the stay of the *Oreto* at Nassau, to her issue from that port, to her enlisting of men, to her supplies, and to her armament, with the co-operation of the British vessel Prince Alfred, at Green Cay, that there was negligence on the part of the British Colonial Authorities;

And whereas, notwithstanding the violation of the neutrality of Great Britain committed by the *Oreto*, this same vessel, later known as the Confederate cruiser *Florida*, was nevertheless on several occasion freely admitted into the ports of British Colonies;

And whereas the judicial acquittal of the *Oreto* at Nassau cannot relieve Great Britain from the responsibility incurred by her under the principles of International Law; nor can the fact of the entry of the *Florida* into the Confederate port of Mobile, and of its stay there during four months, extinguish the responsibility previously to that time incurred by Great Britain. For these reasons, the tribunal, by a majority of four voices to one, is of opinion—That Great Britain has in this case failed, by omission, to fulfil the duties prescribed in the first, in the second, and in the third of the rules established by Article VI, of the Treaty of Washington.

And whereas, with respect to the vessel called the *Shenandoah*, it results from all the facts relative to the departure from London of the merchant-vessel the *Sea King*, and to the transformation of that ship into a Confederate cruiser under the name of the *Shenandoah*, near the Island of Madeira, that the Government of Her Britannic Majesty is not chargeable with any failure, down to that date, in the use of due diligence to fulfil the duties of neutrality. But whereas it results from all the facts connected with the stay of the *Shenandoah* at Melbourne, and especially with the augmentation which the British Government itself admits to have been clandestinely effected of her force, by the enlistment of men within that port, that there was negligence on the part of the authorities at that place: For these reasons, the Tribunal is unanimously of opinion—that Great Britain has not failed by any act or omission, to fulfil any of the duties prescribed by the three rules of Article VI in the Treaty of Washington erent State during the progress of a war, in the same manner as would have been the case under

---

or by the principles of International Law not inconsistent therewith, in respect to the vessel called the *Shenandoah*, during the period of time anterior to her entry into the port of Melbourne. And, by a majority of three to two voices, the Tribunal decides that Great Britain has failed, by omission, to fulfil the duties prescribed by the second and third of the rules aforesaid, in the case of this same vessel, from and after her entry into Hobson's Bay, and is therefore responsible for all acts committed by that vessel after her departure from Melbourne, on the 18th day of February, 1865.

And so far as relates to the vessels called the *Tuscaloosa* (tender to the *Alabama*), the *Clarence*, the *Tacony*, and the *Archer* (tenders to the *Florida*), the Tribunal is unanimously of opinion—That such tenders or auxiliary vessels being properly regarded as accessories must necessarily follow the lot of their principals, and be submitted to the same decision which applies to them respectively.

And so far as relates to the vessel called *Retribution*, the Tribunal by a majority of three to two voices, is of opinion—That Great Britain has not failed by any act or omission to fulfil any of the duties prescribed by the three rules of Article VI in the Treaty of Washington, or by the principles of International Law not inconsistent therewith.

And so far as relates to the vessels called the *Georgia*, the *Sumter*, the *Nashville*, the *Tallahassee*, and the *Chickamauga*, respectively, the Tribunal is unanimously of opinion—That Great Britain has not failed, by any act or omission, to fulfil any of the duties prescribed by the three rules of Article VI in the Treaty of Washington, or by the principles of International Law not inconsistent therewith.

And so far as relates to the vessels called—The *Sallie*, the *Jefferson Davis*, the *Muzic*, the *Boston*, and the *V. H. Joy*, respectively, the Tribunal is unanimously of opinion:—that they ought to be excluded from consideration for want of evidence.

And whereas, so far as relates to the particulars of the indemnity claimed by the United States, the costs of pursuit of the Confederate cruisers are not, in the judgment of the Tribunal, properly distinguishable from the general expenses of the war carried on by the United States:

The Tribunal is, therefore, of opinion, by a majority of three to two voices—That there is no ground for awarding to the United States any sum by way of indemnity under this head.

And whereas prospective earnings cannot properly be made the subject of compensation, inasmuch as they depend in their nature upon future and uncertain contingencies:

The Tribunal is unanimously of opinion—That there is no ground for awarding to the United States any sum by way of indemnity under this head.

And whereas, in order to arrive at an equitable compensation for the damages which have been sustained, it is necessary to set aside all double claims for the same losses, and all claims for 'gross freights' so far as they exceed 'nett freights;' and whereas it is just and reasonable to allow interest at a reasonable rate; and whereas, in accordance with the spirit and letter of the Treaty of Washington, it is preferable to adopt the form of adjudication of a sum in gross, rather than to refer the subject of compensation for further discussion ordinary circumstances, such proceedings are not regarded as a breach of neutrality when the loan

---

and deliberation to a Board of Assessors, as provided by Article X of the said Treaty: The Tribunal, making use of the authority conferred upon it by Article VII of the said Treaty, by a majority of four voices to one, awards to the United States the sum of 15,500,000 dollars in gold as the indemnity to be paid by Great Britain to the United States for the satisfaction of all the claims referred to the consideration of the Tribunal, conformably to the provisions contained in Article VI of the aforesaid Treaty. And, in accordance with the terms of Article XI of the said Treaty, the Tribunal declares that all the claims referred to in the Treaty as submitted to the Tribunal are hereby fully perfectly, and finally settled. Furthermore it declares, that each and every one of the said claims, whether the same may or may not have been presented to the notice of, or made, preferred, or laid before the Tribunal, shall henceforth be considered and treated as finally settled, barred, and inadmissible.

In testimony whereof this present Decision and Award has been made in duplicate, and signed by the Arbitrators who have given their assent thereto, the whole being in exact conformity with the provisions of Article VII of the said Treaty of Washington.

Made and concluded at the Hôtel-de-Ville of Geneva, in Switzerland, the 14th day of the month of September, in the year of our Lord, 1872.

(Signed) C. F. ADAMS.
FREDERICK SCLOPIS.
STAEMPFELI.
VICOMTE D'ITAJUBA.

Considerable difference of opinion, says Sir Sherston Baker, prevails among jurists as the effect which the decision of the Arbitrators has made on the general principles of International Law. It should be remembered that Austria, Holland, Germany, Russia, Spain, and other States, were not represented at the Conference, and both in Great Britain and on the Continent the better opinion seems to be that oppressive and impracticable obligations, hitherto unknown to International Law, would be imposed on neutral Nations if the principles seth forth as the basis of the award, and the interpretation placed on the three rules of the 6th Article of the above treaty, by the majority of the arbitrators, were acceded to in future cases. In reply to Mr. Hardy, on March 21, 1873, Mr. Gladstone, as Prime Minister, stated in the House of Commons, that in bringing these rules to the knowledge of other Maritime Powers, and inviting them to accede to the same, you have a right to expect that we should take care that our recommendation of these rules does not carry with it, in whole or in part, in substance or even in shadow, so far as we (the British Government) are concerned, the recitals of the Arbitrators as being of any authority in this matter.

Further, some considerable correspondence passed between the British Government and the Government of the United States during the years 1871–74, with respect to communicating to other maritime Governments the above rules, but it was not found possible to draft a note which could meet the respective views of the two Governments. (HALLECK'S. International Law. Note of Sir Sherston Baker, p. 189).

in question is negotiated in the market of a neutral State without any aid or guarantee or any interference whatever on the part of the Government.

If a neutral Power lends money to one belligerent and refuses it to another, there is no breach of neutrality, provided this be for reasons of purely financial credit and solidity of one party above the other, the loan being a purely economico-financial operation in the ordinary channels of commerce. But if the neutral does not lend his money for the purpose of getting good interest for it, or if he lends it without charging interest, there is reasonable ground then to conclude that the loan is intended to serve the purpose of placing the belligerent in a more favourable condition of making war and it loses the character of neutrality accordingly. *

6°. *Relations of Neutrality with regard to parties of a Civil War.*

Belligerent character in civil war.

§ 234. Civil or internal wars, which aim at the destruction of the unity of a State, give rise to belligerent rights of the contending parties when the movement becomes serious and lasting. Belligerent rights are granted to parties of a civil war for the sake of humanity and justice and to secure the rights of third parties or neutrals.

The recognition of parties in a civil war is a question of international policy, but the contend-

---

* VATTEL. Liv. III. Chapt. VII. § 110. PHILLIMORE. Vol. III. Edit. 1873. p. 247, et seq. HALLECK. Edit. Sherston Baker. Vol. II. p. 195. W. E. HALL. p. 519.

It is contrary to the law for persons residing in Great Britain to enter into engagements to raise money, by way of loan, for the purpose of supporting subjects of a foreign State in arms against a Government in alliance with Great Britain.—*De Wurtz* v. *Hendricks*, 9. Moore, C.P., 586.

In the judgment in this case, Mr. Justice Best observed that the Court of Chancery had decided, under circumstances of a precisely ing parties having been once acknowledged as belligerents, the relations of the parties with regard to neutrals are the same as those of a war between States. A foreign Power may assist a friendly State to repress rebellion and is

---

similar nature, in the same manner. British Courts of Justice will not take notice of, or afford any assistance to, persons who set about raising loans for subjects of a foreign Government, to enable them to prosecute war against that Government. At all events such loans cannot be raised without the licence of the Crown. See also *Josephs* v. *Pebrer*, 1 Car., and Pay, N. Pri. C., 341. The two following opinions of the British law officers relate to the above question:—

To the Right Hon. George Canning, M.P., etc.

Doctors' Commons, June 17, 1823.

SIR,—We have been honoured with your commands, signified in Mr. Planta's letter of the 12th inst., stating that you were desirous that we should report our opinion upon the following questions:—

1. Whether subscriptions for the use of one of two belligerent States by individual subjects of a Nation professing and maintaining a strict neutrality between them, be contrary to the Law of Nations, and constitute such an offence as the other belligerent would have a right to consider as an act of hostility on the part of the neutral Government?

2. If such individual voluntary subscriptions in favour of one belligerent would give such just cause of offence to the other, whether loans for the same purpose would give the like cause of offence?

3. And, if not, where is the line to be drawn between a loan at an easy or mere nominal rate of interest, or a loan with a previous understanding that interest would never be exacted, and a gratuitous voluntary subscription?

In obedience to your commands, we beg leave to report that we have taken the same into our consideration, and we are of opinion that subscriptions of the nature above alluded to, for the use and avowedly for the support of one of two belligerent States against the other, entered into by individual subjects of a Government professing and maintaining neutrality, are inconsistent with that neutrality, and contrary to the Law of Nations; but we conceive that the other belligerent would not have a right to consider such subscriptions as constituting an act of hostility on the part of the Government, although they might afford just ground of complaint, if carried to any considerable extent. With respect to loans, if entered into merely with commercial views, we think, according to the opinions of writers on the Law of Nations and the practice which has prevailed, they would not be an infringement of neutrality; but if, under colour of loan, a gratuitous contribution was afforded without interest, or with mere nominal interest, we think such a transaction would fall within the opinion given in answer to the first question.

We have the honour to be, &c.
CHRISTOPHER ROBINSON (King's Advocate).
R. GIFFORD (Attorney-General).
J. S. COPLEY (Solicitor-General).

not allowed to aid rebels, but when the insurgent party has succeeded in creating a Government of its own choice, the foreign State may enter into neutrality relations with the seceding party without unfriendliness to the original Government.

Lincoln's Inn, June 21, 1823.

SIR,—We have been honoured with your commands, signified to us by Mr. Planta in his letter dated 18th instant, in which he states, with reference to the queries proposed to His Majesty's law officers in his letter of the 13th instant, he was directed by you further to ask for our opinion whether, having regard to the municipal law of this country, there exists any, and what, means of proceeding legally against individuals and corporations engaged in such subcriptions as were described in those queries.

We have accordingly taken the same into consideration, and beg leave to report that, reasoning upon general principles, we should be inclined to say that such descriptions in favour of one of two belligerent States, being inconsistent with the neutrality declared by the Government of the country and with the Law of Nations, would be illegal, and subject the parties concerned in them to prosecution for a misdemeanour, on account of their obvious tendency to interrupt the friendship subsisting between this country and the other belligerent, and to involve the State in dispute, and possibly in the calamities of war. It is proper, however, to add that subcriptions of a similar nature have formerly been entered into (particularly the subscription in favour of the people of Poland in 1792 and 1793), without any notice having been taken of them by the public authorities of the country, and without any complaint having, as far as we can learn, been made by the Powers whose interests might be supposed to have been affected by such subscriptions. Neither can we find any instance of a prosecution having been instituted for an offence of this nature, or any hint at such a proceeding in any period of our history. We think, therefore, even if it could be proved that the money had been actually sent in pursuance of the subscription, it is not likely that a prosecution against the individuals concerned in such a measure would be successful. But, until the money be actually sent, the only mode of proceeding, as we conceive, would be for counselling or conspiring to assist with money one of the belligerents in the contest with the other, a prosecution attended with still greater difficulty.

We beg leave further to report that no criminal proceeding can be instituted against a corporation for contributing its funds to such a subscription, but that the individual members who may be proved to have acted in the transaction can alone be made criminally responsible.

R. GIFFORD.
J. S. COPLEY.

"Until the fact of a new State is decided by the issue of the struggle, says Dr. Woolsey, the position of neutrals is a delicate one, and one to which little attention has been paid by writers on the Law of Nations. Theoretically we say, (1.) the relation, if the foreign Power stands aloof, is not that of neutrality between States, but of neutrality between parties, one of which is a State and the other trying to become a State. (2.) The foreign Power, therefore, cannot plead the laws of neutrality for treating both parties alike, for the one is an acknowledged State, the other is not. Thus whatever favours it has granted to the cruisers of the friendly State, it is not bound to grant to the revolters, or rather, it is bound not to grant to them the same privileges, for by so doing it admits their right to prey on the commerce of its friends,—which only States can do. (3.) In a certain sense the foreign Power must regard the revolters, as belligerents, entitled to all those rights which humanity demands, as that of asylum for troops or vessels in distress, or fleeing from a superior power,—the same sorts of rights which would be granted to political exiles. The vessels of such revolters cannot be regarded as piratical, for their motive is to establish a new State, while that of pirates is plunder. A pirate never ends his war with mankind. They fight for peace." * (Comp. § 98).

7°. *Colonial and Coasting Trade.*

Colonial and coasting trade as a question of neutrality.

§ 235. Formerly it was regarded by the policy of convenience that the carrying on, by the neutral, of any trade between the belligerent mother-country and the colonies, and the carrying on of the coasting-trade of the belligerent, when such trade was confined in time of peace

* WOOLSEY. p. 300.

to the belligerent's subjects, was not consistent with neutrality. This policy, called the Rule of 1756 (when it was first applied in the war between Great Britain and France, which at one time much agitated both Europe and America), is stripped of its former importance by modern policy in colonial and coast-trade navigation, especially of Great Britain and the Netherlands, and also by the Declaration of Paris of 1856, by which it adopted, in Rule II, that the neutral flag covers enemy property, with the exception of contraband of war (§ 223).

On the other hand it can be argued, that, while neutrals have the right to continue, during time of war, the trade they were accustomed to engage in with the belligerent parties during the time of peace, yet they have no right to engage in new traffic, established between the mother-country and the colonies, or between the ports of a belligerent State, for the sole purpose of aid during war only and to be discontinued after the cessation of war. As such trade could be regarded as a material help and protection to the belligerent flag, which is incompatible with the impartiality imposed by strict neutrality, the question might arise whether it is lawful for a neutral to carry on, in time of war, with a belligerent a trade, in the case of which the municipal law of the belligerent State forbids foreigners to participate in it in time of peace.

The solution of this question depends mainly on the difference existing in the policy of Nations with regard to their respective coasting trade, colonial systems and navigation laws, and, being dependent upon municipal laws, the question can be regarded as belonging to State policy rather than to the domain of International Law. At all events,—Rule II of the Declaration of Paris, of 1856, by which the neutral flag covers enemy's goods, has left no place in International Law for the principles of the Rule of 1756, for the new rule, being expressed in the most general terms, protects inoffensive neutral trade in all articles which are not contraband of war, whether a certain trade had been opened to neutrals in time of peace or not. * (Comp. §§ 226 & 229).

8°. *Belligerent Right of Visit and Search and Capture.*

Principles of the right of visit and search. What is visit and what is search?

§ 236. As stated above (§ 226), neutrality, being based on the principle of strict impartiality, imposes on neutrals the obligation,—when called upon in certain doubtful cases to prove their impartiality,—of granting belligerents, in these special cases, the right of investigation and adjudication within the sphere of acknowledged usages of war, proceedings which in a normal state of affairs should be strictly confined to the limits of jurisdiction of the respective State. Hence arises the belligerent right of visit and search of neutral vessels or conveyances, in time of war, when these are suspected to be in unfair relations with the enemy.

The right of visit means the right to ascertain by an inspection of the ship's papers and other documents the real national character of the vessel and the nature and destination of the cargo; while the right of search, which is an extension of that of visit, is exercised by inspecting the interior of the vessel and the cargo, when the papers and other indications do not afford sufficient evidence to satisfy the belligerent party, who has a legitimate interest in knowing the truth about vessel and cargo.

* WOOLSEY. p. 349. For the history of the Rule of 1756, see Phillimore, Com. Intern. Law. Vol. III. Edit. 1873. p. 370, et seq.

If the flag, as outward and *primâ facie* token of nationality and neutrality, were always to be trusted, and if neutral vessels were never compromising their neutrality by hostile commerce, the right of approach, as described in § 97, would in time of war as in that of peace, suffice to ascertain the nationality and the inoffensive character of any vessel on the high seas. But it is vain to expect such fair dealing on the part of neutrals, with regard to their commerce, or on the part of any belligerent party, who, for the sake of safety or as a stratagem, assumes the disguise of a neutral.

When and where can this right be exercised and by whom.

§ 237. The right of belligerents to search neutral vessels on the high seas, in order to ascertain the non-hostile character of vessel and cargo, is a right of self-defence and thus a necessary usage of war. With the exception of cases of piracy (§ 98) and of intercepting hostile expeditions on their way to aid a rebellion, as will be noted in paragraph 239, this right of visit and search, is an exclusively belligerent right, and must not be confounded with the right of search, agreed upon by special treaties for the suppression of the slave trade, (as noted above in paragraph 99). Public or State vessels are in no case subject to the right of visit or search; the inviolability of the public vessel as representing the State whose flag it unfurls, and the mode of ascertaining its character, are described in paragraphs 105–109.

As no private or non-commissioned vessel is allowed to exercise any belligerent acts whatever, and belligerent rights at sea being granted exclusively to duly commissioned vessels (comp. §§ 224 & 225), it is obvious that only these latter can exercise the right of visit and search as well as that of capture. The right of visit and search can have effect on the high seas or in the waters of belligerents but never within the territorial waters of a neutral State, as noted above in paragraphs 203–205, and on the same principles as described there with regard to the right of capture. *

Proceedings with regard to visit and search.

§ 238. The belligerent vessel which, meeting a vessel, desires to exercise the right of visiting it, shall summon it for the visit, by means of signals according to the International Code of Signals (see § 118) and by firing a blank shot, called the summons or affirming gun. The vessel thus summoned, if a private or merchant vessel, is bound to bring to and to submit to the visit and, if necessary, to the search.

The belligerent is bound to exercise the right of visit and search with due discretion and in such a manner as to obtain the real object in view and nothing more.

On the other hand, the master of a visited vessel is obliged to allow the visiting officer a fair chance to comply with his duty of properly investigating the character of ship and cargo.

In order to gain the protection against capture, which is due to a neutral vessel, the master must exhibit all documents which are required to prove the national character, the ownership of the vessel and cargo and the nature of the voyage, such proof to be in accordance with the law of the flag under which the vessel sails or with any special convention which may have been made between the Nation to which the vessel belongs and the belligerent. With regard to the documents which must serve to prove the national character of private or merchant vessels, called ship's papers *(papiers de bord ou lettres de mer,*

---

* VATTEL. Liv. III. Chapt. VII. HUBNER. Part II. Chapt. III. ORTOLAN. Vol. II. Edit. 1864. p. 248, et seq. HAUTEFEUILLE. Vol. III. p. 2, et seq. HEFFTER. § 167, et seq. KLUBER. § 293. BLUNTSCHLI. § 819. WOOLSEY. Edit. 1879. p. 367, et seq. W. E. HALL. Edit. 1880. p. 637, et seq.

Schiffs-papiere), and the rules applicable to registration and transfer of sea-going vessels, and the documents serving as proofs of ownership, we must refer the reader to paragraphs 66, 102–104 and 222, where they are described and enumerated.

Search of vessels having hostile intent in time of peace. The case of the "Virginius."

§ 239. In particular cases of necessary self-defence,—and after due notice to the respective foreign State,—a State is authorized, in time of peace and apart from belligerent rights, to order its war vessels to visit and, if necessary, to search certain specified foreign vessels, on the high seas, when there is reasonable ground for believing such vessels to be engaged in a hostile expedition against the Government or the territory of the State. For instance, in a rebellion it may happen that a hostile expedition is fitted out in a foreign country to aid the insurrection, and, if such vessels be on their way to land troops and arms to help the rebel party in upsetting the established Government, this Government ought to be authorized, by its right of self-defence, to intercept such hostile conveyance, wherever it may be found outside the jurisdiction of other States. *

* A noticeable instance with regard to the right of visit and search of foreign vessels in time of peace, when under suspicion of hostility, is the case of the steamer *Virginius*, which was under the flag of the United States of America when captured, in October 1873, by a Spanish war steamer on the high sea, while endeavouring to reach the neutral waters of Jamaica, having been foiled in the attempt to land a party of insurrectionists on the Cuban Coast. Of this case Dr. Woolsey gives the following account. "The capture occurred in the night of 31 October, 1873, but the bulletin officially announcing it was not published at Havana until 5 November. A Court was assembled for the trial of the persons taken on the vessel, one hundred and fifty-nine in number, of whom four were executed on the 4th of November, thirty-seven on the 7th, and sixteen on 8th; and the remainder, one hundred and two in number, were delivered on board a United States steamer, December 18. There were nine executed who belonged to the United States, and a larger number of British subjects. The summary and informal process, the cruel execution of persons belonging to the crew, even of mariners and cabin boys, met with the just indignation of the world; but in addition to this, unless the *Virginius* can be shown to have been a piratical vessel, the mode of trial was a violation of Article 7 of the United States Treaty of 1795 with Spain, which secures a regular trial, the use of solicitors, agents, etc.,

§ 240. The system of convoy, which was much in use about the middle of the last century and in the beginning of the present, has often been the

Convoy. Can convoyed vessels be searched?

and their free access to the subjects or citizens of the one party arrested for offences committed within the jurisdiction of the other."

"The Government of the United States, supposing that their rights on the sea had been violated, as well as that persons illegally captured had been executed cruelly and against Treaty, demanded reperation. As the result of negotiations, on the 29th of November, Spain stipulated to restore the *Virginius* and the survivors, and to salute the flag of the United States on the 25th of December following. If however, before that date Spain should satisfactorily prove that the *Virginius* was not entitled to carry the flag of the United States, the salute should be dispensed with, and only a disclaimer of intent of indignity to the flag should be required. Furthermore, the United States engaged on the same condition, to adopt legal proceedings, etc., against the vessel, and the persons who might have violated the laws in relation to the vessel."

"It was afterwards proved that the *Virginius* was not legally a vessel of the United States. The real owners from the first were Spaniards. The oath of the American in whose name she was registered was false. So says the Attorney General in a letter to the Secretary of State, dated 17 December, 1873, who adds that, in his opinion, she had no right as against the United States, to carry the American flag, because she had not been registered according to law. He adds, 'Spain, no doubt, has a right to capture a vessel with an American register, and carrying the American flag found in her own waters, assisting or endeavouring to assist the insurrection in Cuba; but she has no right to capture such a vessel on the high seas, upon an apprehension that, in violation of the neutrality or navigation laws of the United States, she was on her way to assist said rebellion.'"

"The reasoning and opinion of the Attorney General are examined by Mr. R. H. Dana, the editor of Wheaton, in a Boston journal, of 6 January, 1874. In brief, he takes the unassailable position that actual ownership by a person belonging to a State places a ship on the high seas under the jurisdiction of that State. The *Virginius*, owned really by Spaniards, was really under Spanish jurisdiction; and the register of a foreign Nation is not, and by the law of Nations is not recognized as being, a national voucher and guaranty of national character to all the world."

"Nations, having cause to arrest a vessel, would go behind such a document to ascertain the jurisdictional fact which gives a character to the document, and not the document to the fact. Even a genuine passport, which is an assertion of national character, is not conclusive between Nations on a question of right to arrest. And if the Attorney-General thinks that Spain has no jurisdiction to inquire into violations of the United States' laws, that the question whether or not the register was fraudulently obtained, was a matter of our law and for our decision, it may be replied that, granting this to be true, the fact does not touch the question of jurisdiction, which depends on ownership. All that can fairly be said is, that while the Nation of the owners has a right to arrest, the ostensible ownership, appearing on the register fraudulently obtained, would suggest delay and sequestration of the vessel until the facts could be established. We add that the flag is no protection without a right to use it, and that source of bloody contest. This system originated from the necessity under which neutral Govern-

---

every Nation—for purposes of jurisdiction over vessels of its subjects at sea, as well as for other reasons—has a right to decide by its ships of war whether its own vessels are not wearing a foreign flag. But the Spanish captain, who took the *Virginius,* supposed it to be a veritable American vessel, making an attempt to land men and instruments of war in order to assist the insurrection in Cuba. What was his duty in the premises? It was to defend the coasts of Cuba, to the best of his ability against a vessel which was known to be under the control of the insurgents, for which he had been on the look out, and against which the only effectual security was capture on the high seas. Of course such self-defence on the part of Spain involved a risk, like that which was involved in the case of the *Caroline,* when Mr. Webster admitted that self-defence was in certain cases justifiable, although it might lie beyond the ordinary course of International Law. The writer of this work (Dr. Woolsey) defended the proceedings of the Spanish vessel on this ground in some remarks made at the time, which were widely circulated in the newspapers. Some time afterwards an eminent lawyer, Mr. George T. Curtis, examined the subject at large in "*The case of the Virginius, considered with Reference to the Law of Self-defence,*" and justifies the capture on the same ground. We quote a few words. 'We rest the seizure of this vessel on the great right of self-defence which, springing from the Law of Nature is as thoroughly incorporated into the Law of Nations as any right can be. No state of belligerency is needful to bring the right of self-defence into operation. It existed at all times in peace as well as in war. The only questions that can arise about it relate to the modes and places of its exercise. In regard to these we have only to say that there is no greater inconvenience to be suffered by admitting that this right may be exercised on the ocean, than is constantly suffered by neutrals from an exercise of the belligerent rights of Nations at war. In fact the inconvenience is not nearly so great.'"

The documents may be found in *Executive Document No. 30,* Forty-third Congress, first session, accompanying a message of the President.

The following rules of International Law are illustrated by the case of the *Virginius:*—

1. That the right of self-defence authorizes a Nation to visit and capture a vessel as well on the high seas as in its own waters, when there is reasonable ground to believe it to be engaged in a hostile expedition against the territory of such Nation.

2. That a Nation's right of jurisdiction on the high seas, over vessels owned by its citizens or subjects, authorizes the detention and capture of a vessel found on the high seas, which, upon reasonable grounds, is believed to be owned by its citizens or subjects and to be engaged in violating its laws. The flag or register of another Nation, if not properly belonging to a vessel, does not render its detention unlawful by the cruiser of a Nation to which its owners belong. As, however, the register affords *primâ facie* evidence of nationality, the nation which gave the register by mistake, must be treated with great care, detention on grounds proved to be erroneous must be atoned for, and the question of ownership would naturally be committed, where the evidence is not patent, to a third party. (WOOLSEY. Edit. 1879. p. 376, et seq.).

ments were placed, in those days of irregular maritime warfare caused by commercial jealousy and vindictive reprisals, to dispatch vessels of war for the purpose of escorting merchant vessels of their subjects, in order to protect them against the exactions and irregular proceedings of privateers. From this arose the vexed question, whether neutral vessels, under convoy of public vessels of their State, are bound to submit to visit by belligerent's vessels of war.

The right of visit and search of neutral vessels is such a necessary and generally acknowledged belligerent right, devolving, as noted above (§ 226), from the very principle of neutrality, that no alterations in the mode of exercising this right could legally take place without a previous understanding with the belligerent party concerned. Hence the necessity of treaties with regard to convoys. *

When a neutral State thinks it proper to take under its special protection private acts of commerce or otherwise of its subjects, in the face of indisputable belligerent rights, thus dictating

---

* In the treaties concluded, in 1801 and 1802, between Great Britain, Russia, Sweden and Denmark, these three Powers abandoned the doctrine of immunity of visit in the case of vessels under convoy, and consented that, though visit was not to take place unless ground for suspicion existed, the belligerent commander should have the power of making it at his discretion, in presence, if required, of a neutral officer, and of carrying the suspected vessel into one of the ports of his country if he should see reason to do so. (DE MARTENS, Rec. VII. 264, 273, 276). But the subsequent treaties, concluded in 1812 and 1814, between England and the three above mentioned parties to this compromise, placed matters on their old footing, and left the Baltic Powers free to assert, and Great Britain to refuse, the immunity of convoyed vessels. (DE MARTENS. Nouv. Rec. I. 481 and 666 and III. 227). Since then France has accepted the principle of this freedom from visit in six treaties, all with American republics, viz.:—with Venezuela, 1843 (De Martens, Nouv. Rec. Gen. V. 171); Ecuador, 1843 (id. 409); New Granada, 1844 (id. VII. 620); Chili, 1846 (id. XVI. I. 10); Guatemala, 1848 (id. XII. 10); Honduras, 1856 (id. XVI. II. 154). The United States embodied the same principle in thirteen treaties, of which all, with two exceptions, have also been entered into with States on the same continent, viz.:—with Sweden, 1816 (Nouv. Rec. IV. 258); Columbia, 1824 (id. VI. 1000); Central Ame-

the formalities with which the exercise of these rights must be attended, it is assuming an attitude of armed neutrality. The convoying of merchant vessels by State vessels, with the object of exempting the merchant vessels from the visit or search which is an acknowledged belligerent right, is inconsistent with the principle of neutrality when not regulated by a convention of which the belligerent is a party. All one-sided attempts to introduce into the question the inviolability of the public or State vessel, as representing the State whose flag it bears, only serve to complicate an originally plain question of fair dealing, in conditions in which honesty should be allowed to defend itself. By mixing up the honour of the flag with the dispute, an element is introduced which shuts out all compromise, and unnecessarily irritates parties without bringing any logical argument to the conclusion. If it be once agreed upon that all shall fairly show their hands and turn over their pockets, it is a false notion of honour for one to object and can only serve to create suspicion. Although there may be occasionally reasons for protest and even for positive objection, when proceedings are over-stepping the boundaries of necessity, yet the rights and the dignity of the neutral State are far more efficiently upheld by unsophisticated dealings towards belligerents than by a suspicious

---

rica, 1825 (id. 835); Brazil, 1828 (id. IX. 63); Mexico, 1831 (id. X. 340); Chili, 1832 (id. XI. 446); Venezuela, 1836 (id. XIII. 560); Ecuador, 1839 (id. 23); New Granada, 1848 (Nouv. Rec. Gen. XIII. 663); Guatemala, 1849 (id. 304); San Salvador, 1850 (id. XV. 77); Peru, 1870 (Nouv. Rec. Gen. 2°. Serie I. 103) and Italy, 1871 (Archives de Droit Intern. 1874, p. 136).

In 1864, Denmark, Prussia and Austria announced that they would not visit vessels under convoy. Germany, Austria, Spain and Italy, in addition to the Baltic Powers and France, provided by their naval regulations that the declaration of a conveying officer shall be accepted. CALVO. § 1219. RAYNEVAL. p. 265.

withholding from fair investigation. The rights of all parties would be better served if the system of convoy would remain true to the principle of a conventional guarantee for fair deelings on both sides. Since, however, the searching of neutral vessels by belligerents is now carried on with far more moderate proceedings than formerly, and since privateering with its inherent irregularities can now fairly be classed among the international sins of past generations,—the undue molestation of *bonâ fide* neutral commerce is, under ordinary circumstances, at the present state of maritime warfare, no more to be anticipated, and the convoy question has consequently ceased to have much, if any, practical significance (Comp. §§ 236–238).

§ 241. The belligerent has the right of seizure of vessels under neutral flag, for a subsequent adjudication of the capture by the competent Prize-Court, under the following circumstances. *Seizure of neutral vessels.*

1°. When the visit or the search is resisted with violence.

2°. When there is fair ground for suspecting, upon evidence obtained through the visit or search, that the vessel is engaged in an illicit act or that its cargo is contraband of war.

3°. When it is found impossible to ascertain the true national character of the vessel in the absence of essential proofs.

4°. In the case of fraudulent or ambiguous acts committed by the owner or master, viz.: the possession of double or false documents or the destruction, spoliation or concealment, of papers.

The right of seizure on the ground of resistance to a legal visit or search is the necessary consequence of the right of visit, when exercised by the belligerent in virtue of existing treaties or acknowledged rules of International Law. Another question arises, if the property of third persons is to share the fate of the vessel, in case the latter is found guilty so far as to be liable to confiscation. If the vessel is legal prize by reason of the hostile character attached to it in consequence of the acts of the master who represents the owners, and who must be regarded as having acted on their instructions, there is no justifiable reason to admit that the hostile character of the vessel is attached to the inoffensive goods which happen to be shipped on board in legitimate traffic,—the more so, as by Rule III of the Declaration of Paris, neutral goods, with the exception of contraband of war, are not liable to capture under enemy's flag (§ 223). The decisions of British Prize Courts in this matter are all antecedent to the Rule of 1856, which international rule,—it cannot be doubted,—will have in this case, as well as in other cases, decidedly a weighty influence upon future judicial decisions. By putting his goods on board the vessel, which, during the voyage, becomes a hostile vessel by the sole act of the master, the neutral owner, who never entertained any hostile intentions or has any part whatever in the resistance offered to the visitation or search, cannot be compromised by any illegal acts of the master or the owners of the vessel, over which he, as a mere shipper, has no control whatever. He relied on the innocence of his trade and the neutral character of the vessel. His goods not being hostile, his rights cannot be impaired by the fact that the master has compromised the vessel; the act of resistance is not his because not occasioned through his goods being in the vessel. Thus, the neutral rights of the shipper cannot be set aside, nor does the innocent cargo partake of a hostile character by any individual illegal or hostile act of the master or owners of the neutral vessel, any more than neutral goods can become hostile by being shipped in an enemy vessel. According to Chief Justice Marshall, "the object of the neutral is the transportation of his goods. His connection with the vessel which transports them is the same whether that vessel is armed or unarmed. The act of arming is not his, he meddles not with the armament nor with the war; and the belligerent suffers no injury from his act, for if the property be neutral what mischief is done by its escaping a search?" *

With regard to fraudulent or ambiguous acts, such as the possession of false documents or the destruction or concealment of papers, Mr. Hall makes the following statement.

Mr. Hall's statement.

"That a vessel is furnished with double or false documents, is invariably held to be a sufficient reason for bringing her in for adjudication; and according to Russian practice, at any rate, a false passport, and in Spanish practice, double papers of any kind, entail confiscation of both ship and cargo; but generally falsity of papers is regarded with leniency, and is only considered to be noxious when there is reason to believe that the fictitious documents were framed in order to deceive the capturing belligerent, and that they would therefore fraudulently oust the rights of the captors, if admitted as genuine. The ground of this leniency is that, apart from indications that they are directed against the interest of a particular belligerent, they are as likely to have been provided as a safeguard against the ene-

* The *Atalanta*. 3 Wheat. R. 409. HAUTEFEUILLE. Tit. XI. Ch. 240. ORTOLAN. Dipl. de la Mer. Vol. II. p. 260.

my of the captor as against the captor himself. * The destruction or 'spoliation' of papers, and even, though to a less degree, their concealment, is theoretically an offence of the most serious nature, the presumption being that it is effected for the purpose of fraudulently suppressing evidence which, if produced, would cause condemnation. The French Regulations of 1704, repeated in 1744 and 1778, declared to be good prize all vessels, with their cargoes, on simple proof of the fact that papers had been destroyed, irrespective of what the papers were; but the severity of the rule has been tempered in practice, it being commonly required that the destroyed papers should be proved to be such as, in themselves, to entail confiscation. In England and America a milder practice is in use. Spoliation or concealment of papers, if all the other circumstances are clear, only affects the neutral with loss of freight, but it is a cause of grave suspicion and may shut out the guilty person from any indulgence of the Court, as, for example, from permission to bring further proof if further proof be necessary. If the circumstances are not clear, if, for example, spoliation takes place when the capturing vessel is in sight, or at the time of capture, or subsequently to it without the destroyed papers having been seen by the captor, further proof would probably be shut out as of course, the natural inference from the circumstances being that they have been destroyed because their contents were compromising." †

---

* HALLECK. II. 299; The *Eliza* and *Katy*. VI. Rob. 192; The *St. Nicholas*, I. Wheaton, 417. Rev. de Droit Intern. Vol. X. 611; *Negrin*, 251.

† W. E. HALL. Intern. Law. Edit. 1880. p. 650. The *Rising Sun*, II. Rob. 106; The *Hunter*, I Dodson, 487; Livingston v. The Maryland Ins. Cy., VII. Cranch, 544; The *Commercen*, I Wheaton, 386; The *Pizarro*, II Wheaton, 241; The *Johanna Emilie*, Spinks. 22.

The same principle, as stated above in the case of innocent property of third persons loaded in vessels which offer resistance, holds good in the case of fraudulent acts with regard to documents entailing confiscation.

The duties of the Seizor of neutral property.

§ 242. The duties of the seizor of neutral property are stated in the respective regulations with which every State provides its cruisers, and of which the general principles are laid down in Prize Court regulations (Chapter XXXVII).

"In the absence of proof, says Mr. Hall, that a neutral has rendered himself liable to penalties, he has the benefit of those presumptions in his favour which are afforded by his professed neutrality. His goods are *primâ facie* free from liability to seizure and confiscation. If then they are seized, it is for the captor, before confiscating them or inflicting a penalty of any kind on the neutral, to show that the acts of the latter have been such as to give him a right to do so. Property, therefore, in neutral goods or vessels which are seized by a belligerent, does not vest upon the completion of a capture. It remains in the neutral until judgment of confiscation has been pronounced by the competent Courts, after due legal investigation. The Courts, before which the question is brought whether capture of neutral property has been effected for sufficient cause, are instituted by the belligerent and sit in his territory; but the law which they administer is International Law." *

9°. *The Destruction of Neutral Property in enemy vessel.*

Destruction of neutral property before adjudication.

§ 243. The destruction of neutral vessels, when seized by belligerent cruisers, can be justified only by the most cogent reasons caused by un-

* W. E. HALL. p. 651.

controllable circumstances or for self-preservation. When in such extreme cases the right of the neutral is in conflict with that of the belligerent, and the neutral property is in the power of the belligerent, it is vain to expect the captor to release his prey unscathed. When he has not the power to keep, he assumes the right to destroy. "The practice is a barbarous one, says Dr. Woolsey, and ought to disappear from the history of Nations." * According to the decisions of English Courts, when a neutral vessel is burned wantonly or the necessity of the destruction is not proved, the captor or his Government is responsible. † Prize Courts naturally discountenance all summary disposal of prizes on the captor's own authority, such as the destruction or ransom of vessels, proceedings by which the case is withdrawn from their jurisdiction and their decision supplanted. In the case of neutral goods in enemy's vessels, of which the inviolability is guaranteed by Rule III of the Declaration of Paris (§ 223), there exists a most regrettable instance of inconsistency in the application of this rule of International Law, in the late Franco-German war. Two German vessels were captured and burned by a French cruiser, for the reason that the captor had so many prisoners on board from other captures, that he could not spare any of his own men for prize crews. Neutral property laden on board these vessels was burned, and the owners applied in vain for compensation, the Prize-Court at Bordeaux having decided that the burning of the enemy ships with the neutral goods was authorized. The Council of State, to which the owners of the destroyed neutral property appealed, confirmed the judgment of the Prize Court at

* WOOLSEY. (Ed. 1879) p. 251.

† The *Actæon*. Dodson. Admir. Rep. II. 48. The *William*, Idem. II. 55.

Bordeaux on the following grounds. 1°. That, though Rule III of the Declaration of Paris of 1856 gives to a neutral owner a right to the restitution of his goods or the payment of the price, it does not follow that he can claim indemnity on account of acts of injury caused to him by valid capture, or by acts of war, connected with such capture. 2°. The destruction was due to the fact that the commander of the capturing vessel had so many prisoners on board that he could not spare any of his crew for the purpose of taking these prizes into a French port. 3°. Hence the burning was a continuation of the fact of war, the fitness of which the owners of the cargo could not be allowed to discuss. *

With regard to this judgment, Mr. Hall makes the following remarks.

Mr. Hall's opinion.

" It is to be regretted, says he, that no limits were set in this decision to the right of destroying neutral property embarked in an enemy's ship. That such property should be exposed to the consequences of necessary acts of war is only in accordance with principle, but to push the rights of a belligerent further, is not easily justifiable and might under some circumstances amount to an indirect repudiation of the Declaration of Paris. In the case, for example, of a State the ships of which were largely engaged in carrying trade, a general order given by its enemy to destroy, instead of bringing in for condemnation, would amount to a prohibition addressed to neutrals to employ as carriers vessels, the right to use which was expressly conceded to them by the Declaration in question. It was undoubtedly intended by that Declaration that neutrals should be able to place their goods on board belligerent vessels without, as a rule, incurring further risk

* WOOLSEY. p. 252. CALVO. Vol. II. p. 670.

than that of loss of market and time, and it ought to be incumbent upon a captor who destroys such goods, together with his enemy's vessel, to prove to the satisfaction of a Prize Court, and not merely to allege, that he has acted under the pressure of a real military necessity." *

10°. *Acts of Individuals, constituting Violations of Neutrality.*

Neutrality rights are correlative to neutral duties, with regard to private individuals as well as States.

§ 244. Neutrality rights are correlative to neutral duties. This maxim is applicable to individuals in their private capacity as well as to States as bodies-politic. Neutral States can claim from the belligerents all respect and inviolability for their flag and for the persons and properties of their subjects or citizens, when not employed in acts or pursuits incompatible with a *bonâ fide* state of neutrality. In all cases where the neutral right of the private individual is violated, compensation must follow in due course, but as truly also neutral property is liable to confiscation when it has been used or been placed in conditions infringing on belligerent rights.

Besides the general acts of commerce and intercourse, which are noted in the preceding paragraphs as incompatible with neutrality, individuals belonging to a neutral State are reasonably expected to abstain from rendering those special acts of personal assistance to a belligerent Government, or its officials or agents, which might be of direct influence in the operations of a war waged against a State with which his own Government is in amicable relations.

Foreigners in the military or civil service of a belligerent Government.

§ 245. When the laws of his own State, or existing international treaties between the respective parties, do not forbid it, a private individual

* W. E. HALL. International Law. Edit. 1880. p. 635.

may enter the active military or civil service of a belligerent without forfeiting his nationality, but it is the duty of the Government of a *bonâ fide* neutral State, on the notification of a war between States with which it is at peace, to prohibit its subjects or citizens to take any active part whatever in the warlike operations of either belligerent. In that case, the neutral Government is not compromised by the individual acts of its subject or citizen, while the latter, acting in contravention of the laws of his State, loses all claims on its protection (Comp. § 185).

Neutral conveyance of enemy's troops and dispatches.

§ 246. The obligations of neutrality forbid neutral vessels to convey troops and dispatches in the service of belligerents as well as all articles which have been declared contraband of war. In fact, troops and dispatches or information with regard to warlike operations are sometimes even more hostile than contraband of war, as connecting the neutral more closely with the enemy. The mischievous consequences of such a service, says Sir Robert Phillimore, must be estimated to extend far beyond the effect of any contraband that can be conveyed, for it is manifest that by the carriage of dispatches the most important operations of the enemy may be furthered.

With regard to the transport of troops, several political and commercial treaties contain provisions to the effect that the exemptions in favour of goods on a neutral vessel shall be extended to persons sailing on the same in such wise that, though they be enemies of one or both the parties, they shall not be taken from the free ship unless they be military persons (officers or soldiers) actually in the service of the enemy. It is especially held, that the forwarding of officers of high rank would subject the neutral vessel to seizure. *

With regard to the conveyance of hostile individuals and dispatches, the following rules prevail in the decisions of Prize Courts.

Rules with regard to the conveyance of hostile individuals and dispatches by neutral vessels.

1°. Dispatches, which impress a hostile character upon the carrier, are official communications from official persons regarding the public affairs of the belligerent Government. Letters of such persons concerning their own private affairs, and letters written by unofficial persons, are not dispatches. Communications from a hostile Government to one of its Consuls in a neutral country, unless proved to be of a hostile nature, and dispatches of an enemy's Ambassador resident in a neutral country, are excepted from the rule, on the ground that they relate to intercourse between the hostile State and a neutral, which is lawful, and which the other belligerent may not obstruct. The comparative importance of the dispatches, if within the rule, is immaterial.

2°. In order to make the carrying of enemy's dispatches an offence, the guilt of the master

* Treaty of Utrecht of 1713 between France and Great Britain, Dumont VIII. 1.345. Treaty of 1785 and of 1800 between France and the United States. The Bremen ship *Greta* was condemned, in 1855, by a Prize Court at Hongkong, for carrying 270 shipwrecked Russian officers and seamen from a Japanese to a Russian harbour, during the Crimean War.

For the subjects embraced within this section, see MARQUARDSEN (Prof. at Erlangen), Der Trent-Fall, Erlangen, 1862.—For the conveyance of troops and of dispatches most of the modern text writers may be consulted, as WHEATON, IV. 3. § 25. HEFFTER, § 157 b.; ORTOLAN, II., 213; WILDMAN, II., 234–244; PHILLIMORE, III., § 273. The cases, which have principally determined the law in the matter of dispatches, are those of the *Atalanta*, 6 Robinson's Rep. 440; *Carolina*, ibid., 465; and *Rapid*, Edwards' Rep. 228. The *Atalanta* brought dispatches from the French governor of the Isle of France to the French Minister of Marine, and was condemned; the *Carolina*, from the French ambassador in the United States, a neutral country, to his home Government, and was released. For the course which the United States should have taken, from the first news of the *Trent* affair, in consistency with their past principles, compare Mr. Sumner's speech in the Senate of the United States, in January, 1862. WOOLSEY. Edit. 1879. p. 348. PHILLIMORE. Com. Vol. III. Edit. 1878. p. 456.

must be established. It is competent for those entrusted with the care of the ship, on board of which such dispatches are found, to clear themselves of the imputation of being concerned in the knowledge and management of the transaction. If the dispatches are put on board by fraud, without the knowledge of the master or of those representing him then in charge, no penalty is incurred by the ship. But the presumption is against the ignorance of the master, if he sails from a hostile port, and especially if the letters are addressed to persons in a hostile country, and stronger proof is then needed, that he is not privy to a guilty transaction, than if the voyage began in a neutral country and was to end at a neutral or open port.

3°. If the shipmaster is found guilty of conveying hostile dispatches, the penalty is confiscation of the ship which conveys the dispatches. The ship is liable to condemnation, and the cargo is confiscable *ob continentiam delicti*, if both vessel and cargo belong to the same owners.

4°. Masters of Mailboats *(paquebots-poste, Postdampfer)* and, in general of all vessels, whose ordinary business is to carry passengers and mail bags in a regular mail or ferry-line service, are not held responsible for the hostile dispatches or individuals, found on board in ordinary traffic. *

Dr. Woolsey's opinion. Affair of the Trent.

"These rules, says Dr. Woolsey, in their general form, if not in their harsher features, may be said to have passed into the Law of Nations. Not only the declarations of England and France, made in the spring of 1854, but the contemporaneous ones of Sweden and Prussia, sanction them,

* The *Attalanta*. 6 Rob. Adm. Rep. pp. 440–460 is the leading case on the subject. The *Caroline*. Id. p. 461 notes pp. 462–465. The *Rapid*. Edward's Adm. Rep. 228 & 229. WOOLSEY. Intern. Law. Edit. 1879. p. 346. PHILLIMORE. Comm. Intern. Law. Vol. III. Edit. 1873. p. 456. HALL. p. 595. MARQUARDSEN. Der Trentfall. BERNARD. Hist. Acc. of the Neutr. of Great Britain. pp. 301, 215 & 224.

and the Government of the United States, in one instance, has accepted them as part of the Law of Nations. They are received as such by text-writers of various nationalities, by Wildman and Phillimore, by Wheaton, by Heffter, Marquardsen and other German writers, by Ortolan and Hautefeuille. The last named publicist gives a modification of the rule, which, though of private authority, deserves serious attention. Dispatches can be transported, says he, from one neutral port to another, from a neutral to a belligerent, or from a belligerent to a neutral, or finally from one belligerent port to another. In the three first cases the conveyance is always innocent. In the last it is guilty only when the vessel is chartered for the purpose of carrying the dispatches; but when the master of a packet-boat or a chance vessel takes dispatches together with other mail matter, according to usage, he is doing what is quite innocent, and is not bound to ascertain the character of the letters which are put on board his vessel. Whatever may be thought of this, it may be seriously doubted whether a neutral ship, conveying mails according to usage or the law of its country, can be justly treated as guilty for so doing. The analogy from articles which are contraband of war loses its force here. When a war breaks out, a captain ought to know what articles he has on board, but how can he know the contents of mailed letters?" *

---

* WOOLSEY. p. 346.

It may be useful to note here the affair of the *Trent*, which case has a bearing on this question and on other principles of International Law. "This vessel, says Dr. Woolsey, sailing from one neutral port to another on its usual route as a packet ship, was overhauled by an American captain, and four persons were extracted from it on the high seas, under the pretext that they were ambassadors, and bearers of dispatches from the Confederate Government, so-called, to its agents in Europe. The vessel itself was allowed to pursue its way, by waiver of right, as the officer who made the detention thought, but no dispatches were found. On this transaction we may remark,

§ 247. It is a violation of neutrality, and a neutral vessel acquires a hostile character, when she uses the flag and sailing-pass of the enemy with a view to benefit the owner's interests or those of the enemy. The flag is the most obvious badge of the national character of the ship, and she is liable as against herself to be considered as belonging to the Nation thus indicated. It is, however, only the ship which thus takes its national character from the flag or pass and not the goods. * The colourable title binds the vessel under all circumstances, except when it may be used in her favour, for if the real character happens to be hostile, it can always be pleaded against her. The owner is not allowed to redeem his property, by disclaiming the false character and resuming his actual nationality, any more than he can shelter his real nationality by the assumed foreign character. † *Use of the flag and pass of a belligerent by neutral vessels.*

(1.) That there is no process known to International Law by which a Nation may extract from a neutral ship on the high sea a hostile ambassador, a traitor, or any criminal whatsoever. Nor can any neutral ship be brought in for adjudication on account of having such passengers on board. (2.) If there had been hostile dispatches found on board, the ship might have been captured and taken into port; and when it had entered our waters, these four men, being citizens charged with treason, were amenable to our laws. But there appears to have been no valid pretext for seizing the vessel. It is simply absurd to say that these men were living dispatches. (3.) The character of the vessel as a packet ship, conveying mails and passengers from one neutral port to another, almost precludes the possibility of guilt. Even if hostile military persons had been found on board, it might be a question whether their presence would involve the ship in guilt, as they were going from a neutral country and to a neutral country. (4.) It ill became the United States,—a Nation which had ever insisted strenuously upon neutral rights,—to take a step more like the former British practice of extracting seamen out of neutral vessels upon the high seas, than like any modern precedent in the conduct of civilized Nations, and that too when she had protested against this procedure on the part of Great Britain and made it a ground of war. As for the rest, this affair of the *Trent* has been of use to the world, by committing Great Britain to the side of neutral rights upon the seas." WOOLSEY. p. 347.

* The *Success*. 1 Dodson, 131. the *Vrouw Elizabeth*. 5. C. Rob. Adm. Rep. 2. ARNOULD. Edit. Maclachlan, Vol. II. p. 614.

† The *Francis*. 8 Cranch. R. 418. The *Success*. 1 Dod. R 131. The *Fortuna*. 1 Dod. R. 87.

With regard to goods which happen to be found in such vessels, they are, as a rule, not condemnable if the shipment was made in time of peace and not in contemplation of war. The prize-rule that the action of the master compromises the cargo, which was adopted by Prize-Courts in cases of inoffensive neutral property laden in a *bonâ fide* neutral vessel, the master of which, however, has thought proper to resist the right of visit and search of a belligerent cruiser (§ 239), is here set aside, and the owner of the neutral property is allowed to prove his innocence with regard to the acts of the master or owners of the vessel which implicated him. * While the belligerent flag and pass, says Halleck, are, in all cases, decisive as to the ownership or the character of the ship, a distinction is made by the English Courts in favour of the cargo of such ships, if the shipment was made in time of peace and plainly not in contemplation of war. Even where the goods themselves, for purposes having no relation to a future war, are clothed with a foreign character, which has become hostile, the owner is not liable but is permitted to disprove the colourable title, and upon due proof of his neutral character and actual ownership, his property is restored. †

Opinion of Chancellor Kent.

The remarks of Chancellor Kent on this subject are as follows. "Some countries have gone so far as to make the flag and pass of the ship conclusive on the cargo also; but the English Courts have never carried the principle to that extent, as to cargoes laden before the war. The English rule is to hold the ship bound by the

* The *Elsabe*. 4 Rob. R. 408. The *Catharina Elizabeth*. 5 Rob. 232. The *Fanny*. 1 Dod. Adm. Rep. 443. HALLECK. Edit. Sir Sherston Baker. Vol. II. p. 295.

† HALLECK. p. 319.

character imposed upon it by the authority of the Government from which all the documents issue. But goods which have no such dependence upon the authority of the State, may be differently considered; and if the cargo be laden in time of peace, though documented as foreign property in the same manner as the ship, the sailing under a foreign flag and pass has not been held conclusive as to the cargo. The doctrine of the Federal Courts of the United States has been very strict on this point, and it has been frequently decided, that sailing under the licence and passport of protection of the enemy, in furtherance of his views and interests, was, without regard to the object of the voyage or the port of destination, such an act of illegality as subjected both ship and cargo to confiscation as prize of war." *

11°. *Licence to Trade.*

Neutral vessels under licence to trade granted by belligerents.

§ 248. The rules, noted in the preceding paragraph, are likewise applicable if a neutral vessel accepts a licence or safe-conduct from a belligerent for a trade which is interdicted by the usages of war, and as a dispensation from the penalties entailed by the infringement of belligerent rights with respect to the State granting it. The seizure of such a neutral vessel by the enemy of the belligerent granting the licence results from the presumption that the licence was granted by his enemy for the furtherance of his own interests, and that the neutral who lends himself to the promotion of the enemy's object, by accepting such licence, forfeits his neutral rights.

Licence granted to an enemy.

§ 249. A licence to an alien enemy subject removes his personal disabilities so far as is neces-

* KENT. Com. on Am. Law. Vol. I. p. 85.
A neutral flag cannot protect an enemy's ship, although it may protect the cargo.—*Cidade de Lisboa*, 6 Rob. 358.

sary for his protection in the particular trade which is rendered lawful by the operation of the licence. In respect of the voyage and trade which the licence intended to authorize and cover, he is not to be regarded as an enemy, but has all the legal privileges of a subject. So far as that particular voyage, trade, or cargo is concerned, he has a *persona standi* in all the Courts, and may maintain suits in his own name, in the same manner as a subject. (Compare §§ 218 & 219). *

12°. *Rights of Belligerents with regard to Neutral Persons and Property within the Jurisdiction of Belligerents.*

Principles governing the political status of neutral persons and property in belligerent States.

§ 250. Neutral persons within the jurisdiction of belligerents enjoy during the war the same protection as that to which they were entitled during the time of peace, being treated on the same footing as the national subjects and, though they be personally exempt from military service (as noted above, in paragraphs 40 and 185), their property is, in cases of grave urgency, subject to the same liabilities of the *dominium eminens* (§ 30) which are incumbent, in behalf of the public safety of the State, upon the property of the subjects or citizens of the belligerent State, with the understanding, however, that the neutral subject be completely indemnified for the retention, use or

* HALLECK. Edit. Sir Sherston Baker. Vol. II. p. 374.

Morgan v. *Oswald*, 3 Taunt. R. 555; *Usparicha* v. *Noble*, 13 East. R., 332; *Flindt* v. *Scott*, 5 Taunt. R., 674; 15 East. R. 525; *Fenton* v. *Pearson*, 15 East. R., 419.

His Majesty, says Lord C. B. Comyn, may grant letters of safe-conduct to an enemy, and by this means take him into his keeping and protection; see Com. Dig. Prerog. B. 5; *Wells* v. *Williams*, 1 Satk. 46; and independently of letters of safe-conduct or passports, a person residing in this country by the licence and under the protection of the Sovereign, is not to be regarded as an alien enemy. See *Wells* v. *Williams*, I. Ld. Raym., 282. In like manner, an insurance may be effected upon the interest of an alien enemy under the protection of a licence from the Crown.—*Hullman* v. *Whitmore*, 3 M. and S., 338.

destruction of his property in the service of the belligerent State.

§ 251. On the principles stated in the preceding paragraph, neutral vessels are subjected to the following compulsory services.

Embargo (Arret du prince).

1°. Neutral vessels may be forbidden to leave the port or their anchorage during a certain time. This prohibition is called embargo *(arrêt du prince)*, the different aspects of which are treated in paragraph 166. The object of this arrest or detention is to secure the secrecy of certain measures of war, which may be in preparation or in course of execution. Under such circumstances it may be of the highest importance for the belligerent that the enemy remain ignorant of the measures taken in the belligerent's ports or roadsteads; in which case there is no other means left than to stop all outward traffic for the time necessary for the purpose. As such arbitrary detention of neutral vessels in port is unquestionably done for the benefit of the belligerent State, it is simple justice that the neutral be reasonably indemnified for his loss of time.

Prestation.

2°. Neutral vessels may be hired for employment in the service of the State, by paying freight beforehand, for the transport of soldiers, ammunition and instruments of war. This is what is understood by the belligerent right of prestation.

Droit d'angarie.

Neutral vessels may be appropriated and taken over by the belligerent State, on payment of a reasonable price, with compensation for loss and expenses to be paid by the appropriating State. This belligerent right is called Admiralty right or prestation *(droit d'angarie)*. * In all

* The word was derived from the old Persian by the Greeks and retained in the latin word *engariare*, which denotes compulsory service in carrying messages, and, by extension of the meaning, applied to any compulsory service. *Quicumque te angaria verit mille passus vade cum ello et alia duo*, (Mathew, I. 41). WOOLSEY. Edit. 1879, p. 186. MASSÉ. Vol. I. p. 280.

such cases the owner of the goods or vessels concerned must be indemnified for all damages caused by the interruption of their lawful gains or for the distruction of property. *

---

* PHILLIMORE. Vol. III. Edit. 1873. p. 51. W. E. HALL. p. 655. This belligerent right, or the *droit d'angarie*, was acted upon by Prussia when, in the last war with France, the Prussians seized in Alsace for military use between six and seven hundred railway carriages belonging to the Central Swiss Railway Company and kept them in use for some time. Another instance, in the same war, was the seizure by the Prussian First Army Corps of neutral vessels under British flag, which they sank in the Seine, at Duclair, to prevent French gunboats from getting up the river and interfering with the German operations on the two banks of the Seine. Count Bismarck wrote to Count Bernstorff, the Prussian Ambassador at London, as follows:—

"Versailles, January 25, 1871."

"I do myself the honour of transmitting to your Excellency, in pursuance of my preliminary communication of the 4th, and my telegram of the 8th instant, a copy of the Report from the First Army Corps, on the sinking of English ships in the Seine, near Duclair, the preparation of which has been delayed by the manifold movements of the Corps concerned. Your Excellency will find therein, with the same satisfaction as myself, that the measure in question, however exceptional its nature, did not overstep the bounds of international warlike usages. The report shows that a pressing danger was at hand, and every other means of averting it was wanting; the case was, therefore, one of necessity, which, even in time of peace, may render the employment or destruction of foreign property admissible under reservation of indemnification. I take the opportunity of calling to mind that a similar right in time of war has become a peculiar institute of law, the *jus angariæ*, which so high an authority as Sir Robert Phillimore defines thus: that a belligerent Power demands and makes use of foreign ships, even such as are not in inland waters, but in ports and roadsteads within its jurisdiction, and even compels the crews to transport troops, ammunition, or implements of warfare. I hope the negotiation with the owners, for which you are already authorized, will lead to an understanding as to the indemnification for the damage; if not, it would have to be submitted to an arbitrator's award. In the negotiation, also, the difference in the statements of the First Army Corps and of the English Consul at Dieppe, as to the number of English ships sunk, will be explained."

"I respectfully request your Excellency to communicate this dispatch, with its enclosure, to the Secretary of State of Her Britannic Majesty, and to be so good as to express, at the same time, my apology for the delay, as well as my thanks to Her Majesty's Government, for the just appreciation of the military necessity with which Lord Granville has apprehended and treated this matter."

"(Signed) "BISMARCK."

A proper indemnification was subsequently made *(d'Angeberg*. Nos. 914, 920, 957; State Papers, 1871. LXXXI. C. 250).

§ 252. On the principles noted in the preceding paragraph, goods laden in neutral private vessels can be appropriated by the belligerent State in whose waters the vessel is found. In such a case the full market value of the goods is due to the owner. This is called the belligerent right of pre-emption and is applicable to all goods which fall within the range of the exigencies of warfare. (Comp. § 266). * *Right of pre-emption.*

13°. *Relation between the Neutral Diplomate and the belligerent Government. Protection of the Subjects of the Enemy State by the Representative of a Neutral Government.*

§ 253. The representatives of neutral States maintain their relations with the belligerent Government unchanged during the war, and on the same footing as in time of peace, with regard to the ordinary interests of their country, but in the troubled political atmosphere in which they are then guiding the affairs of their State, their vigilance must necessarily be augmented in proportion to circumstances, by watching the course of the storm with careful attention, in order to keep clear from being drawn into the contention on one side or the other. If in the normal state of international intercourse the principal quality of the diplomate is judicious discretion in his dealings with the Government to which he is accredited, this quality is put to the severest test when he is to guide the interests of his country in a belligerent State. *The attitude of a neutral Representative at the belligerent Court.*

§ 254. At the outbreak of hostilities, and on suspension of diplomatic relations, or when the resident Representatives are recalled by the re- *Protection of the subjects of the enemy State by the Representative of a neutral Government.*

* HALLECK. Vol. II. p. 263. WHEATON. Elem. Intern. Law, Pt. IV. Ch. III. § 24. KENT. Com. on Am. Law, Vol. I. pp. 138 & 139. DEBRETT, State Papers, p. 380. MANNING. Law of Nations, pp. 287–316.

spective Governments, each belligerent takes the necessary steps to get his subjects or citizens and their interests and properties, which may be within the other belligerent's jurisdiction, placed under the diplomatic protection of the Representative of some friendly neutral Government, and to have the archives of his legation and those of the closed consulates entrusted to the keeping of such neutral legation. This relation, which must be sanctioned by the belligerent Government within whose jurisdiction it is to have effect, does not entail any political liabilities whatever, nor does it, *per se*, bring the State thus rendering the one belligerent certain services with consent of the other belligerent party, into the position of a mediator between these parties. Its neutrality and impartial attitude remain intact with regard to all parties concerned. The protection is simply administrative and diplomatic, and does not extend to the political status of the protected individuals, as created or affected by political measures of war. Thus, if the belligerent might think it proper to decree that all or certain specified subjects or citizens of the enemy State shall leave the country, the protecting Representative cannot interfere, although he is bound to protest against all unjust or cruel acts committed against resident individuals and their property under his protection, or against the property of those who have left the country. On the other hand, he must also be prepared to answer for their conduct during their tolerated residence in the enemy State, in the same way, and to the same extent, as is customary in the case of his own neutral countrymen. *

* In the Franco-German war, 1870–71, Great Britain undertook the protection of French subjects in Germany. The United States of America were charged with the interests of German subjects of the then existing North-German Confederation, of Saxony and the Grand Duchy of Hessen in France, and those of Bavaria and Baden

14°. *The Inviolability of Neutral Territory. Refuge and Asylum.*

§ 255. The respect of neutral territory and its adjacent jurisdiction is the first duty which the belligerent owes to neutrals. On the other hand, an independent neutral State is bound to prohibit all passage of belligerent troops through its territory, and the stationing of vessels of war of belligerents in its territorial waters, as well as to prohibit the carrying on of any enlistment for foreign service or other aid to belligerent forces within its jurisdiction. When free from special treaty obligations, a neutral State is moreover bound to apply this same prohibition equally to both belligerents, in order to preserve its impartial neutrality intact. The doctrine that impartiality is practised when the same privilege is granted to both parties, is not consistent with the principle of neutrality in warfare, for it is rarely possible that one and the same class of privileges be found of equal value to one as to the other belligerent party. (Comp. §§ 226–233).

Obligation of belligerents to respect neutral territory. The case of the Caroline.

As regards this general rule, there exist but few exceptions, which are dictated by the obligations of humanity and left at the discretion of the neutral State concerned.

---

were under the protection of Russia. Mr. Washburne, the United States Minister at Paris, instructed the Consuls under his control to render to the protected belligerent subjects all assistance compatible with their official position. Their appellation, with regard to these attributes, was as follows :—"*Le Consul des Etats Unis d'Amerique, chargé des affaires des sujets de la Confédération de l'Allemagne du Nord, a* .... "

The very interesting correspondence of this Representative of a neutral protectorate with regard to the performance of his difficult task, under most trying circumstances, during that war, is found in the Papers relating to the foreign relations of the United States, transmitted to Congress with the annual message of the President, December 5, 1870. Washington Government Printing Office, 1870.

The admission of belligerent troops into neutral territory, as a refuge from the enemy after defeat or when, retreating before superior forces in such condition that the pressure of circumstances leaves them but the alternative of unconditional capitulation to the enemy or internation in neutral territory, has been treated above (paragraph 190).

We have also treated before (§§ 89–94) the jurisdiction of a State with regard to its maritime domain and territorial waters, and the rights and duties relating thereto are described. In §§ 112–114 were treated the cases in which asylum and extradition, with regard to vessels in territorial waters are applicable in time of peace, while in §§ 203 & 204 the belligerent right of capture is defined with regard to the inviolability of neutral territorial waters, and the duty of the neutral State whose territorial waters have been illegally used by belligerents.

Vessels pursued on the high seas entering neutral territorial waters are safe, as noted in paragraph 205. *

---

* ABREU. Sobre las Presas. Pt. I. C. IV. § 15. VALIN. Traité des Prises. Ch. IV. § 3. AZUNI. Droit Maritime, Pt. I. C. IV. § 1. VATTEL. Droit des Gens. Liv. III. Ch. VII. §§ 132–133; the *Anna Catharina*, 5 Rob. R. p. 15. MARTENS. Précis du Droit des Gens, §§ 310, et seq. PHILLIMORE. On Int. Law. Vol. III. § 154. MANNING. Law of Nations, pp. 186 & 386.

The case of the Caroline. The question of capture in neutral waters was illustrated in the case of the steamer *Caroline*, which was captured and destroyed by British armed forces, while in American territory, in the winter of 1838. "This vessel, says Mr. Halleck, had been employed by a body of Canadian insurgents, in conveying passengers and munitions of war from the frontier of the State of New York to the British ground of Navy Island. The commander of the expedition, from the Canada side, sent to capture this vessel, expected to find her within British territory, but on coming round the point of the island in the night, he first discovered that the vessel was moored on the American shore. He nevertheless proceeded to make the capture and to destroy the vessel, although then within the neutral territory, and his conduct was approved by his Government. This led to remonstrance on the part of the United States.

§ 256. As noted above (§ 90), a State cannot interdict the innocent use of its littoral seas or territorial waters which are considered open to the peaceable traffic of sea-going vessels of all Nations and as close to the land as necessary for a safe course or shortest route for vessels using these natural water-ways to proceed to their respective destination. On the other hand, a State may, for purposes of controlling its revenue, or for reasons of self-defence, forbid foreign vessels hovering around or anchoring on its coast, when they are not compelled to do so by weather, tide or accident. (Comp. §§ 269–273 on blockade).

Difference between the Right of Refuge and Asylum.

It was said that if, upon a full investigation of all the facts, it should appear that the owner of the vessel had been governed by a hostile intent, or had made common cause with the occupants of Navy Island, the United States would prosecute no claim to indemnity for the destruction of this boat; but that the lawfulness, or unlawfulness of the employment in which the *Caroline* was engaged, however settled, in no manner involved the higher consideration of the violation of territorial sovereignty and jurisdiction. In the discussion which followed, Mr. Webster, while claiming absolute immunity of neutral territory against aggression from either of the belligerents, admitted that the necessity of self-defence might justify hostility in the territory of a neutral Power; but that it was required of the English Government, as the aggressor in this case, to show a necessity of self-defence, instant, overwhelming, leaving no choice of means and no moment of deliberation. It will be for it to show, also, that the local authorities of Canada, even supposing the necessity of the moment authorized them to enter the territories of the United States at all, did nothing unreasonable or excessive; since the act, justified by the necessity of self-defence, must be limited by that necessity and kept clearly within it. Lord Ashburton agreed with Mr. Webster on the inviolability of neutral or independent territory, and on the possible exception to which that principle was liable—the necessity of self-defence, as the first law of our nature—and that the suspension of that great principle must be for the shortest possible period, during the continuance of an admitted overruling necessity, and strictly confined within the narrowed limits imposed by that necessity. He, however. contended that there was that necessity of self-defence, instant, overwhelming, leaving no choice of means, and no moment for deliberation, which preceded the destruction of the *Caroline* while moored to the shore of the United States, that 'it must be admitted that there was, in the hurried execution of the necessary seizure, a violation of territory,' and that it was 'to be regretted that some explanation and apology for this occurrence was not immediately made' to the United States by the British Government.' These acknowledgments and assurances were received as satisfactory by the United States, and the subject was not further discussed by the two Governments. (HALLECK, II. 180. WEBSTER. Dipl. and off. Papers. pp. 112–120).

The right of refuge is different from the asylum which a neutral State may grant to belligerent vessels. The right of asylum (*droit d'asyle*) is a prerogative of the neutral State, which is exercised under special political considerations. But when stress of weather, or any accidents beyond its control, oblige a foreign vessel to take refuge in the nearest shelter of land or harbour of a neutral State, such vessel has a claim on the humanity of the neutral State which is called the right of refuge *(droit de relâche forcée)* and is a maritime international usage recognized by all civilized Nations, being the same for belligerents and neutrals. (Comp. § 93).

Belligerent vessels of war and their prizes are entitled to seek shelter, under the right of refuge, in neutral ports, from casualties of the sea and land, or in order to avoid the danger of a storm or the attacks of an enemy. Belligerent vessels may enter a neutral port in quest of asylum, to supply themselves with water, provisions and other articles of pressing necessity, and also for the purpose of undergoing all strictly necessary repairs, according to the discretion of the Sovereign, who may refuse the asylum absolutely, or grant it under such conditions of duration, place, and other circumstances, as he shall see fit; provided, however, that such restrictions are impartially imposed upon both belligerent parties, so that neither have any cause to complain.

So long as the neutral State has not signified its determination, by proclamation or otherwise, prohibiting belligerent vessels with their prizes and prisoners of war from entering its ports, either belligerent has a right to assume the existence of the privilege of asylum, and to imply from the absence of any such prohibition the right to enter for the purposes indicated, subject to such regulations and limitations as the neutral State may please to prescribe for its own neutrality and peace.

Privateering having been abolished by almost all civilized States, privateers have ceased to occupy any international position, and can therefore not claim asylum in neutral waters. (Comp. § 224). *

The public vessels of a belligerent State, entering neutral waters under the privilege of asylum, retain their right of ex-territoriality for themselves and their prizes of war.

Although a neutral State does not allow armed bodies of troops to traverse its territory on their way to the scene of war, yet the asylum, as noted above, is generally granted to belligerent vessels with troops and transports on board. This seeming anomaly in the duties of neutrals is explained through the principle that the public vessel of a State is regarded as representing its State or as forming part of it. Hence its immu-

---

* In May 1865, the United States declared that, if, after a reasonable time should have elapsed for the proclamation to become known in the ports of Nations claiming to be neutral, the insurgent cruisers should continue to receive hospitality in such ports, the Government would deem itself justified in refusing hospitality to the public vessels of such Nations in ports of the United States, and in adopting such other measures as might be deemed advisable for vindicating the national sovereignty.

During the American civil war, ships of war were only permitted to be furnished with so much coal in English ports as might be sufficient to take them to the nearest port of their own country, and were not allowed to receive a second supply in the same or any other port, without special permission, until after the expiration of three months from the date of receiving such coal. Earl Russell to the Lords Commissioners of the Admiralty, Jan. 31, 1862. The regulations of the United States in 1870 were similar; no second supply being permitted for three months, unless the vessel requesting it had put into a European port in the interval. State Papers, 1871. LXXI. 167. HALLECK. Vol. II. Edit. 1878. pp. 173–183. ORTOLAN. Vol. II. p. 283, et seq. HEFFTER. §§ 146–150. CALVO. § 1083. W. E. HALL. pp. 525 & 529. KENT. Comm. on American Law. Vol. I. p. 120, et seq. CUSHING. Opinion of U. S. Attorney General Vol. VII. p. 123. HAUTEFEUILLE. Droit d. N. neutres. Tit. VI. Chapt. II.

nity from all interference of the neutral State with its internal organization and with all acts beginning and ending within ship-board and not touching the neutral soil. (Compare § 105, and, with regard to prisoners of war of belligerent vessels in neutral waters, § 257). *

Halleck's statement. "The rights of war, says Halleck, can be exercised only within the territory of the belligerent Powers, upon the high seas or in territory belonging to no State. Hostilities cannot be lawfully exercised within the territorial jurisdiction of the neutral State which is the common friend of both parties. To grant any such right to one, would be a detriment to the other, and to extend the privilege to both would necessarily make the neutral territory the theatre of hostile operations and involve the State in the consequences of the war. Hence, every voluntary entrance into neutral territory, with hostile purposes, is absolutely unlawful, and the party so trespassing is liable to be treated as an enemy, unless full satisfaction is made for such violation of neutral rights." †

Prisoners of war on neutral territory. § 257. In paragraph 190 we noted the rules with regard to the reception of belligerent combatants who take refuge in neutral territory and the transport across such territory of the sick and wounded belonging to belligerent armies, such as adopted by the Brussels Conference of 1874 (§ 182).

Public vessels of a belligerent State enjoy, whilst in the territorial waters of a neutral State,

* HEFETER. Droit Intern. Edit. Bergson. §§ 147–149. HALLECK. Edit. Sir Sherston Baker. Vol. II. p. 183. W. E. HALL. p. 550. DE MARTENS. Ed. Vergé. Vol. II. p. 309.

† AZUNI. Droit Maritime, tome II. pp. 53, 69. TETENS. Considerations sur les Droits, etc., p. 34. ORTOLAN. Diplomatie de la Mer. Tome II. Chapt. VIII. RIQUELME. Derecho Pub. Int. Lib. I. Tit. II. Chapt. XIV. WHEATON. Elem. Int. Law. Pt. IV. Ch. III. § 7. WOLFIUS. Jus Gentium, § 687. MARTENS. Précis du Droit des Gens, §§ 310, 311. HAUTEFEUILLE. Des Nations Neutres. Tit. VI. Chapt. I. HALLECK. Vol. II. p. 177.

the same exemption from local jurisdiction with regard to the vessel, the captain, officers and all persons belonging to the crew, and the passengers, as noted in paragraph 105, for the normal state of peace. But they are also subject to the principle of extradition, described in paragraph 44, and political offences being excluded from the list of crimes for which extradition can be claimed, it follows that, apart from special treaty, the captain of a belligerent vessel cannot claim the extradition of prisoners of war when these have regained their liberty by reaching the soil of the neutral State. No use of neutral territory, says Sir Robert Phillimore, for purposes of war is allowed. Neither can a belligerent, without leave, carry prisoners or booty into a neutral territory, because such an act is an immediate continuation of hostilities. *

Illegality of captures within neutral jurisdiction.

§ 258. As stated above (§§ 203–205), it is not competent for a belligerent to exercise any right of warfare within the territorial jurisdiction of a neutral State. The inviolability of the neutral territory is a guarantee for the impartiality of the neutral State and naturally devolves from the principle of neutrality, as noted in § 226. This inviolability being thus in the interest of belligerents themselves, the obligation to respect it is equally incumbent upon both parties. Thus also it is the duty of the neutral State to enforce this respect as far as its power reaches. In case the neutral State should be too weak to resist the

* PHILLIMORE. Vol. III. Edit. 1873. p. 562. The Neutrality Ordinance of Austria, of 1803, contains the following with regard to prisoners of war. "Il ne sera pas permis aux Puissances belligérantes de mettre à terre dans nos ports, etc., aucun individu comme prisonnier de guerre : car aussitôt que de tels prisonniers auraient mis le pied sur le territoire d'un souverain neutre ou ami de leur gouvernement, ils devront être regardés comme libres, et toutes les autorités civiles et militaires leur devront, sous ce rapport, protection et assistance." DE MARTENS. Rec. VIII. III ; and the Neutrality Edict of Venice. 1779. Art. XX. Ib. III. 84.

violation of its territory, the neutral Government should not yield except under formal protest, and is even justified in calling for the aid of other neutral States in support of its threatened neutrality, by forming a neutrality alliance or armed neutrality, as stated in paragraph 228.

Hostilities committed within neutral territories are illegal acts which must be redressed, and as much as possible be atoned for by the culpable belligerent.

Reparation to be made by belligerent for the violation of neutral territory. The case of the Emily St. Pierre.

On the same principle, a capture made by a boat or launch, which was sent out from a belligerent vessel, lying, stationed or cruising within neutral waters, is invalid, for nothing in the shape of proximate acts of war can be permitted to originate in neutral territory. This principle applies even when the capture by such boat or launch is made outside the respective neutral territory, for no belligerent is allowed to use neutral territory as a basis of operation. *

---

* In 1793 the United States of America acted upon this principle by causing the restoration of the ship *Grange*, seized in Delaware Bay; and the English Courts did the same by annulling a capture which took place within the mouth of the Mississippi. Mr. Jefferson's letter to Mr. Ternant. Am. State Papers. I. p. 77. The Anna. 5 Robinson's Adm. Rep. 373.

The issuing from neutral ground of a directly hostile act was declared illegal by Lord Stowell, in a case in which a British Frigate, lying within Prussian waters, sent out her boats to make captures among vessels anchored in the neighbouring roads at the entrance of the Dollart.

The *Twee Gebroeders*. 3 Rob. Adm. R. p. 163. HALLECK. Vol. II. p. 183. W. E. HALL. p. 526.

The case of the Emily St. Pierre. The case of this vessel, captured, in 1862, near the American coast, illustrates the principles noted above, in paragraphs 257 & 258. Some of the crew, being left on board, got possession of the vessel and carried her into Liverpool. The United States' Government claimed her on the ground that the rescue was fraudulent and an act of violence towards a lawful cruiser. It is remarkable that a similar case occurred in 1800, only that Great Britain then was the claimant, and that the United States' Government rebutted the claim, on grounds which the British Government used again in their turn in 1862. · Prof. Bernard says, "there can be no doubt that the American Government was right in 1800 and wrong in 1862, and the English Government wrong in 1800 and right in 1862. The enforcement of blockades is left.........by the Law of Na-

§ 259. Prizes, made by a belligerent outside the territorial waters of the neutral State in whose port they are subsequently brought by the captor, receive the same amount of hospitality as the captor to whom they belong, and they enjoy the asylum afforded by the neutral Government on the same conditions as described in the preceding paragraphs for the belligerent vessels of war. The belligerent is, however, not allowed to sell or dispose in any way of his prizes within neutral jurisdiction, without the special consent of the respective neutral Government.

Naval prizes of war within neutral jurisdiction.

With respect to the captured property of its own subjects, brought within the limits of its jurisdiction, a neutral State is authorized to have the affair brought before its own Prize or Admiralty Court, for investigation and adjudication. This jurisdiction is conceded to the neutral State in acknowledgment of the asylum granted to the captor and his prize.*

Captured property of subjects of the neutral State, within whose jurisdiction the prize is subsequently voluntarily brought by the captor, is to be adjudicated by the Courts of the respective neutral State.

If any vessel, whether belligerent or neutral, is captured within the territorial waters of a neutral State, and the captor subsequently takes refuge with his illegally captured prize within the jurisdiction of the State whose neutrality he has violated, the prize is *de jure* free, the moment it re-enters the violated neutral waters.

Property illegally captured within neutral jurisdiction is to be restored by the neutral Government within whose jurisdiction the illegal act was committed.

---

tions to the belligerent alone. They are enforced by the exercise of the belligerent right of capture; and this right is the weapon which International Law places in his hands for that express purpose. Capture is an act of force, which has to be sustained by force until the property in the vessel has been changed by a sentence of condemnation. If the vessel escapes meanwhile from the captor's hands, it is not for the neutral to restore her to him. Resistance or a rescue is.........a distinct offence, drawing after it a distinct and appropriate penalty, —confiscation. But here, again, it is for the belligerent to inflict the penalty, and it is not the business of the neutral to help him to do this, either by recovering his prize for him or by treating the act as a crime." Prof. BERNARD. British Neutrality pp. 325–329. TWISS. Law of Nations in War. p. 496. WOOLSEY. § 208.

* KENT. Comm. Vol. I. p. 121. VALIN. Comm. Vol. II. p. 274. PHILLIMORE. Comm. Vol. III. Edit. 1873. p. 286.

The neutral Government, within whose territory the illegal capture was made, can call into action its own Courts, when the prize comes within its jurisdiction, even if the case has been decided by the belligerent's Prize-Court. In the case, however the prize has been transferred into a duly commissioned State's vessel, by the belligerent Government, the neutral Government has to confine itself to international means for obtaining redress.

The doctrine that the territory and waters of the neutral State are inviolable and that no hostility can be exercised therein, is thus stated by Lord Stowell. "When the fact of neutral territory is established, it overrules every other consideration; the capture being done away with, the property must be restored, notwithstanding that it may actually belong to the enemy." *

On this sound doctrine the neutral Government is bound to act, with regard to captures illegally made within its jurisdiction, by restoring the property to its lawful owner and by causing prisoners of war made within its jurisdiction to be released.

The admittance in their ports of prizes, seeking asylum, is not obligatory to the neutral, and sound policy demands that no admittance should be granted to captures of private enemy property, except in cases of danger through stress of wea-

---

* The *Vrouw Anna Catharina*, 5 Rob. Adm. Rep. p. 15. WOOLSEY. Ed. 1879. § 174. HALLECK. Edit. Sir Sherston Baker. Vol. II. p. 207. W. E. HALL. p. 543, et seq. ORTOLAN. Dipl. de la Mer. Edit. 1864 Vol. II. p. 298, et seq.

"When a captured vessel is brought or voluntarily comes *infra præsidia* of the neutral Power, that Power has the right to inquire whether its own neutrality has been violated by the capture and, if so, it is bound to restore the property." *La Estrella*. IV. WHEATON. 298.

ther *(relâche forcée)* and only as long as the necessity lasts.*

§ 260. The naval forces of both belligerents might enjoy asylum in a neutral port at one and the same time. During their stay in neutral waters, however, their mutual enemy character remains suspended, through the principles of the Law of War and those of Neutrality combined, which forbid the one enemy attacking the other, while both are enjoying the hospitality of a third friendly Power. The usages of civilized warfare forbid the destruction of neutral life and property, which may be placed at hazard by acts of war within or near the neutral's territory, because, on the part of the neutral thus insulted, the attitude of a strict impartiality, which is the basis of neutrality, could then not be properly maintained. Thus acts of war are only legal within the territory of either of the belligerent parties, on the high seas, or in regions not under the jurisdiction of any civilized Nation. † *The 24-hours rule.*

The general principle of the inviolability of the neutral territory being a necessary condition for the neutral's impartiality, this principle requires that such territory remain free, not alone from actual acts of war, but also, as stated before, from all immediate preparations for proximate acts, and it is the right of the neutral to prevent his territory being used as such by any belligerent party. From this principle is derived the rule

---

* "That is, captures of private property in war ought to be attended with so many inconveniences as to check the spirit of plunder." WOOLSEY. Edit. 1879. p. 283.

During the American Civil War, Great Britain prohibited, by an order of June 1, 1861, the bringing of prizes by vessels of war and privateers of both parties into the waters of the British Kingdom and its colonies. France, by a declaration of June 10, 1861, made the same prohibition. In both instances, of course, *relâche forcée*, cases appealing to simple humanity, were excepted.

† BYNKERSHOEK. Quaest. Jur. Pub. Lib. I. Chapt. 8.

adopted by all civilized Nations, to comply with the request and to follow the directions of the neutral Government, within whose territory belligerent war-vessels are enjoying asylum, with regard to all those measures and precautions which may be proposed by the respective local authorities of that Government, with a view to prevent hostile collisions between the belligerent parties within the neutral territory, or to prevent their using the neutral asylum in order to lay in wait and attack a weaker antagonist when the latter is leaving the neutral territory. For this reason a certain fixed time,—which usually consists of twenty-four hours,—is required to elapse between the departure of each belligerent party, so that the weaker one might have sufficient time, after leaving the neutral asylum, to get clear of his enemy and escape the ambush which thus might have been prepared for him from out of the neutral territory within which both had received shelter. *

The decision with regard to the party which has to leave first and thus has the advantage of the twenty-four hours, is, by the common

---

* ORTOLAN. Dipl. de la Mer. Edit. 1864. Vol. II. p. 291. DE MARTENS. Edit. Vergé. Vol. II. p. 310. PHILLIMORE. Vol. III. Ed. 1873. p. 577. W. E. HALL. p. 552. BERNARD. Hist. Acc. of the Neutr. of Great Britain. pp. 270–273. Neutr. Laws Commissioners Rep. App. No. VI. State Papers LXXI. 167. 1871.

This principle often forms the object of municipal regulations, fixing the time which must elapse between the two departures.

During the war of 1718 the neutral States of Italy adopted certain rules for the guidance of their neutral trade and navigation, of which Rule III had reference to this question and read as follows.

"Aucun vaisseau des nations en guerre qui serait à l'ancre dans les ports de Livourne, de Porto-Ferrajo ou de tout autre de la Toscane, ne pourra sortir lorsqu'il y aura des bàtiments signalés au fanal, ou qui, sans être signalés, seraient aperçus à la vue : et si les vaisseaux des nations en guerre étaient déjà à la voile et que l'on fît des signaux au fanal ou que l'on aperçût des batiments à la mer avant qu'ils soient entiérement sortis du port, on les rappellera d'un coup de canon, et ils seront obligés de rentrer et de mouiller jusqu' à ce que les batiments signalés soient entrés ou hors de vue."

usages of war, left to the highest neutral local authority, whose decision should be given after having heard both parties. If one party consists of unconvoyed or unarmed merchant vessels, such party should always have the preference of first departure. In the absence of any obvious difference in strength between the two parties, such as would naturally suggest giving the preference of first departure to the weaker one, it is usual that the party which notified its intended departure first should be allowed to leave first. In that case the other party is then not allowed to follow the enemy sooner than twenty-four hours after the latter has left the neutral waters. If, however, the party which first announced its intention to depart at a certain time has not left at the time so specified, the party in question loses its turn and the first departure is then given to the other party. The latter, however, is also bound to leave within a reasonable time fixed by himself, and his enemy is then to be retained for the same space of twenty-four hours after his departure. The time within which any party announcing his departure is to leave, is usually fixed at twenty-four hours, and each party has, by turns, the alternative of twenty-four hours to leave before the other. *

---

* A remarkable historical instance of such alternative in time of departure of two opposing belligerent parties from a neutral refuge, is noted by ORTOLAN (Dip. de la Mer. Edit. 1864. pp. 292, et seq.), in the correspondence between the Captain of the French vessel of war *Fantasque* and the Spanish Governor of Cadix, in December 1759, which we insert here.

Report of Captain de Castillon commanding the "Fantasque" to the French Minister of Foreign Affairs.

"A bord du vaisseau du Roy, le Fantasque, Baye de Cadix.
18 Décembre 1759."

"Monseigneur,

"J'ay eu l'honneur de vous rendre compte, par le courrier passé, du parti que j'avois pris en conséquence de la relâche de l'escadre angloise dans cette baye, de demander au gouverneur de Cadix l'assurance d'en pouvoir partir avec vingt-quatre heures d'avance sur

The 24 hours rule could be dispensed with, in the case the commanding officer of the belligerent vessel or fleet deliver to the highest local authority of the neutral port a written

---

les Anglois, en vertu du droit des gens. La réponse du gouverneur me parut satisfaisante; vous en avez pu juger par la traduction que je vous en ai envoyée. Je ne m'occupai plus en conséquence que des moyens de profiter du premier vent favorable pour m'éloigner de ce port, et pouvoir ensuite me déterminer conformément aux ordres contenus dans la lettre de Sa Majesté, du 27 novembre, que vous m'avez fait parvenir par le dernier courrier. Depuis ce temps, la constance des vents de sud et sud-ouest, les mêmes qui ont failli faire péril l'escadre angloise à l'entrée de ce port, m'ont empêché d'en sortir.

"L'escadre angloise ayant profité de ce retardement forcé pour se remettre en état de sortir, l'admiral Broderic envoya hier, à midy un quart, un officier au gouverneur de Cadix pour luy notifier son départ pour aujourd'huy à midy un quart.

"Le gouverneur de Cadix m'en fit part, par une lettre en espagnol, dont je crois devoir vous envoyer la copie non traduite que voicy:

"Mui señor mio, en consecuencia de lo que tengo comunicado á "V. S., en fecha de este mes, sobre la respuesta del vice-almirante "Broderic, en asunto á que veinte i quatro horas antes de salir con "su escuadra avisaria, para que si en ellas quisiere V. S. executarlo "con la suia lo pudiese practicar, prevengo á V. S. que en este punto "acabo de tener un oficio del expresado vice-almirante, en que me "participa que dentro de veinte i quatro horas piensa partir; á fin "de que yo passe á V. S. esta noticia i pueda V. S. executarlo ahora "si gustase, en intelligencia de que no verificandose la salida de V. S. "con sus navios no podré embarazar, pasadas estas veinte i quatro "horas, su viage al referido vice-almirante; i espero en caso de no "determinar V. S. hacerse á la vela, observara lo que previenen los "tratados de paces, i lo que practicaran los Ingleses si V. S. resolviere "salir luego tocante á la seguridad de las veinte quatro horas." *

"Je reçus, monseigneur, cette lettre à trois heures après midi, et fis sur ce qu'elle contient les réflexions suivantes:

1° En faisant quadrer les deux lettres du gouverneur de Cadix, il me parut que je ne pouvois compter sur les vingt-quatre heures qu'à

---

* Monsieur, en conséquence de la communication que j'ai faite à votre seigneurie, en date de ce mois, touchant la réponse faite par le vice-amiral Broderic, que vingt-quatre heures avant de mettre à la voile avec son escadre, il donnerait avis de son départ, afin que vous puissiez mettre le vôtre à exécution si vous le désiriez, j'ai l'honneur de vous prévenir qu'en ce moment même je viens de recevoir une dépêche du dit amiral, par laquelle il m'informe qu'il est dans l'intention de partir dans vingt-quatre heures. Je vous fais part de cette nouvelle afin que vous puissiez mettre vous-même à la voile avec votre escadre si cela vous convient; vous faisant observer que dans le cas où votre départ et celui de vos vaisseaux n'auraient pas lieu, je ne pourrais empêcher celui du vice-amiral après ces vingt-quatre heures. J'espère que dans le cas où vous vous détermineriez à ne pas appareiller, vous observerez ce que commandent les traités de paix et ce que pratiqueront les Anglais touchant la sûreté des vingt-quatre heures, si vous vous décidez à partir tout de suite.

statement of his intentions, pledging his word of honour not to commit any acts of hostility within a reasonable fixed time against, or not to follow the same course as, the enemy leaving the

---

compter du moment où l'amiral anglois avoit donné avis de son départ au dit gouverneur, en sorte que le dit amiral n'étoit point engagé à demeurer vingt-quatre heures après mon départ, mais seulement après sa demande.

"2° Je trouvai extraordinaire qu'ayant demandé à partir le premier, et n'ayant pu en aucune sorte, sans risquer l'escadre du roy, effectuer mon départ, le gouverneur de Cadix me mit dans le cas de recevoir l'heure des ennemis du roy.

"Enfin, le temps étoit tout gâté, je ne pouvois sortir dans la journée, la nuit venant ensuite, et la marée devant m'être contraire toute la matinée. Je setis toute l'adresse du vice-amiral anglois, qui me donnoit vingt-quatre heures dont je ne pouvois profiter; je me déterminay en conséquence à répondre au gouverneur la lettre suivante:

"Monsieur, il est vray qu'il y plusieurs jours je vous ay fait de- "mander de retenir l'escadre angloise dans cette baye pendant l'es- "pace de vingt-quatre heures après mon départ avec mon escadre, "que je comptois effectuer au premier instant où le vent me permet- "troit de sortir. La réponse dont vous m'avez honoré à cet égard "étant conforme à ce que j'avois lieu d'attendre, je ne me suis occupé "que des moyens de profiter du premier souffle de vent favorable "pour sortir de la baye; les mouvements que vous avés pu apercevoir "dans mon escadre doivent vous en convaincre. Je vous fais remar- "quer cela particulèrement, parce qu'il importe fort à mon honneur "que vous soyez convaincu que je ne vous ay pas fait cette demande "par un ésprit de chicane et pour n'en pas user; rien n'est plus "certain, Monsieur, que l'impossibilité où j'ay été de l'effectuer.

"Si l'escadre angloise demande à sortir aujourd'huy, c'est à vous "de décider pour la préference; ce n'est point aux ennemies du roy "mon maitre à décider du sort de son escadre et à me préscrire une "heure; c'est à vous, Monsieur, qui, dans la place où vous êtes, est "revêtu de l'authorité de Sa Majesté Catholique, la seule qui doive "parler en cette occasion. Je vous prie de me faire savoir sur quoi "je dois compter, en conséquence des traités entre Sa Majesté Catho- "lique et le roy d'Angleterre. Je vous demande de me déclarer ce "que vous exigez de moi si l'escadre angloise obtient la préférence "pour sortir la première, et de m'avertir aussy de l'heure à laquelle "mon tour reviendra si l'escadre angloise ne sort pas pendant les "vingt-quatre heures qu'elle a demandées, ayant lieu d'espérer que "vous établires à cet égard au moins une alternative entre nous."

"Le gouverneur de Cadix demanda de pouvoir s'expliquer avant de résoudre mes questions, ce qui n'a pu se faire que ce matin; et ce matin même il est entré dans cette baye un vaissau anglois à deux batteries, qui, joint à ceux que je compte actuellement en état de sortir, porte cette escadre à six vaisseaux et trois frégates.

"Comme je fis dire hier au soir au dit gouverneur qu'il étoit important que j'eusse sa réponse de bon matin, il a donné ordre à l'officier qu'il a envoyé à l'amiral anglois de me communiquer sa réponse. Elle à été lue et m'a été expliquée par M. de Beauval, enseigne sur mon bord, faisant fonctions de major, qui entend fort bien l'anglois;

neutral waters shortly in advance of him or before the expiration of the 24 hours fixed for his detention in port.

The false notion that neutral vessels of war can exercise the right of asylum on the open sea.

§ 261. Before closing our remarks on the right of asylum, we must refer to a false notion which is some times met with, viz., that every vessel of war on the high seas is surrounded by a neutral zone of a breadth equal to the cannon-range, within which a vessel, chased on the high seas by a belligerent or an enemy, should be allowed to take refuge and to seek protection against the attacks of her pursuer, as if she were enjoying a legal asylum in the territorial waters of the State to which the protecting war-vessel belongs.

It is obvious that such a theory is entirely inconsistent with the principles of the Law of War as well as with those of Neutrality, but none the less also with the natural freedom of the open sea, as noted in paragraph 88. That no portion of the open sea can be appropriated by any State to the exclusion of others, is the undeniable principle of the *mare liberum.*

If the commanding officer of a war-vessel or fleet takes under his protection any vessel which is chased at the time by a belligerent on the high

---

cet officier m'a assuré que l'admiral reconnoissoit le droit que nous avions de demander l'alternative, mais qu'il ne s'expliquoit pas sur le point essentiel du jour de notre alternative et sur l'assurance des vingt-quatre heures à commencer du moment de mon départ.

" Cependant, le temps qui avoit paru se mettre au beau s'est tout à fait regâté, ce qui m'a donné le moyen de m'expliquer encore à ce sujet avec le gouverneur de Cadix. Il m'a fait dire qu'il me répondoit des vingt-quatre heures après mon départ, pourvu que je partisse dans les vingt-quatre heures de mon alternative, qui, ayant fini aujourd'huy à midi et un quart, recommencera demain à pareille heure.

" Avec cette assurance, vous ne devés pas douter, Monseigneur, de ma vigilance pour saisir le premier instant favorable.

" Je viens dans le moment de recevoir une lettre du gouverneur de Cadix, dans laquelle il m'assure ce qu'il m'avoit fait dire tant sur l'alternative que sur la protection du port.

" Je suis avec respect..., &c.

" Le chevalier de CASTILLON.

seas, he is acting in contravention of the neutrality of his State, and, by thus forfeiting his neutrality, he places himself in the position of an enemy with all its consequences,—for he has no right to interfere and to bar the right of the belligerent where he himself has no exclusive right of jurisdiction. If the chased vessel belong to his own nationality but not to his convoy, his duty is to closely watch the proceedings of the belligerent party, but it depends entirely upon the discretion of the latter to admit or resist the neutral's interference or mediation.

It need scarcely be said that the above stated principles do not, in any way, prevent the commanding officer of a neutral war-vessel or fleet ascertaining, in the usual way, by signals or otherwise, the real character of an aggressor, when his protection is claimed by the pursued vessel, of whatever nationality this latter may be. Such proceedings would be perfectly consistent with his neutral character, for it belongs to the duty of the public vessels of every civilized State to prevent piracy on the high seas. (As to convoys, see § 240). *

Rules binding belligerent vessels when claiming asylum under neutral jurisdiction.

§ 262. The conditions on which asylum is granted to belligerent vessels of war in neutral waters, may be reduced, on the basis of the foregoing statements, to the following rules.

1°. Belligerent vessels, while in asylum, are bound to abstain from all acts of hostility toward the subjects, vessels or other property of their enemy within the neutral's jurisdiction, and to prevent hostile collisions between the individuals landed from the respective belligerent vessels (§ 255).

---

* MASSÉ. Le Droit Commercial, etc. Vol. I. Edit. 1874. p. 314, et seq.

2°. Prisoners of war are not to be restored after they have touched the neutral soil, nor can they be arrested by the belligerent within neutral jurisdiction (§ 257).

3°. No recruiting or enlistment whatever is allowed within neutral jurisdiction, and no military stores, ammunition or any description of implements of war can be shipped in neutral waters.

4°. Belligerent vessels, while in asylum, are not allowed to use the neutral port or waters as a basis of operation, nor to issue therefrom to strike the enemy an unexpected blow, or to prepare for immediate violence or proximate acts of war (§ 258).

5°. Within neutral jurisdiction all means employed, whether by stratagem, threat or violence, to capture or to recover prizes, or to take or to rescue prisoners of war, are illegal. All property thus illegally captured or retaken must be delivered to the neutral local authorities to be restored to the rightful owners, and the prisoners of war thus made must be set free (§ 259).

6°. Belligerents are not allowed to sell or dispose of or to destroy any prizes of war within neutral jurisdiction, unless it be done with the express and special consent of the neutral local authorities (§ 259).

7°. Belligerents are bound to conform with the regulations made by the neutral local authorities with regard to the twenty-four hours' rule, to prevent the hostile following up or pursuing of an enemy leaving the neutral asylum, and in general to abide by the decisions which the Government of the neutral State, by virtue of its sovereignty right of police over its ports, harbours, coasts and territorial waters, may deem necessary to impose in behalf of its own security, neutrality and peace (§ 260).

CHAPTER XXXV.

CONTRABAND OF WAR.

General Principles of the Law of Contraband.

§ 263. In paragraphs 229–232 we noted the principles of neutral trade and the distinction which, by the Law of Neutrality, is to be made between State acts and commercial acts of private individuals. These principles naturally govern also the trade in those articles by means of which the war is carried on and which, in conformity with the particular circumstances of each belligerent party, are more or less indispensable for warlike operations. These articles consist of two classes of goods, viz., implements of warfare and materials which are always indispensable for the carrying on of war, called contraband of war, and those objects which, though not of direct use for actual warlike operations, are yet always welcome to belligerents as being calculated to facilitate such operations. These might be called the commodities of war, and as such they are particularly obnoxious to a belligerent when carried to his enemy, as giving thereby to the latter an indirect advantage over him. For this reason such classes of goods are generally also called contraband of war, though they are as necessary to the peaceable labourer or manufacturer as they are useful for belligerent forces. Hence the distinction which divides contraband of war into two classes,—articles which are intrinsically contraband and those commodities which are only contraband by implication.

§ 264. The term contraband *, being a designation used, since time immemorial, to express certain prohibited objects of trade, has been adopted by writers on the usages of war to denote those articles of commerce which one belligerent prohibits being supplied to the other, and the trade in which, when conducted by neutrals, is regarded as constituting a violation of their neutral obligations. In order to arrive at a clear understanding with regard to contraband of war, Grotius divides all articles of trade into the following three great categories. 1°. Objects which are of use in war alone, as arms and all implements and materials which, by their nature, are ready for warlike purposes. 2°. Those articles of commerce which are exclusively intended for peaceable use and useless in war, being articles of taste and luxury, such as books, paintings, etc. 3°. Articles which can be indiscriminately employed both in war and in peace, as money, provisions, horses, ships, naval stores and articles of naval equipment. Articles of the first class are absolutely contraband of war, and their supply to a belligerent always constitutes a breach of neutrality. Those of the second class give rise to no dispute as being never contraband. With regard to the third class, which includes those objects or articles of commerce, which may or may not be contraband according to the particular circumstances of the respective belligerent, Grotius says, if seizure is necessary for defence, the necessity of the case confers a right of arresting the goods, under the condition, however, that they shall be restored unless some sufficient reason interferes. † *Doctrine of Grotius.*

* Contrabandum or *contra bannum*, "against the interdict." *Bannus* or *bannum* is represented by the English *ban* and the Italian *bando*, an interdict.

† GROTIUS. De Jure Belli ac Pacis. Lib. III. Cap. I. § 5. W. E. HALL. p. 564.

Rules of Contraband of War, as based on the classification of Grotius.

§ 265. On the classification of Grotius the following theory can be based.

Absolute contraband subject to confiscation.

I. Objects used in war alone, viz., arms and ammunition of all descriptions, and all articles manufactured expressly for military purposes, when these are destined for a belligerent State or for any place occupied by belligerent forces, are absolute contraband of war and always liable to confiscation by the opposing belligerent party, whenever found, outside neutral jurisdiction, on their way to the hostile destination.

Occasional contraband subject to the Right of Pre-emption.

II. Articles which are styled simply commodities of war, and which may be and are used for purposes of peace as well as of war (§ 263), are occasional contraband or contraband according to circumstances, that is, when they are conveyed so that their actual destination is to supply the enemy's army or navy. The list of these articles of ambiguous use must be naturally variable; for which reason they have often been enumerated in treaties. While neutrals have the right to continue, during the time of war, the trade they were accustomed to engage in with the belligerent parties during the time of peace, the opposing party, on the other hand, cannot allow them to supply his enemy with commodities without which the latter would not be able to continue the war; hence the right of the opposing party to interfere with such trade. In cases where the goods are not confiscable, that is when not destined for a besieged or blockaded port or not compromised by other prominent characteristics of a manifestly hostile nature, the opposing belligerent, in order to prevent their being used by his enemy for warlike operations is, by the belligerent right of pre-emption, entitled to take over, by purchase, these commodities of war, when found on their way to his enemy. In this case, the purchase is effected at the mercantile value of the goods including a reasonable profit, usually of ten per cent. of the amount, and full freight is paid to the owners of the vessel carrying the goods, and indemnity for detention. *

Commerce between neutrals and belligerents, in articles of exclusively peaceful purposes is free, excepting trade with besieged or blockaded places.

III. The commerce between neutrals and belligerents in articles exclusively used for peaceful purposes, in provisions and in all other objects directly necessary for the sustenance of life, is permitted, and such goods are not liable to seizure and condemnation as contraband, unless destined for a besieged or blockaded place. (See §§ 269–273).

The enumeration of articles belonging to the first class,—viz., goods of exclusively warlike nature,—is simple enough. They are limited to objects made and fashioned exclusively for use in war, including materials formed for the direct fabrication of arms, implements and munitions of war. Also vessels expressly fitted out or built for use as war vessels, guncotton, dynamite, torpedos and all electric gear connected with them or with artillery.

The enumeration of the second class,—viz., goods which may or may not be applicable to warlike purposes,—is more complex and variable and is generally made known by belligerents at the beginning of the war, as circumstances and the state of war must be taken into consideration,

* W. E. HALL. p. 585. ORTOLAN. Dipl. de la Mer Vol. II. p. 190. The English practice, in cases of pre-emption, is to pay a reasonable indemnification and a fair profit on the commodity intercepted, but not to pay the price which could be obtained in the enemy's ports. In a treaty with Sweden of 1803, it was arranged, that in seizures of this kind the price of the merchandise should be paid, either as valued in Great Britain or in Sweden, at the option of the proprietor, with a profit of ten per cent. and an indemnity for freight and expenses of detention. WOOLSEY. p. 340. PHILLIMORE. Vol. III. Edit. 1873. p. 451.

as well as the character and the destination of the goods.

This class includes all raw materials suited for the manufacture of arms and munitions of war, and their ingredients, as saltpeter, sulphur, etc., vessels not originally built or fitted out for use as war-vessels, money, horses, timber for naval construction, clothing, saddles and bridles, sail-cloth, iron plates, brass, steel, all sorts of marine engines, screw-propellers, cylinders, shafts, boilers, boiler plates, tubes, fire bars and every other component part of a marine engine or boiler, also pitch, tar, rosin, cordage and other naval stores and coal. *

Mr. Hall's statement with regard to the principles of classification of contraband of war.

With regard to the classification of contraband of war, Mr. Hall lays down the following principles. "The principle, that the right to class a particular object as contraband is intimately bound up with the fact of its possession being essential to the belligerent for his warlike purposes, will scarcely be contested by any publicist. The belief that no article except munitions of war can be so essential as to warrant interference with trade, appears to underlie the doctrine of one school of writers; the statement that the contrary is true, is explicitly made by the adherents of the opposite opinion; but these are mere differences of opinion as to the value of facts; upon the question of theory there is general agreement. The policy of Nations, on the other hand, has been governed by no principle. The wish to keep open their own or a foreign market, has usually been a motive quite as powerful as the hope of embarrassing an enemy, and

* ORTOLAN. Dip. de la Mer. Vol. II. Edit. 1864. p. 190. BLUNTSCHLI. Droit Intern. §§ 803–805. HEFFTER. Le Droit Intern. § 160. CALVO. § 1111. *State Papers.* Franco-German War. 1870. No. 3. PHILLIMORE. Vol. III. p. 421. British Order in Council of February 18. 1854. HALLECK. Edit. Sir Sherston Baker Vol. II. p. 257.

it has led to a thoroughly confused practice. Usage does not conform to principle, and at the same time no sufficient rule can be extracted from it. In such a state of things it is evidently best to appeal to principle in the first instance and to regard practice as of secondary value. If this be done, although no great precision can from the nature of things be obtained, it will be possible to classify articles other than munitions of war, to some extent, according to the greater or less intimacy of their association with warlike operations, and consequently, according to the less or greater urgency of the circumstances under which a belligerent may fairly prevent their access to his enemy; it being in all cases understood, that if any usage is strong enough to weigh in favour of a particular custom, it shall receive its full value." *

The right of pre-emption exercised by belligerents on goods deemed occasional contraband.

§ 266. In paragraph 252 we have described the right of pre-emption as it is exercised by belligerents, on the strength of the *dominium eminens*, within their own territory. The belligerent right of pre-emption, as applicable to neutral property on the high seas, is only admissible when the goods to which this right is applied have been declared before-hand to be contraband of war by the particular circumstances of the war, and only when such goods are bound for an enemy port. It is a compromise between the belligerent Power on the sea and the neutral carrying on trade in those goods which are occasional contraband. †

* W. E. HALL. Edit. 1880. p. 579.

† By 27 & 28 Vict. Chapt. 25. § 38, passed in 1864, it is enacted that where a ship of a foreign Nation, passing the seas laden with naval or victualling stores intended to be carried to a port of any enemy of Great Britain, is taken and brought into a port of the United Kingdom, and the purchase for the service of Her Majesty of the stores on board the ship appears to the Lords of the Admiralty ex-

The belligerent having the right of stopping neutral trade in contraband of war with an enemy, the former is bound to announce beforehand, clearly and positively, what he intends to include in the classification of contraband of war besides those articles of undoubtedly hostile nature, noted under the first category in the preceding paragraph. This right, of defining the articles which he deems noxious when carried to his enemy, being conceded to the belligerent, he is thus brought under the obligation to treat this kind of occasional contraband with mildness.

As the goods, to be classed as occasional contraband or contraband according to circumstances, are not by common usage sufficiently defined to cause this distinction to be regarded as part of the Law of Nations, it is obvious that neutrals must know beforehand from belligerents, what articles such belligerents do regard as affording assistance to the enemy or to the enemy's military operations, and with regard to which they are compelled by the Law of War, to apply the right of pre-emption, as noted above.

Dr. Woolsey's opinion.

"The harshness of the doctrine of occasional contraband, says Dr. Woolsey, brought into favour the rule of pre-emption, which was a sort of compromise between the belligerents (if masters of the sea) and the neutrals. The former claimed that such articles should be confiscated, the latter that they should go free. Now, as the belligerent often wanted these articles, and at least could hurt his enemy by forestalling them, it came nearest to suiting both parties if, when they were

---

pedient, without the condemnation thereof in a prize court, in that case the Lords of the Admiralty may purchase on the account or for the service of Her Majesty, all or any of the stores on board the ship and the Commissioners of Customs may permit the stores purchased to be entered and landed within any port.

intercepted on the ocean, the neutral was compensated by the payment of the market price, and a fair profit." *

"Before the treaty of Münster, says Sir Robert Phillimore, or about the middle of the seventeenth century, the custom of pre-emption by the belligerent of the property of the subjects of another State, which was thus prevented from reaching its original destination, had a much wider operation than has been in more modern times allowed to it. All cargos without distinction were then subjected to pre-emption, and various treaties acknowledge and regulate, or prohibit, the exercise of this belligerent right; † and even as late as 1810, a treaty between England and Portugal, after stipulating that military and naval stores seized by Portugal are to be paid for at the price fixed by the proprietors, adds, that if the Portuguese Government takes possession of any cargo whatever, or of any part of a cargo, with the intention of purchasing it, or otherwise, they shall be held liable for the damage which the goods may sustain while under the custody of the Portuguese officers. ‡ But according to general modern usage, the doctrine of pre-emption rests upon the distinction between articles which are contraband universally, and those which, being *ambigui usûs*, are contraband only in the particular circumstances of the case. ‖ The carrying of the former class alone is punishable, and entails the penalty of

Sir Robert Phillimore's statement with regard to pre-emption.

---

* WOOLSEY. Edit. 1879. p. 339. HEFFTER. § 160. WARD. Of contraband, p. 196.

† MANNING. p. 313, e. g., Denmark and Spain, 1641.—VI. Dumont, i. 210. England and Portugal, 1642; ib. 239. Denmark and Holland, 1645; ib. 313. Spain and Holland, 1648. Treaty of Münster; ib. p. 431. England and Holland, 1654; ib. ii. p. 76. England and Portugal, 1654; ib. p. 83.

‡ *De Martens, Suppl.* Vol. VII. p. 207.

‖ See §. 55 of 55 Geo. III. C. 160, A.D. 1815.

confiscation either of ship or cargo, or both. The latter class are subject to the milder belligerent right of pre-emption, which is considered as a fair compromise between the right of the belligerent to seize, and the claim of the neutral to export his native commodities, though immediately subservient to the purposes of hostility." *

Mr. Hall's opinion.

Mr. Hall says:—"In strictness every article, which is either necessarily contraband or which has become so from the special circumstances of the war, is liable to confiscation; but it is usual for those Nations which vary their list of contraband, to subject the latter class to pre-emption only, which by the English practice means purchase of the merchandise at its mercantile value together with a reasonable profit, usually calculated at ten per cent. on the amount. This mitigation of extreme belligerent privilege is also introduced in the case of products native to the exporting country, even when they are affected by an inseparable taint of contraband." †

Penalty on the trade in absolute contraband.

§ 267. The absolute contraband articles, included in the first category of paragraph 265, are sufficiently defined by International Law to be known. If these articles are clearly intended for an enemy port, and when more in quantity than necessary for ship's use, they are subject to seizure and confiscation and no freight is paid to the vessel.

In conformity with the modern practice of European and American Prize Courts, the vessel and other goods, not being contraband, are generally set free, unless the vessel—(in cases where the freedom of the ship is not expressly stipulated by treaty)—is implicated in the hostile act, or under

* The *Sarah Christina*, 1 Rob. Adm. Rep. p. 241. WOOLSEY. § 195. PHILLIMORE. Vol. III. Edit. 1873. p. 450.

† W. E. HALL. p. 585. PHILLIMORE. Vol. III. §§ 268–270.

circumstances of fraud or bad faith on the part of the master or owner of the vessel. *

Dr. Woolsey's statement.

"If the contraband articles, says Dr. Woolsey, are clearly intended for the enemy's use, especially if they are more in quantity than the ship's company need, they are subject to confiscation on being captured, and no freight is paid for them to the transporter. Ancient French ordinances, before the ordinance of 1681, prescribed a much milder course: the value of the contraband articles, at the estimate of the admiral or his lieutenant, was to be paid after bringing the ship so freighted into port. Ancient usage, in general, made the ship also liable to confiscation. The commercial treaty of Utrecht, in 1713, points at this where it says, that 'the ship itself, as well as the other goods found therein, are to be esteemed free, neither may they be detained on pretense of their being, as it were, infected by the prohibited goods, much less shall they be

---

* The cases in which the vessel and the non-offending part of the cargo have been condemned by British Prize Courts, are quoted by Sir Robert Phillimore, as follow:—

1°. Cases in which there are circumstances of aggravation.

2°. Cases in which the contraband belongs to the owner of the vessel.

Among the circumstances of aggravation are to be mentioned:—

a. A false destination, which, with contraband on board, subjects both ship and cargo to condemnation. (The *Franklin* 3. Rob. Adm. Rep. p. 217. The *Ranger*, 6, ib. p. 125. The *Edward*, 4, ib. p. 68).

b. The carriage of contraband, with the privity of the owner and in violation of a Treaty. (The *Neutralitat*, 3, ib. p. 295).

c. A concealment of contraband in the outward cargo, which has been holden to render the ship, on her return, subject to condemnation; and the misconduct of the super-cargo—the agent of the owner—has been holden to affect the owner's interest. (The *Baltic*, 1 Acton, p. 25).

d. A private vessel has been forfeited by the contraband traffic of an officer placed in command by the Board of Admiralty. *Belwitt v. Hill*, 13 *East's Report*, p. 13).

In cases in which the ship belongs to the owner of the contraband, condemnation always follows. If the owner of the contraband own a share only in the vessel, his share will be condemned; and this effect will be produced by the contraband articles, though unclaimed confiscated as lawful prize.' The modern rule, pretty uniformly acknowledged, seems to be, that the ship and the goods that are not contraband go free, except where one or both pertain to the owner of the contraband articles, or where false papers show a privity in carrying them. * The justice of confiscating the ship in both these cases is plain enough, for there is an evident intention of violating, by means of the vessel, the duties of neutrals. Whether, when the rest of the cargo belongs to the same owner, it should be thus severely dealt with, may be fairly doubted. Bynkershoek ('Quæst. J. P.,' I. 12) decided in favour of confiscation, *ob continentiam delicti;* and Sir William Scott gives, as his reason for a similar opinion, 'that where a man is concerned in an illegal transaction, the whole of his property involved in that transaction is liable to confiscation.' The penalty ceases after the objectionable goods have been conveyed to their port. In two

---

if they appear by the evidence to belong to such part-owner. (The *Floreat Commercium*, 3 Rob. Adm. Rep. p. 178. The *Franklin*, ib. p. 217).

With respect to the effect of contraband upon the rest of the cargo, it is to be observed that the penalty of contraband extends to all the property of the same owner involved in the same unlawful transaction. (The *Sarah Christina*, 1 Rob. Adm. p. 242. The *Neptunus*, 6 ib. p. 409.) And therefore, if the same owner possess articles of which some are and some are not contraband, all will be alike condemned. To escape from the contagion of contraband, the innocent articles must be the property of a different owner. (The *Stadt Embden*, 1 Rob. Adm. p. 28).

In a case in which the ship was condemned for carrying of despatches, the penalty was not extended to the cargo, though the property of the same owner, it being shown that he was ignorant of the shipment, and it not being shown that the master had been appointed agent for the cargo. (The *Susan*. The *Hope*. Notes to the *Caroline*, 6 Rob. Adm. Rep. pp. 462–463).

A neutral ship cannot claim exemption from the penalty of carrying contraband, because there exists between her and the country of her seizors a Treaty stipulating that free ships make free goods (The *Asia*, cited in Index to 6 Rob. Adm. Rep. p. 483.) or because a permission has been given to her to trade with the enemy in innocent articles. (The *Eleonora Wilhelmina*, ib. p. 331).

* Of course, where the ship is fitted for the naval warfare of the enemy, it is liable to confiscation on another ground.

other cases the confiscation of the ship has sometimes been enforced, when the contraband goods make up three quarters of the value of the cargo, and when the owner of the vessel is bound, by special treaties of his Government with that of the captor, to abstain from a traffic of this description. The first resolves itself into a rule of evidence in regard to the complicity of the ship, and needs not to be made a distinct case; the other assumes without reason, that the owner of the vessel must have a knowledge of the cargo, and is not generally acknowledged." *

§ 268. With regard to the duration of the delictum and the liability to penalty, Sir William Scott gives the rule that "the articles must be taken *in delicto*, in the actual prosecution of a voyage to an enemy's port. Under the present understanding of the Law of Nations, says he, you cannot take the proceeds in the return voyage. From the moment of quitting a hostile port, indeed, the offence is complete." † In a subsequent case, the liability to capture of a ship carrying contraband articles with the help of false papers, was held to continue until the end of the return voyage, and Sir W. Grant pronounced, in this case, the principle to be that, "if a vessel carried contraband on the outward voyage, she is liable to condemnation on the return voyage. It is by no means necessary that the cargo should have been purchased by the proceeds of the contraband." From these two decisions it appears that false papers extend the vessel's guilt. ‡ *Duration of liability to penalty.*

By another English decision, a neutral Danish vessel, stopping at the Cape of Good Hope on her way to a Danish settlement, Tranquibar,

---

* WOOLSEY. Edition 1879. p. 341.

† The *Imina*. 3 Rob. Rep. 168.

‡ The *Margaret*. I Acton's Rep. 334.

with both contraband and innocent articles on board, the latter of which she intended to sell at the Cape, as well as to deliver letters to Dutch magistrates, was exempted from penalty on the ground that meanwhile the Cape Colony had surrendered to the English, and was now in their possession. *

Treaty between the United States and Prussia with regard to contraband of war.

In the treaty between the United States and Prussia, negotiated by Franklin in 1875 there is an article relating to the subject of contraband and inserted in the new treaty of 1799, which provided, with regard to military stores, that the vessels having them on board may be detained 'for such length of time as the captors may think necessary to prevent the inconvenience or damage that might ensue from their proceeding paying, however, a reasonable compensation for the loss such arrest shall occasion to the proprietors; and it shall further be allowed to use, in the service of the captors, the whole or any part of the military stores so detained, paying the owners the full value of the same, to be ascertained by the current price at the place of its destination. But in a case supposed of a vessel stopped for articles of contraband, if the master of the vessel stopped will deliver up the goods supposed to be of a contraband nature, he shall be permitted to do it, and the vessel shall not in that case be carried into any port, nor further detained, but shall be allowed to proceed on her voyage.' †

---

* The *Trende Sostre.* 6 Rob. Rep. 391 note.

† This treaty was terminable in twelve years or afterwards on twelve months' notification. A similar provision was made in the treaty of 1800 between the United States and France, but expired in 1808. Several like treaties between the United States and the Spanish American republics are still in force. If the goods are such in quantity that they can be handed over, the neutral can go on his way. Otherwise the ship must go to the nearest safe port. WOOLSEY. p. 342.

CHAPTER XXXVI.

MILITARY OCCUPATION, SIEGE AND BLOKADE.

Military Occupation, Siege and Blockade are acts of war based on the same principles of the Law of War.

§ 269. The rights of military occupation, siege and blockade, are analogous belligerent rights, based on the same principles of the Law of War. In conformity with these principles, the attacking belligerent, having acquired an actual *de facto* jurisdiction over the invested territory or the occupied territorial waters, he has the right, so long as he is in actual possession of the territory of his enemy or the latter's territorial waters, with an adequate force, to forbid all egress and ingress from or into a besieged or blockaded place, while, by virtue of the impartiality imposed upon neutrals by the Law of Neutrality, neutrals are bound to respect all legally established sieges and blockades (§270). This right of jurisdiction and blockade over the territorial waters of the enemy ceases the moment the occupation comes *de facto* to an end. Hence the necessity of a continually sufficient force to make the occupation an actual fact and the blockade a belligerent act binding on neutrals. On this principle is based Rule IV. of the Declaration of Paris of 1856, noted in the next paragraph. *

The relations of belligerents and neutrals with regard to occupations and sieges.

The usages of war, with regard to the duties of belligerents whilst exercising the rights of occupation, siege or blockade, are noted in paragraphs 187, 188 and 223. The relations between

* ORTOLAN. Vol. II. Edit. 1864. p. 326, et seq. HAUTEFEUILLE. Des Nations Neutres. Tit. IX. IDEM. Hist. du Droit Mar. Int. P. III. Ch. I. § 1. MASSÉ. Vol. I. p. 249, et seq. CAUCHY. Vol. I. p. 419.

belligerents and neutrals and neutral commerce, during military occupation and sieges or blockades on land, have likewise been noted, in the above named paragraphs, as well as in paragraphs 220 and 250, dealing with the effect of domiciliation in belligerent countries and the rights of belligerents with regard to neutral persons and property within belligerent jurisdiction.

As noted above (§§ 40 and 220), with regard to the effect of domiciliation in the enemy country, neutral individuals within an enemy State, being subject to the jurisdiction of the enemy, must share the fate of war equally with the subjects of that State. Thus neutral subjects, found in an occupied territory of the enemy, are, on the same footing as the national inhabitants, placed under the temporary jurisdiction, military or civil, of the occupying Power, and are subject to the same liabilities, with regard to exceptional taxation in cases of exigency of warfare, as the subjects of the enemy State.

Definition of the term blockade.

§ 270. By a blockade is more especially understood the obstruction of the passage leading into and out of a seaport, river, roadstead or line of coast of the enemy, without any special intention of getting possession of the blockaded place, but with the determined view to cut off all commercial communication by water with the blockaded place. It must be understood, however, that the innocent use of the water way, when this is internationally free (*see* § 93), cannot be withheld in the case of neutral vessels.

The conditions which constitute a valid blockade.

The conditions to be fulfilled in order to make a blockade valid under the Law of Nations and under the declaration of Paris, (§ 223) are the following.

Blockades must be effective.

1°. Blockades, to be binding, must be effective; that is to say, they must be maintained by a force sufficient actually to prevent access to the shores of the enemy, so that there may exist real danger, through the efficiency of the blockading forces, for any party engaged in the act of forcing the blockade, be it by ingress or by egress. To maintain a blockade, the belligerent must be present and able to defend it. *

Blockades of river estuaries, straits or canals, cannot impede international free neutral passage to neutral places or to non-blockaded enemy ports without contraband of war.

2°. When the right of blockade is applied to a river estuary, strait, or canal, the passage of neutral vessels, not bound to the blockaded territory, cannot be impeded if the banks or shores of the blockaded river, strait or canal, do not entirely and exclusively belong to the enemy, or, even when this is the case, if the invested river, strait,

* Rule IV. of the Declaration of Paris.

" Pour déterminer ce qui caractérise un port bloqué, on n'accordera cette denomination qu'a celui où il y a, par la disposition de la puissance qui l'attaque avec des vaisseaux arrêtés et suffisamment proches, danger evident d'entrer." Declaration of the Armed Neutrality of 1780, Art. 27, of the Treaty between France and Russia, of 11 January, 1789. Art. 18, of the Treaty between Russia and the Kingdom of the Two Sicilies, of 17 January, 1789.

The Treaty between France and Denmark, concluded in 1742, established, in Art. 20, the rule, "that no port could be considered really blockaded, if the entrance were not defended by, at least, two vessels of war and a battery of cannon planted on shore, so that no vessel could enter without manifest danger." (WENCK. Codex Jur. Gent. I. 613).

In the Treaty of commerce between the United Provinces of the Netherlands and the Two Sicilies of 1753, it was stipulated that no ports or places should be regarded as besieged or blockaded, if they were not invested, either, by sea, with at least six war-vessels, stationed at short distances beyond the range of the batteries of the blockaded place, or, by land, with batteries and other works, fixed in such manner, that egress is impossible without crossing the fire of the besiegers or the blockaders. (MOSER. Versuch. VII. 588).

In the Treaty between Prussia and Denmark of 1818, Art. 18, it is stated that a port must be blockaded by at least two vessels of war.

The Treaty concluded between Great Britain and Russia, on the 17 June, 1801, to which Sweden and Denmark subsequently adhered, formally states, that no port shall be recognized as blockaded except those before which the attacking Power has stationed war-vessels sufficiently close to constitute an evident danger when entering such ports in violation of the blockade."

KLUBER. Edit. Ott. § 297. MASSÉ. Edit. 1874. p. 245, et seq. WHEATON. Part IV. Ch. III. § 28. ORTOLAN. Vol. II. p. 287, et seq. HAUTEFEUILLE. Vol. II. p. 189, et seq. GERARD DE RAYNEVAL. De la Liberté des Mers. 1811.

or canal serves to unite two parts of the open sea or two navigable internationally free waters. Such a passage, being *de facto* established and universally acknowledged as an international highway, cannot legally be closed for neutral vessels bound to neutral territory or, without contraband of war, to non-blockaded enemy ports. (Comp. §§ 90–93). The blockading belligerent has, however, in this case as in other military operations, the right of visit and search and of exercising such control over the innocent passage of neutral vessels, as he may deem necessary to secure the accomplishment of the blockade. *

Blockades must be explicitly defined.

3°. The places blockaded must be explicitly, positively and comprehensively defined; no extension of blockade by construction can be legal. †

The existence of a blockade must be properly notified by the competent authority.

4°. The blockade must be properly notified to neutrals, by the competent belligerent authority, whether civil or military. In this case it is supposed to exist until publicly repealed by the competent authority or otherwise expired *de facto*, in a credible manner. (Comp. § 272).

After suspension or interruption the resumed blockade must be de novo notified.

5°. When a blockade is *de facto* suspended by the blockading squadron being driven off by a force of the enemy and effectually interrupted, but resumed by the blockading Power, proper notification must be *de novo* proceeded with in order to keep off the neutrals. The blockade must be renewed by notification, in conformity with its nature, and the same measures are required for a recommencement as were required

---

* On this principle, for instance, the Suez Canal could be blockaded by an enemy of Egypt, with free passage to neutrals not touching at any Egyptian place.

MASSÉ. Vol. I. p. 255. ORTOLAN. Vol. II. p. 293. HAUTEFEUILLE. Vol. II. p. 211. CAUCHY. Vol. II. p. 423. CALVO. Vol. II. §§ 1161–1163.

† Opinion of Chief Justice CHASE, in the case of the *Peterhoff*. 5 Wallace (Amer.) Rep. pp. 49–54.

for the original imposition of the blockade. (Comp. § 274). *

§ 271. We have noted, in paragraph 167, that when two Nations are in a state of reprisals, as described in Chapter xxv, the right of blockade is sometimes exercised by the one State as a measure of constraint on the commerce of the other, without entering upon actual warfare. This sort of blockade is called pacific blockade, in contradistinction from the belligerent blockade which is applicable in time of war.

The two sorts of belligerent blockade, viz., siege blockade and maritime or commercial blockade.

There are two species of effective belligerent blockades viz.: the siege blockade and the maritime or commercial blockade.

---

* The *Hoffnung*, 6 Rob. Adm. Rep. p. 120. PHILLIMORE, Vol. III. p. 487.

The *Napoleonic Continental System.* During the six years' war between Great Britain and Napoleon I, the history of blockade had its greatest epoch. Napoleon established what was then known as the Continental system, the object of which was to exclude Great Britain and its Colonies from the trade of the Continent of Europe. The continental system was created by the Decrees of Berlin, in 1806, by which the British Islands were declared to be in a state of blockade, until Great Britain should recognize the French Maritime Law. This decree was met by the British Orders in Council of January 7, 1807, by which all ships were forbidden to enter any French port or any place under French occupation or influence under pain of confiscation. Napoleon retaliated by the decree of Warsaw, January 25, 1807, which declared the confiscation of all British commodities in the Hanseatic cities then newly occupied by the French troops. The British having established a strict blockade of the Elbe and Weser, declared, by two orders in Council, March 11, 1807 and November 11, 1807, all those ports from which the British flag was excluded to be in a state of blockade, and that all ships proceeding thither should be captured, unless they had touched at a British port and paid duty to the British Government. Napoleon replied to this by the Decree of Milan (1807), which declared every ship submitting to the British conditions to be denationalized and a lawful prize, and further that every vessel, to whatever nation she might belong, fitted out from or going to England or the British Colonies, or any country occupied by British troops, should be captured and confiscated.

By these blockade skirmishes, the neutral commerce and navigation, pressed and threatened on all sides, were entirely suppressed and did not revive until Great Britain, remitting that part of the Order in Council by which the countries of the Allies of France were included under the proclamation of blockade, Napoleon, on his side, revoked the Decrees of Berlin and Milan, in 1812; whereupon the British Orders in Council were all instantly declared cancelled.

1°. Siege blockades are those which, forming part of the scheme of the campaign *(plan de campagne)*, are established as a part of the actual military operations, and are thus combined with military expeditions by land, either in the form of invasion, military occupation or siege, or sometimes in the form of a simple investment, having for its object the surrender or conquest of the place thus blockaded or the embarrassment of the movements of the enemy's land forces. By this blockade, which is sometimes maintained as a substitute for bombardment, all communication with the places under blockade is completely forbidden, by land as well as by water.

2°. Maritime or commercial blockades are those which are solely intended to distress the enemy by intercepting its maritime commerce, without any direct military end in view or any direct object of reducing the places thus blockaded or of committing direct acts of hostility on land.

During a maritime or commercial blockade, which is sometimes extended over all those coasts of the enemy which can be guarded by the fleet of the belligerent, the trade of a neutral to or from the blockaded country, is prohibited by sea but lawful by inland navigation or transportation.

It does not follow from this rule that, when a port is besieged by land but not blockaded by sea, the trade might be lawfully carried on by sea. This would be an infringement on the belligerent's right of siege. The primary object of a siege being the reduction of the besieged place, all communication of neutrals with such a place, whether by water or by land, is a violation of neutrality. *

* PHILLIMORE. Vol. III. Edit. 1873. p. 475. HALLECK. Vol. II. p. 222. The *Stert.* 4 Rob. Adm. Rep. p. 66. The *Peterhoff.* 5 Wallace (Amer.) Rep. p. 56.

Both of these species of blockades are belligerent rights, which must be respected by those desiring to maintain impartial neutrality. The neutral has no right to interfere with the military operations of the belligerent by holding intercourse with a place which the latter has besieged or blockaded, and a purely maritime or commercial blockade may sometimes be of as much importance for the general warlike policy of a belligerent as a siege or military occupation. *

§ 272. The notification is the official announcement to neutrals of the institution of an effectual blockade and must contain the following particulars :— *The notification of blockade and its contents.*

1°. The authority from which the declaration emanates, when this does not issue direct from the supreme Government.

2°. The reasons for the blockade, viz., whether it is instituted in consequence of war or as a measure of constraint or reprisal, and whether it is intended to prevent both ingress and egress, or either alone. †

---

* "The line of separation between a military and a commercial blockade, says Mr. Hall, is in some cases extremely fine, and occasionally a blockade, which in its origin is of the latter character, is insensibly transformed into the former. Thus the blockade of the whole coast of the Confederate States during the American Civil War, which began by being no more than the largest commercial blockade ever instituted, was ultimately of considerable military importance, and aided directly in carrying out a plan of operations which had for its object to stifle the enemy by compression on every side." W. E. HALL. p. 557.

† During the Crimean War, the English and French Admirals in the Black Sea, in order to prevent the importation of provisions to the Russian forces occupying the Danube borders, issued, on June 2, 1854, a Notification of Blockade, in which it was stated that the Commanders in Chief of the Allied Naval Forces had established an effective blockade of the Danube, in order to stop all supplies to the Russian Armies. The blockade was defined to include all those mouths of the Danube which communicated with the Black Sea, and vessels of all Nations were notified that they would not be allowed to enter the river until further orders *(qu'ils ne pourront entrer dans ce fleuve jus qu'a nouvel ordre)*. A vessel coming out of the Danube was arrested by the blockading squadron, but the British Court held, hat if the vessel had no notice of the blockade, she was on that

3°. The time at which the blockade will commence.

4°. Definition of every place under blockade, with exact geographical description.

5°. The time allowed for private vessels, overtaken in port by a blockade, to leave the place, which is fixed in conformity with local situations but usually at not less than fifteen days, and a decision of the question whether neutral vessels, if loaded and ready to sail, may go out with their cargo, or not. *

The Notification, to be binding, must be clear. Ambiguous or insidious terms, calculated to mislead neutrals, make the blockade illegal and void. †

In the case of siege blockades and those connected with military operations, the notification is issued by the officer in command under the authority of his Government.

The state of blockade is notified, in the case of a siege blockade, by the fact itself, that is, by the presence of the blockading force, accompanied by a public notification or declaration of the highest local military or naval authority. Military or naval occupation and sieges are purely acts of war and, as such, directly emanating from the officer in command of the invading force, acting under authority of his Government. This is also the case with blockades forming part of the actual military operations on land.

---

general ground entitled to bring out her cargo. If she had notice, she could never suppose that, according to the words of the Notification, she could be liable to capture. The *Gerasimo*. 11 Moo. P. C. p. 88. DEANE. The Law of Blockade. p. 27.

* The period allowed for vessels to leave a blockaded place, is usually fixed at not less than *fifteen days*, during which time it is allowed to issue freely in ballast or with a cargo bought before the commencement of the blockade. This period is sufficient for ordinary sea ports, but for places situated on large rivers, sometimes several hundred miles above the blockaded estuaries, this period must be regulated in conformity with local circumstances and the means of communication with the up-river ports.

† DE MARTENS. Nouv. Rec. XV. 503. HEFFTER. § 157. BLUNTSCHLI. § 837. W. E. HALL. p. 624. The *Vrouw Judith*, 1 Rob. 152. The *Francisca*, Spinks, 122. HALLECK. Vol. II. p. 228.

Whether the blockaded ports are at the same time also besieged by land or not, in all cases in which the blockade by sea forms part of the plan of the campaign, it is natural that this part of the operation be subject to the authority in direct command of the expedition, and must follow the established usages of war, on the same principles as sieges generally. It is therefore expedient that such blockades be notified by the highest officer in command, whether of the army or the fleet, acting under the authority and responsibility of his Government.

The notification of a maritime or commercial blockade emanates directly from the Government of the blockading Power.

In the case of maritime or commercial blockades, the notification or declaration emanates directly from the Government of the blockading Power, which communicates it to the Government of each neutral State, whether before or simultaneously with the enforcement of the blockade.

In all cases, and with regard to all description of blockades, the places blockaded must be distinctly defined in the declaration or notification of the blockade.

Notification of the blockade to be published among the inhabitants of the blockaded coast or port.

It is also the duty of the blockading Power to send, through the Consulate of a friendly Power, a general notice of the places brought under the blockade and the date of its commencement to the local authorities of the blockaded places and to publish the notification at all the blockaded places, for due notice to all concerned, especially with regard to the period allowed for the exit of vessels.

Evidence of notification of the blockade.

§ 273. Besides the above noted formality of declaration and notification, it is the duty of the blockading belligerent to give notice of the blockade, by signal, to any approaching neutral vessel and to warn her off, before taking any action against her.

In case the approaching neutral vessel is visited by the belligerent, the visiting officer shall make a note of this warning of the state of blockade in the log-book of the neutral private vessel.

In the treaty between Great Britain and the United States of America, of 1794, it is provided, "that, whereas vessels frequently sail for a port or place belonging to an enemy, without knowing that the same is either besieged, blockaded or invested, it is agreed that every vessel so circumstanced may be turned away from such port or place; but she shall not be detained nor her cargo, if not contraband, be confiscated, unless, after notice, she shall again attempt to enter." This principle was acted upon in the declaration of the blockade of the Confederate ports, by President Lincoln, of the 19th April, 1864. *

This special warning at the seat of the blockade, notwithstanding and besides the formal declaration between the respective Government authorities, is by no means superfluous. Blockades, being positive acts, are often suspended and repeated, while, by reason of the fact that the nature of a blockade is that of a temporary measure, uncertainty with regard to its existence is a natural consequence. It is, therefore, not too much to require from belligerents, in view of the heavy punishment inflicted in case of a breach of blockade, to give to neutrals the benefit, by ample and generous means, of obtaining due notice of the existence of the state of blockade.

---

* Several treaties have established this rule of warning approaching neutral vessels at the seat of the blockade, as in that of Great Britain and the United States of 1794, those of France with Brazil (1828), with Bolivia (1834), Texas (1839), Venezuela (1843), Ecuador (1848), etc. WHEATON. IV. 3. § 28. ORTOLAN. Vol. II. Edit. 1864. p. 339. WOOLSEY. § 203.

Notification of the discontinuance of a blockade is a duty of belligerents towards neutrals.

§ 274. A blockade ceases, *de jure* as well as *de facto*, whenever the blockading forces are withdrawn or are proved inefficient to constitute an effective blockade, whether these forces be driven away by the enemy or the operation be abandoned by the blockading belligerent.

Notification of the discontinuance of a blockade, whenever the belligerent has abandoned the undertaking, whether temporarily or indefinitely, is a duty which he owes to neutrals, as it would be an infringement on the right of neutrals to leave them to find out for themselves whether the blockade is in existence or not.

In case the blockade has been broken by a force of the enemy, the belligerent, who has raised the blockade, should not fail to give due notice of the fact and of the free access of neutrals to his ports.

Observation Blockade.

§ 275. There is another form of blockade, or, rather, a peculiar phase in which this act of war sometimes presents itself, which requires special attention. When the belligerent is in the act of observing the coasts of his enemy, by means of his vessels of war, to reconnoitre the situation or to determine upon a proper position, whether for a landing or for the establishment of a maritime blockade, it is obvious that he is under the necessity of preventing neutral vessels having any communication with the enemy places under observation. This necessity establishes a belligerent right, which may be called the right of observation blockade. This right, derived from the necessity under which the belligerent is placed of seeking to prevent all communication with the enemy, whose seacoasts or ports he places under observation in preparation of an investment or blockade, is naturally confined within the strictest limits. Such observation blockade, being virtually a blockade in the process of formation, is naturally incomplete and can therefore not claim all the rights of an efficient valid blockade. While it is still incomplete, the right derived from it, with regard to neutrals, cannot be legally enforced with the vigour of a complete blockade. In the case of an observation blockade, the belligerent can, accordingly, do no more than cause neutral vessels, which may be sailing towards the enemy places under observation, the entrance of which he is going to blockade, to return or to leave the enemy's coast, and although the belligerent's right of visit and search, as described above (§§ 236–242), remains in this case, as under other circumstances, intact, he has no right of arresting, nor, *a fortiori*, of confiscating neutral vessels for any violation of an incomplete blockade or observation blockade. *

Licence to public vessels of neutral States to have communication with blockaded places. Ministers and Consuls of neutral States resident in a blockaded port are allowed the same privilege.

§ 276. During the continuance of the state of blockade, no vessels are allowed to enter or leave the blockaded place without special licence or consent of the blockading authority. Public vessels or vessels of war of neutral Powers are all equally bound by the same obligation, to respect the blockade. When the public vessel of a neutral State is allowed to have communication with a blockaded place, the neutral commanding officer is obliged to observe strict neutrality and to comply with the conditions under which such permission has been granted to cross the lines of the blockading belligerent. The impartiality, which must be the prevailing feature of an effective blockade, prohibits that, except to public vessels, permission to enter the blockaded place be given than in extreme cases of positive necessity. Diplomatic Agents and Consular

* N. TETENS. Droit récipr. des Belligerents et Neutres sur mer. Copenhagen. 1805.

Officers of a neutral State are also allowed the amount of communication necessary for the fulfilment of their official duties.

§ 277. From the principles noted above, as forming the basis of the belligerent's right of blockade, it follows that, to constitute a delict under the law of blockade, the following three essential points are necessary:—

The delict of a breach of blockade. Judicial principle of the delict. The doctrine of continuous voyage.

1°. The actual existence of a blockade at the time of the alleged delict;

2°. The knowledge of such blockade by the wrong-doer;

3°. The undoubted intention to violate the blockade, by some overt act.

Hence it is obvious that, so long as neutral vessels remain outside the lines occupied by the belligerent vessels of war, which are engaged in the act of blockading an enemy's territory, no right of blockade is violated, and that only by willfully and knowingly attempting to break the blockade, by forcing through the lines of the blockading forces, whether by egress from or ingress into the blockaded place, the delict of a breach of blockade is accomplished. In that case the belligerent is justified chasing the criminal on the high seas and arresting him there for infringing on his rights. Furthermore, by virtue of the belligerent right of visit and search, any suspicion of offences taking their commencement in the neighbouring waters beyond the lines of the blockading forces, will authorize the detention and examination of the supposed criminal, wherever found outside the jurisdiction of neutral States.

The criteria of the delict which constitute a breach of blockade, like those of all delicts, ought, *in judice*, to be based on acts, which have actually commenced, and not on mere intention without

The doctrine of continued voyage.

any commencement of execution. The intention to break a blockade cannot constitute a delict before there is a beginning of execution of the intention by some overt act. The delict has, however, often been construed out of mere supposed intention without any commencement of execution, and in this usage of maritime warfare, as in that of capturing inoffensive property of private individuals of the enemy State at sea, the theory of might being right has often settled the question without any judicial basis whatever. The inclination of belligerents to extend their rights at the expense of neutrals, appears very prominently also in the attempt to stretch the law of blockade so as to cover spheres within which such law cannot be judicially maintained. This is most conspicuous in the so-called doctrine of continued voyage. *

* The doctrine of continuous voyage or continued voyage was first originated by British Prize Courts in reference to the colonial trade of belligerents carried on by neutrals. The neutral tried to evade the British rule of 1756, by which all trade, especially the colonial, which was not allowed to foreigners in time of peace, was deemed illegal in time of war between neutrals and an enemy, (see § 235), by stopping at a neutral port and, after landing and reloading the cargo, proceeded with the same goods to the belligerent mother country of the colony. The British Courts held that, if the original intention of carrying on the goods could be proved, the continued voyage was as illegal as if the voyage had been completed in a direct manner without any interruption. This rule was also applied by English and afterwards by American Courts, in cases of carrying contraband of war to enemy country or any goods to a blockaded port. The principle that, if an intention to enter a blockaded port can be proved, the vessel and the cargo are subjected to capture from the time of setting sail, has been stretched by the British and American Courts to be applicable in the sense, that even if the goods were unloaded and duly entered at a neutral port, and another vessel should then convey them to a blockaded port, the ship which originally set out with the goods to the intermediate neutral port is held to be liable to confiscation on any part of its return voyage; the cargo, having been landed or not, being, in all cases, confiscable. Furthermore, if the master of the vessel was ordered to stop at the neutral port to ascertain what the danger was before continuing the voyage to the blockaded harbour, still guilt rested on the parties to the transaction as before. "All this, says Dr. Woolsey, seems a natural extention of the English principle of continued voyages as at first given out; but there is danger that Courts will infer intention on insufficient grounds." (WOOLSEY. Edit. 1879. 366).

§ 278. Breach of blockade may be committed by egress as well as by ingress. Breach by ingress is committed when a vessel passes or attempts to pass, either in ballast or with cargo, into a blockaded port. She is regarded as attempting a breach of blockade when, though not having actually passed through the lines of the blockading forces, she keeps hovering about or comes at anchor so near that she could have no other intention than that of watching her chance for slipping into the port or getting under cover of its forts. * *Breach of blockade. By ingress. By egress.*

Breach by egress is committed by attempting to leave the blockaded port without permission, and after the time fixed for neutral vessels to clear the port (§ 272), either in ballast or with cargo, unless such a vessel can prove that it was absolutely impossible for her to leave the port in due time, or if she entered port during an interval in the course of which the blockade was relaxed, the master having had no knowledge of its renewal.

Breaches of blockade by implication exist if a vessel, though remaining outside, sent in her cargo by lighters into the blockaded port. Likewise if a vessel, having legally passed outward, takes, whilst lying outside the line of blockade,

---

The British bark *Springbok* was captured in 1862 and condemned by the American Prize Court at New York, on the principle of the continued voyage as above described. Several highly distinguished authorities on International Law, such as Sir William Vernon Harcourt, Sir Robert Phillimore, Calvo, W. Beach Lawrence, and Bluntschli, have severely condemned the decision of the American Court. The Commission on prize affairs of the Institut de Droit International have given their opinion and protested against the application of the principles laid down in the case of the Springbok, in a consultation and conclusion signed by Professors Arntz, Asser, De Martens, Pierantoni, Renault, Rolin (Albéric), Sir Travers Twiss, Q. C., and Mr. W. E. Hall. The document is published in the Revue de Droit International, Vol. XIV. 1882, p. 328, et seq. This subject was previously treated in the said Revue, Vol. VII. 1875, pages 236–255, Papers of Mr. GESSNER; followed by Observations of Mr. WESTLAKE on pages 258–260 of the same volume.

* The *Neutralitet*. 6 Rob. Adm. Rep. p. 31.

cargo on board from lighters or other vessels which have forced the blockade, she becomes thereby guilty of the delict of breach of blockade. If, however, the cargo is brought to such vessel overland or by inland navigation, at a portion of the coast which is not under blockade—the latter being a mere maritime one, confined to another part of the coast—no delict is committed, because, in the case of a purely maritime blockade, trade by overland routes or by inland navigation is lawful (§ 271).

Excuses for entering a blockaded port.

Excuses for entering a blockaded port have always been allowed by Prize Courts in cases of absolute necessity, whether by stress of weather, or want of provision, provided that the blockaded port was the only accessible port under the circumstances. Also in case the master of a neutral vessel has been misinformed as to facts, by authorities of belligerent forces competent to give such information, be it that he was induced to believe that the blockade had been raised whilst it afterwards proves to be still existing, or be it that he was misled as to the real limits of the blockade which turned out to be more extensive than indicated to the master. Incorrect information, furnished by any authorities not directly connected with the blockade nor competent to give such information, cannot give any ground for a valid excuse of having been misled as to facts. *

* "The want of provisions, says Lord Stowell, is not an excuse which will, on light grounds, be received, because an excuse, to be admissible, must show an imperative and over-ruling compulsion, to enter the particular port under blockade. It may induce the master of a ship to seek a neighbouring port, but it can hardly ever force a person to resort exclusively to a blockaded port. What is said with respect to wind, is of a different nature. I will not say that cases of necessity may not occur, which would afford a sufficient justification. If a party can show, that he was under very great necessity, and that for four or five days he could get into no other port, I would certainly admit such an excuse, if well supported." (The *Hurtige Hanse*, 2 Rob. Adm. Rep. p. 124).

Misleading advice as to established points of International Law regarding blockades, such as, for instance, that the master is always entitled to a warning before capture, does not afford an excuse for steering towards the blockaded port.

Neither can it be regarded as a valid excuse, if a master pleads that he was approaching the blockaded port only to ascertain for himself the existence of the blockade, but with the intention of retiring if he should find that the port was blockaded. The neutral merchant, acting *bonâ fide*, ought not to speculate on the existence or non-existence of a blockade, but should know beforehand, with certainty, the actual state of things, before risking his vessel and goods. To instruct a ship's master to go to a port and, if he finds it blockaded, to ask for warning and to retire, but, in case he should not be stopped, then to enter, is a practice not very far removed from fraud. *

Actual entrance into the blockaded place is not necessary to constitute the delict. If the vessel hovers near the approaches of a blockaded place, without any palpable reason for the non-continuance of her voyage, she is liable to capture for intended breach of blockade.

Knowledge of the existence of the blockade is necessary to constitute the delict.

§ 279. Knowledge of the existence of the blockade must be in the wrong-doer, to constitute the delict. The effect of an official notification of the blockade, forwarded to a neutral Government, can reasonably be expected to include all its subjects or citizens, provided sufficient time has elapsed to enable such authorities to communicate the notification to the subjects or citizens of their State. Such a notification, therefore, establishes sufficient presumption of the knowledge of the blockade, to justify the detention of the implicated vessel be-

* The *Spes* and *Irene*. 5. Rob. Adm. Rep. p. 77.

longing to the respective State and to constitute the principal element of a constructive notice. This supposition, however, does not bar the right of the accused to prove *bonâ fide* ignorance, and to plead his innocence before the Court of the belligerent. If he be condemned, while being really ignorant of the actual existence of the blockade, for want of sufficient time intervening between the notification and his detention, his ignorance may fairly be the subject of diplomatic representation through his Government, which may raise a claim for compensation.

Constructive Notice.

When the proof of personal knowledge of the blockade cannot be established by undeniable facts, then the accused's own proceedings and acts at the time of the alleged breach of the blockade, combined with the facts and circumstances connected with the actual state of the blockade or its notification, and which, at the time, surrounded his proceedings or gave birth to them, must form, in such cases, the legal tests of his guilt or innocence. But in all cases of constructive notice of blockade, it is the sound maxim of justice, that, if there be room for reasonable doubt as to knowledge of the blockade, the neutral is entitled to the benefit of the doubt. *

* HALLECK. Vol. II. p. 226, et seq.

"Where there are no legal or probable grounds for imputing to the master of a neutral vessel the knowledge of the existence of a blockade, which he is charged to have violated, it rests upon the captor to establish the fact of this knowledge by positive evidence. To warrant a condemnation, the proof must be clear and definite, that such vessel had been duly notified of the blockade, and had undertaken or prosecuted the voyage in defiance of the notice or warning. To be binding, the notice or warning must be clear, and not so ambiguous or insidious as to be calculated to mislead the neutral master, otherwise it is illegal and void. Where it is expressed in such general terms as to embrace other ports not blockaded, it is not even valid as to the blockaded port, although included in the general language. Where the notice is irregular and insufficient, no penalty is incurred by its contravention. Proof of the actual knowledge of the party at the inception of the voyage, supersedes, in all cases, the necessity of a warning, nor is it of any importance by what means or in what form he received the information, if the information was credible in its nature

Temporary relaxation of the blockade.

§ 280. Temporary relaxation of the rigour of a blockade is not always sufficient to excuse the master of a vessel from the penalty for a breach, when full knowledge of an efficient blockade has existed at the outset of the voyage.

But when a relaxation of the blockade has really caused reports to be spread and generally circulated in newspapers, that the blockade was raised, and have led innocent merchants, who are naturally eager to profit by the first rush to the re-opened port, to dispatch their vessels and goods to such port, then the relaxation of the blockade, whatever might have been its cause or duration, must, undoubtedly, plead in their favour. Otherwise a temporary relaxation of a blockade, through neglect or otherwise of the blockading forces, might at any time establish a trap in which innocent neutral commerce could easily be ensnared.

Penalty and Duration of the liability of the delict.

§ 281. The penalty for the violation of a blockade is generally confiscation of the vessel and cargo. In cases of breach by egress, the cargo is not implicated, if the owner can prove that the shipper of the cargo or his agent over whom he, at the time, could exercise no control, was not expressly authorized to ship the goods. Such is also the case with regard to a breach by ingress, if it be clearly established by proofs, found on board at the time of capture, that at the inception of the voyage the owners of the

---

and came in such a form and from such a source as to leave no reasonable doubt on his mind as to its authenticity; he is not permitted to aver that he placed no confidence in a communication that had just claims on his belief. Again, if the voyage was commenced without a knowledge of the blockade, but he was afterward notified of its existence by a cruiser, or officer of the blockading State, and if he continues his voyage with the evident intention of entering the blockaded port, he is liable to condemnation." HALLECK. Vol. II. Edition of Sir Sherston Baker p. 227. KENT. Com. on Am. Law, Vol. I. pp. 147–148. DUER. On Insurance, Vol. I. p. 663; the *Henrike* and *Maria*, 1 Rob., 146; the *Vrow Judith*, 1 Rob., 150; the *Apollo*, 5 Rob. 286; the Columbia, 1 Rob., 156. PHILLIMORE. On Int. Law, Vol. III. § 302. HEFFTER. Droit International, § 155.

cargo were innocent as to the intention of violating the blockade and that the illegality consisted solely of the misconduct of the master or owners of the vessel.

The offence committed by breach of blockade continues during the voyage and a vessel taken in any port of that voyage is taken *in delicto.* *

The delict ceases with the raising and termination of the blockade to which it had reference, and after the blockade has ceased to exist no vessel can be seized, for acts committed during a terminated blockade. After notice has been given of the cessation of the blockade, no vessel can be captured for a previous breach. The fact of the blockade having no existence, the *delictum* at the time of capture, has wholly ceased. †

---

* HALLECK. Edit. Sir Sherston Baker. Vol. II. p. 238, et seq. DUER. On Insurance. Vol. I. p. 683, et seq. The *Exchange*, 1 Edwards R. 43. The *Alexander*, 4 Rob. 93. The *Mercurius*, 1 Rob. 80. The *Neptunus*, 3 Rob. 173. The *Adelaide*, 3 Rob. 281. The *Manchester*, 2 Rob. R. 687. The *Lisette*, 6 Rob. Rep. p. 387. HALLECK. Vol. II. p. 241.

† "To justify a capture for the violation of a blockade, says Duer, or the attempt to violate it, the offence must continue to exist at the time of seizure. In technical language, the ship must be then *in delicto.* In cases where the ship has violated the blockade by egress, the *delictum* continues during her whole voyage, till she has reached her final port of destination. Until then, as the offence consists, not in the mere attempt, but in an actual breach, no change of circumstances, or subsequent repentance, can efface the guilt. It is not cancelled by a mere interruption of the voyage, such as the stopping of the ship at an intermediate port, either from necessity or design; when she resumes her voyage, she becomes again subject to the penalty of the law. But when a ship sails for a blockaded port, with a knowledge of the blockade and the intention to violate it, the offence is so far complete as to justify her immediate capture ; yet, as it exists only in an attempt, the *delictum* does not necessarily continue during the whole of her subsequent voyage. If, previous to her capture, the blockade had ceased to exist, or the master, from the information of a ship of war of the blockading State, had just grounds for believing that such was the fact, or had altered his destination, with the intention of not proceeding at all to the blockaded port, the offence no longer exists, and that which had existed is no longer punishable. To constitute the offence, three circumstances must be found to co-exist: the fact of a blockade, the party's knowledge of its existence, and his intention to violate it ; and in each of the above cases, an indispensable circumstance is wanting. The *delictum*, therefore, at the time of capture, had wholly ceased, and both ship and cargo will be restored." (DUER. On Insurance. Vol. I. p. 688, et seq. and Vol. II. p. 463, et seq.

CHAPTER XXXVII.

PRIZE COURTS.

§ 282. Property in private goods or vessels, seized by belligerent vessels, by virtue of the belligerent rights, described in chapters XXXI & XXXVI, does not vest, upon the completion of a capture, until judgment of confiscation has been pronounced by the competent Prize Court. The captor, while acting on his own responsibility during the seizure, is obliged to conform with the rules by which this responsibility is to gain legal sanction, and he cannot obtain a complete title to the object seized except through the sentence of the Prize Court. The latter, after examination and legal investigation of the circumstances under which the seizure has taken place, is to pronounce on the validity of the prize, that is, whether the capture has been effected in conformity with the acknowledged rules of International Law or otherwise. These rules have been explained in the preceding chapters as constituting the laws and usages of war and neutrality. *Principles on which the institution of Prize Courts is based.*

Modern usages have extended the adjudication of Prize Courts to all captures of private property at sea whether of the enemy or of neutrals, and to all captures by naval forces on land or by naval forces in combined action with land forces. In all such captures, the investigation and decision, with regard to the legality of the seizure and the ownership of private property in goods or vessel, rest with the judicial authority of the Prize Court, in conformity with established rules, as noted above in paragraphs 203–222.

The institution of Prize Courts is based on the principle that belligerent States, in whose name the captures are made, are bound to give solemn guarantee that the proceedings of their agents shall be thoroughly investigated by impartial judges, who are to watch against any abuse or violence committed in the exercise of belligerent rights. This guarantee regarding control of the exercise of belligerent rights is obtained, may be, as yet more or less in an imperfect manner,—through the Prize Court.

This Court, which is instituted by the public law of the belligerent State, sits in its territory and has jurisdiction in matters appertaining to naval prizes of war, whether with or without other jurisdiction. The Prize Court institutes proceedings under the authority of the captor's sovereign, but the law it administers is International Law. *

Duties of captors. § 283. In chapter XXXII (§§ 202–222) are noted the usages of war with regard to maritime captures and, in chapter XXXIV (§§ 236–242), the belligerent right of visit and search and of seizure of neutral vessels on the high seas; it remains now more particularly to point out the

---

* W. E. HALL. p. 652. WOOLSEY. Edit. 1879, p. 252.

In Great Britain and its dominions the Prize Courts are the Admiralty and Vice-Admiralty Courts, from which appeal lies to a committee of members of the Privy Council, known as the Judicial Committee. (See Appendix C, British Laws relating to Naval Prizes of war). In the United States of America the Prize Courts are the District and Circuit Courts of the United States, with appeal up through the Circuit to the Supreme Court of the Union. (See note to § 283, Instructions for Captors). In France there is, since 1659, the Conceil des Prizes with appeal to the Conceil d'Etat. By the regulation of 1796 France allowed its Consuls and Vice-Consuls in neutral ports to investigate questions of prizes in a preparatory form. The German Regulations on Prize Affairs are to be found under Appendix G. See also MANNING. p. 381. HEFFTER. § 138.

proceedings of the belligerent captor in conformity with the rules laid down for maritime captures, so far as these have been gradually modified and established by the decisions of the Prize Courts of various maritime Nations.

In the case of maritime prizes, a title can be acquired only after the condemnation by the competent Prize Court, through which the acts and proceedings of the captor are in the first place to be adjudicated. The rules established with regard to the duties of the captor form, therefore, the basis of the *litis decisoria* of Prize Courts (Comp. § 52).

These duties and proceedings can be grouped together under the following rules.

The Prize-Master.

1°. The belligerent captor, in order to manifest his intention of retaining a seized vessel and to secure his right in the prize, must place a competent prize master and prize crew on board, to whose care the prize is to be entrusted. The hatches and passages leading to the cargo must be secured and sealed. The log-book and all papers relating to the vessel and cargo are to be sealed up, for delivery with the vessel.

The prize to be brought under the jurisdiction of the Prize-Court with due diligence and proper care.

2°. The captor is obliged to bring his prize, as speedily as practicable, within the jurisdiction of a competent Prize Court, which is to pronounce judgment upon it, exercising due care to preserve captured vessel and goods against loss. The captor is liable to penalties for negligence. For loss by re-capture or by dangers of the sea, he is not liable. *

* Restitution in value or damages are given for loss or injury received by a vessel in consequence of a refusal of nautical assistance by the captor. *Der Mohr*, 4 Rob. 314; *Die Fire Damer*, 5 Rob. 357.

The principle that a captor must not wilfully expose property to danger of capture by the other belligerent, by bringing it to England when he may resort to Admiralty Courts in the Colonies, was admitted in the *Nicholas* and *Jan*, 1 Rob. 97, though in the particular case the Court decided against the claimant of restitution in value, on the ground that due discretion had not been exceeded. W. E. HALL, p. 653.

The report of the captor, (procès-verbal). The ship's papers.

3°. The captor shall deliver his prize, together with a report *(procès verbal)*, the preliminary examination of the master, officers and crew and all the ship's papers, to the competent authority, as prescribed by the respective prize laws. Where no ship's papers are delivered up or found on board the captured vessel, the fact must be mentioned in the report.

The report *(procès verbal)* must contain an exact and explicit narrative of all the proceedings, from the moment the captured vessel came in sight, up to the time of her delivery to the competent authority. It is also requisite to describe the measures taken with regard to the sealing of the hatches and passages and all other measures which were deemed necessary for the preservation of the cargo.

When the captor does not accompany his prize himself, the report *(procès verbal)* and all the papers are delivered, in his name, by the prize master.

Persons detained to give evidence before the Prize-Court.

4°. The master of the captured or seized vessel, and as many of the officers and crew as are required to give information, especially the mate and the supercargo, shall be detained by the captor, to be examined before the Prize Court. These persons, detained as witnesses, are not to be treated as prisoners of war.

Who are prisoners of war?

5°. Of the persons found on board a captured vessel, only those belonging to the military forces of the enemy, those who have been helping the enemy or who are under actual suspicion of helping or serving the enemy, can be legally detained as prisoners of war. The rules to be followed with regard to prisoners of war, are noted above in paragraph 189.

All are entitled to retain their personal effects.

6°. All persons found on board a captured vessel shall have the right to retain their personal effects.

7°. The captor shall take the necessary measures, that those persons who are not prisoners of war, and not required at the investigation before the Court, shall be properly landed at an inhabited and civilized place, or put on board a neutral vessel to land them safely in their country. *All who are not prisoners of war and not required as witnesses to be liberated.*

8°. The commanding officers and prize masters are personally responsible for the proper treatment of the master, officers and crew and passengers of a captured vessel. If any person is maltreated, the responsible party is liable for damages due to the injured individuals, as the Court may decide. *Responsibility of captor for proper treatment of all the persons found on board the prize.*

9°. A neutral vessel, when seized, is to keep the flag of her own country, until she is condemned by the competent Court. The flag of the captor's State may, however, be exhibited at the fore, to indicate that she is for the time in the possession of the captor. * *The neutral vessel retains her own flag until the decision of the competent Prize Court.*

---

* The following regulations were issued by the Navy Department of the United States of America, with regard to the duties of captors.

"August 7, 1876, Chapter XX."

2. When a vessel is seized as a prize, it shall be the duty of the commanding officer of the vessel making the capture, to cause all the hatches and passages leading to the cargo to be secured and sealed, except such as it may be indispensably necessary to keep open. The log-book and all papers relating to the vessel and cargo, shall also be sealed up. and placed in charge of the prize-master, for delivery with the vessel and cargo.

3. Should it be necessary to take out of a vessel, seized as a prize, any property, either for its better preservation or for the use of the vessels or armed forces of the United States, a correct inventory, and a careful appraisement of its value, by suitable officers qualified to judge, shall be made. This inventory and appraisement to be made in duplicate, one of which is to be transmitted to the Secretary of the Navy and the other to the judge or the United States' attorney of the district to which the prize may be sent.

4. If it should become necessary to sell any portion of captured property, a full report of the facts must be made to the United States' attorney or judge of the district court to which the prize is sent, and any proceeds of sale shall be held subject to the order of the said judge.

Destruction of neutral vessels.

§ 284. As a rule, a neutral vessel cannot be destroyed. The principle that, even in cases of absolute necessity, destruction must be followed by compensation is adopted by all Prize Courts.

---

5. The prize-master will vigilantly guard the property intrusted to his care from spoliation and theft, these offences leading to a forfeiture of prize-money and such other punishment as a prize-court may inflict, both of the crew and the prize-master.

6. The commanding officer of any vessel making a capture shall report to the Navy Department, and to the judge of the court to which the prize is sent, all the material facts, including the names of all vessels within signal distance at the time, with all the circumstances of their position.

7. The commanding officers of all vessels claiming to share in a prize will cause the prize-list to exhibit not only the name and rank or rating, but also the rate of the annual or monthly pay of each person borne on the books at the time of the capture to which the list refers. They will also forward a statement of their claims, with the grounds upon which they are based, to the Navy Department, and to the judge of the district court to which the prize is sent.

8. The master of the captured or seized vessel, and as many of the officers and crew as can properly be taken care of, shall be sent in custody of the prize-master, who will report immediately on his arrival to the United States' attorney, as well as to the Navy Department. The mate and supercargo, after the master, are the most important witnesses before a prize-court, and should always be sent with the vessel, or carried into the port to which she may be sent for adjudication without delay.

9. In time of war the commanding officer of a vessel is to exercise constant vigilance to prevent supplies of arms, munitions, and contraband articles being conveyed to the enemy, yet under no circumstance is he to seize any vessel within the waters of a friendly Nation.

10. A commanding officer in time of war is to exercise the right of visitation and search on all suspected vessels other than neutral men-of-war, but in no case is he authorized to fire at a vessel without showing colours and giving her notice of a desire to speak and to visit her; first, a blank cartridge is to be fired; second, a shot fired wide of her; third, a shot fired at the vessel; nor is he to fire at any such vessel or commit an act of hostility or of authority within a marine league of any foreign country with which the United States is at peace.

11. When a visit is made, a vessel, if neutral, is not to be seized unless a search renders it reasonable to believe that she is engaged in carrying contraband of war for or to the enemy, and to his ports, directly or indirectly, or unless she is attempting to violate a blockade established by the United States. If after any visitation and search, it shall appear that the vessel is, in good faith and without contraband, actually bound and passing from one neutral port to another, and not bound or proceeding to or from a port in the possession of the enemy, then she cannot be lawfully seized. It is the duty of the officer making the search to indorse upon the ship's register or licence the fact of the visit, the nature of the search, by what vessel made, the name of her commanding officer, the latitude and longitude, the time of detention, and when released.

"The act of destruction, says Lord Stowell, cannot be justified to the neutral owner by the gravest importance of such an act to the public service of the captor's own State; to the neutral it can

---

12. In order to avoid difficulty and error in relation to papers found on board a neutral vessel that may have been seized, the commanding officer will take care that official seals, or fastenings of foreign authorities, are in no case broken, and that parcels covered by them are never read by any naval authorities; but that all bags or other covering of such parcels are remitted to the prize-court.

13. The officers and crew of a neutral vessel seized are not to be confined except by detention on board, unless by their own conduct they should render further restraint necessary. Their personal property is to be respected, and a full and proper allowance of provisions is to be distributed to them. If any cruelty or unnecessary force is used towards such crew, a prize-court will decree damages to the injured parties.

14. A neutral vessel seized is to wear the flag of her own country until she is adjudged to be a lawful prize by a competent court. The flag of the United States, however, may be exhibited at the fore, to indicate that she is, for the time, in the possession of officers of the United States.

15. The form of a letter of instructions to be given to prize-masters is as follows:—

'United States S———
'Off———

'SIR,—You will take charge of the———, captured on the——— day of———, 18—, by———, and proceed with the said prize to the port of———, and there deliver her with the accompanying papers (which were all that were found on board), and the persons sent as witnesses, to the judge of the United States district court, or to the United States prize commissioners at that place, taking his or their receipt for the same. You will not deliver either the vessel, the papers, or the witnesses to the order of any other person or parties unless directed to act otherwise by the Navy Department or flag officer commanding the squadron to which you are attached.

On your arrival at ———you will immediately report in person to the commanding or senior navy officer of the navy yard or station thereat, and show him these instructions; and you will report also, by letter, to the Secretary of the Navy, stating in full the particulars of your passage home, and transmit to him, through the commandant or senior officer, the names of the officers and men composing your prize crew, and any communications for the Department with which you may be charged. You will on your arrival allow no person to leave the vessel without permission from the commandant of the station, nor go on shore yourself except on your necessary duty. You will not sleep out of the vessel while in charge, nor allow any but officials boats to approach and only official persons on duty to come on board. You will without delay after reporting call upon the United States attorney at———, show him these instructions which are issued by order of the Secretary of the Navy, and give him all the information in your power respecting the circumstances connected with the capture of the ———. You will then report and show these instructions to the only be justified under any such circumstances by a full restitution in value." * With regard to the destruction of neutral property in war, we refer further to paragraph 243.

---

naval prize commissioner of the district, who is hereby directed to ascertain and notify you of the earliest date at which your attendance shall no longer be required by the court, and to endorse the notification on this paper. You will on being discharged from attendance, if not in the meantime instructed, and whenever you need instructions respecting yourself, officers, or prize crew, immediately report to the commandant of the nearest yard or station or senior officer for such instructions. You will particularly bear in mind and strictly observe the injunctions of the law and of the department respecting captured property or persons under your charge, and recollect that you will be held rigorously responsible for any mismanagement of the trust confided to you. You, your officers, and prize crew are hereby detached from the——— and you will be careful to apply for and take with you their pay accounts and your own, to be presented to the paymaster of the yard or station at or nearest to the port to which you are ordered. The sea pay of yourself and officers will continue while in charge of the prize or under the orders of a flag officer or senior navy officer afloat, but your name will not be borne on the books of the vessel from which you are detached, and you will not be entitled to share in prizes made by such vessel after your detachment.

(Signed)———,

To——— Commanding the United States———.'

16. The prize-master in whose charge instruments are placed, or to whom arms are intrusted, will be held strictly accountable for their condition, and in case of loss or damage by neglect, or other cause not satisfactorily explained, the value will be charged to his account. The officer appointing a prize-master will require him to give a receipt in duplicate for the instruments and arms with which he may be furnished, one to be forwarded to the commanding officer of the station to which the prize vessel is bound, and the other to be retained by such appointing officer; and in case of any deficiency in the delivery of, or palpable abuse of them, the commanding officer of the station will at once have the matter investigated, and report the result to the Navy Department.

17. Prisoners of war are to be treated with humanity; their personal property is to be carefully protected; they shall have a proper allowance of provisions, and every comfort of air and exercise which circumstances will permit of. Every precaution must be taken to prevent any hostile attempt on their part, and, if necessary or expedient, they may be ironed or closely confined. If officers give their parole not to attempt any hostile act on board the vessel, and to conform to such requirements as the commanding officer may consider necessary, they may be permitted any privileges he may deem proper.

18. If any vessel shall be taken acting as a vessel of war, or a privateer, without having a proper commission so to act, the officers and crew shall be considered as pirates, and treated accordingly.

* The *Zee Star*, 4 Rob. 71. The *Felicity*, 2 Dodson. 383. The *Leucade*, Spinks. 221.

§ 285. When any seizures of vessels or goods are made by joint action of allies, the Prize Court of one of the capturing Powers, which is the nearest to the scene of the capture, shall have jurisdiction and shall have power, after condemnation, to apportion the due share of the proceeds to each of the joint captors, as may be regulated by the treaty of alliance. *Prizes taken in joint action with allies.*

§ 286. The international usages with regard to ransom, recapture, *jus postliminii* and salvage, have been treated above in paragraphs 206–210. Prize money is paid to commanding and other officers and crews of public vessels, for the capturing of private property at sea, in conformity with the municipal regulations of the respective State, and the respective amount is adjusted by the Prize Court in proportion to the amount of assets realized by the captured property. *Prize money and Prize bounty.*

Remuneration for the capturing or destroying of public vessels of the enemy is called prize bounty. This is apportioned at a fixed rate, in proportion to the strength of the enemy engaged, and payment is made from the State treasury, the capturing or destroying of public enemy vessels being a direct State affair.

The international rules for naval prizes of war, as proposed by the Institut de Droit International in its session held at Turin, in September, 1882, will be found recited in the note appended to this chapter. *

---

* The questions connected with naval prizes of war have long occupied the serious attention of the *Institut de Droit International.* A very elaborate report, made by Prof. Bulmerincq, appeared in the *Revue de Droit International,* the valuable organ of the Institute, together with a draft by the same able author, of International Regulations for Naval Prizes of War and Prize-Courts, which, after deliberation and modification resolved upon at the session of the Institute of 1880 at Wiesbaden, was finally adopted in the session of 1882, at Turin. *Revue de Droit International et de Legislation*

Comparée. Vol. XIV 1882, pages 173–190, 207–212 and 601–609. The valuable articles of Professor Bulmirincq, on the Law of Maritime Prizes, have been successively published in the Revue de Droit Int. Vol. X–XIV, 1879–1882.

The following are the International Rules for Naval Prizes of War, as proposed by the Institut de Droit International, by a resolution passed at the session of Turin, in September, 1882.

RÈGLEMENT INTERNATIONAL DES PRISES MARITIMES.

I.—DISPOSITIONS GÉNÉRALES.

§ 1.—Les navires de guerre et les forces militaires des États belligérants sont seuls autorisés à exercer le droit de prise, c'est-à-dire l'arrêt, la visite, la recherche et la saisie des navires de commerce pendant une guerre maritime.

§ 2.—La course est interdite.

§ 3.—L'armement en course demeure permis à titre de rétorsion contre les belligérants qui ne respectent pas le principe du § 2. En ce cas, il est interdit de délivrer des commissions à des étrangers.

§ 4.—La propriété privée est inviolable, sous la condition de réciprocité et sauf les cas prévus au § 23.

§ 5.—Le droit de prise à l'égard des belligérants ne s'ouvre qu'après le commencement des hostilités. Il cesse durant l'armistice et avec les préliminaires de la paix. A l'égard des neutres, le droit de prise ne peut être exercé qu'après que les belligérants leur ont notifié l'existence de la guerre.

§ 6.—Le droit de prise ne peut être exercé sur les navires et leurs cargaisons que s'ils ont eu connaissance de l'existence de la guerre. Il n'y a pas lieu d'exercer le droit de prise, si le patron du navire, ou le propriétaire de la cargaison, prouve qu'il n'a pas eu cette connaissance.

§ 7.—Si l'État belligérant qui somme les navires de commerce ennemis de quitter ses ports, leur permet de décharger auparavant les marchandises qu'ils ont à bord et d'en charger de nouvelles, il doit fixer exactement le délai qui leur est accordé à cet effet, et le faire connaître au public. Dans ce cas, le belligérant ne peut laisser exercer un droit de prise contre ces navires avant l'expiration du dit délai.

§ 8.—Le droit de prise ne peut être exercé que dans les eaux des belligérants et en haute mer; il ne peut pas être exercé dans les eaux qui sont expressément, par traité, mises à l'abri des faits de guerre. Le belligérant ne peut pas non plus poursuivre dans les eaux des deux dernières espèces une attaque commencée.

§ 9.—Les prises faites dans les eaux neutres, ou dans les eaux qui sont mises par traité à l'abri des faits de guerre, sont nulles. Les navires ou objets capturés doivent être livrés à l'État neutre ou riverain pour être restitués par cet État à leur propriétaire primitif. En outre, l'État du capteur est responsable de tous les dommages et pertes.

II.—DISPOSITIONS SPÉCIALES.

1. *De l'arrêt.*

§ 10.—Les navires de guerre d'un État belligérant sont autorisés à arrêter, dans les cas prévus par le règlement, tout navire de commerce ou privé qu'ils rencontrent dans les eaux de leur État, ou en haute mer, et ailleurs qu'en des eaux neutres ou soustraites aux faits de guerre.

§ 11.—Le navire de guerre du belligérant, pour inviter le navire de commerce à s'arrêter, se servira comme signal d'un coup de canon de semonce à boulet perdu ou à poudre. Avant ou en même temps, le navire de guerre hissera son pavillon, au-dessus duquel en temps de nuit un fanal sera placé. A ce signal, le navire arrêté hissera son pavillon et se mettra en panne pour attendre la visite. Le navire de guerre enverra alors au navire arrêté une chaloupe montée par un officier accompagné d'un nombre suffisant d'hommes, dont deux ou trois seulement monteront avec l'officier à bord du navire arrêté.

§ 12.—Le navire arrêté ne pourra jamais être requis d'envoyer à bord du navire de guerre son patron ou une personne quelconque, pour montrer ses papiers ou pour tout autre cause.

§ 13.—Le navire de commerce est obligé de s'arrêter: il lui est interdit de continuer sa route. S'il le fait néanmoins, le navire de guerre a le droit de le poursuivre et de l'arrêter de force.

2. *De la visite.*

§ 14.—Le droit de visite s'exerce dans les eaux des belligérants, en tant qu'elles ne sont pas mises par traité à l'abri des faits de guerre, et en haute mer; il s'exerce à l'égard des navires de commerce, mais non à l'égard des navires de guerre d'un État neutre, ni à l'égard d'autres navires appartenant ostensiblement à un tel État, ni à l'égard des navires de commerce neutres qui sont convoyés par un navire de guerre de leur État.

§ 15.—Le droit de visite s'exerce, soit en vue de vérifier la nationalité du navire arrêté, soit pour constater s'il fait un transport interdit, soit pour constater une violation de blocus.

§ 16.—Lorsque des navires de commerce neutres sont convoyés, ils ne seront pas visités si le commandant du convoy remet au navire du belligérant qui l'arrête, une liste des navires convoyés et une déclaration signée par lui et portant qu'il ne se trouve à leur bord aucune contrebande de guerre et quelles sont la nationalité et la destination des navires convoyés.

§ 17.—Lorsque le navire à visiter est un paquebot-poste, il ne sera pas visité, si le commissaire du gouvernement dont il porte le pavillon, se trouvant à son bord, déclare par écrit que le paquebot ne transporte ni dépêches ni troupes pour l'ennemi, ni de la contrebande de guerre pour le compte ou à destination de l'ennemi.

§ 18.—La visite, à laquelle doit se soumettre tout navire qui n'en est pas exempt en vertu des dispositions des articles 16 et 17, commence par l'examen des papiers de bord du navire arrêté. Si ces papiers sont trouvés en règle, ou s'il ne se présente rien de suspect, le navire arrêté peut continuer sa route. Pourront de même continuer leur route, les navires neutres destinés à des expéditions scientifiques, à condition qu'ils observent les lois de la neutralité.

3. *De la recherche.*

§ 19.—Si les papiers de bord ne sont pas en ordre, ou si la visite opérée a fait naître un soupçon fondé comme il est dit en l'article qui suit, l'officier qui a opéré la visite est autorisé à procéder à la recherche. Le navire ne peut s'y opposer; s'il s'y oppose néanmoins, la recherche peut être opérée de force.

§ 20.—Il y a soupçon fondé dans les cas suivants:

1. Lorsque le navire arrêté n'a pas mis en panne sur l'invitation du navire de guerre;

2. Lorsque le navire arrêté s'est opposé à la visite des cachettes supposées recéler des papiers de bord ou de la contrebande de guerre;

3. Lorsqu'il a des papiers doubles, ou faux, ou falsifiés, ou secrets, ou que ses papiers son insuffisants, ou qu'il n'a point de papiers;

4. Lorsque les papiers ont été jetés à la mer ou détruits de quelque autre façon, surtout si ces faits se sont passés après que le navire a pu s'apercevoir de l'approche du navire de guerre ;

5. Lorsque le navire arrêté navigue sous un pavillon faux.

§ 21.—Il n'est pas permis aux personnes qui sont chargées d'opérer la recherche, d'ouvrir ni de rompre des armoires, réduits, caisses, cassettes, tonnes, futailles, ou autres cachettes pouvant renfermer une partie de la cargaisson ; ni d'examiner arbitrairement les objets faisant partie de la cargaison qui se trouvent répandus à découvert dans le navire.

§ 22.—Dans les cas de soupçon mentionnés au § 20, s'il n'y a pas de résistance à la recherche, l'officier qui y procède doit faire ouvrir les réduits par le patron, et faire la recherche dans la cargaison à découvert sur le navire avec le concours du patron.

4. *De la saisie.*

§ 23.—La saisie d'un navire ou d'une cargaison, ennemi ou neutre, n'a lieu que dans les cas suivants :

1. Lorsqu'il résulte de la visite que les papiers de bord ne son pas en ordre ;

2. Dans tous les cas de soupçon mentionnés au § 20 ;

3. Lorsqu'il résulte de la visite, ou de la recherche, que le navire arrêté fait des transports prohibés pour le compte et à destination de l'ennemi ;

4. Lorsque le navire a été pris en violation de blocus :

5. Lorsque le navire a pris part aux hostilités, ou est destiné à y prendre part.

5. *De la nationalité du navire, de la cargaison et de l'equipage.*

§ 24.—La nationalité du navire, de sa cargaison, de son équipage doit être constatée par les papiers de bord, trouvés sur le navire saisi, sans exclusion, toutefois, d'une production ultérieure devant les tribunaux des prises.

§ 25.—La question de savoir si les conditions de nationalité sont remplies, est décidée selon la législation de l'État auquel le navire est ressortissant.

§ 26.—L'acte juridique constatant la vente d'un navire ennemi faite durant la guerre, doit être parfait, et le navire doit être enregistré conformément à la législation du pays dont il acquiert la nationalité, avant qu'il quitte le port de sortie. La nouvelle nationalité ne peut être acquise au navire par une vente faite en cours de voyage.

§ 27.—Les papiers de bord requis en vertu du droit international sont les suivants :

1. Les documents relatifs à la propriété du navire ;

2. Le connaissement ;

3. Le rôle d'équipage, avec l'indication de la nationalité du patron et de l'équipage ;

4. Le certificat de nationalité, si les documents mentionnés sous le chiffre 3 n'y suppléent ;

5. Le journal de bord.

§ 28.—Les documents énoncés au précédent article doivent, pour avoir force probante, être rédigés clairement et sans équivoque.

§ 29.—Si, dans la constatation d'une circonstance déterminante pour la saisie, il y a évidence quant à la nationalité ou la destination du navire, ou quant à la nature de cargaison, ou quant à la nationalité du patron et de l'équipage, suivant le fait dont il s'agit,—et qu'un papier de bord ordinairement relatif à l'une de ces questions manque, la seule absence de ce papier n'est pas un motif de saisie, pourvu toutefois que les autres papiers de bord soient parfaitement d'accord entre eux sur le point en question.

6. *Des transports interdits durant la guerre.*

§ 30.—Sont sujets à saisie, durant la guerre, les objets susceptibles d'être employés à la guerre immédiatement, qui sont transportés par des navires de commerce nationaux, neutres ou ennemis, pour le compte ou à destination de l'ennemi (contrebande de guerre). Les gouvernements belligérants auront à déterminer d'avance, à l'occasion de chaque guerre, les objets qu'ils tiendront pour tels.

§ 31.—Les objets de contrebande de guerre doivent être réellement à bord au moment de la recherche.

§ 32.—Ne sont pas réputés contrebande de guerre les objets nécessaires à la défense de l'équipage et du navire, pourvu que le navire n'en ait pas fait usage pour résister à l'arrêt, à la visite, à la recherche ou à la saisie.

§ 33.—Le navire arrêté pour cause de contrebande de guerre, peut continuer sa route, si sa cargaison ne se compose pas exclusivement, ou en majeure partie, de contrebande de guerre et que le patron soit prêt à livrer celle-ci au navire du belligérant et que le déchargement puisse avoir lieu sans obstacle, selon l'avis du commandant du croiseur.

§ 34.—Sont assimilés au transport interdit de contrebande de guerre (§ 30), les transports de troupes pour les opérations militaires, sur terre et sur mer, de l'ennemi, ainsi que les transports de la correspondance officielle de l'ennemi par les navires de commerce nationaux, neutres ou ennemis.

7. *Du blocus.*

§ 35.—Le blocus déclaré et notifié est effectif, lorsqu'il existe un danger imminent pour l'entrée ou la sortie du port bloqué, à cause d'un nombre suffisant de navires de guerre stationnés ou ne s'écartant que momentanément de leur station.

§ 36.—La déclaration du blocus doit déterminer, non seulement les limites du blocus par leur latitude et longitude, et le moment précis où le blocus commencera, mais encore, éventuellement, le délai qui peut être accordé aux navires de commerce pour décharger, recharger et sortir du port (§ 7).

§ 37.—Le commandant du blocus doit, en outre, notifier la déclaration du blocus aux autorités et aux consuls du lieu bloqué. Les mêmes formalités seront remplies lors du rétablissement d'un blocus qui a cessé d'être effectif, et lorsque le blocus sera étendu à des points nouveaux.

§ 38.—Si les navires bloquants s'éloignent de leur station pour un motif autre que le mauvais temps constaté, le blocus est considéré comme levé ; il doit alors être de nouveau déclaré et notifié.

§ 39.—Il est interdit aux navires de commerce d'entrer dans les places et ports qui se trouvent en état de blocus effectif, et d'en sortir.

§ 40.—Cependant, il est permis aux navires de commerce d'entrer, pour cause de mauvais temps, dans le port bloqué, mais seulement après constatation, par le commandant du blocus, de la persistance de la force majeure.

§ 41.—S'il est évident qu'un navire de commerce, approchant du port bloqué, n'a pas eu connaissance du blocus déclaré et effectif, le commandant du blocus l'en avertira, inscrira l'avertissement dans les papiers de bord du navire averti, tout au moins dans le certificat de nationalité et dans le journal de bord, en marquant la date de l'avertissement ; et invitera le navire à s'éloigner du port bloqué, en l'autorisant à continuer son voyage vers un port non bloqué.

§ 42.—On admet l'ignorance du blocus, lorsque le temps écoulé depuis la déclaration du blocus est trop peu considérable pour que le navire en cours de voyage, qui a tenté d'entrer dans le port bloqué, en ait pu être instruit.

§ 43.—Un navire de commerce sera saisi pour violation de blocus lorsqu'il a essayé par force ou par ruse de pénétrer à travers la ligne de blocus ; ou si après avoir été renvoyé une première fois, il a essayé de nouveau de pénétrer dans le même port bloqué.

§ 44.—Ni le fait qu'un navire de commerce est dirigé sur un port bloqué, ni le simple affrètement, ni la seule destination du navire pour un tel port ne justifient la saisie pour violation de blocus. En aucun cas la supposition d'un voyage continué ne peut justifier la condamnation pour violation de blocus.

8. *Des formalités qui suivent la saisie.*

§ 45.—Après la saisie, le capteur fermera les écoutilles et la soute aux poudres du navire saisi, et y apposera ses scellés. Il fera de même à l'égard de la cargaison, après que celle-ci aura été inventoriée.

§ 46.—Il ne sera rien vendu, ni déchargé, ni échangé, ni en général distrait, consommé ou détérioré de la cargaison.

Si cependant la cargaison consiste en choses pouvant se gâter facilement, ou si ces choses sont avariées, le capteur prendra les mesures les plus convenables pour la conservation de la cargaison, du consentement et en présence du patron, ainsi qu'en présence d'un consul de la nationalité du navire saisi, s'il s'en trouve un dans le voisinage du lieu de le capture. Le commandant du navire capteur procédera, à cet effet, à l'inspection de la cargaison.

§ 47.—Le capteur dressera l'inventaire du navire saisi et de la cargaison, ainsi que la liste des personnes trouvées á bord, et fera passer à bord du navire saisi un équipage suffisant pour s'assurer du navire et y maintenir l'ordre.

§ 48.—Le capteur saisira tous les papiers de bord, documents et lettres qui se trouvent sur le navire saisi. Ces papiers, documents et lettres seront réunis dans un paquet revêtu du cachet du commandant du navire de guerre et de celui du patron du navire saisi ; il sera dressé inventaire de ces papiers, documents et lettres, et le commandant du navire de guerre déclarera par écrit, dans le procès-verbal, que ce sont là *tous* les papiers trouvés sur le navire : il y ajoutera une mention indiquant quels papiers manquaient au moment de la saisie, et dans quel état se trouvaient les papiers saisis, notamment s'ils paraissent avoir avoir été altérés.

§ 49.—Le capteur dressera procès-verval de la saisie, ainsi que de l'état du navire et de la cargaison, en y mentionnant le jour et l'heure de la saisie ; à quelle hauteur elle a eu lieu ; la circonstance qui l'a motivée ; le nom du navire et celui du patron ; le nombre d'hommes composant l'équipage ; la nationalité du navire, du patron et de l'équipage ; sous quel pavillon naviguait le navire au moment de l'arrêt, et s'il y a eu résistance de la part du navire, et de quelle nature a été la résistance. Seront joints au procès-verbal les inventaires du navire, de la cargaison et des papiers de bord, avec mention au procès-verbal que ces inventaires ont été dressés. Copie du procès-verbal sera transmise à l'autorité militaire supérieure de laquelle relève le navire capteur.

§ 50.—Il sera permis au capteur de brûler ou de couler bas le navire saisi, après avoir fait passer sur le navire de guerre les personnes qui se trouvaient à bord et déchargé autant que possible la cargaison, et après que le commandant du navire capteur aura pris à sa charge les papiers de bord et les objets importants pour l'enquête judiciaire et pour les réclamations des propriétaires de la cargaison en dommages et intérêts, dans les cas suivants :—

1. Lorsqu'il n'est pas possible de tenir le navire à flot, à cause de son mauvais état, la mer étant houleuse ;

2. Lorsque le navire marche si mal qu'il ne peut pas suivre le navire de guerre et pourrait facilement être repris par l'ennemi ;

3. Lorsque l'approche d'une force ennemie supérieure fait craindre la reprise du navire saisi ;

4. Lorsque le navire de guerre ne peut mettre sur le navire saisi un équipage suffisant sans trop diminuer celui qui est nécessaire à sa propre sûreté ;

5. Lorsque le port où il serait possible de conduire le navire saisi, est trop éloigné.

§ 51.—Il sera dressé procès-verbal de la destruction du navire saisi et des motifs qui l'ont amenée; ce procès-verbal sera transmis à l'autorité supérieure militaire et au tribunal d'instruction le plus proche, lequel examinera, et au besoin complétera, les actes y relatifs et les transmettra au tribunal des prises.

§ 52.—Des personnes se trouvant à bord du navire saisi, les seules qui seront considérées comme prisonniers de guerre sont celles qui font partie de la force militaire de l'ennemi, et celles qui ont assisté l'ennemi, ou sont soupçonnées de l'avoir assisté.

§ 53.—Le patron, le sobrécargue, le pilote et les autres personnes qu'il pourra être nécessaire d'entendre pour la constatation des faits, seront retenus à bord provisoirement. Ces personnes ne seront autorisées à quitter le bord, après leurs dépositions, qu'en vertu d'une décision du tribunal instructeur.

§ 54.—Les personnes trouvées et retenues à bord seront nourries, et au besoin vêtues et soignées, par le gouvernement de l'État auquel appartient le navire capteur. Le patron fournira caution pour les frais qui en résulteront, lesquels pourront être remboursés en vertu du jugement.

§ 55.—On laissera aux hommes de l'équipage leurs effets servant à leur usage personnel.

§ 56.—Il n'est pas permis au capteur de débarquer les hommes de l'équipage qui ne sont pas nécessaires pour l'enquête et qu'il y a lieu de renvoyer immédiatement faute de place sur le navire capteur ou faute de vivres, sur des terres incultes et inhabitées, ni sur des terres où leur vie et leur liberté seraient en danger. Mais il sera permis au capteur de faire passer ces hommes à bord de navires neutres ou alliés qu'il pourra recontrer, et de les débarquer sur des territoires cultivés et habités.

§ 57.—Le commandant du navire capteur répond du bon traitement et du bon entretien des personnes trouvées à bord du navire saisi, par l'équipage du navire capteur et par celui qui conduit le navire saisi ; il ne doit pas tolérer que celles mêmes d'entre ces personnes qui sont prisonniers de guerre soient employées à des travaux avilissants.

9 *Du transport du navire saisi en un port.*

§ 58.—Le navire saisi sera conduit dans le port le plus voisin de l'État capteur ou dans un port d'une puissance alliée ou se trouvera un tribunal pour instruire à l'égard du navire saisi.

§ 59.—Le navire saisi ne pourra être conduit dans un port d'une puissance neutre que pour cause de péril de mer, ou lorsque le navire de guerre sera poursuivi par une force ennemie supérieure.

§ 60.—Lorsque, pour cause de péril de mer, le navire de guerre s'est réfugié avec le navire saisi dans un port neutre, ils devront quitter ce port aussitôt que possible, après que la tempête aura cessé. L'État neutre a le droit et le devoir de surveiller le navire de guerre et le navire saisi durant leur séjour dans le port.

§ 61.—Lorsque le navire de guerre s'est réfugié avec le navire saisi dans un port neutre parce qu'il était poursuivi par une force ennemie supérieure, la prise sera relâchée.

§ 62.—Le navire saisi et la cargaison seront, autant que possible conservés intacts durant le voyage au port ; la cargaison sera close et scellée, sauf dans le cas où la levée des scellés et l'ouverture de la cargaison seraient jugées nécessaires dans l'intérêt de la conservation de celle-ci, avec le consentement du patron.

These 62 Rules were submitted to the august consideration of the Governments of all Maritime Powers.

CHAPTER XXXVIII.

TREATIES ANTECEDENT TO THE DECLARATION OF PARIS OF 1856, BEARING ON THE QUESTION OF NEUTRAL GOODS IN ENEMY VESSELS AND ENEMY GOODS IN NEUTRAL VESSELS.

Treaties establishing Maritime International Law.

§ 287. In chapter XVII (Vol. I. p. 490) we gave a brief historical sketch of the ancient maritime and commercial codes, which are the sources of the present maritime and commercial International Law and constitute the *lex mercatoria* of all civilized States. In chapter XX (Vol. II. p. 76) will be found the principal treaties and agreements between Nations which can be viewed as historical land marks, indicating the general development of the International Spirit of Law in the mutual intercourse of Nations, when moulding into shape the usages which we now call International Law. In the present chapter we propose to conclude the historical notes of our work by mentioning those treaties antecedent to the Declaration of Paris, of 1856, which made special reference to rules of maritime warfare, or have any bearing on the question of neutral goods in enemy ships and enemy goods in neutral vessels, the Declaration of Paris itself having been treated in chapter XXXIII.

Owing to the development of commerce and navigation, most European wars, especially those of the seventeenth and eighteenth centuries, arose from causes connected with the jealous competition existing between the maritime commercial and colonial Powers of Europe. The treaties, which terminated the respective wars, were generally followed by new commercial conventions containing fresh agreements with regard to the ever shifting questions of neutral commerce and navigation and with regard to the definition of the term contraband of war.

As the stipulations of these treaties constitute an important contribution to the history of maritime International Law, we will briefly note the most important treaties from the commencement of the seventeenth century down to the Declaration of Paris of 1856.

Treaties of the 17th century.

§ 288. The seventeenth century opens with a most liberal concession of the Ottoman Porte to Henry IV. of France, allowing, by the capitulation of 1604, the French flag to protect the enemy's goods. This concession the Porte extended by treaty to Holland, in 1612, and, subsequently, to other Powers.

The treaty of Westphalia, of 1648, the turning point of the policy followed by European States and the greatest epoch in general history, did not contain a special solution of any question of maritime International Law, but the Treaty of the Pyrenees in 1659 (renewed at Aix-la-Chapelle, in 1668) *, which terminated the war between France and Spain, settled the principle established (in Art. XIX) between the contracting parties, that enemy's goods in neutral vessels should be free, but neutral property in the enemy's vessel should follow the fate of the vessel, that is to say :—free ship free goods, enemy's ship enemy's goods, or, as the French put it:—*la robe d'ennemi confisque celle d'ami.* Holland became a party to this treaty in 1661. †

---

* *Schmauss.* I. 690.

† *Dumont.* VI. 11, 84.

The treaties, concluded in the latter half of the seventeenth century, by which Great Britain acknowledged the principle of "free ship free goods," *(la robe d'ennemi confisque celle d'ami)*, were those with Portugal of 1654 (Art. 23), * with France and Spain in 1667 and 1677 (Art. VIII), † with Sweden and with Denmark in 1670, and those with Holland of 1667, concluded at Breda and renewed in 1668 ‡, the treaty of 1674 (Art. VIII) and that of 1689. ||

In 1655, the treaty of commerce and navigation, previously concluded between France and the German Hanseatic towns, was renewed. It embodied the new stipulation (Art. 3), that neutral goods found in enemy's vessel should be free, in the words: "*la robe de l'ennemi ne confisquait pas la robe de l'ami*," and asserted the principle of "free ship free goods," contraband of war being, in both cases, excepted. This concession, however, was revoked by the treaty of 1716, which returned to the old practice, admitting the principle of "free ship free goods" but nothing more.

The treaties of peace signed at Utrecht in 1713 were followed by special treaties of commerce and navigation, concluded between the four great maritime Powers of Europe, viz., France, Spain, England and Holland, which adopted the rules "free ship free goods" and "enemy's ship enemy's goods."

In 1739 a convention was signed between France and Holland, renewing the treaty of commerce and navigation of 1713, by which the two rules "free ship free goods," and "enemy ship enemy goods," were established as a conventional law to be observed between the parties.

---

* *Dumont.* VII. 1. 329.
† *Idem.* VII. 1, 49.
‡ *Schmauss.* 1,979.
|| *Dumont.* VII. 11. 236.

The convention signed in 1742 between France and Denmark was based on the same principle.

The rules "free ship free goods" and "enemy ship confiscable goods" remained thus, ever since the peace of Utrecht (1713), the generally adopted principle, though it was often disregarded by belligerents.

The seven years war. Hübner.

§ 289. The principal point of maritime International Law, raised during the 'Seven Years' War (1756-1763), was the question on what principle neutral vessels and goods could be confiscated by belligerents. The able work of Hübner, on the seizure of neutral vessels, gives ample information with regard to the state of maritime International Law during that period. *

Principles of the armed neutrality.

§ 290. The famous Russian manifest, called the Declaration of Armed Neutrality of 1780, issued by the Empress Catharine, on the 26 February, 1780, during the war between France and Spain against England, contains the following rules for neutral commerce and navigation. †

1°. Neutral vessels can trade freely between the ports and along the coasts of Nations at war.

2°. Enemy's goods in neutral vessels are free, with the exception of contraband of war.

3°. With regard to what is understood to be contraband of war, Russia adhered to her treaty of commerce with Great Britain of 1766, by which, in articles 10 & 11, contraband of war was declared to mean only munitions of war, consisting of cannon, mortars, fire-arms, gun-matches, gunpowder, saltpetre, sulphur, cuirasses, pikes,

* HÜBNER. "De la saisie des batiments neutres, ou du droit qu'ont les nations belligérantes d'arreter les navires des peuples amis," etc. La Haye. 1759. Martin Hübner (born in 1725, died in 1795) was Ambassador of Denmark to England. His "Essai sur l'Histoire du Droit Naturel," published in London in 1757, is also worth consulting.

† *De Martens.* Rec. III. p. 158. Actes relatifs à la Neutralité armée. *De Flasson.* VII. p. 273. note 1.

swords, belts, cartridge-boxes, saddles and bridles. The same obligations were extended to all belligerents.

4°. Only those ports are treated as blockaded ports the entering of which is accompanied with evident danger through the presence of the belligerent's vessels.

5°. These principles to serve as law for the guidance of Prize Courts. *

Russia invited all the maritime Powers of Europe to adhere to the foregoing rules and, in case of need, to defend their neutrality by force, and Russia promised to apply a considerable part of her forces for this purpose. Hence arose the term "armed neutrality" by which these rules are designated. Denmark, Sweden, Holland, the United States of America, Russia, Austria, Portugal, Naples, France and Spain joined in this declaration of armed neutrality and subsequently Prussia and the German Empire, and the Two Sicilies also gave in their adherence. Great Britain kept to her old system of special convention and, where no such convention existed, to the old rules of the *Consolado del Mar*, which was that of "capturing as prize the goods of the enemy at sea, though in neutral vessels, and also contraband of war, though belonging to neutrals, but allowing other innocent neutral goods, though on board hostile vessels, to pass free." †

The declaration of armed neutrality opened a new epoch in the history of maritime International Law by establishing the rights of neutrals. Until then neutral commerce was in every war harrassed by the belligerents on both sides and

* M. DE MARTENS. Rec. Vol. I. p. 145. and Vol. II. pp. 73–76. GESSNER. Le Droit des neutres sur Mer. Edit. 1865. p. 39. WHEATON. Histoire Vol. I. p. 358.

† JAMES REDDIE. Researches Hist. and Critic. on Mar. Intern. Law. Edit. 1844. Vol. I. pp. 92–94, 157 & 162.

suffered nearly as much as if in actual state of war.

The French wars. § 291. During the French war waged in Europe by the First Republic and Napoleon I., there was little chance for the practical development of sound principles of International Law. The doctrine of starving the enemy out, by cutting off all supply of provisions from his ports, was prevalent and the right of pre-emption was in full practice on both sides. The continental system of Napoleon, declaring the British Isles and all the Colonies of Great Britain in a state of blockade, by Decrees dated from Berlin, 21 November, 1806, and from Milan, 11th December, 1807, and the declaration of blockade by England of all the ports and rivers of the Continent, from the Elbe to Brest included, reduced all principles of maritime International Law to their lowest ebb-tide in the history of Europe. (See note on § 270).

Period from the Congress of Vienna to the Declaration of Paris. § 292. The Congress of Vienna, at the end of the Napoleonic period, had no particular influence on the maritime branch of International Law. The dawning of a new and happier period came with the Declaration of Great Britain, of 28 March, 1854, at the beginning of the Crimean war, recognizing that a blockade must be effected with an adequate naval force, and adopting the principle of "free ship free goods," coupled with the promise not to confiscate neutral property found in the enemy's vessels (in both cases contraband of war excepted) and not to issue commissions to privateers. *

This was followed, after the war, by the Declaration of Paris, of 16 April, 1855, which we treated above in chapter XXXIII.

---

* London Gazette of 20 March, 1854.

CHAPTER XXXIX.

THE GENEVA CONVENTION AND THE RED-CROSS SOCIETIES.

I. *Origin of the Red-Cross Societies.*

§ 293. The thrilling sketches, given by Henri Dunant, of the battle of Solferino, awoke civilized mankind to a sense of its duty. *Henri Dunant.*

After having exposed, in a heart-rending style, the horrors of a battle-field, where more than 300,000 men fought for fifteen hours on the 24th of June, 1859, and the consequences of the conflict, during two days after, when the fields, which had sustained the ravages of arms, were yet strewn with the wounded and the dying, without help or shelter,—which the best organized military-medical services of three of the best armies of Europe were not able to render, at the proper time, to all the sufferers,—the citizen of Geneva proposes the following question to Humanity:—

"What do you think of a general association of private individuals, who will make it a voluntary but sacred duty, to give succour to the wounded warriors on the battle-fields, when the military-medical service falls short in this duty, to nurse the desolate sick and wounded, to assist the dying in their last moments and finally to bury the dead?"—In other terms:

"Do you not think it the duty of Humanity to soothe, as much as possible, the calamities of war?"

The heart of good men bled, when they contemplated the ghastly figure of the genius of war, at once sprung up before them, in all its terrible reality,—when the proposition of Dunant was brought before the tribunal of mankind,—and the answer of all civilized nations was: "We *must* help!"

And yet, it was not the first time, that the pen of an able writer, guided by a generous and sympathizing heart, called the attention of civilized mankind to the horrors of a battle-field. Besides many other writers, at different times, Robert Hall, an eminent English preacher and author, wrote in 1802, the following lines, in his *Reflections on War*:—

. . . . . "To confine our attention to the number of the slain would give us a very inadequate "idea of the ravages of the sword. The lot of "those who perish instantaneously, may be considered, apart from religious prospects, as comparatively happy, since they are exempt from "those lingering diseases and slow torments, to "which others are liable. We cannot see an "individual expire, though a stranger or an "enemy, without being sensibly moved, and "prompted by compassion to lend him every assistance in our power. Every trace of resentment "vanishes in a moment: every other emotion "gives way to pity and terror. In these last "extremities, we remember nothing but the respect and tenderness due to our common nature. "What a scene, then, must a field of battle present, where thousands are left without assistance, and without pity, with their wounds "exposed to the piercing air, while the blood, "freezing as it flows, binds them to the earth, "amidst the trampling of horses, and the insults "of an enraged foe! If they are spared by the "humanity of the enemy, and carried from the "field, it is but a prolongation of torment. Con-"veyed in uneasy vehicles, often to a remote "distance, through roads almost impassable, they "are lodged in ill-prepared receptacles for the "wounded and the sick, where the variety of "distress baffles all the efforts of humanity and "skill, and renders it impossible to give to each "the attention he demands. Far from their na-"tive home, no tender assiduities of friendship, "no well-known voice, no wife, or mother or "sister is near to soothe their sorrows, relieve "their thirst, or close their eyes in death. Un-"happy man! and must you be swept into the "grave unnoticed and unnumbered, and no "friendly tear be shed for your sufferings, or "mingled with your dust?"

We quoted the words of this writer, in preference, for, in this picture of woe, is pointed out, to heart and mind, the urgent need in war, of that help, which our Red-Cross Societies of the present time are called to supply. Could there be a more ardent request for neutral voluntary aid on the field of battle and for the inviolable protection of the wounded soldier? And yet, on this, and on even more direct appeals to the civilized world, to lessen the calamities of the battle-fields, by declaring neutral and inviolable the sick and wounded, the medical *personnel* and the ambulances,—as proposed in the eloquent writings of Doctor Palasciano of Naples and of Mr. Henri Arnault of Paris,—no measures were taken by the Nations, for efficient help, till, through alliance of interests and conformity of views, real practical means were suggested, to secure the efficacy of philanthropic ardour.

Dunant's plan was based on the principle, that benevolence without judgment will rarely avail, and, for the guidance of charity in war, he proposed to establish, in time of peace, permanent Societies, which can prepare themselves, in good season, to encourage and guide the philanthropic spirit, which exhibits itself so manifestly in all civilized Nations at the outburst of a war, and to make use of this benevolent tendency, by wise and practical measures, for the speedy and efficient help of wounded soldiers on the battle-fields.

The Genevese Society "For Public Utility" first took up the matter, in its session of the 9th of February 1863, and resolved to convoke an international conference, in order to deliberate upon the course to be taken, for the realization of this humane design. On the 1st of September of the same year, a circular to that effect was issued and published, but particularly brought under discussion at the International Statistical Congress, which met about the same time at Berlin.

The favourable report, given of the Genevese plan, by eminent members of this congress, produced such general sympathy, as was principally the cause, that, at the International Conference, which met at Geneva on the 26th of October of the same year, at the invitation of the Society "For Public Utility," to discuss this international question, almost all the nationalities of Europe were represented.

In this conference, resolutions were adopted on the following measures:—

1°. The establishment, in every country, of Aid-Societies, with the object of being ready in time of war, to give help to the wounded and sick soldiers on the fields of battle, when the official medical help of the armies might be found insufficient, and, as such, to form a powerful auxiliary to the Military-Medical Service.

2°. The regulations by which these national Societies and their committees are to be governed, while organizing themselves in the most useful and convenient way.

3°. The co-operation of these Aid-Societies, which, each by the peculiar ways and means prepared by its own national tendency and customs, may join together into a cordial international alliance, for the surer and speedier realization of their common benevolent purpose.

4°. The following applications to be made to the Governments of all civilized Nations, viz.:—

a. That the Governments may grant their high protection to the Aid-Societies.

b. That, in time of war, the ambulances and the hospitals, be proclaimed neutral, with the adoption of the same flag for all. That neutrality be admitted, in the most complete manner, for the official medical *personnel* and for all who give voluntary personal aid to the sick and wounded. Also neutrality for the wounded or sick warriors, who must be taken up and nursed, without regard to nationality.

c. The adoption of a badge of neutrality, to be worn as a band round the arm, by all the military medical *personnel* and its official, as well as its voluntary or private helpers.

d. Special protection for those inhabitants of the scenes of war, who might give proof of their benevolence, by taking up and nursing sick and wounded soldiers.

The task of this international conference, as may be judged by the results, was, by no means, an easy one, for there were to be brought into harmony, two contradictory elements, Humanity and War. Fundamental regulations were framed, suitable for all Nations and on which the Aid-Societies could be formed, and, the voluntary aid, being naturally of an independent character, had to be brought in agreement with the disciplinary regulations of the armies to secure its acceptance by the military commanders. However, the large experience of most of the members of this conference and the truly philanthropic spirit, possessed by all of them, overcame the difficulties and they succeeded in framing a Charter, by which all the present Red-Cross Societies of the different Nations are guided ;—and, the civilized world can boast of one Constitution at least, in which surely good men and angels rejoice.

Eminent men rose up in every country, to show their countrymen, by writings and speeches, the deficiency of the help thus far tendered to the warrior, who valiantly sheds his blood for his country's honour and defence, and to prove the benevolence of *neutral aid* in war. We shall lack sufficient space, to record here the works of all those just, good and influential citizens, in every civilized country, whose hearts and minds, a merciful God has inspired, to induce their countrymen to undertake a work, so much needed, but which requires so much sacrifice and labour.

When men use the best of their knowledge and faculties, to strive in ambition and vain glory, the success of one might cause wrong or grief to a great part of his fellow-creatures, but when Science and Benevolence join hands, in assiduous labours, to lessen the great sum of human miseries, the success is a blessing to *all*, for it is a step made towards that higher standard in morals, in philanthropy and religion, which alone can justify our hopes of a final universal peace among civilized mankind.

II. *The International Convention of Geneva.*

The Convention of Geneva, its additional articles and those concerning the Navy.

§ 294. After the International Conference held at Geneva (1863), which gave birth to our present Red-Cross Societies, the question of neutralizing the ambulances, military hospitals and their *personnel* was brought on diplomatic ground, by the Swiss Government, under the auspices of the Emperor Napoleon III. The result was an International Convention, concluded at Geneva, on the 22nd of August, 1864, to which almost all the European Governments adhered, "*as being equally animated with the desire to soften as much as possible the calamities inseparable from war, to suppress all useless severity in warfare and to ameliorate the lot of wounded warriors on the fields of battle.*"

The International Convention of Geneva, of the 22nd of August, 1864, as supplemented by the Addional Articles of the 20th of October, 1868, established rules with regard to the manner in which the sick and the wounded, of the armies of the contracting Powers, the staff and other *personnel* employed in ministering to the sick and wounded, and the military hospitals and ambulances with their *materiel* are to be respectively dealt with, in the case of two or more of these Powers waging war with each other.

Although the Geneva Convention makes special mention only of the belligerents, military hospitals and ambulances, with their *personnel* and *materiel*, and although its articles do not provide, in express terms, for the volunteer or independent Red-Cross Societies belonging to neutral nationalities, yet the privileges granted to an enemy for his military ambulances and hospitals, with their belongings, can never be refused to neutral Red-Cross Societies duly organized under the auspices of a friendly Government. The neutral Red-Cross Society is on this ground entitled to the protection of the belligerents, but it should, in the first instance, apply to the chiefs of the belligerent army, to whose wounded and sick it proposes to minister, for official sanction to act, not as an independent body invested with special rights and privileges of its own, but as a hospital reserve for help to sick and wounded of belligerent forces ; following, as far as practicable with its own neutral status, the directions of the belligerent chiefs under whose recognition and sanction it is fulfilling its neutral benevolent duties. Under these conditions the neutral Red-Cross Societies can claim the privileges, accorded by Art. IV & VI and the *3rd add. art.* of the Geneva Convention to the military *ambulances* of belligerents, and by the *13th add. art.* to private hospital-ships (see rules 1°., 4°., 6°. & 16°, stated below).

The International Convention of Geneva and its Additional Articles above quoted, establish the following rules.

Rules of the Geneva Convention and its Additional Articles.

1°. The Ambulances and Military Hospitals are acknowledged as neutral, and, as such, protected and respected by the belligerents, as long as they contain any sick or wounded soldiers. The neutrality ceases, if these ambulances or hospitals are held by a military force *(Conv. Art. I)*.

Under the denomination *Ambulance* are comprehended all sorts of field-hospitals and other temporary establishments, which follow the armies on the battle-fields, to receive the sick and wounded *(3rd add. art.)*

2°. The *personnel* of the hospitals and ambulances, comprehending the staff required for superintendence, medical service, for the administration, and for the transporting of the wounded, and also the chaplains, shall participate in the benefit of neutrality, while executing their duty and so long as there are wounded men to be taken care of. *(Conv. Art. II.)*

3°. The persons designated in the foregoing article, shall continue to give their care to the sick and wounded of the ambulance or hospital where they are officiating, in proportion to the need of help, even after the occupation of the place by the enemy.

When such persons ask for permission to retire, the Commander of the occupying forces shall fix the moment of their departure, which he may postpone only in case of military exigency, and then only for a short time. They shall then be delivered by the occupying army to the outposts of the enemy. *(Conv. Art. III, 1st add. art.)*

All necessary arrangements shall be made by the belligerent Powers, to secure to the neutral *personnel* falling into the hands of the enemy, the full enjoyment of their salaries. *(2nd add. art.)*

4°. The *materiel* of the military hospitals, remaining subject to the Law of War, the persons attached to these hospitals, on leaving, can only carry with them those articles which are their personal property. The ambulances, however, shall retain their *materiel*. *(Conv. Art. IV.)*

In this case also are comprehended, by the denomination *ambulance*, all field-hospitals and other temporary establishments for the sick and wounded, which follow the armies to the battlefields. *(3rd add. art.)*

5°. The inhabitants of the country, who afford aid to the wounded, shall remain free and be respected. The generals of the belligerent Powers shall be instructed to notify to the inhabitants the appeal made to their humanity and the neutrality which they can derive from it. Every wounded man, received and nursed in a house, shall be a safeguard to that dwelling. *(Conv. Art. V.)*

In apportioning the charges, relative to the quartering of troops and the war-contributions, the charitable zeal exhibited by those inhabitants who have taken in wounded soldiers, shall be taken, in an equitable manner, into account. *(4th add. art.)*

6°. Every wounded or sick soldier shall be received and nursed, without regard to nationality. The wounded, who after recovery may be found incapable of bearing arms, shall be sent to their own country.

The means employed in the removal of the wounded, and the persons attached thereto, shall always be covered by absolute neutrality. *(Conv. Art. VI.)*

With the exception of the officers, whose detention could influence the course of the war, the commanders in chief have the power,—with the consent of both parties, and when circumstances allow it,—to send back to their country, the wounded prisoners of war, after their recovery or, if possible, to hand them over sooner, at the outposts: even those who are not found incapable of bearing arms; but these always on the condition of not serving during the war. *(5th add. art.)*

7°. A uniform *distinctive flag* shall be adopted for the hospitals, the ambulances and the means of removal of the sick and wounded. This flag shall always be accompanied by the national colours.

A band round the arm *(brassard)* shall also be worn by the neutral *personnel.* The use of this badge must, however, be authorized by the military authorities.

The flag and the band on the arm exhibit *a red-cross on a white field. (Conv. Art. VII.)*

8°. The details for the execution of this convention, shall be regulated by the Commanders in Chief of the belligerent armies, according to the instructions given by their respective Governments and in conformity with the general principles, laid down in this Convention. *(Conv. Art. VIII.)*

(Articles concerning the Navy.)

9°. The vessels which, at their own risk and peril, are occupied, during or after the action, in picking up the wounded, or which, having taken in wounded, are carrying them on board a neutral or hospital-ship, shall enjoy, during the accomplishment of their task, all the benefits of neutrality, which the circumstances of the battle and the position of the fighting vessels will permit to be granted to them. The appreciation of the said circumstances is intrusted to the humanity of the fighting parties. *Articles concerning the Red-Cross Society in naval warfare.*

The shipwrecked and the wounded, rescued or received by the said neutral vessels, cannot serve again during the war. *(6th add. art.)*

10°. The *personnel* of the religious, medical, and hospital-services of all captured vessels are declared neutral. When leaving the vessel, they carry with them, those articles and surgical instruments, which are their personal property. *(7th add. art.)*

11°. The persons designated in the preceding rule *(7th add. art.)* must continue to fulfil their functions on the captured vessel, till the removal of the wounded, to be ordered by the conqueror, and to assist at this removal. After this they are at liberty to return to their own country. When they ask for leave to withdraw, the Commander-in-Chief shall fix the time of their departure, which can only be postponed,—and then with the shortest delay,—in cases of military exigences (see above, rule 3°.)

The belligerent Powers shall make the necessary arrangements to secure to the neutral *personnel*, which falls into the hands of the enemy, the full enjoyment of its pay. *(1st, 2nd & 8th add. art.)*

12°. The Military Hospital-Ships remain subject to the Law of War, with regard to their *materiel*. They become the property of the captor, who, however, shall not use them, during the war, for any other purpose, than that for which they were destined at the capture. *(9th add. art.)*

Nevertheless vessels unfit for fighting purposes *(impropres au combat)*, which, during the time of peace, have been officially declared, by the respective Governments, to be destined to serve as floating naval-hospitals, shall enjoy, during time of war, a complete neutrality, for their *materiel*, as well as for their *personnel*, provided, that their equipment be exclusively appropriated to their special destination. *(Add. Paragr. to the 9th add. art.)*

13°. Any private vessel, to whatever nationality she may belong, exclusively charged with the removal of the sick and wounded, shall be protected by neutrality; but having been visited by a cruiser of the enemy, this single fact, notified on the log-book of the neutral vessel, shall render the sick and wounded on board incompetent to serve during the war. The cruiser shall have the right to place a commissioner on board the removing vessel, to accompany the convoy, in order to verify the good faith of the operation.

If the said vessel has any cargo on board, the neutrality shall cover this also, provided that the cargo be not of a nature making it liable to be confiscated by the belligerents.

The belligerents reserve to themselves the right to interdict, to any neutral vessel, any communication or direction, which they may judge to be prejudicial to the secrecy of their operations. In urgent cases, particular conventions can be made between the Commanders-in-Chief, for an immediate and temporary neutralisation, in a specified manner, of the vessels destined for the removal of the sick and wounded. *(10th add. art.)*

14°. All the wounded or sick sailors and soldiers on board a captured vessel shall be protected and cared for, by the captor, to whatever nation such wounded or sick may belong.

The wounded, who, after recovery, may be found incapable of service, shall be sent to their own country.

With the exception of the officers, whose detention may influence the course of the war, the Commanders-in-Chief have the authority,—with the consent of both parties, and when circumstances will allow it,—to send the wounded prisoners to their own country, after their recovery, or, if possible, sooner; even those who are not found incapable of serving, on the condition, however, that they shall not serve again during the war. *(11th add. art.* See also above rule 6°.)

15°. The distinctive flag, to be hoisted, together with the national colours, to indicate a ship, boat, or any sort of vessel, which claims the privilege of neutrality by virtue of the principles of this Convention, shall be *a white flag with the red cross.*

The belligerents have the right to exercise, with regard to this claim, every mode of verification they may deem necessary.

The Military Hospital-Ships shall be distinguished by the outside painting being *white with green battery. (12th add. art.)*

16°. The Hospital-Ships *(navires hospitaliers)*, fitted out at the expense of the Red-Cross Societies *(Sociétés de secours)*, recognized by the Governments which have signed the Convention, provided with a commission, emanating from the Sovereign who shall have given express authorisation for their equipment, and with a certificate from the competent naval-officer, stating that the said vessels have been submitted to his control, during the term of their equipment and at their final departure, and that they were then exclusively appropriated to the purpose of their mission, shall be considered as neutral and their crew also. They shall be respected and protected by the belligerents. They shall make themselves recognized by hoisting, together with their national colours, the *white flag with the red cross.* The distinctive badge for their *personnel*, in the exercise of their functions, shall be a band round the arm, with the same colours. Their outer painting shall be *white with red battery.*

These vessels shall give succour and assistance to the wounded and the shipwrecked of the belligerents, without distinction of nationality. They shall not obstruct, in any way, the movements of the combatants. During and after the battle they shall act at their own risk and peril.

The belligerents shall have the right of search and control over these vessels. They can refuse their co-operation, enjoin them to withdraw or detain them, if important circumstances demand.

The wounded and shipwrecked, taken on board these vessels, cannot be reclaimed by any of the belligerents, and they shall be charged not to serve again during the war. *(13th add. art.)*

17°. In naval wars, every strong presumption that one of the belligerents is profiting by the benefit of neutrality, in any other interest than that of the wounded and sick, gives the other belligerent the right to suspend the Convention at his option, untill the contrary is proved. If the presumption is found to be a fact, the Convention may even be suspended, with regard to such belligerent, for the whole duration of the war. *(14th add. art.)*

These are the concessions, which the exigencies of warfare have, up to this time, allowed the Military Powers to make for the sake of Humanity.

The Convention of Geneva and its additional act, together with the Declaration of Paris of the 16th of April 1856 (abolishing privateering) and the Convention of St. Petersburg of the 4th and 16th of November 1868 (prohibiting the use of explosive musket-balls)—are glorious conquests gained by the civilization of our century over the prejudices of former ages, whose laws of war were based on the principle *that the utmost possible injury ought to be inflicted on the enemy and that all means were allowed for this end that the life of the defeated was at the mercy of the victor and that the victory of arms gave an unlimited right to the property of the vanquished.* It is true, history records, at different periods, some solitary instances of conventions, made between the chiefs of belligerent armies, for the neutralisation of the hospitals, the medical service and of the sick and wounded, received in the hospitals, * but these contracts were mere temporary agreements, depending on the momentary disposition of the belligerent powers of the chiefs in command, and which, at all events, ended with the campaign, for which they were made. Such is not the case with a Convention claimed by Justice and Humanity and concluded in time of peace, between independent Powers, moved by charitable and generous sentiments, which give to the contract the character of a general and voluntary international alliance, with the tendency to bring into actual performance the theory of Montesquieu, that the Law of Nations is based on the principle: *that Nations, in their intercourse, be, in peace, of the greatest mutual advantage, and, in war, do the least possible injury to one another.*" †

---

* At the time of the Crusades, Sultan Saladin allowed his enemies, the Hospital-Knights of St. John, to remain tending and nursing their comrades in the City of Jerusalem, which he had conquered.

In 1743, during the Austrian Succession-war, an agreement was signed at Aschaffenburg, between the Austro-Hanoverian (Pragmatic) army under George II, represented by Gen. Count de Stair and the French Army under Marshal de Noailles; the belligerents agreed, to regard the hospitals as neutral and to give protection to the wounded.

A similar convention was made in 1759, during the seven-years war, and signed by the English General Sir Henry Seymour Conway, and the French Commander, Marquis du Barrail.

A Convention, between Louis XV and Frederik the Great, stipulating the neutrality of the Hospitals of the wounded and of all the persons belonging to the Hospital-service, was signed at Brandenburg, the 7th of September 1759, by the French Marshal de Rougé and the Prussian General von Buddenbrock.

† The Plan of Mobilisation of the North German Army (*Mobilmachung's Plan für das Nord-deutsche Bundesheer*) contained the following regulations with regard to the Geneva Convention and its addition articles, as established by Royal Decree of 29 April 1869, and by the German Army Medical Field Regulations (*Instruktion über das Sanitäts-wesen der Armee im Felde*).

1. The Royal Decree contains, as an appendix, a reprint of the Articles of the Geneva Convention.

2. A section of this Decree headed "Instructions for the Army Medical Department in the Field," (*a*) has been supplied by the War

---

(*a*.) Instruktion über das Sanitätswesen der Armee im Felde.

III. *The Red-Cross Societies at Sea.*

§ 295. At the last naval-battle, between the Austrian and Italian Fleets (1866), the want of neutral aid, which,—by virtue of the Geneva Convention,—was enjoyed by the warriors of the same Nations, on land, was bitterly felt by the Navy, and, if we wish to know what unnecessary loss of human lives this want of the Red-Cross aid at sea has caused, let us take a glance at a scene in this battle, yet fresh in our memory.

The necessity for neutral vessels of the Red-Cross Society proved at the naval-battle off Lissa. See Essay on the application of the Geneva Convention to Naval battles in Appendix I.

Office to all Officers commanding troops; and it is assumed that all combatant and medical Officers are thus acquainted with the instructions and with the Articles of the Geneva Convention. The troops also are made acquainted with them through the authorized courses of instruction given by Officers to the Serjeants and men at fixed intervals.

3. These Instructions contain the following passages :—

a. All persons belonging to the Army Medical Department must be provided, as soon as war commences, with the Neutrality-badge; Surgeons, Military and Civil Officers connected with hospitals, Hospital Orderlies and Bearers of Wounded being comprised in this category.

b. All ambulance conveyances, field hospital carts, waggons, and hospital tents, have to be marked with the neutrality sign.

4. The Directing Surgeon of each army corps, or, as representing him, the Surgeon in charge of a detached body of troops, is required to designate beforehand the Surgeon, or Assistant-Surgeons, Orderlies, proportion of ambulance stores, and transport which, on events requiring it, such as wounded having to be left on the ground, &c., are permitted to take their risk of falling temporarily into the hands of the enemy under the protection of the Geneva Convention.

Further extracts from the Instructions for the Army Medical Department, before named, bearing on the subject of the Geneva Convention are :—

Para. 2. The sick and wounded of allied troops, as also sick and wounded prisoners of war, are equally entitled to medical treatment.

Para. 7. During minor engagements the wounded will be taken to the temporary places for dressing wounds by the assistant sick bearers. As far as possible four men per company will be selected for this purpose from the men who have already been trained to this duty in time of peace. They will be distinguished by the white armlet with red cross worn on the left arm.

Para. 13. Temporary hospitals are to be denoted by the National Flag, and by a flag with red cross; after dark by a red lanthorn.

Para. 19. In the event of a retreat, the Commander of the Sanitary Detachment must arrange that both men and *matériel* follow the Army. The Principal Medical Officer determines who of the surgeons

In the Adriatic Sea, near the island of Lissa, the Austrian Fleet under Admiral Tegethoff and the Italian, under command of Admiral Persano, —both able commanders,—are fighting together. All the late improvements in war vessels, of the latest invention, were, on both sides, nearly equally divided; the battle is a test of modern warfare at sea. The weather is stormy, with a heavy sea caused by the northern gales; the atmosphere thick with the smoke of the thundering ironclads in furious *mêlée.*

All at once, the *Ferdinand-Max* (the Austrian flag-ship) and the *Ré d'Italia,*—both ironclad vessels,—met each other. The captain of the

---

and their assistants, with the necessary appliances, are to remain with the wounded under the protection of the Geneva Convention. (*a.*)

Para. 24. The hospital buildings will be distinguished by the National Flag, and a white flag with a red cross.

Para. 25. In the event of a retreat, the Principal Surgeon of a field hospital is responsible that the transport as well as men and *matériel* not required, follow the Army, if possible, in conjunction with the nearest sanitary detachment. The personal assistance required by the sick who have to be left behind, will be determined by the Principal Medical Officer, and only follows the Army after assisting in the further treatment and care of the sick.

Para. 79. The armlets with red cross issued to persons belonging to the volunteer establishments, must bear the stamp of the Royal Commissioner, who is further required to furnish each person, to whom an armlet is issued, with a certificate of authorisation to wear the Badge of Neutrality.

List of persons taken from the Dress Regulations, who are to wear the *brassard,* or arm-badge, in time of war. (*b.*)

During war the following are entitled, and respectively obliged, to wear the white armlet with red cross, the Badge of Neutrality of the Geneva Convention :—

1°. Medical Officers in charge, and their assistants.

2°. All persons belonging to Sanitary Detachments, Field Hospitals and Hospital Reserve Depôts, as also the Hospital Reserves.

3°. The Medical Cfficers, Hospital Assistants, Assistant Sick Bearers and train soldiers, with the regimental cars, and the train soldiers of the Medical Officers.

The armlets, which are to bear the mark of the regiments or corps in the middle of the joining, will be worn on the left sleeve of the coat or cloak in the middle of the upper arm.

(*a.*) The Articles of the Geneva Convention are appended in extenso to this paragraph. (Beilage 4. Instruktion, &c., page 110.)

(*b.*) Beilage 17. Nachweisung der Uniformen und Abzeichen des Sanitäts-Korps. (Instruktion, &c., page 159.)

Ferdinand-Max, discerning the gray colour of the enemy's vessel, amidst the smoke, and perceiving her in a favourable position for being rammed, orders the bold manoeuvre, and, with courageous self-reliance, runs right on towards the enemy's broadside. The *Ré d'Italia* tried to escape, by steaming backwards, but too late she saw the danger, in consequence of the thick clouds of smoke around her. The *Ferdinand-Max* put on full speed, and, with the momentum of its whole weight and a speed of eleven miles, ran its steel spur right into the flank of its enemy. The collision of the huge masses caused a most terrible crash to be heard. The shock was so violent, that the *Ré d'Italia* fell entirely on beams-ends, while the *Ferdinand-Max* was raised over her, by the sea, smashing the iron plates, ribs and beams of the unfortunate vessel. The *Ferdinand-Max* quickly backing, immediately after the collision—(which is strictly necessary for the ramming vessel, to prevent her being locked and drawn down with her foe)—drew back, and the *Ré d'Italia* totally broken up, with a breach of 62 square feet—(as was ascertained later, by the mark left on the painted spur and stern of the *Ferdinand-Max*, where the hard friction had nearly polished the iron)—turned over again; the water streaming through the breach; the crew struggling through the hatches and port-holes and clinging to the masts and rigging. Thus, while the *Ferdinand-Max* was slowly drawing backwards, the *Ré d'Italia* was fast sinking;—and, speedily and surely, the work of destruction was accomplished.

The Austrian officers contemplated with horror their work, while the *Ré d'Italia* was sinking in the deep, amidst the agonized cry for help of its crew. The firing had ceased and all eyes were fixed on the water, which was ingulfing the once proud and powerful sea-castle and its inmates. For a moment all was silent; at this time the ship had sunk entirely; the water closing over her, while thousands of whirlpools carried down, for an instant, all, the living and the dead. Then, all of a sudden, while every eye was strained towards the place, where the *Ré d'Italia* had disappeared, the surface of the sea was covered with human beings, given up again from the deep, on the point of being drowned, and struggling for life with the stormy element. Now no time was to be lost, in saving, what could yet be saved. Admiral Tegethoff ordered his vessel to be stopped and the boats to be put out, and the *Elisabeth*, an Austrian paddle-wheel tender, hastened to the spot, to give assistance. But, what horror! Furious for revenge, the Italians had renewed the combat, and two large Italian frigates came up, on both sides, to attack the *Ferdinand-Max;* —Humanity had to give place to self-preservation; and, the *Ferdinand-Max* being itself somewhat damaged by the action of ramming, had just time enough to manoeuvre itself free, in order not to undergo the same fate as the *Ré d'Italia.* In the mean time, the *Elisabeth*, which came up to save the lives, which were yet to be saved, was fired upon by the Italian frigates, which, not comprehending her object, attacked her and compelled the tender to withdraw.

At the end of the battle the *Palestro* blew up, and, had the battle been carried on longer, several Italian and Austrian vessels might have shared the fate of the *Ré d'Italia* and the *Palestro*.

In impartial statistics it was stated, that more than 400 men were drowned uselessly in this battle, while they might have been easily saved.

Of what efficient help a neutral vessel would have been here!

On land, the main object of battles in the open field is the dispersing of the battalions of the enemy, and, consequently, more lives must be exposed and sacrificed; for there the loss of human lives must determine the conflict. But not so in a sea-battle, the object being here to destroy the war vessels, the lives can always be spared, as much as possible, without prejudice to any war-objects or tactics. Thus the firing on boats and unarmed vessels, which are trying to rescue the drowning men, is as unnecessary in warfare at sea, as it is a horror to humanity. A vessel distinguished by the *neutral flag*, will henceforth, thanks to the humane principles, put forward in the additional articles of the Geneva Convention, incur no danger of being deliberately fired upon, while trying to rescue the unfortunate drowning victims of war, without regard to their nationality. She is now intrusted to the honour of the naval Commanders; her safeguard is the humanity of civilized nations.—God grant, that no Captain may ever dishonour his flag, by showing himself unworthy of this sacred trust!

We have seen, by the history of this naval action what can be henceforth expected from modern warfare at sea, and if the tactic of running down a hostile vessel in open sea already suggests, to the private individual, the idea of whole sale assassination, like smoking the enemy in a cave or discharging poisonous compounds, the more painful it is to humanity to conceive that, as yet, no practical measures have been taken to counteract the disasters of this dreadful military practice at sea, which war imposes but which philanthropy must try to mitigate.

But this is only one part of the double danger to which a warrior at sea is exposed, that of being drowned, and we have seen what, in the first place, is requisite for this part of our object, viz., help outside the vessel. Let us now take a glance inside a war vessel during the fight, and we shall observe, what is wanting for the other part of our duty, viz., the nursing of the sick and wounded.

Dr. Moriz-Bernstein, chef-arzt on board the line-of-battle ship *Kaiser*, gives a description of the action of Lissa, from a naval-medical point of view. He complains of the inconvenience of the localities, reserved for the medical-service, on board the vessels of war, as being too small and not always free from danger. This inconvenience was greatly felt by Dr. Bernstein, even on board one of the largest vessels of the fleet. The battle lasted two hours. In that time the place for the wounded was overfilled and the patients were, for want of space, placed so closely together, that it was impossible to get in between, to give them proper help and refreshment.

When the *Kaiser* ran against the *Rè di Portogallo*, losing its fore-mast and bowsprit, the shock was so violent, that it threw down the doctor together with the patient on whom he was performing an operation. At that moment more wounded were brought in from the batteries, who reported that the ship had caught fire. All was in confusion in this dreadful space, which was to serve as an hospital. Men, who, a moment before, were full of health and strength, in the prime of life, were now lying prostrated, with torn limbs, one upon the other, and surrounded by the bruised and mashed flesh, dripping with blood; wringing their hands and groaning in agony, crying, in the most pitiful way, for help. Such a scene, says Dr. Bernstein, cannot be described and the liveliest imagination has only an imperfect conception of the horrors of such an hospital on board a fighting ship.

After stating the different cases of the wounded, caused by the explosions of bombs, which were of the most dangerous kinds, and amounted, on board the *Kaiser*, to the number of eighty-three, Dr. Bernstein gives his opinion concerning the Hospital-Ship, to be fitted out exclusively for that purpose, in the following terms:—

"The *Hospital-Ship*, in reality to be regarded as an integral part of the Fleet of War, ought never to be wanting and must follow the fleet, as the ambulance or the field-hospital the army. It cannot be depended upon, that battles at sea will always take place in sight of land, like the battles of Helgoland and Lissa; that only the large vessels will have wounded, and that, as was the case with the last battle, there will be found hospitals ashore, ready to receive the wounded. On the contrary, in war, and particularly at sea, all sorts of unexpected eventualities may arise. Suppose, that the ship *Kaiser*, with its crew of 1,000 men, had 300, instead of 83 wounded; that on board of all the vessels, which took part in the battle, the wounded were augmented in the same proportion, in which case there would be 600 to 800 wounded men. And, if these could not have been put ashore at Lissa, where nothing might have been prepared to receive them;—what then? Or, if wind and weather prevented the fleet, which was damaged, from reaching the nearest neutral harbour or friendly port, whilst the enemy was yet in sight, whence it was to be expected that the battle would recommence the next day;—what then? What is to be done, in such cases, with these unfortunate wounded men, who are begging for a resting place and to whom no peace or comfort, so justly due to them, can be affor-ed?" By this it will be sufficiently proved, that Hospital-vessels are highly necessary to a fleet or squadron, and that, as long as they are wanting, the naval-medical service will be incomplete.

From the two preceding sketches, we are able to conceive, of what utility the Aid-Societies, with their neutral Hospital-Ships and Rafts, would be in a sea-battle, and, while bemoaning the loss of life and the misery, which the absence of neutral aid has caused, we feel so much the more strong-ly, that it is the duty of all civilized Nations, to try to overcome all difficulties, in procuring the benefit of the Red-Cross to the neglected warrior at sea. *

* Prompted by the above described sentiments and reflections, the author of this work wrote an essay on the Prize-Questions, which were proposed, at the International-Conference of 1869, by the Central-Committee of the Prussian Aid-Society, in which he tried to suggest practical measures, for the accomplishment of the object of the Red-Cross Societies at Sea. This essay, to which the Prize was graciously allotted, by the Central-Committee at Berlin, on the 30th of September 1870, is reprinted as Appendix I to the present work.

PART VI.

RE-ESTABLISHMENT OF PEACE.

CHAPTER XL.

The Termination of War and the Re-establishment of Peace.

§ 296. The abnormal state of war must cease and the normal state of peace be re-established, as soon as the causes which produced that monstrosity of the Moral Law of Nature, called war, have ceased to affect the moral-mental organism of the human beings concerned, as observed above in paragraph 171, with regard to the place which war occupies in International Law. (Comp. also §§ 155 & 169). *General Principles.*

The obligation to accept peace as soon as its acceptation is sufficiently safe, is laid down by Grotius as a moral principle. * But there is a legal as well as a moral obligation which demands that, with the ceasing of the causes which led to the war, the war itself should cease. Every civilized State is interested in the re-establishment of peace, as every State, whether neutral or belligerent, is more or less injured by war.

" In the event of a war unlawfully continued, though lawfully begun, says Sir Robert Phillimore, it would be morally and legally competent to States which have taken no part in the conduct of the contest, to combine for the purpose of compelling the termination of war and the restoration of peace. The State which continues the evils and horrors of war unrighteously, is

* Grotius. De jure belli ac pacis. Lib. III. Chap. XXV. §§ 2 & 3.

but little, if at all, less an offender against the Society of Societies, against the great commonwealth of States, than the original wrongdoer." *

The cessation of hostilities.

§ 297. War is *de facto* terminated by the cessation of hostilities on the part of both belligerents, or by the complete conquest of one belligerent State by the other, entailing unconditional submission of the conquered State. But peace is not formally and *de jure* established until a treaty of peace is actually concluded. The proceedings which are going on during the interval between the cessation of hostilities and the conclusion of the treaty of peace, are the preliminaries described in the next paragraph.

The preliminaries of peace.

§ 298. The final conclusion of a treaty of peace is often preceded by various sorts of preliminary arrangements, establishing the basis on which the negotiations of peace may be carried on. The form of these preliminaries depends upon the means by which a reconciliation between the belligerent parties is attempted. The belligerents may treat with each other directly or indirectly through friendly mediation. Again, the treaty of peace may be settled by negotiations carried on exclusively between the principal parties concerned or between them and their allies, or the treaty may be settled by a congress consisting of all the parties to the war in consultation with other Powers more or less indirectly concerned in the conclusion of peace.

The principles on which the peace negotiations are based, should be plainly stipulated beforehand, as also the place where and the time when such negotiations are to commence, and whether the treaty of peace is to be settled by congress or by negotiations confined to the parties themselves.

* PHILLIMORE. Vol. III. p. 771.

When the primary conditions of peace are agreed upon, it may happen that there remain yet to be settled some secondary points. But if there is reason to expect that a proper settlement of such secondary points can be arrived at, a preliminary treaty of peace is at once signed, settling the essential conditions, while the questions of minor importance are left open to await settlement by the proposed final negotiations. The preliminary treaty of peace must be duly ratified, and is in all respects binding as long as the final treaty of peace is under negotiation. *The preliminary treaty of peace.*

§ 299. The conclusion of the preliminary treaty of peace is preceded or accompanied by a convention of general suspension of hostilities, called armistice, as described in paragraphs 131 & 195. *The convention of general suspension of hostilities. (Armistice).*

A general suspension of hostilities having been agreed upon between competent representatives of the belligerent Powers, as noted in paragraph 131, the news of it cannot arrive at the same moment at all points where the armies and naval forces of belligerents are actively engaged. It cannot be expected, therefore, that hostilities should cease along the whole line of operations at the same time. The difficulties in the way of simultaneous cessation of hostilities are greatest in cases where naval forces are actively engaged at great distance from the territorial waters of their respective States. It is, therefore, necessary to fix, in the preliminary treaty of peace or in the preceding convention of armistice, a definite period of time after the lapse of which the convention shall be assumed to have become known to all parties concerned.

All acts of war done subsequently to this period, although done in ignorance of the existence of the suspension of hostilities, are necessarily invalid. *Acts of war done subsequently to the general suspension of hostilities.*

Thus, places captured and territories occupied must be given up and evacuated, and all damages done to the public as well as to private property ought to be compensated for.

Naval prizes during a general armistice.

All naval prizes of war made after the expiration of said period of time shall reciprocally be regarded as null and void, even in case the captor was, at the time of the capture, ignorant of the agreement concerning the cessation of hostilities. But, notwithstanding such stipulation, or in cases where no such term is included in the convention, in general, all captures, made at any time with the knowledge that cessation of hostilities had been agreed upon and duly signed between the parties, are null and void. This rule holds good even when the capture took place before the time had expired which was fixed for the fact of the convention to become generally known, for it is a naturally obvious principle that all captures made after the signature of the convention for the cessation of hostilities, that is after the suspension of the belligerent rights, are *de jure* illegal and therefore not acceptable by any Prize Court. This principle is applicable to all captured property, to enemy property as well as to neutral property. An exception to this rule would be the case of a captured vessel belonging to an aggressive party which, with a knowledge of the cessation of hostilities, took the initiative in an attack and was thereupon conquered. In such a case the capture would be valid. *

Rule of conduct with regard to military operations during a truce.

During the continuance of the armistice, each belligerent is bound to abstain from all warlike operations or military acts, which he would not have been able to carry on without direct oppo-

* VALIN. Des Prizes, pp. 46 & 47. EMERIGON. Des Assurances. Chap. XIII. Sec. XIX. MASSÉ. Vol. I. pp. 322–326. VATTEL. Liv. III. Ch. XVI. § 239. HAUTEFEUILLE. Vol. III. p. 291.

sition by the military forces of the enemy, if the hostilities had been continued on the same scale on which they were carried on before the truce was concluded. With regard to the question, what can be done during a truce, Dr. Woolsey sums up the opinions of different authors as follows.

"The following rule, if we are not deceived, expresses the views of most text-writers; that the state, in which things were before the truce, is so far to be maintained, that nothing can be done to the prejudice of either party by the other which could have been prevented in war, but which the truce gives the power of doing. But may a besieged place, during a truce, repair its walls and construct new works? This, which Wheaton, after Vattel, denies, is affirmed by Heffter, after Grotius and Puffendorf. * Heffter also declares it to be unquestioned that the besieger cannot continue his works of siege; by this he gives to the besieged, in any partial truce, the advantage over his foe. The question is whether to strengthen works of offence or of defence is an act of hostility, and is consistent with a promise to suspend hostilities. It would appear that neither party can act thus in good faith, unless it can be shown that the usages of war have restricted the meaning of truce to the suspension of certain operations. The rule then laid down by Vattel, and which he is obliged to qualify by several others, namely, that each may do among themselves, that is, within their own territories or where they are respectively masters, what they would have the right to do in peace, is true only of the general operations of war. A

* GROTIUS. Liv. III. Ch. 21. § 7. PUFFENDORF. VIII. 7. § 10. COCCEIUS, in his notes on Grotius, § 10, denies it, so also VATTEL, III. 16. § 247. and WHEATON, Elements. IV. 2. § 22.

Power may use the interval in collecting its forces, strengthening its works which are not attacked, and the like. But, when we come to the case of besieged towns, the question is, of what are the two parties masters, and various quibbles might be devised to allow either of them to do what he pleased. The governor of a town, says Vattel, may not repair breaches or construct works which the artillery of the enemy would render it dangerous to labour upon during actual siege, but he may raise up new works or strengthen existing ones to which the fire or attacks of the enemy were no obstacle. Why, if he may do this, may not the besiegers strengthen their works which are not exposed to the guns of the fortress? Much the same may be said of revictualling besieged places. The garrison cannot rightfully make use of the truce in ways which the besiegers could have prevented, if the siege had gone on in its course. In the case of besieged towns, arrangements are sometimes made allowing a certain amount of provisions to enter them. Calvo would distinguish between a besieged town and an army blocked up outside of a town. In the last case, but for the truce, the army could have made use of the rights of war to help themselves to provisions, and the revictualling would change nothing in the relative position of the adversaries. In a proposed armistice, in 1870, the neutral Powers urged on Prussia to allow a revictualling of Paris then besieged, proportional to the length of the truce; but these terms were not accepted, and so the truce fell through. (Calvo. II., § 980.)" *

When a truce is concluded for a specified time, no notice is necessary of the recommencement of

* WOOLSEY. Edit. 1879. p. 266.

hostilities. Every one who lingers freely in the enemy's country or within his lines, after this date, is obnoxious to the law of war. But forced delay on account of illness, or other imperative reason, would exempt such a one from harsh treatment. *

* WOOLSEY. p. 268.

CHAPTER XLI.

THE TREATY OF PEACE.

The principle of the treaty of Peace.

§ 300. Every treaty of peace is necessarily a compromise, for to postpone the settlement of every dispute until strict justice can be enforced, is to make the restoration of peace impossible. The general effect of the treaty of peace is to remove the difficulties which caused the war. "It leaves the contracting parties, says Vattel, without any right of committing hostility, either on account of the subject matter which gave rise to the war, or of anything that was done during its continuance; therefore they cannot take up arms again for the same subject. Accordingly, in such treaties, the contracting parties reciprocally engage to preserve perpetual peace, which is not to be understood as if they promised never to make war on each other for any cause whatever. The peace in question relates to the war which it terminates; and it is in reality perpetual, in as much as it does not allow them to renew the same war by taking up arms again for the same subject which had originally given birth to it." * "The peace, says Wheaton, relates to the war, which it terminates; and is perpetual, in the sense that the war cannot be revived for the same cause. This will not, however, preclude the right to claim and resist, if the grievances

* VATTEL. Droit des Gens. Liv. I. Ch. XX. § 244; Chap. XXI. § 262. Liv. IV. Ch. II. §§ 11 & 12. The *Eliza Ann*, 1 Dods. R., 249; the *Molly*, 1 Dods. R., 396.

which originally kindled the war be repeated,—for that would furnish a new injury, and a new cause of war, equally just with the former. If an abstract right be in question between the parties, on which the treaty of peace is silent, it follows that all previous complaints and injury arising under such claim are thrown into oblivion by the amnesty, necessarily implied, if not expressed; but the claim itself is not thereby settled either one way or the other. In the absence of express renunciation or recognition, it remains open for future discussion." * "Peace, says Kent, leaves the contracting parties without any right of committing hostility, for the very cause which kindled the war, or for what has passed in the course of it. It is, therefore, no longer permitted to take up arms for the same cause. But this will not preclude the right to complain and resist, if the same grievances which kindled the war be renewed and repeated, for that would furnish a new injury, and a new cause of war equally just with the former war. If an abstract right be in question between the parties, the right, for instance, to impress at sea one's own subjects from the merchant vessels of the other, and the parties make peace without taking any notice of the question, it follows, of course, that all past grievances, damages and injury, arising under such claim, are thrown into oblivion by the amnesty which every treaty implies, but the claim itself is not thereby settled either one way or the other. It remains open for future discussion, because the treaty wanted an express concession or renunciation of the claim itself." †

---

* WHEATON. Elem. Part IV. Chapt. IV. § 3.

† KENT. Com. on Am. Law. Vol. I. pp. 168 & 169.

The amnesty clause.

§ 301. An essential point in all treaties of peace is the amnesty. When this point is not expressly mentioned in the treaty by what is called the amnesty clause, it is tacitly implied by virtue of the general peace re-established between parties *(lex oblivionis)*. The amnesty is declared between the reconciled parties with the expressed or implied promise to regard reciprocally the state of enmity at an end and completely abolished.

With regard to amnesty, Mr. Hall makes the following statements.

Mr. Hall's statement.

"As between the contracting States, a treaty of peace is a final settlement of all matters connected with the war to which it puts an end. If, therefore, any acts have been done during the course of hostilities, in excess or irrespectively of the rights of war, under the authority of one of the belligerent States, the enemy State cannot urge complaints or claims from the moment that a treaty is signed, either on its own behalf or on behalf of its subjects. It is possible, however, that ordinary acts of war may have been done without sufficient authority, that wrongful acts may have been done wholly without authority, and that subjects of one of the two belligerent States, without having committed treason, may yet have compromised themselves with their own Government by dealings with the enemy. In order to bury the occurrences of the war in oblivion, and to prevent ill-feeling from being kept alive, in order also to protect men who may only have been guilty of a technical wrong, or who may at any rate have been carried away by the excitement of hostilities, and finally in the common interests of belligerents who may be in occupation of an enemy's country, it is understood that persons, acting in any of the ways above mentioned, are exempt, by the conclusion of peace, from all civil or criminal processes to which they might otherwise be exposed in consequence of their conduct in the war, except civil actions arising out of private contracts, and criminal prosecutions for acts recognized as crimes by the law of the country to which the doer belongs, and done under circumstances which remove them from the category of acts having relation to the war. Actions, for example, can be brought on ransom bills; if a prisoner of war borrows money or runs into debt, he may be sued; or if a prisoner of war or a soldier on service commits a common murder he may be tried and punished. The immunity thus conceded is called an amnesty. Usually, but far from invariably, the rule of law is fortified by express stipulation and a clause securing an amnesty is inserted in treaties of peace. Though unnecessary for other purposes, it is required as a safe guard for subjects of a State who, having had distinctly treasonable relations with an enemy, are not protected by an amnesty which is only implied." *

§ 302. The power to make peace is, like the power of waging war, regulated by the public laws of every State. On the question whether the sovereign or chief magistrate of a State, having been taken prisoner, can make a treaty of peace, Vattel makes the following remarks. "Every legitimate Government, whatever it may be, is established solely for the good and welfare of the State. This incontestable principle being once laid down, the making of peace is no longer the peculiar province of the king: it belongs to the Nation. Now, it is certain that a captive

The power to make peace.

* W. E. HALL. Intern. Law. p. 487.

prince cannot administer the Government, or attend to the management of public affairs. How shall he, who is not free, command a Nation? How can he govern it in such a manner as best to promote the advantage of the people, and the public welfare? He does not, indeed, forfeit his rights; but his captivity deprives him of the power of exercising them, as he is not in a condition to direct the use of them to its proper and legitimate end. He stands in the same predicament as a king in his minority or labouring under a derangement of his mental faculties. In such circumstances it is necessary that the person or persons whom the laws of State designate for the regency, should assume the reins of government. To them it belongs to treat of peace, to settle the terms on which it shall be made, and to bring it to a conclusion, in conformity to the laws. The captive sovereign may himself negotiate the peace, and promise what personally depends on him; but the treaty does not become obligatory on the Nation, till ratified by itself, or by those who are invested with the public authority during the prince's captivity, or finally, by the sovereign himself after his release." *

---

* VATTEL. Droit des Gens. Lib. IV. Chapt. II. § 13. Consent to a treaty, whether written or oral, must be distinct. No supposition or *consensus fictus* is sufficient. A treaty is not binding which is made by a king when a prisoner. Thus Pope Clement VII. refused to ratify a treaty with the Duke of Ferrara, which he had made when a prisoner, saying that it was a dishonourable thing for a man in life to ratify a matter done in his name when dead, not consistent with his honour and interest. Again, Francis I. excused himself from ratifying the treaty of Madrid, on account of the inhumanity done to him by the permission of Charles V. Some of the ancient treaties of alliance were recited to be made between king and king, subjects and subjects, such as this—"that there be an universal and perpetual, true and sincere peace and amity between the most Christian king of France and the king of Great Britain, their heirs and successors, and between the kingdoms, States, and subjects of both." PHILLIMORE. Comm. Lib. II. Cap. 8. HALLECK. Edit. Sir Sherston Baker. Vol. I. p. 254.

CHAPTER XLII.

EFFECTS OF THE TREATY OF PEACE.

§ 303. The treaty of peace puts an end to all claims between parties. From the moment of signature the treaty has binding force upon all parties concerned, with regard to all matters affecting military operations (§ 131), but with regard to political affairs, the rules commonly accepted in the case of all other international agreements, as described above in paragraphs 132–139, apply also to the political clauses of the treaty of peace. *The stipulation of the treaty of peace.*

The definite treaty of peace contains two distinct classes of articles, viz., the general provisions, which are clauses always to be found in a well arranged treaty of peace terminating a general war, and the special stipulations, which regulate all details concerning the settlement of those disputes which gave rise to the war and concerning the particular condition in which the disputants find themselves placed in consequence of the war. *General provisions and special stipulations.*

The general provisions of a treaty of peace are embodied in the introduction, which states the motives of the treaty and the fact of formal re-establishment of peace and of relations of amity. These general provisions are generally understood to imply, even without special mention, the re-establishment of all treaties concerning commerce and postal communications and of all other previous treaties, provided that the breach of such neither provoked the war, nor caused special contention at the outset or in the course of the war. The effect of war upon treaties and conventions has been noted above, in paragraph 138.

The general provisions include also the proclamation of a general amnesty. This point is often particularly mentioned and the amnesty declared to comprehend all individual subjects of the treaty Powers who, on either side, acted in violation of the duties of allegiance arising from their respective political nationality.

In the absence of a preliminary treaty of peace or armistice, the stipulations concerning the general cessation of hostilities and the exchange of prisoners of war are inserted among the general provisions of the final treaty.

The general provisions are followed by the special stipulations, dealing with the special points which remain to be settled and with the conditions necessary for carrying them out. The most difficult points to be settled are generally those regarding the final fate of the territories occupied, during the war, by the forces of one belligerent operating within the dominions of the other.

These questions are regulated on the basis of a distinction made between two separate features of the so-called *status quo*.

There is, in the first instance, the *status quo ante bellum*, that is to say, each party might return within the limits and possessions occupied by either before the beginning of hostilities, in which case the possessions which have been disturbed by the war are to be reciprocally restored.

There is, however, in the second instance, another feature of the *status quo* which might be adopted as a basis. This is generally termed the principle of *uti possidetis* and designates the *status quo* occupied by the respective armies on the day of the general suspension of hostilities. These two features of the *status quo* are often modified by what is called general compensation, that is to say, an arrangement regulating the different possessions and rights on a special basis of compromise between the former and the actual *status quo*.'*

The parties interested in the treaty of peace.

§ 304. When more than two States participated in a war, all have to be parties to the treaty of peace, the form of which accordingly varies in conformity with the following conditions.

1°. Each party may conclude a separate treaty with every individual member of the opposing contracting parties. In this case the effect of every treaty with regard to all particular stipulations, is confined exclusively to the two parties of one and the same treaty contracted independently of the others; whilst the general clauses, being the same in all, form the means of establishing reciprocally a sort of unity between the different treaties concluded separately (§ 203).

2°. A general treaty may be drawn up, including collectively all the parties concerned, which form then two opposite contracting groups, while the particular stipulations are contained in the separate articles setting forth the various conditions, individually insisted upon, regarding special reciprocal rights and obligations.

3°. The treaty being concluded between any two parties concerned, a third equally interested party can subsequently accede to the agreement adopting its stipulations by means of a separate instrument. In this case the acceding party

* GROTIUS. Liv. III. Chap XX. 11. § 2.

enters into all rights and obligations as if it had been actually an original party to the pactum.

Besides the above stated modes admissible in the construction of a treaty of peace, there are also to be considered cases of Powers which took no direct part in the warlike operations but were either auxiliaries, or had at least an essential interest in the war or in the re-establishment of peace. In such case the treaty of peace may be constructed in one or other of the following ways. 1°. One of the principal contracting Powers stipulates something in favour of such third parties whether by including them in the enumeration of those to whom the treaty applies,—so that the peace and amity established by the treaty shall extend to them without thereby rendering them principal contracting Powers,—or by inserting a particular clause in their favour; in which latter case it is not necessary that they formally signify their acceptance. 2°. To the treaty may be added separate conventions concluded with or between such third parties above mentioned, which conventions are declared to be part of the principal instrument. 3°. Such third parties may be invited to accede, either with a view to secure their co-operation or consent or simply as a matter of courtesy due to great Powers. The particular mode of participation in a treaty of peace to be allotted to such third parties depends upon the amount of direct or indirect interest they actually possess or exhibit in the conclusion of the peace.

On the other hand it sometimes happens that third parties formally protest against a treaty of peace as a whole or against one or more of its stipulations. *

* Thus the Pope protested against the treaty of Westphalia, and, with the King of Spain, against the final act of the Congress of Vienna. DE MARTENS. Précis de Droit des Gens. § 336. MARTENS. Nouv. Rec. Vol. II. pp. 446–475.

§ 305. The clause of general amnesty involves the right of *post-liminii*, the meaning of which has been noted above in paragraph 209. *General Amnesty*

Persons protected by the general amnesty are entitled to resume their properties and rights as possessed and exercised by them before the war.

§ 306. Public or State rights follow the rule of *uti possidetis*, that is the state in which the war actually leaves the parties, if not otherwise expressly stipulated by the treaty of peace. With regard to the principle of *uti possidetis*, Mr. Hall makes the following statements. *The rule of uti possidetis.*

"By the principle, commonly called that of *uti possidetis*, it is understood that the simple conclusion of peace, if no express stipulation accompanies it, or in so far as express stipulations do not extend, vests in the two belligerents, as absolute property, whatever they respectively have under their actual control in the case of territory and things attached to it, and, in the case of movables, whatever they have in their legal possession at the moment. Occupied territory, for example, is transferred to the occupying Power, and movables, on the other hand, which have been in the territory of an enemy during the war, without being confiscated, remain the property of the original owner. The doctrine is not altogether satisfactory theoretically, but it supplies a practical rule for the settlement of such matters relating to property and sovereignty, as may have been omitted in a treaty, or for covering concessions which one or other party has been unwilling to make in words. This advantage could evidently not be claimed by the necessarily alternative doctrine that, except, in so far as expressly provided, all things should return to their state before the war.* When a stipulation to the latter effect is made, it is to be understood, if couched in general terms, to mean only that any territory belonging to one party, which may be occupied by the other party, with the buildings, &c., on it, is to be handed back, without any further changes than such as may have been brought about by the operations of war, or by acts legitimately done during the course of hostilities." This clause does not refer to property which has been appropriated, destroyed or damaged, in accordance with the laws of war.†

Effect of the Treaty of Peace on private or individual rights.

§ 307. Private or individual rights, and claims contested between individual members of the two countries or between private individuals of the one State and the Government of the other, the prosecution of which were interrupted by the war, as noted above in paragraphs 175 and 180, revive, as a matter of course, with the re-establishment of peace and amicable intercourse between the respective States, although nothing may be said upon the subject in the respective treaty of peace (Comp. § 181). "The treaty of peace, says Wheaton, does not extinguish claims founded upon debts contracted, or injuries inflicted, previously to the war, and unconnected with its causes, unless there be an express stipulation to that effect. Nor does it affect private rights acquired antecedently to the war, or private injuries unconnected with the causes which produced the war. Hence, debts previously contracted between the respective subjects, though the remedy for their recovery is suspended during the war, are revived on the restoration of peace, unless actual-

---

* VATTEL. Liv. IV. Ch. II. § 21. HEFFTER. § 181. PHILLIMORE. III. § DLXXXVI. BLUNTSCHLI. § 715; The *Nuestra Señora de los Dolores*, I. Edwards, 60.

† VATTEL. Liv. IV. Ch. II. § 22, and Ch. III. § 31. PHILLIMORE. III. § DLXXXIV. W. E. HALL. p. 483.

ly confiscated in the mean time, in the rigorous exercise of the strict rights of war, contrary to the milder practice of recent times." * With reference to acts done before the war, says Mr. Hall, the treaty of peace has the effect to revive all private rights and to restore the remedies which have been suspended during the war; contracts, for example, are revived if they are not of such a kind as to be necessarily put an end to by war, and if their fulfilment has not been rendered impossible by such acts of a belligerent Government as the confiscation of debts due by subjects to those of its enemy; the Courts also are re-opened for the enforcement of claims of every kind. †

Effect of the Treaty of Peace on military occupation and war-contributions.

§ 308. The effect of the treaty of peace being to replace the belligerent States in their normal condition towards each other, they enter at once into all the rights and obligations which are the natural results of the relation of peaceable intercourse. Thus, as a consequence of the principle that with the restoration of peace all belligerent rights must cease which are permitted only in war, all military occupations also and all sorts of war contributions, must be abandoned, and the territories of opponents, reciprocally, exempted from anything like belligerent invasion. (Comp. § 187).

But the former enemy may be authorized, by specific stipulations of the treaty of peace, to remain in occupation of certain territories, until some special conditions have been fulfilled, in which case such occupation is devoid of all belligerent rights as regards levies of war contributions or requisitions of money, during the time which may elapse before the evacuation of the country is completed. Neither can, at the conclusion of peace, any demand for arrears of any

* WHEATON. Elem. Part IV. Ch. IV. § 3.

† W. E. HALL. p. 486. HEFFTER. § 180.

sort of war contributions be enforced against the inhabitants of an occupied district. *

Effect of the Treaty of Peace on conquests.

§ 309. The title to conquered territories is complete, in the first instance, by the treaty of peace, either by express cession or by the implied condition of the principle of *uti possidetis;* or, in the second instance, by complete subjugation.

Conquest confirmed by cession.

When stipulations concerning the cession of territory are introduced in the treaty of peace, they are always accompanied by a special agreement with respect to the inhabitants of the ceded conquered territory, in order to secure to them the right, in case they wish to adhere to their original allegiance, of emigrating without injury to their properties. When the treaty of peace is silent with regard to territories occupied by the former enemy, the conqueror's title is complete by the principle of *uti possidetis*, as this is the basis of every such treaty, for unless the contrary is expressed, the conquered territory remains with the conqueror, and his title cannot afterwards be called in question. (Comp. § 31).

By entire subjugation.

By entire subjugation of the conquered State, the right of conquest is confirmed by the fact that, the whole conquered country being incorporated with the conquering State, the power of the former is destroyed, so that there can be no occasion for a treaty of cession or confirmation, because the former owner is no longer in existence as a sovereign State.

---

* Art. 3 of the additional convention (of 26 February 1871) to the General Armistice of 28 January 1871, terminating the hostilities between Germany and France, contained the following with regard to the occupied territories :

"Art. 3. Les troupes allemandes s'abstiendront à l'avenir de prélever des contributions en argent dans les territoires occupés. Les contributions de cette catégorie dont le montant ne serait pas encore payé seront annulées de plein droit, celles qui seraient versées ultérieurement par suite d'ignorance de la présente stipulation devront être remboursées. Par contre, les autorités allemandes continueront à prélever les impôts de l'État dans les territoires occupés."

With regard to the effect of conquest, Halleck makes the following statements.

"The conqueror, who acquires a province or town from the enemy, acquires thereby the same rights which were possessed by the State from which it is taken. If it formed a constituent part of the hostile State, and was fully and completely under its dominion, it passes into the power of the conqueror upon the same footing. It is united with the new State upon the same terms on which it belonged to the old one; that is, with only such political rights as the constitution and laws of the new State may see fit to give it. It retains no political privileges or immunities, but may acquire those it never possessed before. In political rights it may be the gainer or the loser by the change; if, from being a part of an absolute monarchy, it becomes a part of a republic, its liberties will be enlarged, or, if the reverse, they will be restricted. But such restriction, in any case, must be in conformity with the rights of conquest and the laws of war. When New-Mexico formed a part of the Mexican Republic, it enjoyed the right of representation in the Mexican Congress; on the conquest of that territory by the arms of the United States, under General Kearny, a clause was introduced into the new organic law for sending a representative to the Congress of the United States. This part of the organic law was disapproved by the President, and, even without such disapproval, it was utterly inoperative, for this right of representation was a political right, which was lost by the very act of conquest, and could be restored to it only by the action of Congress, after its permanent incorporation into the conquering republic. The case, however, is different where the enemy possessed only a quasi-sovereignty, or limited political rights, over the conquered province or town. The conqueror acquires no other rights than such as belonged to the State against which he has taken up arms." "War, says Vattel, authorizes the conqueror to possess himself of what belongs to his enemy. If he deprives that enemy of the sovereignty of a town or province, he acquires it, such as it is, with all its limitations and modifications. Accordingly, care is usually taken to stipulate, both in particular capitulations and in treaties of peace, that the towns and countries ceded shall retain all their liberties, privileges and immunities. But where such conquered provinces and towns have themselves taken up arms against him, thus making themselves directly his enemies, the conqueror may regard them as vanguished foes and treat them precisely as he would treat other conquered territory." *

Individual righ of he inhabitants of a ceded country.

It is incontestably the principle of modern International Law that inhabitants of a ceded country have a right of adhering to their original allegiance. Therefore it is requisite to insert in treaties of peace a clause securing, during a certain period of time, the liberty of the inhabitants of the ceded territory to emigrate with their property within the jurisdiction of their original political nationality, allowing them, further, with regard to immovable properties left behind, all the right of ordinary non-resident proprietors.

Breach of a treaty of peace.

§ 310. The breach of a treaty of peace, says Vattel, consists in violating the engagements annexed to it, either by doing what it prohibits or by not doing what it prescribes. The engagement contracted by treaty may be violated in

---

* *Cross* v. *Harrison*, 16 How. R., 194 ; *American Ins. Co.* v. *Canter*, 1 Peters R., 542 ; MARCY to KEARNY, Jan. 11, 1847, Ex. Doc., No. 17, 31st Cong., 1st Sess. H.R. HALLECK. Edit. Sir Sherston Baker. Vol. II. p. 482. VATTEL. Liv. III. Ch. XIII. § 201.

three different ways,—by a conduct that is repugnant to the nature and essence of every treaty of peace in general,—by proceedings which are incompatible with the particular nature of the treaty in question,—or, finally, by the violation of any article expressly contained in it. Affected delays in performing the conditions of a treaty of peace are equivalent to an express denial, and differ from it only by the artifice with which he who practices them seeks to palliate his want of faith; he adds fraud to perfidy, and actually violates the article which he should fulfil. But if an impediment stands in the way, time must be allowed, for no one is bound to perform impossibilities. If the obstacle be utterly insurmountable, the other party should accept an indemnification, if the case will admit of it and indemnification be practicable. But if no equivalent can be offered, the intervening impossibility undoubtedly cancels the particular obligation. *

"There is, says Kent, a very material and important distinction made by the writers on public law, between a new war for some new cause, and a breach of a treaty of peace. In the former case, the rights acquired by the treaty subsist, notwithstanding the new war; but in the latter case, they are annulled by the breach of the treaty of peace on which they were founded. A new war may interrupt the exercise of the rights acquired by the former treaty, and, like other rights, they may be wrested from the party by the force of arms. But then they become newly acquired rights, and partake of the operation and result of the new war. To recommence a war by breach of the articles of a treaty of peace, is deemed much more odious than to pro-

* VATTEL. Droit des Gens. Liv. IV. Ch. IV. §§ 50 & 51.

voke a war by some new demand and aggression, for the latter is simply injustice, but, in the former case, the party is guilty both of perfidy and injustice." *

The conditions of the treaty of peace to be scrupulously complied with.

Things stipulated to be restored by the treaty of peace, must be restored in the condition in which they were, at the moment of the cessation of hostilities which immediately preceded the peace, unless there be an express stipulation with regard to the state and condition in which they shall be ceded. A fortress, town, or port to be ceded by capitulation, armistice or treaty, must be ceded in the state in which the agreement of evacuation finds it. There is no obligation to repair the damages caused by the operations of war. To lay waste a country, to dismantle a fortress or to block up a river or a port, after its cession in *status quo* has been agreed upon, is an act of perfidy, for the basis of all moral and legal intercourse, in the case of Nations as well as individuals, is good faith, *i.e.* the respect which the civilized man owes to the word of promise given. (§ 128).

* KENT. Com. on Am. Law. Vol. I. p. 175; the Schooner *Sophie*, 6 Rob., 143; MOSER, F. F. Vermischte Abhandl., No. 1. HALLECK. Edit. Sir Sherston Baker. Vol. I. p. 268.

APPENDICES.

Appendix A.

INSTRUCTIONS FOR THE GOVERNMENT OF ARMIES OF THE UNITED STATES IN THE FIELD.*

SECTION I.

Martial law—Military jurisdiction—Military necessity—Retaliation.

1. A place, district, or country occupied by an enemy stands, in consequence of the occupation, under the martial law of the invading or occupying army, whether any proclamation declaring martial law, or any public warning to the inhabitants, has been issued or not. Martial law is the immediate and direct effect and consequence of occupation or conquest.

The presence of a hostile army proclaims its martial law.

2. Martial law does not cease during the hostile occupation, except by special proclamation, ordered by the commander-in-chief, or by special mention in the treaty of peace concluding the war, when the occupation of a place or territory continues beyond the conclusion of peace as one of the conditions of the same.

3. Martial law in a hostile country consists in the suspension, by the occupying military authority, of the criminal and civil law, and of the domestic administration and government in the occupied place or territory, and in the substitution of military rule and force for the same, as well as in the dictation of general laws, as far as military necessity requires this suspension, substitution, or dictation.

The commander of the forces may proclaim that the administration of all civil and penal law shall continue, either wholly or in part, as in times of peace, unless otherwise ordered by the military authority.

* These instructions were prepared by the celebrated jurist FRANCIS LIEBER, and revised by a board of officers, of whom Major-General E. A. HITCHCOCK was president. Having been approved by the President of the United States, they were issued from the Adjutant-General's office at Washington, April 24, 1863, and used during the war. They have served as a basis for most of the subsequent compilations.

4. Martial law is simply military authority exercised in accordance with the laws and usages of war. Military oppression is not martial law; it is the abuse of the power which that law confers. As martial law is executed by military force, it is incumbent upon those who administer it to be strictly guided by the principles of justice, honour, and humanity—virtues adorning a soldier even more than other men, for the very reason that he possesses the power of his arms against the unarmed.

5. Martial law should be less stringent in places and countries fully occupied and fairly conquered. Much greater severity may be exercised in places or regions where actual hostilities exist, or are expected and must be prepared for. Its most complete sway is allowed even in the commander's own country—when face to face with the enemy, because of the absolute necessities of the case, and of the paramount duty to defend the country against invasion.

To save the country is paramount to all other considerations.

6. All civil and penal law shall continue to take its usual course in the enemy's places and territories under martial law, unless interrupted or stopped by order of the occupying military power; but all the functions of the hostile government—legislative, executive, or administrative—whether of a general, provincial, or local character, cease under martial law, or continue only with the sanction, or, if deemed necessary, the participation of the occupier or invader.

7. Martial law extends to property, and to persons, whether they are subjects of the enemy or aliens to that government.

8. Consuls, among American and European nations, are not diplomatic agents. Nevertheless, their offices and persons will be subjected to martial law in cases of urgent necessity only: their property and business are not exempted. Any delinquency they commit against the established military rule may be punished as in the case of any other inhabitant, and such punishment furnishes no reasonable ground for international complaint.

9. The functions of ambassadors, ministers, or other diplomatic agents, accredited by neutral Powers to the hostile government, cease, so far as regards the displaced government; but the conquering or occupying Power usually recognizes them as temporarily accredited to itself.

10. Martial law affects chiefly the police and collection of public revenue and taxes, whether imposed by the expelled government or by the invader, and refers mainly to the support and efficiency of the army, its safety, and the safety of its operations.

11. The law of war does not only disclaim all cruelty and bad faith concerning engagements concluded with the enemy during the war, but also the breaking of stipulations solemnly contracted by the

belligerents in time of peace, and avowedly intended to remain in force in case of war between the contracting Powers.

It disclaims all extortions and other transactions for individual gain; all acts of private revenge, or connivance at such acts.

Offences to the contrary shall be severely punished, and especially so if committed by officers.

12. Whenever feasible, martial law is carried out in cases of individual offenders by military courts; but sentences of death shall be executed only with the approval of the chief executive, provided the urgency of the case does not require a speedier execution, and then only with the approval of the chief commander.

13. Military jurisdiction is of two kinds: first, that which is conferred and defined by statute; second, that which is derived from the common law of war. Military offences under the statute law must be tried in the manner therein directed; but military offences which do not come within the statute must be tried and punished under the common law of war. The character of the courts which exercise these jurisdictions depends upon the local laws of each particular country.

In the armies of the United States the first is exercised by courts-martial; while cases which do not come within the "Rules and Articles of War," or the jurisdiction conferred by statute on courts-martial, are tried by military commissions.

14. Military necessity, as understood by modern civilised nations, consists in the necessity of those measures which are indispensable for securing the ends of the war, and which are lawful according to the modern law and usages of war.

15. Military necessity admits of all direct destruction of life or limb of *armed* enemies, and of other persons whose destruction is incidentally *unavoidable* in the armed contests of the war; it allows of the capturing of every armed enemy, and every enemy of importance to the hostile government, or of peculiar danger to the captor; it allows of all destruction of property, and obstruction of the ways and channels of traffic, travel, or communication, and of all withholding of sustenance or means of life from the enemy; of the appropriation of whatever an enemy's country affords necessary for the subsistence and safety of the army, and of such deception as does not involve the breaking of good faith either positively pledged, regarding agreements entered into during the war, or supposed by the modern law of war to exist. Men who take up arms against one another in public war do not cease on this account to be moral beings, responsible to one another, and to God.

16. Military necessity does not admit of cruelty—that is, the infliction of suffering for the sake of suffering or for revenge, nor of maiming or wounding except in fight, nor of torture to extort confessions. It does not admit of the use of poison in any way, nor of the wanton devastation of a district. It admits of deception, but disclaims acts of

perfidy; and, in general, military necessity does not include any act of hostility which makes the return to peace unnecessarily difficult.

17. War is not carried on by arms alone. It is lawful to starve the hostile belligerent, armed or unarmed, so that it leads to the speedier subjection of the enemy.

18. When the commander of a besieged place expels the non-combatants, in order to lessen the number of those who consume his stock of provisions, it is lawful, though an extreme measure, to drive them back, so as to hasten on the surrender.

19. Commanders, whenever admissible, inform the enemy of their intention to bombard a place, so that the non-combatants, and especially the women and children, may be removed before the bombardment commences. But it is no infraction of the common law of war to omit thus to inform the enemy. Surprise may be a necessity.

20. Public war is a state of armed hostility between sovereign nations or governments. It is a law and requisite of civilised existence that men live in political, continuous societies, forming organised units, called States or nations, whose constituents bear, enjoy, and suffer, advance and retrograde together, in peace and in war.

21. The citizen or native of a hostile country is thus an enemy, as one of the constituents of the hostile State or nation, and as such is subjected to the hardships of the war.

22. Nevertheless, as civilisation has advanced during the last centuries, so has likewise steadily advanced, especially in war on land, the distinction between the private individual belonging to a hostile country and the hostile country itself, with its men in arms. The principle has been more and more acknowledged that the unarmed citizen is to be spared in person, property, and honour as much as the exigencies of war will admit.

23. Private citizens are no longer murdered, enslaved, or carried off to distant parts, and the inoffensive individual is as little disturbed in his private relations as the commander of the hostile troops can afford to grant in the overruling demands of a vigorous war.

24. The almost universal rule in remote times was, and continues to be with barbarous armies, that the private individual of the hostile country is destined to suffer every privation of liberty and protection, and every disruption of family ties. Protection was, and still is, with uncivilised people, the exception.

25. In modern regular wars of the Europeans, and their descendants in other portions of the globe, protection of the inoffensive citizen of the hostile country is the rule; privation and disturbance of private relations are the exceptions.

26. Commanding generals may cause the magistrates and civil officers of the hostile country to take the oath of temporary allegiance

or an oath of fidelity to their own victorious government or rulers, and they may expel every one who declines to do so. But whether they do so or not, the people and their civil officers owe strict obedience to them as long as they hold sway over the district or country, at the peril of their lives.

27. The law of war can no more wholly dispense with retaliation than can the law of nations, of which it is a branch. Yet civilised nations acknowledge retaliation as the sternest feature of war. A reckless enemy often leaves to his opponent no other means of securing himself against the repetition of barbarous outrage.

28. Retaliation will therefore never be resorted to as a measure of mere revenge, but only as a means of protective retribution, and, moreover, cautiously and unavoidably; that is to say, retaliation shall only be resorted to after careful inquiry into the real occurrence, and the character of the misdeeds that may demand retribution. Unjust or inconsiderate retaliation removes the belligerents farther and farther from the mitigating rules of a regular war, and by rapid steps leads them nearer to the internecine wars of savages.

29. Modern times are distinguished from earlier ages by the existence, at one and the same time, of many nations and great governments related to one another in close intercourse.

Peace is their normal condition; war is the exception. The ultimate object of all modern war is a renewed state of peace.

The more vigorously wars are pursued, the better it is for humanity. Sharp wars are brief.

30. Ever since the formation and coexistence of modern nations, and ever since wars have become great national wars, war has come to be acknowledged not to be its own end, but the means to obtain great ends of state, or to consist in defence against wrong; and no conventional restriction of the modes adopted to injure the enemy is any longer admitted; but the law of war imposes many limitations and restrictions on principles of justice, faith, and honour.

Section II.

Public and private property of the enemy—Protection of persons, and especially women; of religion, the arts and sciences—Punishment of crimes against the inhabitants of hostile countries.

31. A victorious army appropriates all public money, seizes all public movable property until further direction by its government, and sequesters for its own benefit or that of its government all the revenues of real property belonging to the hostile government or nation. The

title to such real property remains in abeyance during military occupation, and until the conquest is made complete.

32. A victorious army, by the martial power inherent in the same, may suspend, change, or abolish, as far as the martial power extends, the relations which arise from the services due, according to the existing laws of the invaded country, from one citizen, subject, or native of the same to another.

The commander of the army must leave it to the ultimate treaty of peace to settle the permanency of this change.

33. It is no longer considered lawful—on the contrary, it is held to be a serious breach of the law of war—to force the subjects of the enemy into the service of the victorious government, except the latter should proclaim, after a fair and complete conquest of the hostile country or district, that it is resolved to keep the country, district, or place permanently as its own, and make it a portion of its own country.

34. As a general rule, the property belonging to churches, to hospitals, or other establishments of an exclusively charitable character, to establishments of education, or foundations for the promotion of knowledge, whether public schools, universities, academies of learning, or observatories, museums of the fine arts, or of a scientific character—such property is not to be considered public property in the sense of paragraph 31; but it may be taxed or used when the public service may require it.

35. Classical works of art, libraries, scientific collections, or precious instruments, such as astronomical telescopes, as well as hospitals, must be secured against all avoidable injury, even when they are contained in fortified places whilst besieged or bombarded.

36. If such works of art, libraries, collections, or instruments belonging to a hostile nation or government, can be removed without injury, the ruler of the conquering State or nation may order them to be seized and removed for the benefit of the said nation. The ultimate ownership is to be settled by the ensuing treaty of peace.

In no case shall they be sold or given away, if captured by the armies of the United States, nor shall they ever be privately appropriated, or wantonly destroyed or injured.

37. The United States acknowledge and protect, in hostile countries occupied by them, religion and morality; strictly private property; the persons of the inhabitants, especially those of women; and the sacredness of domestic relations. Offences to the contrary shall be rigorously punished.

This rule does not interfere with the right of the victorious invader to tax the people or their property, to levy forced loans, to billet soldiers, or to appropriate property, especially houses, land, boats or ships, and churches, for temporary and military uses.

38. Private property, unless forfeited by crimes or by offences of the owner, can be seized only by way of military necessity, for the support or other benefit of the army of the United States.

If the owner has not fled, the commanding officer will cause receipts to be given, which may serve the spoliated owner to obtain indemnity.

39. The salaries of civil officers of the hostile government who remain in the invaded territory, and continue the work of their office, and can continue it according to the circumstances arising out of the war—such as judges, administrative or police officers, officers of city or communal governments—are paid from the public revenue of the invaded territory, until the military government has reason wholly or partially to discontinue it. Salaries or incomes connected with purely honorary titles are always stopped.

40. There exists no law or body of authoritative rules of action between hostile armies, except that branch of the law of nature and nations which is called the law and usages of war on land.

41. All municipal law of the ground on which the armies stand, or of the countries to which they belong, is silent and of no effect between armies in the field.

42. Slavery, complicating and confounding the ideas of property (that is of a *thing*), and of personality (that is of *humanity*), exists according to municipal law or local law only. The law of nature and nations has never acknowledged it. The Digest of the Roman law enacts the early dictum of the pagan jurist, that "so far as the law of nature is concerned, all men are equal." Fugitives escaping from a country in which they were slaves, villeins, or serfs, into another country, have, for centuries past, been held free and acknowledged free by judicial decisions of European countries, even though the municipal law of the country in which the slave had taken refuge acknowledged slavery within its own dominions.

43. Therefore, in a war between the United States and a belligerent which admits of slavery, if a person held in bondage by that belligerent be captured by or come as a fugitive under the protection of the military forces of the United States, such person is immediately entitled to the rights and privileges of a freeman. To return such person into slavery would amount to enslaving a free person, and neither the United States nor any officer under their authority can enslave any human being. Moreover, a person so made free by the law of war is under the shield of the law of nations, and the former owner or State can have, by the law of post-liminy, no belligerent lien or claim of service.

44. All wanton violence committed against persons in the invaded country, all destruction of property not commanded by the authorized officer, all robbery, all pillage or sacking, even after taking a place by main force, all rape, wounding, maiming, or killing of such inhabitants,

are prohibited under the penalty of death, or such other severe punishment as may seem adequate for the gravity of the offence.

A soldier, officer or private, in the act of committing such violence, and disobeying a superior ordering him to abstain from it, may be lawfully killed on the spot by such superior.

45. All captures and booty belong, according to the modern law of war, primarily to the government of the captor.

Prize money, whether on sea or land, can now only be claimed under local law.

46. Neither officers nor soldiers are allowed to make use of their position or power in the hostile country for private gain, not even for commercial transactions otherwise legitimate. Offences to the contrary committed by commissioned officers will be punished with cashiering or such other punishment as the nature of the offence may require; if by soldiers, they shall be punished according to the nature of the offence.

47. Crimes punishable by all penal codes, such as arson, murder, maiming, assaults, highway robbery, theft, burglary, fraud, forgery, and rape, if committed by an American soldier in a hostile country against its inhabitants, are not only punishable as at home, but in all cases in which death is not inflicted, the severer punishment shall be preferred.

Section III.

Deserters—Prisoners of war—Hostages—Booty on the battle-field.

48. Deserters from the American army, having entered the service of the enemy, suffer death if they fall again into the hands of the United States, whether by capture, or being delivered up to the American army; and if a deserter from the enemy, having taken service in the army of the United States, is captured by the enemy, and punished by them with death or otherwise, it is not a breach against the law and usages of war, requiring redress or retaliation.

49. A prisoner of war is a public enemy armed or attached to the hostile army for active aid, who has fallen into the hands of the captor, either fighting or wounded, on the field or in the hospital, by individual surrender or by capitulation.

All soldiers of whatever species of arms; all men who belong to the rising *en masse* of the hostile country; all those who are attached to the army for its efficiency and promote directly the object of the war, except such as are hereinafter provided for; all disabled men or officers on the field or elsewhere, if captured; all enemies who have thrown away their arms and ask for quarter, are prisoners of war, and as such exposed to the inconveniences as well as entitled to the privileges of a prisoner of war.

50. Moreover, citizens who accompany an army for whatever purpose, such as sutlers, editors, or reporters of journals, or contractors, if captured, may be made prisoners of war, and be detained as such.

The monarch and members of the hostile reigning family, male or female, the chief, and chief officers of the hostile government, its diplomatic agents, and all persons who are of particular and singular use and benefit to the hostile army or its government, are, if captured on belligerent ground, and if unprovided with a safe-conduct granted by the captor's government, prisoners of war.

51. If the people of that portion of an invaded country which is not yet occupied by the enemy, or of the whole country, at the approach of a hostile army, rise under a duly authorized levy, *en masse* to resist the invader, they are now treated as public enemies, and if captured, are prisoners of war.

52. No belligerent has the right to declare that he will treat every captured man in arms of a levy *en masse* as a brigand or bandit.

If, however, the people of a country, or any portion of the same, already occupied by an army, rise against it, they are violators of the laws of war, and are not entitled to their protection.

53. The enemy's chaplains, officers of the medical staff, apothecaries, hospital nurses and servants, if they fall into the hands of the American army, are not prisoners of war, unless the commander has reasons to retain them. In this latter case, or if, at their own desire, they are allowed to remain with their captured companions, they are treated as prisoners of war, and may be exchanged if the commander sees fit.

54. A hostage is a person accepted as a pledge for the fulfilment of an agreement concluded between belligerents during the war, or in consequence of a war. Hostages are rare in the present age.

55. If a hostage is accepted, he is treated like a prisoner of war, according to rank and condition, as circumstances may admit.

56. A prisoner of war is subject to no punishment for being a public enemy, nor is any revenge wreaked upon him by the intentional infliction of any suffering, or disgrace, by cruel imprisonment, want of food, by mutilation, death, or any other barbarity.

57. So soon as a man is armed by a sovereign government and takes the soldier's oath of fidelity, he is a belligerent; his killing, wounding, or other warlike acts, are no individual crimes or offences. No belligerent has a right to declare that enemies of a certain class, colour, or condition, when properly organised as soldiers, will not be treated by him as public enemies.

58. The law of nations knows of no distinction of colour; and if an enemy of the United States should enslave and sell any captured

persons of their army, it would be a case for the severest retaliation, if not redressed upon complaint.

The United States cannot retaliate by enslavement; therefore death must be the retaliation for this crime against the law of nations.

59. A prisoner of war remains answerable for his crime against the captor's army or people, committed before he was captured, and for which he has not been punished by his own authorities.

All prisoners of war are liable to the infliction of retaliatory measures.

60. It is against the usage of modern war to resolve, in hatred and revenge, to give no quarter. No body of troops has the right to declare that it will not give, and therefore will not expect, quarter; but a commander is permitted to direct his troops to give no quarter, in great straits, when his own salvation makes it *impossible* to cumber himself with prisoners.

61. Troops that give no quarter have no right to kill enemies already disabled on the ground, or prisoners captured by other troops.

62. All troops of the enemy known or discovered to give no quarter in general, or to any portion of the army, receive none.

63. Troops who fight in the uniform of their enemies, without any plain, striking, and uniform mark of distinction of their own, can expect no quarter.

64. If American troops capture a train containing uniforms of the enemy, and the commander considers it advisable to distribute them for use among his men, some striking mark or sign must be adopted to distinguish the American soldier from the enemy.

65. The use of the enemy's national standard, flag, or other emblem of nationality, for the purpose of deceiving the enemy in battle, is an act of perfidy by which they lose all claim to the protection of the laws of war.

66. Quarter having been given to an enemy by American troops, under a misapprehension of his true character, he may, nevertheless, be ordered to suffer death if, within three days after the battle, it be discovered that he belongs to a corps which gives no quarter.

67. The law of nations allows every sovereign government to make war upon another sovereign State, and therefore admits of no rules or laws different from those of regular warfare, regarding the treatment of prisoners of war, although they may belong to the army of a government which the captor may consider as a wanton and unjust assailant.

68. Modern wars are not internecine wars, in which the killing of the enemy is the object. The destruction of the enemy in modern war, and, indeed, modern war itself, are means to obtain that object of the belligerent which lies beyond the war.

Unnecessary or revengeful destruction of life is not lawful.

69. Outposts, sentinels, or pickets are not to be fired upon, except to drive them in, or when a positive order, special or general, has been issued to that effect.

70. The use of poison in any manner, be it to poison wells, or food, or arms, is wholly excluded from modern warfare. He that uses it puts himself out of the pale of the law and usages of war.

71. Whoever intentionally inflicts additional wounds on an enemy already wholly disabled, or kills such an enemy, or who orders or encourages soldiers to do so, shall suffer death, if duly convicted, whether he belongs to the army of the United States, or is an enemy captured after having committed his misdeed.

72. Money and other valuables on the person of a prisoner, such as watches or jewellery, as well as extra clothing, are regarded by the American army as the private property of the prisoner, and the appropriation of such valuables or money is considered dishonourable, and is prohibited.

Nevertheless, if *large* sums are found upon the persons of prisoners, or in their possession, they shall be taken from them, and the surplus, after providing for their own support, appropriated for the use of the army, under the direction of the commander, unless otherwise ordered by the government. Nor can prisoners claim as private property, large sums found and captured in their train, although they had been placed in the private luggage of the prisoners.

73. All officers, when captured, must surrender their side-arms to the captor. They may be restored to the prisoner in marked cases, by the commander, to signalise admiration of his distinguished bravery, or approbation of his humane treatment of prisoners before his capture. The captured officer to whom they may be restored cannot wear them during captivity.

74. A prisoner of war being a public enemy, is the prisoner of the government, and not of the captor. No ransom can be paid by a prisoner of war to his individual captor, or to any officer in command. The government alone releases captives, according to rules prescribed by itself.

75. Prisoners of war are subject to confinement or imprisonment such as may be deemed necessary on account of safety, but they are to be subjected to no other intentional suffering or indignity. The confinement and mode of treating a prisoner may be varied during his captivity according to the demands of safety.

76. Prisoners of war shall be fed upon plain and wholesome food whenever practicable, and treated with humanity.

They may be required to work for the benefit of the captor's government, according to their rank and condition.

77. A prisoner of war who escapes may be shot, or otherwise killed in his flight; but neither death nor any other punishment shall be inflicted upon him simply for his attempt to escape, which the law of war does not consider a crime. Stricter means of security shall be used after an unsuccessful attempt at escape.

If, however, a conspiracy is discovered, the purpose of which is a united or general escape, the conspirators may be rigorously punished, even with death; and capital punishment may also be inflicted upon prisoners of war discovered to have plotted rebellion against the authorities of the captors, whether in union with fellow-prisoners or other persons.

78. If prisoners of war, having given no pledge nor made any promise on their honour, forcibly or otherwise, escape, and are captured again in battle, after having rejoined their own army, they shall not be punished for their escape, but shall be treated as simple prisoners of war, although they will be subjected to stricter confinement.

79. Every captured wounded enemy shall be medically treated, according to the ability of the medical staff.

80. Honourable men, when captured, will abstain from giving to the enemy information concerning their own army; and the modern law of war permits no longer the use of any violence against prisoners, in order to extort the desired information, or to punish them for having given false information.

Section IV.

Partisans—Armed enemies not belonging to the hostile army—Scouts—Armed prowlers—War-rebels.

81. Partisans are soldiers armed and wearing the uniform of their army, but belonging to a corps which acts detached from the main body for the purpose of making inroads into the territory occupied by the enemy. If captured, they are entitled to all the privileges of the prisoner of war.

82. Men, or squads of men, who commit hostilities, whether by fighting, or inroads for destruction or plunder, or by raids of any kind, without commission, without being part and portion of the organised hostile army, and without sharing continuously in the war, but who do so with intermitting returns to their homes and avocations, or with the occasional assumption of the semblance of peaceful pursuits, divesting themselves of the character or appearance of soldiers,—such men, or squads of men, are not public enemies, and therefore, if captured, are not entitled to the privileges of prisoners of war, but shall be treated summarily as highway robbers or pirates.

83. Scouts or single soldiers, if disguised in the dress of the country, or in the uniform of the army hostile to their own, employed in obtaining information, if found within or lurking about the lines of the captor, are treated as spies, and suffer death.

84. Armed prowlers, by whatever names they may be called, or persons of the enemy's territory, who steal within the lines of the hostile army, for the purpose of robbing, killing, or of destroying bridges, roads, or canals, or of robbing or destroying the mail, or of cutting the telegraph wires, are not entitled to the privileges of the prisoner of war.

85. War-rebels are persons within an occupied territory who rise in arms against the occupying or conquering army, or against the authorities established by the same. If captured, they may suffer death, whether they rise singly, in small or large bands, and whether called upon to do so by their own, but expelled, government or not. They are not prisoners of war; nor are they, if discovered and secured before their conspiracy has matured to an actual rising, or to armed violence.

Section V.

Safe-conduct—Spies—War-traitors—Captured messengers—Abuse of the flag of truce.

86. All intercourse between the territories occupied by belligerent armies, whether by traffic, by letter, by travel, or in any other way, ceases. This is the general rule, to be observed without special proclamation.

Exceptions to this rule, whether by safe-conduct, or permission to trade on a small or large scale, or by exchanging mails, or by travel from one territory into the other, can take place only according to agreement approved by the government, or by the highest military authority.

Contraventions of this rule are highly punishable.

87. Ambassadors, and all other diplomatic agents of neutral Powers, accredited to the enemy, may receive safe-conducts through the territories occupied by the belligerents, unless there are military reasons to the contrary, and unless they may reach the place of their destination conveniently by another route. It implies no international affront if the safe-conduct is declined. Such passes are usually given by the supreme authority of the State, and not by subordinate officers.

88. A spy is a person who secretly, in disguise or under false pretence, seeks information with the intention of communicating it to the enemy.

The spy is punishable with death, by hanging by the neck, whether or not he succeed in obtaining the information or in conveying it to the enemy.

89. If a citizen of the United States obtains information in a legitimate manner, and betrays it to the enemy, be he a military or civil officer, or a private citizen, he shall suffer death.

90. A traitor under the law of war, or a war-traitor, is a person in a place or district under martial law, who, unauthorized by the military commander, gives information of any kind to the enemy, or holds intercourse with him.

91. The war-traitor is always severely punished. If his offence consists in betraying to the enemy anything concerning the condition, safety, operations or plans of the troops holding or occupying the place or district, his punishment is death.

92. If the citizen or subject of a country or place invaded or conquered gives information to his own government, from which he is separated by the hostile army, or to the army of his government, he is a war-traitor, and death is the penalty of his offence.

93. All armies in the field stand in need of guides, and impress them if they cannot obtain them otherwise.

94. No person having been forced by the enemy to serve as guide is punishable for having done so.

95. If a citizen of a hostile and invaded district, voluntarily serves as a guide to the enemy, or offers to do so, he is deemed a war-traitor, and shall suffer death.

96. A citizen serving voluntarily as a guide against his own country commits treason, and will be dealt with according to the law of his country.

97. Guides, when it is clearly proved that they have misled intentionally, may be put to death.

98. All unauthorized or secret communication with the enemy is considered treasonable by the law of war.

Foreign residents in an invaded or occupied territory, or foreign visitors in the same, can claim no immunity from this law. They may communicate with foreign parts, or with the inhabitants of the hostile country, so far as the military authority permits, but no further. Instant expulsion from the occupied territory would be the very least punishment for the infraction of this rule.

99. A messenger carrying written despatches or verbal messages from one portion of the army, or from a besieged place, to another portion of the same army, or its government, if armed, and in the uniform of his army, and if captured while doing so, in the territory occupied by the enemy, is treated by the captor as a prisoner of war,

If not in uniform, nor a soldier, the circumstances connected with his capture must determine the disposition that shall be made of him.

100. A messenger or agent who attempts to steal through the territory occupied by the enemy, to further, in any manner, the interests of the enemy, if captured, is not entitled to the privileges of the prisoner of war, and may be dealt with according to the circumstances of the case.

101. While deception in war is admitted as a just and necessary means of hostility, and is consistent with honourable warfare, the common law of war allows even capital punishment for clandestine or treacherous attempts to injure an enemy, because they are so dangerous, and it is so difficult to guard against them.

102. The law of war, like the criminal law regarding other offences, makes no difference on account of the difference of sexes, concerning the spy, the war-traitor, or the war-rebel.

103. Spies, war-traitors, and war-rebels, are not exchanged according to the common law of war. The exchange of such persons would require a special cartel, authorized by the government, or, at a great distance from it, by the chief commander of the army in the field.

104. A successful spy or war-traitor, safely returned to his own army, and afterwards captured as an enemy, is not subject to punishment for his acts as a spy or war-traitor, but he may be held in closer custody as a person individually dangerous.

Section VI.

Exchange of prisoners—Flags of truce—Flags of protection.

105. Exchanges of prisoners take place—number for number—rank for rank—wounded for wounded—with added condition for added condition—such, for instance, as not to serve for a certain period.

106. In exchanging prisoners of war, such numbers of persons of inferior rank may be substituted as an equivalent for one of superior rank as may be agreed upon by cartel, which requires the sanction of the government, or of the commander of the army in the field.

107. A prisoner of war is in honour bound truly to state to the captor his rank ; and he is not to assume a lower rank than belongs to him, in order to cause a more advantageous exchange ; nor a higher rank, for the purpose of obtaining better treatment.

Offences to the contrary have been justly punished by the commanders of released prisoners, and may be good cause for refusing to release such prisoners.

108. The surplus number of prisoners of war remaining after an exchange has taken place is sometimes released either for the payment

of a stipulated sum of money, or, in urgent cases, of provision, clothing, or other necessaries.

Such arrangement, however, requires the sanction of the highest authority.

109. The exchange of prisoners of war is an act of convenience to both belligerents. If no general cartel has been concluded, it cannot be demanded by either of them. No belligerent is obliged to exchange prisoners of war.

A cartel is voidable so soon as either party has violated it.

110. No exchange of prisoners shall be made except after complete capture, and after an accurate account of them, and a list of the captured officers, has been taken.

111. The bearer of a flag of truce cannot insist upon being admitted. He must always be admitted with great caution. Unnecessary frequency is carefully to be avoided.

112. If the bearer of a flag of truce offer himself during an engagement, he can be admitted as a very rare exception only. It is no breach of good faith to retain such a flag of truce, if admitted during the engagement. Firing is not required to cease on the appearance of a flag of truce in battle.

113. If the bearer of a flag of truce, presenting himself during an engagement, is killed or wounded, it furnishes no ground of complaint whatever.

114. If it be discovered, and fairly proved, that a flag of truce has been abused for surreptitiously obtaining military knowledge, the bearer of the flag thus abusing his sacred character is deemed a spy.

So sacred is the character of a flag of truce, and so necessary is its sacredness, that while its abuse is an especially heinous offence, great caution is requisite, on the other hand, in convicting the bearer of a flag of truce as a spy.

115. It is customary to designate by certain flags (usually yellow), the hospitals in places which are shelled, so that the besieging enemy may avoid firing on them. The same has been done in battles, when hospitals are situated within the field of the engagement.

116. Honourable belligerents often request that the hospitals within the territory of the enemy may be designated, so that they may be spared.

An honourable belligerent allows himself to be guided by flags or signals of protection as much as the contingencies and the necessities of the fight will permit.

117. It is justly considered an act of bad faith, of infamy or fiendishness, to deceive the enemy by flags of protection. Such act of bad faith may be good cause for refusing to respect such flags.

118. The besieging belligerent has sometimes requested the besieged to designate the buildings containing collections of works of art,

scientific museums, astronomical observatories, or precious libraries, so that their destruction may be avoided as much as possible.

Section VII.

The parole.

119. Prisoners of war may be released from captivity by exchange, and, under certain circumstances, also by parole.

120. The term *parole* designates the pledge of individual good faith and honour to do, or to omit doing, certain acts after he who gives his parole shall have been dismissed, wholly or partially, from the power of the captor.

121. The pledge of the parole is always an individual but not a private act.

122. The parole applies chiefly to prisoners of war whom the captor allows to return to their country, or to live in greater freedom within the captor's country or territory, on conditions stated in the parole.

123. Release of prisoners of war by exchange is the general rule; release by parole is the exception.

124. Breaking the parole is punished with death when the person breaking the parole is captured again.

Accurate lists, therefore, of the paroled persons must be kept by the belligerents.

125. When paroles are given and received, there must be an exchange of two written documents, in which the name and rank of the paroled individuals are accurately and truthfully stated.

126. Commissioned officers only are allowed to give their parole, and they can give it only with the permission of their superior, as long as a superior in rank is within reach.

127. No non-commissioned officer or private can give his parole except through an officer. Individual paroles not given through an officer are not only void, but subject the individual giving them to the punishment of death as deserters. The only admissible exception is where individuals, properly separated from their commands, have suffered long confinement without the possibility of being paroled through an officer.

128. No paroling on the battle-field, no paroling of entire bodies of troops after a battle, and no dismissal of large numbers of prisoners, with a general declaration that they are paroled, is permitted, or of any value.

129. In capitulations for the surrender of strong places or fortified camps, the commanding officer, in cases of urgent necessity, may agree

that the troops under his command shall not fight again during the war, unless exchanged.

130. The usual pledge given in the parole is not to serve during the existing war, unless exchanged.

This pledge refers only to the active service in the field, against the paroling belligerent or his allies actively engaged in the same war. These cases of breaking the parole are patent acts, and can be visited with the punishment of death; but the pledge does not refer to internal service, such as recruiting or drilling the recruits, fortifying places not besieged, quelling civil commotions, fighting against belligerents unconnected with the paroling belligerents, or to civil or diplomatic service for which the paroled officer may be employed.

131. If the government does not approve of the parole, the paroled officer must return into captivity; and should the enemy refuse to receive him, he is free of his parole.

132. A belligerent government may declare, by a general order, whether it will allow paroling, and on what conditions it will allow it. Such order is communicated to the enemy.

133. No prisoner of war can be forced by the hostile government to parole himself, and no government is obliged to parole prisoners of war, or to parole all captured officers if it paroles any. As the pledging of the parole is an individual act, so is paroling, on the other hand, an act of choice on the part of the belligerent.

134. The commander of an occupying army may require, of the civil officers of the enemy, and of its citizens, any pledge he may consider necessary for the safety or security of his army; and upon their failure to give it, he may arrest, confine, or detain them.

Section VIII.

Armistice—Capitulation.

135. An armistice is the cessation of active hostilities for a period agreed upon between belligerents. It must be agreed upon in writing, and duly ratified by the highest authorities of the contending parties.

136. If an armistice be declared, without conditions, it extends no further than to require a total cessation of hostilities along the front of both belligerents.

If conditions be agreed upon, they should be clearly expressed, and must be rigidly adhered to by both parties. If either party violates any express condition, the armistice may be declared null and void by the other.

137. An armistice may be general, and valid for all points and lines of the belligerents; or special—that is, referring to certain troops or certain localities only.

An armistice may be concluded for a definite time; or for an indefinite time, during which either belligerent may resume hostilities on giving the notice agreed upon to the other.

138. The motives which induce the one or the other belligerent to conclude an armistice, whether it be expected to be preliminary to a treaty of peace, or to prepare during the armistice for a more vigorous prosecution of the war, do in no way affect the character of the armistice itself.

139. An armistice is binding upon the belligerents from the day of the agreed commencement; but the officers of the armies are responsible from the day only when they receive official information of its existence.

140. Commanding officers have the right to conclude armistices binding on the district over which their command extends; but such armistice is subject to the ratification of the superior authority, and ceases so soon as it is made known to the enemy that the armistice is not ratified, even if a certain time for the elapsing between giving notice of cessation and the resumption of hostilities should have been stipulated for.

141. It is incumbent upon the contracting parties of an armistice to stipulate what intercourse of persons or traffic between the inhabitants of the territories occupied by the hostile armies shall be allowed, if any.

If nothing is stipulated, the intercourse remains suspended, as during actual hostilities.

142. An armistice is not a partial or a temporary peace; it is only the suspension of military operations to the extent agreed upon by the parties.

143. When an armistice is concluded between a fortified place and the army besieging it, it is agreed by all the authorities on this subject that the besieger must cease all extension, perfection, or advance of his attacking works, as much so as abstain from attacks by main force.

But as there is a difference of opinion among martial jurists, whether the besieged have the right to repair breaches, or to erect new works of defence within the place during an armistice, this point should be determined by express agreement between the parties.

144. So soon as a capitulation is signed, the capitulator has no right to demolish, destroy, or injure the works, arms, stores, or ammunition, in his possession, during the time which elapses between the signing and the execution of the capitulation, unless otherwise stipulated in the same.

145. When an armistice is clearly broken by one of the parties, the other party is released from all obligation to observe it.

146. Prisoners, taken in the act of breaking an armistice, must be treated as prisoners of war, the officer alone being responsible who

gives the order for such a violation of an armistice. The highest authority of the belligerent aggrieved may demand redress for the infraction of an armistice.

147. Belligerents sometimes conclude an armistice while their plenipotentiaries are met to discuss the conditions of a treaty of peace; but plenipotentiaries may meet without a preliminary armistice; in the latter case the war is carried on without any abatement.

Section IX.

Assassination.

148. The law of war does not allow proclaiming either an individual belonging to the hostile army, or a citizen, or a subject of the hostile government, an outlaw, who may be slain without trial by any captor, any more than the modern law of peace allows such international outlawry; on the contrary, it abhors such outrage. The sternest retaliation should follow the murder committed in consequence of such proclamation, made by whatever authority. Civilised nations look with horror upon offers of rewards for the assassination of enemies, as relapses into barbarism.

Section X.

Insurrection—Civil war—Rebellion.

149. Insurrection is the rising of people in arms against their government, or a portion of it, or against one or more of its laws, or against an officer or officers of the government. It may be confined to mere armed resistance, or it may have greater ends in view.

150. Civil war is war between two or more portions of a country or State, each contending for the mastery of the whole, and each claiming to be the legitimate government. The term is also sometimes applied to war of rebellion, when the rebellious provinces or portions of the State are contiguous to those containing the seat of government.

151. The term *rebellion* is applied to an insurrection of large extent, and is usually a war between the legitimate government of a country and portions or provinces of the same who seek to throw off their allegiance to it, and set up a government of their own.

152. When humanity induces the adoption of the rules of regular war towards rebels, whether the adoption is partial or entire, it does in no way whatever imply a partial or complete acknowledgment of their government, if they have set up one, or of them, as an independent or sovereign power. Neutrals have no right to make the adoption of the

rules of war by the assailed government toward rebels the ground of their own acknowledgment of the revolted people as an independent power.*

153. Treating captured rebels as prisoners of war, exchanging them, concluding of cartels, capitulations, or other warlike agreements with them; addressing officers of a rebel army by the rank they may have in the same; accepting flags of truce; or, on the other hand, proclaiming martial law in their territory, or levying war-taxes or forced loans, or doing any other act sanctioned or demanded by the law and usages of public war between sovereign belligerents, neither proves nor establishes an acknowledgment of the rebellious people, or of the government which they may have erected, as a public or sovereign power. Nor does the adoption of the rules of war towards rebels imply an engagement with them extending beyond the limits of these rules. It is victory in the field that ends the strife, and settles the future relations between the contending parties.

154. Treating, in the field, the rebellious enemy according to the law and usages of war, has never prevented the legitimate government from trying the leaders of the rebellion or chief rebels for high treason, and from treating them accordingly, unless they are included in a general amnesty.

155. All enemies in regular war are divided into two general classes—that is to say, into combatants and non-combatants or unarmed citizens of the hostile government.

The military commander of the legitimate government, in a war of rebellion, distinguishes between the loyal citizen in the revolted portion of the country and the disloyal citizen. The disloyal citizens may further be classified into those citizens known to sympathise with the rebellion, without positively aiding it, and those who, without taking up arms, give positive aid and comfort to the rebellious enemy, without being bodily forced thereto.

156. Common justice and plain expediency require that the military commander protect the manifestly loyal citizens, in revolted territories, against the hardships of the war, as much as the common misfortune of all war admits.

The commander will throw the burden of the war, as much as lies within his power, on the disloyal citizens of the revolted portion or province, subjecting them to a stricter police than the non-combatant enemies have to suffer in regular war; and if he deems it appropriate, or if his government demands of him, that every citizen shall, by an oath of allegiance, or by some other manifest act, declare his fidelity to

---

* The recognition of belligerent rights by England and France was grounded, not on the conduct of the North to the South, but on the proclamation of blockade. (Prof. LORIMER's remark in his work Institutes of the Law of Nations. Vol. II. App. p. 335).

the legitimate government, he may expel, transfer, imprison, or fine the revolted citizens who refuse to pledge themselves anew as citizens obedient to the law, and loyal to the government.

Whether it is expedient to do so, and whether reliance can be placed upon such oaths, the commander or his government has the right to decide.

157. Armed or unarmed resistance by citizens of the United States against the lawful movements of their troops, is levying war against the United States, and is therefore treason.

Appendix B.

THE LAWS OF WAR,

AS PROPOSED BY THE INSTITUT DE DROIT INTERNATIONAL.

(Being adopted at the session of the Institut, held at Oxford in September, 1880).

The names of the members of the Commission which drew up the Manual were :—

The Right Honourable Mountague Bernard (Great Britain).
Professor Bluntschli (Germany).
Colonel Den Beer Poortugael (Holland).
Mr. W. E. Hall (Great Britain).
Professor T. E. Holland, D.C.L. (Great Britain).
M. N. de Landa (Spain).
M. Ch. Lucas (France).
Professor De Martens (Russia).
Professor Neumann, Mèmber of the Upper House of the Reichsrath (Austria).
Professor Pierantoni, Member of the Italian Parliament (Italy).
Professor Rivier (Switzerland).
Professor Schulze, Member of the Upper House of the Landtag (Germany).
M. G. Moynier (Switzerland), *Secretary.*

THE LAWS OF WAR AS CONDUCTED ON LAND.

PART I.—GENERAL PRINCIPLES.

1. The state of war admits of the performance of acts of violence on the part only of the armed forces of the belligerent States.

Persons not forming part of a belligerent armed force must abstain from the performance of such acts.

A distinction being implied in the above rule between the individuals of whom the armed force of a State is composed and other subjects of a State, it becomes necessary to define an "armed force."

2. The armed force of a State comprehends—

1 §. The army properly so called, including militia.

2 §. National Guards, Landsturm, and all corps which satisfy the following requirements:

(a) That of being under the direction of a responsible leader.

(b) That of wearing a uniform or a distinctive mark, which latter must be fixed, and capable of being recognized at a distance.

(c) That of bearing arms openly.

3 §. Crews of vessels of war, and other members of the naval forces of the country. (naval volunteers).

4 §. Inhabitants of a territory not militarily occupied by the enemy, who, on the approach of his army, take up arms spontaneously and openly for the purpose of combating it. Such persons form part of the armed force of the State, even though, owing to want of time, they have not organised themselves militarily.

3. Every belligerent armed force is bound to conform to the laws of war.

The sole object during war to which States can legitimately direct their hostilities being the enfeeblement of the military strength of the enemy.—(Declaration of St. Petersburg of the 4/16th November, 1868.)

4. The laws of war do not allow belligerents an unlimited freedom of adopting whatever means they may choose for injuring their enemy. Especially they must asbtain from all useless severity, and from disloyal, unjust, or tyrannical acts.

5. Military conventions made between belligerents during war—such as armistices and capitulations—must be scrupulously observed and respected.

6. No invaded territory is considered to be conquered until war is ended. Until then the occupying State only exercises a *de facto* control of an essentially provisional nature.

Part II.—Application of the General Principles.

I. of hostilities.

A. Rules of Conduct with respect to Persons.

(a) *Of the inoffensive population.*

Acts of violence being permissible only between armed forces (Art. 1).

7. It is forbidden to maltreat the inoffensive portion of the population.

(b) *Of means of injuring the enemy.*

Loyalty of conduct being enjoined (Art. 4).

arms must conquer arms).

8. It is forbidden—

(a) To employ poison in any form.

(b) To endeavour to take the life of an enemy in a traitorous manner—*e. g.*, by employing assassins, or by simulating surrender.

(c) To attack the enemy while concealing the distinctive marks of an armed force.

(d) To make improper use of the national flag, of signs of military ranks, or of the uniform of the enemy, of a flag of truce, or of the protective marks prescribed by the Convention of Geneva (see Arts. 17 and 40).

It being obligatory to abstain from useless severities (Art. 4).

9. It is forbidden—

(a) To use arms, projectiles, or substances calculated to inflict superfluous suffering, or to aggravate wounds, particularly projectiles which, being explosible, or charged with fulminating or inflammable substances, weigh less than 400 grammes.—(Declaration of St. Petersburg).

(b) To mutilate or kill an enemy who has surrendered at discretion, or is disabled, and to declare that quarter will not be given, even if the force making such declaration does not claim quarter for itself.

(c) *Of wounded, sick, and the hospital staff.*

The wounded, the sick, and the hospital staff are exempted from unnecessary severities, which might otherwise touch them, by the following rules (Arts. 10 to 18), drawn from the Convention of Geneva.

10. Wounded and sick soldiers must be brought in and cared for, to whatever nation they belong.

11. When circumstances permit, officers commanding in chief, immediately after a combat, may send in enemy soldiers wounded during it to the advanced posts of the enemy, with the consent of the latter.

12. The operation of moving sick and wounded is a neutral act, and the staff engaged in it is neutral.

13. The staff of the hospitals and ambulances—namely, surgeons, clerks, hospital orderlies, and other persons employed in the sanitary, administrative, and transport departments, as well as chaplains, and members and agents of societies duly authorized to assist the official

hospital staff—is considered to be neutral while exercising its functions, and so long as there are wounded to remove or succour.

14. The staff specified in the preceding Article must continue after occupation by an enemy has taken place to give its attention to the sick and wounded, to such extent as may be needful, in the ambulance or hospital which it serves.

15. When such staff applies for leave to retire, it falls to the officer commanding the occupying troops to fix the date of departure. After request, however, has been made, the departure of the staff can only be postponed for a short time, and for reasons of military necessity.

16. Measures must, if possible, be taken to secure to the neutralised staff fitting maintenance and allowance when it falls into the hands of the enemy.

17. The neutralised hospital staff must wear a white armlet with a red cross on it. The armlet can be issued only by the military authorities.

18. It is the duty of the generals of the belligerent Powers to appeal to the humanity of the inhabitants of the country in which they are operating, for the purpose of inducing them to succour the wounded, pointing out to them at the same time the advantages which result to themselves therefrom (Arts. 36 and 59). Those who respond to any such appeal are entitled to special protection.

(d) *Of the dead.*

19. It is forbidden to strip and mutilate the dead lying on the field of battle.

20. The dead must never be buried before such indications of their identity (especially "livrets, numeros," &c.) as they may have upon them have been collected. The indications thus gathered upon enemy dead are communicated to their army or government.

(e) *Who can be made prisoners of war.*

21. Persons forming part of the armed force of belligerents, on falling into the power of the enemy, must be treated as prisoners of war, conformably to Article 61, and those following it.

This rule applies to messengers openly carrying official despatches, and to civil aeronauts employed to observe the enemy or keep up communication between different parts of the army or territory.

22. Persons who follow an army without forming part of it, such as correspondents of newspapers, sutlers, contractors, &c., on falling into the power of the enemy, can only be detained for so long a time as may be required by military necessity.

(f) *Of spies.*

23. Persons captured as spies cannot demand to be treated as prisoners of war.

But

24. Persons belonging to a belligerent armed force are not to be considered spies on entering, without the cover of a disguise, within the area of the actual operations of the enemy. Messengers, also, who openly carry official despatches, and aeronauts (Act. 21) are not to be considered spies.

To guard against the abuses to which accusations of acting as a spy give rise in time of war, it must clearly be understood that

25. No person accused of being a spy can be punished without trial.

It is moreover admitted that

26. A spy who succeeds in quitting a territory occupied by the enemy, cannot be held responsible for acts done before so leaving, if he afterwards falls into the enemy's hands.

(g) *Of flags of truce.*

27. A person who is authorized by one of the belligerents to enter into communication with the other belligerent, and presents himself to the latter with a white flag, is inviolable.

28. He may be accompanied by a trumpeter or drummer, by a flag-bearer, and, if necessary, by a guide and an interpreter, all of whom are also inviolable.

The necessity of this privilege is evident, especially as its exercise is frequently required in the simple interests of humanity. I must not, however, be so used as to be prejudicial to the opposite party.

Hence

29. The commander to whom a flag of truce is sent is not obliged to receive its bearer under all circumstances.

Besides

30. The commander who receives a flag of truce has the right to take all necessary measures to prevent the presence of an enemy within his lines from being prejudicial to him.

The bearer of a flag of truce, and those who accompany him, are bound to act with good faith towards the enemy who receives them (Art. 4).

31. If the bearer of a flag of truce abuse the confidence which is accorded to him, he may be temporarily detained; and if it be proved that he has made use of his privileges to suborn to traitorous practices, he loses his right of inviolability.

B. Rules of Conduct with regard to Things.

(a) *Of the means of exercising violence. Of bombardment.*

Mitigations of the extreme rights of violence are necessarily consequent upon the rule that useless severity shall not be indulged in (Art. 4). It is thus that

32. It is forbidden—

(a) To pillage, even in the case of towns taken by assault.
(b) To destroy public or private property, unless its destruction is required by an imperative necessity of war.
(c) To attack and bombard undefended places.

The right of belligerents to have recourse to bombardment against fortresses and other places in which the enemy is intrenched is not contestable, but humanity requires that this form of violence shall be so restrained as to limit as much as possible its effects to the armed forces of the enemy and to their defences.

33. The commander of an attacking force must do everything in his power to intimate to the local authorities his intention of bombarding, before the bombardment commences, except when bombardment is coupled with assault.

34. In cases of bombardment, all necessary measures ought to be taken to spare, so far as possible, buildings devoted to religion, the arts, sciences, and charity, hospitals, and places in which sick and wounded are kept; provided always that such buildings are not at the same time utilised, directly or indirectly, for defence.

It is the duty of the besieged to indicate these buildings by visible signs, notified to the besieger beforehand.

(b) *Of the sanitary* matériel.

The rules (Arts. 10 and those following) for the protection of the wounded would be insufficient if special protection were not also given to hospitals. Consequently, in accordance with the the Convention of Geneva,

35. The ambulances and hospitals used by armies are recognized as being neutral, and must be protected and respected as such by the belligerents, so long as there are sick and wounded in them.

36. A like rule applies to private buildings, or parts of private buildings, in which sick and wounded are collected and cared for.

Nevertheless

37. The neutrality of ambulances and hospitals ceases to exist if they are guarded by a military force, a police post being alone permissible.

38. The *matériel* of military hospitals remains subject to the laws of war; persons attached to the hospitals can only, therefore, carry away their private property on leaving. Ambulances, on the other hand, preserve their *matériel.*

39. Under the circumstances contemplated in the foregoing paragraph the term ambulance is applicable to field hospitals and other temporary establishments which follow the troops to the field of battle for the purpose of receiving sick and wounded.

40. A distinctive flag and uniform, bearing a red cross upon a white ground, is adopted for hospitals, ambulances, and things and persons connected with the movement of sick and wounded. It must always be accompanied by the national flag.

II. OF OCCUPIED TERRITORY.

A. DEFINITION.

41. A territory is considered to be occupied when, as the result of its invasion by an enemy's force, the State to which it belongs has ceased in fact to exercise its ordinary authority within it, and the invading State is alone in a position to maintain order. The extent and duration of the occupation are determined by the limits of space and time within which this state of things exists.

B. RULES OF CONDUCT WITH REGARD TO PERSONS.

Since new relations arise from the provisional change of government,

42. It is the duty of the occupying military authority to inform the inhabitants of the occupied territory as soon as possible of the powers which it exercises, as well as of the local extent of the occupation.

43. The occupier must take all measures in his power to re-establish and to preserve public order.

With this object

44. The occupier must, so far as possible, retain the laws which were in vigour in the country in time of peace, modifying, suspending, or replacing them only in case of necessity.

45. The civil functionaries of every kind who consent to continue the exercise of their functions are under the protection of the occupier. They may be dismissed, and they may resign at any moment. For failing to fulfil the obligations freely accepted by them, they can only be subjected to disciplinary punishment. For betraying their trust, they may be punished in such manner as the case may demand.

46. In emergencies the occupier may require the inhabitants of an occupied district to give their assistance in carrying on the local administration.

As occupation does not entail a change of nationality on the part of the inhabitants,

47. The population of an occupied country cannot be compelled to take an oath of fidelity or obedience to the enemy's power. Persons doing acts of hostility directed against the occupier are, however, punishable (Art. 1).

48. Inhabitants of an occupied territory who do not conform to the orders of the occupier can be compelled to do so.

The occupier cannot, however, compel the inhabitants to assist him in his works of attack of defence, nor to take part in military operations against their own country (Art. 4).

Moreover,

49. Human life, female honour, religious beliefs, and forms of workship must be respected. Interference with family life is to be avoided (Art. 4).

C. Rules of Conduct with respect to Things.

(a) *Public property.*

Although an occupier, for the purpose of governing the occupied territory, takes the place in a certain sense of the legitimate government, he does not possess unrestricted powers. So long as the ultimate fate of the territory is undecided—that is to say, until the conclusion of peace —the occupier is not at liberty to dispose freely of such property of his enemy as is not immediately serviceable for the operations of war.

Hence

50. The occupier can appropriate only money and debts (including negotiable instruments) belonging to the State, arms, stores, and in general such movable property of the State as can be used for the purposes of military operations.

51. Means of transport (State railways and their rolling stock, State vessels, &c.), as well as land telegraphs and landing cables, can only be sequestrated for the use of the occupier. Their destruction is forbidden, unless it be required by the necessities of war. They are restored at the peace in the state in which they then are.

52. The occupier can only enjoy the use of, and do administrative acts with respect to, immovable property, such as buildings, forests, and agricultural lands belonging to the enemy State (Art. 6).

Such property cannot be alienated, and must be maintained in good condition.

53. The property of municipal and like bodies, that of religious, charitable, and educational foundations, and that appropriated to the arts and sciences, are exempt from seizure.

All destruction or intentional damage of buildings devoted to the above purposes, of historical monuments, of archives, and of works of art or science, is forbidden, unless it be imperatively demanded by the necessities of war.

(b) *Private property.*

If the powers of an occupier are limited with respect to the property of the enemy State, *a fortiori* they are limited with respect to the property of private persons.

54. Private property, whether held by individuals or by corporations, companies, or other bodies, must be respected, and cannot be confiscated, except to the extent specified in the following Articles.

55. Means of transport (railways and their rolling stock, vessels, &c.), telegraphs, stores of arms and munitions of war, may be seized by the occupier, notwithstanding that they belong to individuals or companies; but they must be restored if possible at the conclusion of peace, and compensation for the loss inflicted on their owners must be provided.

56. Supplies in kind (requisitions) demanded from districts or individuals must correspond to the generally recognized necessities of war, and must be proportioned to the resources of the country.

Requisitions can only be made by express authorisation of the officer commanding in the occupied locality.

57. The occupier can only levy such taxes and duties as are already established in the occupied State. He uses them to satisfy the expenses of administration to the extent that they have been so used by the legitimate government.

58. The occupier can only levy contributions in money as the equivalent of unpaid fines, or unpaid taxes, or of supplies in kind, which have not been duly made.

Contributions in money can only be imposed by the order, and on the responsibility, of the general in chief or of the supreme civil authority established in the occupied territory; and their incidence must as far as possible correspond to that of the taxes already in existence.

59. In apportioning the burdens arising from the billeting of troops and contributions of war, zeal shown by individuals in caring for the wounded is to be taken into consideration.

60. Receipts are to be given for the amount of contributions of war, and for articles requisitioned when payment for them is not made. Measures must be taken to secure that these receipts shall be given always, and in proper form.

III. OF PRISONERS OF WAR.

A. THE STATE OF CAPTIVITY.

Captivity is neither a punishment inflicted on prisoners of war (Art. 21) nor an act of vengeance; it is merely a temporary detention which is devoid of all penal character. In the following Articles, regard is had both to the consideration due to prisoners of war and to the necessity of keeping them in safe custody.

61. Prisoners of war are at the disposal of the enemy government, not of the individuals or corps which have captured them.

62. They are subjected to the laws and rules in force in the enemy army.

63. They must be treated with humanity.

64. All that belongs to them personally, except arms, remains their property.

65. Prisoners are bound to state, if asked, their true name and rank. If they do not do so, they can be deprived of all or any of the mitigations of imprisonment enjoyed by other prisoners circumstanced like themselves.

66. Prisoners can be subjected to internment in a town, fortress, camp, or any other place, definite bounds being assigned which they are not allowed to pass; but they can only be confined in a building when such confinement is indispensable for their safe detention.

67. Insubordination justifies whatever measures of severity may be necessary for its repression.

68. Arms may be used against a fugitive prisoner after summons to surrender.

If he is retaken before he has rejoined his army, or has escaped from the territory under the control of his captor, he may be punished, but solely in a disciplinary manner, or he may be subjected to more severe surveillance than that to which prisoners are commonly subjected. But if he be captured afresh, after having accomplished his escape, he is not punishable unless he has given his parole not to escape, in which case he may be deprived of his rights as prisoner of war.

69. The government detaining prisoners in charged with their maintenance.

In default of agreement between the belligerents on this point, prisoners are given such clothing and rations as the troops of the capturing State receive in time of peace.

70. Prisoners cannot be compelled to take part in any manner in the operations of the war, nor to give information as to their country or army.

71. They may be employed upon public works which have no direct relation to the operations carried on in the theatre of war, provided that labour be not exhausting in kind or degree, and provided that the employment given to them is neither degrading with reference to their military rank, if they belong to the army, nor to their official or social position, if they do not so belong.

72. When permission is given to them to work for private employers, their wages may be received by the detaining government, which must either use it in procuring comforts for them, or must pay it over to them on their liberation, the cost of their maintenance being if necessary first deducted.

B. TERMINATION OF CAPTIVITY.

The reasons which justify the detention of a captured enemy last only during the continuance of war.

Consequently

73. The captivity of prisoners of war ceases as of course on the conclusion of peace ; but the time and mode of their actual liberation is a matter for agreement between the governments concerned.

In virtue of the Convention of Geneva,

74. Captivity ceases as of course, before the date fixed upon for general liberation, in case of wounded or sick prisoners who, after being cured, are found to be incapable of further service.

The captor must send these back to their country so soon as their incapacity is established.

During the war,

75. Prisoners can be released by means of a cartel of exchange negotiated between the belligerent parties.

Even without exchange,

76. Prisoners can be set at liberty on parole, if the laws of their country do not forbid it. The conditions of their parole must be clearly stated. If so set at liberty, they are bound, on their honour, to fulfil scrupulously the engagements which they have freely entered into. Their government, on its part, must neither require nor accept from them any service inconsistent with their pledged word.

77. A prisoner cannot be compelled to accept his liberty or parole. In the same way the enemy government is not obliged to accede to a request made by a prisoner to be released on parole.

78. Prisoners liberated on parole and retaken in arms against the government to which they are pledged, can be deprived of the rights of prisoners of war, unless they have been included among prisoners exchanged unconditionally under a cartel of exchange negotiated subsequently to their liberation.

IV. PERSONS INTENDED IN NEUTRAL TERRITORY.

It is universally admitted that a neutral State cannot lend assistance to belligerents, and especially cannot allow them to make use of its territory without compromising its neutrality. Humanity, on the other hand, demands that a neutral State shall not be obliged to repel persons who beg refuge from death or captivity. The following rules are intended to reconcile these conflicting requirements—

79. The neutral State, within the territory of which bodies of troops or individuals belonging to the armed force of the belligerents take refuge, must intern them at a place as distant as possible from the theatre of war.

It must do the same with persons using its territory as a means of carrying on military operations.

80. Interned persons may be kept in camps, or may be shut up in fortresses or other places of safety.

The neutral State decides whether officers may be left free on parole on an engagement being entered into by them not to leave the neutral territory without authorisation.

81. In default of special convention regulating the maintenance of interned persons, the neutral State supplies them with rations and clothes, and bestows care upon them in other ways to such extent as is required by humanity.

It also takes care of the *matériel* of war which the interned persons may have had with them on entering the neutral territory.

On the conclusion of peace, or sooner if possible, the expenses occasioned by the internment are repaid to the neutral State by the belligerent State to which the interned persons belong.

82. The provisions of the Convention of Geneva of the 22nd August, 1864 (see above, Articles 10 to 18, 35 to 40, and 74), are applicable to the hospital staff, as well as to the sick and wounded who have taken refuge in, or been carried into, neutral territory.

Especially

83. Sick and wounded who are not prisoners may be moved across neutral territory, provided that the persons accompanying them belong solely to the hospital staff, and that any *matériel* carried with them is such only as is required for the use of sick and wounded. The neutral State, across the territory of which sick and wounded are moved, is bound to take whatever measures of control are required to secure the strict observance of the above conditions.

Part III.—Penal Sanction.

When infractions of the foregoing rules take place, the guilty persons should be punished, after trial, by the belligerent within whose power they are.

84. Persons violating the laws of war are punishable in such way as the penal law of the country may prescribe.

But this mode of repressing acts contrary to the laws of war being only applicable when the guilty person can be reached, the injured party has no resource other than the use of reprisals when the guilty person cannot be reached, if the acts committed are sufficiently serious to render it urgently necessary to impress respect for the law upon the enemy. Reprisals, the occasional necessity of which is to be deplored, are an exceptional practice, at variance with the general principles that the innocent must not suffer for the guilty, and that every belligerent ought to conform to the laws of war even without reciprocity on the part of the enemy. The right to use reprisals is tempered by the following restrictions:—

85. Reprisals are forbidden whenever the wrong which has afforded ground of complaint has been repaired.

86. In the grave cases in which reprisals become an imperative necessity, their nature and scope must never exceed the measure of the infraction of the laws of war committed by the enemy.

They can only be made with the authorisation of the commander-in-chief.

They must, in all cases, be consistent with the rules of humanity and morality.

Appendix C.

BRITISH LAWS, RELATING TO NAVAL PRIZES OF WAR.

I.

27 & 28 Vict., C. 25.

An Act for regulating Naval Prize of War. Passed 23rd June, 1864.

Whereas it is expedient to enact permanently, with amendments, such provisions concerning naval prize, and matters connected therewith, as have heretofore been usually passed at the beginning of a war.

Be it therefore enacted, &c.

Preliminary.

1. This Act may be cited as The Naval Prize Act, 1864.
2. In this Act—

The term 'the Lords of the Admiralty' means the Lord High Admiral of the United Kingdom, or the Commissioners for executing the office of Lord High Admiral.

The term 'the High Court of Admiralty' means the High Court of Admiralty of England.

The term 'any of Her Majesty's ships of war' includes any of Her Majesty's vessels of war, and any hired armed ship or vessel in Her Majesty's service.

The term 'officers and crew,' includes flag officers, commanders, and other officers, engineers, seamen, marines, soldiers, and others on board any of Her Majesty's ships of war.

The term 'ship' includes vessel, and boat, with the tackle, furniture, and apparel of the ship, vessel, or boat.

The term 'ship papers' includes all books, passes, sea briefs, charter-parties, bills of lading, cockets, letters, and other documents and writings delivered up or found on board a captured ship.

The term 'goods' includes all such things as are by the course of Admiralty and law of nations the subject of adjudication as prize (other than ships).

I.—Prize Courts.

3. The High Court of Admiralty and every Court of Admiralty or of Vice-Admiralty, or other Court exercising Admiralty jurisdiction in Her Majesty's dominions, for the time being authorized to take cognizance of and judicially proceed in matters of prize, shall be a Prize Court within the meaning of this Act.

Every such Court, other than the High Court of Admiralty, is comprised in the term 'Vice-Admiralty Prize Conrt,' when hereafter used in this Act.

High Court of Admiralty.

4. The High Court of Admiralty shall have jurisdiction throughout Her Majesty's dominions as a Prize Court.

The High Court of Admiralty as a Prize Court shall have power to enforce any order or decree of a Vice-Admiralty Prize Court, and any order or decree of the Judicial Committee of the Privy Council in a Prize Appeal.

Appeal; Judicial Committee.

5. An appeal shall lie to Her Majesty in Council from any order or decree of a Prize Court, as of right in case of a final decree, and in other cases with the leave of the Court making the order or decree.

Every appeal shall be made in such manner and form and subject to such regulations (including regulations as to fees, costs, charges, and expenses) as may for the time being be directed by Order in Council, and in the absence of any such order, or so far as any such order does not extend, then in such manner and form and subject to such regulations as are for the time being prescribed or in force respecting maritime causes of appeal.

6. The Judicial Committee of the Privy Council shall have jurisdiction to hear and report on any such appeal, and may therein exercise all such powers as for the time being appertain to them in respect of appeals from any Court of Admiralty jurisdiction, and all such powers as are under this Act vested in the High Court of Admiralty, and all such powers as were wont to be exercised by the Commissioners of Appeal in prize causes.

7. All processes and documents required for the purposes of any such appeal shall be transmitted to and shall remain in the custody of the registrar of Her Majesty in prize appeals.

8. In every such appeal the usual inhibition shall be extracted from the registry of Her Majesty in prize appeals within three months after the date of the order or decree appealed from, if the appeal be from the High Court of Admiralty, and within six months after that date if it be from a Vice-Admiralty Prize Court.

The Judicial Committee may, nevertheless, on sufficient cause shown, allow the inhibition to be extracted and the appeal to be prosecuted after the expiration of the respective periods aforesaid.

Vice-Admiralty Prize Courts.

9. Every Vice-Admiralty prize court shall enforce within its jurisdiction all orders and decrees of the Judicial Committee in prize appeals and of the High Court of Admiralty in prize causes.

10. Her Majesty in Council may grant to the Judge of any Vice-Admiralty Prize Court a salary not exceeding five hundred pounds a year, payable out of money provided by Parliament, subject to such regulations as seem meet.

A Judge to whom a salary is so granted shall not be entitled to any further emolument, arising from fees or otherwise, in respect of prize business transacted in his Court.

An account of all such fees shall be kept by the registrar of the court, and the amount thereof shall be carried to and form part of the Consolidated Fund of the United Kingdom.

11. In accordance, as far as circumstances admit, with the principles and regulations laid down in the Superannuation Act, 1859, Her Majesty in Council may grant to the Judge of any Vice-Admiralty Prize Court an annual or other allowance, to take effect on the termination of his service, and to be payable out of money provided by Parliament.

12. The Registrar of every Vice-Admiralty Prize Court shall, on the first day of January and first day of July in every year, make out a return (in such form as the Lords of the Admiralty from time to time direct) of all cases adjudged in the Court since the last half-yearly return, and shall with all convenient speed send the same to the Registrar of the High Court of Admiralty, who shall keep the same in the registry of that Court, and who shall, as soon as conveniently may be, send a copy of the returns of each half year to the Lords of the Admiralty, who shall lay the same before both Houses of Parliament.

General.

13. The Judicial Committee of the Privy Council, with the Judge of the High Court of Admiralty, may from time to time frame general orders for regulating (subject to the provisions of this Act) the procedure and practice of Prize Courts, and the duties and conduct of the officers thereof and of the practitioners therein, and for regulating the fees to be taken by the officers of the Courts, and the costs, charges, and expenses to be allowed to the practitioners therein.

Any such general orders shall have full effect, if and when approved by Her Majesty in Council, but not sooner or otherwise.

Every Order in Council made under this section shall be laid before both Houses of Parliament. Every such Order in Council shall be kept exhibited in a conspicuous place in each Court to which it relates.

14. It shall not be lawful for any registrar, marshal, or other officer of any Prize Court, or for the registrar of Her Majesty in prize appeals, directly or indirectly to act or be in any manner concerned as advocate, proctor, solicitor, or agent, or otherwise, in any prize cause or appeal, on pain of dismissal or suspension from office, by order of the Court or of the Judicial Committee (as the case may require).

15. It shall not be lawful for any proctor or solicitor, or person practising as a proctor or solicitor, being employed by a party in a prize cause or appeal, to be employed or concerned, by himself or his partner or by any other person, directly or indirectly, by or on behalf of any adverse party in that cause or appeal, on pain of exclusion or suspension from practice in prize matters, by order of the Court or of the Judicial Committee (as the case may require).

II.—Procedure in Prize Causes.

Proceedings by Captors.

16. Every ship taken as prize, and brought into port within the jurisdiction of a Prize Court, shall forthwith, and without bulk broken, be delivered up to the marshal of the Court.

If there is no such marshal, then the ship shall be in like manner delivered up to the principal officer of customs at the port.

The ship shall remain in the custody of the marshal, or of such officer, subject to the orders of the Court.

17. The captors shall, with all practicable speed after the ship is brought into port, bring the ship papers into the registry of the Court.

The officer in command, or one of the chief officers of the capturing ship or some other person who was present at the capture, and saw the ship papers delivered up or found on board, shall make oath that they are brought in as they were taken, without fraud, addition, subduction, or alteration, or else shall account on oath to the satisfaction of the Court for the absence or altered condition of the ship papers, or any of them.

Where no ship papers are delivered up or found on board the captured ship, the officer in command, or one of the chief officers of the capturing ship, or some other person who was present at the capture shall make oath to that effect.

18. As soon as the affidavit as to ship papers is filed, a monition shall issue, returnable within twenty days from the service thereof, citing all persons in general to show cause why the captured ship should not be condemned.

19. The captors shall, with all practicable speed after the captured ship is brought into port, bring three or four of the principal persons belonging to the captured ship before the Judge of the Court, or some person authorized in this behalf, by whom they shall be examined on oath on the standing interrogatories.

The preparatory examinations on the standing interrogatories shall, if possible, be concluded within five days from the commencement thereof.

20. After the return of the monition, the Court shall on production of the preparatory examinations and ship papers, proceed with all convenient speed either to condemn or to release the captured ship.

21. Where, on production of the preparatory examinations and ship papers, it appears to the Court doubtful whether the captured ship is good prize or not, the Court may direct further proof to be adduced, either by affidavit or by examination of witnesses, with or without pleadings, or by production of further documents; and on such further proof being adduced the Court shall, with all convenient speed, proceed to adjudication.

22. The foregoing provisions, as far as they relate to the custody of the ship, and to examination on the standing interrogatories, shall not apply to ships of war taken as prize.

Claim.

23. At any time before final decree made in the cause, any person claiming an interest in the ship may enter in the registry of the Court a claim, verified on oath.

Within five days after entering the claim, the claimant shall give security for costs in the sum of sixty pounds; but the Court shall have power to enlarge the time for giving security, or to direct security to be given in a larger sum, if the circumstances appear to require it.

Appraisement.

24. The Court may, if it thinks fit at any time, direct that the captured ship be appraised.

Every appraisement shall be made by competent persons sworn to make the same according to the best of their skill and knowledge.

Delivery on Bail.

25. After appraisement, the Court may, if it thinks fit, direct that the captured ship be delivered up to the Claimant, on his giving security to the satisfaction of the Court to pay to the captors the appraised value thereof in case of condemnation.

Sale.

26. The Court may at any time, if it thinks fit, on account of the condition of the captured ship, or on the application of a claimant, order that the captured ship be appraised as aforesaid (if not already appraised), and be sold.

27. On or after condemnation the Court may, if it thinks fit, order that the ship be appraised as aforesaid (if not already appraised), and be sold.

28. Every sale shall be made by or under the superintendence of the marshal of the Court or of the officer having the custody of the captured ship.

29. The proceeds of any sale, made either before or after condemnation, and after condemnation the appraised value of the captured ship, in case she has been delivered up to a claimant on bail, shall be paid under an order of the Court either into the Bank of England to the credit of Her Majesty's Paymaster General, or into the hands of an official accountant (belonging to the Commissariat or some other department) appointed for this purpose by the Commissioners of Her Majesty's Treasury or by the Lords of the Admiralty, subject in either case to such regulations as may from time to time be made, by Order in Council, as to the custody and disposal of money so paid.

Small armed ships.

30. The captors may include in one adjudication any number, not exceeding six, of armed ships not exceeding one hundred tons each, taken within three months next before institution of proceedings.

Goods.

31. The foregoing provisions relating to ships shall extend and apply, *mutatis mutandis*, to goods taken as prize on board ship; and the Court may direct such goods to be unladen, inventoried, and warehoused.

Monition to captors to proceed.

32. If the captors fail to institute or to prosecute with effect proceedings for adjudication, a monition shall, on the application of a claimant, issue against the captors, returnable within six days from the service thereof, citing them to appear and proceed to adjudication; and on the return thereof the Court shall either forthwith proceed to adjudication or direct further proof to be adduced as aforesaid, and then proceed to adjudication.

Claim on Appeal.

33. Where any person, not an original party in the cause, intervenes on appeal, he shall enter a claim, verified on oath, and shall give security for costs.

III.—Special Cases of Capture.

Land Expeditions.

34. Where, in an expedition of any of Her Majesty's naval or naval and military forces against a fortress or possession on land, goods belonging to the state of the enemy or to a public trading company of the enemy exercising powers of government are taken in the fortress or possession, or a ship is taken in waters defended by or belonging to the fortress or possession, a Prize Court shall have jurisdiction as to the goods or ship so taken, and any goods taken on board the ship, as in case of prize.

Conjunct Capture with Ally.

35. Where any ship or goods is or are taken by any of Her Majesty's naval or naval and military forces while acting in conjunction with any forces of any of Her Majesty's allies, a prize Court shall have jurisdiction as to the same as in case of Prize, and shall have power, after condemnation, to apportion the due share of the proceeds to Her Majesty's ally, the proportionate amount and the disposition of which share shall be such as may from time to time be agreed between Her Majesty and Her Majesty's ally.

Joint Capture.

36. Before condemnation, a petition on behalf of asserted joint captors shall not (except by special leave of the Court) be admitted, unless and until they give security to the satisfaction of the Court to contribute to the actual captors a just proportion of any costs, charges, or expenses, or damages that may be incurred by or awarded against the actual captors on account of the capture and detention of the prize.

After condemnation, such a petition shall not (except by special leave of the Court) be admitted unless and until the asserted joint captors pay to the actual captors a just proportion of the costs, charges, and expenses incurred by the actual captors in the case, and give such security as aforesaid, and show sufficient cause to the Court why their petition was not presented before condemnation.

Provided, that nothing in the present section shall extend to the asserted interest of a flag officer claiming to share by virtue of his flag.

Offences against Law of Prize.

37. A Prize Court, on proof of any offence against the law of nations, or against this Act, or any Act relating to naval discipline, or against any Order in Council or royal proclamation, or of any breach of Her Majesty's instructions relating to prize, or of any act of disobedience to the orders of the Lords of the Admiralty, or to the com-

mand of a superior officer, committed by the captors in relation to any ship or goods taken as prize, or in relation to any person on board any such ship, may, on condemnation reserve the prize to Her Majesty's disposal, notwithstanding any grant that may have been made by Her Majesty in favour of captors.

Pre-emption.

38. Where a ship of a foreign nation passing the seas laden with naval or victualling stores intended to be carried to a port of an enemy of Her Majesty is taken and brought into a port of the United Kingdom, and the purchase for the service of Her Majesty of the stores on board the ship appears to the Lords of the Admiralty expedient without the condemnation thereof in a Prize Court, in that case the Lords of the Admiralty may purchase, on the account or for the service of Her Majesty, all or any of the stores on board the ship; and the Commissioners of Customs may permit the stores purchased, to be entered and landed within any port.

Capture by Ship other than a Ship of War.

39. Any ship or goods taken as prize by any of the officers and crew of a ship other than a ship of war of Her Majesty, shall, on condemnation, belong to Her Majesty in her office of Admiralty.

IV.—Prize Salvage.

40. Where any ship or goods belonging to any of Her Majesty's subjects, after being taken as prize, by the enemy, is or are retaken from the enemy by any of Her Majesty's ships of war, the same shall be restored, by decree of a Prize Court to the owner, on his paying as prize salvage one-eighth part of the value of the prize to be decreed and ascertained by the Court, or such sum not exceeding one-eighth part of the estimated value of the prize as may be agreed on between the owner and the receptors, and approved by order of the Court: Provided, that where the recapture is made under circumstances of special difficulty or danger, the Prize Court may, if it thinks fit award to the recaptors as prize salvage a larger part than one-eighth part, but not exceeding in any case one-fourth part, of the value of the prize.

Provided also, that where a ship, after being so taken is set forth or used by any of Her Majesty's enemies as a ship of war, this provision for restitution shall not apply, and the ship shall be adjudicated on, as in other cases of prize.

41. Where a ship belonging to any of Her Majesty's subjects, after being taken as prize by the enemy, is retaken from the enemy by any of Her Majesty's ships of war, she may, with the consent of the recaptors, prosecute her voyage, and it shall not be necessary for the recaptors to proceed to adjudication till her return to a port of the United Kingdom.

The master or owner, or his agent, may, with the consent of the recaptors, unload and dispose of the goods on board the ship before adjudication.

In case the ship does not, within six months, return to a port of the United Kingdom, the recaptors may nevertheless institute proceedings against the ship or goods in the High Court of Admiralty, and the Court may thereupon award prize salvage as aforesaid to the recaptors, and may enforce payment thereof, either by warrant of arrest against the ship or goods, or by monition and attachment against the owner.

V.—Prize Bounty.

42. If, in relation to any war, Her Majesty is pleased to declare, by proclamation or Order in Council, her intention to grant prize bounty to the officers and crews of her ships of war, then such of the officers and crew of any of Her Majesty's ships of war as are actually present at the taking or destroying of any armed ship of any of Her Majesty's enemies shall be entitled to have distributed among them as prize bounty a sum calculated at the rate of five pounds for each person on board the enemy's ship at the beginning of the engagement.

43. The number of the persons so on board the enemy's ship shall be proved in a Prize Court, either by the examinations on oath of the survivors of them, or of any three or more of the survivors, or if there is no survivor by the papers of the enemy's ship or by the examinations on oath of three or more of the officers and crew of Her Majesty's ship, or by such other evidence as may seem to the Court sufficient in the circumstances.

The Court shall make a decree declaring the title of the officers and crew of Her Majesty's ship to the prize bounty, and stating the amount thereof.

The decree shall be subject to appeal as other decrees of the Court.

44. On production of an official copy of the decree the Commissioners of Her Majesty's Treasury shall, out of money provided by Parliament, pay the amount of prize bounty decreed, in such manner as any Order in Council may from time to time direct.

VI.—Miscellaneous Provisions.

Ransom.

45. Her Majesty in Council may from time to time, in relation to any war, make such orders as may seem expedient, according to circumstances, for prohibiting or allowing, wholly or in certain cases, or subject to any conditions or regulations or otherwise, as may from time to time seem meet, the ransoming or the entering into any contract or agreement for the ransoming of any ship or goods belonging to any of Her Majesty's subjects, and taken as prize by any of Her Majesty's enemies.

Any contract or agreement entered into, and any bill, bond, or other security given for ransom of any ship or goods, shall be under the exclusive jurisdiction of the High Court of Admiralty as a Prize Court (subject to appeal to the Judicial Committee of the Privy Council), and if entered into or given in contravention of any such Order in Council, shall be deemed to have been entered into or given for an illegal consideration.

If any person ransoms or enters into any contract or agreement for ransoming any ship or goods, in contravention of any such Order in Council, he shall for every such offence be liable to be proceeded against in the High Court of Admiralty at the suit of Her Majesty in Her office of Admiralty, and on conviction to be fined, in the discretion of the Court, any sum not exceeding five hundred pounds.

Convoy.

46. If the master or other person having the command of any ship of any of Her Majesty's subjects, under the convoy of any of Her Majesty's ships of war, wilfully disobeys any lawful signal, instruction, or command of the commander of the convoy, or without leave deserts the convoy, he shall be liable to be proceeded against in the High Court of Admiralty at the suit of Her Majesty in her office of Admiralty, and upon conviction to be fined, in the discretion of the Court, any sum not exceeding five hundred pounds, and to suffer imprisonment for such time, not exceeding one year, as the Court may adjudge.

Customs Duties and Regulations.

47. All ships and goods taken as prize and brought into a port of the United Kingdom shall be liable to and be charged with the same rates and charges and duties of customs as under any Act relating to the customs may be chargeable on other ships and goods of the like description; and

All goods brought in as prize which would on the voluntary importation thereof be liable to forfeiture or subject to any restriction under the laws relating to the customs, shall be deemed to be so liable and subject, unless the Commissioners of Customs see fit to authorize the sale or delivery thereof for home use or exportation unconditionally or subject to such conditions and regulations as they may direct.

48. Where any ship or goods taken as prize is or are brought into a port of the United Kingdom, the master or other person in charge or command of the ship which has been taken, or in which the goods are brought, shall, on arrival at such port, bring to at the proper place of discharge, and shall, when required by any officer of customs, deliver an account in writing under his hand concerning such ship and goods, giving such particulars relating thereto as may be in his power, and shall truly answer all questions concerning such ship or goods asked by

any such officer, and in default shall forfeit a sum not exceeding one hundred pounds, such forfeiture to be enforced as forfeitures for offences against the laws relating to the customs are enforced, and every such ship shall be liable to such searches as other ships are liable to, and the officers of the customs may freely go on board such ship and bring to the Queen's warehouse any goods on board the same, subject, nevertheless, to such regulations in respect of ships of war belonging to Her Majesty as shall from time to time be issued by the Commissioners of Her Majesty's Treasury.

49. Goods taken as prize may be sold either for home consumption or for exportation; and if in the former case the proceeds thereof, after payment of duties of customs, are insufficient to satisfy the just and reasonable claims thereon, the Commissioners of Her Majesty's Treasury may remit the whole or such part of the said duties as they see fit.

Perjury.

50. If any person wilfully and corruptly swears, declares, or affirms falsely in any prize cause or appeal, or in any proceeding under this Act, or in respect of any matter required by this Act to be verified on oath, or suborns any other person to do so, he shall be deemed guilty of perjury, or of subornation of perjury (as the case may be), and shall be liable to be punished accordingly.

Limitation of Actions, &c.

51. Any action or proceeding shall not lie in any part of Her Majesty's dominions against any person acting under the authority or in the execution or intended execution or in pursuance of this Act for any alleged irregularity or trespass, or other Act or thing done or omitted by him under this Act, unless notice in writing (specifying the cause of the action or proceeding) is given by the intending plaintiff or prosecutor to the intended defendant one month at least before the commencement of the action or proceeding, nor unless the action or proceeding is commenced within six months next after the act or thing complained of is done or omitted, or, in case of a continuation of damage within six months next after the doing of such damage has ceased.

In any such action the defendant may plead generally that the act or thing complained of was done or omitted by him when acting under the authority or in the execution or intended execution or in pursuance of this Act, and may give all special matter in evidence; and the plaintiff shall not succeed if tender of sufficient amends is made by the defendant before the commencement of the action; and in case no tender has been made, the defendant may, by leave of the Court in which the action is brought, at any time pay into Court such sum of money as he thinks fit, whereupon such proceeding and order shall be had and made in and by the Court as may be had and made on the payment of money into Court in an ordinary action; and if the plaintiff does not succeed in the action, the defendant shall receive such full and reasonable indemnity, as to all costs, charges and expenses incurred in and about the action as may be taxed and allowed by the proper officer subject to review; and though a verdict is given for the plaintiff in the action he shall not have costs against the defendant, unless the judge before whom the trial is had certifies his approval of the action.

Any such action or proceeding against any person in Her Majesty's naval service, or in the employment of the Lords of the Admiralty, shall not be brought or instituted elsewhere than in the United Kingdom.

Petitions of Right.

52. A petition of right, under The Petitions of Right Act 1860, may, if the suppliant thinks fit, be intituled in the High Court of Admiralty, in case the subject matter of the petition or any material part thereof arises out of the exercise of any belligerent right on behalf of the Crown, or would be cognizable in a Prize Court within Her Majesty's dominions if the same were a matter in dispute between private persons.

Any petition of right under The last-mentioned Act, whether intituled in the High Court of Admiralty or not, may be prosecuted in that Court, if the Lord Chancellor thinks fit so to direct.

The provisions of this Act relative to appeal, and to the framing and approval of general orders for regulating the procedure and practice of the High Court of Admiralty, shall extend to the case of any such petition of right intituled or directed to be prosecuted in that Court; and, subject thereto, all the provisions of The Petitions of Right Act, 1860, shall apply, *mutatis mutandis,* in the case of any such petition of right; and for the purposes of the present section the terms 'Court' and 'Judge' in that Act shall respectively be understood to include and to mean the High Court of Admiralty and the Judge thereof, and other terms shall have the respective meanings given to them in that Act.

Orders in Council.

53. Her Majesty in Council may from time to time make such Orders in Council as seem meet for the better execution of this Act.

54. Every Order in Council under this Act shall be published in the London Gazette, and shall be laid before both Houses of Parliament within thirty days after the making thereof, if Parliament is then sitting, and if not, then within thirty days after the next meeting of Parliament.

Savings.

55. Nothing in this Act shall—

(1) Give to the officers and crew of any of Her Majesty's ships of war any right or claim in or to any ship or goods taken as prize or the proceeds thereof, it being the intent of this Act that such officers and crews shall continue to take only such interest (if any) in the proceeds of prizes as may be from time to time granted to them by the Crown; or

(2) Affect the operation of any existing treaty or convention with any foreign Power; or

(3) Take away, or abridge the power of the Crown to enter into any treaty or convention with any foreign Power containing any stipulation that may seem meet concerning any matter to which this Act relates; or

(4) Take away, abridge, or control, further or otherwise than as expressly provided by this Act, any right, power, or prerogative of Her Majesty the Queen in right of Her Crown, or in right of her office of Admiralty, or any right or power of the Lord High Admiral of the United Kingdom, or of the Commissioners for executing the Office of Lord High Admiral; or

(5) Take away abridge, or control further or otherwise than as expressly provided by this Act, the jurisdiction or authority of a Prize Court to take cognizance of and judicially proceed upon any capture, seizure, prize, or reprisal of any ship or goods, and to hear and determine the same, and according to the course of Admiralty and the law of nations, to adjudge and condemn any ship or goods, or any other jurisdiction or authority of or exercisable by a Prize Court.

Commencement.

56. This Act shall commence on the commencement of the Naval Agency and Distribution Act, 1864.

II.

27 & 28 Vict., C. 24.

"An Act to provide for the appointment, duties, and remuneration of agents for ships of war, and for the distribution of salvage, bounty, prize, and other money among the officers and crews thereof."—Passed 23rd June, 1864.

Be it enacted, &c.

Preliminary.

1. This Act may be cited as the Naval Agency and Distribution Act, 1864.

2. In this Act—

The term 'the Lords of the Admiralty' means the Lord High Admiral of the United Kingdom, or the Commissioners for executing the office of Lord High Admiral.

The term 'the High Court of Admiralty' means the High Court of Admiralty of England.

The term 'ship of war' includes vessel of war.

The term 'officers and crew' includes all flag officers, commanders, and other officers, engineers, seamen, marines, soldiers, and others on board any of Her Majesty's ships of war.

3. Any ship or vessel belonging to Her Majesty, and in actual service (other than a ship of war), may be declared by the Lords of the Admiralty to be a ship of war for the purposes of this Act; and all the provisions of this Act shall thereupon apply to such ship or vessel, and shall continue to so apply, as long as she then continues in actual service, but no longer.

Appointment of Ship's Agent.

4. Each of Her Majesty's ships of war shall at all times while in commission have, for the purposes of this Act, an agent styled the ship's agent, to be appointed in the first instance as soon as may be after the ship is put in commission, and afterwards from time to time as a vacancy in the office or other occasion may require.

5. The ship's agent shall be appointed from time to time at pleasure by the commanding officer of the ship for the time being, by an instrument signed and attested in the form given in the schedule to this Act.

6. Any such instrument shall not have effect unless and until it is filed in the registry of the High Court of Admiralty, having been previously registered in the office of the Accountant-General of the Navy.

An official copy of any such instrument under the seal of the High Court of Admiralty shall be conclusive evidence thereof.

7. A person holding any office or employment in Her Majesty's service or under the crown, or a proctor, attorney, or solicitor, shall not be capable of being a ship's agent.

If any person being a ship's agent accepts any such office or employment, or becomes a proctor, attorney, or solicitor, his appointment as ship's agent shall be thereby vacated.

8. A partnership body, not incorporated, may be appointed a ship's agent; and in that case the partners for the time being, or any one or

more of them, may act as the agent; and any change of partners shall not affect the appointment.

The names of the partners shall at the time of appointment, and from time to time on any change happening, be registered in the office of the Accountant-General of the Navy, and in the registry of the High Court of Admiralty.

9. The appointment of the ship's agent shall not be affected by a change of the commanding officer of the ship.

10. The ship's agent shall at all times have an office or place of business within five miles of the General Post Office, London.

11. The ship's agent shall be subject to the jurisdiction and authority of the High Court of Admiralty as if he were an officer of the Court, and in case of any neglect or misconduct on his part shall be liable to be proceeded against and punished accordingly.

Duties of Ship's Agents.

12. It shall be the duty of the ship's agent, by himself or by a proper sub-agent appointed and remunerated by him, to take or cause or procure to be taken all steps and proceedings, and do or cause or procure to be done all things, that may be necessary or proper to be taken or done for any purpose on behalf or in the name of the ship or of the officers and crew thereof, or any of them, in the several cases following.

In case of salvage services rendered to any ship or cargo, or otherwise, within the meaning of the enactments for the time being in force relating to merchant shipping:

In case of any breach of any law respecting national character or otherwise relating to merchant shipping:

In case of any seizure for breach of any law relating to the customs:

In case of any seizure or capture under any Act relating to the abolition of slave-trade:

In case of any matter arising out of an attack on or engagement with persons alleged to be pirates, afloat or on shore:

In case of any capture, re-capture, or destruction of any ship, goods or thing in time of war or hostilities:

In case of any special service or other matter in respect whereof any grant, reward, or remuneration is payable.

Distribution of Salvage, Bounty, Prize and other Money.

13. Where in any of the several cases aforesaid any money is distributable among the officers and crew of any of Her Majesty's ships of war, the costs, charges and expenses of the officers and crew and of the ship's agent, and all other (if any) costs, charges, or expenses properly

chargeable against that money, shall be paid thereout before distribution thereof, all such costs, charges, and expenses being first taxed and allowed by the proper officer of the Court having jurisdiction in the case, and if there is no such Court, then by the registrar of the High Court of Admiralty.

14. In the several cases aforesaid, money distributable among the officers and crew of any of Her Majesty's ships of war, so far as full provision respecting the distribution thereof is not made by or under any Act of Parliament other than this Act, shall be distributed under the direction of the Lords of the Admiralty in the shares in that behalf specified in any royal proclamation or Order in Council.

15. The several shares of any such money as aforesaid shall be paid to the persons entitled thereto in such manner, and subject and according to such restrictions, conditions, and provisions, as may from time to time be directed by Order in Council.

Any assignment, sale or contract of or relating to any such money as aforesaid, payable in respect of the services of any petty officer or seaman, non-commissioned officer of Marines or Marine, other than such as may be made or entered into under the authority of and in conformity with any such Order in Council, shall be void.

16. All bills, orders, receipts, and other instruments drawn, given, or made under the authority or in pursuance of any such Order in Council by, to, or upon any officer or person in the service of Her Majesty or of the Lords of the Admiralty, shall be exempt from stamp duty.

17. All forfeited and unclaimed shares and balances of prize money, and a per-centage of five pounds in every one hundred pounds out of the proceeds of all prizes, and out of all grants to the Royal Navy and Marines, and out of all bounty money, and also out of all other money distributable in the several cases aforesaid among the officers and crew of any of Her Majesty's ships of war out of which such per-centage is at the commencement of this Act by law deducted, shall, under the direction of the Lords of the Admiralty, continue to be carried to and to form part of the naval prize cash balance.

So much of the naval prize cash balance as the Lords of the Admiralty think expedient shall from time to time by Her Majesty's Paymaster General, under the authority and direction of the Lords of the Admiralty, be paid and transferred to the Consolidated Fund of the United Kingdom.

In case at any time a claim in respect of prize or bounty money is made which the naval prize cash balance is not sufficiently to meet, there shall be paid out of the said Consolidated Fund a sufficient sum to meet such claim.

18. A ship's agent shall be entitled, on request, and on payment of reasonable expenses, to be furnished with copies of or extracts from any

official accounts kept under or for the purposes of this Act in relation to any of Her Majesty's ships of war for which he is agent.

Remuneration of Ship's Agent.

19. Before any such money as aforesaid is distributed among the officers and crew of any of Her Majesty's ships of war, there shall be paid, under the direction of the Lords of the Admiralty, to the ship's agent a per-centage of two and half per centum on the net amount actually distributable, as the sole and full remuneration of the ship's agent for his services in the case.

20. In the following cases :—

Where more than one of Her Majesty's ships of war are entitled to participate in any such money,—

Where the ship's agent is changed pending proceedings,—

The ships agent's per-centage shall, in case of difference, be apportioned between or among the respective agents of the several ships, or the several persons having been and being the ship's agent (as the case may be), in such manner as the Registrar of the High Court of Admiralty thinks just, having regard to the duration and character of the services of the several agents in the case, subject to objection to the Registrar's award to be taken before the Judge of the Court.

Investment of Salvage, Bounty, Prize, and other Money.

21. Any money for the time being awaiting distribution, but for any reason not immediately distributable as aforesaid, may under the direction of the Lords of the Admiralty, be invested in or on any proper stocks, funds, or securities ; and the proceeds of those stocks, funds, or securities, and any dividends or interest accrued due thereon, shall be distributed as the money invested would have been distributed if an investment had not been made :

Provided that no such investment shall be made of any money pending any adverse claim thereto, except with the consent of the claimant.

Decision as to Distribution or Investment.

22. Where any question (whether in respect of asserted joint capture, or in respect of flag shares, or in respect of any other matter) arises concerning the distribution of any money distributable as aforesaid or concerning any investment thereof, actual or intended, the High Court of Admiralty shall have exclusive jurisdiction to hear and determine the same; and any person, claiming and interest in such money, or the Lords of the Admiralty, may apply to the High Court of Admiralty for a judgment on that question ; and the Court, after hearing the parties interested, shall decide thereon, and such decision shall be final, and shall be binding on all persons concerned.

Miscellaneous.

23.—Nothing in this Act shall,—

(1) Authorize a ship's agent or his sub-agent to practise or act as a proctor, attorney, solicitor, or other legal practitioner in any Court; or

(2) Affect the right or power of the officers and crew of any of Her Majesty's ships of war as salvors, seizors, captors, re-captors, or otherwise, or of any of such officers and crew, to take or cause or procure to be taken any step or proceeding, or do or cause or procure to be done any thing, that may be necessary or proper to be taken or done for any purpose in any Court or elsewhere, in case of the absence or default of the ship's agent; or

(3) Affect any right or power of control, or other authority, that Her Majesty has or may exercise in any prize cause or other proceeding.

24.—Nothing in this Act shall invalidate an appointment of an agent made before the commencement of this Act under The Navy Prize Agents Act, 1863; but every agent so appointed shall, from the commencement of this Act, be subject to this Act as if he were appointed under it.

25.—Her Majesty in Council may from time to time make such orders as seem meet for the better execution of this Act.

26.—Every Order in Council under this Act shall be published in the London Gazette, and shall be laid before both Houses of Parliament within thirty days after the making thereof, if Parliament is then sitting, and if not, then within thirty days after the next meeting of Parliament.

27.—This Act shall commence on such day, not later than the first day of January One thousand eight hundred and sixty five, as Her Majesty in Council thinks fit to direct.

Form of Appointment of Ship's Agent.

I, * Commanding Officer of Her Majesty's † hereby appoint ‡ of ‖ to be the Ship's Agent for the purposes of The Naval Agency and Distribution Act, 1864.

Dated the Day of (Signed) *A. B.*

Witness, (Signed) *C. D.*

* Name of Officer.

† Description and Name of Ship.

‡ Name of Agent.

‖ Address of Agent.

Appendix D.

TERRITORIAL WATERS OF THE BRITISH EMPIRE.

I

Territorial Waters Jurisdiction Act.

41 & 42 Vict. C. 73. (16 August 1878.)

In the case (A.D. 1876) of Regina v. Keyn, known as the Franconia case,* the prisoner was a foreigner in command of a foreign ship on a voyage from one foreign port to another. Whilst passing within three miles of the English coast, his ship ran into a British ship and sank her. A passenger on board the British ship was drowned, and the prisoner, having been indicted at the Central Criminal Court, was found guilty of manslaughter. The question whether that Court had jurisdiction, was reserved for the Court for Crown Cases Reserved.

After the case had been twice argued, it was holden by a majority of one,† that the Central Criminal Court had no jurisdiction to try the prisoner for the offence charged. ‡

In consequence of the decision in this case, an Act was passed in the session of 1878, which, after a preamble reciting that "the rightful jurisdiction of Her Majesty, her heirs and successors extends and has always extended over the open seas adjacent to the coasts of the United Kingdom, and of all other parts of Her Majesty's dominions to such a distance as is necessary for the defence and security of such dominions," and that "it is expedient that all offences committed on the open sea within a certain distance of the coasts of the United Kingdom and of all other parts of Her Majesty's dominions, by whomsoever committed, should be dealt with according to law," proceeds to enact as follows:—

1. This Act may be cited as the Territorial Waters Jurisdiction Act, 1878.

---

* Law Reports, 2 Ex. Div., p. 63.

† The majority consisted of Cockburn, C. J., Kelly, C.B., Bramwell, J. A., Lush and Field, J. J., Sir R. Phillimore and Pollock, B.; the dissentients were Lord Coleridge, C. J., Brett and Amphlett, J. J. A., Grove, Denman, and Lindley. J. J., Archibald, J., agreed with the majority, but died before the judgment was delivered.

‡ See Judgment given by Sir Robert Phillimore, Law Reports, 2 Ex. Div. p. 81.

2. An offence committed by a person, whether he is or is not a subject of Her Majesty, on the open sea within the territorial waters of Her Majesty's dominions, is an offence within the jurisdiction of the Admiral, although it may have been committed on board or by means of a foreign ship, and the person who committed such offence may be arrested, tried, and punished accordingly.

3. Proceedings for the trial and punishment of a person who is not a subject of Her Majesty, and who is charged with any such offence as is declared by this Act to be within the jurisdiction of the Admiral, shall not be instituted in any Court of the United Kingdom, except with the consent of one of Her Majesty's Principal Secretaries of State, and on his certificate that the institution of such proceedings is in his opinion expedient, and shall not be instituted in any of the dominions of Her Majesty out of the United Kingdom, except with the leave of the Governor of the part of the dominions in which such proceedings are proposed to be instituted, and on his certificate that it is expedient that such proceedings should be instituted.

4. On the trial of any person who is not a subject of Her Majesty for an offence declared by this Act to be within the jurisdiction of the Admiral, it shall not be necessary to aver in any indictment or information on such trial that such consent or certificate of the Secretary of State or Governor as is required by this Act has been given, and the fact of the same having been given shall be presumed, unless disputed by the defendant at the trial; and the production of a document purporting to be signed by one of Her Majesty's Principal Secretaries of State as respects the United Kingdom, and by the Governor as respects any other part of Her Majesty's dominions, and containing such consent and certificate, shall be sufficient evidence for all the purposes of this Act of the consent and certificate required by this Act.

Proceedings before a justice of the peace or other magistrate previous to the committal of an offender for trial or to the determination of the justice or magistrate that the offender is to be put upon his trial, shall not be deemed proceedings for the trial of the offence committed by such offender for the purposes of the said consent and certificate under this Act.

5. Nothing in this Act contained shall be construed to be in derogation of any rightful jurisdiction of Her Majesty, her heirs or successors, under the Law of Nations, or to affect or prejudice any jurisdiction conferred by Act of Parliament or now by law existing in relation to foreign ships or in relation to persons on board such ships.

6. This Act shall not prejudice or affect the trial in manner heretofore in use of any act of piracy as defined by the Laws of Nations, or affect or prejudice any law relating thereto; and where any act of piracy as defined by the Law of Nations is also any such offence as is declared by this Act to be within the jurisdiction of the Admiral, such

offence may be tried in pursuance of this Act, or in pursuance of another Act of Parliament, law, or custom relating thereto.

In this Act, unless there is something inconsistent in the context, the following expressions shall respectfully have the meanings hereinafter assigned to them, that is to say—

The jurisdiction of the Admiral, as used in this Act, includes the jurisdiction of the Admiralty of England and Ireland, or either of such jurisdictions as used in any Act of Parliament; and for the purpose of arresting any person charged with an offence declared by this Act to be within the jurisdiction of the Admiral, the territorial waters adjacent to the United Kingdom, or any other part of Her Majesty's dominions, shall be deemed to be within the jurisdiction of any judge, magistrate, or officer having power within such United Kingdom, or other part of Her Majesty's dominions, to issue warrants for arresting or to arrest persons charged with offences committed within the jurisdiction of such judge, magistrate, or officer.

United Kingdom includes the Isle of Man, the Channel Islands and other adjacent islands.

The territorial waters of Her Majesty's dominions, in reference to the sea, means such part of the sea adjacent to the coast of the United Kingdom, or the coast of some other part of Her Majesty's dominions, as is deemed by International Law to be within the territorial sovereignty of Her Majesty; and for the purpose of any offence declared by this Act to be within the jurisdiction of the Admiral, any part of the open sea within one marine league of the coast measured from low-water mark shall be deemed to be open sea within the territorial waters of Her Majesty's dominions.

Governor, as respects India, means the Governor-General or the Governor of any Presidency; and where a British possession consists of several constituent colonies, means the Governor-General of the whole possession or the Governor of any of the constituent colonies; and as respects any other British possession, means the officer for the time being administering the government of such possession; also any person acting for in the capacity of Governor shall be included under the term 'Governor':

'Offence' as used in this Act means an act, neglect, or default of such a description as would, if committed within the body of a county in England, be punishable on indictment according to the law of England for the time being in force. 'Ship' includes every description of ship, boat, or other floating craft. 'Foreign ship' means any ship which is not a British ship.

It is hardly necessary to state, says Sir Robert Phillimore, that this Statute does not affect the general International Law on the subject. *

* Sir ROBERT PHILLIMORE. Com. International Law, Vol. I. Edit. 1879, p. 283.

II.

Discussions in the British House of Lords with regard to the Territorial Waters Jurisdiction.

(Extracts from the 'Times,' February 15th, 1878.)

The Lord Chancellor rose to call the attention of the House to the question of the jurisdiction of the Crown in the territorial waters of the empire, more especially with reference to the recent case of the 'Franconia,'* and to present a bill on the subject. The jurisdiction to which he had to call attention was not over rivers, bays, or harbours, because in respect of that no controversy had ever arisen, but the jurisdiction over the territorial waters in that belt or zone of the high seas which more or less surrounded the shores of the Empire. This, at first sight, would appear to be a question of law. No doubt it was a question of law, but he rather thought of that which had been described as the first law of nature—the law of self-preservation. It was necessary, to some extent and in some measure, that there should be a territorial jurisdiction over the high seas surrounding the sea-board. No empire which had a sea-board could be allowed to remain without some jurisdiction of that kind. If in the case of such an empire it was held that the jurisdiction of the kingdom ended with the dry land, the consequence would be that the subjects of that kingdom in the presence of foreigners would be absolutely without defence from the moment they entered the sea for the purpose of bathing, or fishing, or for any other purpose. Not only so, but when on dry land they would be without protection, because if no jurisdiction from the land extended to the sea surrounding the sea-board, people from all parts of the world might come to the part of the high sea contiguous to the land and resort to practices which might be of the most serious character to people on shore. So, again, in the case of war, hostilities carried on by belligerents outside the shore might expose a neutral Power to the greatest danger. It might be asked whether the question was not solved, so far, at all events, as to the low water mark to which unquestionably the territorial jurisdiction extended. With regard to the low water mark, it must be remembered that there were parts of the coasts where there were considerable intervals between high and low water mark, and also there were in the kingdom, as their lordships knew, many places where the sea came so close to the cliffs that there was absolutely no horizontal interval between high and low water marks. It had been suggested, or might be suggested, that if the jurisdiction of this country extended over the part of the high seas immediately adjoining the shore, inasmuch as the right of passage over that part was allowed to foreign ships, it

* Regina v. Keyn. See No. I of this Appendix.

would be unfair to claim such a jurisdiction as against them. He was quite willing to concede the right of passage contended for, but he had imagined that it was to be conceded on this footing and this footing only,—that those who availed themselves of the right of passage should not expose themselves to any complaint of a violation of the rights of those by whom the right of passage was conceded. In truth, any such exemption would apply to the case of foreign ships coming into one of our bays. What made it necessary for him to bring this matter under the notice of their lordships was a case of considerable interest—that of the collision between the 'Franconia' and the 'Strathclyde' off Dover, by which a number of persons lost their lives. [His Lordship here gave a short history of the facts]. He would endeavour to explain what he understood to be the main ground of the judgment of the majority of the judges in the 'Franconia' case. But before he did so, there was an incident which he wished to mention to their lordships. One of the learned judges, for whom they all had the greatest respect, and whose judgment, from his experience in criminal cases, was of the greatest weight—Mr. Justice Lush—stated that though he concurred with the Lord Chief Justice in that learned judge's view of the case, yet he wished to guard himself in this particular case with respect to the limits of the high seas. He said—

"I wish to guard myself being supposed to adopt any words or expressions which may seem to imply a doubt as to the competency of Parliament to legislate as it may think fit for these waters. I think that usage and the common consent of Nations, which constitute International Law, have appropriated these waters to the adjacent State to deal with them as the State may deem expedient for its own interests. They are, therefore, in the language of diplomacy and of International Law, termed by a convenient metaphor the territorial waters of Great Britain, and the same or equivalent phrases are used in some of our statutes, denoting that the belt of sea is under the exclusive dominion of the State. But the dominion is the dominion of Parliament, not the dominion of Common Law . . . Therefore, although, as between Nation and Nation these waters are British territory, as being under the exclusive dominion of Great Britain, in judicial language they are out of the realm, and any exercise of criminal jurisdiction over a foreign ship in these waters must, in my judgment, be authorized by any Act of Parliament."

As he understood these words, if Sir Robert Lush had found that in the particular place Parliament had stepped in and said that portion of the water was part of the United Kingdom, we would have been of opinion that the Crown had territorial jurisdiction over it, and the conviction ought not to be quashed. It was fortunate for the prisoner in the 'Franconia' case, though not fortunate for the vindication of the law, that Mr. Justice Lush was under the impression that that had not been done which really had been done. It appeared that in an Act of

1848, for the regulation of Customs, there was a provision authorizing the Lords of the Treasury to establish ports in many places where ports were required, and to define their limits. Under that provision the Lords of the Treasury issued a warrant, which was inserted in the London Gazette of the 3rd of March, 1848. In that warrant were these paragraphs:—

'That the limits of the port of Dover shall commence at St. Margaret's Bay aforesaid, and continue along the said coast of Kent to Copt Point in the said county. That the limits of the port of Folkestone shall commence at Copt Point aforesaid, and continue along the coast to Dungeness, in the said county. And we, the said Commissioners of Her Majesty's Treasury, do further declare that the limits seaward of the said ports shall extend to a distance of three miles from low water mark out to sea, and that the limits of such ports shall include all islands, bays, harbours, rivers, and creeks within the same respectively.'

So that under Parliamentary powers the proper authorities had declared long before the 'Franconia' case that the limits of the port of Dover extended three miles out to sea. We understood the view of the majority of the judges to be this, that there was one jurisdiction by land and the other by sea; that the jurisdiction by land was one limited by the limits of counties, taking into the county the low water mark and the harbours and rivers within the county; and the jurisdiction by sea, the old jurisdiction of the Lord High Admiral now exercised by the Central Criminal Court; that the jurisdiction of the Lord High Admiral extended to the high seas, but the persons over whom it was exercised must be British subjects, not foreigners; and that the Central Criminal Court had no jurisdiction over the persons of foreigners beyond the low water mark. That he understood to be the common ground on which the majority of the judges acted in quashing the conviction. And taking that as the *ratio decidendi* of the judges in a decision which he accepted, it would at first sight appear that there was nothing more for him to do than to ask the favourable consideration of their lordships for a bill to amend the law; but there fell some observations from Sir Robert Phillimore, the Lord Chief Baron, and the Lord Chief Justice, whose judgment was the most elaborate, and might be regarded as the leading judgment of the majority, and which contained a principle that seemed to challenge the right of Parliament to legislate on this subject. Expressions of the Lord Chief Justice would certainly seem to imply that we could not legislate with respect to the high seas even within the limits of the belt or zone to which he had referred without the consent of foreign Nations, or until after communication with foreign Nations. That was a very serious question. If the judgments of those learned judges amounted, as they were supposed to do, to a proposition of that kind, of course Parliament would be exceeding its powers if it entered into legislation applying to that belt or zone with the view of making foreigners amenable to our law. But he would ask their lordships to consider whether there was any foundation for that principle. He ventured to think there was not, and he thought it would be a very serious thing if they were. He would lay before their lordships the views of great constitutional writers of this Kingdom and of the United States on this question. Then he would add the views of international jurists on the continent, and next he would show what our own judges had ruled in international cases, and lastly he would direct attention to what their lordships themselves had done in the course of legislation. [His Lordship here referred to the principal English, American, and foreign writers on International Law]. It appeared to be established as a matter of principle that there must be a zone. The only doubt was as to show how far our limits extend. The authorities were clear on this—that if three miles were not found sufficient for the purpose of defence and protection, or if the nature of the trade or commerce in the zone required it, there was a power in the country on the sea-board to extend the zone; but at present there was a consensus of opinion among the authorities that certainly the jurisdiction extended to three miles. If that were not the established law, Nations with a sea-board would be very much worse off than those which had none, because a neighbour on land you could make a treaty with or treat as any enemy, but if a Nation with a sea-board had no control over a zone it would always be liable to dangerous aggression from beyond the sea. (Hear, hear.)

He would now refer their lordships to judicial opinion. In a case in which Prussia claimed restitution of a ship seized by an English man-of-war within three miles of Prussian territory, Lord Stowell said:—

A claim has been given for the Prussian Government, asserting the capture to have been made within the Prussian territory. It has been contended that, although the act of capture itself might not have taken place within the neutral territory, yet that the ship to which the capturing boats belonged was actually lying within the neutral limits. The first fact to be determined is the character of the place where the capturing ship lay, whether she was actually stationed within those portions of land and water, or of something between water and land, which are considered to be within Prussian territory. She was lying within the eastern branch of the Ems, within what I think may be considered at a distance of three miles at most from East Friesland. I am of opinion that the ship was lying within those limits in which all direct operations are by the Law of Nations forbidden to be exercised. No proximate acts of war are in any manner to be allowed to originate on neutral ground, and I cannot but think that such an act as this, that a ship should station herself on neutral territory and send out her boats on hostile enterprises, is an act of hostility much too immediate to be permitted. The capture cannot be maintained.

In another case—that of the 'Maria'—Lord Stowell said:—

It might likewise be improper for me to pass over entirely without notice, as another preliminary observation, though without meaning to lay any particular stress on it, that the transaction in question took place in the British Channel, close upon the British coast, a station over which the Crown of England has from pretty remote antiquity always asserted something of that special jurisdiction which the sovereigns of other countries have claimed and exercised over certain parts of the seas adjoining to their coasts.

He would now refer their lordships to an opinion expressed by Sir John Nicholl, on a claim by a lord of a manor to goods derelict. Sir John said:—

"As to the right of the lord extending three miles beyond low water, it is quite extravagant as a jurisdiction belonging to any manor. As between Nation and Nation, the territorial right may, by a sort of tacit understanding, be extended to three miles; but that rests upon different principles—viz., that their own subjects shall not be disturbed in their fishing, and particularly in their coasting trade and communications between place and place during the war. They would be exposed to danger, if hostilities were allowed to be carried on between belligerents nearer to the shore than three miles."

A case occurred when the Duke of Wellington held the office now held by his noble friend (Earl Granville). In 1829, within three miles of one of the Cinque Ports, some fishermen at sea were fortunate enough to discover a whale valued at £370. A claim to the fish was made by the Lord Warden, and the Admiralty claimed against him. The learned Judge who tried the question came to the conclusion that the office of Lord Warden of the Cinque Ports was more ancient than that of Lord High Admiral, and the Lord Warden of the Cinque Ports succeeded in carrying away the whale. What were the views of Dr. Lushington? He said:—

"What are the limits of the United Kingdom? The only answer I can conceive to that question is—the land of the United Kingdom and three miles from the shore."

Again, the same learned Judge, speaking on the question of compulsory pilotage, said:—

The Parliament of Great Britain, it is true, has not, according to the principles of public law, any authority to legislate for foreign vessels on the high seas, or for foreigners out of the limits of British jurisdiction; though, if Parliament thought fit to do so, this Court, in its instance of jurisdiction at least, would be bound to obey. In cases admitting of doubt, the presumption would be that Parliament intended to legislate without violating any rule of International Law, and the construction has been accordingly. Within, however, British jurisdiction, namely, within British territory, and at sea, within three miles from the coast, and, within all British rivers *intra fauces*, and over foreigners in British ships, I apprehend that the British Parliament has an undoubted right to legislate.

Then he would add to that the opinion of the late Lord Wensleydale in that House, in Gemmell v. The Commissioners of Woods and Forests, a well known Scotch salmon fishery case :—

It may be worth while to observe that it would be hardly possible to extend to seaward beyond the distance of three miles, which, by the acknowledged law of Nations, belongs to the coast of the country, is under the dominion of the country by being within cannon range, and so capable of being kept in perpetual possession.

In advising that House in another case, a noble and learned friend (Lord Chelmsford), whom he was glad to see there to-night, and who held the office which he (the Lord Chancellor) had the honour to hold, said :—

The three miles limit depends upon a rule of International Law, by which every independent State is considered to have territorial property and jurisdiction in the seas which wash their coast within the assumed distance of a cannon shot from the shore.

He would add to that the opinion expressed by another noble and learned friend of his (Lord Hatherley), whom he was also glad to see there. His noble and learned friend, in the case of a collision between a foreign and a British ship, said :—With respect to foreign ships, I shall adhere to the opinion which I expressed in "Cope v. Doherty," that a foreign ship meeting a British ship on the open ocean cannot properly be abridged of her rights by an Act of the British Legislature. Then comes the question, how far our Legislature could properly affect the rights of foreign ships within the limits of three miles from the coast of this country. There can be no possible doubt that the water below low water mark is part of the high sea. But it is equally beyond question that for certain purposes every country may, by the common Law of Nations, exercise jurisdiction over that portion of the high seas which lies within three miles from its shores.

In the case of the Free Fisheries of "Whitstable v. Gann," Sir William Erle said:—

The soil of the sea-shore to the extent of three miles from the beach is vested in the Crown.

Now, these were the opinions—and as far as he was aware there was no opinion in the other way—of the eminent judges who had considered this subject. He said he would inform their Lordships what had been done in the way of legislation. He might refer their Lordships to many Acts of Parliament, but he would only refer to one. He would take the last edition of the Foreign Enlistment Act. That was an Act which, if the words 'deliberation and care,' might ever be applied to the passing of an Act, might be applied to the passing of it. It was brought forward by the Government of the day under the advice of its legal advisers. It had also the gravest consideration from many persons outside the Government. What that Act did was this: it provided that this Act shall extend to all the dominions of Her Majesty, including the adjacent territorial waters. He had troubled their lordships with these references because he felt bound, after the doubts supposed to be cast on the question, to establish the position that their lordships were entitled to legislate as he proposed. The right which we claimed over the high seas was a right which we had always exercised, and he asked their lordships to pass an Act for the purpose of obviating the doubts he had pointed out. Her Majesty's Government did not wish to make any new enactment as regarded the case of British subjects within the territorial waters of this country. No person doubted the full jurisdiction of the Crown over them. It was only in the case of those who were not British subjects that doubts had been expressed. With regard to those who might be foreigners, and temporarily within the three-mile limit, Her Majesty's Government wished that there should not be an absolute necessity of proceeding against them for a breach of our law. They proposed to enact that an offence committed by a person who was not a subject of Her Majesty on the open sea within the territorial waters of Her Majesty's dominions, although the offence might have been committed on board a foreign ship, might, with the consent of one of the principal Secretaries of State, be tried by a British tribunal. He asked their lordships to read the Bill a first time, and he proposed the second reading for this day week.

Lord Selborne said, that as far as the case connected with the 'Franconia' proceeded on a technical ground for the trial of a criminal offence on the high seas, within the territorial waters of this country, he did not profess to entertain an opinion which would entitle him to criticise the judgment of the majority of the Judges; but he must say that on reading that judgment some doubt was entertained as to the existence in principle of the territorial right properly so-called in the sovereign of this country over waters which all writers on International Law had regarded as territorial waters. It was by the general consent of Nations that the three-mile limit had been fixed, and within that limit other Nations claimed exactly the same jurisdiction and rights that we ourselves claimed. The Bill proposed, very properly, to assert our right to punish criminal offences committed within that limit, and much prudence was shown in not seeking to extend by this measure our jurisdiction for this purpose beyond the three-mile limit. It had been argued that, in consequence of the increase in the range of artillery, that limit should be extended to five or even six miles; but although that might be a very sensible alteration to make in International Law, it should only be affected by the general consent of all Nations.

Appendix E.

FOREIGN ENLISTMENT ACT, 1870.

33 & 34 Vict. C. 90.

An Act to regulate the conduct of Her Majesty's subjects during the existence of hostilities between foreign States with which Her Majesty is at peace. (9th August, 1870).

Whereas it is expedient to make provision for the regulation of the conduct of Her Majesty's subjects during the existence of hostilities between foreign States with which Her Majesty is at peace.

Be it enacted by the Queen's most Excellent Majesty, by and with the advice and consent of the Lords Spiritual and Temporal, and Commons, in this present Parliament assembled, and by the authority of the same, as follows :

Preliminary.

Short title of Act. 1. This Act may be cited for all purposes as "The Foreign Enlistment Act, 1870."

Application of Act. 2. This Act shall extend to all the dominions of Her Majesty, including the adjacent territorial waters.

Commencement of Act. 3. This Act shall come into operation in the United Kingdom immediately on the passing thereof, and shall be proclaimed in every British possession by the Governor thereof as soon as may be after he receives notice of this Act, and shall come into operation in that British possession on the day of such proclamation, and the time at which this Act comes into operation in any place is, as respects such place, in this Act referred to as the commencement of this Act.

Illegal Enlistment.

Penalty on enlistment in service of a foreign State. 4. If any person, without the license of Her Majesty, being a British subject, within or without Her Majesty's dominions, accepts or agrees to accept any commission or engagement in the military or naval service of any foreign State at war with any foreign State at peace with Her Majesty, and in this Act referred to as a friendly State, or whether a British subject or not within Her Majesty's dominions, induces any other person to accept or agree to accept any commission or engagement in the military or naval service of any such foreign State as aforesaid,—

He shall be guilty of an offence against this Act, and shall be punishable by fine and imprisonment, or either of such punishments, at the discretion of the Court before which the offender is convicted; and imprisonment, if awarded, may be either with or without hard labour.

Penalty on leaving Her Majesty's dominions with intent to serve a foreign State.

5. If any person, without the license of Her Majesty being a British subject, quits or goes on board any ship with a view of quitting Her Majesty's dominions, with intent to accept any commission or engagement in the military or naval service of any foreign state at war with a friendly State, or, whether a British subject or not, within Her Majesty's dominions, induces any other person to quit or to go on board any ship with a view of quitting Her Majesty's dominions with the like intent,—

He shall be guilty of an offence against this Act, and shall be punishable by fine and imprisonment, or either of such punishments, at the discretion of the Court before which the offender is convicted; and imprisonment, if awarded, may be either with or without hard labour.

Penalty on embarking persons under false representations as to service.

6. If any person induces any other person to quit Her Majesty's dominions or to embark on any ship within Her Majesty's dominions under a misrepresentation or false representation of the service in which such person is to be engaged, with the intent or in order that such person may accept or agree to accept any commission or engagement in the military or naval service of any foreign State at war with a friendly State,—

He shall be guilty of an offence against this Act, and shall be punishable by fine and imprisonment, or either of such punishments, at the discretion of the Court before which the offender is convicted; and imprisonment, if awarded, may be either with or without hard labour.

Penalty on taking illegally enlisted persons on board ship.

7. If the master or owner of any ship, without the license of Her Majesty, knowingly either takes on board or engages to take on board, or has on board such ship within Her Majesty's dominions any of the following persons in this Act referred to as illegally enlisted persons; that is to say,

(1.) Any person who, being a British subject, within or without the dominions of Her Majesty, has, without the license of Her Majesty, accepted or agreed to accept any commission or engagement in the military or naval service of any foreign State at war with any friendly State:

(2.) Any person, being a British subject, who, without the license of Her Majesty, is about to quit Her Majesty's dominions with intent to accept any commission or engagement in the military or naval service of any foreign State at war with a friendly State:

(3.) Any person who has been induced to embark under a misrepresentation or false representation of the service in which such person is to be engaged, with the intent or in order that such person may accept or agree to accept any commission or engagement in the military or naval service of any foreign State at war with a frienly State:

Such master or owner shall be guilty of an offence against this Act, and the following consequences shall ensue; that is to say,—

(1.) The offender shall be punishable by fine and imprisonment, or either of such punishments, at the discretion of the Court before which the offender is convicted; and imprisonment, if awarded, may be either with or without hard labour; and

(2.) Such ship shall be detained until the trial and conviction or acquittal of the master or owner, and until all penalties inflicted on the master or owner have been paid, or the master or owner has given security for the payment of such penalties to the satisfaction of two justices of the peace, or other magistrate or magistrates having the authority of two justices of the peace; and

(3.) All illegally enlisted persons shall immediately on the discovery of the offence be taken on shore, and shall not be allowed to return to the ship.

Illegal Shipbuilding and Illegal Expedition.

Penalty on illegal ship-building and illegal expeditions.

8. If any person within Her Majesty's dominions, without the license of Her Majesty, does any of the following acts; that is to say,—

(1.) Builds or agrees to build, or causes to be built any ship with intent or knowledge, or having reasonable cause to believe, that the same shall or will be employed in the military or naval service of any foreign State at war with any friendly State; or

(2.) Issues or delivers any commission for any ship with intent or knowledge, or having reasonable cause to believe that the same shall or will be employed in the military or naval service of any foreign State at war with any friendly State; or

(3.) Equips any ship with intent or knowledge, or having reasonable cause to believe that the same shall or will be employed in the military or naval service of any foreign State at war with any friendly State; or

(4.) Despatches, or causes or allows to be despatched, any ship with intent or knowledge, or having reasonable cause to believe that the same shall or will be employed in the military or naval service of any foreign State at war with any friendly State:

Such person shall be deemed to have committed an offence against this Act, and the following consequences shall ensue:

(1.) The offender shall be punishable by fine and imprisonment, or either of such punishments, at the discretion of the Court before which the offender is convicted; and imprisonment, if awarded, may be either with or without hard labour.

(2.) The ship in respect of which any such offence is committed, and her equipment, shall be forfeited to Her Majesty:

Provided that a person building, causing to be built, or equipping a ship in any of the cases aforesaid, in pursuance of a contract made before the commencement of such war as aforesaid, shall not be liable to any of the penalties imposed by this section in respect of such building or equipping if he satisfies the conditions following; (that is to say),

(1.) If forthwith, upon a proclamation of neutrality being issued by Her Majesty, he gives notice to the Secretary of State that he is so building, causing to be built, or equipping such ship, and furnishes such particulars of the contract and of any matters relating to, or done, or to be done under the contract as may be required by the Secretary of State.

(2.) If he gives such security, and takes and permits to be taken such other measures, if any, as the Secretary of State may prescribe for ensuring that such ship shall not be despatched, delivered, or removed without the license of Her Majesty until the termination of such war as aforesaid.

Presumption as to evidence in case of illegal ship.

9. Where any ship is built by order of or on behalf of any foreign State when at war with a friendly State, or is delivered to or to the order of such foreign State, or any person who to the knowledge of the person building is an agent of such foreign State, or is paid for by such foreign State or such agent, and is employed in the military or naval service of such foreign State, such ship shall, unless the contrary is proved, be deemed to have been built with a view to being so employed and the burden shall lie on the builder of such ship of proving that he did not know that the ship was intended to be so employed in the military or naval service of such foreign State.

Penalty on aiding the warlike equipment of foreign ships.

10. If any person within the dominions of Her Majesty, and without the license of Her Majesty,—By adding to the number of the guns, or by changing those on board for other guns, or by the addition of any equipment for war, increases or augments, or procures to be increased or augmented, or is knowingly concerned in increasing or augmenting the warlike force of any ship,

which at the time of her being within the dominions of Her Majesty was a ship in the military or naval service of any foreign State at war with any friendly State,—

Such person shall be guilty of an offence against this Act, and shall be punishable by fine and imprisonment, or either of such punishments, at the discretion of the Court before which the offender is convicted; and imprisonment, if awarded, may be either with or without hard labour.

Penalty on fitting out naval or military expeditions without license.

11. If any person within the limits of Her Majesty's dominions, and without the license of Her Majesty,—

Prepares or fits out any naval or military expedition to proceed against the dominions of any friendly State, the following consequences shall ensue:

(1.) Every person engaged in such preparation or fitting out, or assisting therein, or employed in any capacity in such expedition, shall be guilty of an offence against this Act, and shall be punishable by fine and imprisonment, or either of such punishments, at the discretion of the Court before which the offender is convicted; and imprisonment, if awarded, may be either with or without hard labour:

(2.) All ships, and their equipments, and all arms and munitions of war, used in or forming part of such expedition, shall be forfeited to Her Majesty.

Punishment of accessories.

12. Any person who aids, abets, counsels, or procures the commission of any offence against this Act, shall be liable to be tried and punished as a principal offender.

Limitation of term of imprisonment.

13. The term of imprisonment to be awarded in respect of any offence against this Act shall not exceed two years.

Illegal Prize.

Illegal prize brought into British ports restored.

14. If during the continuance of any war in which Her Majesty may be neutral, any ship, goods, or merchandise captured as prize of war within the territorial jurisdiction of Her Majesty, in violation of the neutrality of this realm, or captured by any ship which may have been built, equipped, commissioned, or despatched, or the force of which may have been augmented, contrary to the provisions of this Act, are brought within the limits of Her Majesty's dominions by the captor, or any agent of the captor, or by any person having come into possession thereof with knowledge that the same was prize of war so captured as aforesaid, it shall be lawful for the original owner of such prize, or his agent, or for any person authorized in that behalf by the Government of the foreign State to which such owner belongs, to make application to the Court of Admiralty for seizure and detention of such prize, and the Court shall, on due proof of the facts, order such prize to be restored.

Every such order shall be executed and carried into effect in the same manner and subject to the same right of appeal as in case of any order made in the exercise of the ordinary jurisdiction of such Court; and in the meantime, and until a final order has been made on such application, the Court shall have power to make all such provisional and other orders as to care or custody of such captured ship, goods, or merchandise, and (if the same be of perishable nature, or incurring risk of deterioration) for the sale thereof, and with respect to the deposit or investment of the proceeds of any such sale, as may be made by such Court in the exercise of its ordinary jurisdiction.

General Provision.

License by Her Majesty how granted.

15. For the purposes of this Act, a license by Her Majesty shall be under the sign manual of Her Majesty, or be signified by Order in Council or by proclamation of Her Majesty.

Legal Procedure.

Jurisdiction in respect of offences by persons against Act.

16. Any offence against this Act shall, for all purposes of and incidental to the trial and punishment of any person guilty of any such offence, be deemed to have been committed either in the place in which the offence was wholly or partly committed, or in any place within Her Majesty's dominions in which the person who committed such offence may be.

Venue in respect of offences by persons. 24 & 25 Vict. C. 97.

17. Any offence against this Act may be described in any indictment or other document relating to such offence, in cases where the mode of trial requires such a description, as having been committed at the place where it was wholly or partly committed, or it may be averred generally to have been committed within Her Majesty's dominions, and the *venue* or local description in the margin may be that of the country, city, or place in which the trial is held.

Power to remove offenders for trial.

18. The following authorities, that is to say, in the United Kingdom any judge of a superior Court, in any other place within the jurisdiction of any British Court of justice, such Court, or, if there are more Courts than one, the Court having the highest criminal jurisdiction in that place, may, by warrant or instrument in the nature of a warrant in this section included in the term "warrant," direct that any offender charged with an offence against this Act shall be removed to some other place in Her Majesty's dominions for trial in cases where it appears to the authority granting the warrant that the removal of such offender would be conducive to the interests of justice, and any prisoner so removed shall be triable at the place to which he is removed, in the same manner as if his offence had been committed at such place.

Any warrant for the purposes of this section may be addressed to the master of any ship or to any other person or persons, and the person or persons to whom such warrant is addressed shall have power to convey the prisoner therein named to any place or places named in such warrant, and deliver him, when arrived at such place or places, into the custody of any authority designated by such warrant.

Every prisoner shall, during the time of his removal under any such warrant as aforesaid, be deemed to be in the legal custody of the person or persons empowered to removed him.

Jurisdiction in respect of forfeiture of ships for offences against Act.

19. All proceedings for the condemnation and forfeiture of a ship, or ship and equipment, or arms and munitions of war, in pursuance of this Act shall require the sanction of the Secretary of State or such chief executive authority as is in this Act mentioned, and shall be had in the Court of Admiralty, and not in any other Court; and the Court of Admiralty shall, in addition to any power given to the Court by this Act, have, in respect of any ship or other matter brought before it in pursuance of this Act, all powers which it has in the case of a ship or matter brought before it in the exercise of its ordinary jurisdiction.

Regulations as to proceedings against the offender and against the ship.

20. Where any offence against this Act has been committed by any person by reason whereof a ship, or ship and equipment, or arms and munitions of war, has or have become liable to forfeiture, proceedings may be instituted contemporaneously or not, as may be thought fit, against the offender in any Court having jurisdiction of the offence, and against the ship, or ship and equipment, or arms and munitions of war, for the forfeiture in the Court of Admiralty; but it shall not be necessary to take proceedings against the offender because proceedings are instituted for the forfeiture, or to take proceedings for the forfeiture because proceedings are taken against the offender.

Officers authorized to seize offending ships.

21. The following officers, that is to say,—

(1.) Any officer of customs in the United Kingdom, subject nevertheless to any special or general instructions from the Commissioners of Customs, or any officer of the Board of Trade, subject nevertheless to any special or general instructions from the Board of Trade;

(2.) Any officer of customs or public officer in any British possession, subject nevertheless to any special or general instructions from the Governor of such possession;

(3.) Any commissioned officer on full pay in the military service of the Crown, subject nevertheless to any special or general instructions from his commanding officer;

(4.) Any commissioned officer on full pay in the naval service of the Crown, subject nevertheless to any special or general instructions from the Admiralty or his superior officer,

may seize or detain any ship liable to be seized or detained in pursuance of this Act, and such officers are in this Act referred to as the "local authority"; but nothing in this Act contained shall derogate from the power of the Court of Admiralty to direct any ship to be seized or detained by any officer by whom such Court may have power under its ordinary jurisdiction to direct a ship to be seized or detained.

Powers of officers authorized to seize ships.

22. Any officer authorized to seize or detain any ship in respect of any offence against this Act may, for the purpose of enforcing such seizures or detention, call to his aid any constable or officers of police, or any officers of Her Majesty's army or navy or marines, or any excise officers or officers of customs, or any harbour master or dock master, or any officers having authority by law to make seizures of ships, and may put on board any ship so seized or detained any one or more of such officers to take charge of the same, and to enforce the provisions of this Act, and any officer seizing or detaining any ship under this Act may use force, if necessary, for the purpose of enforcing seizures or detention, and if any person is killed or maimed by reason of his resisting such officer in the execution of his duties, or any person acting under his orders, such officer so seizing or detaining the ship, or other person, shall be freely and fully indemnified as well against the Queen's Majesty, her heirs and successors, as against all persons so killed, maimed, or hurt.

Special powers of Secretary of State or chief executive authority to detain ships.

23. If the Secretary of State or the chief executive authority is satisfied that there is a reasonable and probable cause for believing that a ship within Her Majesty's dominions has been or is being built, commissioned, or equipped contrary to this Act, and is about to be taken beyond the limits of such dominions, or that a ship is about to be despatched contrary to this Act, such Secretary of State or chief executive authority shall have power to issue a warrant stating that there is reasonable and probable cause for believing as aforesaid, and upon such warrant the local authority shall have power to seize and search such ship, and to detain the same until it has been either condemned or released by process of law, or in manner hereinafter mentioned.

The owner of the ship so detained, or his agent, may apply to the Court of Admiralty for its release, and the Court shall as soon as possible put the matter of such seizure and detention in course of trial between the applicant and the Crown.

If the applicant establish to the satisfaction of the Court that the ship was not and is not being built, commissioned, or equipped, or intended to be despatched contrary to this Act, the ship shall be released and restored.

If the applicant fail to establish to the satisfaction of the Court that the ship was not and is not being built, commissioned, or equipped, or intended to be despatched contrary to this Act, then the ship shall be detained till released by order of the Secretary of State or chief executive authority.

The Court may, in cases where no proceedings are pending for its condemnation, release any ship detained under this section on the owner giving security to the satisfaction of the Court, that the ship shall not be employed contrary to this Act, notwithstanding that the applicant may have failed to establish to the satisfaction of the Court that the ship was not and is not being built, commissioned, or intended to be despatched contrary to this Act. The Secretary of State or the chief executive authority may likewise release any ship detained under this section, on the owner giving security to the satisfaction of such Secretary of State or chief executive authority, that the ship shall not be employed contrary to this Act, or may release the ship without such security, if the Secretary of State or chief executive authority think fit so to release the same.

If the Court be of opinion that there was not reasonable and probable cause for the detention, and if no such cause appear in the course of the proceedings, the Court shall have power to declare that the owner is to be indemnified by the payment of costs and damages in respect of the detention, the amount thereof to be assessed by the Court, and any amount so assessed shall be payable by the Commissioners of the Treasury out of any monies legally applicable for that purpose. The Court of Admiralty shall also have power to make a like order for the indemnity of the owner, on the application of such owner to the Court, in a summary way, in cases where the ship is released by the order of the Secretary of State or the chief executive authority, before any application is made by the owner or his agent to the Court for such release.

Nothing in this section contained shall affect any proceedings instituted or to be instituted for the condemnation of any ship detained under this section where such ship is liable to forfeiture, subject to this provision, that if such ship is restored in pursuance of this section all proceedings for such condemnation shall be stayed; and where the Court declares that the owner is to be indemnified by the payment of costs and damages for the detainer, all costs, charges, and expenses incurred by such owner in or about any proceedings for the condemnation of such ship shall be added to the costs and damages payable to him in respect of the detention of the ship.

Nothing in this section contained shall apply to any foreign non-commissioned ship despatched from any part of Her Majesty's dominions after having come within them under stress of weather or in the course of a peaceful voyage, and upon which ship no fitting out or equipping of a warlike character has taken place in this country.

Special power of local authority to detain ship.

24. Where it is represented to any local authority, as defined by this Act, and such local authority believes the representation, that there is a reasonable and probable cause for believing that a ship within Her Majesty's dominions has been or is being built, commissioned, or equipped contrary to this Act, and is about to be taken beyond the limits of such dominions, or that a ship is about to be despatched contrary to this Act, it shall be the duty of such local authority to detain such ship, and forthwith to communicate the fact of such detention to the Secretary of State or chief executive authority.

Upon the receipt of such communication the Secretary of State or chief executive authority may order the ship to be released if he thinks there is no cause for detaining her, but if satisfied that there is reasonable and probable cause for believing that such ship was built, commissioned, or equipped or intended to be despatched in contravention of this Act, he shall issue his warrant stating that there is reasonable and probable cause for believing as aforesaid, and upon such warrant being issued further proceedings shall be had as in cases where the seizure or detention has taken place on a warrant issued by the Secretary of State without any communication from the local authority.

Where the Secretary of State or chief executive authority orders the ship to be released on the receipt of a communication from the local authority without issuing his warrant, the owner of the ship shall be indemnified by the payment of costs and damages in respect of the detention upon application to the Court of Admiralty in a summary way in like manner as he is entitled to be indemnified where the Secretary of State having issued his warrant under this Act releases the ship before any application is made by the owner or his agent to the Court for such release.

Power of Secretary of State or executive authority to grant search warrant.

25. The Secretary of State or the chief executive authority may, by warrant, empower any person to enter any dockyard or other place within Her Majesty's dominions and inquire as to the destination of any ship which may appear to him to be intended to be employed in the naval or military service of any foreign State at war with a friendly State, and to search such ship.

Exercise of powers of Secretary of State or chief executive authority.

26. Any powers or jurisdiction by this Act given to the Secretary of State may be exercised by him throughout the dominions of Her Majesty, and such powers and jurisdiction may also be exercised by any of the following officers, in this Act referred to as the chief executive authority, within their respective jurisdictions; that is to say,

(1.) In Ireland by the Lord Lieutenant or other the chief governor or governors of Ireland for the time being, or the chief secretary to the Lord Lieutenant:

(2.) In Jersey by the Lieutenant Governor;

(3.) In Guernsey, Alderney, and Sark, and the dependent islands by the Lieutenant Governor:

(4.) In the Isle of Man by the Lieutenant Governor:

(5.) In any British possession by the Governor.

A copy of any warrant issued by a Secretary of State or by any officer authorized in pursuance of this Act to issue such warrant in Ireland, the Channel Islands, or the Isle of Man shall be laid before Parliament.

Appeal from Court of Admiralty. 27. An appeal may be had from any decision of a Court of Admiralty under this Act to the same tribunal and in the same manner to and in which an appeal may be had in cases within the ordinary jurisdiction of the Court as a Court of Admiralty.

Indemnity to officers. 28. Subject to the provisions of this Act providing for the award of damages in certain cases in respect of the seizure or detention of a ship by the Court of Admiralty no damages shall be payable, and no officer or local authority shall be responsible, either civilly or criminally in respect of the seizure or detention of any ship in pursuance of this Act.

Indemnity to Secretary of State or chief executive authority. 29. The Secretary of State shall not, nor shall the chief executive authority, be responsible in any action or other legal proceedings whatsoever for any warrant issued by him in pursuance of this Act, or be examinable as a witness, except at his own request, in any Court of justice in respect of the circumstances which led to the issue of the warrant.

Interpretation Clause.

Interpretation of terms. 30. In this Act, if not inconsistent with the context, the following terms have the meanings hereinafter respectively assigned to them; that is to say,

Foreign State. "Foreign State" includes any foreign prince, colony, province, or part of any province or people, or any person or persons exercising or assuming to exercise the powers of government in or over any foreign country, colony, province, or part of any province or people:

Military service. "Military service" shall include military telegraphy and any other employment whatever, in or in connection with any military operation:

Naval service. "Naval service" shall, as respects a person, include service as a marine, employment as a pilot in piloting or directing the course of a ship of war or other ship when such ship of war or other ship is being used in any military or naval operation and any employment whatever on board a ship of war, transport, store ship, privateer or ship under letters of marque; and as respects a ship, include any user of a ship as a transport, store ship, privateer or ship under letters of marque:

United Kingdom. "United Kingdom" includes the Isle of Man, the Channel Islands, and other adjacent islands:

British possession. "British possession" means any territory, colony, or place being part of Her Majesty's dominions, and not part of the United Kingdom, as defined by this Act:

The Secretary of State. "The Secretary of State" shall mean any one of Her Majesty's Principal Secretaries of State:

The Governor. "The Governor" shall as respects India mean the Governor General or the governor of any presidency, and where a British possession consists of several constituent colonies, mean the Governor of the whole possession or the Governor of any of the constituent colonies, and as respects any other British possession it shall mean the officer for the time being administering the government of such possession; also any person acting for or in the capacity of a governor shall be included under the term "Governor":

Court of Admiralty. "Court of Admiralty" shall mean the High Court of Admiralty of England or Ireland, the Court of Session of Scotland, or any Vice-Admiralty Court within Her Majesty's dominions:

Ship. "Ship" shall include any description of boat, vessels, floating battery, or floating craft; also any description of boat, vessel, or other craft or battery, made to move either on the surface of or under water, or sometimes on the surface of and sometimes under water:

Building. "Building" in relation to a ship shall include the doing any act towards or incidental to the construction of a ship, and all words having relation to building shall be construed accordingly:

Equipping. "Equipping" in relation to a ship shall include the furnishing a ship with any tackle, apparel, furniture, provisions, arms, munitions, or stores, or any other thing which is used in or about a ship for the purpose of fitting or adapting her for the sea or for naval service, and all words relating to equipping shall be construed accordingly:

Ship and equipment. "Ship and equipment" shall include a ship and everything in or belonging to a ship:

Master. "Master" shall include any person having the charge or command of a ship.

Repeal of Acts and Saving Clauses.

Repeal of Foreign Enlistment Act. 59 *G.* 3 *C.* 69. 31. From and after the commencement of this Act, and Act passed in the fifty-ninth year of the reign of His late Majesty King George the Third, chapter sixty-nine, intituled "An Act to prevent the enlisting or engagement of His Majesty's subjects to serve in foreign service and the fitting out or equipping, in His Majesty's dominions, vessels for warlike purposes, without His Majesty's licence," shall be repealed: Provided that such repeal shall not affect any penalty, forfeiture, or other punishment incurred or to be incurred in respect of any offence committed before this Act comes into operation, nor the institution of any investigation or legal proceeding, or any other remedy for enforcing any such penalty, forfeiture, or punishment as aforesaid.

Saving as commissioned foreign ships. 32. Nothing in this Act contained shall subject to forfeiture any commissioned ship of any foreign State, or give to any British Court over or in respect of any ship entitled to recognition as a commissioned ship of any foreign State any jurisdiction which it would not have had if this Act had not passed.

Penalties not to extend to persons entering into military service in Asia. 59 *G.* 3 *C.* 69, § 12. 33. Nothing in this Act contained shall extend or be construed to extend to subject to any penalty any person who enters into the military service of any prince, State, or potentate in Asia, with such leave or licence as is for the time being required by law in the case of subjects of Her Majesty entering into the military service of princes, States, or potentates in Asia. *

---

* Instructions for the guidance of the Commanders-in-chief, or the senior officers present, as to the course to be pursued in carrying into effect, and in assisting the civil authorities to carry into effect, the provisions of the Foreign Enlistment Act, 1870, will be found in the Queen's Regulations and Admiralty Instructions, 1879, p. 141.

Appendix F.

BRITISH NEUTRALITY REGULATIONS, 1870.

Neutrality Proclamation.

Whereas We are happily at peace with all Sovereigns, Powers, and States;

And whereas, notwithstanding Our utmost exertions to preserve peace between all Sovereigns, Powers, and States, a state of war unhappily exists between His Imperial Majesty the Emperor of the French and His Majesty the King of Prussia, and between their respective subjects and others inhabiting within their countries, territories, or dominions;

And whereas We are on terms of friendship and amicable intercourse with each of these Sovereigns, and with their several subjects, and others inhabiting within their countries, territories, or dominions;

And whereas great numbers of Our loyal subjects reside and carry on commerce, and possess property and establishments, and enjoy various rights and privileges, within the dominions of each of the aforesaid Sovereigns, protected by the faith of Treaties between us and each of the aforesaid Sovereigns;

And whereas We, being desirous of preserving to our subjects the blessings of peace, which they now happily enjoy, are firmly purposed and determined to abstain altogether from taking any part, directly or indirectly, in the war now unhappily existing between the said Sovereigns, their subjects and territories, and to remain at peace with, and to maintain a peaceful and friendly intercourse with each of them, and their respective subjects, and others inhabiting within any of their respective countries, territories, and dominions, and to maintain a strict and impartial neutrality in the said state of war, unhappily existing betweeen them;

We, therefore, have thought fit, by and with the advice of Our Privy Council, to issue this Our Royal Proclamation.

And We do hereby strictly charge and command all Our loving subjects to govern themselves accordingly, and to observe a strict neutrality in and during the aforesaid war, and to abstain from violating or contravening either the laws and statutes of the realm in this behalf, or the Law of Nations in relation thereto, as they will answer to the contrary at their peril.

And whereas in and by a certain Statute made and passed in the fifty-ninth year of His Majesty King George the Third, entitled "An Act to prevent the enlisting or engagement of His Majesty's subjects to serve in a foreign service, and the fitting out or equipping, in His Majesty's dominions, vessels for warlike purposes without His Majesty's licence" it is amongst other things declared and enacted as follows:—

"That if any person within any part of the United Kingdom, or in any part of His Majesty's dominions beyond the seas, shall, without the leave and licence of His Majesty, for that purpose first had and obtained as aforesaid, equip, furnish, fit out, or arm, or attempt or endeavour to equip, furnish, fit out, or arm, or procure to be equipped, furnished, fitted out, or armed, or shall knowingly aid, assist, or be concerned in the equipping, furnishing, fitting out, or arming of any ship, or vessel with intent or in order that such ship or vessel shall be employed in the service of any foreign Prince, State, or Potentate, or of any foreign colony, province, or part of any foreign colony, province, or part of any province or people, or of any person or persons, exercising, or assuming to exercise, any powers of government, in or over any foreign State, colony, province, or part of any province or people, as a transport or store-ship, or with intent to cruise or commit hostilities against any Prince, State or Potentate, or against the subjects or citizens of any Prince, State or Potentate, or against the persons exercising, or assuming to exercise, the powers of government in any colony, province, or part of any province or country, or against the inhabitants of any foreign colony, province, or part of any province or country, with whom His Majesty shall not then be at war, or shall, within the United Kingdom, or any of His Majesty's dominions, or in any settlement, colony, territory, island, or place, belonging or subject to His Majesty, issue or deliver any commission for any ship or vessel, to the intent that such ship or vessel shall be employed as aforesaid, every such person so offending shall be deem guilty of a misdemeanour, and shall, upon conviction thereof, upon any information or indictment, be punished by fine or imprisonment, or either of them, at the discretion of the Court in which such offender shall be convicted; and every such ship or vessel, with the tackle, apparel, and furniture, together with all the materials, arms, ammunition, and stores, which may belong to or be on board of any such ship or vessel, shall be forfeited; and it shall be lawful for any officer of His Majesty's Customs or Excise, or any officer of His Majesty's Navy, who is by law empowered to make seizures for any forfeiture incurred under any of the laws of Customs or Excise, or the laws of trade or navigation, to seize such ships and vessels aforesaid, and in such places, and in such manner in which the officers of His Majesty's Customs or Excise, and the officers of His Majesty's Navy, are empowered respectively to make seizures under the laws of Customs and Excise, or under the laws of trade and navigation; and that every such ship and vessel, with the tackle, apparel, and furniture, together with all the materials, arms, ammunition and stores, which may belong to, or be on board of such ship or vessel, may be prosecuted and condemned in the like manner and in such Courts as ships or vessels may be prosecuted and condemned for any breach of the laws made for the protection of the Revenues of Customs and Excise, or of the laws of trade and navigation."

And it is, in and by the said Act, further enacted, "That if any person in any part of the United Kingdom of Great Britain and Ireland or in any part of His Majesty's dominions beyond the seas, without the leave and licence of His Majesty for that purpose first had and obtained as aforesaid, shall, by adding to the number of the guns of such vessels, or changing those on board for other guns, or by the addition of any equipment for war, increase or augment, or procure to be increased or augmented, or shall be knowingly concerned in increasing or augmenting the warlike force of any ship or vessel of war, or cruizer, or other armed vessel, which, at the time of her arrival in any part of the United Kingdom, or any of His Majesty's dominions, was a ship of war, cruizer or armed vessel, in the service of any foreign Prince, State, or Potentate, or of any person or persons exercising, or assuming to exercise, any powers of government in or over any colony, province, or part of any province or people belonging to the subjects of any such Prince, State, or Potentate, or to the inhabitants of any colony, province, or part of any province or country, under the control of any person or persons so exercising, or assuming to exercise, the powers of government, every such person so offending shall be deemed guilty of a misdemeanour, and shall, upon being convicted thereof, upon any information or indictment, be punished by fine and imprisonment, or either of them, at the discretion of the Court before which such offender shall be convicted."

Now, in order that none of Our subjects may unwarily render themselves liable to the penalties imposed by the said Statue, We do hereby strictly command that no person or persons whatsoever do commit any act, matter, or thing whatsoever contrary to the provisions of the said Statute, upon pain of the several penalties by the said Statute imposed, and of Our high displeasure.

And we do hereby further warn and admonish all Our loving subjects, and all persons whatsoever entitled to Our protection, to observe towards each of the aforesaid Sovereigns their subjects and territories, and towards all belligerents whatsoever, with whom We are at peace, the duties of neutrality; and to respect, in all and each of them, the exercise of those belligerent rights which We and Our Royal Predecessors have always claimed to exercise.

And we do hereby further warn all Our loving subjects, and all persons whatsoever entitled to Our protection, that, if any of them shall presume, in contempt of this Our Royal Proclamation, and of Our high displeasure, to do any acts in derogation of their duty as subjects of a neutral Sovereign, in a war between other Sovereigns, or in violation or contravention of the Law of Nations in that behalf, as more especially by breaking, or endeavouring to break, any blockade lawfully and actually established by or on behalf of either of the said Sovereigns, by carrying officers, soldiers, despatches, arms, ammunition, military stores or materials, or any article or articles considered and deemed to be contraband of war, according to the law or modern usages of Nations, for the use of service of either of the said Sovereigns, that all persons so offending, together with their ships and goods, will rightfully incur, and be justly liable to, hostile capture, and to the penalties denounced by the Law of Nations in that behalf.

And We do hereby give notice, that all Our subjects and persons entitled to Our protection who may misconduct themselves in the premises, will do so at their peril and of their own wrong; and that they will in no wise obtain any protection from us against such capture or such penalties as aforesaid, but will, on the contrary, incur Our high displeasure by such misconduct.

Letter addressed by Earl Granville to the Lords Commissioners of the Admiralty.

FOREIGN OFFICE, *July* 19*th*, 1870.

MY LORDS,—Her Majesty being fully determined to observe the duties of neutrality during the existing state of war between the Emperor of the French and the King of Prussia, and being moreover resolved to prevent, as far as possible, the use of Her Majesty's harbours, ports, and coasts, and the waters within Her Majesty's territorial jurisdiction, in aid of the warlike purposes of either belligerent, has commanded me to communicate to your Lordships, for your guidance, the following rules, which are to be treated and enforced as Her Majesty's orders and directions:—

Her Majesty is pleased further to command that these rules shall be put in force in the United Kingdom, and in the Channel Islands, on and after the 26th of July, instant, and in Her Majesty's territories and possessions beyond the seas, six days after the day when the governor, or other chief authority, of each of such territories or possessions respectively, shall have notified and published the same; stating in such notification that the said rules are to be obeyed by all persons within the same territories and possessions.

1. During the continuance of the present state of war, all ships of war of either belligerent are prohibited from making use of any port or roadstead in the United Kingdom of Great Britain and Ireland, or in the Channel Islands, or in any of Her Majesty's colonies or foreign possessions or dependencies, or of any waters subject to the territorial jurisdiction of the British Crown, as a station, or place of resort, for

any warlike purpose, or for the purpose of obtaining any facilities of warlike equipment; and no ship of war of either belligerent shall hereafter be permitted to sail out of or leave any port, roadstead, or waters subject to British jurisdiction, from which any vessel of the other belligerent (whether the same shall be a ship of war or a merchant ship) shall have previously departed, until after the expiration of, at least, twenty-four hours from the departure of such last-mentioned vessel beyond the territorial jurisdiction of Her Majesty.

2. If any ship of war of either belligerent shall, after the time when this order shall be first notified and put in force in the United Kingdom, and in the Channel Islands, and in the several colonies and foreign possessions and dependencies of Her Majesty respectively, enter any port, roadstead, or waters belonging to Her Majesty, either in the United Kingdom or in the Channel Islands, or in any of Her Majesty's colonies or foreign possessions or dependencies, such vessels shall be required to depart and to put to sea within twenty-four hours after her entrance into such port, roadstead, or waters, except in case of stress of weather, or of her requiring provisions or things necessary for the subsistence of her crew, or repairs; in either of which cases the authorities of the port, or of the nearest port (as the case may be), shall require her to put to sea as soon as possible after the expiration of such period of twenty-four hours, without permitting her to take in supplies beyond what may be necessary for her immediate use; and no such vessel which may have been allowed to remain within British waters for the purpose of repair shall continue in any such port, roadstead, or waters, for a longer period than twenty-four hours after her necessary repairs shall have been completed. Provided, nevertheless, that in all cases in which there shall be any vessel (whether ships of war or merchant-ships) of the said belligerent parties in the same port, roadstead, or waters within the territorial jurisdiction of Her Majesty, there shall be an interval of not less than twenty-four hours between the departure therefrom of any such vessel (whether ship of war or merchant-ship) of the one belligerent, and the subsequent departure therefrom of any ship of war of the other belligerent; and the time hereby limited for the departure of such ships of war respectively shall always, in case of necessity, be extended so far as may be requisite for giving effect to this proviso, but no further or otherwise.

3. No ship of war of either belligerent shall hereafter be permitted, while in any port, roadstead, or waters subject to the territorial jurisdiction of Her Majesty, to take in any supplies, except provisions and such other things as may be requisite for the subsistence of her crew, and except so much coal only as may be sufficient to carry such vessel to the nearest port of her own country, or to some nearer destination, and no coal shall again be supplied to any such ship of war in the same or any other port, roadstead, or waters subject to the territorial jurisdiction of Her Majesty, without special permission until after the

expiration of three months from the time when such coal may have been last supplied to her within British waters as aforesaid.

4. Armed ships of either party are interdicted from carrying prizes made by them into the ports, harbours, roadsteads, or waters of the United Kingdom, or any of Her Majesty's colonies or possessions abroad.—I have, &c.,

GRANVILLE.

Appendix G.

PRUSSIAN INSTRUCTIONS IN PRIZE AFFAIRS.*

I.—Sovereign Decree of 20th June, 1864.

Concerning the Sanction of a Set of Prize Regulations as well as Decisions concerning Proceedings in Prize Affairs.
(G. S. 369, et seq.).

In pursuance of the report of the Ministry of State of 10th instant, I sanction the prize regulations submitted together with the same, as well as the directions submitted at the same time, concerning procedure in prize affairs.

This my decree, together with the set of prize regulations and the directions concerning procedure in prize affairs, both of which are returned as enclosures to this, are to be promulgated through the Collection of Laws.

Karlsbad, 20th June, 1864.

WILLIAM.

v. Bismarck-Shönhausen. *v.* Bodelschwingh. *v.* Roon. *v.* Itzenplitz. *v.* Mühler. Gr. zur Lippe. *v.* Selchow. Gr. zur Eulenburg.

To the Ministry of State.

II.—Prize Regulations.

Section I.

The Bringing up of Hostile or Suspected Vessels.

§ 1.

None but Royal vessels of war are authorized to stop and bring up hostile or suspected ships.

* Translated from an appendix to the work of Mr. F. Perels, Counsellor to the German Admiralty, *Das Internationale Offentliche Seerecht.*

§ 2.

All ships belonging to the hostile State or to its subjects (hostile vessels) are to be stopped and brought up.

§ 3.

Ships of neutral Powers or of their subjects (neutral ships), irrespective of the question to whom the cargo belongs, are not to be brought up, unless it be that the case in hand is one of those mentioned in paragraphs 4–6.

§ 4.

Irrespective of nationality, are to be stopped and brought up,

(1.) Ships, whose cargo consists of contraband of war, destined for the enemy or for a hostile port, but without prejudice to the decision contained in § 7, under sub-section 2.;

(2.) Ships which forcibly resist being stopped.

§ 5.

Irrespective of nationality are further to be stopped and brought up, as suspicious,

(1.) Ships, which carry a double set of or probably false or forged papers;

(2.) Ships, which carry no papers or which have done away with their papers, especially if this has been done only when the cruiser was already in sight;

(3.) Ships which do not heave to or stop on being challenged by the cruiser, or which opposed the search of hold and closets presumably containing contraband of war or papers.

§ 6.

Subject to stoppage and bringing up, irrespective of nationality, are also those ships, which cannot produce proper evidence of nationality. The question as to what ship's papers are requisite as evidence of nationality, depends upon the laws of the country to which the ship belongs.

§ 7.

As valid prizes will be considered:—

(1.) Hostile ships (§ 2), together with their cargo; but neutral goods on board of a hostile ship are, with the exception of contraband of war, free.

(2.) Ships, whose cargo consists of contraband of war (§ 4, sub-section 1), together with the latter; when only part of the cargo consists of contraband of war, the skipper is authorized to discharge the contraband of war either on the spot or in the nearest port, in which case he is exempt from being brought up and may continue his voyage without molestation with the remainder of the cargo.

(3.) Ships which forcibly resist being stopped (§ 4, sub-section 2);

(4.) Ships, brought up as suspicious, provided that the damaging suspicions attaching to them are not removed.

§ 8.

The following articles, so far as destined for the enemy or an enemy's port, are to be considered contraband of war:—

Guns, mortars, all kinds of arms, bombs, shells, balls or bullets, caps, fuzes, gun-powder, cuirasses, armourers' utensils, saddles, bridles and generally all things, which admit of direct application to purposes of war. Supplies of the above mentioned sort which serve the requirements of the ship herself, do not come under the category of contraband of war.

§ 9.

No stopping and bringing up is permissible within the sphere of neutral waters.

§ 10.

Those national ships, which were taken by the enemy and retaken from the same (reconquered), are treated as valid prizes, provided they are not to be considered as a case of recapture.

§ 11.

In stopping and searching a ship, the commander of the cruiser is to observe the following procedure.

The commander gives the vessel a signal to heave to or to stop, whereupon he sends for the skipper to come to him on board with his ship's papers. If herein no cause for objection turns up, he permits the ship forthwith to continue her voyage without molestation. But if he meets with well-founded occasion for any suspicion which would justify his bringing up the ship, he is to send an officer on board the ship to make more detailed inquiry into the circumstances. In making this inquiry, closed compartments, partitions, cupboards, chests, casks, fixtures or other receptacles must not be opened or broken into. But the officer instructed to make this inquiry is rather to get those compartments etc., the search of which he deems necessary, to be opened by the skipper. Even cargo lying loose in the ship is to be searched only in conjunction with the skipper.

§ 12.

Neutral ships, sailing under convoy of the ships of war of a neutral Power, are not subject to search; it is sufficient if the officer in command of the convoy declares that the papers of the ships under convoy are in order, and that they have no contraband of war on board.

§ 13.

The commander of a cruiser who has brought up a ship (prize) must keep strict watch, that nothing of the cargo or ship's effects is discharged, sold, changed or removed or otherwise lost. He should, in conjunction with the skipper or mate of the ship brought up, put all cargo, as far as practicable, under seal or lock. The commander of the cruiser should take the ship's papers, together with an inventory signed by him and by the skipper of the ship brought up, and seal up the whole in one fascicle under the seal of the cruiser and under the seal of the skipper.

§ 14.

The commander of the cruiser should then take the necessary measures, by sending, if need be, an officer with a sufficient crew on board of the vessel brought up, in order to navigate her into a Prussian port, or if this is connected with difficulties, into the port of a Power allied with Prussia where there is a prospect of obtaining military protection. The cargo should not be broached till then, unless the skipper or his deputy should agree to the cargo being opened in order to preserve it.

§ 15.

The navigation of the ship to another port or place is only then permitted when storm, bad weather, scarcity of provisions, pursuit by enemies or any other stress of sea require it. Even in such a case, the ship is to be brought into the port, pointed out in § 34, without broaching cargo, as soon as circumstances permit it.

§ 16.

If the ship cannot be taken any farther on account of damage accruing to ship or cargo, or if the cargo consists of goods which may easily perish, it becomes the duty of the commander of the cruiser or of the officer navigating the prize, to use his best judgment and to take, in conjunction with the skipper and the Prussian Consul if there is one at the respective place, those measures which serve the best interest of ship and cargo.

§ 17.

As soon as a ship is brought into the port, pointed out in § 1, she is to be handed over to the harbour police authorities or to the officers who, according to decisions given in § 39 regarding procedure in prize affairs, are competent in the matter, and proceedings should be taken in accordance with the directions contained in §§ 8 and 39 of those decisions.

§ 18.

The crew of the vessel brought up is maintained and fed at the expense of the State until the case is decided. If the prize is condemned, those of the crew, who are subjects of the enemy, will be treated as prisoners of war. The subjects of friendly or neutral Powers, however, are forwarded to the Consuls of the respective States for further disposal.

§ 19.

The commander of the cruiser, which has brought up a prize, has to submit a detailed report regarding the bringing up of the prize to his superior officers.

Section II.

The Blockade of Hostile Ports.

§ 20.

A port is considered as blockaded if it is so shut up, by one or several vessels of war, that a merchant vessel cannot enter or leave port without apparent danger of being brought up.

§ 21.

The commander who has been entrusted with the carrying out of the blockade, has, on his arrival at the blockade station, to notify in writing all consuls residing at the port, and at the same time to request all neutral ships, lying in the port, to leave it within a suitable term which is to be fixed by the commander after having consulted the proposals of commanders of ships.

§ 22.

Every ship, irrespective of nationality, which attempts to break the blockade is to be brought up and considered a valid prize. A neutral ship, which leaves the blockaded port within the time referred to in § 21, is not to be stopped and brought up as breaking blockade.

§ 23.

An attempt to break blockade is, in the case of a neutral vessel, only then to be construed as such, when the vessel has had knowledge of the blockade.

§ 24.

The question whether the vessel had knowledge of the blockade, is to be judged according to the circumstances of the case, in which respect the longer or shorter period, which has elapsed since announcement and notice of blockade, is an influential point.

If the commander of the respective vessel of war is of opinion that the blockade was not known to the ship, he is to inform the ship of the same, to note the fact of this notice having been given it on the ship's papers, especially on the documents, which serve to give evidence of nationality, as well as in the ship's log-book, and to send the ship back or to cause her to change her course.

§ 25.

The taking out of papers of clearance for a blockaded port or the course of a ship being set for a blockaded port, is not sufficient to construe it as an attempt to break through the blockade.

§ 26.

Further proceedings in the case of a ship brought up for breaking blockade, are determined according to the directions given in section I.

Final Directions.

§ 27.

The commanders and officers of vessels of war, have to adhere carefully to the instructions contained in these regulations. They will be called to account, if acting against them, and they can besides be sentenced to pay amends for the damages and costs arising from any proceedings which are contrary to law.

§ 28.

A copy of these regulations should be found on board of every cruising vessel of war.

III.—Directions concerning procedure in Prize Affairs.

Section I.

The Constitution of the Prize Court.

§ 1.

A special court (prize court), which has its seat in Berlin, is established for the decisions of prize affairs.

§ 2.

The prize court consists of a president and six other members.

Attached to the prize court, is further also a public prosecutor who is to conduct prize affairs in the public interest and to make the requisite motions in the prize court.

§ 3.

The members of the prize court and the public prosecutor attached to it, are nominated by the King.

§ 4.

The president of this prize court, must be competent for the higher branch of judicature; amongst the other members of the prize court there must be a high naval officer, a counsellor of the Ministry of Marine acting as referee, a counsellor of the Ministry of Foreign Affairs acting as referee, and two officials holding an office which has judicial functions.

§ 5

No salary is connected with the office of a member of the prize court nor with the office of the public prosecutor attached to the same.

§ 6.

The prize court is, in accordance with the instructions given concerning the right of control which the Minister of Judicature wields with regard to the tribunals of justice, subject to the joint supervision of the Ministry of Foreign Affairs, of the Ministry of Marine and of the Ministry of Judicature.

§ 7.

In the prize court the presence of at least five members, including the president, is requisite to form a quorum.

Section II.

Proceedings in Prize Affairs.

§ 8.

The commander of the ship by which a prize has been brought up, must, immediately after bringing her into the national port referred to in § 14 of the above given prize regulations, transmit to the court competent to deal with cases of maritime law and in the absence of such a court to the ordinary tribunal of justice of the first instance, to the circuit of which the port belongs, a written statement of the facts of the case which form the basis of the bringing up of the prize. In this statement there are especially to be brought forward the reasons, which led to the bringing up, as well as all facts, which apparently tend to justify the condemnation of the prize. All books, papers, pass-ports, charter parties, bills of lading, letters and other documents which were delivered at or after the bringing up or which were found on board the prize (§ 13, *loco citato*) must be attached.

When the port belongs to the circuit of a deputy court or of a commission of justice, the branch court is to be considered as competent.

§ 9

It is the duty of the court, to break without delay the seals of all ships' documents handed in, in the presence of the commander of the cruiser or of the navigating officer of the prize as also in the presence of the skipper of the ship brought in, and to make a list of them. The court is also to arrange that the skipper of the ship brought up together with the other persons belonging to the crew of the latter and, as far as may be necessary to clear up the circumstances of the case, also the crew which took part in the bringing up and as the case may be the passengers of the ship brought up, be examined regarding everything concerning the bringing up and the facts relating to it, through a judge acting in conjunction with an officer who takes down a protocol of the proceedings. If the depositions of these persons deviate, in important points, from the written statement of the commander or of the officer who navigated the prize, an examination of the latter must also be effected in order to clear up the contradictions.

The court is further bound to ascertain, with the utmost despatch and in accordance with the existing instructions regarding the procedure of examination, the facts bearing on the decision of the question whether the prize has been lawfully brought up and whether she is to be wholly or partially condemned or to be set at liberty.

The court then transmits the statement of the commander or of the officer who navigated the prize, together with all the transactions relating to the bringing up, to the public prosecutor attached to the prize court.

§ 10.

The public prosecutor submits all the transactions forwarded to him to the prize court by means of a written recommendation. If, in examining the papers, he finds, that the prize must be set at liberty, he has to recommend her immediate release. If the prize court considers this recommendation as sufficiently justified, it issues at once, without further debate, the decree of release. The minute ratifying this decision is to be forwarded, together with the depositions, to the public prosecutor who causes the necessary steps to be taken, to release the prize, provided it be without prejudice to the directions given in § 26.

The public prosecutor is authorized, before making his recommendation in the prize court, to effect further inquiries by means of a requisition addressed to the competent authorities.

§ 11.

If the public prosecutor does not consider an immediate release justifiable, he recommends to the prize court a public summons to be issued to all those who have an interest in the prize not being condemned. In this case, likewise, if the prize court does not consider the recommendation of immediate release as appropriate, it issues a decree by which the aforesaid interested parties, as far as they have not sent in a reclamation, are summoned to prove their claims before the prize court, within fourteen days, by means of a written reclamation.

This summons, which need not contain a threat of forfeiture of any rights, is to be published by inserting it once in the *Government Gazette*.

If, after the lapse of the term fixed, it is found that no reclamation has been put in at the prize court before or within the said term, then, upon a written recommendation of the public prosecutor the decision is issued by the prize court without any further transaction and communicated to the public prosecutor according to § 10.

The prize court should, even when no reclamation has been put in release the prize whose condemnation the court does not consider justifiable.

In case of a condemnation there is no need for the preclusion of the known and unknown interested parties, who omitted to put in a written reclamation.

§ 12.

If a reclamation is put in, it is settled in pursuance of the following directions.

§ 13.

Every reclamation without distinction, whether it be put in before or after the issue of the public summons (§ 11), is to be lodged with the prize court in writing, and the document must be signed by a barrister. To the reclamation paper are to be attached all documents relating to anything which is referred to in support of the reclamation and all other means of proving the allegations made must be described in the same.

§ 14.

The prize court decides concerning the reclamation on the basis of verbal transactions, in the course of which a hearing is to be given to both the public prosecutor and to the reclaimant through verbal representations and recommendations. The reclaimant is to be summoned to appear at the time fixed for the transaction, according to the existing instructions concerning judicial summonses, without a threat of forfeiture of any rights. The summons can also be validly placed in the hands of the barrister who has signed the reclamation paper.

The reclaimant is to be allowed, on application being made before the term fixed, to inspect the transactions taken down so far, or a copy of them may be transmitted to him. At the term itself, he may get a barrister, who is to be furnished with power, to represent him.

The papers in the case have to be submitted to the public prosecutor for his inspection at the same time when the term fixed for the hearing of the case is communicated to him.

§ 15.

The hearing of the case is to be opened by a verbal statement of facts on the part of some member of the prize court. Thereupon both the reclaimant and the public prosecutor are heard with their verbal recommendations and representations, on which occasion it is permitted to bring forward new facts and proofs.

§ 16.

After the conclusion of the hearing of the case, the prize court has to pronounce and proclaim the decision. The court is however authorized to reserve judgment, in which case a new term is to be fixed, and to be made known to both the public prosecutor and to the reclaimant. The proclamation is not suspended by the mere fact that only the public prosecutor or only the reclaimant appears on the new term fixed. If neither of them appears, the protocol (§ 19) to be drawn up regarding this fact takes the place of the proclamation. Both the public prosecutor and the reclaimant, are, on application, to be furnished with a formal minute of the decision given.

§ 17.

If the prize court deems it necessary, before drawing up a final decision, to have evidence taken, the taking of the evidence is ordered by a preliminary summons. It is the duty of the public prosecutor to bring about a settlement of the latter by means of a requisition addressed to the competent authorities. After the settlement of the preliminaries, a new term is fixed for the hearing of the case, to which the reclaimant must be summoned according to § 14, and at the same time presented with a copy of the transactions taken down whilst taking the evidence. At the new hearing of the case, also, both the public prosecutor and the reclaimant may bring forward new facts and proofs.

§ 18.

If the reclaimant does not appear at any one term fixed for a hearing of the case, the hearing and the decision of the case are nevertheless to be proceeded with. A re-instatement *in statu quo ante* does not take place. The authority of the prize court to adjourn the hearing of the case either officially or on a recommendation made is not excluded hereby.

§ 19.

The proceedings before the prize court are not public. For every transaction before the prize court a protocol is to be drawn up by a sworn protocol writer, which protocol must contain the substance of the declarations and recommendations of the public prosecutor and the reclaimant, as also the decrees or the decision of the prize court with a statement as to the promulgation of the same. After the portion containing the declarations and recommendations has been read aloud in the presence of the public prosecutor and the reclaimant, and, as the case may be, supplemented and corrected, the protocol is to be signed by the president of the prize court and by the protocol-writer.

§ 20.

Against the decision of the prize court an appeal lies to the supreme prize court.

§ 21.

The supreme prize court, the chairman of which is the president or a vice-president of the supreme tribunal, consists of:—

The president in the Ministry of Marine, the director in the Ministry of Foreign Affairs, the director of the Department for Commerce and Industry in the Ministry of Commerce and of three members of the supreme tribunal.

The president of the supreme prize court and the other members belonging to the supreme tribunal, are appointed by the King.

The direction contained in § 5 applies also to the members of the supreme prize court.

§ 22.

The right of appeal belongs to the public prosecutor as well as to the reclaimant.

§ 23.

The term within which an appeal is to be lodged covers ten days. It begins with the day of promulgation of the decision; but the day of promulgation is not included in this term.

§ 24.

The appeal is lodged by means of a document, to be handed in to the prize court, in which document the complaints are to be specified and argued in detail.

The appeal paper of a reclaimant must be signed by a barrister.

The prize court should communicate the appeal paper of the public prosecutor to the reclaimant and that of the latter to the public prosecutor to be answered in either case within a term of ten days, which term admits of no extension. The reply of the reclaimant must be signed by a barrister. After the term fixed for handing in the reply has elapsed or after the document has been handed in, the papers in the case are sent by the prize court to the supreme prize court.

§ 25.

The supreme prize court issues judgment on the basis of the papers in the case, and on the basis of the written report of a referee to be appointed from among its members, the new facts and proofs which may have been brought forward in the course of the appeal being taken into consideration.

If the supreme prize court considers a more detailed inquiry necessary, the papers in the case are sent back to the prize court. The public prosecutor is to make a motion for the inquiry in the same manner as if the order had been issued by the prize court (§ 17). The supplementary transactions are to be communicated by the prize court to the reclaimant by transmitting to him a written copy, before the papers in the case are again submitted to the supreme prize court.

The decision of the supreme prize court is communicated by the prize court to the public prosecutor and to the reclaimant by the transmission of a formal minute.

The direction contained in § 7 applies also to the supreme prize court.

§ 26.

To the public prosecutor belongs the right, even in the cases mentioned in paragraphs 10 and 11, to lodge against the decision for release of the prize court, an appeal which is to be made in accordance with § 24, within ten days, counting from the day on which the decision is transmitted to him, without however counting the day of transmission. The further proceedings are determined in accordance with paragraphs 24 and 25, as far as the latter do not refer to action in conjunction with the reclaimant.

The decision in favour of condemnation cannot be impugned in the cases mentioned in § 11, by an interested party who has not at the proper time handed in to the prize court a written reclamation either by way of appeal or by means of a petition for re-instatement *in statu quo ante*.

§ 27.

Against the decision of the supreme prize court no further legal redress exists.

§ 28.

The prize court and the supreme prize court are to furnish arguments in support of their decisions.

§ 29.

The prize court and the supreme prize court are not bound by positive rules of proof in giving their decision; they have to form their judgment on the basis of their own free convictions as derived from the whole tenor of the transactions and of the evidence as to how far a fact has been proved or not. As to the question how far a fact or document, regarding which no declaration has been made, should be deemed admitted or recognized, it is also left to them to judge according to the circumstances of the case.

With regard to the judicial rules of decision, the instructions, issued regarding prize law, will serve as a guide, and in their absence, the judges may be guided by any other principles of International Law, without prejudice, however, to the consideration due to treaties concluded with neutral States and without prejudice to the use of retortion in suitable cases.

§ 30.

The recommendations and remarks of consuls and agents of foreign Powers, can be brought to the notice of the prize court and supreme prize court only through the medium of the public prosecutor.

§ 31.

If several reclamations have been put in in a case, they are dealt with and decided all at the same time.

§ 32.

The prize court and supreme prize court are not authorized to decide on the obligation to make amends for damages and costs, especially not in the cases referred to in paragraph 27 of the prize regulations.

§ 33.

Proceedings in prize affairs are exempt from costs and stamp duty.

The cash expenses are, in the case of a prize being condemned, to be paid first of all out of the proceeds of the same.

Section III.

Preliminary Procedures. Execution of the Decisions of the Prize Court.

§ 34.

When the ship brought up has been delivered by the commander or by the officer navigating the prize, according to § 17 of prize regulations, to the harbour police authorities, the latter take, if need be, after consultation with the military authorities of the port, the necessary measures for the safety of ship and cargo, as well as for the custody and maintenance of the crew. As regards ship and cargo an inventory is to be taken by the harbour police authorities acting in conjunction with sworn experts. In taking the inventory of the cargo, the ship's papers relating to the latter should be taken, as far as possible, for a basis, and the compartments of the ship which have been put under seal or closed should be opened as far as necessary.

The skipper and the crew of the vessel brought up are allowed to communicate with the shore, as soon as the evidence, prescribed in § 9, has been taken. The passengers of the ship are forthwith to be released.

§ 35.

Until the final decision of the prize court has been given, any further arrangement, whether changing the situation or not, according to § 34, must be abstained from unless a different course of action is prescribed by the subjoined rules:—

(1.) If it is undoubtedly affirmed that either the whole cargo or that a portion of it cannot be adjudged a valid prize, the cargo or that portion of it, regarding which the presumption holds good, is to be released forthwith. The same rule applies also to the ship, when it is beyond doubt that the cargo only and not the ship can be condemned.

(2.) The ship is to be unloaded entirely or partly and the cargo to be stored or sold, and the proceeds to be deposited in court, provided that such a measure be necessary, to prevent material damages, and especially when the cargo threatens to perish.

(3.) If the ship requires repairs, which cannot be delayed any longer without danger of loss or of a considerable reduction in value, the repairs are to be effected, or the ship, especially if she be unfit for repairs or not worth being repaired, is to be sold and the proceeds to be deposited in court.

(4.) If under the circumstances other measures are requisite to prevent damage, such measures are likewise not excluded.

(5.) If objections arise to giving the crew of the vessel brought up permission to communicate with the shore after having given their evidence, the said communication with the shore can be prohibited or at least limited.

Any of the preceding measures can be ordered only by the court, designated in § 8, on the recommendation of the harbour police authorities or the interested third party. The court has to allow, before giving its decision, as far as there is no danger in delay, a hearing to the parties interested in the matter, as well as to apply for a statement of the public prosecutor attached to the prize court, regarding the recommendation made. Against the decision of the court an appeal may be made to the prize court whose decision is final. The resolution mentioned in § 5 may be issued by the court also *ex officio*; but in this case, also, a complaint against its enactment may be lodged with the prize court.

§ 36.

The prize is after condemnation to be sold publicly by the harbour police authorities on the motion of the public prosecutor attached to the prize court.

The proceeds, after deduction of expenses, flow into the public exchequer. The officers and crew of the vessel of war, which has brought up the prize, have a claim to two thirds of the net proceeds.

The division amongst them is made according to a set of regulations to be issued by the Minister of Marine.

§ 37.

If the prize court has decided on a condemnation, the decision, especially with regard to disposal of the crew and the maintenance of the same (§ 18 of the Prize Regulations), may forthwith be executed provisionally, unless it be that the prize court in making the decision gave directions to the contrary, or that this has been ordered supplementarily by the supreme prize court after having been applied to in the matter. The reclaimant can prevent the execution only if he gives security for costs and damages arising from a suspension of execution, by depositing in court the necessary amount in cash or in valuable papers which have currency anywhere on any national stock exchange. The value of the papers is to be calculated according to current rate of exchange.

The amount of money necessary for giving security is determined by the Prize Court, according to its independent judgment.

The decision of the prize court in favour of release can be carried into execution only after the time allowed for appeal has elapsed or if appeal has been rejected.

Final Directions.

§ 38.

The foregoing directions come, in a corresponding manner, into force also in cases in which not the vessel brought up but only the cargo or the proceeds of ship and cargo have come into port (§ 16 of the Prize Regulations).

On the other hand, the foregoing directions have no application in the case of the capture of a hostile vessel of war.

§ 39.

If a ship brought up is navigated into the port of a Power allied with Prussia (§ 14 of Prize Regulations), the duties incumbent, according to the foregoing directions, upon the court and harbour police authorities, will be undertaken by officials appointed by means of a special order by the Minister of Foreign Affairs and the Minister of Marine.

Appendix H.

EXTRACT FROM THE INSTRUCTIONS, ISSUED FOR THE COMMANDERS OF GERMAN VESSELS OF WAR, AS SANCTIONED BY IMPERIAL ORDER OF 28 SEPTEMBER, 1872.*

(CONDUCT OF COMMANDERS IN FOREIGN COUNTRIES.)

§ 6.

The commander of a ship is a representative of the Emperor. Being cut off from direct intercourse with his superiors, he is therefore obliged, in all cases which the existing decisions and instructions cannot foresee, to act upon his own judgment in accordance with circumstances.

§ 7.

He must at all times permit himself to be guided by the consideration of the interests of the Imperial service and of the Fatherland, and decide accordingly.

§ 8.

His ship represents in foreign countries the armed power of the Fatherland.

§ 9.

On his arrival in any foreign port, the commander is to make himself acquainted with the local police, customs and quarantine regulations; the latter he should study if possible even in the port of departure, and he is to take care that these regulations be observed in all respects.

In answering questions addressed to him by the sanitary officers or by other officials, he should go to work with the greatest attention and exactness, and seek to avoid misunderstandings which might give rise to complaints. Before running into inland waters, he should, so far as they are subject to the sovereignty of foreign Powers, obtain the

---

* Translated from an appendix to the work of Mr. F. PERELS, Counsellor to the German Admiralty, *Das Internationale Oeffentliche Seerecht.*

permission of the authorities of the respective country. In cases of pressing necessity, when this sanction cannot be awaited, he must apply for it retrospectively.

§ 10.

He is to afford protection and to render help, in connection with the consuls, to the subjects of the German Empire and to their commerce, traffic and navigation, but he should at the same time respect and obey the laws of the country in force at the respective place.

§ 12.

The general official instructions for consuls of the German Empire of 6th June, 1871, serve as a guide for intercourse with German consular representatives.

The legal and political responsibility for the consequences of any armed interference of the Imperial German Navy, caused by an Imperial representative, falls solely on the latter. It is his duty to negotiate with the authorities of the respective country, as also especially to examine, whether all peaceful means, to prevent the life, liberty or property of German subjects being imperilled, have been exhausted, whether a delay would cause serious danger, or whether according to the nature of the circumstances in no other way, than by use of physical force, a violation of rights might be prevented or indemnity or satisfaction obtained, for damage suffered or as the case may be for insult offered to the German flag.

If they have no special instructions, or if under the circumstances of the case in question previous communication with an Imperial representative is possible, the commanders of H. I. G. M. vessels of war act only upon request of the latter, and bear entirely themselves the military responsibility for the execution of a requisition accepted by them; they have therefore, on their own part, to examine the material practicability of its execution and will be personally responsible for the maintenance of the honour of the Imperial flag of war, when once engaged. They are however under certain circumstances at liberty to claim, orally or in writing, due consideration on the part of the Imperial representative for any personal objections they may have against a requisition, which runs in the direction of employing physical force, or for any views they may have regarding the propriety or impropriety of any particular mode of procedure, so as to decline undertaking the full responsibility for the same. As to any official investigation and decision regarding the political and juridical aspects of the several points in question, and as to the conduct of negotiations regarding the subject with the authorities of the respective country, or, as the case may be, with the chiefs of uncivilized tribes, commanders have authority for such proceedings in those places only, where there is no regular Imperial representative.

Imperial Order of 28th December, 1875, bearing on § 12. *(M. V. Bl. page 242).*

In pursuance of your report, I decide that in the instructions sanctioned by me under date of 28 September, 1872, for the commander of any of my ships and vessels, the following passage, which is to define the mutual relations between my representatives in foreign parts and the commanders of my ships and to determine the limits of the competence and responsibilities of both parties, in political and military affairs, shall be accepted as a supplement to § 12 page 4 *ad a linea* 2.

In any requisitions to be addressed to commanders of Imperial ships of war by Imperial Embassies or Consulates, it is to be considered a binding rule, that the juridical and political responsibility for the consequences of any armed interference of the Imperial navy caused by an Imperial representative falls solely on the latter. It is therefore likewise only the duty of the latter, to negotiate with the authorities of the respective country, as also especially to examine, whether all peaceful means to prevent the life, liberty or property of subjects of the Empire being imperilled, have been exhausted, whether a delay would cause a serious danger, or whether, according to the position of affairs, only by use of physical force a violation of rights can be prevented, or, for suffered damage or as the case may be for insult offered to the German flag, indemnity and satisfaction can be obtained.

The commanders of Imperial ships of war act, unless they have special instructions or unless previous communication with an Imperial representative is impossible, only on the proposition of the latter and bear exclusively themselves the military responsibility for the execution of an accepted requisition; they have therefore on their own part to examine the physical practicability of it, and to be personally responsible for the maintenance of the honour of the Imperial flag of war, when once engaged. They are however under certain circumstances at liberty to claim, orally or in writing, due consideration on the part of the Imperial representative, for any personal objections they may have against a requisition which runs in the direction of employing physical force, or for any views they may have regarding the propriety or impropriety of any particular mode of procedure, so as to decline undertaking the full responsibility for the same.

As to any official investigation and decision regarding the political and juridical aspects of the several points in question, and as to the conduct of negotiations regarding the subject with the authorities of the respective country, or, as the case may be, with the chiefs of uncivilized tribes, commanders have authority for such proceedings in those places only, where there is no regular Imperial representative.

You have accordingly to cause the further measures to be taken.

To the Chief of the Admiralty.

(Signed) WILLIAM.

§ 13.

If a commander gets into any conflict with the authorities of a foreign State, he has to hand over to the consul or diplomatic representative of the German Empire the further dealing with the affair and to report, as a matter of course, to his superior officers.

§ 14.

If, somehow, an immediate interference is absolutely necessary, he is to take into consideration the precepts of Maritime International Law, and not to omit in his proceedings paying attention to the fact that the entire responsibility for the consequences remains with himself. ....

§ 15.

As it is the interest of the German Empire, that German representatives should be held in as high estimation as possible, it is the duty of every commander to give them the honours to which they are entitled in the handsomest and fullest manner possible according to the flag and salute regulations; it is moreover his duty, to act in the best possible and most free accord with the diplomatic and consular representatives, and to carry out their requisitions as far as practicable.

Finally, the consuls should be taken to be the natural agents for all requisites of the ship. The list of the German envoys, consuls, and vice-consuls officiating in the various countries and places, together with their respective spheres, will be found in the book chest of the ship.

Imperial Order of 7th January, 1879, *bearing on* §§ 12, 13 & 15. *(M. V. Bl. page* 1*).*

As a supplement to the decisions of §§ 12, 13, and 15 of the instructions for commanders, sanctioned by me, I decide, in pursuance of your report, the following to be added as preface to § 15. The commander, in visiting foreign ports, should without loss of time enter into communication with the local Imperial representative (envoy, embassy, consulate) and inform the same of the purpose and probable length of his stay. The commander has moreover to report to the Imperial representative in the capital of the respective country, his arrival, and the purpose and probable length of stay, in all those cases, where it is not merely a matter of supplementing his provisions and stores, but where he is to fulfil definite duties or to apply for the help or as the case may be for the assistance of foreign authorities, even if a mutual relation of requisitions between the Imperial representative and the ship's commander is not involved thereby.

Berlin, 7th January, 1879.

To the Chief of the Admiralty.

(Signed) WILLIAM.

§ 16

For any politico-military action, which the sailing orders, given to the commander, require, or which is connected with the carrying out of requisitions of our ambassadors or political agents, the following rules may be taken as a guide:

(1.) That the honour of the flag must be upheld under any circumstances; that therefore the commander, from the moment when he accepts a requisition takes upon himself the full and sole responsibility for its being carried through, and that an undertaking once commenced must be brought to an end by employing all powers available;

(2.) That every action should be preceded by the most thorough preparation and knowledge of all circumstances, and that one must not commence any more than what can be carried through under favourable circumstances. Nothing is worse with uncivilized or half civilized peoples, than to have to retire, without having accomplished one's aim;

(3.) That the defeated enemy should be treated generously, without a show of weakness.

Appendix I.

ESSAY ON THE PRIZE QUESTIONS, PROPOSED BY THE CENTRAL-COMMITTEE OF THE PRUSSIAN RED-CROSS SOCIETY, IN 1869, WITH REGARD TO THE EXTENSION OF THE SOCIETY'S AID TO THE NAVY.

Prize-Queries of the Prussian Central-Committee, Proposed at the International Conference of the Aid-Societies, held at Berlin, in April 1869, under the presidency of the Honourable R. von Sydow.

I. "Under what circumstances, in what way and with what success, have private individuals, hitherto, tried to participate,—in naval wars,—in the rescuing of the shipwrecked and in the care of the sick and wounded of the Fleets of War?"

II. "To what extent and under what conditions, can the Aid-Societies undertake this task, with probability of success?"

III. "What preparations are necessary, in time of peace, to solve this problem in a manner answerable to the claims of Humanity?"

IV. "In what respect can the solution of this task be advanced and assured, by forming and entertaining relations between the permanent Aid-Societies for the nursing of sick and wounded soldiers in the field, and the existing associations for the rescue of shipwrecked persons?"

Answers to the Questions.

Question I.

It is a characteristic feature of our time, that, while art and science are uniting their utmost skill to invent new instruments of warfare, and the art of killing is attaining a dreadful perfection, Philanthropy is endeavouring, with equal zeal, to alleviate the calamities of war. While peace-apostles are drawing up their theoretical maxims for securing the universal and permanent suspension of bloody conflicts between civilized nations, Humanity is trying to contrive practical means to heal, as much as possible, the disastrous effects of war, which, while they cannot be prevented, can, at least, be made less painful to bear.

Societies for the aid of wounded soldiers on the battle-field have existed throughout all ages. From the Order of the Knights of St. John of Jerusalem,—still subsistent in the two great branches of Christianity, the Roman-Catholic Order of St. John, in Spain, and the Protestant Evangelic, in Prussia,—down to the Sisters of St. Vincent de Paul, the Deaconesses of Kaiserswoerth, and of Bethanien, at Berlin, the Brethren of the Rauhe-Haus at Hamburg, the Grand-Duchess Helena-Paulowna, with her Sisters of the Cross, and Miss Florence Nightingale with her helpers, at Sebastopol,—different religious societies, of all branches of the Christian Church, have been working on this field of Charity. But, each carried out its own benevolent work in its own way, with its own organisation and rules, without that general and voluntary union of strength and design, which gives new youth and vigour to the continuous exertions of Charity.

The Red-Cross Alliance of our days has a wider range. Her badge is the emblem of Peace in the midst of the war-cries, and reminds the nations, that, though fighting, we are all brethren and that human charity is above human passions and prejudices. Although it is apparent, that it will not be the merit of our century to have extinguished warfare between civilized nations, yet, it is to our generation that the honour and the glory belong of those general and practical efforts for ameliorating what cannot be totally avoided.

The treaty of Paris (1856) commenced the work of securing neutrality to private property at sea. The Genevese Convention, with its additional articles, accomplished a work of practical philanthropy, by claiming the right of Humanity to heal the wounds of the human instruments of war, on the fields of conflict, without regard to nation or creed. On this great work, the noble Prussian Central-Committee puts the crowning stone, by her efforts to bring into a practical shape the principles adopted for securing aid to the wounded warrior; not only on land, but also on the ocean, where a double charge is upon our shoulders: the healing of the wounds, inflicted by human hands, and the rescuing from the perils of an element, whose strength it is above our power to control.

If voluntary aid, by private individuals or societies, to soldiers on the battle-field, be a fact often recorded by History, it is not so with the extension of these philanthropic efforts to succour the warrior at sea. This new branch of Charity, this help to the sailors on their own battle-ground, by private corporations, is unprecedented in history: a new task, without a guide.

On the question, as to what has heretofore been done, and with what success, by private individuals or societies, to save the shipwrecked and to nurse the sick and wounded on fleets, engaging in time of war, the history of the naval battles of ancient and modern times, gives no information, and that of the late wars no sufficient answer, to form an experienced guide for our present object. In this case, our present Aid-Societies, bereft as they are, of the necessary enlightenment through historical experienee, will have,—for the aid of the sailor in battles at sea,—to trace their own path of duty, on this new field of glorious labour.

Question II.

Let us then face the difficulties, and, guided by technical knowledge, try to solve the question : to what extent and under what conditions the Aid-Societies can undertake their double task on the Fleet, the rescuing of the shipwrecked and the nursing of the sick and wounded,—and we find that, for this double task, the following conditions are indispensable, to enable the Aid-Societies to carry out their benevolent work to an extent, by which they can secure to the sailor the practical benefit of their labours.

These are :

1°. Suitable *Hospital-Ships (Vereins-Lazarethschiffe, Bâtiments de secours)* for active service with the Fleets, and exclusively fitted out as such, unarmed, but protected by the privilege of neutrality.

2°. *Hospital-Rafts* (as described hereafter), which enjoy the same amount of neutrality, and are used to pick up, even between the engaging vessels, the shipwrecked and those who are cast overboard by explosion or fire, in order to carry them on board the Hospital-ship for medical aid.

3°. A special corps of *Naval nurses and helpers*, accustomed to life on board ship at sea; which can be raised by the local-committees of our present Aid-Societies at the sea-ports, where is established the basis of operations of the fleet or squadron, on which their services is required.

4°. *International regulation* of the state of neutrality of the Hospital-ships and Rafts, their crews and all who are picked up by the Rafts, during action; of the sort and class of Hospital-ships and Rafts, to be used and their position to be kept in the fleet, in motion and during action.

5°. *Naval-Hospitals at the Sea-ports*, under direction of the respective local-committees, where the Hospital-ships can disembark the sick and wounded after a battle at sea.

1°. HOSPITAL-SHIPS.

With regard to Hospital-ships, we must, in the first place, call attention to a deficiency, which exists in the organisation of the Medical-Services on the fleets and squadrons of most nations. This organisation is very expensive and yet it seldom answers the purpose, from want of a sufficient number of surgeons to supply the fleet, and of the necessary room on board a fighting vessel, for taking up the sick and wounded. In a fleet or squadron, each vessel, large or small, has its own medical staff of surgeons and helps, apothecary's shops and full supply of medicaments and hospital-furniture; while, for the sick and wounded on board each vessel, a space is taken from the quarters of the crew, which reduces the comfort of the healthy, without affording sufficient convenience and security for the patients and the surgeons and helpers in attendance, during a battle. In fact, the best medical help, on board an active war-vessel, might fail, in time of action, from want of space and proper security, to exercise its functions. Experienced naval-medical officers have proved, that the Medical Service and Nursing would be far more efficient, if we had attached to each squadron, one or more Hospital-ships, exclusively fitted out for medical service, and quite able to keep with the fleet; where the medical department is established and the principal medical help concentrated. One surgeon, with one or two assistants, on each vessel, would then be sufficient for cases of accidents, and the first dressing of the wounded in a battle; whilst the removable sick and wounded could be transported to the Hospital-ship, where the Chief-surgeon and his assistants are stationed, and full aid and comfort can be afforded to the patient. The wooden Frigates, which, in the present state of warfare, are useless for fighting-services, will afford the principal means to carry out this purpose. As to the internal service and medical administration on board a Hospital-ship, little may be said. Every naval-medical officer of any experience, will be fully aware of the necessaries, required for the wounded and sick on board a vessel at sea. Proper ventilation, beds, linen, good drink-water and nourishment and everything belonging to hygienic regulations and medical help, as well as judicious and prudent regulations and instructions, for the medical service on board a good Hospital-ship, these all ought to be settled questions at the Naval-Medical Department of every civilized nation.

A *Hospital-Ship*, whether fitted out by the Government or by the Aid-Societies, must be a frigate, having a spacious main deck with proper height from deck to beam; propelled by sail and steam and quite sea-worthy. (*) In the internal arrangement it must be observed, that the main or battery-deck be reserved for the sick and wounded, while the lower-deck *(Zwischen-deck)* is destined for the surgeons, helpers, nurses, apothecary and stores, for ship and rafts; objects for rescuing, clothing, provisions and bedding for shipwrecked persons, and objects required for the nursing of the sick and wounded (these objects in proportion to the size of the Hospital-ship and the number of sick and wounded, which she is able to take up). A

(*) Resolution of the Intern. Conf. 1869. Sec: II, 8 and 15.

proper *Ice-cellar* must not be forgotten, for which a fit place will be found in the water-hold *(Wasser-raum)* on the ballast. The captain, ship's officers and crew for ship and rafts, must have their apartments and berths on the upper-deck. There also, the cooking-rooms *(Schiffsherd)*, bakery, slaughter-house, washing-rooms, etc., the capstan *(Spill)* and the running part of anchor-chains, with the bitts *(Bâtinge)*, have their places.

The *Sick-deck (Kranken-deck)* must be a clear deck, fore and aft, without any divisions or partitions, except for the closets *(der Abtritt)*, at the sides, with outside discharges and ventilators. The operating-table, when in use, is temporarily put up, at any convenient place on the sick-deck, fastened to the deck and screened off by a sail. The sick-deck,—whitewashed all over with lime,—is ventilated by port-holes in the sides, fore and aft, and air-tubes (*Luft-löcher*)—(Watson's & Gilmore's patent)—and windsails (*Kühlsegeln*), through the upper-deck, the chimney or the hollow iron masts. The hatchways (*Lücken*) above the engine, and the steps leading from the upper-deck to the engine room, must be incased and shut off from the sick-deck; so that the heat of fire and engine cannot be spread over the sick-deck, but is carried straight up, through the hatches, to the upper-deck. No unnecessary communication over the sick-deck must be allowed; all passages through the hatches to the lower decks and the ship's store-rooms and coal-bunkers (*Kohlenkasten*) must be incased, as above mentioned.

At each side of the vessel, two or more of the port-holes must have suitable dimensions, to take in the sick-transport-cots, which are hoisted, from the Raft alongside, up to the port-hole, by means of a tackle (*Talie*), hanging from a davit (*Taube-jütte*) above the port-hole, and whose running-bight (*laufende Part*) is on the upper-deck, where the hoisting work is to be done. The transport-cot is carried by slings (*Lengen*), attached to the cot, and pendants (*Schinkel*), hooked to the tackle: so that the cot, hanging in one tackle, is hoisted up horizontally and can be turned athwart-ship (*quer-schiffs*), to be taken through the port-holes on the sick-deck. (*)

The *Sleeping-Cots (flache Hangmatten)*,—made of canvas, with square bottoms of wooden frame with springs,—six feet long by two and a half broad (inside dimension), must be hung from brass swinging-hooks, lengthwise in rows, with 3—3½ feet distance at the sides, by one at the head and feet. Above each cot hangs, at the foot-end, a swinging-table, to carry the medicine bottles, food and other necessaries at hand, for the patient in the cot.

(*) A most able description of the fittings of the British ship *Victor Emanuel* as a hospital ship, during the Ashantee war in 1874, is given in the *Lancet* of November 22, December 6, 1873, and April 18, 1874, and,—with all particulars regarding ventilation,—in a paper, read by the distinguished British Admiral A. P. RYDER, at the Royal United Service Institution, Whitehall Yard, on May 29, 1874, and inserted in the Journal of the Institution Vol. XVIII, No. LXXVIII (1874).

As a model cot, for the sick and wounded at sea, we can recommend the cot with suspension-apparatus, of the invention of Dr. van Stockum (Dutch R. N.) in use at the Naval-Hospital at Willemsoord, Holland. The ingenious apparatus of these cots allows the beds and linen to be changed from under the patient, without removing or, in the least, disturbing him; which is of much comfort and safety for a man dangerously wounded at sea.

The *Sick-transport-cot* is a single cot, of the same dimensions as the cots of the sick-deck, and quite fitted to be hung up in the rows, in case the state of the patient does not allow his being removed to the common sleeping-cot, when taken on the sick-deck. At the head and foot-end of the transport-cot, is a fixed sling, with thimble (*Kausse*) where the pendants of the hoisting-tackle are hooked in, to take the cot to the sick-deck as above described.

The Hospital-ships fitted out by the Red-Cross Societies, to follow the fleet, must be placed at the disposal of the Admiral in command. They must be subject to the rules and regulations of the Naval Medical Service. Their destination is to give succour during and after the battle. As soon as the signal of distress is hoisted from any vessel, they proceed with their Rafts to the assistance of the crew, without regard to Nationality. Directly after the battle they indicate, by a signal, that they are able and ready to receive the sick and wounded. (*) The Captain and the First or Executive officer are to be commissioned by the Government at the nomination of the Central-Committee of the Red-Cross Society; by which means the vessel's commission, required by the 13th addit. article of the Convention is also secured. The surgeons, the nurses and helpers and the personnel of the sick-deck service must be procured by the Society,—through the Local-Committee of the sea-port, where the hospital-ship is to be fitted out,—and placed under the direction of the Chief-Surgeon of the Fleet or Squadron. The rest of the ship's officers, the engineers and the crew for ships and rafts, are hired by the Captain, under direction of the said Local-Committee. The medical service and the administration belonging thereto, on board the Hospital-ships of the Red-Cross Societies are to be regulated on the same footing as the Government Hospital-ships, with which the Society's ships must be identical, to procure that analogy and unity in the Medical Service, by which only effectual help can be obtained.

In the present state of the war-navies, with ironclad and submerged war-vessels, the Hospital-ship, as above described, will become, even in time of peace, indispensable for the Naval-Medical Service. A bad kind of fever has been stated to prevail on board the ironclads. Dr. Holden (of the U. S. Navy) gives in his work "*On the causes of*

(*) Resolutions of the Intern. Confer. of 1869. Sec. II. §§ 3, 4 & 5.

certain diseases in ships of war," (1866), (*Archives de Médecine-navale,* 1859)—his experiences of the sort of fever called the "*iron-clad fever,*" which has been observed to be peculiar to these sorts of vessels. And so it will be found, henceforth, impossible to keep sick or wounded people on board these ironclads and monitors for any length of time. For a squadron at sea, this may be of serious consequence

2°. THE HOSPITAL-RAFT.

The Hospital-Raft (*Hospital-flösse*) is to be regarded as the chief-instrument for carrying out the purpose of the Red-Cross Societies at Sea. In the present state of modern warfare, probably only ironclad ram-turret-monitors are to be used as fighting vessels, and in a sea-fight calamities will henceforth occur wholesale, for the battle in open sea must now be decided by the total destruction of one of the parties, if it is to be decided at all. The war-vessels will blow up, be run down, or sink, for the iron and steel improvements will enable them to withstand the force of shot and shell, as long as ammunition lasts, till a great catastrophe puts an end to the conflict. The wounded will be less numerous behind the submerged iron walls, or within the iron shot-proof turrets; but a whole crew, or a great part of those who survive a catasprophe, may be struggling with death in the water at the same time, and would surely perish, if they had to be picked up by common boats, and besides that, where are the boats to be launched at such a moment?

In such disasters, the Hospital-Rafts, neutral, and always ready at hand, are the only means for rescuing a mass of drowning or wounded men between the fighting vessels, and carrying them safely for help to the Hospital-ship.—(A description of the Hospital-Raft, is given hereafter).

As the Hospital-ship, even when viewed in its full meaning as a Rescuing-vessel (*bâtiment de secours*), cannot be expected to be able to introduce itself between the fighting vessels, or to approach closely a sinking vessel or one on the point of blowing up,—so as to give direct help, from the decks to the shipwrecked, by throwing life-buoys or ropes to the persons in danger,—it must necessarily devolve on the Hospital-Rafts, with their peculiar buoyancy, agility and low position, almost on a level with the surface of the sea, to render all direct help, by taking over the crew from vessels in a helpless state, or by hauling up the shipwrecked out of the water, by means of ropes attached to some floating object, of sufficient buoyancy to keep a man afloat, while grasping it. With such means of rescuing, the Rafts, sent on duty, must be amply supplied. The ropes to be used for such purpose must be *Manilla,* which is more buoyant than tarred hemp.

The usefulness of *circular Life-buoys,* to be thrown from the Rafts or the decks of the Hospital-ships,—to support persons, who have fallen into the water, until they can be reached,—will not escape notice, as this is the common practice of rescuing on board every vessel. The most efficient way to give the whole crew of a vessel, immediately after a catastrophe, sure means of keeping afloat till they can be rescued by the Hospital-Rafts, are *Life-belts,* (on the plan of Capt. J. R. Ward, Brit. R. N., Inspector of Lifeboats to the N. L. B. Institution), which every man has to keep on during the whole fight, and besides that the *Cork-Matrasses* (ordinary sized hammock-matrasses, stuffed with buoyant materials, of Messrs. Pellews' patent). * Both of these precautionary means are used in the Russian Navy.

DIRECTIONS FOR RESTORING THE APPARENTLY DROWNED.

In treating of the means for rescuing people from a watery grave, it will not be deemed superfluous to call to mind the directions for the recovery of the apparently dead from drowning. The operations for restoring those rescued from the water, are so mechanical, and easily understood, that it is the imperative duty of everybody engaged in the Red-Cross service, to study the instructions on that subject and, in a case of drowning, to follow them in all their details. Drowning too, like all other accidents, is so unexpected and has, very soon, so many of the symptoms of death, that presence of mind in the bystanders, and promptitude of action, are absolutely necessary to make the doubtful balance incline to life.

The following are the recommendations, given in the instructions, emanating from the Committee of the British *Royal National Life-Boat Institution* :—

1°. Send immediately for medical assistance, blankets and dry clothing, but proceed to treat the patient instantly on the spot, in the open air, with the face downward, whether on shore or afloat, exposing the face, neck and chest to the wind, except in severe weather, and removing all tight clothing from the neck and chest, especially the braces.

The points to be aimed at, are—first and *immediately*, the RESTORATION OF BREATHING; and secondly, after breathing is restored, the PROMOTION OF WARMTH AND CIRCULATION.

The efforts to *Restore Breathing* must be commenced immediately and energetically, and persevered in for one or two hours, or until a medical man has pronounced that life is extinct. Efforts to promote *Warmth* and *Circulation,* beyond removing the wet clothes and drying the skin, must not be made until the first appearance of natural breathing. For, if circulation of the blood be induced before breathing has recommenced, the restoration to life will be endangered.

(*) Resolutions of the Intern. Conf. of 1869. Sec. II. § 14.

2°. *To Restore Breathing.* (*Dr. Marshall Hall's Method of Inducing Respiration*).

To clear the throat.—Place the patient on the floor or deck with the face downwards, and one of the arms under the forehead, in which position all fluids will readily escape by the mouth, and the tongue itself will fall forward, leaving the entrance into the windpipe free. Assist this operation by wiping and cleansing the mouth.

If satisfactory breathing commences, use the treatment described below, to promote warmth. If there be only slight breathing—or no breathing—or if the breathing fail, then :—

3°. *To Excite Breathing.*—Turn the patient well and instantly on the side, (supporting the head)—and :—

Excite the nostrils with snuff, hartshorn and smelling salts, or tickle the throat with a feather, etc. if they are at hand. Rub the chest and face warm, and dash cold water, or cold and hot water alternately, on them.

If there be no success, lose not a moment but instantly :—

To Imitate Breathing.—Replace the patient on his face, raising and supporting his chest well on a folded coat or other article of dress.

Turn the body very gently on the side and a little beyond, and then briskly on the face, back again, repeating these measures cautiously, efficiently and perseveringly about fifteen times in the minute, or once every four or five seconds, occasionally varying the side.

(*By placing the patient on the chest, the weight of the body forces the air out; when turned on the side, this presure is removed, and air enters the chest*).

On each occasion that the body is replaced on the face, make uniform but efficient pressure with brisk movement, on the back between and below the shoulder-blades or bones on each side, removing the pressure immediately before turning the body on the side.

During the whole of the operations, let one person attend solely to the movements of the head, and of the arm placed under it.

(*The first measure increases expiration,—the second commences inspiration.—The result is: Respiration or Natural Breathing;—and, if not too late, Life*).

Whilst the above operations are being proceeded with, dry the hands and feet, and as soon as dry clothing or blankets can be procured, strip the body and cover or gradually re-clothe it, taking care not to interfere with the efforts to restore breathing.

DR. SILVESTER'S METHOD.

Should the above described efforts not prove successful in the course of from two to five minutes, proceed to imitate breathing by Dr. Silvester's method, as follows :—Place the patient on his back on a flat surface, inclined a little upwards from the feet; raise and support the head and shoulders on a small firm cushion or folded article of dress, placed under the shoulder-blades.

Draw forward the patient's tongue, and keep it projecting beyond the lips: an elastic band over the tongue and under the chin will answer this purpose, or a piece of string or tape may be tied round them, or, by raising the lower jaw, the teeth may be made to retain the tongue in that position. Remove all tight clothing from about the neck and chest, especially the braces.

To Imitate the Movements of Breathing.—Standing at the patient's head, grasp the arms just above the elbows, and draw the arms gently and steadily upwards above the head, and *keep them stretched* upwards for two seconds. *By this means, air is drawn into the lungs*). Then turn down the patient's arms, and press them gently and firmly for two seconds against the sides of the chest. (*By this means, air is pressed out of the lungs*).

Repeat these measures alternately, deliberately and perseveringly, about fifteen times a minute, until a spontaneous effort to respire is perceived, immediately upon which cease to imitate the movements of breathing, and proceed to *Induce Circulation and Warmth.*

Treatment after Natural Breathing has been restored.

To promote Warmth and Circulation.—Commence rubbing the limbs upwards, with firm grasping pressure and energy, using handkerchiefs, flannels, etc. (*By this measure the blood is propelled along the veins towards the heart*).

The friction must be continued under the blanket or over the dry clothing.

Promote the warmth of the body by application of hot flannels, bottles or bladders of hot water, heated bricks etc., to the pit of the stomach, the arm-pits, between the thighs and to the soles of the feet. On the restoration of life, a tea-spoonful of warm water should be given, and then, if the power of swallowing have returned, small quantities of wine, warm brandy and water, or coffee, should be administered. The patient should be kept in bed, and a disposition to sleep encouraged.

General Observations.

The above described treatment should be persevered in for some hours, as it is an erroneous opinion, that persons are irrecoverable, because life does not soon make its appearance;—persons having been restored after persevering for many hours.

The *appearances which generally accompany death*, are: breathing and the heart's action cease entirely; the eyelids are generally half closed; the pupils dilated; the jaws clenched; the fingers semi-contracted; the tongue approaches to the under edges of the lips, and these, as well as the nostrils, are covered with a frothy mucus. Coldness and pallor of surface increase.

Cautions. Prevent unnecessary crowding of persons round the body, especially if in an appartment; keep the patient, if possible, in the open air until respiration has been restored;—at all events, be careful to let the air play freely about the room where he is treated.

Avoid rough usage, and do not allow the body to remain on the back unless the tongue is secured. Under no circumstances hold the body up by the feet. On no account place the body in a warm bath, unless under medical direction, and even then it should only be employed as a momentary excitant.

3°. SICK-NURSES AND HELPERS FOR THE HOSPITAL-SHIP'S SERVICE AT SEA.

The speciality of the service, which the Red-Cross Societies are called to perform on the ocean, makes it necessary to establish a separate corps of Nurses and Helpers for the Hospital-Ship's service at sea, and to make them accustomed to the life on board. The peculiar nature of this field of work admits none inexperienced as regards life at sea (*unerfahren*), without the risk of failure.

The *personnel* of the Sick-Deck-service must be trained in time of peace, through the care of the Local-Committees at the Sea-ports. The Red-Cross Societies cannot face their task at sea in time of war in a proper manner, if they do not provide themselves, during peace, with a corps of well trained persons for the work of sick-nurses at sea. In this respect, all that is regarded as requisite for the army, is of no less consequence for the peculiar task at sea. *

When we speak of the necessity for the sea-*personnel* of the Red-Cross Societies to be accustomed to life at sea, we, by no means, intend to exclude female nurses from the Hospital-Ship. On the contrary, the kind treatment and the diligent attendance of our sister-associates in this task of humanity, are of too great a value for the sick and wounded sailor, to be disregarded. In the midst of the ocean, far from home and friends, tender female care will be an uncommon blessing to the sailor, and may revive the courage and hope of many a sinking heart, for the benefit of both body and soul. Let us, then, spare no trouble to gain this powerful auxiliary of the Red-Cross for the wounded warrior at sea. The Hospital-Ships must have the necessary arrangements with this end in view, for which every possibility exists,—and once accustomed on board, experience has proved woman to be as comfortable at sea, as the best sailor.

(*) Resolutions of the Intern. Confer. of 1869. Sec. III. Nos. 12–15.

4°. INTERNATIONAL REGULATIONS.

By the 13th additional article of the International Convention of 1864, stipulated by the Commissioners of the different Governments which signed the Convention, at Geneva, the 20th of October 1868, is regulated the state of neutrality of the Hospital-Ships and other vessels of the Red-Cross Societies, of their crews and *personnel* for the hospital-service, and of all, who are picked up by these vessels during an action. But as the sort of vessels to be used and their movement and position, during action, is left to their own discretion and risk, it would prove of great utility to the common cause, if the different nationalities of the Red-Cross were to come to an agreement,—at an international conference, on these and other points, which it may be found necessary to stipulate, for the common service of the Red-Cross at sea.

For the international regulation of the position and service of the Hospital-Ships and their Rafts and Boats in a sea-fight, the following points have to be settled, at an international conference of the Red-Cross Societies.

1°. *Sort of vessels.*

a. The sort of vessel to be used as Hospital-Ships, by all Nations, so, that no fear can be entertained, that a Hospital-Ship could ever be used for fighting purposes. The best sort of Hospital-Raft. *

b. The Hospital-Ships must be unarmed, but, to afford security for the inmates, their decks may be made bomb-proof.

2°. *Distinguishing Colour, Badge and Signals.*

a. With the national colours at the stern, the Societies' vessels bear the neutrality ensign,—the white flag, with the Red-Cross,—at the main-top-mast.

b. It is necessary to stipulate:—1°. The signal, by which the neutral Hospital-Ship can be recognized *by night*, (*a red light under a white one*), at the main-top-mast. 2°. The *signal of distress* (*yellow flag*, and, *by night*, *a red light*). 3°. The signal of being able and ready to give help (*yellow flag with the Red-Cross*, and, *by night*, *two red perpendicular lights*). †

c. The Hospital-Rafts and the Boats for the manoeuvring of the Rafts, if necessary, are, like the Hospital-Ships, painted white with the red band along the outsides.

d. The crews of Hospital-Ships, Rafts and Boats are to be dressed in white, with the neutrality badge on the arm.

(*) Resolutions of the Intern. Confer. of 1869. Sec. II. No. 14. Idem Nos. 5 & 7.
(†) Resolutions of the Intern. Confer. of 1869. Sec. II. No. 14. Idem Nos. 5 & 7.

They can never be used for any work belonging to the fighting-vessels, but must be strictly kept to their neutral duty.

3°. The place of the Hospital-Ships in the fleet; when in motion out of action; in line of battle; while chasing and while retreating. Their position to be kept out of the line of fire, when the parties are in action. All to be regulated in General Instructions for the Captains of the Hospital-Ships and the Naval Commissioners of the Red-Cross Societies.

4°. The place of the Hospital-Rafts, during action, always ready at hand, to pick up the shipwrecked and the wounded.

5°. General Instructions, for the Surgeons, Nurses, and Helpers of the Societies, with regard to their mutual *international relations* and to *their relations towards the Naval Authorities*. These regulations to be made as uniform as possible, for the different Nationalities of the Red-Cross Societies. *

6°. The rewards to be offered to promote acts of humane bravery during an action. A pension to those, who become disabled, while rescuing or helping the shipwreked and the wounded, and the support to be granted to the families of those, who have lost their lives in these actions. †

7°. The International Signal-Code must be so drawn up as to be readily used among the Hospital-Ships, Rafts and Boats of all parties, for mutual recognition and help of the Red-Cross at sea, by day and by night.

5°. NAVAL HOSPITALS AT THE SEA-PORTS.

As these Hospitals are like those for the Army, no particular description of them need be given here. The management of the Naval Hospitals is intrusted to the respective Local-Committees at the sea-ports. The regulations regarding the medical service and the administration thereof, are the same for the Military-Naval-Hospitals, with which the Society's Naval Hospitals must be identical in working, as the Society's Hospital-Ships are with the Military Hospital-Ships.

At the Military-Naval-Hospitals, the Society's nurses and the *personnel* for the Sick-Deck-service can be trained, through the care of the respectve local-committees.

Question III.

After having regulated the conditions under which the Red-Cross Societies may fulfill their task in time of war, to its utmost extent, so far as human power can reach, we must trace their duty in time of peace, in order to be ever ready when their benevolent aid is required by humanity.

(*) Resolutions of the Intern. Confer. of 1869. Sec. II. No. 11. Idem No. 9.
(†) Idem No. 10.

In the first place, we must entertain, through periodical International Conferences, a cordial mutual understanding between the different Maritime Nationalities of the Red-Cross Societies, with regard to the best measures to be adopted for carrying out their common purposes in time of war. For instance : it is most requisite to agree upon the best model for Hospital-Rafts, in order to facilitate general mutual help in time of action.

The Red-Cross Societies must regulate their respective relations with the Military-Naval-Authorities.

The *Materiel* to be used by the Red-Cross Societies at sea, must be determined upon, by special statements. In time of peace, models must be procured, by purchase or exchange, and notes taken of the manufactures and places of production. The *Materiel* of the Red-Cross Societies, must,—as far as its special destination allows,—be procured in the manner and constructed on the models of the Military Navies.

With the view of general utility, and with the object of encouraging new inventions to alleviate the calamities of war, it is desirable to establish at the place of residence of the respective Central Committees, permanent exhibitions of articles, destined for the rescuing and medical help of the shipwrecked and the wounded. *

The special Corps of Sick-nurses and Helpers for the Hospital-Ship-service at sea, must be organized and instructed. The exercise of the crews of Hospital-Ships and Rafts must not be neglected in time of peace. The Red-Cross Societies must come to an understanding with their respective Military-Naval-Departments, to the effect, that one or more Hospital-Ships, with full complement of crew and nurses, and fitted out for use in time of war, may be attached to every evolution-squadron. To these preparatory measures in time of peace, the Aid-Societies contribute according to their means, and the arrangement made with the respective Naval Departments. The Hospital-Rafts must be tried during the cruise, and the crews of the rafts trained under different circumstances as to weather and sea.

In this way, we shall acquire practical proofs and experience, and be able to judge what is best to be done, in order to be ever prepared to meet the calamities of a naval war.

Although we have here only to do with the affairs of the private Red-Cross Societies, yet we cannot avoid recommending the Naval Departments to profit in time of peace, in fitting out Hospital-Ships, which can enjoy the benefit of *entire neutrality*, as stipulated by the paragraph added to the 9th additional article of the Genevese Convention. The wooden, unprotected and unarmed vessels, with so many vulnerable points, fitted out as described in these pages for Hospital-Ships, cannot be used for fighting, and consequently, as not being

(*) Resolutions of the Intern. Confer. of 1869. Sec. II.

adapted to fighting purposes (*impropers au combat*) and their equipment exclusively appropriated to their special destination as *Floating-Hospitals*,—they will answer all the exigencies of the said 9th additional article and its fortunately adopted paragraph.—

Question IV.

After what has been said with regard to the necessity of experienced helpers at sea, we cannot but answer in the negative the question: "would the object in view be advanced and secured, if the established Red-Cross Societies for the assistance of the medical service of the Army in time of war, were to act in agreement and jointly with the Life-Boat Associations?"

For the reasons already given, the *personnel* of the Army, when not accustomed to life at sea, cannot be useful for the Hospital-Ship service at sea; so that the Local-Committees of the sea-ports will be called upon to supply the wants of the Sick-Deck on board the Hospital-Ships; while the Inland-Committees can support the Naval-Hospitals at the sea-ports, which, at all events, are identical with the hospitals of the Army.

As to the Life-Boat Institutions, they will do their duty during and after action, with regard to shipwrecked warriors on the coast where they are stationed; and, to this duty, they are already bound by their destination and the Rules of their Institution. For the nursing of sick and wounded warriors, who may be rescued by the Life-Boats, during or after a sea-fight, in a harbour or near the coasts, special agreement must be made by the Red-Cross Societies with the respective Life-Boat Institutions. But as to the service in *open sea,* during and after an action, the Red-Cross Societies cannot depend on the Life-Boats, for the field of labour of the latter is limited to sea-coasts and the shoals, and in these waters, their task is arduous enough, for us to give up all hope that their sphere of activity may be extended to battles in open sea. The Life-Boat Institution has another great design; it is on the watch for the victims of wind and weather, and consequently cannot leave its post. To attain practical results, each party must do its own work at the place appropriated to each, by the very nature of the task to be fulfilled in the great work of Humanity.

DESCRIPTION OF AN HOSPITAL-RAFT.

In conclusion we will give a description of the Hospital-Raft, from which we expect the most efficient help in battles in open sea.

The Hospital-Raft is the vessel, by which, under every circumstance of wind and weather, with hollow, chopping and beating seas (*Hohle-see, Stampf-see*) and in the surf (*Brandung*), persons can be picked up out of the sea, in circumstances when this cannot be accomplished by an ordinary or even life-boat, without danger of being swamped or capsized.

This Raft is composed of three or more air-tight (*luft-dicht*) cylinders of gutta-percha or other elastic material 20 to 22 feet long, and 24 to 26 inches in diameter (Engl. measure). These cylinders are encased in strong canvas cylinders, and connected together, by means of heavy canvas-flanges (*Seitenstück*). On the top of, and across these cylinders, are placed 5 to 6 strong planks, 2 inches thick and 14 inches broad, which are lashed, at each end, and between the cylinders, by means of ropes, passed in holes of the planks and through the side-pieces of the canvas cylinders. These planks answer the double purpose of stretchers to keep the cylinders apart and in shape, when inflated and also as seats for passengers. Between these seats are fixed the sick-transport cots, ready to receive the patients, and furnished with the slings, to be hoisted up, through the port-holes on the sick-deck of the Hospital-Ship, as before described. When the Raft is not in use, the cylinders are flattened out and rolled up across these planks, which remain attached to the cylinders.

Across these planks, at each end, and lengthwise of the outer-cylinders, are fastened,—by means of bolts at the end of the planks and rope-lashings to the flanges of the outer-cylinders,—beams of suitable dimensions, which answer the double purpose of gunwale (*Balkwäger, Dollbord*) and for attaching row-locks or tholes (*Ruder-klamp, Dullen*) for the oars, for propelling and manoeuvring the Raft.

To each of the air cylinders is attached an air-valve (*Luft-klappe*) which can be opened and shut at leisure, and when it becomes necessary to use the Raft, an inflating bellows (*Aufblähungs-blasebalg*) which always attends the Rafts,—is attached to each air-valve and the Raft is got in readiness to be launched in the space of eight or ten minutes.

The gutta-percha or inside cylinder is but an air reservoir and has no strain to bear. The canvas or outer cylinder, being of smaller dimensions than the inner or air cylinders, it becomes impossible to inflate the air-cylinder to its full extent or beyond its strength; consequently, the entire wear and strain falls upon the outer or canvas cylinders, which can be repaired by any person, either on board ship or in foreign countries, if necessary. So that, by this method of construction, strength and durability are combined with simplicity and cheapness.

Rafts, composed of floats, constructed of gutta-percha, coated with canvas, will prove of more than ordinary value to Hospital-Ships. The chief qualities of these Rafts are:—1°. They can be cast overboard in the roughest sea, as the raft cannot be stove (*schmoren, unter Wasser drücken*) when alongside of the vessel,—(an accident to which life-boats are liable)—nor be swamped or capsized. 2°. They can be got ready for service in eight or ten minutes. 3°. When not in use, they can be collapsed, rolled up and stowed away in a small space, so that a dozen of these rafts would hardly occupy more room than a good sized life-boat of ordinary construction.

The Raft, of which we have here given a description, as desirable for an Hospital-Raft, is not a new invention of ours. In fact, it bears relation to all classes of floats, constructed of flexible air and water-proof materials coated with canvas ; capable of being collapsed and folded up into a small space ;—as an Hospital-Ship has no room to carry enough life-boats of ordinary size, to answer the exigencies of a catastrophe in a sea-battle. Different sorts of life-saving rafts are used by the North-American vessels ; but, one of the best sort appears to be the patent of Edward L. Perry, (Constructor to the Life-saving Raft-Company at New-York) ; *—which we have here taken for a model.

This 3-cylinder raft, when inflated and ready for use, has a length of 22 feet and a breadth of 13 feet, with a buoyant capacity of ten thousand pounds, and a deck surface for passengers of 264 square feet ; and when rolled and packed up for stowing away, it takes up only a space of about two feet in diameter, by thirteen feet long, with a weight of about five hundred pounds. It is propelled by eight oars. On trial, it was pulled to windward through a heavy sea in a gale of wind, with six oars, at the rate of five miles an hour, making very little or no water and riding the sea to prefection, with thirty men on it. For the object of the Red-Cross at Sea, this raft is to be strongly recommended, with some additions for the special service of a Hospital-Raft.

(*) Resolutions of the Intern. Confer. of 1869. Sec. II. No. 14.

GENERAL INDEX.

Note. The numerals in this Index refer to the respective numbers of the paragraphs, and of the subsections of paragraphs. The paragraphs run in uninterrupted succession through the whole work and are marked at the top of each page.

TABLE OF CONTENTS.

VOL. II.

Part IV.

MUTUAL RIGHTS AND RESPONSIBILITIES OF STATES IN TIME OF PEACE.

CHAPTER XVIII.

GENERAL PRINCIPLES WITH REGARD TO THE MUTUAL DUTIES OF STATES IN THEIR INTERCOURSE.

CHAPTER XIX.

RIGHT OF LEGATION, NEGOTIATION AND TREATY.

CHAPTER XX.

Treaties affecting International Law.

CHAPTER XXI.

International Agents.

Public Ministers, their Rights and Duties.

CHAPTER XXII.

CONSULAR OFFICERS.

Rules for the Consular Office.

CHAPTER XXIII.

Balance of Power and Intervention.

CHAPTER XXIV.

The Laws of Peace.

Settlement of International Differences. Amicable Arrangement and Compromise. Mediation and Arbitration. Political Conferences and International Congresses.

CHAPTER XXV.

The Condition between Peace and War.

Measures of constraint falling short of war.
Retortion and Reprisal.

Part V.

WAR AND ITS APPURTENANCES.

CHAPRER XXVI.

GENERAL OBSERVATIONS WITH REGARD TO WAR BETWEEN NATIONS. PRINCIPLES OF THE LAW OF WAR.

CHAPTER XXVII.

THE CONDITION OF WAR AND ITS EFFECT ON PRIVATE INDIVIDUALS OF THE BELLIGERENT STATES.

CHAPTER XXVIII.

DIFFERENT KINDS OF WAR. LAWFUL AND UNLAWFUL WARS.

CHAPTER XXIX.

DECLARATION OF WAR.

CHAPTER XXX.

THE ENEMY AND HIS ALLIES.

CHAPTER XXXI.

Rights and Duties of Belligerent States with regard to each other. The Usages of War.

1°. General Remarks on the Usages of War (Coutumes de la guerre. Kriegsgebrauch).

2°. Usages of War with regard to the relations between private individuals of enemy States.

3°. Usages of War with regard to Enemy's subjects and Enemy's property within a belligerent country.

4°. Means and Instruments of carrying on war.

5°. The living Instruments of War. Combatants and Non-Combatants.

6°. Of the means of inflicting bodily injury to the enemy.

7°. *Military Occupation.*

8°. *Sieges and Bombardments.*

9°. *Prisoners of War.*

10°. *Belligerent troops on Neutral territory.*

11°. *The Rights of Belligerents with respect to Private Individuals and their property.*

12°. *Spies.*

13°. *Non-hostile relations between belligerents.*

14°. *Capitulation.*

15°. *Armistices.*

16°. *Retaliation in War.*

17°. *Of the sick and wounded. The Geneva Convention.*

CHAPTER XXXII.

Usages of War with regard to the seizure of the Enemy's Private Property on the High Seas.

1°. *The doctrine of Inviolability of the Private Property of Individual Members of the Enemy State on the High Seas.*

2°. *The Right of Capture.*

3°. *Ransom of Captured Vessels.*

4°. *Recapture. Right of the Original Owner. Jus Postliminii.*

5°. *Loans of Money by Neutrals.*

6°. *Relations of Neutrality with regard to parties of a Civil War.*

7°. *Colonial and Coasting Trade.*

8°. *Belligerent Right of Visit and Search and Capture, with respect to neutral vessels.*

9°. *The Destruction of Neutral Property in enemy vessel.*

10°. *Acts of Individuals, constituting Violation of Neutrality.*

11°. *Licence to Trade.*

12°. *Rights of Belligerents with regard to Neutral Persons and Property within the Jurisdiction of Belligerents.*

13°. *Relation between the Neutral Diplomate and the belligerent Government. Protection of the Subjects of the Enemy State by the Representative of a Neutral Government.*

14°. *The Inviolability of Neutral Territory. Refuge and Asylum.*

Pages.

CHAPTER XXXV.

Contraband of War.

CHAPTER XXXVI.

Military Occupation, Siege and Blockade.

CHAPTER XXXVII.

PRIZE COURTS.

CHAPTER XXXVIII.

TREATIES PRECEDING THE DECLARATION OF PARIS, OF 1856, BEARING ON THE QUESTIONS OF NEUTRAL GOODS IN ENEMY VESSELS AND ENEMY GOODS IN NEUTRAL VESSELS.

CHAPTER XXXIX.

THE GENEVA CONVENTION AND THE RED-CROSS SOCIETIES.

I. *Origin of the Red-Cross Societies.*

II. *The International Convention of Geneva.*

III. *The Red-Cross Societies at Sea.*

Part VI.

RE-ESTABLISHMENT OF PEACE.

CHAPTER XL.

THE TERMINATION OF WAR AND THE RE-ESTABLISHMENT OF PEACE.

CHAPTER XLI.

THE TREATY OF PEACE.

CHAPTER XLII.

EFFECTS OF THE TREATY OF PEACE.

Appendices.

END OF THE SECOND AND LAST VOLUME.

Printed in Dunstable, United Kingdom

91222214R00409